Writing and Reading Across the Curriculum

Writing and Reading Across the Curriculum

Fourteenth Edition

Laurence Behrens
University of California Santa Barbara

Leonard J. Rosen
Bentley University

Pearson

330 Hudson Street, NY, NY 10013

Director of English: Karon Bowers
Executive Producer and Publisher: Aron Keesbury
Development Editor: David Kear
Marketing Manager: Nicholas Bolt
Program Manager: Rachel Harbour
Project Manager: Amy Kopperude,
  iEnergizer Aptara®, Ltd.

Cover Designer: Pentagram
Cover Illustration: Christopher DeLorenzo
Manufacturing Buyer: Roy L. Pickering, Jr.
Printer/Binder: LSC Communications, Inc.
Cover Printer: Phoenix Color/Hagerstown

Acknowledgments of third-party content appear on pages 561–564, which constitute an extension of this copyright page.

PEARSON, ALWAYS LEARNING, and Revel are exclusive trademarks owned by Pearson Education, Inc., or its affiliates in the United States and/or other countries.

Unless otherwise indicated herein, any third-party trademarks that may appear in this work are the property of their respective owners and any references to third-party trademarks, logos, or other trade dress are for demonstrative or descriptive purposes only. Such references are not intended to imply any sponsorship, endorsement, authorization, or promotion of Pearson's products by the owners of such marks, or any relationship between the owner and Pearson Education, Inc., or its affiliates, authors, licensees, or distributors.

Library of Congress Cataloging-in-Publication Data

Names: Behrens, Laurence, author. | Rosen, Leonard J., author.

Title: Writing and reading across the curriculum / Laurence Behrens, University of California Santa Barbara; Leonard J. Rosen, Bentley Universssity.

Description: Fourteenth Edition. | Boston : Pearson, [2018] | Includes bibliographical references and index.

Identifiers: LCCN 2017051806| ISBN 9780134668512 (Student Edition : paperback) | ISBN 0134668510 (Student Edition : paperback) | ISBN 0134681932 (ePub3) | ISBN 0134682157 (ePub3) | ISBN 9780134681931 (epub3) | ISBN 9780134682150 (epub3)

Subjects: LCSH: College readers. | Interdisciplinary approach in education—Problems, exercises, etc. | English language—Rhetoric—Problems, exercises, etc. | Academic writing—Problems, exercises, etc.

Classification: LCC PE1417 .B396 2017 | DDC 808/.0427—dc23 LC record available at https://lccn.loc.gov/2017051806

1   17

Rental Edition ISBN 10: 0-13-466851-0
Rental Edition ISBN 13: 978-0-13-466851-2
A la Carte ISBN 10: 0-13-468195-9
A la Carte ISBN 13: 978-0-13-468195-5
Access Code Card ISBN 10: 0-13-468134-7
Access Code Card ISBN 13: 978-0-13-468134-4
Instructor's Review Copy ISBN 10: 0-13-468202-5
Instructor's Review Copy ISBN 13: 978-0-13-468202-0

Pearson www.pearsonhighered.com

Brief Contents

Contents

Part II Brief Takes 215

MUSIC

8 "Over the Rainbow" and
the Art of the Musical Cover 216

*Whose version of "Please Don't Stop the Mu-
sic" do you prefer? Rihanna's or Jamie Cul-
lum's? Such questions are at the heart of this
chapter on the musical "cover," an interpretation by a musician or a band of a previously
recorded song.*

PSYCHOLOGY

SOCIOLOGY

Part III   An Anthology of Readings

LITERATURE AND FILM

COMPUTER SCIENCE

12 Artificial Intelligence 369

SOCIOLOGY

13 Have You Heard This?
The Latest on Rumor   433

FOLKLORE

14 Fairy Tales: A Closer Look at Cinderella   477

BUSINESS

15 Advertising   523

Preface

When *Writing and Reading Across the Curriculum* was first published, more than thirty-five years ago, the response was both immediate and enthusiastic. Instructors found the topics in *WRAC* both interesting and teachable, and students appreciated the links that such topics suggested to the courses they were taking concurrently in the humanities, the social sciences, and the sciences. Readers told us how practical they found our "summary, synthesis, and critique" approach to writing college-level papers, and in later editions welcomed the addition of "analysis" to our coverage in Part I.

In developing each successive edition of *WRAC*, we strive to retain the essential multidisciplinary character of the text while providing ample new topics and individual readings to keep it fresh and timely. Some topics have proven particularly enduring—our "Obedience" chapter has been a fixture, as has "Fairy Tales: A Closer Look at 'Cinderella.'" But we take care to make sure that a substantial portion of the book is completely new every time, both by extensively revising existing chapters and by creating new ones. While we retain an emphasis on summary, critique, synthesis, and analysis, we continue to develop content on topics such as the process of writing and argumentation that address the issues and interests of today's classrooms.

What's New in the 14th Edition

The fourteenth edition of *Writing and Reading Across the Curriculum* represents a major revision of the previous edition.

- We are pleased to offer an altogether new Note to the Student, titled "An Introduction to Thinking and Writing in College," which provides a graphically rich overview of the foundational skills needed for success in college life. These foundational skills include cultivating intellectual curiosity, exploring similarities and differences, arguing with logic and evidence, and challenging arguments. "An Introduction to Thinking and Writing in College" builds on the topic "The Idea of Money," the same topic that forms the basis of the new model synthesis in Chapter 4.

- **Chapter 1** on Summary **now distinguishes between summarizing readily accessible texts and summarizing more difficult ones**, providing examples and strategies for summarizing each. The chapter also includes an **expanded discussion on incorporating quotations** into sentences.

- **Chapter 2** on Critical Reading and Critique **includes a new model critique**: "The Right to Bury the Online Past"—an op-ed arguing that people harmed by the Web's infinite memory should have the right to petition search providers like Google to de-list links to sensitive materials.

- **Chapter 4** on Explanatory Synthesis **includes a new model explanatory synthesis** on "The 'Idea' of Money," a paper on how rectangular pieces of paper in a wallet, dolphin teeth, diamonds, and squirrel pelts—all forms of money at different points in history—hold no inherent value: they're worth only what we agree they're worth. The topic for this new model paper provides the topic for the new "An Introduction to Thinking and Writing in College."

- The **extensively revised and updated Chapter 7** on Locating, Mining, and Citing Sources introduces students to the latest techniques for conducting college-level research. The update includes **the most current citation formats for APA and MLA.**

- **Nearly 50 new readings** throughout the book span the disciplines, representing a range of perspectives and encouraging students to write critical responses, summaries, analyses, and syntheses. Every chapter has been refreshed with new readings.

- **With its new foundational song, the immortal "Over the Rainbow,"** Chapter 8 continues to introduce students to perceptive listening and to writing about popular music.

- **Chapter 11, "First Impressions,"** provides **four new novel openings**: Jane Austen's *Pride and Prejudice*; Robert Louis Stevenson's *The Strange Case of Dr. Jekyll and Mr. Hyde*; L. Frank Baum's *The Wonderful Wizard of Oz*; and Willa Cather's *My Ántonia*. **Also new: additional movies** with fresh Discussion and Writing Suggestions for each opening scene.

- **New to this edition, Artificial Intelligence, Chapter 12, introduces students to rapid advances in AI science and related, potential upheavals in biology, politics, philosophy, and the economy.**

- **Chapter 14 restores** a perennial favorite in WRAC: **Fairy Tales: A Closer Look at Cinderella.** In addition to multiple versions of the tale, we include several new, hard-hitting (brief) critiques as well as readings on the tale's core structure and its feminist implications.

- **Chapter 15, Advertising, offers two portfolios, one directing students to archives of print ads and another to carefully curated television commercials. Students will practice their visual literacy skills by conducting close analyses.**

- **Online text and video sources** are provided throughout, with recommended search terms and strategies.

Structure and Signature Strengths

Structure

Writing and Reading Across the Curriculum is divided into a rhetoric and an anthology of readings. The anthology of readings is further subdivided into two parts, the first of these serving as a kind of bridge between the rhetoric and the anthology.

Part I takes students step-by-step through the process of writing papers based on source material, explaining and demonstrating how summaries, critiques, syntheses, and analyses can be generated from the kinds of readings students will encounter later in the book—and throughout their academic careers.

Part II, "Brief Takes," offers mini-chapters of five to seven readings that are accompanied by a set of sequential writing exercises. We see working on one or more of these brief takes as a kind of "warm-up" exercise for the more intensive intellectual activities involved in tackling the full-length chapters. "The Roar of the Tiger Mom" and "The Art of the Musical Cover" (albeit with a different song to organize the chapter) are carried over from the previous edition. The third chapter, "Obedience to Authority," is distilled from a full-length chapter in the thirteenth edition.

Part III offers full-length anthology chapters of ten or more readings on compelling topics selected to stimulate student interest. Tackling a range of perspectives, voices, and writing and argument strategies, these units immerse students in the kinds of sustained reading and writing required for other college courses.

Signature Strengths

Continued focus on argument in Part I emphasizes the following:

- The Elements of Argument: Claim, Support, Assumption. This section adapts the Toulmin approach to the kinds of readings students will encounter in Parts II and III of the text.

- The Three Appeals of Logos, Ethos, Pathos. This discussion may be used to analyze arguments in the readings in Parts II and III of the book.

- Developing and Organizing Support for Arguments. This section helps students mine source materials for facts, expert opinions, and examples that will support their arguments.

- Annotated Student Papers. Model summaries, critique, explanatory synthesis, and argument synthesis emphasize writing strategies and careful use of sources.

Revel

Revel is an interactive learning environment that deeply engages students and prepares them for class. Media and assessment integrated directly within the authors' narrative lets students read, explore interactive content, and practice in one continuous learning path. Thanks to the dynamic reading experience in Revel, students come to class prepared to discuss, apply, and learn from instructors and from each other.

Learn more about Revel
www.pearson.com/revel

Supplements

Make more time for your students with instructor resources that offer effective learning assessments and classroom engagement. Pearson's partnership with educators does not end with the delivery of course materials; Pearson is there with you on the first day of class and beyond. A dedicated team of local Pearson representatives will work with you to not only choose course materials but also integrate them into your class and assess their effectiveness. Our goal is your goal—to improve instruction with each semester.

Pearson is pleased to offer the following resources to qualified adopters of *Writing and Reading Across the Curriculum*. Several of these supplements are available to instantly download from Revel or on the Instructor Resource Center (IRC); please visit the IRC at www.pearsonhighered.com/irc to register for access.

- **Instructor's Resource Manual** Create a comprehensive roadmap for teaching classroom, online, or hybrid courses. Designed for new and experienced instructors, the Instructor's Manual for the fourteenth edition of *Writing and Reading Across the Curriculum* provides sample syllabi and course calendars, chapter summaries, classroom ideas for writing assignments, introductions to each set of readings, and answers to review questions. Available within Revel and on the IRC.

- **Powerpoint Presentation** Make lectures more enriching for students. The PowerPoint Presentation includes a full lecture outline and photos and figures from the textbook and Revel edition. Available on the IRC.

Acknowledgments

We have benefited over the years from the suggestions and insights of many teachers—and students—across the country. We would especially like to thank these reviewers for the fourteenth edition: Mary Seel, SUNY Broome Community College; Teresa Brandt, Ohlone College; Dylan Parkhurst, Stephen F. Austin State University; Angela Adams, Loyola University Chicago; Marianne Trale, Community College of Allegheny County; Mary Carlin, Salem State University; Valerie Belew, Nashville State Community College; Carlen Donovan, Idaho State University; Tonya Charles, Idaho State University.

We would also like to thank the following reviewers for their help in the preparation of past editions: Dr. Iona Joseph Abraham, Lorain County Community College; Angela Adams,

Loyola University Chicago; James Allen, College of DuPage; Fabián Álvarez, Western Kentucky University; Chris Anson, North Carolina State University; Phillip Arrington, Eastern Michigan University; Anne Bailey, Southeastern Louisiana University; Carolyn Baker, San Antonio College; Joy Bashore, Central Virginia Community College; Nancy Blattner, Southeast Missouri State University; Mary Bly, University of California, Davis; Laurel Bollinger, University of Alabama in Huntsville; David Bordelon, Ocean County College; Bob Brannan, Johnson County Community College; Paul Buczkowski, Eastern Michigan University; Jennifer Bullis, Whatcom Community College; Paige Byam, Northern Kentucky University; Susan Callendar, Sinclair Community College; Anne Carr, Southeast Community College; Jeff Carroll, University of Hawaii; Joseph Rocky Colavito, Northwestern State University; Michael Colonneses, Methodist College; James A. Cornette, Christopher Newport University; Timothy Corrigan, Temple University; Kathryn J. Dawson, Ball State University; Cathy Powers Dice, University of Memphis; Dianne Donnelly, University of South Florida; William Donovan, Idaho State University; Kathleen Dooley, Tidewater Community College; Judith Eastman, Orange Coast College; David Elias, Eastern Kentucky University; Susan Boyd English, Kirkwood Community College; Kathy Evertz, University of Wyoming; Kathy Ford, Lake Land College; University of Wyoming; Wanda Fries, Somerset Community College; Bill Gholson, Southern Oregon University; Karen Gordon, Elgin Community College; Deborah Gutschera, College of DuPage; Derek G. Handley, Community College of Allegheny County; Lila M. Harper, Central Washington University; M. Todd Harper, University of Louisville; Kip Harvigsen, Ricks College; Michael Hogan, Southeast Missouri State University; Sandra M. Jensen, Lane Community College; Deanna M. Jessup, Indiana University; Anita Johnson, Whatcom Community College; Mark Jones, University of Florida; Daven M. Kari, Vanguard University; Kim Karshner, Lorain County Community College; Jane Kaufman, University of Akron; Kerrie Kawasaki-Hull, Ohlone College; Rodney Keller, Ricks College; Walt Klarner, Johnson County Community College; Jeffery Klausman, Whatcom Community College; Alison Kuehner, Ohlone College; Michelle LaFrance, University of Massachusetts Dartmouth; William B. Lalicker, West Chester University; Dawn Leonard, Charleston Southern University; Lindsay Lewan, Arapahoe Community College; Clifford L. Lewis, U Mass Lowell; Signee Lynch, Whatcom Community College; Jolie Martin; San Francisco State University; Meg Matheny, Jefferson Community and Technical College, Southwest; Krista L. May, Texas A&M University; Kathy Mendt, Front Range Community College–Larimer Campus; RoseAnn Morgan, Middlesex County College; David Moton, Bakersfield College; Eliot Parker, Mountwest Community and Technical College; Roark Mulligan, Christopher Newport University; Joan Mullin, University of Toledo; Stella Nesanovich, McNeese State University; Catherine Olson, Lone Star College-Tomall; Denise Paster, Coastal Carolina University; Susie Paul, Auburn University at Montgomery; Thomas Pfau, Bellevue Community College; Jeff Pruchnic, Wayne State University; Aaron Race, Southern Illinois University–Carbondale; Nancy Redmond, Long Beach City College; Deborah Reese, University of Texas at Arlington; Alison Reynolds, University of Florida; Priscilla Riggle, Bowling Green State University; Jeanette Riley, University of New Mexico; Robert Rongner, Whatcom Community College; Sarah C. Ross, Southeastern Louisiana University; Deborah L. Ruth, Owensboro Community & Technical College; Amy Rybak, Bowling Green State University; Raul Sanchez, University of Utah; Mary R. Seel, Broome Community College; Rebecca Shapiro, Westminster College; Mary Sheldon, Washburn University; Horacio Sierra, University of Florida; Philip Sipiora, University of Southern Florida; Joyce Smoot, Virginia Tech;

Ellen Sorg, Owens Community College; Bonnie A. Spears, Chaffey College; Bonnie Startt, Tidewater Community College; R. E. Stratton, University of Alaska–Fairbanks; Katherine M. Thomas, Southeast Community College; Scott Vander Ploeg, Madisonville Community College; Victor Villanueva, Washington State University; Deron Walker, California Baptist University; Jackie Wheeler, Arizona State University; Pat Stephens Williams, Southern Illinois University at Carbondale; and Kristin Woolever, Northeastern University.

The authors wish to thank Robert Krut, of the University of California, Santa Barbara Writing Program, for his contributions to the "Rumor" chapter. We also acknowledge the work of Barbara Magalnick in contributing to the "Summary" chapter. For their numerous comments and suggestions on developing the research chapter, "Locating, Mining, and Citing Sources," we thank Ayanna Gaines, associate librarian at Ventura College; Richard Caldwell, head of library instruction at the University of California, Santa Barbara Library; and Susan Bigelow, Assistant Director of Libraries, Goodwin College.

For his consultation on the model synthesis "Responding to Bullies" in Chapter 4, we gratefully acknowledge the assistance of Philip Rodkin, Professor of Psychology at the University of Illinois at Urbana-Champaign. Tragically, Phil died in May 2014, and he will be sorely missed by all who knew him.

We thank musician Greg Blair for his expertise in writing the model paper on "Stormy Weather" and for creating a series of entertaining and instructive videos to accompany his glossary of musical terms.

Finally, special thanks to David B. Kear, Cynthia Cox, Rachel Harbour, and Amy Kopperude for helping shepherd the manuscript through the editorial and production process.

Laurence Behrens
Leonard J. Rosen

An Introduction to Thinking and Writing in College

 ## Learning Objectives

After completing this introduction, you will be able to:

0.1   Define academic thinking and writing.

0.2   Cultivate intellectual curiosity.

0.3   Explore similarities and differences.

0.4   Understand the importance of arguing with logic and evidence.

0.5   Understand why arguments must be challenged.

0.6   Understand how writing can be a tool for critical thinking.

College may initially seem both overwhelming and bewildering. You may not even be clear, at first, what college is *for*, aside from taking classes you hope will help you to land a better job one day. The statistics are clear: a diploma will significantly boost your employment prospects and earning power. Of course, it's not just the diploma that improves your fortunes; it's the skills and habits of thinking you've developed along the way.

These skills and habits include your ability to

1. cultivate intellectual curiosity;
2. explore similarities and differences;
3. argue, using logic and evidence; and
4. challenge arguments.

This brief introduction to thinking and writing in college will touch on these habits and skills and will suggest some of the ways you'll grow intellectually in the coming years.

Defining Academic Thinking and Writing

0.1 Define academic thinking and writing.

What do people think and write about in college? In a word, everything. Besides teaching your classes, grading papers, and serving on academic committees, your instructors also spend a great deal of time investigating questions that fascinate them. What was the main cause of the Soviet Union's collapse? What gives a poem its beauty and power? How can viruses be used to fight cancer?

Pick a topic, any topic, and you're almost certain to find someone on campus studying it in order to understand more deeply what it is and how it works. To take one example, consider a dollar bill—that is, a piece of money.

What could be more typical or ordinary? Is there any point to studying money in an academic setting? Well, yes, there is. Read this excerpt from a student paper, "The 'Idea' of Money." (You'll find the complete paper in Chapter 4.)

> In a barter-based economy, people traded goods and services they agreed had equal value. In an economy based on money, objects became a substitute for goods and services that would otherwise have been traded. Such substitutes became "currency" or "money." In this new system, the butcher no longer had to trade his meat for beer or shoes if he had no need for them. As long as the butcher, brewer, and shoemaker each valued the same currency—be it stone tools, gold nuggets, or cowry shells—a new kind of exchange could take place. Money emerged across different cultures for the

same reason: convenience. But the *form* money took varied from one society to the next and from one historical period to the next depending on what people considered valuable. This raises an important question: If different forms of money arose in different places and at different times, what, exactly, gives money its value?

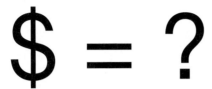

Sheldon Kearney's paper on the origins of money led him to a strange conclusion: the notion that money itself holds no value—that is to say, a nugget of gold is inherently worth no more than a handful of sea shells. More on that in a moment. The point here is that *any* topic, even the most ordinary, can be studied in an academic setting, and inquiries can lead to surprising results.

Academic writing builds on careful study and differs from personal writing and business writing. Personal, expressive writing makes private experience (the "I" experience) public in ways the writer hopes will be meaningful to readers. Business writing, such as e-mails, letters, proposals, advertising brochures, and reports, promotes the interests of a company or corporation. Academic writing involves reading widely, searching for evidence, and thinking logically—all in an effort to understand more deeply and to communicate understanding in books, articles, essays, speeches, blog posts, films, and other media.

Cultivating Intellectual Curiosity

0.2   Cultivate intellectual curiosity.

From high school you'll recall that knowledge is divided among broad areas of study—the humanities, sciences, social sciences, performing arts, and so on. These same divisions hold true in college. Within each broad area we find further divisions called disciplines, such as philosophy, physics, history, and anthropology. A single topic—let's consider money once more—can be studied from multiple disciplinary perspectives. Consider a few of the many ways that researchers might study money in an academic setting:

> *Anthropologists* study the origins of civilization. They might focus on the forms that money has taken over time and ask: What explains the different forms of money we find in different cultures—for instance, wampum and dolphin teeth?

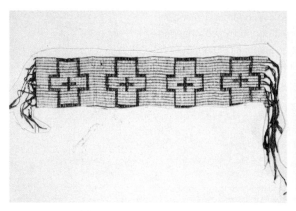

Wampum (Beads)

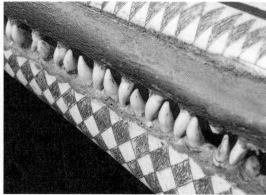

Dolphin Teeth

Historians might investigate when and why state-issued money first became widespread. They might study the Roman Empire, which stretched from present-day Great Britain to North Africa and the Middle East. In an empire spanning such vast territories and comprising so many cultures and languages—each with its own forms of money—a common currency would have helped to promote trade and consolidate central authority. During the rule of Julius Caesar, Rome issued the aureus, examples of which survive today.

Roman Aureus

Metallurgists might wonder how changing technologies for extracting metals from raw ore enabled the production and widespread use of state-issued coins like the aureus. For example, how were early crucibles used for smelting gold constructed?

Crucible

Sociologists might study the financial organization of marriages and ask how and why the tradition of paying dowries (the transfer of wealth from the bride's family to the groom's) emerged. Does that ancient tradition survive today in the customary payment of weddings by a bride's family?

Artists create objects such as paintings, sculptures, stories, and poems that provoke conversations. Think how many books you have read or films you have seen that turn on the goal of acquiring money. Consider, for example, novels like Thackeray's *Vanity Fair* or Fitzgerald's *The Great Gatsby*. Consider films like *Wall Street*, *Ocean's 11*, and *Trading Places*. In what ways do artists provoke conversations? Why are these conversations important?

Gun Wrapped in Money

Economists might ask: What *is* money? How does money get its value? What precisely distinguishes one form of money—say, cowry shells—from other forms like dollars? Why would a grocer accept dollars but *not* cowry shells as payment for a quart of milk? Is one currency inherently more valuable than others? This is the question taken up in the paper "The 'Idea' of Money" in Chapter 4.

Every discipline approaches a topic in characteristic ways, with characteristic questions. You can be sure that each approach fascinates its investigators: the historians, economists, and sociologists who study money, for instance, from their distinctive points of view. Your job in taking courses across the curriculum is to be curious: to ask *why*, to cultivate fascination. In time, your fascination will guide you in choosing a major field of study.

Salt

Curious

- Salt was once used as money? Why?
- The word "salary" is derived from salt? When and why did this use develop?
- Salt has been farmed and mined for profit? Where? When? How?
- How does salt raise blood pressure?

Not so much

This is a pile of salt.

What does it take to be curious?

For the most part, as a freshman or sophomore, you'll be receiving established knowledge in the form of books, articles, lectures, and lab studies. You're not likely to start out creating knowledge the way your instructors do in their own investigations. But they'll be preparing you to create knowledge by teaching you their methods of investigation. That is, they'll be teaching both the *what* of their discipline and the *how*. The *what* is content: the history of Roman money, for instance, or economic theories of money. The *how* is thinking critically about that content. *Critical* in an academic sense doesn't mean *negative* but rather *careful* and *alert*. Thinking critically involves many skills, chief among them the ability to explore similarities and differences, to argue with logic and evidence, and to challenge arguments (especially your own).

Whether you major in finance, nursing, computer science, or literature, the larger goal is to become a careful, disciplined thinker. That's what employers value in college graduates, and that is what is required of you in becoming an informed, engaged citizen. Plenty of biology and philosophy majors end up working in fields that have nothing to do with biology or philosophy. But the skills and habits of thinking they developed in their studies have everything to do with their success.

Let's take a closer look at four important skills that anchor intellectual life at college:

- Exploring similarities and differences
- Arguing with logic and evidence
- Challenging arguments
- Communicating critical thinking through writing

Exploring Similarities and Differences

0.3   Explore similarities and differences.

Academic thinking often involves close study of examples. Any time you gather multiple examples of a topic and study them, you'll have an occasion to make comparisons and contrasts. Examine these images, which are forms of money from different times and places.

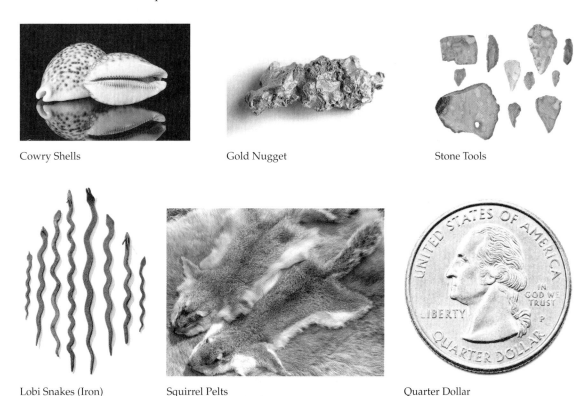

Cowry Shells   Gold Nugget   Stone Tools

Lobi Snakes (Iron)   Squirrel Pelts   Quarter Dollar

In comparing these forms of money, we can observe different materials: worked objects (coins, iron snakes, stone tools) and objects in their natural state (gold nuggets, cowry shells). Squirrel pelts, used as currency in medieval Russia and Finland, are both worked and unworked: squirrels had to be killed and skinned. We can also observe similarities: All these forms of money are portable. People could carry them easily. These forms of money are also divisible: People could accept one cowry shell or many as payment, a smaller lobi snake (once used in Burkina Faso) or a larger one, pennies and nickels in place of a quarter, and so on.

If you were writing a paper about money, you would quickly conclude that money takes no single form. How would you treat the differences and the similarities you found? What conclusions would you draw? In college-level work, you will frequently observe similarities and differences, and you will need to account for them. You can see how Sheldon Kearney handles such comparisons and contrasts in his paper, "The 'Idea' of Money," in Chapter 4.

Arguing with Logic and Evidence

0.4 Understand the importance of arguing with logic and evidence.

In social settings, few people want to be known for arguing all the time. In academic settings, people are *expected* to argue: to use logic and evidence both to present their work and review the work of others.

Later in this text you will learn strategies and techniques for arguing. For now, consider the debatable statement that money is "an idea." Could you convince others that money is not a "thing" but rather an "agreement" among people? Arguing the point would require you to state that gold in itself, as a metal dug from the earth, is no more valuable than the feathers of a goose or chicken. Is it possible? Say you're trapped in an Arctic outpost. Winter is approaching and what you need, urgently, is insulation to keep you from freezing to death. In this case, wouldn't three pounds of feathers (to make a down blanket) be of far more value to you than three pounds of gold? And if that's the case, what can be said about the inherent value of gold, feathers, or *any* form of money? Perhaps money *is* an idea!

Gold Nugget

Feather

We're headed toward strange territory here: the notion that money is valuable not in itself but because people agree to value it. Consider this idea: Money is an *agreement*, not a thing. Feathers could be money, and so could salt, beads, or pieces of paper in our wallets. The particular *form* that money takes is meaningless. All that's needed for the larger economy to function is for everyone to agree that whatever we exchange and call money has value. An economy based on sunflower seeds? Why not—peppercorns were once used as money! If you're not comfortable making this argument, you could look for help in the form of experts who could support your position. That's why Sheldon Kearney quotes this source in his paper, "The 'Idea' of Money":

> [T]he notion that gold is somehow [a] more "real" [form of money] than paper [money] is, well, a mirage. Gold is valuable because we've collectively decided that it's valuable and that we'll accept goods and services in exchange for it. And that's no different, ultimately, from our collective decision that colorful rectangles of paper [in our wallets] are valuable and that we'll accept goods and services in exchange for them. . . .
>
> We cling to the belief that money needs to be backed by something "solid."
>
> —James Surowiecki, IEEE Spectrum, 30 May 2012

In a college setting, our knowledge of the world is built through argument: the ability to examine evidence, reach a conclusion, and convince others that our conclusions are correct or reasonable. Argument will become one of the core skills you'll learn in college.

Challenging Arguments

0.5 Understand why arguments must be challenged.

If arguing is essential in academic settings, so is pushing back against arguments when their logic or evidence is flawed. Consider that the larger intellectual goal in the academy is to build knowledge, and no one is well served when faulty arguments are accepted as true. Later in this text you'll learn how to evaluate and challenge the arguments of others. It goes without saying that others will challenge you when they're not convinced of the soundness of your arguments. So pushing back, respectfully and logically, is essential to your success both in college and beyond.

An example: The enormously influential eighteenth-century thinker Adam Smith is regarded as the first modern economist, and his theory of the emergence of money from barter economies is widely accepted. He believed that people in early societies traded one good for others of equal (mutually agreed upon) value. Eventually, Smith wrote, barter gave way to money when it was no longer convenient or practical to exchange goods in trade. That's the generally accepted view.

The Barter Economy

But in an academic setting, no view of the world, however well regarded, however celebrated its creator, is immune to challenge. Some scholars dispute Smith's theory of how currency emerged in early civilizations. Consider this challenge from anthropologist David Graeber:

> Adam Smith first proposed in *The Wealth of Nations* that as soon as a division of labor appeared in human society, some specializing in hunting, for instance, others making arrowheads, people would begin swapping goods with one another (6 arrowheads for a beaver pelt, for instance). . . . For exchange to be possible, both sides have to have something the other is willing to accept in trade. This was assumed to eventually lead to the people stockpiling items deemed likely to be generally desirable, which would thus become ever more desirable for that reason, and eventually become money. Barter thus gave birth to money. . . .
>
> Anthropologists gradually fanned out into the world and began directly observing how economies where money was not used . . . actually worked. . . . What they never found was any place, anywhere, where economic relations between members of community took the form economists predicted [based on Adam Smith's theory of barter]: "I'll give you twenty chickens for that cow." Hence in the definitive anthropological work on the subject, Cambridge anthropology professor Caroline Humphrey concludes, "No example of a barter economy, pure and simple, has ever been described, let alone the emergence from it of money; all available [studies suggest] that there never has been such a thing."

Graeber is an anthropologist who has used the evidence of field research to challenge the widely accepted views of Adam Smith. Not surprisingly, supporters of Smith's views have pushed back. A debate, an academic conversation about barter and the emergence of money, has developed. (To catch some of its flavor, Google "Graeber Smith barter money debate.") Why does this debate matter? It matters because some scholars believe that a confused understanding of what money is and how it emerged has profound implications for our economy today.

Challenging arguments is as important as making them; at times, mounting a challenge will take a degree of fearlessness. But if your goal is to help the larger community better understand how the world works, in the end people will thank you.

Communicating Critical Thinking Through Writing

0.6   **Understand how writing can be a tool for critical thinking.**

Your writing class, indeed all your classes, will be devoted to improving your skills of critical thinking. By way of demonstration, you have followed an example of how *any* topic—in our case, money—can be studied critically. What distinguishes academic study is not the topic but rather the questions that investigators pose about the topic and the methods they use to investigate.

As a college student, you are now—you are becoming—an investigator. You will think critically whenever you cultivate your intellectual curiosity, question similarities and differences, argue using logic and evidence, and challenge the work of others. If your college diploma means anything, it's that you have developed skills in and a respect for critical thinking.

Writing is one of the main ways of both expressing and developing your knowledge. As you write, you force yourself to clarify ideas before communicating them. In this way, writing itself becomes a tool for learning.

Your writing in college will take five typical forms:

- **Summary** accurately distills what you've read or seen.
- **Evaluation** judges the merits of and responds to the arguments of others.
- **Explanation** defines and describes neutrally, without interpretation.
- **Argument** uses evidence and logic to answer debatable questions, build new knowledge, and influence others.
- **Analysis** studies an object closely, illuminating it to yourself and others.

Your college writing course and this text, *Writing and Reading Across the Curriculum*, will teach you these forms of writing, as well as the broader skills of critical thinking from which they follow.

So what is college *for* aside from your gaining skills to boost your job prospects and earning power? College is for making knowledge through collaboration and argument; it's for teaching both the content and habits of thinking you'll need to be an informed, engaged citizen who understands that learning never ends. You have embarked on a journey, one that will reward you in ways large and small in the years to come. Enjoy the trip!

Part I
Structures and Strategies

Chapter 1
Summary, Paraphrase, and Quotation

 Learning Objectives

After completing this chapter, you will be able to:

1.1 Preview a selection.

1.2 Form a preliminary understanding of topic and purpose based on your preview.

1.3 Reread for content and structure.

1.4 Summarize and paraphrase parts of sources.

1.5 Summarize entire works using a systematic strategy.

1.6 Write a summary of an especially challenging source.

1.7 Write summaries of visual presentations, including graphs, charts, and tables.

1.8 Select effective material to quote directly and indirectly.

1.9 Alter quotations with ellipses and brackets.

1.10 Avoid classic mistakes in using quotations.

1.11 Use six strategies to incorporate quotations, summaries, and paraphrases into your sentences.

1.12 Avoid plagiarism by citing sources and using your own words and sentence structure.

A summary is a brief, objective, and complete restatement of a source. At times, instructors will ask that you summarize an *entire* article or book as a stand-alone assignment. In such cases, your summary will be a paper unto itself (more on this below). More typically, you will read an article or book and identify potentially useful *parts*—a few sentences or paragraphs, perhaps. Later, you might summarize these parts and incorporate them into your papers.

A paraphrase is also an objective restatement of a source, and you use it the same way you do a summary. Paraphrases are more detailed than summaries, however, and sometimes may be the same length of the original passage. Summary and paraphrase are basic to working with sources. Both demonstrate your understanding of what you've read.

Being able to read a passage and summarize or paraphrase what it says is basic to college-level work. But for all kinds of reasons, people don't always read carefully—and in college that's a problem because your academic success depends on your ability to understand source materials: books, scholarly articles, essays and popular articles, research reports, op-eds, and more.

This chapter focuses on reading with attention, so that you will be able to summarize and paraphrase sources as well as quote them in support of the papers you write.

Previewing to Understand the Author's Purpose

1.1 Preview a selection.

Writers of articles and nonfiction books aim to inform, persuade, or some combination of the two. Explanatory writing defines, describes, and is usually information-rich. In explanations, authors do not inject their opinions. By contrast, in persuasive writing, authors attempt to change your thinking about a topic or to convince you that their opinions are the best ones.[1]

Sources will not be all one type or the other. A paper arguing that the government should mandate a reduction in the salt content of commercially prepared foods might first explain how salt intake affects health. The argument would then follow and build on the explanation. In reading any passage of text, determine the extent to which the author is attempting to explain and/or persuade. Imagine placing every source you read somewhere on a continuum:

Explain_____**Persuade**

Ask: Where along this continuum
should I place this source?

---

[1]There is serious academic debate concerning the extent to which *all* writing attempts to persuade. Still, for practical purposes, it is reasonable to say that writing that makes a good-faith effort to emphasize the topic and not the writer's views can be considered explanatory or informational, while writing that promotes the writer's views is persuasive.

Before writing notes on a source, preview it to gain a sense of the whole. Skim the text. Read quickly and identify the author's purpose: to explain and/or persuade.

For an article:
- Read summaries (also called abstracts) if available.
- Read opening and closing paragraphs.
- Read all major headings.
- Read the first line of every paragraph.

For a book:
- Read book jacket information, including the author's biography.
- Read the preface.
- Skim the table of contents.
- Read the first and last paragraph of every chapter.

Let's adapt these strategies to reading and summarizing a single paragraph before applying them to an article-length selection. The following is excerpted from "A Framework for Thinking Ethically."

> **THE UTILITARIAN APPROACH TO ETHICS**
>
> Some [philosophers] emphasize that the ethical action is the one that provides the most good or does the least harm, or, to put it another way, produces the greatest balance of good over harm. The ethical corporate action, then, is the one that produces the greatest good and does the least harm for all who are affected— customers, employees, shareholders, the community, and the environment. Ethical warfare balances the good achieved in ending terrorism with the harm done to all parties through death, injuries, and destruction. The utilitarian approach deals with consequences; it tries both to increase the good done and to reduce the harm done.
>
> —Manuel Velasquez

Let's characterize the author's purpose. To what extent do you find Velasquez explaining? Arguing? Some combination of the two? It should be clear from the first and last sentences as well as from the paragraph's heading (included in the original article) that the author is defining a term: *utilitarianism*. From this brief preview, you've learned enough to write a summary based on your understanding of the author's purpose, topic, and content:

Purpose	to explain
Topic	the philosophy of utilitarianism
Content	maximizing good and minimizing bad
Summary	Utilitarianism is an "[a]pproach to ethics" that seeks to maximize the good effects of our actions over bad effects.

To test the accuracy of this summary, reread the paragraph—this time every word. You'll discover that Velasquez devotes the interior sentences to two examples of utilitarianism, neither of which requires making a change to our summary.

Preview one more paragraph: Read the first and final sentences to determine if you've learned enough to understand the author's purpose, topic, and content.

"Responding to Bullies" [a student paper]

Definitions in antibullying laws are inconsistent, the effectiveness of antibullying programs is unproven, and cyberbullying laws may threaten free speech. Still, bullying persists and we must respond. Each day, 160,000 children skip school because they don't want to confront their tormentors (National). Even bullies are at risk: In one study, over half of the middle-school boys characterized as bullies had court records by their 24th birthday (Fox et al. 2). While bullying in childhood may not be the sole or even main *cause* of later criminal behavior (another possibility: there may be abuse in the home), these statistics provide all the more reason to intervene in the bully/victim relationship. Both victims and bullies require our help.

—Peter Simmons

We learn a great deal from reading the first and last sentences of this paragraph (excerpted from a student paper, which you can find in Chapter 5 on pp. 142–48):

Purpose	to argue—to present data that changes our opinion
Topic	bullying
Content	difficulties dealing effectively with bullies
Summary	The problem of bullying demands an institutional response that has, up to now, been ineffective and has hurt both bullies and their victims.

When you reread the paragraph in full, you find its interior sentences given to evidence that Simmons uses to change our thinking about bullies. Again, what we learn from the interior sentences does not require changes to our summary.

Exercise 1.1

Previewing a Paragraph

Choose a six- to eight-sentence paragraph from an article of interest in a newspaper or magazine (print or online) and preview it as illustrated above. Then summarize that paragraph in a single sentence after noting its purpose, topic, and content.

Now let's apply the previewing strategies to an entire article—concerning the benefits and concerns associated with computer-chip brain implants. For the moment, do not read every word. First, *preview* the article to gain a sense of the author's purpose, topic, and content. Later, you'll return to the selection to read word for word and make notes. As with the paragraphs above, you may be surprised at how much you can learn from a quick preview.

External Enhancements of Memory May Soon Go High-Tech

Jyutika Mehta

December 4, 2015

"Pentagon spurs new work on a brain implant to aid memory problems"

—Headline, *Los Angeles Times*, July 9, 2014

1   Imagine never again forgetting where you parked your car, or that last item you had on your grocery list, or why you walked into this room anyway. If you trust media stories about research currently under way at Defense Advanced Research Projects Agency (DARPA) to build an implantable device to restore memory, you might not have to worry about these memory lapses in the future.

Intro

2   Many neuroscientists share the dream of neuroprosthetic technology that could help damaged brains function. Many such devices are in various stages of experimentation. Beyond helping those with impaired memories, the next step could conceivably be implantable "brain chips" that would improve the memories of the rest of us, ensuring that in the future we never forget anything.

3   But what would it really mean if we were able to remember every single thing?

How brains remember

4   Since the early neurological work on memory in the 1950s and 1960s, studies have demonstrated that memories are not stored in just one part of the brain. They're widely distributed across the whole brain, particularly in an area called the cortex.

To explain

5   Contrary to the popular notion, our memories are not stored in our brains like books on shelves in specific categories. They're actively reconstructed from elements scattered throughout various areas of the cortex by a process called encoding.

6   As we experience the world through our eyes, ears, and so on, various groups of neurons in the cortex fire together to form a neural pathway from each of these senses and encode these patterns into memories. That's why the aroma of cornbread may trigger a Thanksgiving dinner memory at grandmother's house many years ago, or the sound of a car backfiring may trigger a panic attack in a war veteran.

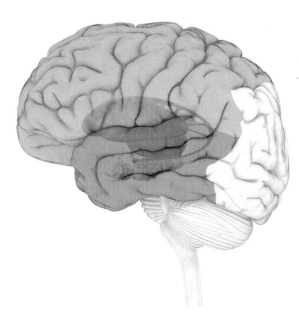

The Human Brain

A structure called the hip- **7** pocampus, located within the cerebral cortex, plays a vital role in memory. We find the hippocampus is damaged in conditions that affect memory such as Alzheimer's disease.

Forgetting, then, is an **8** inability (either temporary or permanent) to retrieve part of the neural pathway that's been encoded in the brain. Increasing forgetfulness is a normal part of the aging process, as the neurons start to lose their connections and pathways start to wither off. Ultimately the brain shrinks and becomes less effective at remembering. The hippocampus is one of the first areas of the brain to deteriorate with age.

Some things are better left forgotten

I believe that forgetting is almost as critical as remembering. **9**

I study the brain and examine how language, communication, and hence memory are **10** represented in the brain and the influence disorders such as stroke and post-traumatic stress disorder (PTSD) have on it. While human memory is dynamic and flexible, it's also susceptible to distortions arising from aging and pathological processes.

But forgetting isn't just a loss that comes with age. It's a normal part of the memory pro- **11** cess. We don't need to remember a lot of what happens to us—what we made for dinner two years ago, where we left the car the last five times we parked in this lot. Those are examples of things that aren't useful to remember anymore.

There's also the question of memories that are actively hindering our lives. Research **12** suggests, and my work with memory-related conditions corroborates, that some people have an inability to forget traumatic events. This characteristic is partially responsible for conditions including depression and PTSD.

When memories of terrible events don't fade naturally, can we move on with our lives? **13**

A patient diagnosed with PTSD-related depression in one of my studies wanted to sup- **14** press all memories of his combat experience. He lost two friends in a particular battle and has had difficulty getting past that experience. It appears that we cannot willfully eliminate memories.

15 **"The mission of the National Center for PTSD is to advance the clinical care and social welfare of America's Veterans and others who have experienced trauma, or who**

16 **suffer from PTSD, through research, education, and training in the science, diagnosis, and treatment of PTSD and stress-related disorders."**

—National Center for PTSD

He tells me that yes, he would like to recall where he put his car keys and would like to remember his children's birthdays, but he would rather eliminate the traumatic memories of his combat experience.

Developing technology for total recall may sound wonderful and time-saving for improving daily living. Never forget an appointment, never spend precious minutes looking for misplaced keys, perhaps never even need a calendar to remember important events. And, of course, an implantable brain chip would be a huge boon for those whose memories have been destroyed by disease or injury. But there's a hitch to total recall that doesn't allow us as individuals and as a society to forget.

17 Perfect memory engenders stasis—the legacy of any failures (personal or in others) won't be allowed to fade and therefore we cannot move past them. Forgetting allows for new beginnings and for personal and societal healing and forgiveness. It is critical for a war veteran to advance past a traumatizing event from the battlefield, or a spouse with hurt feelings to be able to let go of that experience to repair a relationship. We all need to let some memories go; it's part of the process that allows us to appreciate the proverbial forest of our existence while not getting too bogged down with the trees of our daily lives.

18 For better or worse, technology for not ever forgetting may be here sometime soon. Whatever form this imagined external memory enhancement takes, it will be interesting to see how a new way of remembering changes us in return.

19 Perhaps some of us may have to add one more thing to our list—remember to forget.

Forming a Preliminary Understanding of Topic and Purpose

1.2　Form a preliminary understanding of topic and purpose based on your preview.

Based on a quick preview—*skimming,* not word-for-word reading just yet—restate the topic and purpose of the selection in your own words:

> Devices to improve memory and reduce forgetfulness are coming; but we should be cautious in welcoming them because at least some forgetting is a natural part of remembering and may even be beneficial.

Where would you place the article on a continuum ranging from explanatory to persuasive?

Explain_____I_____Persuade

Why did we locate the article at a point *between* Explain and Persuade? As noted earlier, authors often do both in one article, and Jyutika Mehta does so here. Based on a quick preview, we've classified the author's purpose as more explanatory than persuasive. Why?

Even from a brief preview, we can see that Mehta both explains how the brain stores and processes memories and argues that some amount of forgetting is useful. The paragraphs of the selection devoted to storage and processing are informational, while the paragraphs devoted to the usefulness of forgetting express Mehta's opinion. From our brief preview, it's possible to get a clear sense of Mehta's purpose: to both explain *and* argue. Mehta has weighted the article more toward explanation. She is not making a strong argument: for instance, that implanted memory chips are a terrible idea. Rather, she's urging caution. From the preview, then, we can determine purpose, topic, and a general sense of content:

Purpose	to explain *and* argue
Topic	brain implants that enhance memory
Content	pluses and minuses of forgetting and of brain implants that enhance memory
Preliminary Summary	We should respond cautiously to brain implants designed to enhance memory.

Rereading for Content and Structure

1.3   Reread for content and structure.

Once you've previewed a selection, reread it carefully. Read every word, prepared to make notes:

- Label sections. Make margin notes to highlight a reading's main sections—that is, groupings of related paragraphs. (The author may have done this for you by providing headings.)
- Underline or highlight the main idea and supporting ideas of each section.
- Label the thesis. Every selection will have a main point, a thesis. Underline or highlight it.
- Is the author's purpose to inform, to persuade, or both?
  - If the purpose is to inform, identify the topic and its parts. Identify facts, examples, definitions, processes.
  - If the purpose is to persuade, identify the author's claim—the main opinion. Identify reasons and evidence. Is the author arguing based on logic? On emotions?
- Identify what you *don't* understand.

Skim the source once more and review your notes. Distinguish as clearly as you can between what you do and do not understand.

- In two or three sentences, restate the main point.
- Seek other sources to clarify what you do not understand.

Consider how a section of this reading looks after it's been marked up:

How Brains Remember

(4–5) Memory consists of parts distributed throughout brain

4   Since the early neurological work on memory in the 1950s and 1960s, studies have demonstrated that memories are not stored in just one part of the brain. They're widely distributed across the whole brain, particularly in an area called the cortex.

5   Contrary to the popular notion, our memories are not stored in our brains like books on shelves in specific categories. They're actively reconstructed from elements scattered throughout various areas of the cortex by a process called encoding.

(6) Each sense has corresponding brain area to store parts of memories. Connections across parts form memories.

6   As we experience the world through our eyes, ears, and so on, various groups of neurons in the cortex fire together to form a neural pathway from each of these senses and encode these patterns into memories. That's why the aroma of cornbread may trigger a Thanksgiving dinner memory at grandmother's house many years ago, or the sound of a car backfiring may trigger a panic attack in a war veteran.

(7) Disease affects memory

7   A structure called the hippocampus, located within the cerebral cortex, plays a vital role in memory. We find the hippocampus is damaged in conditions that affect memory such as Alzheimer's disease.

(8) Forgetting is natural part of aging. Neural connections break down.

8   Forgetting, then, is an inability (either temporary or permanent) to retrieve part of the neural pathway that's been encoded in the brain. Increasing forgetfulness is a normal part of the aging process, as the neurons start to lose their connections and pathways start to wither off. Ultimately the brain shrinks and becomes less effective at remembering. The hippocampus is one of the first areas of the brain to deteriorate with age.

Exercise 1.2
Marking up a Passage

Reread the opening of the article by Mehta (p. 18) and mark up paragraphs 1–3.

- In the margin, label this opening section "Introduction." Write a few words beneath this label to express the meaning of these paragraphs.
- Underline, circle, or otherwise highlight what you consider important information in these paragraphs.

Reread the end of Mehta's article (p. 20) and mark up paragraphs 18 and 19.

- In the margin, label this section "Conclusion." Write a few words beneath this label to express the meaning of these paragraphs.
- Underline, circle, or otherwise highlight what you consider important information in these paragraphs.

Critical Reading for Summary

- **Examine the context.** Note the credentials, occupation, and publications of the author. Identify the source in which the piece originally appeared. This information helps illuminate the author's perspective on the topic he or she is addressing.

- **Note the title and subtitle.** Some titles are straightforward, whereas the meanings of others become clearer as you read. In either case, titles typically identify the topic being addressed and often reveal the author's attitude toward that topic.

- **Identify the main point.** Whether a piece of writing contains a thesis statement in the first few paragraphs or builds its main point without stating it up front, look at the entire piece to arrive at an understanding of the overall point being made.

- **Identify the subordinate points.** Notice the smaller subpoints that make up the main point, and make sure you understand how they relate to the main point. If a particular subpoint doesn't clearly relate to the main point you've identified, you may need to modify your understanding of the main point.

- **Break the reading into sections.** Notice which paragraphs make up a piece's introduction, body, and conclusion. Break up the body paragraphs into sections that address the writer's various subpoints.

- **Distinguish between points, examples, counterarguments.** Critical reading requires careful attention to what a writer is doing as well as what he or she is saying. When a writer quotes someone else or relays an example of something, ask yourself why this is being done. What point is the example supporting? Is another source being quoted as support for a point or as a counterargument that the writer sets out to address?

- **Watch for transitions within and between paragraphs.** In order to follow the logic of a piece of writing, as well as to distinguish between points, examples, and counterarguments, pay attention to the transitional words and phrases writers use. Transitions function like road signs, preparing the reader for what's next.

- **Read actively and recursively.** Don't treat reading as a passive, linear progression through a text. Instead, read as though you are engaged in a dialogue with the writer: Ask questions of the text as you read, make notes in the margin, underline key ideas in pencil, put question or exclamation marks next to passages that confuse or excite you. Go back to earlier points once you finish a reading, stop during your reading to recap what's come so far, and move back and forth through a text.

Summarizing and Paraphrasing *Parts* of Sources

1.4   **Summarize and paraphrase parts of sources.**

Summarizing *Parts* of Sources

To write a summary of a few sentences or paragraphs, follow these steps:

1. Identify the *part* of the source you want to use.

2. Decide whether you want to summarize, paraphrase, or quote from the source.

3. State as briefly as possible your understanding of the author's point.
   - Condense lists into phrases (a list of governors, for example, could be condensed to *current governors*).
   - Reduce multiple examples to a single example (or eliminate examples altogether).
   - Condense stages of a detailed process to a single, descriptive statement.

4. Use your own words. (Quote an occasional word or brief phrase.)

5. Use your own sentence structure. Do not copy the author's sentence structure, substituting your words for the author's.

6. Credit the author. See Chapter 7 for details on citation format.

Here's a paragraph (from a lengthy article) used as a source for a paper on using computers to rebuild distressed communities:

ORIGINAL PASSAGE

In the United States, communities seem to be deteriorating from a complex combination of causes. In the inner cities of big urban centers, many people fear street crime and stay off the streets at night. In the larger suburban and post-suburban areas, many people hardly know their neighbors and "latch key" children often have little adult contact after school. An African proverb which says that "it takes a whole village to raise a child" refers to a rich community life with a sense of mutual responsibility that is difficult to find in many new neighborhoods. . . . Some advocates believe that computer technology in concert with other efforts could play a role in rebuilding community life by improving communication, economic opportunity, civic participation, and education.

—Rob Kling, "Social Relationships in Electronic Forums"

Here's a summary of the source as it might appear on a digital note card:

COMPUTER POWER TO HELP HEAL BROKEN COMMUNITIES

Using tech tools to communicate may keep people talking within communities that are in decline. A community depends on people acting in the interests of neighbors for the common good. Computers can be part of the solution for rebuilding. (Kling 439)

And here's how this summary (highlighted) might appear in a paper titled "Re-imagining Our Neighborhoods." Notice the citation, which combines the source author's name in the lead-up to the summary and a page reference.

In a pattern that's all too common, the character of a neighborhood can quickly change when good jobs disappear. Neighborhoods once anchored by middle-class manufacturing work disintegrate as homeowners are laid off. Unable to pay the mortgage, people abandon their homes and urban blight sets in, both physical and social. Houses with weed-choked lots and boarded-up windows form the outward signs of decline. Those who remain give up on their neighborhood. They might stop visiting on summer evenings or stop calling to see if everything's okay when a walkway goes unshoveled in winter. Hope may be on the way, however, in programs that introduce computers to marginal neighborhoods. According to sociologist Rob Kling, using computers to communicate may keep people talking within communities that are in decline. A community, after all, is built on people acting in the interests of neighbors for the common good. Computers can be part of the solution for rebuilding (439).

In one neighborhood in Detroit, . . .

CAN A SUMMARY BE OBJECTIVE?   By definition, writing a summary requires you to select and restate some parts of the original source and leave out other parts. Deciding what to select and what to leave out calls for your personal judgment, so a summary is in one sense a work of interpretation. And certainly your interpretation of a passage may differ from another person's.

One factor affecting the nature and quality of your interpretation is prior knowledge. If you're new to the subject of anthropology, say, and you're summarizing a journal article in that field, your summary will likely differ from that of your professor. She's an expert, after all, who will have a much clearer sense of what information is crucial and should be included in a summary.

Still, one must begin somewhere. Every expert at some point was a novice. As you gain experience in a subject area, you'll gain in confidence and accuracy. In most cases it's possible to produce a reasonably objective, and accurate, summary of a passage if you read with attention and make a conscious, good-faith effort to be unbiased—which means not allowing your own feelings on the subject to distort your account of the text.

When to Summarize and Paraphrase

Summarize:

- To present main points of a lengthy passage (article or book)
- To condense long lists or other details

Paraphrase:

- To clarify a short or complex passage
- To emphasize main points

Paraphrasing *Parts* of Sources

Paraphrase a passage when you want to preserve all (or virtually all) the points, major and minor, of a brief original passage and when, for clarity (perhaps the language of the original is especially complex), you want to communicate the ideas in your own words. To avoid plagiarism when paraphrasing, bear two principles in mind:

1. Use your own words. Quote only an occasional word or brief phrase, if needed.

2. Use your own sentence structure. Do not reproduce the author's sentence structure.

ORIGINAL PASSAGE

We have found out that the distortion in dreams which hinders our understanding of them is due to the activities of a censorship, directed against the unacceptable, unconscious wish-impulses.

—Sigmund Freud

Here's a paraphrase as it might appear on a digital note card. As you can see, it is as long as Freud's original passage.

CENSORSHIP OF DREAMS

It is difficult to understand dreams because they contain distortions. Freud believed that these distortions arise from our internal censor, which attempts to suppress unconscious and forbidden thoughts.

You incorporate paraphrases into your writing just as you do summaries, as illustrated above.

Summarizing Entire Works

1.5 Summarize entire works using a systematic strategy.

Sometimes you will be asked to write stand-alone summaries—brief papers that summarize an entire source. For instance, an instructor may ask you to summarize a lecture, an article, or a book in order to assess your level of understanding. Here are three typical assignments that call for a summary:

Film Studies Summarize Harvey Greenberg's essay on the film classic *King Kong*.

Mathematics Read "Structuring Mathematical Proofs" by Uri Leron [*The American Mathematical Monthly* 90 (March 1983): 174–85]. In two to four pages, summarize the concept of linear proof, giving one good example from this course.

Psychology Summarize Leon Festinger's theory of cognitive dissonance.

Guidelines for Writing Summaries

- **Read the passage carefully.** Determine its structure. Identify the author's purpose in writing. (This will help you distinguish between more important and less important information.) Make a note in the margin when you get confused or when you think something is important; highlight or underline points sparingly, if at all.

- **Reread.** This time divide the passage into sections or stages of thought. The author's use of paragraphing will often be a useful guide. Label, on the passage itself, each section or stage of thought. Underline key ideas and terms. Write notes in the margin.

- **Write one-sentence summaries,** on a separate sheet of paper, of each stage of thought.

- **Write a thesis—a one- or two-sentence summary of the entire passage.** The thesis should express the central idea of the passage, as you have determined it from the preceding steps. You may find it useful to follow the approach of most newspaper stories—naming the what, who, why, where, when, and how of the matter. For persuasive passages, summarize in a sentence the author's conclusion. For descriptive passages, indicate the subject of the description and its key feature(s). *Note:* In some cases, a suitable thesis may already be in the original passage. If so, you may want to quote it directly in your summary.

- **Write the first draft of your summary** by (1) combining the thesis with your list of one-sentence summaries or (2) combining the thesis with one-sentence summaries plus significant details from the passage. In either case, eliminate repetition and less important information. Disregard minor details or generalize them (e.g., George W. Bush and Barack Obama might be generalized as "recent presidents"). Use as few words as possible to convey the main ideas.

- **Check your summary against the original passage** and make whatever adjustments are necessary for accuracy and completeness.

- **Revise your summary,** inserting transitional words and phrases where necessary to ensure coherence. Check for style. Avoid a series of short, choppy sentences. Combine sentences for a smooth, logical flow of ideas. Check for grammatical correctness, punctuation, and spelling.

Read, Reread, and Highlight

Here are three goals in writing a stand-alone summary:

1. To state the author's thesis.
2. To state the author's purpose (which will usually be to inform or argue).
3. To state the main ideas that support the thesis.

As we've seen, achieving these goals requires reading with attention. Before summarizing a source, underline key phrases or sentences; circle important words; at each paragraph, write three- to five-word summaries in the margin. If the author has grouped paragraphs according to specific ideas, give these groupings a label. (The writer may already identify such sections for you by providing headings.) See, for example, Jyutika Mehta's article on digital memory enhancements, pages 18–20. Note the use of margin notes and highlights.

Divide into Stages of Thought and Write a Brief Summary of Each Stage of Thought

Before writing a summary, review the sections you've identified and labeled (if the source author has not already provided headings). For each section, convert your margin notes to sentences. Mehta labeled two main sections of her article: "How brains remember" and "Some things are better left forgotten." In addition to these we've labeled the opening and closing sections "Introduction" and "Conclusion." Here are the four sections headings for her article, along with sentences of summary for each:

> Introduction: paragraphs 1–3
>
> | Devices to enhance memory are coming. Just as prosthetic limbs improve the function of people who have lost an arm or leg, "neuroprosthetic technology" holds the potential to improve the function of those with diminished memories.

> Section 1: How brains remember, paragraphs 4–8
>
> | The brain does not store memories whole "like books on shelves." Rather, it "widely distribute[s]" the constituent parts of memories to various areas associated with functions like sight and smell. A memory is "encode[d]" through connections among areas and can be lost when these connections break down due to disease or the natural aging process.

> Section 2: Some things are better left forgotten, paragraphs 9–15
>
> | Mehta claims that "forgetting is almost as critical as remembering" both in terms of what we typically and usefully forget and what we can't forget. We don't need to remember insignificant details (like what we ate for dinner years ago). At the same time, traumas we can't forget can disrupt our lives. Soldiers who can't forget deadly battles can suffer from depression.

> Conclusion: paragraphs 16–19
>
> | Brain chips to enhance memory could benefit people, but we should be cautious because, while forgetting can be useful, perfect memory comes with potential problems. Enhanced memories could relieve us of tedious problems like misplacing keys and could also restore function to people with damaged brains. Yet forgetting has its uses in allowing traumatized people and societies to move on from a painful past to new beginnings. Even as they improve our memories, we may need for our own good to "remember to forget."

Write a Thesis: A Brief Summary of the Entire Passage

The thesis is the statement that announces a paper's subject and the claim that you or—in the case of a summary—a source author will be making about that subject. It is the one-sentence conclusion, or main idea, of the selection. The thesis will be the most general statement of your summary and (absent details, of course) can serve *as* a summary.

Every selection you read will have a thesis, a main point. Begin the summary paper with *your* summary of the author's thesis. The thesis may be located at the beginning of the work. This is called a *deductive* organization: main idea first, supporting details following. The author may locate the thesis at the end of the work: specific details first, leading to the main idea. This is called an *inductive* organization. The author might also locate the thesis anywhere between the beginning and the end.

Here's our summary of Jyutika Mehta's thesis for her article on implantable memory devices:

> **Our Thesis:** In the online journal *The Conversation*, brain and communications researcher Jyutika Mehta reports that devices to reduce forgetfulness are coming and advises that we respond cautiously because at least some forgetting is a natural, beneficial part of remembering.

Your brief restatement of the author's thesis is the most important sentence of your summary, and you should rewrite as necessary until you've accurately distilled the author's main idea. (We revised the thesis of Mehta's article three times before settling on the version above.)

Draft 1:   Forgetting is important to memory.
Problem: Statement makes no mention of devices to enhance memory.

Draft 2:   Devices to improve memory are coming, but we should be cautious in welcoming them.
Problem: Better because it introduces Mehta's caution. But there's no attempt to *explain* the caution.

Draft 3:   Devices to reduce forgetfulness are coming, but we should be cautious in welcoming them because at least some forgetting is a natural, beneficial part of remembering.
Problem: No mention of author or source.

Write Your Summary

To organize your summary, join paragraph or section summaries to your version of the thesis. After placing these sentences into paragraph form, revise to ensure the smooth flow of ideas and to eliminate redundancy. Match the length of your summary to your intended use of the summary. As a general rule, the longest summaries should be no longer than one-fourth the length of the original source. If you are summarizing a book, a book chapter, or an especially long article, your summary should be quite a bit shorter than that.

WRITE A ONE- OR TWO-SENTENCE SUMMARY. The briefest summary would consist of the thesis only—and, possibly, a brief expansion to essential points of the passage. You might use a one-sentence summary to introduce a quotation or to make a brief reference to a source.

WRITE A MIDDLE-LENGTH SUMMARY. When you devote a paragraph or more to discussing a source, you may want to introduce it with a longer summary. Follow the thesis with section summaries. You'll likely need to revise to ensure smooth flow among and to eliminate repetition. Note that we've highlighted transitions.

A Summary of "External Enhancements of Memory May Soon Go High-Tech" by Jyutika Mehta

In the online journal *The Conversation*, brain and communications researcher Jyutika Mehta reports that devices to reduce forgetfulness are coming and advises that we respond cautiously because at least some forgetting is a natural, beneficial part of remembering. The promise of enhanced memory is enormous: Just as prosthetic limbs improve the function of people who have lost an arm or leg, "neuroprosthetic technology" holds out the potential to improve the function of those with diminished memories. The brain, Mehta explains, does not store memories whole "like books on shelves." Rather, it "widely distribute[s]" the constituent parts of memories to various areas associated with functions like sight and smell. A memory is "encode[d]" through connections among areas and can be lost when these connections break down due to disease or the natural aging process. Mehta claims that "forgetting is almost as critical as remembering" both in terms of what we typically and usefully forget and what we can't. We don't need to remember insignificant details like what we ate for dinner years ago. At the same time, traumas we can't forget can disrupt our lives. For instance, soldiers who can't forget deadly battles can suffer from depression or PTSD. Brain chips to enhance memory could benefit many, but we should be cautious about such technology because perfect memory comes with potential problems. True, enhanced memories could relieve us of tedious problems like misplacing keys and could also restore function to people with damaged brains. Yet forgetting has its uses, allowing people and entire societies to move on from painful pasts to new beginnings. Even as technologies that enhance memories improve our memories, for our own good we may need to "remember to forget."

WRITE AN EXPANDED SUMMARY.   A third, more detailed kind of summary consists of a thesis followed by summaries of most of the selection's paragraphs. Use an expanded summary when you intend to devote significant discussion to the source—if, for instance, you are planning to evaluate it. In this case you would summarize more closely, including more details so that you would introduce each point thoroughly (and neutrally) before evaluating it. This is the approach taken by the student who wrote the model critique in Chapter 2. In that paper, the writer devotes three full paragraphs of summary to the article she is evaluating. The point to remember is that a summary has no fixed length (although by definition it is a *brief* restatement); rather, you should expand it and trim it according to your needs.

Where Do We Find Written Summaries?

Here are just a few of the types of writing that involve summary:

Academic Writing

- **Critique papers.** Summarize material in order to critique it.
- **Synthesis papers.** Summarize to show relationships between sources.
- **Analysis papers.** Summarize theoretical perspectives before applying them.
- **Research papers.** Note taking and reporting research require summary.
- **Literature reviews.** Overviews of work presented in brief summaries.
- **Argument papers.** Summarize evidence and opposing arguments.
- **Essay exams.** Demonstrate understanding of course materials through summary.

Workplace Writing

- **Policy briefs.** Condense complex public policy.
- **Business plans.** Summarize costs, relevant environmental impacts, and other important matters.
- **Memos, letters, and reports.** Summarize procedures, meetings, product assessments, expenditures, and more.
- **Medical charts.** Record patient data in summarized form.
- **Legal briefs.** Summarize relevant facts of cases.

Summarizing Challenging Sources

1.6   Write a summary of an especially challenging source.

Inevitably, you will encounter readings that challenge you—that on first glance may seem too difficult or too long for easy comprehension. When you encounter such material, use the skills learned above on attentive reading and the skills learned here to read and understand, and then demonstrate your understanding by writing a summary. Take heart: If you work systematically, you will make progress. Remember that you don't need to read a difficult source all in one sitting. If, in previewing the selection, you can identify sections (or if the author has labeled sections), read and make margin notes for one section at a sitting. Return to the assignment regularly, reading a section (or two) at a time, and soon enough you'll have completed the task.

In "The Baby in the Well," by Paul Bloom, we find a fascinating but challenging essay on the topic of "empathy": the ability to imagine yourself in someone else's circumstance and "feel his or her pain." We've eased the difficulty of the piece in three ways:

- Leading off with a summary
- Providing section headings, which do not appear in the original *New Yorker* essay
- Highlighting the thesis

When encountering challenging selections on your own, you won't have the benefit of these aids—although authors will, on occasion, divide their work with section headings. Still, by reading systematically, you *can* take on difficult material and understand it.

Reading and Summarizing Challenging Sources

- Use your preview skills.

- Realize you may not complete your reading in one sitting.

- Expect to be confused. When you encounter sentences that confuse you, reread them. Place a question mark in the margin. Move on—and when you complete your reading, revisit passages you've highlighted with a question mark.

- Identifying sections as you read—groupings of related paragraphs—is a key to understanding: The better you can divide the whole into parts, distinguishing main ideas from supporting ideas, the clearer the entire piece will be.

Demonstration Summary of Paul Bloom's "The Baby in the Well"

Read this summary of "The Baby in the Well" before reading the essay itself. After reading, you can follow the process of how we wrote section summaries and prepared to write the summary.

In "The Baby in the Well: The Case against Empathy," Paul Bloom argues that, while empathy is important in fostering positive human relationships, we should prefer reason as a guide to social policy because empathy's focus on the distress of one individual may blind us to the suffering of thousands whose names and faces we do not know. Bloom begins with an uncontroversial point: Many believe that what makes us moral beings is empathy, the ability to see the world from others' points of view, to feel their pain and distress, and to feel the impulse to help them. Most people are capable of empathy, a quality Bloom believes is necessary not only for human progress but also for the survival of our species.

There is a downside to empathy, however: Empathy tends to focus on the distress of individuals or relatively small groups of individuals whose names and faces we know, a phenomenon known as the "identifiable victim effect." But the same people who feel empathetic toward individuals can be oblivious to large-scale catastrophes such as genocide, mass starvation, and deaths due to preventable illnesses as well as to routine homicides that occur in the thousands every year. Because our empathetic impulses may overpower our "dispassionate analysis of a situation," empathy can "lead us astray." When we act only on impulses of empathy, we may help a relatively small number of identifiable individuals, but we often ignore many other individuals who don't have "names or stories" or with whose political values we don't sympathize.

> For this reason, good moral judgment often requires us to put empathy aside; to assume that all lives have the same value; and to use qualities like "prudence, reason, fairness [and] self-control" to plan for the well-being of humanity as a whole. Of course, no one wants to live in a world without empathy. As a moral guide, however, empathy should "yield to reason." Our generous assistance to the few is often wasted. But assistance to the many, "guided by deliberation and calculation," is essential for the future well-being of the billions of people who constitute humankind.

Before reading a challenging selection word for word, PREVIEW it.

- Read the title: if you do not understand every word in the title, consult a dictionary. In this example, do not proceed until you understand the word *empathy.*
- Read the entire first paragraph.
- Read the first sentence of every subsequent paragraph.
- Read the full final paragraph.

After you have previewed the selection, reread with attention. This time divide the passage into sections or stages of thought if the author has not already done this. The author's use of paragraphing will often be a useful guide. On the passage itself, label each section or stage of thought. Underline key ideas and terms. Write notes in the margin. *Note:* The section headings we provided to aid your reading do not appear in the original *New Yorker* essay.

The Baby in the Well: The Case against Empathy*

—Paul Bloom

Paul Bloom, professor of psychology and cognitive science at Yale University, is also co-editor-in-chief of the scientific journal Behavioral and Brain Sciences. *He is the author of numerous articles and books, including* How Children Learn the Meaning of Words *(2000) and* How Pleasure Works: The New Science of How We Like What We Like *(2010). This article appeared in* The New Yorker *on May 20, 2013.*

In 2008, Karina Encarnacion, an eight-year-old girl from Missouri, wrote to President-elect Barack Obama with some advice about what kind of dog he should get for his daughters. She also suggested that he enforce recycling and ban unnecessary wars. Obama wrote to thank her, and offered some advice of his own: "If you don't already know what it means, I want you to look up the word 'empathy' in the dictionary. I believe we don't have enough empathy in our world today, and it is up to your generation to change that."

1   SECTION 1: Definition and importance of empathy.

2   This wasn't the first time Obama had spoken up for empathy. Two years earlier, in a commencement address at Xavier University, he discussed the importance of being able "to see the world through the eyes of those who are different from us—the child who's hungry, the steelworker who's been laid off, the family who lost the entire life they built together when the storm came to town." He went on, "When you think like this—when you choose to broaden your ambit of concern and empathize with the plight of others, whether they are close friends or distant strangers—it becomes harder not to act, harder not to help."

3   The word "empathy"—a rendering of the German *Einfühlung*, "feeling into"—is only a century old, but people have been interested for a long time in the moral implications of feeling our way into the lives of others. In "The Theory of Moral Sentiments" (1759), Adam Smith observed that sensory experience alone could not spur us toward sympathetic engagement with others: "Though our brother is upon the rack, as long as we ourselves are at our ease, our senses will never inform us of what he suffers." For Smith, what made us moral beings was the imaginative capacity to "place ourselves in his situation . . . and become in some measure the same person with him, and thence form some idea of his sensations, and even feel something which, though weaker in degree, is not altogether unlike them."

4   In this sense, empathy is an instinctive mirroring of others' experience—James Bond gets his testicles mashed in "Casino Royale," and male moviegoers grimace and cross their legs. Smith talks of how "persons of delicate fibres" who notice a beggar's sores and ulcers "are apt to feel an itching or uneasy sensation in the correspondent part of their own bodies." There is now widespread support, in the social sciences, for what the psychologist C. Daniel Batson calls "the empathy-altruism hypothesis." Batson has found that simply instructing his subjects to take another's perspective made them more caring and more likely to help.

SECTION 2:
Empathy
necessary to
human survival?

5   **"The word 'empathy' . . . is only a century old, but people have been interested for a long time in the moral implications of feeling our way into the lives of others."**

Empathy research is thriving these days, as cognitive neuroscience undergoes what some call an "affective revolution." There is increasing focus on the emotions, especially those involved in moral thought and action. We've learned, for instance, that some of the same neural systems that are active when we are in pain become engaged when we observe the suffering of others. Other researchers are exploring how empathy emerges in chimpanzee and other primates, how it flowers in young children, and the sort of circumstances that trigger it.

6   This interest isn't just theoretical. If we can figure out how empathy works, we might be able to produce more of it. Some individuals stanch their empathy through the deliberate endorsement of political or religious ideologies that promote cruelty toward their adversaries, while others are deficient because of bad genes, abusive parenting, brutal experience, or the usual unhappy goulash of all of the above. At an extreme lie the 1 percent or so of people who are clinically described as psychopaths. A standard checklist for the condition includes "callousness; lack of empathy"; many other distinguishing psychopathic traits, like lack of guilt and pathological lying, surely stem from this fundamental deficit. Some blame the empathy-deficient for much of the suffering in the world. In *The Science of Evil: On Empathy and the Origins of Cruelty* (Basic Books), Simon Baron-Cohen goes so far as to equate evil with "empathy erosion."

In a thoughtful new book on bullying, *Sticks and Stones* (Random House), Emily Bazelon **7**
writes, "The scariest aspect of bullying is the utter lack of empathy"—a diagnosis that she
applies not only to the bullies but also to those who do nothing to help the victims. Few of
those involved in bullying, she cautions, will turn into full-blown psychopaths. Rather, the
empathy gap is situational: Bullies have come to see their victims as worthless; they have
chosen to shut down their empathetic responses. But most will outgrow—and perhaps
regret—their terrible behavior. "The key is to remember that almost everyone has the capacity
for empathy and decency—and to tend that seed as best as we possibly can," she maintains.

Two other recent books, *The Empathic Civilization* (Penguin), by Jeremy Rifkin, and **8**
Humanity on a Tightrope (Rowman & Littlefield), by Paul R. Ehrlich and Robert E. Ornstein,
make the powerful argument that empathy has been the main driver of human progress, and
that we need more of it if our species is to survive. Ehrlich and Ornstein want us "to emotionally
join a global family." Rifkin calls for us to make the leap to "global empathic consciousness." He
sees this as the last best hope for saving the world from environmental destruction, and concludes with the plaintive question "Can we reach biosphere consciousness and global empathy
in time to avoid planetary collapse?" These are sophisticated books, which provide extensive
and accessible reviews of the scholarly literature on empathy. And, as befits the spirit of the
times, they enthusiastically champion an increase in empathy as a cure for humanity's ills.

This enthusiasm may be misplaced, however. Empathy has some unfortunate features— **9**
it is parochial, narrow-minded, and innumerate.[2] We're often at our best when we're smart
enough not to rely on it.

In 1949, Kathy Fiscus, a three-year-old girl, fell into a well in San Marino, California, and **10**
the entire nation was captivated by concern. Four decades later, America was transfixed by
the plight of Jessica McClure—Baby Jessica—the eighteen-month-old who fell into a narrow
well in Texas, in October 1987, triggering a fifty-eight-hour rescue operation. "Everybody in
America became godmothers and godfathers of Jessica while this was going on," President
Reagan remarked.

The immense power of empathy has been demonstrated again and again. It is why **11**
Americans were riveted by the fate of Natalee Holloway, the teenager who went missing in
Aruba, in 2005. It's why, in the wake of widely reported tragedies and disasters—the tsunami
of 2004, Hurricane Katrina the year after, or Sandy [in 2012]—people gave time, money, and
even blood. It's why, last December [2012], when twenty children were murdered at Sandy
Hook Elementary School, in Newtown, Connecticut, there was a widespread sense of grief,
and an intense desire to help. Last month [April 2013], of course, saw a similar outpouring of
support for the victims of the Boston Marathon bombing.

Why do people respond to these misfortunes and not to others? The psychologist Paul **12**
Slovic points out that, when Holloway disappeared, the story of her plight took up far more
television time than the concurrent genocide in Darfur. Each day, more than ten times the
number of people who died in Hurricane Katrina die because of preventable diseases, and
more than thirteen times as many perish from malnutrition.

SECTION 3: The
problem with
empathy: Its
focus on
"babies in
wells."

SECTION 4:
How empathy
operates.

---

[2]By *innumerate,* Bloom means unable to think quantitatively, especially in terms of conceiving or appreciating large numbers. Used in this context, *innumerate* means unable to conceive of the great numbers of
people who are or will become victims of natural or human-made disasters.

13   There is, of course, the attention-getting power of new events. Just as we can come to ignore the hum of traffic, we become oblivious of problems that seem unrelenting, like the starvation of children in Africa—or homicide in the United States. In the past three decades, there were some sixty mass shootings, causing about five hundred deaths; that is, about one-tenth of 1 percent of the homicides in America. But mass murders get splashed onto television screens, newspaper headlines, and the Web; the biggest ones settle into our collective memory—Columbine, Virginia Tech, Aurora, Sandy Hook. The 99.9 percent of other homicides are, unless the victim is someone you've heard of, mere background noise.

14   The key to engaging empathy is what has been called "the identifiable victim effect." As the economist Thomas Schelling, writing forty-five years ago, mordantly observed, "Let a six-year-old girl with brown hair need thousands of dollars for an operation that will prolong her life until Christmas, and the post office will be swamped with nickels and dimes to save her. But let it be reported that without a sales tax the hospital facilities of Massachusetts will deteriorate and cause a barely perceptible increase in preventable deaths—not many will drop a tear or reach for their checkbooks."

15   You can see the effect in the lab. The psychologists Tehila Kogut and Ilana Ritov asked some subjects how much money they would give to help develop a drug that would save the life of one child, and asked others how much they would give to save eight children. The answers were about the same. But when Kogut and Ritov told a third group a child's name and age, and showed her picture, the donations shot up—now there were far more to the one than to the eight.

16   The number of victims hardly matters—there is little psychological difference between hearing about the suffering of five thousand and that of five hundred thousand. Imagine reading that two thousand people just died in an earthquake in a remote country, and then discovering that the actual number of deaths was twenty thousand. Do you now feel ten times worse? To the extent that we can recognize the numbers as significant, it's because of reason, not empathy.

SECTION 5: How empathy leads us astray.

17   In the broader context of humanitarianism, as critics like Linda Polman have pointed out, the empathetic reflex can lead us astray. When the perpetrators of violence profit from aid—as in the "taxes" that warlords often demand from international relief agencies—they are actually given an incentive to commit further atrocities. It is similar to the practice of some parents in India who mutilate their children at birth in order to make them more effective beggars. The children's debilities tug at our hearts, but a more dispassionate analysis of the situation is necessary if we are going to do anything meaningful to prevent them.

18   **"A 'politics of empathy' doesn't provide much clarity in the public sphere."**   A "politics of empathy" doesn't provide much clarity in the public sphere, either. Typically, political disputes involve a disagreement over whom we should empathize *with*. Liberals argue for gun control, for example, by focusing on the victims of gun violence; conservatives point to the unarmed victims of crime, defenseless against the savagery of others. Liberals in favor of tightening federally enforced safety regulations invoke the employee struggling with work-related injuries; their conservative counterparts talk about the small businessman bankrupted by onerous requirements. So don't suppose that if your ideological opponents could only ramp up their empathy they would think just like you.

PART 1

Los Angeles Times

EQUAL — RIGHTS
LIBERTY UNDER THE LAW — TRUE INDUSTRIAL FREEDOM

ALL THE NEWS
ALL THE TIME

VOL. LXVIII | C C ★ | MONDAY MORNING, APRIL 11, 1949 | DAILY, SEVEN CENTS

KATHY'S BODY TAKEN FROM SHAFT

Church Blast Kills Six and Injures 50

Furnace Explosion Pulls Down Roof on Sunday Throng

MARION, S.D., April 10 (AP)—The St. Mary's Catholic Church blew up today while it was partly filled with Palm Sunday worshipers. Six persons were killed and at least 50 injured when the roof and brick walls came tumbling down upon them as they knelt in their pews.

Many more escaped injury because they were in front of the church enjoying the sunshine waiting for the bell to call them to worship. About 75 persons were in their seats.

It was just before the 9 a.m. Mass was to begin.

The Rev. Joseph Zimmerman, 73, pastor for the parish of Marion and Monroe, waited in the sacristy to enter the altar, banked with palm leaves.

Walls Blown Out

Some of the parishioners complained it was cold in the church. Phil Wachendorf, a car dealer who had helped the church obtain a bottle-fuel furnace a few years ago, volunteered to go to the basement and turn it on. The janitor had gone outside to ring the bell.

Wachendorf, speaking from his hospital bed in Sioux Falls, said he threw the furnace's switch and "everything blew out."

The whole building shook, and then bricks and timbers showered down upon the congregation. Wachendorf, badly hurt and his hands burned, managed to crawl out of the basement through a hole in the wreckage.

The force of the blast caved in the roof and blew out the walls. There was a small fire, but it was extinguished quickly.

The sound of the explosion, plus the screams of injured and trapped persons, attracted the attention of nearly every person in this farm town of 775 people.

Bodies Found

They rushed to the crumbled church and began to dig in the rubble. The only part of the building that remained standing was some of the wall around the altar and the choir space.

Father Zimmerman had been trapped by debris falling into the sacristy. Helped out, he escaped with a broken rib and cuts. Then he assisted rescue operations.

Found were the bodies of Mr. and Mrs. John Marson, Mrs. Peter Redding, Mrs. George Bittner and Mrs. Philip Luke, all of Marion, and Charles McGinnis of Monroe. All were in their 60s or 70s.

Hospital Jammed

Ambulances and doctors rushed to from all surrounding communities. Private cars were commandeered to take injured to Sioux Falls and Mitchell, the closest cities with good hospital facilities. Each is about 40 miles from Marion.

The Chicago, Milwaukee, St. Paul & Pacific Railroad provided a special train to carry the injured to Mitchell.

The injured arrived at hospitals so fast, there was no accurate count of the number.

One eyewitness was Miss Agnes

Turn to Page 10, Column 4

FEATURES INDEX

U.S. Troop Increase in Europe Suggested

Secretary of the Army Royall says European leaders stress importance of ground forces in defense planning. They urge necessity of increasing American forces there. See Page 10, Part I.

On Other Pages

AMUSEMENTS: Page 7, Part III.
BRADY: Page 7, Part III.
CLASSIFIED: Pages 10 to 19, Part III.
COLBY: Page 4, Part III.
COMICS: Page 8, Part III.
CROSSWORD: Page 19, Part III.
DICK TRACY CONTEST: Page 4, Part IV.
HOPPER: Page 6, Part III.
M'LEMORE: Page 12, Part I.
POLYROODES: Page 21, Part III.
RADIO: Page 8, Part III.
SHIPPING: Page 20, Part III.
SOUTHLAND: Page 22, Part I.
SPORTS: Part IV.
VITAL RECORD: Page 10, Part III.
WEATHER: Page 19, Part III.
WOMEN: Part III.

LAST TRIP—The body of little Kathy Fiscus is brought to the surface in the tired arms of Bill Yancey—the first man down last night and the last to come up. The fatigued but eager crews still stood ready to render any service for her—even now. *Times Photo*

KATHY—This snapshot, taken last December of the laughing San Marino child, was then of interest mostly to her parents—whose grief the whole nation now shares.

WARMEST DAY OF YEAR KEEPS LIFEGUARDS BUSY

Los Angeles' warmest day since last Oct. 22 sent thousands to the beaches yesterday and gave lifeguards their busiest day in two years.

In the South Bay area, from El Porto Beach to Palos Verdes, 143 rescues were made, according to Lt. Bill Stidham of the Los Angeles County Lifeguards.

Stidham said 23 first-aid cases were treated and 11 lost children returned to their parents.

By midmorning the temperature reached 88 deg.—the maximum. Low was 51. All time record for April 10 is 96 deg., in 1904.

Another warm day is in store for today, the weatherman predicted.

THOUSANDS OF DP'S IN ANTI-RED RIOT

MUNICH, April 10 (AP)—Thousands of displaced persons engaged in a riotous demonstration against Russia today.

American military police dispersed the crowd by using tear gas. An estimated 10,000 persons art in the de-   ation

German police saw the crow∂ was protesting tunn∙l prevention of churches. The demonstrators marched through Munich's streets and attempted, police said, to break into a building housing a Soviet Union mission.

At least five persons were reported injured. Several persons were detained for questioning. The marchers were said to consist mostly of Ukrainians.

Cossacks in Van

The procession was led by seven Cossacks carrying a Cossack flag. Many Ukrainians and Cossacks outside Russia have opposed the Soviet regime since the Bolshevik revolution of 1917.

Witnesses said American military police with armored cars prevented the crowd from breaking into the Soviet mission building. The displaced persons grabbed stones from ruined buildings and threw the Americans. Then the American MPs used tear gas in routing the crowd.

The demonstration started with a mass meeting in Munich's Koe-   nigsplatz. The crowd then was estimated at 10,000, but it had dwindled some by the time the Americans intervened.

The crowd, whipped up by two hours of oratory, set out in an unorganized procession. En route they spotted some "known Communist" agents, a w�tness   said.

After   a   w�   ∙ Sh: went ag∙∂n∂∂   ∂∂∙ hu∙ but word of her plight and ∙∙∙ ∙   each the harb∂s ∂ew until two hours later.

Forty-five persons were aboard the vessel, including refugees bound for the United States from Burma.

SPORTS SECTION IN WHITE TODAY

Due to mechanical limitations involved in publication of an unusually large paper—56 pages—the sports section in today's Times appears in white instead of its customary green. For the convenience of readers it is published as usual in a four-page separate section which can be removed. It will be found inserted between Pages 22 and 23, Part I.

Grounded Ship Awaits Rescue by Coast Guard

A Coast Guard ship and a salvage tug late last night were standing by the SS Steel Chemist, 15,000-ton freighter, aground at the south end of San Nicholas Island, 90 miles off the Southern California coast.

A hole was stove in the Isthmian Line vessel when she struck the rocks in a dense fog, but she was in no grave danger, agents of the company said, although losing fuel.

The Coast Guard buoy tender Diligence and the tug Kanak attempted to float the ship off the rocks at high tide during the night, but the effort was unsuccessful.

Second Tug Due

A second tug, the Viking, was expected to arrive at the scene before dawn today for a second attempt to refloat the freighter.

The 465-foot craft was bound for Los Angeles-Long Beach Harbor from the Far East and Honolulu with a heavy cargo of Ha-   saltp∙, suc∂∙ ∂∂ hol f∙∂∙

Shotgun Blast Kills Man on Fishing Boat

A man identified as Harry Anderson, about 45, of 2165 Clifton Ave. was killed by an accidental shotgun blast aboard a small fishing boat in Pyramid Cove, San Clemente Island, yesterday, Coast Guard radio reported.

According to a terse message received at Long Beach headquarters, Anderson met death aboard the boat Coral King, out of San Pedro.

DARKNESS FALLS

Parents Learn News Their Child Is Lost

It was in a darkened, modest San Marino home that word of their daughter's death came to Mr. and Mrs. David Fiscus.

Behind drawn shades in their bedroom, the ashen-faced, dry-eyed parents were told by Dr. Paul Hanson that 3½-year-old Kathy would be with them no longer.

The news came at 8:45 p.m., shortly after the anxious parents ended the third of their vigils to a police car, parked with its engine running, in front of the house.

Ready to Follow

From 5:55 until 7:35 p.m. they sat in the car—ready to follow an ambulance carrying their little daughter to the hospital should the rescuers find her alive.

They sat calmly and with little conversation the whole time. Mrs. Fiscus sat in the car's back seat with her sister, Mrs. Hamilton Lyon; the father in front with the driver.

Streets leading from the rescue scene past the home and to St. Luke Hospital were blocked and motorcycle officers stood ready to escort the ambulance.

Minister Calls

After Dr. Hanson left the house the parents were visited by a minister.

Down the slope toward the scene of the desperate activity, the nearly incessant glare of news camera flashbulbs whitened the night sky.

But the only one to notice from the Fiscus home was Deeper. Kathy's black and white dog, who kept his watch from the yard.

San Marino's Epic Drama Magnet for Vast Throngs

A great crowd—between 5000 and 10,000, officers estimated—stood under the hot sun throughout the day yesterday—creative and somber, watching tense volunteer workers fight to rescue Kathy Fiscus.

It was a quiet throng.

Few of the onlookers could see or guess what progress the perspiring rescue crews were making. Yet they stayed on, mostly watching.

A great moment might be the supreme one—when the news would come that Kathy had been found. The crowd waited.

The spectators covered every conceivable place of vantage. They pressed 20 deep against the 10-foot steel mesh fence which borders the field on the south and east. They strained against the police-guarded ropes that marked the rescue operation on the north and west.

Few could get a decent look. Even those who had the best spots could see but little. Rugged workers toiling about a 24-inch casing. Men descending into the casing. Buckets filled with earth rising from the top of the rescue pipe. A worker dumping the buckets. Over and over again, hour after hour. That was all.

But as though under a spell the throngs stayed on—to the numbing climax.

THE WEATHER

U.S. Weather Bureau: Scattered high cloudiness today and tomorrow with early morning fog near the coast. Slightly cooler afternoons. High yesterday, 88; lowest, 51.

Doctor Asserts Life Apparently Ended Friday After Fall

[Full page of pictures on Kathy Fiscus rescue operations on Page 3, Part I, and more pictures and stories on Pages 2, 4, 5, 6 and 7, Part I.]

Kathy Fiscus is dead.

She died last Friday after she fell into an abandoned well in a San Marino vacant lot and became wedged in a rusty pipe 94 feet underground.

Dr. Paul Hanson made that official announcement to a hushed throng gathered at the scene of heroic rescue attempts at 8:53 p.m. yesterday.

"Kathy apparently has been dead since she was last heard speaking Friday night," the physician said over a public-address system.

He then read a message from the 3½-year-old child's parents, Mr. and Mrs. David H. Fiscus, 2590 Robles Ave.

"There is nothing we can say to thank the people who helped by their many sacrifices," the message said.

Dr. Hanson asked the crowd of several thousand grouped under the shroud of night to leave as a courtesy to the little girl's family.

Drowning Belief Cited

Mrs. Jeanette Lyon, Kathy's aunt, disclosed that the cause of Kathy's death is believed to be drowning. She said she had asked Dr. Hanson if the youngster had drowned, and he said she had.

An autopsy surgeon will be assigned to the case today and an autopsy probably will be scheduled to determine the exact death cause.

Less than one hour after Dr. Hanson made his public announcement Kathy's body was brought from the earth that had clutched her close.

Bill Yancey, San Gabriel cesspool contractor who was the first man to the bottom of the 94-foot rescue shaft, carried it out—the last man to leave the hole.

A vagrant frill of a pink party dress strayed from the gray blanket that covered it as the body was placed in a black hearse from Turner & Stevens Mortuary in Pasadena. She was wearing the dress when she unaccountably fell through the well opening two inches narrower than this newspaper page.

Hush Greets News

News of Kathy's death was received with hushed frustration by sympathizers who had held a glimmer of hope to the last.

The child's body had been reached in the well pipe at 6:03 p.m. by rescuers who cut through the corroded metal with pneumatic saws.

This was 49 hours and 18 minutes after she dropped into the earth while frolicking in the plowed field.

Her body was grotesquely wedged into a bend in the pipe, her legs jammed hard against the side of the 14-inch-wide well.

Dr. Hanson and Dr. Robert McCulloch, the Fiscus family physician, remained after the announcement of her death to assist in extricating the body.

Last Sound Friday

Kathy's last sound came about 6:30 p.m. Friday. She had answered through sobs the questions of her mother shouting frantically down the well.

Then a rope was dropped. Apparently she held to it while it was pulled up a few feet. But her tiny hands lost their grip on the hemp and she fell back against the jagged sides of her dark tomb.

She cried for a while then, softly. And that was all.

From the physician's analysis this presumably was the time of her death.

From all of the Southland men came with equipment to free Kathy from her cylindrical coffin. The plight of the little blond girl captured the sympathy of the world.

Gargantuan Effort Made

A gargantuan effort to pull her free—and alive—from the earth, grew to epic proportions. Men and machines worked without rest, stubbornly determined to lift Kathy into the sunshine again.

Two days of heroism followed. Men risked their lives for the Kathy who lay dead 94 feet beneath them, but who even in death that was her secret inspired the world to prayer.

And then in a night seared by floodlights came the tragic knowledge that the laughter of Kathy Fiscus was stilled forever.

News Delayed for Over Two Hours

Official word of the child's death was delayed more than two hours by volunteer supervisors who insisted on prolonged secrecy. Her body was reached by O. A. Kelly and H. E. (Whitey) Blickensderfer.

Raymond Hill, engineer nominally in charge of the rescue operations, first announced that Kathy had been found at 6:03 p.m. He refused to say at first whether the child, whose fate held the world in suspense, was alive or dead.

After repeated conferences at the mouth of the rescue shaft, a white canvaslike bag was lowered into the hole.

Rope Pulled With Agonizing Care

Moments later ropes were lowered into the well. Four

Turn to Page 2, Column 1

19   On many issues, empathy can pull us in the wrong direction. The outrage that comes from adopting the perspective of a victim can drive an appetite for retribution. (Think of those statutes named for dead children: Megan's Law, Jessica's Law, Caylee's Law.) But the appetite for retribution is typically indifferent to long-term consequences. In one study, conducted by Jonathan Baron and Ilana Ritov, people were asked how best to punish a company for producing a vaccine that caused the death of a child. Some were told that a higher fine would make the company work harder to manufacture a safer product; others were told that a higher fine would discourage the company from making the vaccine, and since there were no acceptable alternatives on the market the punishment would lead to more deaths. Most people didn't care; they wanted the company fined heavily, whatever the consequence.

20   **"There's a larger pattern here. Sensible policies often have benefits that are merely statistical, but victims have names and stories."**   This dynamic regularly plays out in the realm of criminal justice. In 1987, Willie Horton, a convicted murderer who had been released on furlough from the Northeastern Correctional Center, in Massachusetts, raped a woman after beating and tying up her fiancé. The furlough program came to be seen as a humiliating mistake on the part of Governor Michael Dukakis, and was used against him by his opponents during his run for president the following year. Yet the program may have *reduced* the likelihood of such incidents. In fact, a 1987 report found that the recidivism rate in Massachusetts dropped in the eleven years after the program was introduced, and that convicts who were furloughed before being released were less likely to go on to commit a crime than those who were not. The trouble is that you can't point to individuals who *weren't* raped, assaulted, or killed as a result of the program, just as you can't point to a specific person whose life was spared because of vaccination.

21   There's a larger pattern here. Sensible policies often have benefits that are merely statistical, but victims have names and stories. Consider global warming—what Rifkin calls the "escalating entropy bill that now threatens catastrophic climate change and our very existence." As it happens, the limits of empathy are especially stark here. Opponents of restrictions on CO_2 emissions are flush with identifiable victims—all those who will be harmed by increased costs, by business closures. The millions of people who at some unspecified future date will suffer the consequences of our current inaction are, by contrast, pale statistical abstractions.

22   **"[I]t is impossible to empathize with seven billion strangers, or to feel toward someone you've never met the degree of concern you feel for a child, a friend, or a lover."**   The government's failure to enact prudent long-term policies is often attributed to the incentive system of democratic politics (which favors short-term fixes), and to the powerful influence of money. But the politics of empathy is also to blame. Too often, our concern for specific individuals today means neglecting crises that will harm countless people in the future.

SECTION 6: Empathy isn't enough.

23   Moral judgment entails more than putting oneself in another's shoes. As the philosopher Jesse Prinz points out, some acts that we easily recognize as wrong, such as shoplifting or tax evasion, have no identifiable victim. And plenty of good deeds—disciplining a child for dangerous behavior, enforcing a fair and impartial procedure for determining who should get an organ transplant despite the suffering of those low on the list—require us to put our empathy to one side. Eight deaths are worse than one, even if you know the name of the one;

humanitarian aid can, if poorly targeted, be counterproductive; the threat posed by climate change warrants the sacrifices entailed by efforts to ameliorate it. "The decline of violence may owe something to an expansion of empathy," the psychologist Steven Pinker has written, "but it also owes much to harder-boiled faculties like prudence, reason, fairness, self-control, norms and taboos, and conceptions of human rights." A reasoned, even counterempathetic analysis of moral obligation and likely consequences is a better guide to planning for the future than the gut wrench of empathy.

Rifkin and others have argued, plausibly, that moral progress involves expanding our concern from the family and the tribe to humanity as a whole. Yet it is impossible to empathize with seven billion strangers, or to feel toward someone you've never met the degree of concern you feel for a child, a friend, or a lover. Our best hope for the future is not to get people to think of all humanity as family—that's impossible. It lies, instead, in an appreciation of the fact that, even if we don't empathize with distant strangers, their lives have the same value as the lives of those we love.

24

That's not a call for a world without empathy. A race of psychopaths might well be smart enough to invent the principles of solidarity and fairness. (Research suggests that criminal psychopaths are adept at making moral judgments.) The problem with those who are devoid of empathy is that, although they may recognize what's right, they have no motivation to act upon it. Some spark of fellow feeling is needed to convert intelligence into action.

25 SECTION 7:
Concession:
Where empathy
does matter.

But a spark may be all that's needed. Putting aside the extremes of psychopathy, there is no evidence to suggest that the less empathetic are morally worse than the rest of us. Simon Baron-Cohen observes that some people with autism and Asperger's syndrome, though typically empathy-deficient, are highly moral, owing to a strong desire to follow rules and insure that they are applied fairly.

26

Where empathy really does matter is in our personal relationships. Nobody wants to live like Thomas Gradgrind—Charles Dickens's caricature utilitarian, who treats all interactions, including those with his children, in explicitly economic terms. Empathy is what makes us human; it's what makes us both subjects and objects of moral concern. Empathy betrays us only when we take it as a moral guide.

27

Newtown, in the wake of the Sandy Hook massacre, was inundated with so much charity that it became a burden. More than eight hundred volunteers were recruited to deal with the gifts that were sent to the city—all of which kept arriving despite earnest pleas from Newtown officials that charity be directed elsewhere. A vast warehouse was crammed with plush toys the townspeople had no use for; millions of dollars rolled in to this relatively affluent community. We felt their pain; we wanted to help. Meanwhile— just to begin a very long list—almost twenty million American children go to bed hungry each night, and the federal food-stamp program is facing budget cuts of almost 20 percent. Many of the same kindly strangers who paid for Baby Jessica's medical needs support cuts to state Medicaid programs—cuts that will affect millions. Perhaps fifty million Americans will be stricken next year by food-borne illness, yet budget reductions mean that the FDA will be conducting two thousand fewer safety inspections. Even more invisibly, next year the average American will release about twenty metric tons of carbon dioxide into the atmosphere, and many in Congress seek to loosen restrictions on greenhouse gases even further.

"Many of the same kindly strangers who paid for Baby Jessica's medical needs support cuts to state Medicaid programs—cuts that will affect millions."

28 SECTION 8:
Conclusion:
Empathy should
yield to reason.

29   Such are the paradoxes of empathy. The power of this faculty has something to do with its ability to bring our moral concern into a laser pointer of focused attention. If a planet of billions is to survive, however, we'll need to take into consideration the welfare of people not yet harmed—and, even more, of people not yet born. They have no names, faces, or stories to grip our conscience or stir our fellow feeling. Their prospects call, rather, for deliberation and calculation. Our hearts will always go out to the baby in the well; it's a measure of our humanity. But empathy will have to yield to reason if humanity is to have a future.

Write a Brief Summary of Each Stage of Thought

The purpose of this step is to wean you from the language of the original passage so that you are not tied to it when writing the summary. Here are brief summaries for each stage of thought in the sections of "The Baby in the Well."

Section 1: *Definition and importance of empathy* (paragraphs 1–4).

> Many believe that what makes us moral beings is empathy, the ability to see the world from others' points of view, to feel their pain and distress, and to feel the impulse to help them.

Section 2: *Empathy necessary to human survival* (paragraphs 5–8).

> Empathy research focuses on how our moral impulses are affected when we see or sense others who are in pain. Some people feel no distress at the pain of others, but most are capable of empathy, a quality Bloom believes is necessary not only for human progress but also for the survival of our species.

Section 3: *The problem with empathy: its focus on "babies in wells"* (paragraphs 9–11).

> Empathy is "parochial, narrow-minded, and innumerate."[3] It tends to focus on individuals or relatively small groups of individuals who are in well-publicized distress.

Section 4: *How empathy operates* (paragraphs 12–16).

> Because of the "identifiable victim effect," people care about the effects of highly publicized tragedies on people whose faces they can see. But at the same time, they seem oblivious to large-scale catastrophes such as genocide, mass starvation, and deaths due to preventable illnesses as well as to routine homicides that occur in the thousands every year.

Section 5: *How empathy leads us astray* (paragraphs 17–22).

> So empathy "can lead us astray." Our empathetic impulses may overpower our "dispassionate analysis of a situation." Acting on impulses of empathy may help a relatively small number of identifiable individuals, but it may also hurt many other individuals of whom we are less aware, who don't have "names or stories," or with whose values we don't politically sympathize.

---

[3]See definition of *innumerate* in footnote 3, page 35.

Section 6: *Empathy isn't enough* (paragraphs 23–24).

> Moral judgment often requires us to put empathy aside; to assume that all lives have the same value; and to use qualities like "prudence, reason, fairness [and] self-control" to plan for the well-being of humanity as a whole.

Section 7: *Concession: Where empathy does matter* (paragraphs 25–27).

> No one wants to live in a world without empathy, a quality that is so vital in maintaining our human relationships.

Section 8: *Conclusion: Empathy should yield to reason* (paragraphs 28–29).

> But as a moral guide, empathy should "yield to reason." Assistance to the few is often wasted because it is too much or it is unneeded. But "guided by deliberation and calculation," assistance to the many is essential for the future well-being of the billions of people who constitute humankind.

Write a Thesis: A Brief Summary of the Entire Passage

Probably no two summaries of Bloom's thesis statement (which appears about a third of the way into his essay) would be worded identically. But it is fair to say that any reasonable thesis will indicate that Bloom's subject is the inadequacy of empathy for dealing with large-scale human suffering. This inadequacy results from what he calls the "identifiable victim effect"—our tendency to respond favorably more often to individuals whose names and faces we know than to large numbers of present or future victims who remain anonymous to us. Does Bloom make a statement anywhere in this passage that pulls all this together? Examine paragraph 9 and you will find his thesis—two sentences that sum up the problems with empathy:

> **Bloom's thesis (paragraph 9):** Empathy has some unfortunate features—it is parochial, narrow-minded, and innumerate. We're often at our best when we're smart enough not to rely on it.

You may have learned that a thesis statement must be expressed in a single sentence. We would suggest a slight rewording of this generally sound advice and say that a thesis statement must be *expressible* in a single sentence. For reasons of emphasis or style, a writer might choose to distribute a thesis across two or more sentences. Certainly, the sense of Bloom's thesis can take the form of a single statement.

Here is our summary of Bloom's thesis:

> **Our summary of Bloom's thesis:** In "The Baby in the Well: The Case against Empathy," Paul Bloom argues that, while empathy is important in fostering positive human relationships, we should prefer reason as a guide to social policy because empathy's focus on the distress of one individual may blind us to the suffering of thousands whose names and faces we do not know.

The author and title reference could also be indicated in the summary's title (if this were a freestanding summary), in which case their mention could be dropped from the thesis statement. Bear in mind that writing an accurate thesis for a summary takes time. In this case, it took four drafts, roughly ten minutes, to compose a thesis and another few minutes of fine-tuning after a draft of the entire summary was completed. It's fair to say that if you can't express the thesis in your own words, you do not (yet) understand the passage:

> **Draft 1:** In "The Baby in the Well: The Case against Empathy," Paul Bloom argues that we should not rely on empathy.
> **Problem:** Vague. It's not clear from this statement why Bloom thinks we should not rely on empathy.
>
> **Draft 2:** In "The Baby in the Well: The Case against Empathy," Paul Bloom argues against empathy because of its focus on the distress of the individual rather than on the suffering of large numbers of people.
> **Problem:** Better, but the thesis should note that Bloom acknowledges the value of empathy and indicates what he sees as a preferable alternative to empathy.
>
> **Draft 3:** In "The Baby in the Well: The Case against Empathy," Paul Bloom argues that, while empathy has its place, we should prefer reason because empathy's focus on the distress of one individual may blind us to the suffering of thousands of individuals.
> **Problem:** Close—but a better thesis would formulate a more precise phrase than "has its place" and would introduce the crucial idea of the "identifiable victim effect"—one indicated in the final thesis by the phrase "whose names and faces we do not know."

Write a Draft by Combining Thesis, Section Summaries, and Selected Details

Combining your thesis for the selection and your section summaries will give you a rough draft of your summary. At this point, you'll need to reread and make adjustments by inserting transitions, for instance, or eliminating redundancies. Your final draft of the summary should read as any finished paper.

You've read a summary of Bloom's essay before reading the selection itself, on page 32–33. Now, knowing how it was put together—by combining individual summaries of Bloom's sections and our summary of his main point—you may want to reread it. If you have reason to write an expanded summary, add details from the selection according to which part(s) of the article you want to emphasize.

Summarizing Graphs, Charts, and Tables

1.7 **Write summaries of visual presentations, including graphs, charts, and tables.**

In your reading in the sciences and social sciences, you will often find data and concepts presented in nontext forms—as figures and tables. Such visual devices offer a snapshot, a pictorial overview of material that is communicated more quickly and clearly in graphic form than as a series of (often complicated) sentences. Note that, in essence, graphs, charts, and tables are themselves summaries. The writer uses a graph, which in an article or book is often labeled as a numbered figure, and presents the quantitative results of research as points on a line or a bar or as sections ("slices") of a pie. Pie charts show relative proportions, or percentages. Graphs, especially effective in showing patterns, relate one variable to another: for instance, income to years of education or sales figures of a product over a period of three years.

Writers regularly draw on graphs, charts, and tables to provide information or to offer evidence for points they are arguing. In the following pages, we present graphs, charts, and tables from a variety of sources, all focused on the subject of U.S. immigration.

Bar Graphs

Figure 1.1 is a *bar graph* indicating the countries that have sent the highest number of immigrants to the United States in the decades from 1901–1910 through 2001–2010. The horizontal—or *x*—axis indicates the decades from 1901 through 2010.

Figure 1.1 Top Sending Countries: Selected Periods[4]

Percent of All Immigrants

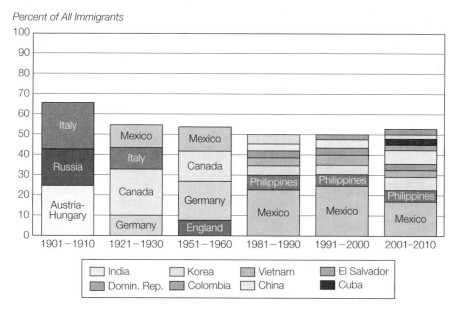

[4]Figure 2. "Top Sending Countries Comprising at Least Half of All L[egal] P[ermanent] R[esidents]. Selected Periods." Ruth Ellen Wasem [Specialist in Immigration Policy], "U.S. Immigration Policy: Chart Book of Key Trends, C[ongressional] R[esearch] S[ervice]: Report for Congress," p. 3. Source: CRS Analysis of Table 2, Statistical Yearbook of Immigration, U.S. Department of Homeland Security, Office of Immigration Statistics, FY2010. www.crs.gov, http://www.fas.org/sgp/crs/homesec/R42988.pdf.

The vertical—or *y*—axis on the left indicates the percentage of immigrants represented by each country. Each vertical bar for each decade is subdivided into sections representing the countries that sent the most immigrants in that decade. Note that in the decade from 1901 to 1910, the three top sending countries were Italy, Russia, and Austria-Hungary. A hundred years later, in the decade from 2001 through 2010, the top sending countries were Mexico, the Philippines, and China. (Note that the decades from 1931 through 1950 and from 1961 through 1980 are not represented in the graph.)

Here is a summary of the information presented in Figure 1.1:

> Between 1900 and 2010, the flow of immigration to the United States has dramatically shifted from Europe to Asia and the Americas. In the decade from 1901 to 1910, three European countries—Italy, Russia, and Austria-Hungary—accounted for most of the immigrant flow to this country. Starting in the next decade, however, two countries in the Americas—Mexico and Canada—became the top sources of immigrants to the United States. Mexico has remained a top sending country for most of the twentieth century and into the present century, currently accounting for more immigrants than any other nation. At the same time, immigration from Mexico dropped off slightly in the decade from 2001 to 2010. All of the other top sending countries during this decade are in Asia and South and Central America. The top sending Asian countries are Korea, India, Vietnam, China, and the Philippines; those from the Americas include—in addition to Mexico—Colombia, Cuba, El Salvador, and the Dominican Republic. Collectively, immigrants from the Asian and American countries represented on the chart in the 2001–2010 decade account for slightly more than 50 percent of all immigrants admitted.

Figure 1.2 is a horizontal bar graph summarizing the results of the U.S. Census Bureau census of 2000, showing the fifteen largest ancestries among U.S. citizens. The data corroborate what we have learned in grade school: that America is a nation of immigrants. In this type of graph, the shaded portion of the bar represents a particular value (in this case, millions of people responding to the U.S. Census). We also find percentages at the beginning of each bar, in parentheses. Finally, the length of each portion of the bar is proportional to the percentage.

Exercise 1.3
Summarizing Graphs

Write a brief summary of the data in Figure 1.2. Use our summary of Figure 1.1 as a general model.

Figure 1.2 Fifteen Largest Ancestries: 2000 (In millions. Percentage of total population in parentheses.)

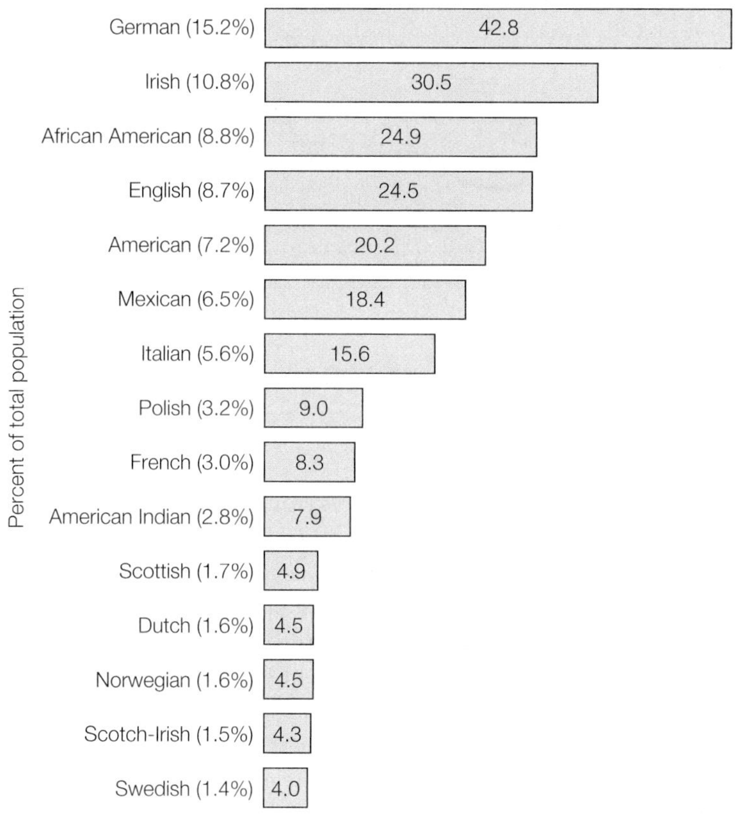

Percent of total population

German (15.2%)	42.8
Irish (10.8%)	30.5
African American (8.8%)	24.9
English (8.7%)	24.5
American (7.2%)	20.2
Mexican (6.5%)	18.4
Italian (5.6%)	15.6
Polish (3.2%)	9.0
French (3.0%)	8.3
American Indian (2.8%)	7.9
Scottish (1.7%)	4.9
Dutch (1.6%)	4.5
Norwegian (1.6%)	4.5
Scotch-Irish (1.5%)	4.3
Swedish (1.4%)	4.0

Source: U.S. Census Bureau, Census 2000 special tabulation.

Line Graphs

Line graphs are useful for showing trends over a period of time. Usually, the horizontal axis indicates years, months, or shorter periods, and the vertical axis indicates a quantity: dollars, barrels, personnel, sales, anything that can be counted. The line running from left to right indicates the changing values, over a given period, of the object of measurement. Frequently, a line graph features multiple lines (perhaps in different colors, perhaps some solid, others dotted, etc.), each indicating a separate variable to be measured. Thus, a line graph could show the changing approval ratings of several presidential candidates over the course of a campaign season. Or it could indicate the number of iPads versus Android tablets sold in a given year.

Figure 1.3 is a line graph indicating the fluctuations in the number of nonimmigrant ("legal temporary") visas issued by the U.S. State Department from 1987

Figure 1.3 Nonimmigrant Visas Issued by the U.S. Department of State[5]

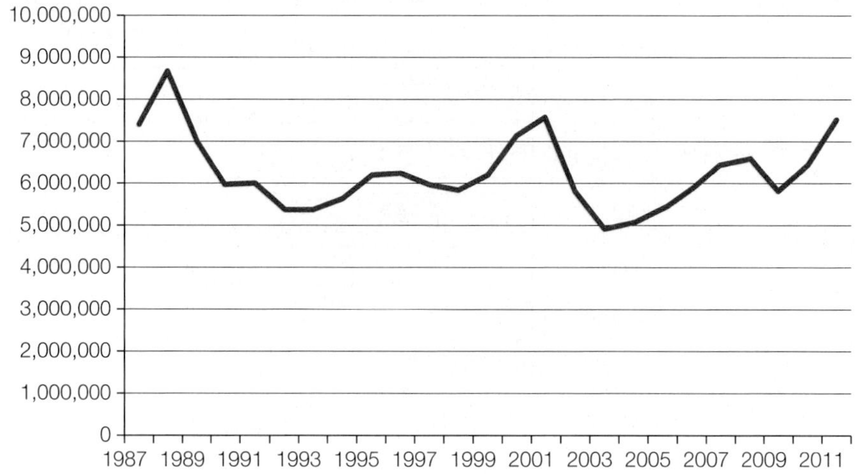

through 2013. The number of such visas reached its highest level—nearly 9 million—in 1988 and 1989. The lowest number of visas—fewer than 5 million—was issued in 2004. Following the line allows us to discern the pattern of nonimmigrant migration. By combining the information gleaned from this figure with other information gathered from other sources, you may be able to make certain conjectures or draw certain conclusions about the patterns of immigration.

In Figure 1.4, we have a quadruple line graph, which allows us to view at the same time the changes in "Average Weekly Earnings of Full-Time Foreign-Born Workers, Ages 25 to 64, by When They Came to the United States to Stay, 2009." With two lines representing men and women from Mexico and Central America, and two lines representing men and women from the rest of the world, the reader can easily make comparisons about earning power relative to nation-groups of origin and year of arrival in the United States. These four simple lines show dramatic evidence concerning the earning power of immigrants who have been in the United States the longest.

Exercise 1.4

Summarizing Line Graphs

Write a brief summary of the key data in Figure 1.4. Use our summary of Figure 1.1 (or your summary of Figure 1.2) as a model.

---

[5] "Figure 6. Nonimmigrant Visas Issued by the U.S. Department of State." Source: CRS presentation of data from Table XVIII of the annual reports of the U.S. Department of State Office of Visa Statistics. Ruth Ellen Wasem [Specialist in Immigration Policy], "U.S. Immigration Policy: Chart Book of Key Trends, C[ongressional] R[esearch] S[ervice]: Report for Congress," p. 7. www.crs.gov, http://www.fas.org/sgp/crs/homesec/R42988.pdf.

Figure 1.4 Average Weekly Earnings of Full-Time Foreign-Born Workers, Ages 25 to 64, by When They Came to the United States to Stay, 2009

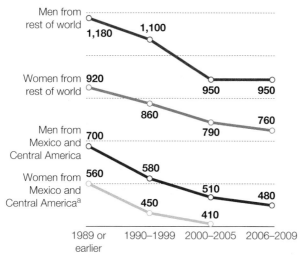

a The sample of women from Mexico and Central America, Current Population Survey, Outgoing Rotation Groups, 2009.

Pie Charts

Bar and line graphs are useful for visually comparing numerical quantities. *Pie charts*, on the other hand, are useful for visually comparing percentages of a whole. The pie represents the whole; the individual slices represent the relative sizes of the parts.

Figure 1.5 is a pie chart indicating the major categories of immigrants who were classified as legal permanent residents (LPRs) in fiscal year 2011. At a glance, you are able to perceive percentages that are visually larger or smaller slices of a pie.

Exercise 1.5

Summarizing Pie Charts

Write a brief summary of the data in Figure 1.5. Use our summary of Figure 1.1 (or your summary of Figure 1.2) as a model.

Figure 1.5 Breakdown of Legal Permanent Residents (LPRs) in Fiscal Year 2011[6]

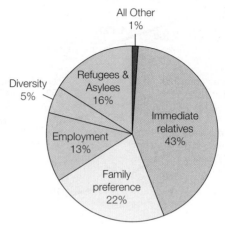

1.1 Million LPRs in FY2011

Other Charts: Bubble Maps, Pictograms, and Interactive Charts

A *bubble map* is a type of chart characterized by disks of various sizes placed on a map of the world, a country, or a smaller region. The relative sizes of the disks represent various percentages or absolute numbers, making it easy to see at a glance which countries or regions have larger or smaller numbers of whatever variable is represented by the disk.

Figure 1.6 depicts a bubble map in which variously sized bubbles, placed over particular cities and regions in the United States, represent numbers of foreign-born students who have secured visas for studying in the United States. A quick look at the map reveals three main destinations for foreign-born students: the Northeast corridor from Washington to Boston, and the Los Angeles and San Francisco metropolitan areas.

Pictograms are charts that use drawings or icons to represent persons or objects. For example, a pictogram depicting the resources available to a particular nation engaged in a war might use icons of soldiers, tanks, planes, artillery, and so on, with each icon representing a given number of units.

Figure 1.7 is a pictogram depicting three categories of immigrant visas issued in 2012: temporary worker visas (including those "H" visa workers who have high-level or other specialized skills), permanent immigrant visas, and a third (miscellaneous) category, consisting of intracompany transferees and their families, along with other temporary workers and their families.

---

[6]Ruth Ellen Wasem [Specialist in Immigration Policy], "U.S. Immigration Policy: Chart Book of Key Trends, C[ongressional] R[esearch] S[ervice]: Report for Congress." www.crs.gov, http://www.fas.org/sgp/crs/homesec/R42988.pdf, p. 5 (second chart—pie).

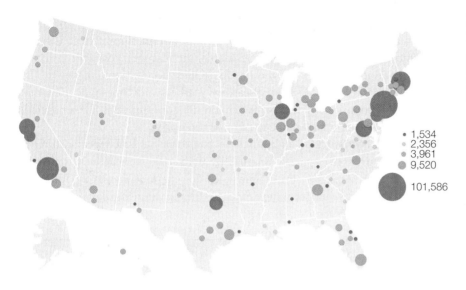

Figure 1.6 Map: 118 U.S. Metro Areas with at Least 1,500 Foreign Students, 2008–2012[7]

- 1,534
- 2,356
- 3,961
- 9,520
- 101,586

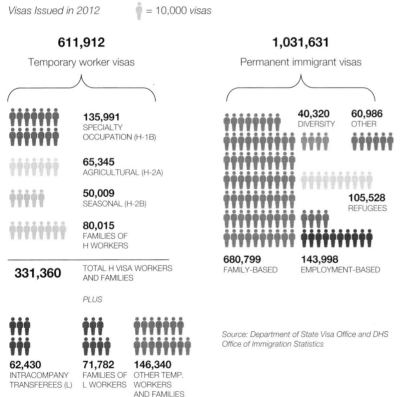

Visas Issued in 2012   = 10,000 *visas*

Figure 1.7 U.S. Visas Issued in 2012[8]

611,912
Temporary worker visas

1,031,631
Permanent immigrant visas

135,991
SPECIALTY OCCUPATION (H-1B)

65,345
AGRICULTURAL (H-2A)

50,009
SEASONAL (H-2B)

80,015
FAMILIES OF H WORKERS

331,360   TOTAL H VISA WORKERS AND FAMILIES

PLUS

62,430
INTRACOMPANY TRANSFEREES (L)

71,782
FAMILIES OF L WORKERS

146,340
OTHER TEMP. WORKERS AND FAMILIES

40,320
DIVERSITY

60,986
OTHER

105,528
REFUGEES

680,799
FAMILY-BASED

143,998
EMPLOYMENT-BASED

Source: Department of State Visa Office and DHS Office of Immigration Statistics

[7]Brookings Institute. 2014. http://www.brookings.edu/research/interactives/2014/geography-of-foreign-students#/M10420

[8]"Visas Issued in 2012." Jill H. Wilson, Brookings Institute, "Immigration Facts: Temporary Foreign Workers," 18 June 2013. Pictogram under paragraph 2. http://www.brookings.edu/research/reports/2013/06/18-temporary-workers-wilson.

In this particular figure, each icon of an individual represents approximately 10,000 immigrants. Each of the three major classes of immigrant visas is subdivided into several categories. So, for example, the temporary worker visa category is subdivided into those who have specialty occupations, those who are agricultural workers, those who are seasonal workers, and those who are family members of the workers. The other two main categories of visas are subdivided in other ways, based on the makeup of those categories.

Interactive charts, found online, allow you to bring up concealed data by moving your cursor over particular areas. (If all the data were actually shown on the chart, it would overwhelm the graphic.) For example, locate the following two interactive maps, one from the Center for Immigration Studies and the other from the *New York Times*.

Go to: Google or Bing

Search terms: *"CIS Growth Immigrant Population snapshot counties"*

"immigration explorer new york times"

The "County Map: Growth of Adult Immigration Population, 1990 to 2014" offers "detailed information on the nation's immigrant population (legal and illegal) at the county level in 1990, 2000, and 2014." Locate any of the shaded 232 counties across the United States and click for data on four maps.

The immigration explorer map depicts the immigrant component of every county in the United States. Moving your cursor over any particular county reveals the number of foreign-born residents of that county, along with its total population in the year 2000. A simple calculation reveals the percentage of foreign-born residents in each county.

Tables

A table presents numerical data in rows and columns for quick reference. If the writer chooses, tabular information can be converted to graphic information. Charts and graphs are preferable when the writer wants to emphasize a pattern or relationship; tables are preferable when the writer wants to emphasize numbers. While the charts in Figures 1.1 to 1.7 are focused on a relatively small number of countries and other variables, the table in Figure 1.8 breaks down immigration into numerous countries and several regions.[9] Note that this table is divided into two sets of data: immigration by world region and immigration by country. The regional component of the table allows us to focus on the big picture. In terms of sources of immigrants to the United States, the longer

---

[9]Randall Monger and James Yankay, Table 3: "Legal Permanent Resident Flow by Region and Country of Birth: Fiscal Years 2010 to 2012." *U.S. Legal Permanent Residents 2012*, March 2013, p. 4. Department of Homeland Security, Office of Immigration Statistics Policy Directorate. http:// www.dhs.gov/sites/default/files/publications/ois_lpr_fr_2012_2.pdf.

Figure 1.8 Legal Permanent Resident Flow by Region and Country of Birth, Fiscal Years 2010 to 2012

Region and Country of Birth	2012 Number	2012 Percent	2011 Number	2011 Percent	2010 Number	2010 Percent
REGION						
Total	**1,031,631**	**100.0**	**1,062,040**	**100.0**	**1,042,625**	**100.0**
Africa	107,241	10.4	100,374	9.5	101,355	9.7
Asia	429,599	41.6	451,593	42.5	422,063	40.5
Europe	81,671	7.9	83,850	7.9	88,801	8.5
North America	327,771	31.8	333,902	31.4	336,553	32.3
Caribbean	127,477	12.4	133,680	12.6	139,951	13.4
Central America	40,675	3.9	43,707	4.1	43,951	4.2
Other North America	159,619	15.5	156,515	14.7	152,651	14.6
Oceania	4,742	0.5	4,980	0.5	5,345	0.5
South America	79,401	7.7	86,096	8.1	87,178	8.4
Unknown	1,206	0.1	1,245	0.1	1,330	0.1
COUNTRY[a]						
Total	**1,031,631**	**100.0**	**1,062,040**	**100.0**	**1,042,625**	**100.0**
Mexico	146,406	14.2	143,446	13.5	139,120	13.3
China, People's Republic	81,784	7.9	87,016	8.2	70,863	6.8
India	66,434	6.4	69,013	6.5	69,162	6.6
Philippines	57,327	5.6	57,011	5.4	58,173	5.6
Dominican Republic	41,566	4.0	46,109	4.3	53,870	5.2
Cuba	32,820	3.2	36,452	3.4	33,573	3.2
Vietnam	28,304	2.7	34,157	3.2	30,632	2.9
Haiti	22,818	2.2	22,111	2.1	22,582	2.2
Colombia	20,931	2.0	22,635	2.1	22,406	2.1
Korea South	20,846	2.0	22,824	2.1	22,227	2.1
Jamaica	20,705	2.0	19,662	1.9	19,825	1.9
Iraq	20,369	2.0	21,133	2.0	19,855	1.9
Burma	17,383	1.7	16,518	1.6	12,925	1.2
El Salvador	16,256	1.6	18,667	1.8	18,806	1.8
Pakistan	14,740	1.4	15,546	1.5	18,258	1.8
Bangladesh	14,705	1.4	16,707	1.6	14,819	1.4
Ethiopia	14,544	1.4	13,793	1.3	14,266	1.4
Nigeria	13,575	1.3	11,824	1.1	13,376	1.3
Canada	12,932	1.3	12,800	1.2	13,328	1.3
Iran	12,916	1.3	14,822	1.4	14,182	1.4
All other countries	354,270	34.3	359,794	33.9	360,377	34.6

[a](Countries ranked by 2012 LPR flow)

SOURCE: U.S. Department of Homeland Security, Computer Linked Application Information Management System (CLAIMS), Legal Immigrant Data, Fiscal Years 2010 to 2012.[10]

[10]"Legal Permanent Resident Flow by Region and Country of Birth, Fiscal Years 2010 to 2012." Source: U.S. Department of Homeland Security, Computer Linked Application Information Management System (CLAIMS), Legal Immigrant Data, Fiscal Years 2010 to 2012. Department of Homeland Security, "U.S. Legal Permanent Residents 2012," p. 4. http://www.dhs.gov/sites/default/files/publications/ois_lpr_fr_2012_2.pdf.

country component allows us to draw finer distinctions among the countries that make up these regions.

A table may contain so much data that you would not want to summarize *all* of it for a particular paper. In this case, you would summarize the *part* of a table that you find useful. Here is a summary drawn from the information from Figure 1.8, focusing primarily on those regions and countries that provide the largest numbers and the smallest numbers of immigrants, but also pointing out other interesting data points. Notice that the summary requires the writer to read closely and discern which information is significant. The table reports raw data and does not speak for itself. Toward the end of the summary the writer, who draws on data from other sources (such as the bar graph in Figure 1.1) and who also calculates percentages, speculates on the reason for the changing numbers of immigrants from Pakistan and then sums up her overall impression of the data in the table:

> During the years 2010 to 2012, by far the largest number of legal immigrants to the United States came from Asian countries, primarily the People's Republic of China, India, and the Philippines. After Asia, North America—chiefly Mexico, the Caribbean countries, and Central America—provided the greatest number of immigrants. Together, these two regions accounted for more than 73 percent of the more than 1,031,000 immigrants who entered the United States legally in 2012. By contrast, the region of Oceania—made up of Melanesia, Micronesia, and Polynesia, islands in the tropical Pacific—accounted during the same year for only half of 1 percent of total U.S. legal immigration. Europe in 2012 provided about 8 percent of the total—a far cry from a century ago when this region provided more than 60 percent of total U.S. immigrants.
>
> In terms of individual countries during the period 2010–2012, Mexico, by a huge margin, provided more immigrants to the United States than any other country, with the number rising at a small but steady rate in all three years. As indicated above, China was second after Mexico as the source country of the highest numbers of immigrants, though the pattern in these three years does not indicate a trend: There were 17,000 more Chinese immigrants in 2011 than there were in 2010, but in 2012 the number dropped by more than 5,000. On the other hand, immigration from the Dominican Republic shows a steady drop: from 53,780 in 2010 to 46,109 in 2011, to 42,566 in 2012. Pakistan also provided 20 percent fewer immigrants in 2012 than it did in 2010, a significant decline possibly related to the war against the Taliban and to American military strikes in that country. On the whole, however, during this three-year period, there were no major shifts in total numbers of immigrants, with increases or decreases no greater than 3 percent.

Exercise 1.6
Summarizing Tables

Focus on other data in Figure 1.8 and write a brief summary of your own. Or use a search engine to locate another table on the general topic of immigration and summarize its data.

Choosing Quotations

1.8   Select effective material to quote directly and indirectly.

You have seen that *summary* is an objective, brief restatement of what someone else has said or written and that *paraphrase* is another kind of restatement, though one that is often as long as the original source. Summaries and paraphrases use your words, not the source author's. A *quotation*, by contrast, records the *exact* language used by someone in speech or writing. Almost all academic pursuits build on the writing and research of others, and you will regularly refer to that work by quoting, summarizing, and paraphrasing.

Quotations can be direct or indirect. A *direct* quotation precisely records the language of another. An *indirect* quotation is one in which you report what someone has said without repeating the words exactly as spoken (or written):

Direct quotation   Franklin D. Roosevelt said, "The only thing we have to
                          fear is fear itself."

Indirect quotation   Franklin D. Roosevelt said that we have nothing to fear
                          but fear itself.

Direct quotations are indicated by a pair of quotation marks (" "); a direct quotation must reproduce exactly the wording of the original passage. When using an indirect quotation, you have the liberty of changing words (although not meaning).

Every time you use a quotation—or a summary or paraphrase—you must *credit your source* by identifying both the author and, in combination with a Works Cited page, information on where to find the referenced material. Citations work in two parts. The first appears in your sentence (an in-text citation). Here, you provide the author's name and a specific page reference. Here are two versions of an in-text citation:

- From the beginning, the AIDS antibody test has been "mired in controversy" (Bayer 101).
- From the beginning, Bayer claims that the AIDS antibody test has been "mired in controversy" (101).

The second part of a citation appears in an alphabetized Works Cited list (in the sciences called a References list):

Bayer, Ronald. "Ethics and Public Policy: Engaging the Moral Challenges Posed by AIDS." *AIDS Patient Care and STDs*, vol. 20, no. 7, 2006, pp. 456–60.

See Chapter 7, pages 208–13, to learn more on citing sources.

When to Quote

- To capture another writer's particularly memorable language
- To capture another writer's clear, concise language
- To lend authority and credibility to your own writing

Quote Memorable Language

Quote when source material is worded so eloquently or powerfully that to summarize or paraphrase would diminish much of its impact and significance. Here, for example, is historian of magic Jim Steinmeyer on why the illusions of great magicians succeed:

> The success of a magician lies in making a human connection to the magic, the precise focus that creates a fully realized illusion in the minds of the audience. The simple explanation is that seldom do the crude gimmicks in a magic show—those mirrors, threads, or rubber bands—deceive people. The audience is taken by the hand and led to deceive themselves.
>
> —from *Hiding the Elephant*

No summary or paraphrase could do justice to the evocative power of Steinmeyer's words about audiences deceiving themselves. If you were writing a paper, say, on the evolution of magic from early religious rituals to stage shows, you might very well want to quote Steinmeyer.

Quote Clear, Concise Language

Quote particularly clear and economical language when your words of summary or paraphrase, by contrast, would be wordy. Read this passage from the online academic journal *The Conversation*. (You've read the complete piece earlier in the chapter, pp. 18–20.)

> Since the early neurological work on memory in the 1950s and 1960s, studies have demonstrated that memories are not stored in just one part of the brain. They're widely distributed across the whole brain, particularly in an area called the cortex.
>
> Contrary to the popular notion, our memories are not stored in our brains like books on shelves in specific categories. They're actively reconstructed from elements scattered throughout various areas of the cortex by a process called encoding.
>
> As we experience the world through our eyes, ears, and so on, various groups of neurons in the cortex fire together to form a neural pathway from each of these senses and encode these patterns into memories. That's why the aroma of cornbread may trigger a Thanksgiving dinner memory at grandmother's house many years ago, or the sound of a car backfiring may trigger a panic attack in a war veteran.
>
> — Jyutika Mehta, *from* "External Enhancements of Memory May Soon Go High-Tech"

Assume that you're writing a paper on memory and decide to refer to Mehta's paragraphs on brain function and memory. You might quote specific words or phrases or entire sentences.

> The brain does not store whole memories "like books on shelves." As brain and communications researcher Jyutika Mehta explains, it "widely distribute[s]" the constituent parts of memories to various areas associated with functions like sight and smell. A memory is "encode[d]" through connections among areas and can be lost when these connections break down due to disease or the natural aging process.

The brackets in the quoted material alert readers that we've altered Mehta's original language to fit the flow of our sentence. (You'll find more below on altering quotations for this purpose.)

Quote Authoritative Language

When you quote experts or prominent political, artistic, or historical figures, you enhance the credibility of your own work. You might quote to help explain or define or to support an argument. In this next example, student writer Peter Simmons quotes the author of a well-reviewed book on bullying to help him clarify the *mis*use of the term:

> "[A]t least ten different definitions" are being used in state laws, according to Emily Bazelon, author of *Sticks and Stones: Defeating the Culture of Bullying*—and, for her, that's a problem. A frequent commentator on the subject, Bazelon argues that "bullying isn't the same as garden-variety teasing or a two-way conflict. The word is being overused," she writes, "expanding accordionlike, to encompass both appalling violence or harassment and a few mean words."

Altering Quotations

1.9   Alter quotations with ellipses and brackets.

At times, you may need to alter a quotation in order to integrate it effectively into your writing. Two of the ways to do so are to use ellipses and to use brackets.

Use Ellipses to Indicate Omissions

At times you may decide to omit some words from a quotation—possibly for reasons of length, possibly because you want to emphasize only one part of a quoted passage. When you omit words from a quotation, alert readers to the change by using ellipses, three spaced periods (. . .). Consider the following:

> It's hard to pinpoint the invention of the electric car to one inventor or country. Instead it was a series of breakthroughs—from the battery to the electric motor—in the 1800s that led to the first electric vehicle on the road.
>
> —U.S. Department of Energy, "Timeline: History of the Electric Car"

Here is one way to quote this sentence, leaving out the parenthetical remark "from the battery to the electric motor." The ellipses indicate that you have altered quoted material by removing words.

> "It's hard to pinpoint the invention of the electric car to one inventor or country. Instead it was a series of breakthroughs . . . in the 1800s that led to the first electric vehicle on the road."

Online you will readily find advice on using ellipses to:

- omit the beginning of a sentence;
- omit the end of a sentence;

- quote the opening of a paragraph, omit sentences, and resume quoting the end of the paragraph; or

- omit one or more paragraphs when quoting a lengthy passage.

The details of punctuation vary somewhat in these cases, but the point to remember is clear: Show omissions with ellipses.

Use Brackets to Add or Substitute Words

Sometimes you must *add* words to a quotation both for clarity and to integrate another person's language into the flow of your own sentence. When doing so, use brackets, which distinguish your words from those of the source author's. For instance, when a quoted pronoun's reference (such as "she" or "he") would be unclear, delete the pronoun and substitute an identifying word or phrase in brackets. In making the substitution, no ellipses are needed.

Assume you've decided to quote the underlined sentence:

> Young teens need to learn that not everything they hear or see is true. Let your child know that the TV show or movie he sees, the radio station or music he listens to, and the magazine he reads may have a definite point of view. <u>Talk with him about how the media can promote certain ideas or beliefs, which may differ from those of your family</u>. If your child wants to watch, listen to, or read something that you believe is inappropriate, let him know exactly why you object.
>
> —U.S. Department of Education: "Media—Helping Your Child through Early Adolescence"

In quoting this sentence, you need to identify the pronoun *him*. If you don't, readers won't understand the reference. You can make the substitution inside or outside the quotation. If inside, use brackets:

> "Talk with [your young teen] about how the media can promote certain ideas or beliefs, which may differ from those of your family."

If you clarify the reference outside the quotation (and, hence, do not alter the quotation), you do not need to use brackets:

> The U.S. Department of Education urges parents to talk with their young teen "about how the media can promote certain ideas or beliefs."

At times, you may need to change verb tense, number (plural versus singular), or some other point of grammar in order to integrate a quotation into your sentence:

> "If your [children want] to watch, listen to, or read something that you believe is inappropriate, let [them] know exactly why you object."

You should also add clarifying, bracketed information to quoted material when a reference essential to the sentence's meaning is implied but not stated directly. Consider the following:

How do we know that we are all originally from Africa? <u>Twenty years ago the proposition was mostly guesswork</u>.

—Nayan Chanda, *Bound Together*

If you wanted to quote the underlined sentence, you would use brackets to clarify the meaning of "the proposition":

> "Twenty years ago the proposition [that we are all originally from Africa] was mostly guesswork."

As with ellipses, there are numerous variations on when and how to use brackets to note altered quotations, and you will readily find advice online. Here is the principle to remember: *Any time* you add to a quotation, use brackets to distinguish your words from the source author's.

Avoiding Classic Mistakes in Quoting

1.10 Avoid classic mistakes in using quotations.

Avoid Quoting Too Much

Quoting just the right source at the right place can significantly improve your papers. The trick is knowing when to quote (discussed above) and how much to quote. A common error is quoting too much.

The language and intellectual content of your papers should primarily be yours: *your* language, *your* thesis, *your* conclusion. You can and should refer to the work of others to support and improve your work, but when you borrow too much—whether by quoting, summarizing, or paraphrasing—you risk giving away intellectual ownership. Use quotations sparingly as you would a piquant spice. Quote only the words you need, and no more.

Quote Only What You Need

- When you can quote a sentence or two, do not quote a paragraph.

- When you can quote a phrase, do not quote a sentence.

- When you can quote a word or two, do not quote a phrase.

Avoid Freestanding Quotations

Avoid using quotations without a lead-in that sets a context for understanding. Freestanding quotations can be jarring, as in this example:

AVOID

> Many in higher education believe athletic programs distort what ought to be the primary objective of college life. "It sends the wrong message when football coaches earn multiples of what full professors earn." Others are less concerned with symbols than with actual dollars, arguing that money spent on football deprives deserving academic programs of much-needed support.

Even if it were followed by a parenthetical citation, a freestanding quotation like this one ("It sends the wrong message") jars the reader. Introduce quotations with a *signal phrase* (as highlighted here) that prepares readers:

BETTER

> Many in higher education believe athletic programs distort what ought to be the primary objective of college life. As Rhode Island's Assistant Commissioner for Post-Secondary Learning, Anne Sachs, argues, "It sends the wrong message when football coaches earn multiples of what full professors earn." Others are less concerned with symbols. . . .

Understand When to Use First and Last Names

Mention an author's first name only on initial use:

> Many in higher education believe athletic programs distort what ought to be the primary objective of college life. Anne Sachs, Rhode Island's Assistant Commissioner for Post-Secondary Learning, objects to the pay scales of athletic staff: "It sends the wrong message when football coaches. . . ."

All subsequent references to Anne Sachs would be limited to her last name, Sachs. In no event would you refer to the author of your source as "Anne."

> Sachs is particularly offended that some schools pay their head football coach far more than they do their president.

Don't Introduce Well-Known Names

When your readers are college students and instructors, some names—for instance, those of presidents and well-known people like Einstein, Freud, and Picasso—need no introduction and should not be introduced with an identifying (or signal) phrase.

AVOID

> As Albert Einstein, a famous physicist, wrote, . . .
>
> The famous painter Pablo Picasso once said, . . .

BETTER

> As Einstein wrote, . . .
>
> Picasso once said, . . .

Figures such as Einstein and Picasso are part of the cultural landscape. In an academic setting, it is expected that everyone knows who they are. Even if you didn't know at first that Eleanor Roosevelt was the influential and much-admired wife of President Franklin Delano Roosevelt, you would not (on learning that fact during your research) begin a sentence, "Eleanor Roosevelt, wife of Franklin Delano Roosevelt, . . ." As a general rule, write identifying phrases only for source authors who are likely to be unknown to your readers.

Exercise 1.7
Incorporating Quotations

[1]Since the early neurological work on memory in the 1950s and 1960s, studies have demonstrated that memories are not stored in just one part of the brain. [2]They're widely distributed across the whole brain, particularly in an area called the cortex.

[3]Contrary to the popular notion, our memories are not stored in our brains like books on shelves in specific categories. [4]They're actively reconstructed from elements scattered throughout various areas of the cortex by a process called encoding.

[5]As we experience the world through our eyes, ears, and so on, various groups of neurons in the cortex fire together to form a neural pathway from each of these senses and encode these patterns into memories. [6]That's why the aroma of cornbread may trigger a Thanksgiving dinner memory at grandmother's house many years ago, or the sound of a car backfiring may trigger a panic attack in a war veteran.

—Jyutika Mehta, *from* "External Enhancements of Memory May Soon Go High-Tech"

Quote from this passage as follows, using ellipses and/or brackets:

1. Quote sentence 2, providing a clear reference for the word *they're*.

2. Quote sentence 3, from "our memories are" through to the end of sentence 4, deleting the words from *not stored* through *They're.*

3. Quote sentence 6, providing a clear reference for the word *That's.*

Using Signal Phrases

1.11 Use six strategies to incorporate quotations, summaries, and paraphrases into your sentences.

When you incorporate quotations, summaries, or paraphrases into your work, do so in ways that ensure the smooth flow of your sentences. (In "Avoiding Free-standing Quotations" above, you've seen a jarring example of what happens when you *don't* prepare readers for a quotation.) Let's assume that, while conducting research for a paper on foreign aid—particularly, the logic by which the United States gives aid to other countries—you come across the following, written by ecologist Garrett Hardin:

If we divide the world crudely into rich nations and poor nations, two thirds of them are desperately poor, and only one third comparatively rich, with the United States the wealthiest of all. Metaphorically each rich nation can be seen as a lifeboat full of comparatively rich people. In the ocean outside each lifeboat swim the poor of the world, who would like to get in, or at least to share some of the wealth. What should the lifeboat passengers do?

First, we must recognize the limited capacity of any lifeboat. For example, a nation's land has a limited capacity to support a population and as the current [early 1970s] energy crisis has shown us, in some ways we have already exceeded the carrying capacity of our land.

Suppose you want to refer to Hardin's essay by quoting the underlined sentence or by summarizing or paraphrasing his metaphor concerning the lifeboat. We have already noted the importance of introducing references with a *signal phrase*. At the heart of all such phrases is the verb, which characterizes what is to come and sets the reader's expectations. You have options in choosing these verbs. Consider using the ones listed in this box.

Signal Verbs to Introduce Quotations, Summaries, and Paraphrases

Choose from the following list the verb that best characterizes what your source author says. The present tense is typically used in introducing sources.

adds	considers	illustrates	says
agrees	contends	implies	sees
argues	declares	insists	shows
asks	defends	maintains	speculates
asserts	denies	notes	states
believes	derides	observes	suggests
claims	disagrees	points out	thinks
comments	disputes	rejects	warns
compares	emphasizes	relates	writes
concedes	explains	reports	
concludes	finds	responds	
condemns	holds	reveals	

Signal Verbs and Tense

Use signal verbs in the "historical" present tense when introducing quotations, summaries, and paraphrases. The logic: The content of a quotation, summary, or paraphrase is always "present" to you and readers in the way, say, a movie is present every time you watch it, regardless of when it was filmed.

But when referring generally to a source written in the past, one you are not immediately quoting, summarizing, or paraphrasing, use the past tense.

Present tense   Jefferson *writes* that "all men are created equal."

Past tense   Jefferson *wrote* many drafts of the Declaration of Independence.

Six Strategies for Using Signal Phrases (or Sentences)

You can incorporate sources into the flow of your sentences in a variety of ways. Here's how we would introduce and then quote, summarize, and paraphrase Garrett Hardin. In each case, we've highlighted the signal phrase (or sentence):

1. IDENTIFYING PHRASE AT THE BEGINNING

Quotation

> As Garrett Hardin argues, "Metaphorically each rich nation can be seen as a lifeboat full of comparatively rich people" (26).

2. IDENTIFYING PHRASE IN THE MIDDLE

Summary

> To explore the logic of helping the poor, Garrett Hardin uses the metaphor of a lifeboat—comparing those who are safely on board and alive versus those who are not and at risk of drowning (26).

3. IDENTIFYING PHRASE AT THE END

Paraphrase

> The logic by which the United States gives aid to other nations can be explored through the metaphor of a lifeboat. Those in the boat are like the wealthy nations of the world with resources enough to feed their citizens. Those swimming in the ocean beyond the boat are like poor nations struggling for survival. Poor nations want to climb aboard to share the resources of the wealthy and live. But the boat can only support so many passengers without sinking itself. As Garrett Hardin, the ecologist who developed this metaphor, asks, should those in the boat help those outside and risk hurting (or killing) themselves by sharing limited resources (26)?

4. REFERENCE TO A SOURCE PRECEDED BY THAT

Quotation [no comma + bracketed lowercase initial word]

> The ecologist Garrett Hardin suggests that "[m]etaphorically each rich nation can be seen as a lifeboat full of comparatively rich people" (26).

5. IDENTIFYING SENTENCE AT THE BEGINNING—WITH A COLON

Summary

> Garrett Hardin suggests we use a metaphor to examine the logic of foreign aid: With food and resources enough to support their citizens, the wealthy nations of the world are like passengers on a lifeboat who face the question of using limited resources to help those outside the boat, according to Garrett Hardin (26).

Punctuation note: If the words following a colon form a complete sentence, capitalize the first letter of the first word.

6. BLOCK QUOTATION   Use a sentence and colon to introduce quotations longer than four lines.

> Garrett Hardin uses the metaphor of a lifeboat to examine the logic by which the United States gives aid to other nations:
>
>> If we divide the world crudely into rich nations and poor nations, two thirds of them are desperately poor, and only one third comparatively rich, with the United States the wealthiest of all. Metaphorically each rich nation can be seen as a lifeboat full of comparatively rich people. In the ocean outside each lifeboat swim the poor of the world, who would like to get in, or at least to share some of the wealth. What should the lifeboat passengers do? (26)

Incorporating Quotations into Your Sentences

- **Quote only the part of a sentence or paragraph that you need.** Use no more of the writer's language than necessary to make or reinforce your point.

- **Incorporate the quotation into the flow of your own sentence.** The quotation must fit, both syntactically and stylistically, into your surrounding language.

- **Avoid freestanding quotations.** A quoted sentence should never stand by itself. Use a *signal phrase*—at the beginning, the middle, or the end of the sentence—to attribute the source of the quotation.

- **Use ellipsis marks.** Indicate deleted language in a quoted sentence with ellipsis marks.

- **Use brackets to add or substitute words.** Use brackets to add or substitute words in a quoted sentence when the meaning of the quotation would otherwise be unclear.

Exercise 1.8

Summarizing, Paraphrasing, and Quoting a Brief Passage

Read the following paragraph from Lincoln's Second Inaugural Address. Make use of the paragraph in three ways: First, write and introduce a summary. Second, write and introduce a paraphrase. Third, quote and introduce the underlined words. When quoting Lincoln, you need to use brackets. Model your three references to this paragraph on any of the six strategies discussed in this section. Remember to use an appropriate signal phrase (including verb) and quotation marks, as needed.

In the opening sentence, Lincoln is referring to his first inauguration:

> On the occasion corresponding to this four years ago all thoughts were anxiously directed to an impending civil war. <u>All dreaded it, all sought to avert it</u>. While the inaugural address was being delivered from this place, devoted altogether to *saving* the Union without war, insurgent agents were in the city seeking to *destroy* it without war—seeking to dissolve the Union and divide effects by negotiation. Both parties deprecated war, but one of them would *make* war rather than let the nation survive, and the other would *accept* war rather than let it perish, and the war came.
>
> —Abraham Lincoln,
> *Second Inaugural Address*, March 4, 1865

How to Use Sources to Build Paragraphs

These guidelines can help you to introduce sources into your paragraphs. Be flexible in applying the guidelines. At times, you may need to invert or skip steps.

1. Write a topic sentence establishing the main idea of the paragraph. On occasion, you might quote or summarize a source to establish this idea.

2. Move your reader toward the source. Follow the topic sentence with another sentence (or two) that introduces the particular fact, example, statistic, or opinion you're calling attention to in the source.

3. Directly introduce the source. If you are stating the author's name in your sentence (as opposed to not-ing it in a citation), use a signal phrase (According to Smith . . .) and/or a descriptive verb (Smith argues that . . .).

4. Quote, summarize, or paraphrase the source using techniques.

5. Cite the source.

6. *Use* the source: Comment, respond, explain its significance.

7. (Optional) Introduce additional sources into the paragraph to create a conversation, but do so only if you prepare for each new source by following some version of steps 1–6.

Avoiding Plagiarism

1.12 Avoid plagiarism by citing sources and using your own words and sentence structure.

Plagiarism is generally defined as the attempt to pass off the work of another as one's own. Whether born out of calculation or desperation, plagiarism is the least tolerated offense in the academic world. The fact that most plagiarism is unintentional—arising from an ignorance of the conventions rather than deceitfulness—makes no difference to many professors.

The ease of cutting and pasting whole blocks of text from Web sources into one's own paper makes it tempting for some to take the easy way out and avoid doing their own research and writing. But, apart from the serious ethical issues involved, the same technology that makes such acts possible also makes it possible for instructors to detect them. Software marketed to instructors allows them to conduct Web searches, using suspicious phrases as keywords. The results often provide irrefutable evidence of plagiarism. You can avoid plagiarism and charges of plagiarism by following the basic rules provided in the box on page 64.

Following is a passage from an article by Richard Rovere on Senator Joseph P. McCarthy, along with several student versions of the ideas represented.

> McCarthy never seemed to believe in himself or in anything he had said. He knew that Communists were not in charge of American foreign policy. He knew that they weren't running the United States Army. He knew that he had spent five years looking for Communists in the government and that—although some

> must certainly have been there, since Communists had turned up in practically every other major government in the world—he hadn't come up with even one.[11]

One student version of this passage reads:

> McCarthy never believed in himself or in anything he had said. He knew that Communists were not in charge of American foreign policy and weren't running the United States Army. He knew that he had spent five years looking for Communists in the government, and although there must certainly have been some there, since Communists were in practically every other major government in the world, he hadn't come up with even one.

Clearly, this is intentional plagiarism. The student has copied the original passage almost word for word.

Here is another version of the same passage:

> McCarthy knew that Communists were not running foreign policy or the Army. He also knew that, although there must have been some Communists in the government, he hadn't found a single one, even though he had spent five years looking.

This student has attempted to put the ideas into her own words, but both the wording and the sentence structure are so heavily dependent on the original passage that even if it *were* cited, most professors would consider it plagiarism.

In the following version, the student has changed the wording and sentence structure sufficiently, and she uses a *signal phrase* (a phrase used to introduce a quotation or paraphrase, signaling to the reader that the words to follow come from someone else) to credit the information to Rovere properly so that there is no question of plagiarism:

> According to Richard Rovere, McCarthy was fully aware that Communists were running neither the government nor the Army. He also knew that he hadn't found a single Communist in government, even after a lengthy search (192).

And although this is not a matter of plagiarism, as noted above, it's essential to quote accurately. Do not change any part of a quotation or omit any part of it without using brackets or ellipses. (For more on ellipses and brackets, see pages 55–56.)

Rules for Avoiding Plagiarism

- Cite *all* quoted material and *all* summarized and paraphrased material, unless the information is common knowledge (e.g., the Civil War was fought from 1861 to 1865).

- Make sure that both the *wording* and the *sentence structure* of your summaries and paraphrases are substantially your own.

---

[11]Richard Rovere, "The Most Gifted and Successful Demagogue This Country Has Ever Known," *New York Times Magazine*, April 30, 1967.

Chapter 2
Critical Reading and Critique

Learning Objectives

After completing this chapter, you will be able to:

2.1 Understand the connection between critical reading and critique.

2.2 Analyze the informative and persuasive strategies authors use to achieve their purpose.

2.3 Identify points of agreement and disagreement with an author and evaluate assumptions.

2.4 Write a critique of an article, editorial, or chapter.

Critical Reading

2.1   Understand the connection between critical reading and critique.

In college work, you read to learn and use new information. But sources are not equally valid or equally useful, so you must learn to distinguish critically among them by evaluating them. Through evaluation, you determine the extent to which sources are reliable.

There is no ready-made formula for determining reliability. Critical reading and its written equivalent—the *critique*—require discernment; sensitivity; imagination; knowledge of the subject; and, above all, willingness to become involved in what you read. These skills are developed only through repeated practice. But you must begin somewhere, and so we recommend that you start by posing two broad questions about passages, articles, and books that you read:

1. To what extent does the author succeed in his or her purpose?
2. To what extent do you agree with the author?

Where Do We Find Written Critiques?

Here are just a few of the types of writing that involve critique:

Academic Writing

- **Research papers** critique sources in order to establish their usefulness.
- **Position papers** stake out a position by critiquing other positions.
- **Book reviews** combine summary with critique.
- **Essay exams** demonstrate understanding of course material by critiquing it.

Workplace Writing

- **Legal briefs and legal arguments** critique previous arguments made by or anticipated from opposing counsel.
- **Business plans and proposals** critique other less cost-effective, efficient, or reasonable approaches.
- **Policy briefs** communicate strengths and weaknesses of policies and legislation through critique.

Question 1: To What Extent Does the Author Succeed in His or Her Purpose?

2.2 Analyze the informative and persuasive strategies authors use to achieve their purpose.

All critical reading *begins with an accurate summary.* Before attempting an evaluation, you must be able to locate an author's thesis and identify the selection's content and structure. You must also understand the author's *purpose.*

Authors write to inform, to persuade, and to entertain. A given piece may be primarily *informative* (a summary of the research on cloning), primarily *persuasive* (an argument on what the government should do to alleviate homelessness), or primarily *entertaining* (a play about the frustrations of young lovers). Or it may be all three (as in John Steinbeck's novel *The Grapes of Wrath,* about migrant workers during the Great Depression). But if the finished piece is coherent, it will have a primary reason for having been written. Identifying this primary reason—this purpose—is your first job as a critical reader.

Your next job is to determine how successful the author has been in achieving this objective. As a critical reader, you bring different criteria, or standards of judgment, to bear when you read pieces intended to inform, persuade, or entertain.

Writing to Inform

A piece intended to inform provides definitions, describes or reports on a process, recounts a story, gives historical background, and/or provides facts and figures. An informational piece responds to questions such as these:

What (or who) is _____?

How does _____ work?

What is the controversy or problem about?

What happened?

How and why did it happen?

What were the results?

What are the arguments for and against _____?

To the extent that an author answers such questions and you could (if you had the time) confirm these answers, the selection is intended to inform. Having determined this, you can organize your response by considering three criteria: accuracy, significance, and fair interpretation of information.

EVALUATING INFORMATIVE WRITING

Accuracy of Information   It is your responsibility as a critical reader to determine if information is trustworthy. You should check facts against other sources. Government publications are often good resources for verifying facts about political legislation, population data, crime statistics, and the like. You can also search key terms in library databases and on the Web.

Web Sites and the Trust Factor: Know What Sort of Site You're On

- *Some Web-based sources* are identical to print-based counterparts.

  These sites—for instance, the Web-based version of major newspapers and magazines—will be as authoritative as their edited, fact-checked counterparts in print. They differ only in their medium of publication. You should try to verify information found on such sites (by checking against other sources), but the likelihood is high that this information is reliable.

- *Many Web-based sources* are self-published.

  Self-published Web sites present a greater challenge in terms of accuracy because distorted "facts," unsupported opinion, and hidden agendas are often offered as reliable. Beware! It will often be difficult to verify what you find on such sites.

Significance of Information   One useful question that you can put to a reading is "So what?" In the case of selections that attempt to inform, you may reasonably wonder whether the information makes a difference. What can the reader gain from this information? How is knowledge advanced by the publication of this material? Is the information of importance to you or to others in a particular audience? Why or why not?

Fair Interpretation of Information   At times you will read reports whose sole purpose is to relate raw data or information. More frequently, once authors present information, they will attempt to evaluate or interpret it. Distinguish between the author's presentation of facts and figures and his or her attempts to evaluate them. Watch for shifts from straightforward descriptions of factual information ("20 percent of the population") to assertions about what this information means ("a mere 20 percent of the population"), what its implications are, and so on. You may find that the information is valuable but the interpretation is not.

Questions to pose for interpreted facts:

- Could you offer a contrary explanation for the same facts?
- Does more information need to be gathered before firm conclusions can be drawn? Why?

Writing to Persuade

Writing is frequently intended to persuade—that is, to influence the reader's thinking. To make a persuasive case, the writer must begin with an assertion that is arguable, some statement about which reasonable people could disagree. Such an assertion is called a *thesis*. Here are two examples:

1. Because they do not speak English, many children in this affluent land are being denied their fundamental right to equal educational opportunity.

2. Bilingual education, which has been promoted by a small group of activists with their own agenda, is detrimental to the very students it is supposed to serve.

Thesis statements such as these represent conclusions that authors have drawn as a result of researching and thinking about an issue. You go through the same process yourself when you write persuasive papers or critiques. And just as you are entitled to evaluate critically the assertions of authors you read, so your professors—as well as other students—are entitled to evaluate *your* assertions.

Keep in mind that writers organize arguments by arranging evidence to support one conclusion and to oppose (or dismiss) another. You can assess the validity of an argument and its conclusion by determining whether the author has (1) clearly defined key terms, (2) used information fairly, and (3) argued logically and not fallaciously (see pp. 74–78).

EVALUATING PERSUASIVE WRITING   On July 7, 2015, Consumer Watchdog, a consumer protection organization, petitioned the Federal Trade Commission

Exercise 2.1
Informative and Persuasive Thesis Statements

With a partner from your class, identify at least one informative and one persuasive thesis statement from two passages of your own choosing. Photocopy these passages and highlight the statements you have selected.

As an alternative, and also working with a partner, write one informative and one persuasive thesis statement for *three* of the topics listed at the end of this exercise. For example, for the topic of prayer in schools, your informative thesis statement could read:

> Both advocates and opponents of school prayer frame their position as a matter of freedom.

Your persuasive thesis statement might be worded as follows:

> As long as schools don't dictate what kinds of prayers students should say, then school prayer should be allowed and even encouraged.

Don't worry about taking a position that you agree with or feel you could support; this exercise doesn't require that you write an essay. Here are the topics:

Immigration policy

Stem cell research

Grammar instruction in English class

Violent lyrics in music

Teaching computer skills in primary schools

Curfews in college dormitories

Course registration procedures

(FTC) to argue that U.S. citizens should enjoy the right to be forgotten online: the right to ask search engine companies, like Google, to delist—that is, to remove from search engine results—links to Web sites that are irrelevant, embarrassing, or damaging.

A fascinating debate ensued, as you'll discover in the following brief selections. As you read, consider the merits of each argument and take a position. What do *you* think about the "Right to Be Forgotten" online—and why? Crucially, you must understand the reasons for your conclusions. In the model critique that follows the third selection, you'll see how student Ethel Weiss develops her response.

Here is a list of the readings:

- The opening two paragraphs from Consumer Watchdog's complaint to the FTC
- The *Washington Post*'s (negative) response to Consumer Watchdog's position
- An editorial in support of Consumer Watchdog's position

Consumer Watchdog

July 7, 2015

Chairwoman Edith Ramirez

Commissioner Julie Brill

Commissioner Maureen K. Ohlhausen

Commissioner Joshua D. Wright

Commissioner Terrell McSweeny

Federal Trade Commission

600 Pennsylvania Avenue, N.W.

Washington, D.C. 20580

Re: Complaint Regarding Google's Failure to Offer "Right to Be Forgotten" in the U.S.

Dear Chairwoman Ramirez and Commissioners Brill, Ohlhausen, Wright, and McSweeny:

I am writing on behalf of Consumer Watchdog, a nationally recognized nonprofit, nonpartisan consumer education and advocacy organization, to formally lodge a complaint about Google's failure to offer U.S. users the ability to request the removal of search engine links from their name to information that is inadequate, irrelevant, no longer relevant, or excessive. In Europe the ability to make this request is popularly referred to as the Right To Be Forgotten. As Commissioner Brill has suggested it may more accurately be described as the Right Of Relevancy or the Right To Preserve Obscurity. Google's refusal to honor the right and consider such removal requests in the United States while holding itself out to be concerned about users' privacy is both unfair and deceptive, violating Section 5 of the Federal Trade Commission Act. We urge the Commission to investigate and act.

Here is why the Right To Be Forgotten—or Right of Relevancy—is so important to protecting consumers' privacy in the digital age: Before the Internet if someone did something foolish when they were young—and most of us probably did—there might well be a public record of what happened. Over time, as they aged, people tended to forget whatever embarrassing things someone did in their youth. They would be judged mostly based on their current circumstances, not on information no longer relevant. If someone else were highly motivated, they could go back into paper files and folders and dig up a person's past. Usually this required effort and motivation. For a reporter, for instance, this sort of deep digging was routine with, say, candidates for public office, not for Joe Blow citizen. This reality that our youthful indiscretions and embarrassments and other matters no longer relevant slipped from the general public's consciousness is Privacy By Obscurity. The Digital Age has ended that. Everything—all our digital footprints—are instantly available with a few clicks on a computer or taps on a mobile device.

—John M. Simpson

Americans Shouldn't Demand a "Right to Be Forgotten" Online

Washington Post*

By the Editorial Board, August 28, 2015

Should the Federal Trade Commission force Google to respect people's "right to be forgotten"?

No.

Last year a European court ordered the online search giant to bow to people's interest in obscurity, and ever since the company has had to take requests from European citizens who want their Google results purged of unflattering links. European judges reasoned that privacy concerns should take precedence over public access to online speech.

Now Consumer Watchdog, a U.S. nonprofit, wants to bring these sorts of limits on freedom of expression to the United States: The group petitioned the FTC to force Google to offer U.S. citizens similar treatment. It's an understandable but misguided request.

First, any FTC action likely would run afoul of the First Amendment. The FTC wouldn't mandate the removal of information from the Internet; Web sites wouldn't be taken down. But they would become much harder to locate, with the FTC effectively prescribing what speech should be findable and what should not. The government shouldn't entangle itself.

Consumer Watchdog's request also would create an incentive for tech companies to suppress information, as they would face regulatory scrutiny for permitting unflattering information to remain accessible while facing little countervailing pressure to keep information findable. Google has acceded to only about 40 percent of delisting requests it has received in Europe since it lost its case there. But the company could decide in the future that carefully evaluating delisting requests isn't worth the time, and other companies might, too.

Even without FTC action, Europe's regulatory overreach may affect the whole Internet: French privacy authorities are pressing Google to remove links from all its search sites, not just those most Europeans use.

If government mandates are a bad idea, what about voluntary action? Google says it wants its search results to reflect "the whole Web," not just what search subjects want viewable. That's the right instinct. As much as possible, there should not be two worlds of public information online—an attenuated one that is accessible to all, and a wider realm that is accessible to those with more time, know-how, or money. Moreover, online norms should not tilt the system against small-time publishers in favor of larger ones who have more capacity to make a fuss when their links are delisted. After pushback from major European media organizations, Google restored links to some of their material. It seems unlikely a local blogger writing on a no-name site would get equal consideration, or even know how to press for it.

There's room for compromise with people who worry that one slip-up saved on a Web site somewhere will haunt them for the rest of their lives. Google announced in June that it will deny people easy access to "revenge porn," for example, since its only purpose is to degrade. And when it comes to information people voluntarily surrender about themselves, whether for public circulation or not, Web services' privacy policies should be clear about what information users are handing over and how they can purge it later.

These would be modest improvements. But unspectacular progress is better than starting down the road of stifling the Internet's remarkably free flow of information.

The Right to Bury the (Online) Past

Washington Post, September 13, 2015

By Liza Tucker

Liza Tucker is a consumer advocate with the nonprofit group Consumer Watchdog.

Imagine your 18-year-old daughter is decapitated in a car accident. Gruesome police photographs of her body are leaked onto the Internet. Every time someone searches your family's name, the photos pop up at the top of the page. That's what happened to Christos and Lesli Catsouras because in the United States, unlike in Europe, search engines are not required to act on requests by individuals to remove such links.

That's why our nonprofit consumer group has petitioned the Federal Trade Commission to grant every American "the right to be forgotten," a position the [*Washington*] *Post* criticized in an August 28 editorial, "Stifling the Internet," for potentially opening the door to the purging of "unflattering" links upon request. We believe that families such as the Catsourases should have the right to ask the Internet's corporate gatekeepers to stop elevating deeply disturbing, unauthorized, irrelevant, excessive, or distorted personal information to the top of search results associated with their names.

Extending the right to be forgotten to Americans would not mean that government would limit freedom of expression, as the *Post* suggested. True suppression of speech happens when a government reviews all media and suppresses those parts it deems objectionable on moral, political, military, or other grounds. With a right to be forgotten, Google, Yahoo, and other corporations—not the government—would decide what material should not be provided in response to search requests, while the material would still remain on any Web sites that posted it.

Google may be battling this right in the United States, but in Europe it has shown that it is perfectly capable of separating the wheat from the chaff. Google reports that it has evaluated more than 310,000 requests to remove more than 1.1 million URLs. It has removed about 42 percent and left 58 percent alone.

The sorts of requests that Google had denied involve people who want embarrassing, but still relevant, information excised from the Web. For example, Google did not remove links to recent articles reporting on the arrest and conviction of a Swiss financial professional for financial crimes. He's still in that business, so those who might deal with him should know. Google denied a request from a man in Britain to remove references to his dismissal for sexual crimes committed on the job. Such information is relevant to his next employer.

Requests that Google has honored also make sense. A rape victim in Germany asked it to remove a link to a newspaper article about the crime. A woman in Italy asked for the removal of links to a decades-old article about the murder of her husband in which her name was used. Google rightly complied as the widely accessible information victimized individuals all over again.

Such readily accessible material can be devastating, unjustly foreclosing economic and social opportunities. The more prominent the result, the more credible, accurate, and relevant it can seem, even if the opposite is true.

For example, a Florida doctor locked herself into a bedroom to avoid a violent boyfriend. After he jimmied the lock with a knife, she scratched his chest with her fingernails. He told police she had used the knife on him. Police arrested them both and charged her with aggravated assault with a deadly weapon. The charges against her were soon dropped, but she had to pay thousands to Web sites to remove her mug shot.

A middle-aged school guidance counselor disclosed the fact that she modeled lingerie in her late teens when she was hired, but she still was fired after the photos surfaced on the Web. It made no difference that the photos were irrelevant to her job.

U.S. law already recognizes that certain information should become irrelevant after the passage of time has demonstrated that an individual is not likely to repeat a mistake. The Fair Credit Reporting Act, which is enforced by the FTC, dictates that debt collections, civil lawsuits, tax liens, and even arrests for criminal offenses in most cases be considered obsolete after seven years and so excluded from credit reports.

This concept is not lost on Google. When a teacher in Germany who was convicted for a minor crime over 10 years ago contacted the company, it removed links to an article about the conviction from search results for the individual's name. But public figures are a different matter. When a high-ranking public official asked to remove recent articles discussing a decades-old criminal conviction, Google declined.

Google touts its privacy principles, claiming that it strives to offer its diverse users "meaningful and fine-grained choices over the use of their personal information." It's deceptive and unfair for Google to make this claim but not to honor the privacy it purports to protect.

Google makes money off online searches. It has an obligation not to exploit or appropriate the salacious details of people's lives in the pursuit of clicks and money without considering petitions to have such details removed.

The Catsouras family and others have the right not to be traumatized forever by images or information that never belonged in the public domain. They deserve the right to bury the past and move on. Google's refusal to answer the family's pleas without a law in place compelling it to do so shows exactly why the FTC needs to act.

Exercise 2.2
Critical Reading Practice

Look back to Chapter 1, pages 21–22, for the section titled "Rereading for Content and Structure." Use each of the guidelines listed there to examine the argument by Liza Tucker. Note in the margins of the selection, or on a separate sheet of paper, the argument's main point, subpoints, and use of examples.

PERSUASIVE STRATEGIES

Clearly Defined Terms   The validity of an argument depends to some degree on how carefully an author has defined key terms. Take the assertion, for example, that American society must be grounded in "family values." Just what do people who use this phrase mean by it? The validity of their argument depends on whether they and their readers agree on a definition of "family values"—as well as what it means to be "grounded in" family values. The success of the argument—its ability to persuade—hinges on the definition of a key term. In responding to an argument, be sure you (and the author) are clear on what exactly is being argued.

Note that, in addition to their *denotative* meaning (their specific or literal meaning), many words carry a *connotative* meaning (their suggestive, associative, or emotional meaning). For example, the denotative meaning of "home" is simply the house or apartment where one lives. But the connotative meaning— with its associations of family, belongingness, refuge, safety, and familiarity— adds a significant emotional component to this literal meaning. (See more on connotation in "Emotionally Loaded Terms," p. 75.)

In the course of her argument, Tucker writes the following: "We believe that families such as the Catsourases should have the right to ask the Internet's corporate gatekeepers to stop elevating deeply disturbing, unauthorized, irrelevant, excessive, or distorted personal information to the top of search results associated with their names." In part, agreement with Tucker depends on whether or not readers share her definition of what counts as "irrelevant" information. As a newspaper in the business of guarding our rights to free speech, the *Post* believes that all information has value (is "relevant") and should not be suppressed. Not surprisingly, the *Post* and Tucker disagree over the right to be forgotten online.

As the writer of a critique, you should identify and discuss any undefined or ambiguous term that might give rise to confusion.

Fair Use of Information   Information is used as evidence in support of arguments. When you encounter such evidence, ask yourself two questions: (1) "Is the information accurate and up-to-date?" At least a portion of an argument becomes invalid when the information used to support it is wrong or stale. (2) "Has the author cited *representative* information?" The evidence used in an argument must be presented in a spirit of fair play. An author is less than ethical when he presents only the evidence favoring his own views even though he is well aware that contrary evidence exists. For instance, it would be dishonest to argue that an economic recession is imminent and to cite only indicators of economic downturn while ignoring and failing to cite contrary (positive) evidence.

"The Right to Bury the (Online) Past" is not an information-heavy essay. The success of the piece turns on the author's powers of persuasion, not on her use of facts and figures. Tucker does, however, discuss Google's (self-) published track record of reviewing petitions for delisting information. Her discussion of this material extends only as far as Google's self-published examples. Yet more than a month prior to publication of her op-ed in the *Post*, Google suffered a data leak concerning its delisting policies, and newspapers like *The Guardian* found reasons to be skeptical that Google was doing all it could, or should, in transparently considering petitions for delisting. This information casts doubt on Google's ability to handle delisting well. The information was available to Tucker, though it went unused—a point raised in the model critique of her argument because it raises questions about her assumption that we can trust Google to make the right delisting decisions.

LOGICAL ARGUMENTATION: AVOIDING LOGICAL FALLACIES

At some point, you'll need to respond to the logic of the argument itself. To be convincing, an argument should be governed by principles of *logic*—clear and orderly thinking. This does *not* mean that an argument cannot be biased. A biased argument—that is, an argument weighted toward one point of view and against others, which is in fact the nature of argument—may be valid as long as it is logically sound.

Let's examine several types of faulty thinking and logical fallacies you will need to watch for.

Emotionally Loaded Terms   Writers sometimes attempt to sway readers by using emotionally charged words. Words with positive connotations (e.g., "family values") are intended to sway readers to the author's point of view; words with negative connotations (e.g., "paying the price") try to sway readers away from an opposing point of view. The fact that an author uses emotionally loaded terms does not necessarily invalidate an argument. Emotional appeals are perfectly legitimate and time-honored modes of persuasion. But in academic writing, which is grounded in logical argumentation, they should not be the *only* means of persuasion. You should be sensitive to *how* emotionally loaded terms are being used. In particular, are they being used deceptively or to hide the essential facts?

Tucker uses her share of emotionally loaded words, part of her strategy of securing the reader's support for her position. Certainly no one would want "gruesome" photos of our deceased loved ones readily available online. No one would want others to gawk at personal information we regard as "deeply disturbing, . . . irrelevant, excessive, or distorted." Tucker wants us on her side, and her emotionally loaded language works—to an extent. Still, critical readers must recognize these words for what they are: part of an emotional strategy for argument. For the logic of her argument we must look elsewhere. Above all, do not let an emotional appeal blind you to shortcomings of logic, ambiguously defined terms, or a misuse of facts.

Ad Hominem **Argument**   In an *ad hominem* argument, the writer rejects opposing views by attacking the person who holds them. By calling opponents names, an author avoids the issue. Consider this excerpt from a political speech:

> I could more easily accept my opponent's plan to increase revenues by collecting on delinquent tax bills if he had paid more than a hundred dollars in state taxes in each of the past three years. But the fact is, he's a millionaire with a millionaire's tax shelters. This man hasn't paid a wooden nickel for the state services he and his family depend on. So I ask you: Is *he* the one to be talking about taxes to *us*?

It could well be that the opponent has paid almost no state taxes for three years, but this fact has nothing to do with, and is used as a ploy to divert attention from, the merits of a specific proposal for increasing revenues. The proposal is lost in the attack against the man himself, an attack that violates principles of logic. Writers (and speakers) should make their points by citing evidence in support of their views and by challenging contrary evidence.

Faulty Cause and Effect   The fact that one event precedes another in time does not mean that the first event has caused the second. An example: Fish begin dying by the thousands in a lake near your hometown. An environmental group immediately cites chemical dumping by several manufacturing plants as the cause. But other causes are possible: A disease might have affected the fish, the growth of algae might have contributed to the deaths, or acid rain might be a factor. The origins of an event are usually complex and are not always traceable to a single cause. You must carefully examine cause-and-effect reasoning when you find a writer using it. In Latin, this fallacy is known as *post hoc, ergo propter hoc* ("after this, therefore because of this").

Tucker argues that federal regulation is needed to force Google into considering petitions to delist offensive, irrelevant Web sites. Even allowing for agreement on what counts as "irrelevant," Tucker assumes that a FTC rule would lead to the outcome she desires. Essentially, she's arguing cause and effect: do this (set a rule) to cause that (responsible delisting). Yet there are problems that may cloud these effects. First, she's not considering the potential conflicts Google faces each time it considers a petition to delist. Might financial concerns—money to be made from advertising—complicate Google's ability to make ethical decisions? Second, should Google be making these decisions at all? Do its employees have the training or interest to make sound, consistent decisions about delisting sites? True, an FTC rule would force an "effect," and some sites would be delisted. But would this be the best possible, fairest, and most consistent effect? (You'll find more on this line of critique in the model paper.)

Either/Or Reasoning   Either/or reasoning also results from an unwillingness to recognize complexity. If in analyzing a problem an author artificially restricts the range of possible solutions by offering only two courses of action and then rejects the one that he opposes, he cannot logically argue that the remaining course of action, which he favors, is therefore the only one that makes sense. Usually, several other options (at least) are possible. For whatever reason, the author has chosen to overlook them. As an example, suppose you are reading a selection on genetic engineering in which the author builds an argument on the basis of the following:

> Research in gene splicing is at a crossroads: Either scientists will be carefully monitored by civil authorities and their efforts limited to acceptable applications, such as disease control; or, lacking regulatory guidelines, scientists will set their own ethical standards and begin programs in embryonic manipulation that, however well intended, exceed the proper limits of human knowledge.

Certainly, other possibilities for genetic engineering exist beyond the two mentioned here. But the author limits debate by establishing an either/or choice. Such a limitation is artificial and does not allow for complexity. As a critical reader, you need to be on the alert for reasoning based on restrictive either/or alternatives.

Tone

Tone refers to the overall emotional effect produced by a writer's choice of language. Writers might use especially emphatic words to create a tone: A film reviewer might refer to a "magnificent performance," or a columnist might criticize "sleazeball politics."

These are extreme examples of tone; tone can also be more subtle, particularly if the writer makes a special effort *not* to inject emotion into the writing. As we indicated in the section on emotionally loaded terms, the fact that a writer's tone is highly emotional does not necessarily mean that the writer's argument is invalid. Conversely, a neutral tone does not ensure an argument's validity.

Many instructors discourage student writing that projects a highly emotional tone, considering it inappropriate for academic or preprofessional work. (One sure sign of emotion: the exclamation mark, which should be used sparingly.)

Hasty Generalization   Writers are guilty of hasty generalization when they draw their conclusions from too little evidence or from unrepresentative evidence. To argue that scientists should not proceed with the Human Genome Project because a recent editorial urged that the project be abandoned is to make a hasty generalization. That lone editorial may be unrepresentative of the views of most individuals—both scientists and laypeople—who have studied and written about the matter.

False Analogy   Comparing one person, event, or issue to another may be illuminating, but it can also be confusing or misleading. Differences between the two may be more significant than their similarities, and conclusions drawn from one may not necessarily apply to the other. A candidate for governor who argues that her experience as CEO of a major business would make her effective in governing a state is assuming an analogy between the business and the political/civic worlds that may not hold up to examination. Most businesses are hierarchical, or top-down: When a CEO issues an order, he or she can expect it to be carried out without argument. But governors command only their own executive branches.

They cannot issue orders to independent legislatures or courts (much less private citizens); they can only attempt to persuade. In this case, the thoughtful reader or listener is entitled to challenge the implied analogy.

Begging the Question   To beg the question is to assume as proven fact the very thesis being argued. To assert, for example, that the United States does not need a new healthcare delivery system because it currently has the best healthcare in the world does not prove anything: It merely repeats the claim in different—and equally unproven—words. This fallacy is also known as *circular reasoning*.

Non Sequitur   *Non sequitur* is Latin for "it does not follow"; the term is used to describe a conclusion that does not logically follow from the premise. "Because minorities have made such great strides in the past few decades," a writer may argue, "we no longer need affirmative action programs." Aside from the fact that the premise itself is arguable (*have* minorities made such great strides?), it does not follow that because minorities *may* have made great strides, there is no further need for affirmative action programs.

Oversimplification   Be alert for writers who offer easy solutions to complicated problems. "America's economy will be strong again if we all 'buy American,'" a politician may argue. But the problems of the U.S. economy are complex and cannot be solved by a slogan or a simple change in buying habits. Likewise, a writer who argues that we should ban genetic engineering assumes that simple solutions ("just say no") will be sufficient to deal with the complex moral dilemmas raised by this new technology.

Exercise 2.3
Understanding Logical Fallacies

List the nine logical fallacies discussed in the preceding section. Briefly define each one in your own words. Then, in a group of three or four classmates, review your definitions and the examples we've provided for each logical fallacy. Collaborate with your group to find or invent additional examples for each of the fallacies. Compare your examples with those generated by the other groups in your class.

Writing to Entertain

Authors write not only to inform and persuade but also to entertain. One response to entertainment is a hearty laugh, but it is possible to entertain without encouraging laughter: A good book or play or poem may prompt you to reflect, grow wistful, become elated, get angry. Laughter is only one of many possible reactions. Like a response to an informative piece or an argument, your response to an essay, poem, story, play, novel, or film should be precisely stated and carefully developed.

Question 2: To What Extent Do You Agree with the Author?

2.3   Identify points of agreement and disagreement with an author and evaluate assumptions.

A critical evaluation consists of two parts. The first part, which we just discussed, assesses the accuracy and effectiveness of an argument in terms of the author's logic and use of evidence. The second part, discussed here, responds to the argument—that is, agrees or disagrees with it.

Identify Points of Agreement and Disagreement

Be precise in identifying where you agree and disagree with an author. State as clearly as possible what *you* believe in relation to what the author believes as presented in the piece. Whether you agree enthusiastically, agree with reservations, or disagree, you can organize your reactions in two parts:

- Summarize the author's position.
- State your own position and justify why you believe as you do. This elaboration becomes an argument itself, regardless of the position you take.

Any opinion that you express is effective to the extent that you support it by supplying evidence from your reading, your observation, or your personal experience. Without such evidence, opinions cannot be authoritative. "I thought the article on inflation was lousy." Or "It was terrific." Why? "I just thought so, that's all." Such opinions have no value in an academic setting because the criticism is imprecise: The critic has taken neither the time to read the article with care nor the time to explore his or her own reactions.

Exercise 2.4

Exploring Your Viewpoints—in Three Paragraphs

Go to a Web site that presents short persuasive essays on current social issues, such as reason.com or drudgereport.com. Or go to an Internet search engine like Google or Bing and type in a social issue together with the word "articles," "editorials," or "opinion," and see what you find. Locate a selection on a topic of interest that takes a clear, argumentative position. Print the selection on which you choose to focus.

- Write one paragraph summarizing the author's key argument.

- Write two paragraphs articulating your agreement or disagreement with the author. (Devote each paragraph to a *single* point of agreement or disagreement.)

    Be sure to explain why you think or feel the way you do and, wherever possible, cite relevant evidence—from your reading, experience, or observation.

Explore Reasons for Agreement and Disagreement: Evaluate Assumptions

One way of developing your responses to a reading is to explore the underlying *reasons* for agreement and disagreement. Your reactions are based largely on assumptions that you hold and how those assumptions compare with the author's. An *assumption* is a fundamental statement about the world and its operations that you take to be true. Often, a writer will express an assumption directly, as in this example:

1. One of government's most important functions is to raise and spend tax revenues on projects that improve the housing, medical, and nutritional needs of its citizens.

In this instance, the writer's claim is a direct expression of a fundamental belief about how the world, or some part of it, should work. The argumentative claim *is* the assumption. Just as often, an argument and its underlying assumption are not identical. In these cases, the assumption is some other statement that is implied by the argumentative claim—as in this example:

2. Human spaceflight is a waste of public money.

The logic of this second statement rests on an unstated assumption relating to the word *waste*. What, in this writer's view, is a *waste* of money? What is an effective or justified use? In order to agree or not with statement 2, a critical reader must know what assumption(s) it rests on. A good candidate for such an assumption would be statement 1. That is, a person who believes statement 1 about how governments ought to raise and spend money could well make statement 2. This may not be the only assumption underlying statement 2, but it could well be one of them.

Inferring and Implying Assumptions

The words *infer* and *imply* are important in any discussion of hidden, or unstated, assumptions. You should be clear about their meanings. A critical reader *infers* what is hidden in a statement and, through that inference, brings what is hidden into the open for examination. Thus, the critical reader infers from statement 2 on human spaceflight the writer's assumption (statement 1) on how governments should spend money. At the same time, the writer of statement 2 *implies* (hints at but does not state directly) an assumption about how governments should spend money. There will be times when writers make statements and are unaware of their own assumptions.

Writers *imply*. Readers *infer*.

Assumptions provide the foundation on which entire presentations are built. You may find an author's assumptions flawed—that is, not supported by factual evidence. You may disagree with value-based assumptions underlying an author's position. For instance, you may not share a writer's assumption of what counts as "good" or "correct" behavior. You may disagree with the conclusions that follow from such assumptions. At the same time, you should be willing to examine the validity of your own assumptions. When your beliefs about the world and how it works are contradicted by actual experience, you may be forced to rethink these beliefs.

Determining the Validity of Assumptions

Once you have identified an assumption—either implied or stated directly—how do you test its soundness, its validity? Start by considering how well the author's assumptions stack up against your own experience, observations, reading, and values—while remaining honestly aware of the limits of your own personal knowledge. Readers will want to examine two assumptions at the heart of Liza Tucker's essay:

1. People have a right to anonymity.
2. For-profit companies are (or should be) equipped to make difficult decisions concerning ethics.

At the very least, readers should be aware of competing assumptions:

3. A free and open society should avoid limiting information.
4. For-profit companies are in business to make money, not arbitrate ethical disputes.

Whether you agree or disagree with an author's assumptions (statements 1 and 2) or the competing assumptions (statements 3 and 4), it is your job to recognize them, whether they are stated or not. In developing your critical response to a source, you should spell out assumptions as best you can and then accept or reject them. Ultimately, your agreement or disagreement with an author will rest on your agreement or disagreement with that author's assumptions.

Critique

2.4 Write a critique of an article, editorial, or chapter.

A *critique* is a *formalized, critical reading of a passage*. It is also a personal response, but writing a critique is considerably more rigorous than saying that a movie is "great" or a book is "fascinating" or "I didn't like it." These are all responses, and, as such, they're a valid, even essential, part of your understanding of what you see and read. But such responses don't illuminate the subject—even for you—if you don't explain how you arrived at your conclusions.

Your task in writing a critique is to turn your critical reading of a passage into a systematic evaluation in order to deepen your reader's (and your own) understanding of that passage. When you read a selection to critique, determine the following:

- What an author says
- How well the points are made

- What assumptions underlie the argument
- What issues are overlooked
- What implications can be drawn from such an analysis

When you write a critique, positive or negative, include the following:

- A fair and accurate summary of the passage
- Information and ideas from other sources (your reading or your personal experience and observations) if you think these are pertinent
- A statement of your agreement or disagreement with the author, backed by specific examples and clear logic
- A clear statement of your own assumptions

Remember that you bring to bear on any subject an entire set of assumptions about the world. Stated or not, your assumptions underlie every evaluation you make. You therefore have an obligation, both to the reader and to yourself, to clarify your standards by making your assumptions explicit. The process of writing a critical assessment forces you to examine your own knowledge, beliefs, and assumptions. Ultimately, the critique is a way of learning about yourself.

How to Write Critiques

You may find it useful to organize a critique into five sections: introduction, summary, assessment of the presentation (on its own terms), your response to the presentation, and conclusion.

The box that follows offers guidelines for writing critiques. These guidelines are not a rigid formula. Most professional authors write critiques that do not follow the structure outlined here. Until you are more confident and practiced in writing critiques, however, we suggest you follow these guidelines. They are meant not to restrict you but rather to provide an initial, workable sequence for formally evaluating the work of others.

Guidelines for Writing Critiques

- **Introduce.** Introduce both the passage under analysis and the author. State the author's main argument and the point(s) you intend to make about it.

  Provide background material to help your readers understand the relevance or appeal of the passage. This background material might include one or more of the following: an explanation of why the subject is of current interest, a reference to a possible controversy surrounding the subject of the passage or the passage itself, biographical information about the author, an account of the circumstances under which the passage was written, and a reference to the intended audience of the passage.

- **Summarize.** Summarize the author's main points. Make sure to state the author's purpose for writing.

- **Assess the presentation.** Evaluate the validity of the author's presentation, distinct from your points of agreement or disagreement. Comment on the author's success in achieving his or her purpose by reviewing three or four specific points. You might base your review on one or more of the following criteria:

> Is the information accurate?
>
> Is the information significant?
>
> Has the author defined terms clearly?
>
> Has the author used and interpreted information fairly?
>
> Has the author argued logically?

- **Respond to the presentation.** Now it is your turn to respond to the author's views. With which views do you agree? With which do you disagree? Discuss your reasons for agreement and disagreement; when possible, tie these reasons to assumptions—both the author's and your own. Where necessary, draw on outside sources to support your ideas.

- **Conclude.** State your conclusions about the overall validity of the piece—your assessment of the author's success at achieving his or her aims and your reactions to the author's views. Remind the reader of the weaknesses and strengths of the passage.

Demonstration: Critique

The critique that follows is based on Liza Tucker's op-ed piece "The Right to Bury the (Online) Past" (pp. 83–86), which we have already begun to examine. In this formal critique, you will see that it is possible to agree with an author's main point—in this case, that we should enjoy a right to be forgotten—yet disagree with how she argues in support of her point. Critiquing a different selection, you could just as easily accept the author's facts and figures but reject the conclusion he or she draws from them. As long as you articulate the author's assumptions and your own carefully, explaining in some detail your agreement and disagreement, the critique is yours to take in whatever direction you see fit.

Model Critique

Ethel Weiss
Professor Alex Neill
Writing 2
11 February 2017

Critique of
"The Right to Bury the (Online) Past"
by Liza Tucker

    Should people have the right to selectively erase their digital past? It's a fact of cyber-life that the Web has an endless memory, possibly a record of everything we've written or viewed online. Who hasn't regretted posting an awkward (or worse) comment or photo, wondering if a bad moment will come back to haunt us? As Internet writer and editor Jason Feifer remarks, "If every regrettable thing we did became part of a permanent social record, we'd all end up bitter and friendless."

1

1 Intro: raising key questions, making the issue real for readers, setting context for the critique.

2 Intro: setting more focused context: European Court's ruling on right to be forgotten (RTBF).

2   It's understandable that people might want relief from damaging or embarrassing online cyber materials. Residents of Europe got that relief in May 2014 when the European Court of Justice ruled:

> European citizens have a right to request that commercial search firms, such as Google, that gather personal information for profit, should remove links to private information when asked, provided the information is no longer relevant. . . . The Court found that the fundamental right to privacy is greater than the economic interest of the commercial firm and, in some circumstances, the public interest in access to Information. (Right to Be)

3 Intro: steering reader to Tucker by way of *Washington. Post.* In last (highlighted) sentence, thesis: both agree and disagree with Tucker.

3   In a recent editorial, the *Washington Post* argued that this right "to be forgotten" should *not* be extended to Americans. The *Post* was responding to a request by the advocacy group Consumer Watchdog that the Federal Trade Commission (FTC) issue a ruling similar to the European Court's. Liza Tucker responded with an editorial of her own defending Consumer Watchdog. In her view, Americans should have the right to "ask the Internet's corporate gatekeepers to stop elevating deeply disturbing, unauthorized, irrelevant, excessive, or distorted personal information to the top of search results." At stake in this debate is a question crucial to democracy: Should the free flow of information and ideas ever be restricted? Tucker says *yes*. She has the best of intentions, but her desire to impose a European Court–like solution in this country raises issues of trust, freedom of speech, and conflict of interest.

4–5 Summary of Tucker.

4   Tucker wants the FTC to require Google (and other search companies), when asked, to consider delisting links to embarrassing online materials that are no longer relevant or newsworthy. She cites the disturbing example of a middle-aged woman who lost her job as a social worker because years earlier, as a teenager, she posed as a lingerie model. Should decades-old photos be allowed to ruin a woman's career when these photos have no bearing on her present work? With the links removed from search lists, these materials would still exist on the Internet but would be difficult (or impossible) to find.

5   Both the *Post* and Tucker agree that, for the moment, Google (Europe) is responding well to requests for delisting links. As of November 3, 2015, the company received 337,132 requests to delist URLs and agreed to do so 42% of the time (Transparency Report). That left 58% of requested materials listed and easily available—links, for instance, to news reports about a man convicted of financial irregularities who wanted references to those irregularities delisted even though he continued to work in the financial industry. Tucker believes the delisting system in Europe has led to a responsible outcome that could be duplicated in the United States. Yet the *Post*, pointing to these same statistics, worries that Google could eventually choose to "suppress information, . . . [concluding] that carefully evaluating delisting requests isn't worth the time."

6 Summary of Tucker continues, using *Washington Post* to make key distinction.

Post: Google should act voluntarily. Tucker: Rules are needed.

6   Still, the *Post* recognizes the need to delist some materials. But instead of forcing Google to act, the *Post* believes that the company should act voluntarily. In fact, Google has already shown a willingness to do so by delisting links to so-called "revenge porn." The *Post* believes rule-free, "unspectacular progress is better than starting down the road of stifling the Internet's remarkably free flow of information." Tucker doesn't want to wait for Google and other companies to police themselves. She wants the FTC to act now.

Tucker is fighting the right battle but advocating the wrong approach in demanding the FTC give Americans a right to be forgotten. Google's business is to scour the Web and deliver search results in the form of a list. As an indexer of Web links, Google is (or should be) blind to the content of this list. In no event is it responsible for this content, which it didn't create. Google's role in the Web-searching experience is to make content available to us, ensuring our right to read and a publisher's right to create any content we want, no matter how offensive to some. In this capacity, Google plays an important role in maintaining the free, unrestricted flow of digital information. The *Post* argues correctly that no matter how "unflattering" online material may be to a particular individual, the danger posed by selectively removing links to that material is potentially *more* damaging because it places the First Amendment freedoms of the larger society at risk.

Tucker believes that forcing Google to consider delisting requests would avoid this danger because the First Amendment applies only to restrictions on speech imposed by governments, not by companies. Technically, this is a valid distinction. The European Court is not dictating which materials can and can't be listed in Google's search results. The Court leaves that decision to Google as it responds to each and every request to delist. Companies can set whatever policies they want along these lines. For instance, if Google wanted to delist every Web site that displayed the word "orange," it would be within its rights to do so. Still, the cumulative result of delisting is the loss of easy access to certain Web sites. When an organization makes previously public information unavailable, that begins to look like censorship *even if* the government is not dictating which links get suppressed. The first problem with Tucker's argument is that she supports a rule that, as the *Post* writes, could "stifl[e] . . . the Internet's remarkably free flow of information."

The second problem is that even if Google agreed to consider requests for delisting certain links, such decisions should not be left in the hands of for-profit companies because of possible conflicts of interest. One conflict, suggested by the *Post*: In deciding cases, Google might consider the size of the media outlet whose content is getting delisted. The smaller the outlet, the less likely it will have the resources to fight a delisting. This calculation might favor larger outlets, which Google might shy away from for fear of getting sued. A second possible conflict: In deciding cases, Google might be motivated by financial considerations—and it would be within its rights to do so as a for-profit company. What would happen, for instance, if links to photos someone wants removed earned Google a significant amount of advertising revenue? In its delisting decision, Google would be forced to weigh ad revenues against requests to delist. There should be no place for either type of conflict when making decisions like these.

While Google seems to be following the European Court's ruling, we have no real way of knowing, and this is the third problem with Tucker's argument: She takes Google at its word that it's doing the right thing. After all, the company has published a Transparency Report about its delisting decisions, which essentially claims: "Look, we're doing well! We're complying with the law!" Maybe not. *The Guardian* (UK) reports that before a Web leak in July 2015, Google had "refused to make public" its data on right-to-be-forgotten requests. The information exposed in that leak led one Dutch researcher to state that Google "is becoming almost like a court or government, but without the fundamental checks on its power." *The Guardian* determined that "Google's data leak reveals flaws in making it judge and jury over our rights." The newspaper has called on Google to be "much more transparent" in its policies for delisting links.

7

7 (Highlighted) transition to critique is a version of the thesis.

First critique of Tucker: *Washington Post*'s position on freedom of speech is correct.

8

8 Critique above continues re: censorship and argues Tucker wrong in claiming RTBF won't involve censorship.

9

9 Second critique of Tucker: two conflicts of interest:

(1) Google might avoid delisting links to big media companies;

(2) Google faces possible conflict between profit and delisting.

10

10 Third critique of Tucker: We don't know if Google is making ethical RTBF decisions.

Two problems: transparency + concentration of power.

11 Critique turns
to writer's
suggestion for
resolving
problem: take
decision out of
Google's hands.

11   Of course, Google invited none of this scrutiny. It fought a losing legal battle with the European Court, and it would fight any attempt to grant U.S. citizens a similar right to be forgotten. But whether in Europe or in the U.S., the decision to grant or deny delisting requests should be taken out of Google's hands because the company is a commercial enterprise not geared to making complicated ethical decisions based on standards it refuses to share. Not that businesses are inherently *un*ethical, and not that Google hasn't been reasonable: according to one report, Google has spent "sizeable resources towards achieving the correct balance in its decisions" and "has been more active and transparent than any competitor" (Powles). But given its for-profit nature and lack of dedicated focus on ethics, there is no reason to trust Google's judgments in granting or refusing a petitioner's request to delist search results. Indeed, after the data leak, *The Guardian* wrote that the company "probably shouldn't be making these decisions without much finer-grained guidance and worked examples from the democratic organs of Europe" (Powles).

12 Conclusion.
Writer agrees
with Tucker that
a need exists.
Disagrees that
Google should
take charge of
solution.

Writer doesn't
offer specific
solution but
points in
direction of
possibilities.

12   Tucker is right: people need relief from damaging online materials. But Google should not be the entity providing that relief. Some other entity—neither the government (for fear of censorship) nor search companies (for fear of conflicts of interest)—should undertake the task of handling delisting requests. Perhaps neutral mediators or arbitrators could help resolve such requests. Whatever the solution, Tucker is correct in arguing that Americans, along with Europeans, should have a "right to be forgotten" online. But she and Consumer Watchdog are wrong to insist that the FTC force Google into making delisting decisions. We need a delisting process that both preserves the free flow of necessary information and allows search engine companies [to] do what they do best.

Works Cited

"Americans Shouldn't Demand a 'Right to Be Forgotten' Online." *Washington Post,* 28 Aug. 2015, www.washingtonpost.com/opinions/americans-shouldnt-demand-a-right-to-be-forgotten-online/2015/08/28/dbc8c262-4aaa-11e5-8e7d-9c033e6745d8_story.html.

Feifer, Jason. "I Wanted to Shame an Accused Con Man. I Didn't Realize How Much Power I Had over Him." *Washington Post,* 30 Oct. 2015, www.washingtonpost.com/opinions/i-wanted-to-shame-an-accused-con-man-i-didnt-realize-how-much-power-i-had-over-him/2015/10/30/e00a7084-72a3-11e5-8248-98e0f5a2e830_story.html.

Powles, Julia. "Google's Data Leak Reveals Flaws in Making It Judge and Jury over Our Rights." *The Guardian,* 14 July 2015, www.theguardian.com/technology/2015/jul/14/googles-data-leak-right-to-be-forgotten.

"The Right to Be Forgotten (*Google v. Spain*)." Epic.org, 2015, https://epic.org/privacy/right-to-be-forgotten/.

"Transparency Report: European privacy requests for search removals." *Google*, 12 Nov. 2015, www.google.com/transparencyreport/removals/government/.

Tucker, Liza. "The Right to Bury the (Online) Past." *Washington Post,* 13 Sept. 2015, www.washingtonpost.com/opinions/the-right-to-bury-the-online-past/2015/09/13/414793bc-5892-11e5-b8c9-944725fcd3b9_story.html.

Exercise 2.5
Informal Critique of the Model Critique

Write an informal response to this critique. What are its strengths and weaknesses? To what extent does the critique follow the general Guidelines for Writing Critiques that we outlined on pages 82–83? To the extent that it varies from the guidelines, speculate on why. Jot down ideas for a critique that takes a different approach to Tucker's op-ed.

Critical Reading for Critique

- *Understand the selection.* Examine the context; note the title and subtitle; identify the main point; identify the subpoints; break the reading into sections; distinguish between points, examples, and counterarguments; watch for transitions within and between paragraphs; and read actively.

- *Establish the writer's primary purpose in writing.* Is the piece meant primarily to inform, persuade, or entertain?

- *Evaluate informative writing. Use these criteria (among others):*

  Accuracy of information

  Significance of information

  Fair interpretation of information

- *Evaluate persuasive writing. Use these criteria (among others):*

  Clear definition of terms

  Fair use and interpretation of information

  Logical reasoning

- *Evaluate writing that entertains. Use these criteria (among others):*

  Interesting characters

  Believable action, plot, and situations

  Communication of theme

  Use of language

- *Decide whether you agree or disagree with the writer's ideas, position, or message.* Once you have determined the extent to which an author has achieved his or her purpose, clarify your position in relation to the writer's.

Chapter 3
Thesis, Introduction, and Conclusion

 ## Learning Objectives

After completing this chapter, you will be able to:

3.1 Write a thesis that makes an assertion about your topic and provides a structure for your paper.

3.2 Write introductions that provide a context for your readers.

3.3 Write conclusions that move beyond a summary of your paper.

Three features of your paper deserve particular attention: your *thesis*, which presents the paper's underlying rationale; your *introduction*, which draws readers into the world of your subject matter; and your *conclusion*, which leaves readers thinking about your particular take on the subject matter. Here we take a closer look at each of these crucial components.

Writing a Thesis

3.1 Write a thesis that makes an assertion about your topic and provides a structure for your paper.

A thesis is a one- or two-sentence summary of a paper's content. Whether explanatory, mildly argumentative, or strongly argumentative, the thesis is an assertion about that content—for instance, what the content is, how it works, what it means, if it is valuable, if action should be taken, and so on. A paper's thesis is similar to its conclusion, but it lacks the conclusion's concern for broad implications and significance. The thesis is the product of your thinking; it therefore represents *your* conclusion about the topic on which you're writing. So you have to have spent some time thinking about this conclusion (that is, during the invention stage) in order to arrive at the thesis that will govern your paper.

For a writer in the drafting stages, the thesis establishes a focus, a basis on which to include or exclude information. For the reader of a finished product, the thesis forecasts the author's discussion. A thesis, therefore, is an essential tool for both writers and readers of academic papers.

The Components of a Thesis

Like any other sentence, a thesis includes a subject and a predicate that together make an assertion about the subject. In the sentence "Lee and Grant were different kinds of generals," "Lee and Grant" is the subject and "were different kinds of generals" is the predicate. What distinguishes a thesis from any other sentence with a subject and a predicate is that *the thesis presents the controlling idea of the paper*. The subject of a thesis, and the assertion about it, must present the right balance between the general and the specific to allow for a thorough discussion within the allotted length of the paper. The discussion might include definitions, details, comparisons, contrasts—whatever is needed to illuminate a subject and support the assertion. (If the sentence about Lee and Grant were a thesis, the reader would assume that the rest of the paper contained comparisons and contrasts between the two generals.)

Bear in mind when writing theses that the more general your subject and the more complex your assertion, the longer your discussion must be to cover the subject adequately. The broadest theses require book-length treatments, as in this case:

> Meaningful energy conservation requires a shrewd application of political, financial, and scientific will.

You couldn't write an effective ten-page paper based on this thesis. The topic alone would require pages just to define what you mean by "energy conservation" and "meaningful." Energy can be conserved in homes, vehicles, industries, appliances, and power plants, and each of these areas would need consideration. Having accomplished this first task of definition, you would then turn your attention to the claim, which entails a discussion of how politics, finance, and science individually and collectively influence energy conservation. Moreover, the thesis requires you to argue that "shrewd application" of politics, finance, and science is required. The thesis may very well be accurate and compelling, yet it promises entirely too much for a ten-page paper.

So to write an effective thesis and therefore a controlled, effective paper, you need to limit your subject and your claims about it. This narrowing process should help you arrive at a manageable topic for your paper. You will convert that topic to a thesis when you make an assertion about it—a *claim* that you will explain and support in the paper.

MAKING AN ASSERTION

Thesis statements make an assertion or claim *about* your paper's topic. If you have spent enough time reading and gathering information and brainstorming ideas about the assignment, you'll be knowledgeable enough to have something to say based on a combination of your own thinking and the thinking of your sources.

If you have trouble coming up with such an assertion, devote more time to invention strategies: Try writing your subject at the top of a page and then listing everything you now know and feel about it. Often, from such a list you'll venture an assertion you can then use to fashion a working thesis. One good way to gauge the reasonableness of your claim is to see what other authors have asserted about the same topic. Keeping good notes on the views of others will provide you with a useful counterpoint to your own views as you write and think about your claim, and you may want to use those notes in your paper.

Next, make several assertions about your topic, in order of increasing complexity, as in the following:

1. Fuel-cell technology has emerged as a promising approach to developing energy-efficient vehicles.
2. To reduce our dependence on nonrenewable fossil fuel, the federal government should encourage the development of fuel-cell vehicles.
3. The federal government should subsidize the development of fuel-cell vehicles as well as the hydrogen infrastructure needed to support them; otherwise, the United States will be increasingly vulnerable to recession and other economic dislocations resulting from our dependence on the continued flow of foreign oil.

Keep in mind that these are *working theses.* Because you haven't begun a paper based on any of them, they remain *hypotheses* to be tested. You might choose one and use it to focus your initial draft. After completing a first draft, you would revise it by comparing the contents of the paper to the thesis and making adjustments as necessary for unity. The working thesis is an excellent tool for planning broad sections of the paper, but—again—don't let it prevent you from pursuing related discussions as they occur to you.

STARTING WITH A WORKING THESIS

A thesis is a summary, yet it's difficult to summarize a presentation yet to be written—especially if you expect to discover what you want to say during the process of writing. Even if you know your material well, the best you can do at first is to formulate a *working* thesis—a hypothesis of sorts, a well-informed hunch about your topic and the claim you intend to make about it. After completing a draft, you can evaluate the degree to which your working thesis accurately summarizes the content of your paper. If the match is a good one, the working thesis becomes the final thesis. But if sections of the paper drift from the focus of the working thesis, you'll need to revise the thesis and the paper itself to ensure that the presentation is unified.

USING THE THESIS TO PLAN A STRUCTURE

A working thesis will help you sketch the structure of your paper, because an effective structure flows directly from the thesis. Consider, for example, the third thesis on fuel-cell technology:

> The federal government should subsidize the development of fuel-cell vehicles as well as the hydrogen infrastructure needed to support them; otherwise, the United States will be increasingly vulnerable to recession and other economic dislocations resulting from our dependence on the continued flow of foreign oil.

This thesis is *strongly argumentative,* or *persuasive.* The economic crises mentioned suggest urgency in the need for the solution recommended: the federal subsidy of a national hydrogen infrastructure to support fuel-cell vehicles. A well-developed paper based on this thesis would require you to commit yourself to explaining (1) why fuel-cell vehicles are a preferred alternative to gasoline-powered vehicles; (2) why fuel-cell vehicles require a hydrogen infrastructure (i.e., you must explain that fuel cells produce power by mixing hydrogen and oxygen, generating both electricity and water in the process); (3) why the government needs to subsidize industry in developing fuel-cell vehicles; and (4) how continued reliance on fossil fuel technology could make the country vulnerable to economic dislocations.

This thesis, then, helps you plan the paper, which should include a section on each of the four topics. Assuming that the argument follows the organizational plan we've proposed, the working thesis would become the final thesis. Based on this thesis, a reader could anticipate sections of the paper to come. A focused thesis therefore becomes an essential tool for guiding readers.

At this stage, however, your thesis is still provisional. It may turn out that as you do research or begin drafting, the paper to which this thesis commits you looks to be too long and complex. As a result, you may decide to drop the second clause of the thesis (concerning the country's vulnerability to economic dislocations) and focus instead on the need for the government to subsidize the development of fuel-cell vehicles and a hydrogen infrastructure, relegating the economic concerns to your conclusion (if used at all). With such a change, your final thesis might read: "The federal government should subsidize the development of fuel-cell vehicles as well as the hydrogen infrastructure needed to support them."

How Ambitious Should Your Thesis Be?

Writing tasks vary according to the nature of the thesis.

- The *explanatory thesis* is often developed in response to short-answer exam questions that call for information, not analysis (e.g., "How does James Barber categorize the main types of presidential personality?").

- The *mildly argumentative thesis* is appropriate for organizing reports (even lengthy ones), as well as for essay questions that call for some analysis (e.g., "Discuss the qualities of a good speech").

- The *strongly argumentative thesis* is used to organize papers and exam responses that call for information, analysis, *and* the writer's forcefully stated point of view (e.g., "Evaluate the proposed reforms of health maintenance organizations").

The strongly argumentative thesis, of course, is the riskiest of the three, because you must state your position forcefully and make it appear reasonable—which requires that you offer evidence and defend against logical objections. But such intellectual risks pay dividends; and if you become involved enough in your work to make challenging assertions, you will provoke challenging responses that enliven classroom discussions as well as your own learning.

This revised thesis makes an assertive commitment to the subject even though the assertion is not as complex as the original. Still, it is more argumentative than the second proposed thesis:

> To reduce our dependence on nonrenewable fossil fuel, the federal government should encourage the development of fuel-cell vehicles.

Here we have a _mildly argumentative_ thesis that enables the writer to express an opinion. We infer from the use of the words "should encourage" that the writer endorses the idea of the government's promoting fuel-cell development. But a government that "encourages" development is making a lesser commitment than one that "subsidizes," which means that it allocates funds for a specific policy. So the writer who argues for mere encouragement takes a milder position than the one who argues for subsidies. Note also the contrast between the second thesis and the first one, in which the writer is committed to no involvement in the debate and suggests no government involvement whatsoever:

> Fuel-cell technology has emerged as a promising approach to developing energy-efficient vehicles.

This, the first of the three thesis statements, is _explanatory_, or *informative*. In developing a paper based on this thesis, the writer is committed only to explaining how fuel-cell technology works and why it is a promising approach to energy-efficient vehicles. Given this thesis, a reader would *not* expect to find the writer strongly recommending, for instance, that fuel-cell engines replace internal combustion engines in the near future. Neither does the thesis require the writer to defend a personal opinion; he or she need only justify the use of the relatively mild term "promising."

In sum, for any topic you might explore in a paper, you can make any number of assertions—some relatively simple, some complex. On the basis of these assertions, you set yourself an agenda for your writing—and readers set for themselves expectations for reading. The more ambitious the thesis, the more complex will be the paper and the greater the readers' expectations.

Exercise 3.1
Drafting Thesis Statements

Working individually or in small groups, select a topic of current interest on your campus: perhaps the administration's dormitory visitor policy or the role of fraternities and sororities. Draft three theses on this topic: one explanatory, one mildly argumentative, and one strongly argumentative.

Introductions

3.2 Write introductions that provide a context for your readers.

Writing introductions and conclusions is usually difficult. How to start? What's the best way to approach your topic? With a serious tone, a light touch, an anecdote? And how to end? How to leave the reader feeling satisfied, intrigued, provoked?

Often, writers avoid such decisions by putting them off—and productively so. Bypassing careful planning for the introduction and conclusion, they begin writing the body of the piece. Only after they've finished the body do they go back to write the opening and closing paragraphs. There's a lot to be said for this approach: Because you've presumably spent more time thinking and writing about the topic itself than about how you're going to introduce or conclude it, you're in a better position to set out your ideas. Often it's not until you've actually seen the text on paper or on screen and read it over once or twice that a natural or effective way of introducing or concluding it occurs to you. Also, you're generally in better psychological shape to write both the introduction and the conclusion after the major task of writing is behind you and you've already set down the main body of your discussion or argument.

An effective introduction prepares the reader to enter the world of your paper. It makes the connection between the more familiar world inhabited by the reader and the less familiar world of the writer's topic; it places a discussion in a context that the reader can understand. If you find yourself getting stuck on an introduction at the beginning of a first draft, skip over it for the moment. State your working thesis directly and move on to the body of the paper.

Here are some of the most common strategies for opening a paper:

Quotation

Consider the two introductory paragraphs to an article titled "Blinded by the War on Terrorism," from journalist Sarah Chayes's article in the *Los Angeles Times*:

> "This is a great time to be a white-collar criminal."

> An assistant U.S. attorney I know startled me with this remark in 2002. The bulk of her FBI investigators, she explained, had been pulled off to work on terrorism, which left traditional crime investigations sorely understaffed.[1]

Chayes uses a provocative remark by a U.S. attorney to grab our attention. Our assumption, perhaps naïve, is that in a stable society governed by laws there should *never* be a good time to be a white-collar (or any other kind of) criminal. But we learn that this is apparently not the case, as Chayes pivots on the quotation to open her report on the stretched resources at the U.S. Department of Justice. Quoting the words of others offers many points of departure for your paper: You can agree with the quotation. You can agree and expand. You can sharply disagree. Or you can use the quotation to set a historical context or establish a tone.

Historical Review

Often the reader will be unprepared to follow the issue you discuss without some historical background. Consider this introduction to a comparative essay on the two world wars:

> World War I (1914–1918) and World War II (1939–1945) were the most catastrophic and destructive conflicts in human history. For those who believed in the steady but inevitable progress of civilization, it was impossible to imagine that two wars in the first half of the twentieth century could reach levels of barbarity and horror that would outstrip those of any previous era. Historians estimate that more than 22 million people, soldiers and civilians, died in World War I; they estimate that between 40 and 50 million died in World War II. In many ways, these two conflicts were similar: They were fought on many of the same European and Russian battlegrounds, with more or less the same countries on opposing sides. Even many of the same people were involved: Winston Churchill and Adolf Hitler figured in both wars. And the main outcome in each case was the same: total defeat for Germany. However, in terms of the impact on cities and civilian populations, the military aspects of the two wars in Europe, and their aftermaths, the differences between World Wars I and II considerably outweigh the similarities.

This introductory review sets a context for the writer's thesis, the final sentence of the paragraph: that the differences between the wars, as determined by comparing three criteria, were greater than the similarities. Setting a historical context requires familiarity with a topic and, for most student writers, this will involve research. Readers will appreciate this research—you did it for them, after all!

Review of a Controversy

A particular type of historical review provides the background on a controversy or debate. Consider this introduction:

---

[1]Sarah Chayes, "Blinded by the War on Terrorism." *Los Angeles Times*, 28 July 2013.

Is America a melting pot or a salad bowl? How people answer this question should indicate whether they support or oppose bilingual education programs. First established in 1968, such programs mandate that students who are non-native speakers of English be taught in their own language until they become proficient in English. Proponents of bilingual education believe that the programs provide a vital period of transition for ethnic, non-English speaking students who would otherwise fall behind in their academic work and eventually drop out of school in discouragement. Opponents argue that the sooner non-English speaking students "immerse" themselves in English, the sooner they will master their studies and integrate themselves into the American mainstream. Which side is right? The answer is clear-cut, depending on your political point of view—which is exactly the problem. The decades-old debate over bilingual education cannot be resolved until antagonists can find at least some area of agreement on the role and significance of ethnic cultures in the American life.[2]

The writer sets out a controversy by reviewing the main arguments for and against bilingual education. Instead of taking sides in the debate, however, the writer argues (in the thesis, the final sentence of the paragraph) that a *prior* issue—the role of ethnicity in America—must be addressed before taking on bilingual education.

From the General to the Specific

Another way of providing a transition from the reader's world to the less familiar world of the paper is to work from a general subject to a specific one. The following is the first paragraph of a paper that evaluates an argument about the ways in which the media has idealized body types in American culture.

Most freshmen know how it feels to apply to a school and be rejected. Each year, college admissions officers mail out thousands of thin letters that begin: "Thank you for your application. The competition this year was unusually strong. . . ." We know we will not get into every college on our list or pass every test or win every starring role after every audition, but we believe we deserve the chance to try. And we can tolerate rejection if we know that we compete on a level playing field. When that field seems to arbitrarily favor some candidates over others, however, we take offense. At least that's what happened when an ambitious mother took offense, bringing to court a suit that claimed her eight-year-old daughter, Fredrika Keefer, was denied admission to [the] prestigious San Francisco Ballet School because she had the wrong "body type."[3]

[2]Leslie Weingarten, unpublished paper.
[3]Ron Labare, unpublished paper.

Anecdote and Illustration: From the Specific to the General

The following three paragraphs each offer an anecdote that moves the reader from a specific case to a more general subject:

> On April 13 of this year, a Wednesday, my wife got up later than usual and didn't check her e-mail until around 8:30 a.m. The previous night, she had put her computer to "sleep," rather than shutting it down. When she opened it that morning to the Gmail account that had been her main communications center for more than six years, it seemed to be responding very slowly and jerkily. She hadn't fully restarted the computer in several days, and thought that was the problem. So she closed all programs, rebooted the machine, and went off to make coffee and have some breakfast.
>
> When she came back to her desk, half an hour later, she couldn't log into Gmail at all. By that time, I was up and looking at e-mail, and we both quickly saw what the real problem was. In my inbox I found a message purporting to be from her, followed by a quickly proliferating stream of concerned responses from friends and acquaintances, all about the fact that she had been "mugged in Madrid." The account had seemed sluggish earlier that morning because my wife had tried to use it at just the moment a hacker was taking it over and changing its settings—including the password, so that she couldn't log in again. . . .
>
> It was at about this time that I started thinking about the ramifications of this problem beyond our own situation. . . .[4]

This introduction moves from the specific (a particular instance of computer hacking) to the general (the ramifications of trusting critical electronic information to storage in the "cloud"). The anecdote is one of the most effective means at your disposal for capturing and holding your reader's attention. It's also one of the most commonly used types of introduction in popular articles. For decades, speakers have begun their remarks with a funny, touching, or otherwise appropriate story. (In fact, plenty of books are nothing but collections of such stories, arranged by subject.)

Question

Frequently you can provoke the reader's attention by posing a question or a series of questions:

> Why is the sky blue? Countless children have asked, and countless adults have fumbled the answer. The sky is blue because Earth's atmosphere scatters sunlight into its component colors (red, orange, yellow, green, blue), with blue light scattering most "because it travels as shorter, smaller waves" (NASA). What's a light wave? What's scattering? What's visible light as opposed to nonvisible light energy? If you want to be humbled quickly, try explaining any of the above to a curious five-year-old! In fact, our best teachers do precisely this all the time:

---

[4]James Fallows, "Hacked!" *The Atlantic*, Nov. 2011.

present complex information to kids in age-appropriate ways. While instinct surely forms one part of great teaching—the sixth sense of knowing what students need from one instructional moment to the next—teaching is also a science built on skills that can be studied, understood, and taught. On a per-student basis, other nations invest far more in this science than America does. If we intend to keep pace with rising educational standards in the rest of the world, it is long past time we match that commitment.

Opening your paper with a question invites readers to formulate a response and then to test that response against the one you will develop in your paper. How *do* we answer the question "Why is the sky blue?" With difficulty! It is our acknowledgment of this difficulty that the writer uses to introduce her thesis: America should invest more heavily in teacher training.

Statement of Thesis

Perhaps the most direct method of introduction is to begin immediately with the thesis:

> Nuclear power was beginning to look like a panacea—a way to lessen our dependence on oil, make our energy supply more self-sufficient and significantly mitigate global warming, all at the same time. Now it looks more like a bargain with the devil.
>
> I wish this were not so. . . .[5]

This selection begins with a two-sentence general assertion—that reliance on nuclear fission is inherently dangerous (as any "bargain with the devil" is bound to be). This is Eugene Robinson's thesis for an article titled "Japan's Nuclear Crisis Might Not Be the Last," in which he addresses what he thinks is a naïve enthusiasm for nuclear power as a route to energy independence. Beginning with a thesis statement (as opposed to a quotation, question, or anecdote) works well when, as in this case, a debate is well understood (there's no need to provide context for readers) and you want to settle immediately into making your argument. Opening with your thesis also works well when you want to develop an unexpected, or controversial, argument. If, for example, you open with the provocative assertion that "Reading is dead" in a paper examining the problem of declining literacy in the digital age, the reader is bound to sit up and take notice, perhaps even protest: "No, it's not—I read all the time!" This strategy "hooks" a reader, who is likely to want to find out how you will support such an emphatic thesis.

One final note about our model introductions: They may be longer than introductions you have been accustomed to writing. Many writers (and readers) prefer shorter, snappier introductions. The ideal length of an introduction depends on the length of the paper it introduces, and it may also be a matter of personal or corporate style. There is no rule concerning the correct length of an

---

[5]Eugene Robinson, "Japan's Nuclear Crisis Might Not Be the Last." *Washington Post*, 14 Mar. 2011.

introduction. If you feel that a short introduction is appropriate, use one. Conversely, you may wish to break up what seems like a long introduction into two paragraphs.

Exercise 3.2
Drafting Introductions

Imagine that you are writing a paper using the topic you selected in Exercise 3.1. Conduct some preliminary research on the topic, using an Internet search engine such as Google or Bing, or an article database available at your college. Choose one of the seven types of introductions we've discussed—preferably one you have never used before—and draft an introduction that would work to open a paper on your topic. Use our examples as models to help you draft your introduction.

Conclusions

3.3   Write conclusions that move beyond a summary of your paper.

You might view your conclusion as an introduction in reverse: a bridge from the world of your paper back to the world of your reader. The simplest conclusion is a summary of the paper, but at this point you should go beyond mere summary. You might begin with a summary, for example, and then extend it with a discussion of the paper's significance or its implications for future study, for choices that individuals might make, for policy, and so on. You could urge readers to change an attitude or modify a behavior. Certainly, you're under no obligation to discuss the broader significance of your work (and a summary, alone, will satisfy the formal requirement that your paper have an ending); but the conclusions of effective papers often reveal that their authors are "thinking large" by placing their limited subject into a larger social, cultural, or historical context.

Two words of advice: First, no matter how clever or beautifully executed, a conclusion cannot salvage a poorly written paper. Second, by virtue of its placement, the conclusion carries rhetorical weight: It is the last statement a reader will encounter before turning from your work. Realizing this, writers who expand on the basic summary conclusion often wish to give their final words a dramatic flourish, a heightened level of diction. Soaring rhetoric and drama in a conclusion are fine as long as they do not unbalance the paper and call attention to themselves. Having labored long hours over your paper, you may be inclined at this point to wax eloquent. But keep a sense of proportion and timing. Make your points quickly and end crisply.

Summary (Plus)

Concluding paragraphs that summarize the article as a whole are useful if the article is lengthy or if the writer simply wants to reemphasize the main point. In his article "Wind Power Puffery," H. Sterling Burnett argues that the benefits of wind power have been considerably exaggerated and the drawbacks considerably downplayed. He explains why wind is an unreliable source of steady power and how conventional power plants must, at considerable expense, supplement the electrical energy derived from wind farms. Wind power also creates its own environmental problems, Barnett argues, and wind towers pose deadly hazards to birds and other flying creatures. He concludes with a summary of his main points—and an opinion that follows from these points:

> Wind power is expensive, doesn't deliver the environmental benefits it promises and has substantial environmental costs. In short, wind power is no bargain. Accordingly, it doesn't merit continued government promotion or funding.[6]

The final sentence goes beyond summary to articulate the main conclusion Barnett draws from the arguments he has made.

Statement of the Subject's Significance

One of the more effective ways to conclude a paper is to discuss the larger significance of your subject. Here you move from the specific concern of your paper to the broader concerns of the reader's world. A paper on the Wright brothers might end with a discussion of air travel as it affects economies, politics, or families; a paper on contraception might end with a discussion of its effect on sexual mores, population, or the church. But don't overwhelm your reader with the importance of your remarks. Keep your discussion focused.

In this paragraph, folklorist Maria Tatar concludes the introduction to her book *The Annotated Classic Fairy Tales* (2002):

> Disseminated across a wide variety of media, ranging from opera and drama to cinema and advertising, fairy tales have become a vital part of our cultural capital. What keeps them alive and pulsing with vitality and variety is exactly what keeps life pulsing: anxieties, fears, desires, romance, passion, and love. Like our ancestors, who listened to these stories at the fireside, in taverns, and in spinning rooms, we remained transfixed by stories about wicked stepmothers, bloodthirsty ogres, sibling rivals, and fairy godmothers. For us, too, the stories are irresistible, for they offer endless opportunities to talk, to negotiate, to deliberate, to charter, and to prattle on endlessly as did the old wives from whom the stories are thought to derive. And from the tangle of that talk and chitchat, we begin to define our own values, desires, appetites, and aspirations, creating identities that will allow us to produce happily-ever-after endings for ourselves and our children.[7]

After a lengthy discussion of what fairy tales are about and how they work, Tatar concludes with a theory about why these ancient stories are still important: They are "a vital part of our cultural capital." They deal with "what keeps life

---

[6]H. Sterling Barnett, "Wind Power Puffery." *Washington Times*, 4 Feb. 2004.
[7]Maria Tatar, "An Introduction to Fairy Tales." *The Annotated Classic Fairy Tales* (2002), ed. and trans. by Maria Tatar. W. W. Norton & Company, Inc.

pulsing," and in the way that they encourage opportunities to talk about these classic motifs, they serve to connect our ancestors' "values, desires, appetites, and aspirations" with our own and our children's. Ending the paper with a statement of the subject's significance is another way of saying, "The conclusions of this paper matter." If you have taken the trouble to write a good paper, the conclusions *do* matter. Don't be bashful: State the larger significance of the point(s) you have made. (But avoid claiming too great a significance for your work, lest by overreaching you pop the balloon and your reader thinks, "No, the subject's not *that* important.")

Call for Further Research

Scientists and social scientists often end their papers with a review of what has been presented (as, for instance, in an experiment) and the ways in which the subject under consideration needs to be further explored. *A word of caution:* If you raise questions that you call on others to answer, make sure you know that the research you are calling for hasn't already been conducted.

The following conclusion ends an article titled "Toward an AIDS Vaccine" by Bruce D. Walker and Dennis R. Burton:

> With few exceptions, even the most critical and skeptical of scientists, who have stressed the difficulties of developing an HIV vaccine, feel that this is no time to give up. However, far more selectivity than hereto in advancing immunogens to large-scale clinical trials is required. The mantra of "the only way we will know if it is likely to be effective is to try it in humans" is not appropriate given the current state of knowledge. Trust in science, making full use of the tool kit that is provided by modern molecular biology, immunology, virology, structural biology, chemistry, and genomics is crucial. There is a critical need to understand how other vaccines work with a level of detail that has never been necessary for pathogens less adapted to immune evasion. The way forward is without question very difficult and the possibility of failure high, but the global need is absolutely desperate, and this is an endeavor that must be pursued, now with greater passion than ever.[8]

Notice how this call for further research emphasizes both the difficulty of the task ahead and the critical nature of pursuing that task. The authors point to some of the pitfalls ahead and, in their plea to "[t]rust in science," point to a way forward.

Solution/Recommendation

The purpose of your paper might be to review a problem or controversy and to discuss contributing factors. In such a case, after summarizing your discussion, you could offer a solution based on the knowledge you've gained while conducting

---

[8]From "Toward an AIDS Vaccine" by Bruce D. Walker and Dennis R. Burton. *Science*, 9 May 2008: 760–64. DOI: 10.1126/science.1152622. Reprinted with permission from AAAS. http://www.sciencemag.org/content/320/5877/760.abstract.

research, as in the following conclusion. Of course, if your solution is to be taken seriously, your knowledge must be amply demonstrated in the body of the paper. Here's the concluding paragraph from a student paper titled "Balancing Privacy and Safety in the Wake of Virginia Tech."

> What happened at Virginia Tech was a tragedy. Few of us can appreciate the grief of the parents of the shooting victims at Virginia Tech, parents who trusted that their children would be safe and who were devastated when that faith was betrayed. We cannot permit lone, deranged gunmen to exorcise their demons on campus. We should support changes that involve a more proactive approach to student mental health and improvements in communication between departments that can identify students at risk of becoming violent. But we must also guard against allowing a few isolated incidents, however tragic, to restrict the rights of millions of other, law-abiding students. Schools must not use Virginia Tech as a pretext to bring back the bad old days of resident assistants snooping into the personal lives of students and infringing on their privacy—all in the name of spotting the next campus killer. Both the federal courts and Congress have rejected that approach and for good reason have established the importance of privacy rights on campus. These rights must be preserved.[9]

In this conclusion, the author recommends dealing with violence on campus not by infringing on student privacy but by supporting improvements to mental health services and communication among departments to spot potentially troubled students. Her recommendation urges a balanced approach to addressing the problem of campus violence.

Anecdote

As we've seen in our discussion of introductions, an anecdote is a briefly told story or joke, the point of which is to shed light on your subject. The anecdote is more direct than an allusion. With an allusion, you merely refer to a story ("We would all love to go floating down the river like Huck . . . "); with the anecdote, you retell the story. The anecdote allows readers to discover for themselves the significance of a reference to another source—an effort most readers enjoy because they get to exercise their creativity.

The following anecdote concludes an article by Newton Minow, former chairman of the Federal Communications Commission, who, more than fifty years ago, gained instant celebrity by declaring that television was a "vast wasteland." In his article, "A Vaster Wasteland," Minow discusses "critical choices about the values we want to build into our 21st-century communications system—and the public policies to support them." He explains how we should commit to six major goals and concludes:

> As we think about the next 50 years, I remember a story President Kennedy told a week before he was killed. The story was about French Marshal Louis-Hubert-Gonzalve Lyautey, who walked one morning through his garden with his gardener.

---

[9]Alison Tucker, unpublished paper.

He stopped at a certain point and asked the gardener to plant a tree the next morning. The gardener said, "But the tree will not bloom for 100 years." The marshal replied, "In that case, you had better plant it this afternoon."[10]

Minow doesn't bother to explain the significance of the anecdote, which he assumes should be clear: The task ahead will not see fruit for a long time, but unless we get to work immediately, it will take even longer.

Quotation

A favorite concluding device is the quotation—the words of a famous person, an authority in the field on which you are writing, or simply someone in a position to know a great deal about the subject. By quoting another, you link your work to that person's, thereby gaining authority and credibility. The first criterion for selecting a quotation is its suitability to your thesis. But consider carefully what your choice of sources says about you. Suppose you are writing a paper on the American work ethic. If you could use a line either by the comedian Jon Stewart or by the current secretary of labor to make the final point of your conclusion, which would you choose and why? One source may not be inherently more effective than the other, but the choice would affect the tone of your paper.

The following paragraph concludes an article called "Tiger Mom vs. Tiger Mailroom." The author, Patrick Goldstein, who writes about the film industry for the *Los Angeles Times*, joined the "Tiger Mom" debate, sparked by Amy Chua. In an earlier article titled "Chinese Mothers Are Superior," Chua explained why she forbade her children to engage in normal childhood recreational and after-school activities (except for learning the piano or violin), insisting that they work as hard as possible to earn grades no lower than A. Goldstein argues that in most professions, drive and initiative are more important than grade point averages: "charm, hustle, and guile are the aces in the deck." He concludes:

> In Hollywood, whether you were a C student or a *summa cum laude*, it's a level playing field. "When you're working on a movie set, you've got 50 film professors to learn from, from the sound man to the cinematographer," says producer David Permut, who dropped out of UCLA to work for [independent filmmaker] Roger Corman. "I've never needed a resume in my whole career. All you need is a 110-page script that someone is dying to make and you're in business."[11]

Goldstein's quotation from Permut drives home his point that, in the real world, it's not grades but talent, connections, and old-fashioned "hustle" that are the crucial elements in professional success.

---

[10]Newton S. Minow, "A Vaster Wasteland." *The Atlantic*, Apr. 2011, p. 52.
[11]Patrick Goldstein, "Tiger Mom vs. Tiger Mailroom." *Los Angeles Times*, 6 Feb. 2011.

Question

Just as questions are useful for opening papers, they are useful for closing them. Opening and closing questions function in different ways, however. The introductory question promises to be addressed in the paper that follows, but the concluding question leaves issues unresolved, calling on readers to assume an active role by offering their own answers. Consider the following paragraph, written to conclude a critique of an argument by columnist Charles Krauthammer on the importance of refunding the National Aeronautics and Space Administration (NASA) and returning to the moon:

> In "The Moon We Left Behind," Charles Krauthammer stirs the emotions with his call for the United States to return to the moon; and, in terms of practical spinoffs, such a return could benefit this country in many ways. Krauthammer's argument is compelling, even if he too easily discounts the financial and political problems that will pose real obstacles to a renewed lunar program. Ultimately, what one thinks of Krauthammer's call to renew moon exploration depends on how one defines the human enterprise and the purpose of collective agreement and collective effort—what we call "government." To what extent should this purpose be to solve problems in the here and now? To what extent should it be to inquire and to push against boundaries for the sake of discovery and exploration, to learn more about who we are and about the nature of our universe? There have always been competing demands on national budgets and more than enough problems to justify spending every tax dollar on problems of poverty, social justice, crime, and the like. Krauthammer argues that if we are to remain true to our spirit of inquiry, however, we cannot ignore the investigation of space because scientific and technological progress is also a human responsibility. He argues that we can—indeed, we must—do both: look to our needs here at home and also dream, look to the sky, and ask: What is out there?

The writer poses three questions. The first two form a pair and appear mid-paragraph to establish the poles in a philosophical debate: Before we can respond to suggestions to spend billions on space exploration, we must answer *prior* questions on the proper role of government. These questions challenge readers to consider that purpose themselves. The paragraph concludes on another question that directs the reader's gaze outward, to space. The strategy here is to inspire wonder as we turn away from the critique.

Speculation

When you speculate, you consider what might happen as well as what has happened. Speculation involves a spinning out of possibilities. It stimulates readers by immersing them in your discussion of the unknown, implicitly challenging them to agree or disagree. The following paragraphs conclude a student paper on the effects of rising sea levels.

The fate of low-lying coastal cities like Tacloban in the Philippines or Pacific island nations like Tuvalu can now be plotted, and the news is not good either for them or for coastal dwellers in more developed areas of the world. We have seen numerous examples of how rising sea levels have resulted in storm surges responsible for destroying dwellings and farms and for killing thousands. According to a recent United Nations report, sixty million people now live in low-lying coastal areas "within one meter of sea level," and by the end of the century that number is likely to double (United Nations Radio). We know enough to understand the risks of concentrating populations by the oceans. Yet even after devastating storms, governments continue to rebuild communities, indeed whole villages and towns, in the same vulnerable areas.

Over time, Nature generally doesn't lose contests like these, and sooner or later we will find ourselves contemplating the unthinkable: abandoning great coastal cities like New York, Calcutta, and Tokyo for higher ground. If the potential human destruction isn't enough to force policy makers to relocate whole populations away from the coasts, in time the loss of money will. Insurance companies, the ones who pay out on billion-dollar losses from major storms, may simply stop insuring cities and businesses that insist on living and working by the sea. When people can no longer insure themselves against heavy losses from climate-related events, the inevitable course of action will be clear: to build on higher ground, further from danger. In two hundred years, the coastal maps of the world will look very different than they do today.[12]

The prospect of nations abandoning great coastal cities like New York and Tokyo might seem extreme, but it is the author's intent to suggest a scenario that challenges readers to agree or not. If you have provided the necessary information prior to your concluding speculation, you will send readers back into their lives (and away from your paper) with an implicit challenge: Do they regard the future as you do? Whether they do or not, you have set an agenda. You have got them thinking.

Exercise 3.3
Drafting Conclusions

Choose one of the eight types of conclusions we've discussed—preferably one you have never used before—and draft a conclusion for the topic you chose in Exercises 3.1 and 3.2. Use our examples as models to help you draft your conclusion.

---

[12] Allen Hawkins, unpublished student paper.

Chapter 4
Explanatory Synthesis

 Learning Objectives

After completing this chapter, you will be able to:

4.1 Define synthesis as a purposeful discussion of relationships inferred among sources.

4.2 Distinguish between explanatory and argument syntheses.

4.3 Explain the process involved in writing a synthesis.

4.4 Write and revise an explanatory synthesis.

What Is a Synthesis?

4.1 Define synthesis as a purposeful discussion of relationships inferred among sources.

A *synthesis* is a written discussion that draws on two or more sources. It follows that your ability to write syntheses depends on your ability to infer relationships among sources like these:

- Essays
- Fiction
- Interviews
- Articles
- Lectures
- Visual media

This process is nothing new for you because you infer relationships all the time—say, between something you've read in the newspaper and something you've seen for yourself, or between the teaching styles of your favorite and least favorite instructors. In fact, if you've written research papers, you've already written syntheses.

In a *synthesis,* you make explicit the relationships that you have inferred among separate sources.

Using Summary and Critique as a Basis for Synthesis

The skills you've already learned and practiced in previous chapters will be vital in writing syntheses. Before you're in a position to draw relationships among two or more sources, you must understand what those sources say; you must be able to *summarize* those sources. Readers frequently benefit from at least partial summaries of sources in your synthesis essays. At the same time, you must go beyond summary to make judgments—judgments based on your *critical reading* of your sources: what conclusions you've drawn about the quality and validity of these sources, whether you agree or disagree with the points made in your sources, and why you agree or disagree.

Using Inference as a Basis for Synthesis: Moving Beyond Summary and Critique

In a synthesis, you go beyond the critique of individual sources to determine the relationships among them. Is the information in source B, for example, an extended illustration of the generalizations in source A? Would it be useful to compare and contrast source C with source B? Having read and considered sources A, B, and C, can you infer something else—in other words, D (not in a source, but your own idea)?

Because a synthesis is based on two or more sources, you will need to be selective when choosing information from each. It would be neither possible nor desirable, for instance, to discuss in a ten-page paper on the American Civil War every point that the authors of two books make about their subject. What you as a writer must do is select from each source the ideas and information that allow you to achieve your purpose in the best way possible.

Identifying Your Purpose

Your purpose in reading source materials and then drawing on them to write your own material is often reflected in the wording of an assignment. For instance, consider the following assignments on the Civil War:

Economics   Argue the following proposition, in light of your readings: "The Civil War was fought not for reasons of moral principle but for reasons of economic necessity."

Government   Prepare a report on the effects of the Civil War on Southern politics at the state level between 1870 and 1917. Focus on one state.

Each of these assignments creates a particular purpose for writing. Having located sources relevant to your topic, you would select for possible use in a paper only the parts of those sources that helped you in fulfilling this purpose. And how you used those parts—how you related them to other material from other sources—would also depend on your purpose.

EXAMPLE: SAME SOURCES, DIFFERENT USES   If you were working on the government assignment, you might draw on the same source as a student working on a literature assignment by referring to Robert Penn Warren's novel *All the King's Men,* about Louisiana politics in the early part of the twentieth century. But because the purposes of the two assignments are different, you and the other student would make different uses of this source. The parts or aspects of the novel that you find worthy of detailed attention might be mentioned only in passing—or not at all—by the other student.

Where Do We Find Written Syntheses?

Here are just a few of the types of writing that involve synthesis:

Academic Writing

- **Analysis papers** synthesize and apply several related theoretical approaches.

- **Research papers** synthesize multiple sources.

- **Argument papers** synthesize different points into a coherent claim or position.

- **Essay exams** demonstrate understanding of course material through comparing and contrasting theories, viewpoints, or approaches in a particular field.

Workplace Writing

- **Newspaper and magazine articles** synthesize primary and secondary sources.

- **Position papers and policy briefs** compare and contrast solutions for solving problems.

- **Business plans** synthesize ideas and proposals into one coherent plan.

- **Memos and letters** synthesize multiple ideas, events, and proposals into concise form.

- **Web sites** synthesize information from various sources to present in Web pages and related links.

Using Your Sources

Your purpose determines not only what parts of your sources you will use but also how you will relate those parts to one another. Because the very essence of synthesis is the combining of information and ideas, you must have some basis on which to combine them. *Some relationships among the material in your sources must make them worth synthesizing.* It follows that the better able you are to discover such relationships, the more easily you will be able to use your sources in writing syntheses.

Types of Syntheses: Explanatory and Argument

4.2 Distinguish between explanatory and argument syntheses.

In this and the next chapter, we categorize syntheses into two main types: *explanatory* and *argument*. The easiest way to recognize the difference between the two types may be to consider the difference between a news article and an editorial on the same subject.

For the most part, we'd say that the main purpose of the news article is to convey *information* and that the main purpose of the editorial is to convey *opinion* or *interpretation*. Of course, this distinction is much too simplified: News articles often convey opinion or bias, sometimes subtly, sometimes openly; editorials often convey unbiased information along with opinion. But as a practical matter we can generally agree on the distinction between a news article that primarily conveys information and an editorial that primarily conveys opinion. Consider the balance of explanation and argumentation in the following two selections.

Seau Suffered from Brain Disease

by Mary Pilon and Ken Belson*
New York Times
January 10, 2013

The former N.F.L. linebacker Junior Seau had a degenerative brain disease linked to repeated head trauma when he committed suicide in the spring [2012], the National Institutes of Health [NIH] said Thursday.

The findings were consistent with chronic traumatic encephalopathy [CTE], a degenerative brain disease widely connected to athletes who have absorbed frequent blows to the head, the N.I.H. said in a statement. Seau is the latest and most prominent player to be associated with the disease, which has bedeviled football in recent years as a proliferation of studies has exposed the possible long-term cognitive impact of head injuries sustained on the field.

"The type of findings seen in Mr. Seau's brain has been recently reported in autopsies of individuals with exposure to repetitive head injury," the N.I.H. said, "including professional and amateur athletes who played contact sports, individuals with multiple concussions, and veterans exposed to blast injury and other trauma."

Since C.T.E. was diagnosed in the brain of the former Eagles defensive back Andre Waters after his suicide in 2006, the disease has been found in nearly every former player whose brain was examined posthumously. (C.T.E. can be diagnosed only posthumously.)

Researchers at Boston University, who pioneered the study of C.T.E., have found it in 33 of the 34 brains of former N.F.L. players they have examined.

Concussion Problem Not Unique to U-M

The State News (Michigan State University)

October 13, 2014

By the Editorial Board

Officials, coaches and fans alike have been discussing the issue of football players' concussions for a long, long time. But incidents like what happened when U-M [University of Michigan] quarterback Shane Morris was concussed during this year's game against Minnesota are still part of a fervent national conversation.

But isn't the solution fairly obvious?

If there's even the slightest suspicion that a player has suffered a head injury, remove him from the game. Period.

After Shane Morris was hit against Minnesota, it was clear he had no business playing. He could barely stay on his feet, and had to lean on a fellow player to stay upright. Nonetheless, he went back in the same game for two more plays, inciting public outrage.

Though U-M football head coach Brady Hoke said he didn't believe Morris had been concussed, U-M's athletic director Dave Brandon later confirmed that Morris had in fact suffered a mild concussion injury.

And while U-M claims the medical team didn't see the hit, it was pretty [d***] clear to spectators. Even ESPN announcer Dave Cunningham, who was calling the game, was quick to express his shock.

"I gotta tell you right now, that No. 7 (Morris) is still in this game is appalling," Cunningham said. "It is appalling that he was left in on that play to throw the ball again as badly as he was hit by Cockran . . . that is terrible looking after a young player."

The dangers of continuing to play after a concussion are pretty well-known at this point, so how did Morris's re-entry somehow slip through the cracks? How many officials does it take to notice a player can't stand up, and suggest he be evaluated before returning to the field?

"We now understand that, despite having the right people on the sidelines assessing our student-athletes' well-being, the systems we had in place were inadequate to handle this unique and complex situation properly," Brandon said in a statement. . . .

[T]his isn't just U-M's problem. It's important to recognize this kind of rash decision making could happen at any college football game, putting any player's health at risk, even in Spartan Stadium.

So to those on the sidelines, pay attention. And remember that you are ultimately deciding if a game win is worth more than a man's health and well-being.

Both of these passages address the topic of concussions. The first, excerpted from a 2013 news report in the *New York Times,* is informational, focusing only on evidence of chronic traumatic encephalopathy (CTE) in the brain of National Football League player Junior Seau, who committed suicide earlier that year (2012). The article quotes a statement from the National Institutes of Health on the association between CTE and repeated head injuries among athletes, professional and amateur, and also veterans. The article makes no interpretive statements, states no arguable claim, concerning the topic. By contrast, the second passage, written by the student editorial board of the *State News* (at Michigan

State University), takes a forceful stance in response to the continued play of a University of Michigan student athlete after being concussed in a game against rival University of Minnesota. The first passage is informative, an explanation; the second passage is an argument. As an alert, critical reader, you should be able to determine whether authors are explaining or arguing.

How to Write Syntheses

4.3   Explain the process involved in writing a synthesis.

Although writing syntheses can't be reduced to a lockstep method, the guidelines listed in the accompanying box should be helpful. In this chapter, we focus on explanatory syntheses. In the next chapter, we'll discuss the argument synthesis.

Guidelines for Writing Syntheses

- **Consider your purpose in writing**. What are you trying to accomplish in your paper? How will this purpose shape the way you approach your sources?

- **Select and carefully read your sources** according to your purpose. Then reread the passages, mentally summarizing each. Identify those aspects or parts of your sources that will help you fulfill your purpose. When rereading, *label* or *underline* the sources' main ideas, key terms, and any details you want to use in the synthesis.

- **Take notes on your reading.** In addition to labeling or underlining key points in the readings, you might write brief one- or two-sentence summaries of each source. This will help you in formulating your thesis statement and in choosing and organizing your sources later.

- **Formulate a thesis.** Your thesis is the main idea that you want to present in your synthesis. It should be expressed as a complete sentence. You might do some predrafting about the ideas discussed in the readings in order to help you work out a thesis. If you've written one-sentence summaries of the readings, looking over the summaries will help you to brainstorm connections between readings and to devise a thesis.

   When you write your synthesis drafts, you will need to consider where your thesis fits in your paper. Sometimes the thesis is the first sentence, but more often it is *the final sentence of the first paragraph*. If you are writing an *inductively arranged* synthesis (see Chapter 5, pp. 129–30), the thesis sentence may not appear until the final paragraphs.

- **Decide how you will use your source material.** How will the information and the ideas in the passages help you fulfill your purpose?

- **Develop an organizational plan,** according to your thesis. How will you arrange your material? It is not necessary to prepare a formal outline, but you should have some plan that will indicate the order in which you will present your material and the relationships among your sources.

- **Draft the topic sentences for the main sections.** This is an optional step, but you may find it a helpful transition from organizational plan to first draft.

- **Write the first draft** of your synthesis, following your organizational plan. Be flexible with your plan, however. Frequently, you will use an outline to get started. As you write, you may discover new ideas and make room for them by adjusting the outline. When this happens, reread your work frequently, making sure that your thesis still accounts for what follows and that what follows still logically supports your thesis.

- **Document your sources.** You must do this by crediting sources within the body of the synthesis—citing the author's last name and the page number from which the point was taken—and then providing full citation information in a list of Works Cited at the end. Don't open yourself to charges of plagiarism! (See Chapter 1.)

- **Revise your synthesis,** inserting transitional words and phrases where necessary. Make sure that the synthesis reads smoothly, logically, and clearly from beginning to end. Check for grammatical correctness, punctuation, and spelling.

NOTE: You should accept a certain amount of backtracking and reformulating when writing a synthesis. For instance, in developing an organizational plan (step 6 of the process), you may discover a gap in your presentation that sends you scrambling for other sources—back to step 2. Our recommendations here will give you a structure for starting, but be flexible and expect discontinuity.

Writing an Explanatory Synthesis

4.4 Write and revise an explanatory synthesis.

Many of the papers you write in college will be more or less explanatory in nature. An explanation helps readers understand a topic. Writers explain when they divide a subject into its component parts and present them to the reader in a clear and orderly fashion. Explanations may entail descriptions that re-create in words some object, place, emotion, event, sequence of events, or state of affairs.

- As a student reporter, you may need to explain an event—to relate when, where, and how it took place.

- In a science lab, you may observe the conditions and results of an experiment and record them for review by others.

- In a political science course, you might review research on a particular subject—say, the complexities underlying the electoral college and our selection of presidents—and then present the results of your research to your professor and the members of your class.

Your job in writing an explanatory paper—or in writing the explanatory portion of an argumentative paper—is not to argue a particular point but rather *to present the facts in a reasonably objective manner.* Of course, explanatory papers, like other academic papers, should be based on a thesis (see Chapter 3). But the purpose of a thesis in an explanatory paper is less about advancing a particular opinion and more about focusing on the various facts contained in the paper.

Demonstration: Explanatory Synthesis—The "Idea" of Money

To illustrate how the process of synthesis works, we'll begin with a number of short extracts from several articles on the same subject.

Suppose you were writing a paper on an intriguing idea that occurred to you as you stood in a checkout line at the grocery, waiting to buy a loaf of bread: that the pieces of paper you hand over to the cashier have no real value. That is, a dollar bill is just a rectangular piece of paper. For that matter, a gold nugget is just a lump of mineral. You wonder as you receive your change: What gives money its value?

Fascinated by the possibility that money is not worth anything at all—except the value we mutually attach to it—you decide to conduct some research with the goal of *explaining* what you discover to interested classmates.

Exercise 4.1
Exploring the Topic

Read the selections that follow on the subject of money and how its value is established. After you read the selections and before resuming our discussion, make some observations for yourself. Consider these questions: What is money? What makes money valuable? What makes money lose its value? Share your observations with other students.

In the following pages we present excerpts from the kinds of source materials you might locate during the research process.

Note: To save space and for the purpose of demonstration, we offer excerpts from two sources only; a full list of sources appears in the Works Cited of the model synthesis on pages 120–125. In preparing your paper, of course, you would draw on the entire articles from which these extracts were taken. The discussion of how these passages can form the basis of an explanatory synthesis resumes on page 114.

A Brief History of Money: Or, How We Learned to Stop Worrying and Embrace the Abstraction
IEEE Spectrum
by James Surowiecki
May 30, 2012

In the 13th century, the Chinese emperor Kublai Khan embarked on a bold experiment. China at the time was divided into different regions, many of which issued their own coins, discouraging trade within the empire. So Kublai Khan decreed that henceforth money would take the form of paper.

It was not an entirely original idea. Earlier rulers had sanctioned paper money, but always alongside coins, which had been around for centuries. Kublai's daring notion was to make paper money (the chao) the dominant form of currency. And when the Italian merchant Marco

Polo visited China not long after, he marveled at the spectacle of people exchanging their labor and goods for mere pieces of paper. It was as if value were being created out of thin air.

Kublai Khan was ahead of his time: He recognized that what matters about money is not what it looks like, or even what it's backed by, but whether people believe in it enough to use it. Today, that concept is the foundation of all modern monetary systems, which are built on nothing more than governments' support of and people's faith in them. Money is, in other words, a complete abstraction—one that we are all intimately familiar with but whose growing complexity defies our comprehension.

Apple, Banks in Talks on Mobile Person-to-Person Payment Service

*Wall Street Journal**

November 11, 2015

Robin Sidel and Daisuke Wakabayashi

Apple Inc. is in discussions with U.S. banks to develop a payment service that would let users zap money to one another from their phones rather than relying on cash or checks, according to people familiar with the matter.

The move would put the tech giant in competition with an increasing number of Silicon Valley firms trying to persuade Americans to ditch their wallets in favor of digital options.

A small but growing number of Americans are already starting to embrace such services allowing consumers to pay baby sitters, split dinner checks, and share other bills.

The talks with banks are continuing and it is unclear if any of the firms have struck an agreement with Apple, these people said. Key details remain in flux, including technical aspects that would determine how the service would tie into the banking industry's existing infrastructure, they said.

If Apple's plans go forward, the service would likely be similar to PayPal Holdings Inc.'s Venmo platform, which is popular among younger consumers to do things such as pitch in on gifts and share rent payments with roommates.

Consider Your Purpose

We asked a student, Sheldon Kearney, to read these two selections and to use them (and others) as sources in an explanatory paper on money as an idea. (We also asked him to write additional comments describing the process of developing his thoughts into a draft.) His paper (the final version begins on p. 120) drew on nineteen selections on the history and philosophy of money. How did he—how would you—go about synthesizing the sources?

First, remember that before considering the *how* you must consider the *why*. In other words, what is your *purpose* in synthesizing these sources? You might use them for a paper dealing with a broader issue: the move to all-electronic forms of payment, for instance. If this were your purpose, any sources on the history and uses of paper money would likely be used in only one section.

For a business or finance course, you might search for sources on the gold standard, the principle that the United States and other nations could convert money on demand to gold. (This is no longer the case in the United States.) Several of the sources you located on the idea of money might prove useful for such an assignment, but you would need to search for other, more specific sources on the reasons gold was chosen to back the monetary supply. Again, your *purpose* in writing governs your choice of sources.

Assume that your goal is to write an explanation of money as an *idea*: an account of how money came to be; how it is used; and why, in and of itself, it is worthless aside from the value we mutually attach to it. The goal: to present information but not advance a particular opinion on the subject.

Exercise 4.2
Critical Reading for Synthesis

Review the two readings on money and list the ways they suggest that money is less a thing than an idea. Make your list as specific and detailed as you can. Assign a source to each item on the list.

Formulate a Thesis

The difference between a purpose and a thesis is primarily a difference of focus. Your purpose provides direction to your research and gives a focus to your paper. Your thesis sharpens this focus by narrowing it and formulating it in the words of a single declarative statement. (Chapter 3 has more on formulating thesis statements.)

Kearney's purpose in this case was to explain, to synthesize source material with little or no comment. He asked the following of his sources: Taken as a whole, what do they mean? Here Kearney discusses how he devised a thesis for his explanatory synthesis:

> I began my writing process by looking over all the readings and noting the main points of each reading.
>
> Then I reviewed all of these points and identified the ideas, history, and examples in the readings. These I recorded underneath my list of main points: All the readings focus on the origins, definition, or uses of money.
>
> Looking over these points, I drafted a preliminary thesis. This thesis summed up for me the information I found in my sources:

> Whatever form it takes, from sea shells to paper and even to pixels on a screen, money is valuable only to the extent people believe it is.

I intended to use this statement to guide my first draft, but in the actual writing I got stuck on the origins of money: barter, the direct exchange of goods like apples and oranges *without* the use of money. Money grew out of barter, and I unbalanced my draft by discussing barter more than what should have been my focus: money as an idea valuable only to the extent people think it is. I reminded myself of that focus in the last sentence:

> All the money used around the world might lead one to conclude that money is the solid foundation of the global economy, but look a little closer and we find that this foundation is an unsteady idea.

This statement seemed more promising, and my instructor suggested I use some version of it as my thesis for a revision. This is exactly what I did, though in revision I ended up filling out the statement and expanding it to two sentences. Still, the statement—that money is an idea—remained the basis of my final thesis:

> With millions of transactions paid for each day in cash, credit, stocks and other "instruments," money appears to be the rock-solid foundation of the global economy. But look a little closer at the origins and the uses of money and we find that this foundation, far from being a definite, stable thing like rock, is only an idea.

Decide How You Will Use Your Source Material

To begin, you will need to summarize your sources—or at least be *able* to summarize them. That is, the first step to any synthesis is understanding what your sources say. But because you are synthesizing *ideas* and *information* rather than sources, you will have to be more selective than if you were writing a simple summary. In your synthesis, you will not use *all* the ideas and information in every source, only the ones related to your thesis. Write brief phrases in the margin of the sources, underline key phrases or sentences, or take notes on a separate sheet of paper or in a word-processing file or electronic data-filing program. Decide how your sources can help you achieve your purpose and support your thesis. As you begin clarifying your thoughts, consider whether you need additional sources. For example, how might you use images to explain the thesis that money is an idea?

Develop an Organizational Plan

An organizational plan is your map for presenting material to the reader. What material will you present? To find out, examine your thesis. Do the content and structure of the thesis (that is, the number and order of statements) suggest an organizational plan for the paper? For example, consider Kearney's revised thesis—the one he used in his final draft:

> With millions of transactions paid for each day in cash, credit, stocks, and other "instruments," money appears to be the rock-solid foundation of the global economy. But look a little closer at the origins and the uses of money and we find that this foundation, far from being a definite, stable thing like rock, is only an idea.

Without knowing anything about the origins and uses of money, a reader of this thesis could reasonably expect an account of:

- Forms of money
- Origins of money
- Uses of money
- Money as an idea

Study your thesis, and let it help suggest an organization. Expect to devote at least one paragraph of your paper to developing each section that your thesis promises. After examining the thesis closely and identifying likely sections, think through the possibilities of arrangement. Ask yourself: What information does the reader need to understand first? How do I build on this first section—what block of information will follow? Think of each section in relation to others until you have placed them all and have worked your way through to a plan for the whole paper.

Bear in mind that any one paper can be written—successfully—according to a variety of plans. Your job before beginning your first draft is to explore possibilities. Sketch a series of rough outlines:

- Arrange and rearrange your paper's likely sections until you develop a plan that both enhances the reader's understanding and achieves your objectives as a writer.
- Think carefully about the logical order of your points: Does one idea or point lead to the next?
- If one idea does not lead to the next, can you find a more logical place for the point, or are you just not clearly articulating the connections between the ideas?

Your final paper may well deviate from your final sketch; in the act of writing you may discover the need to explore new material, omit planned material, refocus, or reorder your entire presentation. Just the same, a well-conceived organizational plan will encourage you to begin writing a draft.

Organize a Synthesis by Idea, Not by Source

A synthesis is a blending of sources organized by *ideas*. The following rough sketches suggest how to organize and how *not* to organize a synthesis. The sketches assume you have read seven sources on a topic, sources A to G.

Incorrect: Organizing by Source plus Summary

Thesis

Summary of source A in support of the thesis.

Summary of source B in support of the thesis.

Summary of source C in support of the thesis.

(etc.)

Conclusion

This is *not* a synthesis because it does not blend sources. Each source stands alone as an independent summary. No dialogue or connection among sources is possible.

Correct: Organizing by Idea

Thesis

First idea: Refer to and discuss *parts* of sources (perhaps A, C, F) in support of this idea.

Second idea: Refer to and discuss *parts* of sources (perhaps B, D) in support of this idea.

Third idea: Refer to and discuss *parts* of sources (perhaps A, E, G) in support of this idea.

(etc.)

Conclusion

This *is* a synthesis because the writer blends and creates a dialogue among sources in support of an idea. Each organizing idea, which can be a paragraph or group of related paragraphs, in turn supports the thesis.

Write Your Synthesis

Here is the first draft of Kearney's explanatory synthesis. Thesis and topic sentences are highlighted.

Alongside this first draft we have included comments and suggestions for revision from Kearney's instructor. For purposes of demonstration, these comments are likely to be more comprehensive than the selective comments provided by most instructors.

Explanatory Synthesis: First Draft

Kearney 1

Sheldon Kearney

Professor Leslie Davis

Technology and Culture

October 1, 2016

The "Idea" of Money

1   Does money buy happiness? People have been debating this question for centuries, but they have been less concerned with the question of what, exactly, money is. Money takes many forms: coin, paper, plastic cards, electronic accounts, traveler's checks, stocks, and bonds being the most common. Whatever form it takes, money is valuable only to the extent people believe it is.

2   Basic to any understanding of money is the notion of exchange. In the first stages of civilization, goods were exchanged by people through a system of bartering—a form of trade in which two people exchange possessions of equal "value," where the value of the items traded away is equal to the value of the items received. Value is a purely subjective term because people who will use an item determine its worth to them. For example, while an apple and an orange may seem to be of equal value to the passive observer, Anne may prefer apples to oranges and thus be willing to trade more oranges for fewer apples. Likewise, Mark may prefer oranges to apples, and thus be willing to trade more apples for fewer oranges. If Anne's and Mark's relative preferences for fruit coincide, then they will trade, and each will be happy.

(1) Your title is intriguing—but your first paragraph is skimpy! Set more of a context. Your thesis may be too narrow.

Also rethink your opening sentence—a fine philosophical question but irrelevant to subject of paper. Gives misleading impression of where discussion is headed.

(2) You use Anne + Mark to define exchange. Okay here but don't overuse. You risk a superficial discussion.

(3) This would be a useful spot for an authoritative source on "exchange." Look to classic economists.

(4) Good content—cowrie shells, etc. But too much Anne/Mark.

Could a few images help the paper—forms money has taken?

(5) Suggest reworking the last sentence to avoid weak "There is . . ." opening.

(6) In stating money is an idea, you assume what you explain. Too much Anne/Mark. Paper needs a solid example of hyperinflation. Develop here mention of Germany between world wars in para. 4?

(7–8) Avoid freestanding quotation: "Paper money was . . ." Use signal phrase.

Excellent use of gold standard, introduced then removed. If gold didn't back currency, what did?

Gold standard a great setup for the key word in your paper (in para. 9): faith.

3   In a barter system, exchanges like these were based on mutual need. A farmer who grew wheat may have valued chickens and thus traded wheat for chickens because he had none. Meanwhile, a farmer who raised chickens might not have had any wheat and therefore traded chickens for the wheat that he needed. Now each farmer was better off. Instead of having an excess of one food item, each had some of both. Equal exchange was the foundation of the barter system, and the barter system was the precursor of the currency system.

4   Currency grew out of exchanges of goods and, particularly, the need for convenience in these exchanges. If Mark valued oranges but had no apples to offer Anne, then Mark needed to offer something else that both he and Anne valued. Currency was born. Objects that were easy to exchange, durable, and relatively common—such as cowrie shells, precious metals, and tools—became popular substitutes for goods and services that would have been traded in a barter system. In time, currency took the form of coins. Because different regions issued different coins, exchanges between regions became difficult. In the thirteenth century, Kublai Khan solved this problem and unified his empire by introducing a single paper currency (Surowiecki). Over time, currency has taken many forms and, today, has even become invisible in mobile-to-mobile phone apps like Apple Pay (Sidel and Wakabayashi). All that's required for currency to work is widespread confidence that, visible or not, it has value. When that confidence is lost, entire economies can collapse, which is what happened in Germany between the world wars (Jung).

5   From its creation, then, money served the process of economic exchange. People used cowrie shells (or their currency of choice) to satisfy the demands of political, religious, and personal relationships as well as economic relationships. There is a likelihood that these relationships increased the development and spread of a common currency.

6   That money is more an idea or an agreement than it is a thing is no less true today than it was in ancient times. Money was—and remains—a fragile social construct, holding value only because the economic community agrees that it does. If enough people come to doubt that value and say, in effect, that "money isn't worth the paper it's printed on," an entire economy could falter as people refuse to accept previously agreed-on amounts of money in exchange for goods and services. An economy will quickly become unstable if Anne refuses Mark's cowrie shells or dollars in exchange for her oranges because she has lost confidence in those currencies, or if she demands that Mark pay twice or four times the amount of cowrie shells because, in her view, they are worth less today than they were yesterday.

7   In March 1900, the United States government passed the Gold Standard Act, fixing the exchange rate between gold and paper currency. This act, which mirrored similar policies of the British and was instituted after decades of currency instability, established that all the paper money issued by the United States would be backed by—could be traded for—a given amount of gold. In the United States, this gold was kept in a central location at Fort Knox. "[P]aper money was a convenience, but it was acceptable only if it could be converted into precious metal by bringing it into the bank or government agency that printed it" (p. 219). Paper money in this system was a promise, or an exchangeable IOU.

8   With the Gold Standard Act, the government sought to reassure citizens and business interests that the pieces of paper in their wallets and bank accounts were actually worth something and that the foundation of the economy was solid. Confident consumers could

Kearney 3

spend dollars and merchants could accept dollars, everyone agreeing that the currency in use provided a fair exchange. By 1929, however, the basic logic of the gold standard was undermined when the amount of currency in circulation, $4.46 billion, exceeded the amount of gold held in reserve to back that currency, $2.3 billion (St. Louis Federal Reserve, 2001). The gap widened over the years until, in 1971, President Nixon ended the gold standard. For the last 45 years, the United States has held no precious metals in reserve to back its currency. What, then, is the foundation of our economy?

In a word, faith. The economy of the United States rests on a good-faith agreement people are willing to make that its currency has value, even if it isn't backed by gold. That's the same agreement the Russians make regarding rubles, the Japanese with yen, the British with pounds, and the Europeans with euros. All the money used around the world might lead one to conclude money is the solid foundation of the global economy, but look a little closer and we find that this foundation is an unsteady idea.

9

(9) (1) Do more with "invisible" digital money mentioned in para. 4. (2) Use your sources more. Thus far, weak effort at synthesis. (3) Draft wanders from your original thesis. Final sentence could be good start for revision. Also cite sources!

Revise Your Synthesis

Many writers plan for three types of revision: global, local, and surface.

Global revisions affect the entire paper: the thesis, the type and pattern of evidence employed, and the overall organization. A global revision may also emerge from a change in purpose—say, when a writer realizes that a paper works better as an argument than as an explanation. In this case, Kearney decided to revise globally based on his instructor's suggestion to use a statement from the conclusion as a thesis in the second draft. Kearney needed to:

- Support the revised thesis by explaining more clearly why money is an idea.
- Extend money as an idea into the digital age.
- Summarize, quote, or paraphrase more sources to lend the paper authority.

Local revisions affect paragraphs: topic and transitional sentences; the type of evidence presented within a paragraph; evidence added, modified, or dropped within a paragraph; and logical connections from one sentence or set of sentences within a paragraph to another. Kearney needed to:

- Find a good historical example of hyperinflation.
- Explain the concept of exchange without relying on the analogy of Anne and Mark.
- Clarify and expand his introduction.

Surface revisions deal with sentence style and construction; word choice; and errors of grammar, mechanics, spelling, and citation form.

Sheldon Kearney revised based on his instructor's comments and based on his own assessment of what he wanted to achieve in his paper. His final draft/ revision represents two revisions: the first, to put large elements in place, like moving the thesis from the last paragraph to the first and better clarifying what he meant by the "idea" of money; the second, to better support individual paragraphs with fresh examples and references to authoritative sources. Along the way, he fixed sentence-level problems.

Exercise 4.3
Revising the Explanatory Synthesis

Read Kearney's revision that follows and answer these questions:

- How effective is the paper?

- What makes this paper an explanation?

- To what extent did Kearney follow his instructor's advice?

- Did you learn from this paper?

Explain each answer with a brief paragraph.

Model Explanatory Synthesis

Kearney 1

Sheldon Kearney

Professor Leslie Davis

Technology and Culture

October 20, 2016

The "Idea" of Money

1   Money takes many forms: coins, paper, plastic cards, electronic accounts, PayPal transactions, discount coupons, stocks, bonds, and poker chips being some of the most common. In U.S. currency alone, there was $1.34 trillion in circulation in September 2015 ("How much"). Add trillions more in Chinese yuan, euros, British pounds and Russian rubles needed to transact business every day throughout the world, and it appears that money is the rock-solid foundation of the global economy. But look a little closer at the origins and the uses of money and we find that this foundation, far from being a definite, stable thing like rock, is only an idea.

2   Basic to any understanding of money is the notion of exchange. Once economies developed to the point where labor became specialized—some people brewed beer while others made shoes or grew wheat—people exchanged goods through a system of bartering, according to Adam Smith. Where there's a division of labor, Smith explained in *The Wealth of Nations* (1776), butchers who sell meat have all the meat they need for personal consumption. So, too, brewers have all the beer they need, and more. Quite naturally, an exchange would arise between them as they traded some of their "commodities" (meat and beer) with each other so each could enjoy both. In an economy based on barter, wrote Smith, "[e]very man thus lives by exchanging, or becomes in some measure a merchant, and the society

itself grows to be what is properly a commercial society" (Book 1, Chapter 4). Smith went on to observe that barter has its limits:

> [W]hen the division of labour first began to take place, this power of exchanging must frequently have been very much clogged and embarrassed in its operations. One man, we shall suppose, has more of a certain commodity than he himself has occasion for, while another has less. The former consequently would be glad to dispose of, and the latter to purchase, a part of this superfluity. But if this latter should chance to have nothing that the former stands in need of, no exchange can be made between them. The butcher has more meat in his shop than he himself can consume, and the brewer and the baker would each of them be willing to purchase a part of it. But they have nothing to offer in exchange, except the different productions of their respective trades, and the butcher is already provided with all the bread and beer which he has immediate occasion for. No exchange can, in this case, be made between them. He cannot be their merchant, nor they his customers; and they are all of them thus mutually less serviceable to one another. (Book 1, Chapter 4)

To deal with this problem, currency was born. Objects that were "divisible, portable, **3** acceptable, scarce, durable, and stable" (Hill) became a substitute for goods and services that would have been traded in a barter system. In a currency-based economy, the butcher didn't need to trade his meat for beer or shoes, if he needed neither. As long as the butcher, brewer, and farmer each valued the same currency—be it stone tools, gold nuggets, or cowrie shells—a new kind of exchange could take place. Money emerged across cultures for the same reason: convenience. The *form* money took varied from one society to the next.

Cowrie Shells · Gold Nugget · Stone Tools

As Glyn Davies points out in *The History of Money*, factors other than economics were **4** also involved in the creation of money: fees, called a "tribute," paid to kings or generals, dowries provided by families of a bride, "blood-money" demanded by families to keep the peace when someone was hurt or killed, and money in the form of precious metals and jewels to be formed into religious ornaments (iv). That is, money emerged for social reasons as well as economic ones.

From its creation, then, money served the process of economic and social exchange. **5** People used cowrie shells (or their currency of choice) to satisfy the demands of political, religious, and personal relationships as well as economic relationships. All these relationships likely influenced the development and spread of a common currency, which was needed to bring economic order to vast empires: Rome, for instance, introduced a single currency to be used throughout its empire, extending from Great Britain to North Africa to the Middle East (Cottrell xiii).

Roman (Gold) Coin: Aureus

6   Whether ancient like the aureus (above) or modern like a U.S. quarter, currency in the form of minted coins may look to us like legitimate money that holds "real" value as compared to cowrie shells. But when we think about what, exactly, gives gold, whether a raw nugget or a minted aureus, its value, we end up inevitably having to accept a strange and difficult concept: nothing about gold (or diamonds or silver or rubies) is valuable other than the value we are mutually willing to give it. That is, gold derives its value from the same agreement between people that gave cowrie shells value or stone tools value among ancient humans. Gold is relatively scarce—and it meets the other five generally accepted characteristics of money: it can be divided, and it's portable, widely accepted, durable, and stable (Hill). Yet none of these qualities gives gold any more inherent value than cowrie shells or the paper bills we place in our wallets, which have the same characteristics. Business journalist James Surowiecki puts it this way:

> [T]he notion that gold is somehow [a] more "real" [form of money] than paper is, well, a mirage. Gold is valuable because we've collectively decided that it's valuable and that we'll accept goods and services in exchange for it. And that's no different, ultimately, from our collective decision that colorful rectangles of paper [money] are valuable and that we'll accept goods and services in exchange for them. . . . We cling to the belief that money needs to be backed by something "solid."

Andreas Antonopoulus, author of *Mastering Bitcoin*, claims that money is a form of language "that allows us to express . . . value between people. It's a technology that's older than the wheel. It's as old as fire" (qtd. in *Bitcoin*).

7   Money's being more an idea or an agreement than it is a thing is no less true today than it was in ancient times. Money was—and remains—a fragile social construction, holding value only because the economic community agrees that it does. People *trust* that money can "be converted at any time into concrete goods" (Trigilia 38). If enough people come to doubt a currency's ability to do that, an entire economy could collapse as people refuse to accept previously agreed-on amounts of money in exchange for goods and services. This is exactly what happens in times of hyperinflation—as in Germany in 1922-1923. After World War I, Germans placed so little value in their own currency that a theater

ticket cost one billion marks and a cup of coffee that cost 5,000 marks rose to 9,000 by the time a customer ordered and drank a second cup. When the man complained, "he was told he should have ordered the coffees at the same time because the price had gone up in between" (Jung).

In March 1900, the United States government passed the Gold Standard Act, fixing the **8** exchange rate between gold and paper currency. This act, which mirrored similar policies of the British and was instituted after decades of currency instability, established that all the paper money issued by the United States would be backed by—could be traded for—a given amount of gold. In the United States, this gold was kept in a central location at Fort Knox. Jacob Deroy explains that "paper money was a convenience, but it was acceptable only if it could be converted into precious metal by bringing it into the bank or government agency that printed it" (219). Paper money in this system was a promise, or an exchangeable IOU. In theory, people would accept the value of the paper money because it could be converted into "real" money—that is, gold.

With the Gold Standard Act, the government sought to reassure citizens and business **9** interests that the pieces of paper in their wallets and bank accounts were actually worth something and that the foundation of the economy was solid. Confident consumers could spend dollars and merchants could accept dollars, everyone agreeing that the currency in use provided a fair exchange. By 1929, however, the basic logic of the gold standard was undermined when the amount of currency in circulation, $4.46 billion, exceeded the amount of gold held in reserve to back that currency, $2.3 billion ("Currency"). The gap widened over the years until, in 1971, President Nixon ended the gold standard. For the last 45 years, the United States has held no precious metals in reserve to back its currency. What, then, is the foundation of our economy?

Faith. **10**

Whether the butcher is buying beer from the brewer or a car from a local dealer, all con- **11** cerned trust that the dollars he pays have value. And they do, as long as everyone believes they do and continues to buy and sell goods and services based on that belief. The ending of the gold standard was like a trumpet blast announcing that money is a belief system, not a physical thing.

For anyone needing a louder blast, the perfect expression of this belief system may be **12** seen in two digital developments that promise to upend the way we use and think of money: The first, invented in 2009, is Bitcoin, a digital currency that has *no* physical form. The second, released in 2014 (and after), is Apple Pay and similar mobile payment systems. Though the Apple product is linked to bank accounts and, hence, dollars (a traditional currency), the connection to actual money seems remote at points of sale where *no* cash is exchanged or credit-card information recorded. Instead, the buyer launches an app on her iPhone, which transmits a digital "token" to the seller's computer, at which point the buyer can leave the shop with a fresh pizza or a new pair of jeans (Evans). Apple's Chief Executive Tim Cook predicts "that digital-payments systems like Apple Pay will become so pervasive in the future that 'your kids will not know what' cash is" (qtd. in Sidel). When that happens, we'll have come a long way from bartering and the use of cowrie shells or gold coins, trusting instead that the new digital systems will exchange dollars, invisibly, at the speed of light between the computer servers at Apple and vendors who accept their mobile payment system.

13   As remote as physical money is from such mobile app transactions, actual dollars in a bank (somewhere) back the exchange. An even more radical development can be found in Bitcoins, which exist not as digital versions of dollars or any other currency but as strings of numbers in computers linked over the Internet. Anyone conducting business electronically can choose to pay in Bitcoins as long as the person, or company, they are buying from accepts Bitcoins as legitimate payment. In this system, a person's wealth as expressed in Bitcoins exists as encrypted files in a massive computer network. If the butcher and his neighbor, Anne, agree that her used car is worth five hundred Bitcoins, then the butcher sends Anne a string of numbers—computer to computer. The ownership of that string of numbers moves across the network from the butcher's digital "wallet" to Anne's. The butcher drives Anne's car away, and Anne can use her new Bitcoins to pay for a new car or rent on her apartment or anything she pleases, as long as the person with whom she's doing business next agrees that Bitcoins have value. On what, exactly, is this value based? Again, the strange word that applies to all forms of money: faith.

> The value of a Bitcoin is . . . derived from the faith that you have in the value of what you can procure with that Bitcoin. It's just like you [derive value] for a dollar, a Euro, or a Yen. The faith that you have in that currency's value is how you value that currency. (Kahn)

14   Bitcoins bring the socially constructed, or invented, nature of money into the open, exploding the belief that the value of gold or diamonds somehow exists *in* the gold or diamonds. It does not. If enough of us agreed, we could restore the use of peppercorns as common currency: from ancient times through the Middle Ages, peppercorns were used as money (Hunt 314). All we would need is a mutual belief in their value. It's exactly the same agreement humans have made concerning stones, cowrie shells, and tools; it's the same agreement we continue to make concerning gold, silver, digital payment apps, and Bitcoins. Because the goods and services we buy with money are solid and real, it can be difficult and strange to admit that money is not and never has been a *thing*. Money is an idea, an ancient one as crucial to the development of civilization as the controlled use of fire, or the wheel.

Works Cited

"Aureus." Image 26959520. *Dreamstime*, 2016, www.dreamstime.com/photos-images/aureus.html.

Bitcoin: The End of Money as We Know It. Directed by Torsten Hoffmann and Michael Watchulonis. 3D Content Hub, 2015, *Netflix*, www.netflix.com/.

Cottrell, Philip, et al., editors. *From the Athenian Tetradrachm to the Euro: Studies in European Monetary Integration*. Ashgate, 2007.

"Cowrie Shells." Image 9819406. *Dreamstime*, 2016, www.dreamstime.com/photos-images/cowrie-shells.html.

"*Currency Statistics 1929.*" *Economic Research,* Federal Reserve Bank of St. Louis, 18 Apr. 2001, https://research.stlouisfed.org/fred2/series/CURRCIR.

Davies, Glyn. *A History of Paper Money from Ancient Times to the Present Day*. Wales UP, 2002.

Deroy, Jacob. *Economic Literacy: What Everyone Needs to Know About Money and Markets*. Crown, 1995.

Evans, Jonny. "Apple Pay: What You Need to Know." *Computerworld*, 10 Sept. 2014, www.computerworld.com/article/2605321/apple-pay-what-you-need-to-know.html.

"Gold Nugget." Image15891596. *Dreamstime*, 2016, www.dreamstime.com/photos-images/gold-nugget.html.

Hill, Andrew. "Functions and Characteristics of Money." *Federal Reserve Bank of Philadelphia*, 2013, www.philadelphiafed.org/.

"How Much U.S. Currency Is in Circulation?" Federalreserve.gov, Board of Governors of the Federal Reserve System, 29 Feb. 2016, www.federalreserve.gov/faqs/currency_12773.htm.

Hunt, Lynn, et al. *The Making of the West, Combined Volume: People and Cultures*. 4th ed., vol. 1, Bedford, 2012. *Google Books*, https://books.google.com/books?isbn=0312672683.

Jung, Alexander. "Germany in the Era of Hyperinflation." *Spiegel Online*, 14 Aug. 2009, www.spiegel.de/international/germany/millions-billions-trillions-germany-in-the-era-of-hyperinflation-a-641758.html.

Kahn Academy. "Bitcoin: What Is It?" Minutes: 00:3:10–00:3:18. *Kahn Academy*, May 2013, https://www.khanacademy.org/economics-finance-domain/core-finance/money-and-banking/bitcoin/v/bitcoin-what-is-it.

Sidel, Robin, and Daisuke Wakabayashi. "Apple, Banks in Talks on Mobile Person-to-Person Payment Service." *Wall Street Journal*, 11 Nov. 2015, www.wsj.com/articles/apple-in-talks-with-u-s-banks-to-develop-mobile-person-to-person-payment-service-1447274074.

Smith, Adam. *The Wealth of Nations*. 1776. *Project Gutenberg*, www.gutenberg.org/files/3300/3300-8.txt.

"Stone Tools." Image 36733032. *Dreamstime*, 2016, www.dreamstime.com/photos-images/stone-tools.html.

Surowiecki, James. "A Brief History of Money: Or, How We Learned to Stop Worrying and Embrace the Abstraction." *IEEE Spectrum*, 30 May 2012, http://spectrum.ieee.org/at-work/innovation/a-brief-history-of-money.

Trigilia, Carlo. *Economic Sociology: State Market, and Society in Modern Capitalism*. Wiley, 2008.

Critical Reading for Synthesis

- **Understand each source you will draw on in writing your synthesis.** Examine its context; note the title and subtitle; identify the main point; identify the subpoints; break the reading into sections; distinguish between points, examples, and counterarguments; watch for transitions within and between paragraphs; and read actively and recursively.

- **Establish the writer's primary purpose.** Use some of the guidelines discussed in Chapter 2. Is the piece primarily informative, persuasive, or entertaining? Assess whether the piece achieves its purpose.

- **Read to identify a key idea.** If you begin reading your source materials with a key idea or topic already in mind, read to identify what your sources have to say about the idea.

- **Read to discover a key idea.** If you begin the reading process without a key idea or topic in mind, read to discover if your sources suggest one.

- **Read for relationships.** Regardless of whether you already have a key idea or you are attempting to discover one, note the ways in which the readings relate to each other, to a key idea, and to your purpose in writing the synthesis.

Chapter 5
Argument Synthesis

 ## Learning Objectives

After completing this chapter, you will be able to:

5.1   Apply the elements of argument to the writing of an argument synthesis.

5.2   Write an argument synthesis.

5.3   Use various strategies to develop and support your arguments.

5.4   Use comparison and contrast, where appropriate, to develop your argument synthesis.

5.5   Use your purpose to guide your choice of writing an explanatory synthesis, argument synthesis, or comparison-and-contrast synthesis.

What Is an Argument Synthesis?

5.1   **Apply the elements of argument to the writing of an argument synthesis.**

An argument is an attempt to persuade a reader or listener that a specific debatable claim is true and worthy of support. Writers argue in order to establish facts, to make statements of value, and to recommend policies. For instance, answering the question "What role does compromise play in the legislative process?" would involve making an argument. You might support your answer by interviewing experts, referring to historical evidence, and drawing on data gleaned from social science experiments.

Would readers accept your conclusions? That depends on the quality of your supporting evidence and the care and logic with which you have argued your case.

What we are calling an *argument synthesis* draws on evidence from a variety of sources in an attempt to persuade others of the truth or validity of a debatable claim.

By contrast, the explanatory synthesis, as we have seen, is fairly modest in purpose. It emphasizes the sources themselves, not the writer's use of sources to persuade others. The writer of an explanatory synthesis aims to inform. Here, for example, is a thesis devised for an explanatory synthesis on the ubiquity of smartphones in contemporary life:

> Smartphones make it possible for us to be always within reach, though many people would prefer *not* to be always within reach.

This thesis summarizes two observations about the impact of smartphones, arguing neither for nor against the validity of either observation.

An argument thesis, however, is *persuasive* in purpose. A writer working with the same source material might conceive and support a very different thesis:

> Smartphones create an illusion of meaningful connection with others and have ruined our abilty, perhaps even our desire, to be content while alone.

The thesis of an argument synthesis, also called a *claim*, is a debatable statement about which reasonable people could disagree. It is a statement that you support with logic and evidence in order to persuade others that your view is true or desirable.

The Elements of Argument: Claim, Support, and Assumption

One way of understanding argument is to see it as an interplay of three essential elements:

- Claim
- Support
- Assumption

A *claim* is a proposition or conclusion that you are trying to prove. You prove this claim by using *support* in the form of fact, statistics, or expert opinion. Linking your supporting evidence to your claim is your *assumption* about the subject. This assumption, also called a *warrant*, is an underlying belief or principle about some aspect of the world and how it operates (see our discussion of assumptions in Chapter 2, pp. 79–81). By their nature, assumptions (which are often unstated) tend to be more general than either claims or supporting evidence.

Here are the essential elements of an argument that parents should restrict the amount of television that their teenagers watch:

Claim

> High school students should watch no more than two hours of TV per day.

Support

> An important new study and the testimony of educational specialists reveal that students who watch more than two hours of TV a night have, on average, lower grades than those who watch less TV.

Assumption

> Excessive TV viewing adversely affects academic performance.

As another example, here are the essential elements of an argument about smartphone technology:

Claim

> The use of smartphones threatens to undermine human intimacy, connection, and ultimately community.

Support

- People are spending increasing amounts of time on smartphones: In 2015, owners of smartphones spent, on average, 7.7 hours per day on their devices.
- College health officials report that excessive smartphone use threatens many college students' academic and psychological well-being.
- To encourage direct human-to-human interaction, some restaurants have begun offering discounts to patrons who turn off their smartphones during the meal.
- New kinds of relationships fostered on smartphones can pose challenges to preexisting relationships.

Assumptions

- The communication skills used and the connections formed during smartphone interactions fundamentally differ from those used and formed during face-to-face contact.
- "Real" connection and a sense of community are sustained by face-to-face contact, not by digital interactions.

For the most part, construct arguments logically so that assumptions link evidence (supporting facts, statistics, and expert opinions) to claims. As we'll see, however, logic is only one component of effective arguments.

Exercise 5.1

Practicing Claim, Support, and Assumption

Devise two sets of claims, support, and assumptions. First, in response to the example above about smartphone interactions, write a one-sentence claim addressing the positive impact (or potentially positive impact) of smartphones on relationships—whether you personally agree with the claim or not. Then list the supporting statements on which such a claim might rest and the assumption that underlies them. Second, write a claim that states your own position on any debatable topic you choose. Again, devise statements of support and relevant assumptions.

The Three Appeals of Argument:
Logos, Ethos, Pathos

Speakers and writers have never relied on logic alone in advancing and supporting their claims. More than 2,000 years ago, the Athenian philosopher and rhetorician Aristotle explained how speakers attempting to persuade others to adopt their point of view could achieve their purpose by relying on one or more *appeals,* which he called *logos, ethos,* and *pathos.*

Since we frequently find these three appeals employed in political argument, we'll use political examples in the following discussion. All three appeals are also used extensively in advertising, legal cases, business documents, and many other types of argument. Bear in mind that in academic writing, the appeal to logic (*logos*) is by far the most commonly used appeal.

LOGOS   *Logos* is the rational appeal, the appeal to reason. Academic presentations, including the papers you will write across the curriculum, build almost exclusively on appeals to logic and evidence. If writers and speakers expect to persuade their audiences, they must argue logically and must supply appropriate evidence to support their case. Logical arguments are commonly of two types (often combined): deductive and inductive.

Deductive Reasoning   The *deductive* argument begins with a generalization, then cites a specific case related to that generalization from which follows a conclusion. An example of a deductive argument may be seen in President John F. Kennedy's address to the nation in June 1963 on the need for sweeping civil rights legislation. Kennedy begins with the generalizations that it "ought to be possible . . . for American students of any color to attend any public institution they select without having to be backed up by troops" and that "it ought to be possible for American citizens of any color to register and vote in a free election without interference or fear of reprisal." Kennedy then provides several specific examples (primarily recent events in Birmingham, Alabama) and statistics to show that segregation had prevented many from enrolling in public colleges and from registering to vote. He concludes:

> We face, therefore, a moral crisis as a country and a people. It cannot be met by repressive police action. It cannot be left to increased demonstrations in the streets. It cannot be quieted by token moves or talk. It is time to act in the Congress, in your state and local legislative body, and, above all, in all of our daily lives.

Underlying Kennedy's argument is this reasoning:

All Americans should enjoy certain rights. (*assumption*)

Some Americans do not enjoy these rights. (*support*)

We must take action to ensure that all Americans enjoy these rights. (*claim*)

Inductive Reasoning   Another form of logical argumentation is *inductive* reasoning. A speaker or writer who argues inductively begins not with a generalization but with several pieces of specific evidence. The speaker then draws a conclusion from this evidence. For example, in a debate on gun control, former senator Robert C. Byrd cited specific examples of rampant crime involving guns: "I read of young men being viciously murdered for a pair of sneakers, a leather jacket, or $20." He also offered statistical evidence of the increasing crime rate: "in 1951, there were 3.2 policemen for every felony committed in the United States; this year nearly 3.2 felonies will be committed per every police officer." He concluded, "Something has to change. We have to stop the crimes that are distorting and disrupting the way of life for so many innocent, law-respecting Americans. The bill that we are debating today attempts to do just that."

Maintaining a Critical Perspective   Of course, the mere piling up of evidence does not in itself make the speaker's case. As Donna Cross explains in "Politics: The Art of Bamboozling,"[1] politicians are very adept at "card-stacking"—lining up evidence in favor of a conclusion without bothering to mention (or barely mentioning) contrary evidence. And statistics can be selected and manipulated to prove anything, as demonstrated in Darrell Huff's landmark book *How to Lie with Statistics* (1954). Moreover, what appears to be a logical argument may in fact be fundamentally flawed. (See Chapter 2 for a discussion of logical fallacies and faulty reasoning.)

On the other hand, the fact that evidence can be distorted, statistics can be misused, and logic can be fractured does not mean that these tools of reason should be dismissed. It means only that audiences have to listen and read critically, and question the use of statistics and other evidence.

Exercise 5.2
Using Deductive and Inductive Logic

Choose an issue currently being debated at your school or a college-related issue about which you are concerned. Write a claim about this issue. Then write two paragraphs addressing your claim—one in which you organize your points deductively (beginning with your claim and following with support) and one in which you organize them inductively (presenting supporting evidence and following with a claim). Possible issues might include college admissions policies, classroom crowding, or grade inflation. Alternatively, you could base your paragraphs on a claim generated in Exercise 5.1.

ETHOS   *Ethos,* or the ethical appeal, is based not on the ethics relating to the subject under discussion but rather on the ethical status of the person making the argument. A person making an argument must have a certain degree of credibility: That person must be of good character, have sound sense, and be qualified to argue based either on expert experience with the subject matter or on carefully conducted research. Students writing in academic settings establish

---

[1]Donna Cross, *Word Abuse: How the Words We Use Use Us* (New York: Coward, 1979).

their appeal to *ethos* by developing presentations that are well organized, carefully reasoned, and thoroughly referenced with source citations. These are the hallmarks of writers and speakers who care deeply about their work. If you care, your audience will care and consider your argument seriously.

Appeals to *ethos* are usually most explicit in political contests. For example, Elizabeth Cervantes Barrón, running for senator as the Peace and Freedom Party candidate, establishes her credibility this way: "I was born and raised in central Los Angeles. I grew up in a multiethnic, multicultural environment where I learned to respect those who were different from me. . . . I am a teacher and am aware of how cutbacks in education have affected our children and our communities." On the other end of the political spectrum, the American Independent gubernatorial candidate Jerry McCready also begins with an ethical appeal: "As a self-employed businessman, I have learned firsthand what it is like to try to make ends meet in an unstable economy being manipulated by out-of-touch politicians." Both candidates are making an appeal to *ethos,* an appeal based on the strength of their personal qualities for the office they seek. Both argue, in effect, "Trust me. My experience makes me a credible, knowledgeable candidate."

As a "consumer" of political arguments—that is, as a voter—ask, "Does this appeal to personal qualifications matter?" "Do I *agree* that this candidate is of upstanding character?" "Am I persuaded that personal traits will translate to policies that I support?"

Exercise 5.3
Using *Ethos*

Return to the claim you used for Exercise 5.2 and write a paragraph in which you use an appeal to *ethos* to make a case for that claim.

PATHOS Finally, speakers and writers appeal to their audiences by using *pathos,* an appeal to the emotions. Writers in academic settings rely heavily on the force of logic and evidence, and rarely make appeals to *pathos.* Beyond academic settings, however, appeals to the emotions are commonplace. Nothing is inherently wrong with using an emotional appeal. Indeed, because emotions often move people far more successfully than reason alone, speakers and writers would be foolish not to use emotion. And it would be a drab, humorless world if human beings were not subject to the sway of feeling as well as reason. The emotional appeal becomes problematic only when it is the *sole* or *primary* basis of the argument.

President Ronald Reagan was a master of emotional appeal. He closed his first inaugural address with a reference to the view from the Capitol to the Arlington National Cemetery, where lie thousands of markers of "heroes":

> Under one such marker lies a young man, Martin Treptow, who left his job in a small-town barbershop in 1917 to go to France with the famed Rainbow Division. There, on the western front, he was killed trying to carry a message between battalions under heavy artillery fire. We're told that on his body was found a diary. On the flyleaf under the heading, "My Pledge," he had written these words: "America must win this war. Therefore, I will work, I will save, I will sacrifice, I will endure, I will fight cheerfully and do my utmost, as if the issue of the whole struggle depended on me alone." The crisis we are facing today does not require of us the kind of sacrifice that Martin Treptow and so many thousands of others were called upon to make. It does require, however, our best effort and our willingness to believe in ourselves and to believe in our capacity to perform great deeds, to believe that together with God's help we can and will resolve the problems which now confront us.

Surely, Reagan implies, if Martin Treptow can act so courageously and so selflessly, we can do the same. His logic is somewhat unclear because the connection between Martin Treptow and ordinary Americans of 1981 is rather tenuous (as Reagan concedes), but the emotional power of the heroism of Martin Treptow, whom reporters were sent scurrying to research, carries the argument.

Exercise 5.4
Using *Pathos*

Return to the claim you used for Exercises 5.2 and 5.3 and write a paragraph in which you use an appeal to *pathos* to argue for that claim.

The Limits of Argument

Our discussion of *ethos* and *pathos* indicates a potentially troubling but undeniable reality: Arguments are not won on the basis of logic and evidence alone. In the real world, arguments don't operate like academic debates. If the purpose of argument is to get people to change their minds or to agree that the writer's or speaker's position on a particular topic is the best available, then the person making the argument must be aware that factors other than evidence and good reasoning come into play when readers or listeners are considering the matter.

These factors involve deep-seated cultural, religious, ethnic, racial, and gender identities; moral preferences; and the effects of personal experiences (either pleasant or unpleasant) that are generally resistant to logic and evidence, however well framed. You could try—using the best available arguments—to convince someone who is pro-life to agree with the pro-choice position (or vice versa). Or you could try to persuade someone who opposes capital punishment to believe that state-endorsed executions are necessary for deterrence (or for any other reason). You might even marshal your evidence and logic to try to persuade someone whose family members have had run-ins with the law that police efforts are directed at protecting the law-abiding.

On such emotionally loaded topics, however, it is extremely difficult, if not impossible, to get people to change their minds because they are so personally invested in their beliefs. As Susan Jacoby, author of *The Age of American Unreason*, notes, "Whether watching television news, consulting political blogs, or (more rarely) reading books, Americans today have become a people in search of validation for opinions that they already hold."[2] Put Jacoby's claim to the test: On any given evening, watch a half-hour of Fox News and MSNBC News. The news coverage of at least a few stories will likely overlap. Can you detect a slant, or bias, in this coverage? Which program would a political conservative be inclined to watch? A liberal? Why?

FRUITFUL TOPICS FOR ARGUMENT   The tenacity with which people hold onto longtime beliefs does not mean, however, that they cannot change their minds or that subjects like abortion, capital punishment, and gun control should be off limits to reasoned debate. The past twenty years has seen some contentious issues, like gay marriage, resolved both in the courts and through elections; and reasoned argument—as well as appeals to *pathos* and *ethos*—has played a significant role. Still, you should be aware of the limits of argument. The most fruitful topics for argument in a freshman composition setting tend to be those on which most people are persuadable, either because they know relatively little about the topic or because deep-rooted cultural, religious, or moral beliefs are not involved. At least initially in your career as a writer of academic papers, it's probably best to avoid hot-button topics that are the focus of broader cultural debates and to focus instead on topics in which *pathos* plays less of a part.

For example, most people are not emotionally invested in plug-in hybrid or hydrogen-powered vehicles, so an argument on behalf of the more promising technology for the coming decades will not be complicated by deep-seated beliefs. Similarly, most people don't know enough about the mechanics of sleep to have strong opinions on how to deal with sleep deprivation. Your arguments on such topics, therefore, will provide opportunities both to inform your readers or listeners and to persuade them that your arguments, if well reasoned and supported by sound evidence, are at least plausible, if not entirely convincing.

---

[2]Susan Jacoby, "Talking to Ourselves: Americans Are Increasingly Closed-Minded and Unwilling to Listen to Opposing Views," *Los Angeles Times*, 20 Apr. 2008: M10.

How to Write Argument Syntheses

5.2 Write an argument synthesis.

Demonstration: Developing an Argument Synthesis—Responding to Bullies

To demonstrate how to plan and draft an argument synthesis, let's suppose that your composition instructor has assigned a research paper and that in pondering possible topics you find yourself considering what can be done to discourage widespread bullying in American schools. Perhaps you have a personal motivation to write on this topic: You were bullied as a child or recall watching others being bullied but did nothing to intervene. So you do some preliminary reading and discover that the problem of bullying is widespread and that all fifty states have adopted antibullying legislation. Still, however, the problem persists. What can be done to solve it?

You have a topic, and you have a guiding question for a paper.

Suppose, in preparing to write a paper in which you will argue for a workable solution to the problem of bullying, you locate (among others) the following sources:

- "Bullying Statistics" (a Web site)
- *The 2015 National School Climate Survey: The Experiences of Lesbian, Gay, Bisexual, Transgender, and Queer Youth in Our Nation's Schools* (a report)
- *Olweus Bullying Prevention Program: Scope and Sequence* (a publisher's catalog description of a widely adopted antibullying program)
- "Bullying—And the Power of Peers" (a scholarly article also delivered as a paper at a White House conference on bullying)

Carefully read these sources (which follow), noting the kinds of evidence—facts, expert opinions, and statistics—you could draw on to develop an *argument synthesis*. These passages are excerpts only; in preparing your paper, you would draw on the entire articles, reports, and Web sites from which these passages were taken. And you would draw on more sources than these in your search for supporting materials (as the writer of the model synthesis has done). But these four sources provide a good introduction to the subject. Our discussion of how these passages can form the basis of an argument synthesis resumes on page 139.

Bullying Statistics

—Pacer.org

General Statistics

- One out of every four students (22%) report being bullied during the school year (National Center for Educational Statistics, 2015).

- 19.6% of high school students in the U.S. report being bullied at school in the past year. 14.8% reported being bullied online (Centers for Disease Control, 2014).

- 64 percent of children who were bullied did not report it; only 36 percent reported the bullying (Petrosina, Guckenburg, DeVoe, and Hanson, 2010).

- More than half of bullying situations (57%) stop when a peer intervenes on behalf of the student being bullied (Hawkins, Pepler, and Craig, 2001).

- School-based bullying prevention programs decrease bullying by up to 25% (McCallion and Feder, 2013).

- The reasons for being bullied reported most often by students were looks (55%), body shape (37%), and race (16%) (Davis and Nixon, 2010).

Statistics about bullying of students with disabilities

- Only 10 U.S. studies have been conducted on the connection between bullying and developmental disabilities, but all of these studies found that children with disabilities were two to three times more likely to be bullied than their nondisabled peers (Marshall, Kendall, Banks, and Gover, 2009).

- Researchers discovered that students with disabilities were more worried about school safety and being injured or harassed by other peers compared to students without a disability (Saylor and Leach, 2009).

- The National Autistic Society reports that 40% of children with autism and 60% of children with Asperger's syndrome have experienced bullying.

- When reporting bullying, youth in special education were told not to tattle almost twice as often as youth not in special education (Davis and Nixon, 2010).

The 2015 National School Climate Survey: The Experiences of Lesbian, Gay, Bisexual, Transgender, and Queer Youth in Our Nation's Schools

—*Joseph G. Kosciw, Ph.D., Emily A. Greytak, Ph.D., Noreen M. Giga, M.P.H., Christian Villenas, Ph.D., David J. Danischewski, M.A.*

In 1999, [the Gay, Lesbian & Straight Education Network] (GLSEN) identified that little was known about the school experiences of lesbian, gay, bisexual, transgender, and queer (LGBTQ) youth and that LGBTQ youth were nearly absent from national studies of adolescents. We responded to this national need for data by launching the first National School Climate Survey, and we continue to meet this need for current data by conducting the study every two years. Since then, the biennial National School Climate Survey has documented the unique challenges LGBTQ students face and identified interventions that can improve school climate. The survey documents the prevalence of anti-LGBT language and victimization, such as experiences of harassment and assault in school. In addition, the survey examines school policies and practices that may contribute to negative experiences for LGBTQ students and make them feel as if they are not valued by their school communities. The survey also explores the effects that a hostile school climate may have on LGBTQ students' educational outcomes and well-being. Finally, the survey reports on the availability and the utility of LGBT-related school resources and supports that may offset the negative effects of a hostile school climate and promote a positive learning experience. In addition to collecting this critical data every two years, we also add and adapt survey questions to respond to the changing world for LGBTQ youth. For example, in the 2015 survey we expanded upon the types of discriminatory practices we explore by including questions related to extracurricular activities, school athletics, and gender segregation in school activities. The National School Climate Survey remains one of the few studies to examine the school experiences of LGBTQ students nationally, and its results have been vital to GLSEN's understanding of the issues that LGBTQ students face, thereby informing our ongoing work to ensure safe and affirming schools for all.

In our 2015 survey, we examine the experiences of LGBTQ students with regard to indicators of negative school climate:

- Hearing biased remarks, including homophobic remarks, in school;
- Feeling unsafe in school because of personal characteristics, such as sexual orientation, gender expression, or race/ethnicity;
- Missing classes or days of school because of safety reasons;
- Experiencing harassment and assault in school; and
- Experiencing discriminatory policies and practices at school.

We also examine:

- The possible negative effects of a hostile school climate on LGBTQ students' academic achievement, educational aspirations, and psychological well-being;
- Whether or not students report experiences of victimization to school officials or to family members and how these adults address the problem; and
- How the school experiences of LGBTQ students differ by personal and community characteristics.

In addition, we demonstrate the degree to which LGBTQ students have access to supportive resources in school, and we explore the possible benefits of these resources:

- Gay-Straight Alliances (GSAs) or similar clubs;
- School anti-bullying/harassment policies;
- Supportive school staff; and
- Curricular resources that are inclusive of LGBT-related topics.

Given that GLSEN has been conducting the survey for over a decade, we also examine changes over time on indicators of negative school climate and levels of access to LGBT-related resources in schools.

Olweus Bullying Prevention Program

Publisher Catalogue Description

The Olweus Bullying Prevention Program (OBPP) is the most researched and best-known bullying prevention program available today. With over thirty-five years of research and successful implementation all over the world, OBPP is a whole-school program that has been proven to prevent or reduce bullying throughout a school setting.

All Students and Adults Participate

The Olweus Bullying Prevention Program is designed for students in elementary, middle, and junior high schools (students ages five to fifteen years old). Research has shown that OBPP is also effective in high schools, with some program adaptation. All students participate in most aspects of the program, while students identified as bullying others, or as targets of bullying, receive additional individualized interventions.

Program Goals

The Olweus Bullying Prevention Program is designed to improve peer relations and make schools safer, more positive places for students to learn and develop. Goals of the program include:

- reducing existing bullying problems among students
- preventing the development of new bullying problems
- achieving better peer relations at school

Outcomes of the Program

Statistics show how successful implementation of the Olweus Bullying Prevention Program can reduce school bullying. Outcomes have included:

- Fifty percent or more reductions in student reports of being bullied and bullying others. Peer and teacher ratings of bullying problems have yielded similar results.
- Significant reductions in student reports of general antisocial behavior such as school bullying, vandalism, school violence, fighting, theft, and truancy.
- Significant improvements in the classroom social climate as reflected in students' reports of improved order and discipline, more positive social relationships, and more positive attitudes toward schoolwork and school.
- Greater support for students who are bullied, and stronger, more effective interventions for students who bully.

White House Report/Bullying—And the Power of Peers

Promoting Respectful Schools
Philip Rodkin

Using Peers to Intervene

In a review of bullying-reduction programs, Farrington and Ttofi (2009) found that interventions that involve peers, such as using students as peer mediators or engaging bystanders to disapprove of bullying and support victims of harassment, were associated with *increases* in victimization! In fact, of 20 program elements included in 44 school-based programs, work with peers was the *only* program element associated with significantly *more* bullying and victimization. (In contrast, there were significant and positive effects for parent training and school meetings in reducing bullying.) Still other reviews of bullying intervention programs have found generally weak effects (Merrell, Gueldner, Ross, and Isava, 2008).

These disheartening results speak to the fact that peer influences can be a constructive or destructive force on bullying and need to be handled with knowledge, skill, and care. Antisocial peer groups can undermine behavioral interventions. For peer mediation to be effective, students who are chosen to be peer mediators should probably be popular and prosocial (Pellegrini et al., 2010; Pepler et al., 2010; Vaillancourt et al., 2010).

Some of the most innovative, intensive, grassroots uses of peer relationships to reduce bullying, such as the You Have the Power! program in Montgomery County, Maryland, have not been scientifically evaluated. The final verdict awaits on some promising programs that take advantage of peer relationships to combat bullying, such as the Finnish program KiVa (Salmivalli et al., 2010), which has a strong emphasis on influencing onlookers to support the victim rather than encourage the bully, and the Steps to Respect program (Frey et al., 2010), which works at the elementary school level.

Teachers can ask what *kind* of bully they face when dealing with a victimization problem. Is the bully a member of a group, or is he or she a group leader? How are bullies and victims situated in the peer ecology? Educators who exclusively target peripheral, antisocial cliques as the engine of school violence problems may leave intact other groups that are more responsible for mainstream peer support of bullying. A strong step educators could take would be to periodically ask students about bullying and their social relationships. (See "What Teachers Can Do.")

* * *

The task ahead is to better integrate bullies and the children they harass into the social fabric of the school and better inform educators of how to recognize, understand, and help guide children's relationships. With guidance from caring, engaged adults, youth can organize themselves as a force that makes bullying less effective as a means of social connection or as an outlet for alienation.

What Teachers Can Do

- **Ask students about bullying.** Survey students regularly on whether they are being harassed or have witnessed harassment. Make it easier for students to come to an adult in the school to talk about harassment by building staff-student relationships, having suggestion boxes where students can provide input anonymously, or administering school-wide surveys in which students can report confidentially on peers who bully and on the children whom they harass. Consider what bullying accomplishes for a bully. Does the bully want to gain status? Does the bully use aggression to control others?

- **Ask students about their relationships.** Bullying is a destructive, asymmetric relationship. Know whom students hang out with, who their friends are, and whom they dislike. Know whom students perceive to be popular and unpopular. Connect with students who have no friends. School staff members vary widely in their knowledge of students' relationships and tend to underestimate the level of aggression among peers.

- **Build democratic classroom and school climates.** Identify student leaders who can encourage peers to stand against bullying. Assess whether student social norms are *really* against bullying. Train teachers to better understand and manage student social dynamics and handle aggression with clear, consistent consequences. Master teachers not only promote academic success but also build relationships, trust, and a sense of community.

- **Be an informed consumer of antibullying curriculums.** Antibullying interventions can be successful, but there are significant caveats. Some bullies would benefit from services that go beyond bullying-reduction programs. Some programs work well in Europe but not as well in the United States. Most antibullying programs have not been rigorously evaluated, so be an informed consumer when investigating claims of success. Even with a well-developed antibullying curriculum, understanding students' relationships at your school is crucial.

- **Remember that bullying is also a problem of values.** Implement an intellectually challenging character education or socioemotional learning curriculum. Teach students how to achieve their goals by being assertive rather than aggressive. Always resolve conflicts with civility among and between staff and students. Involve families.

Exercise 5.5
Critical Reading for Synthesis

Having read the selections related to bullying on pages 134–39, write a one-sentence summary of each. On the same page, list two or three topics that you think are common to several of the selections. Beneath each topic, list the authors who have something to say on that topic and briefly note what they have to say. Finally, for each topic, jot down what *you* have to say.

Now regard your effort: With each topic you have created a discussion point suitable for inclusion in a paper. (Of course, until you determine the claim of such a paper, you won't know to what end you might direct the discussion.) Write a paragraph or two in which you introduce the topic and then conduct a brief conversation among the interested parties (including yourself).

Consider Your Purpose

Your specific purpose in writing an argument synthesis is crucial. What exactly you want to do will affect your claim and how you organize the evidence. Your purpose may be clear to you before you begin research, or it may not emerge until after you have completed your research. Of course, the sooner your purpose is clear to you, the fewer wasted motions you will make. On the other hand, the more you approach research as an exploratory process, the likelier that your conclusions will emerge from the sources themselves rather than from preconceived ideas. Each new writing project will have its own rhythm in this regard. Be flexible in your approach.

Let's say that while reading these four (and additional) sources related to bullying, you share the concern of many who believe that bullies traumatize too many vulnerable children and prevent them from feeling safe at school. Perhaps you believe that bullying is fundamental to human nature, or at least to some people's human nature, and that laws will do little to change the behavior. Perhaps you believe that laws shape, or at least constrain, human behavior all the time: the laws against murder or theft, for instance, or, more mundanely, speeding. You may believe that laws *do* have a role to play in lessening if not preventing bullying and that we should be willing to sacrifice some freedom of speech to prevent bullies from menacing their victims through text messages and online postings.

Most people will bring at least some personal history to this topic, and personal history is often a good place to begin. Mine that history for insights, and use them if they can guide you in posing questions and in developing arguments. Your purpose in writing, then, emerges from these kinds of responses to the source materials you find.

Making a Claim: Formulate a Thesis

Match your claim to your purpose. If your purpose is to convince others that bullies can learn to moderate their behavior, then write a claim to that effect. Your claim (generally expressed in one-sentence form as a *thesis*) lies at the heart of your argument. You will draw support from your sources as you argue logically for your claim.

Not every piece of information in a source will be useful for supporting a claim. You must read with care and select the opinions, facts, and statistics that best advance your position. You may even find yourself drawing support from sources that make claims entirely different from your own. For example, in researching the subject of bullying prevention, you may come across an antibullying program that you know has been proven ineffective by researchers, yet that source's presentation of statistics concerning the prevalence of bullying may be sound and useful for your own argument.

You might use one source as part of a *counterargument*—an argument opposing your own—so that you can demonstrate its weaknesses and, in the process, strengthen your own claim. On the other hand, you might find a source with an opposing thesis so convincing that you end up adopting it or modifying your own thesis. The point is that *the argument is in your hands.* You must devise it yourself and use your sources in ways that will support the claim you present in your thesis.

Based on your reactions to sources, you may find yourself thinking as follows:

1. Despite being required by the states' antibullying laws, programs to combat bullying do not work because they prescribe a one-size-fits-all approach to a complex problem.
2. At the same time, the suffering bullies cause is too great to do nothing.
3. A local approach to bullying makes sense, one that builds on the wisdom and experience of parents, teachers, and community leaders.

You review your sources and begin working on a thesis. After a few tries, you develop this thesis:

> A blend of local, grassroots strategies and state-mandated programs and laws promises to be the best approach to dealing with bullying in American schools.

Decide How You Will Use Your Source Material

Your claim commits you to introducing the problem of bullying, explaining top-down antibullying legislation and its advantages and limitations, explaining grassroots strategies and their advantages and limitations, and arguing for a combined approach to changing the behavior of bullies. The sources (some provided here, some located elsewhere) offer information and ideas—evidence—that will allow you to support your claim. For instance, the catalog description of the Olweus Bullying Prevention Program (OBPP) establishes the principles of a widely adopted one-size-fits-all approach to bullying prevention. Yet the "White House Report" by Rodkin cautions that "some programs [like Olweus] work well in Europe but not as well in the United States." (These and several other sources not included in this chapter will be cited in the model argument paper.)

Develop an Organizational Plan

After establishing your overall purpose and your claim, developing a thesis (which may change as you write and revise the paper), and deciding how to draw on your source materials, how do you logically organize your paper? In many cases, a well-written thesis will suggest an organization. In the case of the antibullying project, the first part of your paper would define the problem of bullying and discuss the legislative response. The second part would argue that problems are associated with antibullying legislation. The third part would introduce a solution to these problems. After sorting through your material and categorizing it by topic and subtopic, you might compose the following outline:

I. Introduction
  A. Graphic example of bullying
  B. Background: Who is bullied
  C. Cyberbullying
    1. Definition
    2. Suicides
  D. Antibullying laws
    1. Laws criminalize bullying
    2. Laws mandate education to reduce bullying

Thesis

II. Problems with antibullying laws
  A. Laws implemented in a rush (after Columbine)
  B. Elements of some laws unconstitutional
  C. Laws don't follow standard definitions
  D. Effectiveness of antibullying programs uneven

III. An alternate solution to the problem of bullying
  A. Rationale and blueprint for alternate approach

   B. A local, grassroots solution
    1. Emily Bazelon
    2. Lee Hirsch and Cynthia Lowen
    3. Philip Rodkin
   C. Concession
    1. Local solutions possibly flawed
    2. Local solutions should be evaluated
  IV. Conclusion: Blended approach needed

Draft and Revise Your Synthesis

The final draft of an argument synthesis, based on the outline above, follows. Thesis and topic sentences are highlighted. A note on documentation: While the topic leans more toward the social sciences than it does the humanities, the writer—completing a research assignment for a freshman composition class—has used Modern Language Association (MLA) documentation style as his instructor requested. MLA style is used most often in the humanities.

A cautionary note: When writing syntheses, it is all too easy to become careless in properly crediting your sources. Before drafting your paper, review the section on Avoiding Plagiarism in Chapter 1.

Model Argument Synthesis

Simmons 1

Peter Simmons
Professor Lettelier
Composition 201
8 November 2016

Responding to Bullies

1 Opens with an anecdote that appeals to our emotions. (*Pathos*) An effective strategy for a paper on bullying.

1 On the school bus the nerdy kid with glasses tries to keep his head down. A group of older, bigger kids gets on. One of the older kids sits next to the nerdy kid, who asks, hopefully, "You're my buddy, right?" The other kid turns to him and says, "I'm not your buddy. I will f—g end you. I will shove a broomstick up your a—. You're going to die in so much pain." Another day, the nerdy kid is repeatedly punched by a kid across the aisle, who then jabs him in the arm with the point of a pencil. These scenes from the recent documentary film *Bully* are repeated in some form or other thousands of times every day.

2 Statistics establish bullying as a major problem. Prepares ground for argument to follow.

2 According to some estimates, more than thirteen million school-age children, one in four students, are bullied each year in the United States. Nearly two-thirds of bullying behavior goes unreported, and of those who suffer, a disproportionate number are the most vulnerable of children, those with learning disabilities or those who dare to break social norms, such as LGBT [lesbian, gay, bisexual, and transgender] youth (Pacer's; Kosciw et al.). At one time, victims could find some relief at home or in the summer—away from school buses, corridors, and playgrounds where bullies lurk. The Internet has taken even that refuge away. Bullies now follow their victims online with hateful instant messages and postings on Facebook. Tyler Clementi, a Rutgers freshman, jumped off the George Washington Bridge after his roommate

Simmons 2

remotely recorded and posted online a private, consensual, same-sex encounter. In another horrifying case, a twelve-year-old girl jumped from an abandoned silo to her death after two classmates, twelve and fourteen, urged her to "drink bleach and die." Subsequently, one of the harassers posted a message on Facebook admitting, "Yes, I bullied Rebecca and she killed herself but IDGAF [I don't give a ----]." Bullying is a harsh and routine fact of life for school-age kids all over the country. What do we, as a society, propose to do about this? Are tough antibullying laws the answer?

Over the last fifteen years, responding to bully-related suicides and the horrors of Columbine, state governments have passed two-part antibullying laws. The first part of the law makes it a crime to commit especially vicious behaviors associated with bullying; the second, educational part requires school districts to implement antibullying programs. On its face, a two-part program that punishes bullies and teaches behaviors designed to reduce bullying seems sensible. But is it effective? The answer, unfortunately, is no—at least for the moment. Laws that punish the worst offenders with prison time or juvenile detention may make parents and legislators feel as if they're getting tough. But, in fact, bullying remains widespread, and relatively few cases rise to the level of criminal behavior. At the same time, several key initiatives introduced in local school districts seem to be showing some promise in addressing this difficult problem. In the end, a blend of local, grassroots strategies and state-mandated programs and laws promises to be the best approach to dealing with bullying in American schools.

3
3 Thesis stated clearly in last sentence of paragraph.

The first state to adopt antibullying legislation was Georgia, in 1999, in response to the Columbine tragedy earlier that year when Dylan Klebold and Eric Harris killed a teacher and twelve classmates and left twenty-one wounded. The assault triggered a national outcry and a demand to understand what happened. Eva Porter, author of *Bully Nation*, argues that the media too quickly (and incorrectly) pegged the shooters as young men who'd been bullied and retaliated with lethal force. "The nation," she writes, "fearing a repeat of the tragedy—adopted a zero-tolerance attitude toward many normal, albeit painful, aspects of childhood behavior and development, and defined them as bullying."

4
4-5 A critique of state laws passed in wake of Columbine— laws could be flawed.

Critique sets expectation re: how responses to bullying can be improved.

Understandably, legislators wanted to prevent bullied kids from becoming Klebold- and Harris-like killers. In the eleven years following the attack, a span that included several highly publicized teen suicides associated with bullying, forty-nine state legislatures adopted 120 antibullying bills ("School"). (The fiftieth state, Montana, adopted antibullying legislation in 2015.) The post-Columbine rush to action was so hasty that experts began wondering about the extent to which these legislative measures were "informed by research, not singular high profile incidents" like Columbine (Patchin) or prompted by "the perceived urgent need to intervene" (Smith et al.).

5

No one can doubt the good intentions of legislators who want to reduce bullying. Yet the laws they enacted may be too blunt an instrument to deal with the most common forms of bullying. Civil rights activists are concerned that anti-cyberbullying laws, in particular, could curtail freedom of speech (Bazelon, "Anti"). In 2011, responding to the bully-related suicide of fourteen-year-old Jamey Rodemeyer, the Make It Better Project argued that "[c]riminalizing bullying is not the answer" (Gay-Straight Alliance). Writing about the case, Daniel Villarreal explains why: "While some . . . bullying could even rise to the level of criminal harassment, criminalizing bullying overall could result in over-reaching laws that punish any student who

6
6–10 Five paragraphs devoted to problems with current antibullying laws.

6 Problem 1—Antibullying laws may violate free speech.

'causes emotional harm' or 'creates a hostile environment'—two vague, subjective criteria that could well qualify any online insult or cafeteria put down as a criminal offense." Villarreal could have been predicting the future. In 2012, the Missouri Supreme Court struck down part of an antibullying law (enacted after a bullying-related suicide) that violated free speech ("Mo. High Court"). LGBT youth are easy targets for bullies. When a national organization that supports LGBT youth opposes antibullying laws intended to help them, the wisdom of such laws is put into serious question.

7–8 Problem 2—
Antibullying laws
misunderstand
definition of
bullying.

7　　The second problem with antibullying legislation is that states do not generally follow "research-based definitions of bullying" (Sacco 3–8), even though most researchers have adopted a definition crafted by Dan Olweus, the Norwegian psychologist credited with conducting the first large-scale, controlled study of bullying in 1978. According to Olweus, a "person is bullied when he or she is exposed, repeatedly and over time, to negative actions on the part of one or more other persons, and he or she has difficulty defending himself or herself." Olweus introduced the element of an "imbalance of power" that results from bullies using their physical strength or social position to inflict emotional or physical harm ("Bullying").

8　　"[A]t least ten different definitions" are being used in state laws, according to Emily Bazelon, author of *Sticks and Stones: Defeating the Culture of Bullying*—and, for her, that's a problem. A frequent commentator on the subject, Bazelon argues that "'bullying' isn't the same as garden-variety teasing or a two-way conflict. The word is being overused," she writes, "expanding, accordionlike, to encompass both appalling violence or harassment and a few mean words" ("Defining"). Antibullying researchers at Harvard and New York University note that teens take care to distinguish "drama"—the more typical verbal and emotional jousting among teenagers—from bullying. Drama can be more easily shrugged off as "so high school" and helps teens avoid thinking of themselves as hapless victims (Boyd and Marwick). Yet when school-based programs fail to realize that what some students dismiss as "drama" is really "bullying," the effectiveness of antibullying programs is in doubt as schools may miss a lot of hurtful behaviors. "To me this is an issue about reporting, underreporting specifically," says educational psychologist Philip Rodkin. "It's also about teenagers wanting to diminish the importance of some negative interaction, which sometimes is exactly the right thing to do, sometimes not at all the right thing" (Personal). At the same time, there is also the danger that too many harmless behaviors can be labeled as bullying. As one superintendent who is implementing the tough, new antibullying law in New Jersey says: "[S]tudents, or their parents, will find it easier to label minor squabbles bullying than to find ways to work out their differences" (Dolan, qtd. in Hu).

9–10 Problem
3—School
districts reaching
for one-size-fits-
all solutions that
don't work for
every situation.

Argument
supported with
data from
studies.

9　　A third problem with antibullying laws—and perhaps the most serious—is that they require school districts to adopt antibullying programs of unproven value. Educators are rushing to comply with these laws, and they are adopting premade, one-size-fits-all programs that have not been shown to work. In an analysis of forty-two studies, researchers at Texas A&M International University evaluated the effectiveness of school-based antibullying efforts. The combined studies involved 34,713 elementary, middle, and high school students and "measure[d] some element of bullying behavior or aggression toward peers" (Ferguson et al. 407). The researchers concluded that "school-based anti-bullying programs are not practically effective in reducing bullying or violent behaviors in the schools" (410). Another review of sixteen antibullying studies involving 15,386 K–12 students concluded "that school bullying interventions may produce modest positive outcomes . . . [but] are more likely to influence knowledge, attitudes, and self-perceptions rather than actual bullying behaviors" (Merrell et al.). These are "disheartening" results (Swearer et al. 42; Rodkin).

The world's most well-known antibullying program, the Olweus Bullying Prevention Program (OBPP), is a "whole-school" approach that "is used at the school, classroom, and individual levels and includes methods to reach out to parents and the community for involvement and support" (Hazelden). Backed by thirty-five years of research, Olweus has demonstrated the effectiveness of his approach in Norwegian schools. Schools worldwide, including many in the United States, have used OBPP. But researchers have been unable to show that the Olweus program is consistently effective outside Norway. A University of Washington study found that in American schools OBPP had "no overall effect" in preventing bullying (Bauer, Lozano, and Rivera). With their larger class sizes and racial, ethnic, and economic diversity, American schools may differ too greatly from Norwegian schools for OBPP to succeed. Or the Olweus program may need to be adapted in ways that have not yet been developed.

10 10 Even most well-known antibullying program doesn't work consistently across cultures.

To sum up, definitions in antibullying laws are inconsistent, the effectiveness of antibullying programs is unproven, and cyberbullying laws may threaten free speech. Still, bullying persists and we must respond. Each day, 160,000 children skip school because they don't want to confront their tormentors (National). Even bullies are at risk: In one study, over half of the middle-school boys characterized as bullies had court records by their 24th birthday (Fox et al. 2). While bullying in childhood may not be the sole or even main *cause* of later criminal behavior (another possibility: there may be abuse in the home), these statistics provide all the more reason to intervene in the bully/victim relationship. Both victims and bullies require our help.

11 11 Transitional paragraph summarizes three problems with existing antibullying laws.

Paragraph pivots paper to next section: potential solutions.

Fresh approaches to the problem of bullying are needed, and Rodkin suggests a sensible, potentially fruitful direction: "The task ahead," he writes in a report presented at a 2011 White House Conference on Bullying Prevention, "is to better integrate bullies and the children they harass into the social fabric of the school and better inform educators of how to recognize, understand, and help guide children's relationships." Rodkin's recommendations favor an on-the-ground, local approach with individual students rather than a broad, mandated program. Mary Flannery of the National Education Association agrees that, ultimately, bullies and their victims must be engaged one on one:

12 12–14 Three paragraphs turn the paper toward local solutions (versus one-size statewide solutions).

> Many bullying programs apply a one-size-fits-all approach to problems on campus. They train teachers and support professionals to be watchful and consistent (often at a high price). But while it's critically important for every adult on campus to recognize and stop bullying, Colby College professor Lyn Mikel Brown, co-director of the nonprofit Hardy Girls, Healthy Women, believes most of these "top-down" programs look promising, but don't go far enough.
>
> "You really have to do this work with students," Brown says. "Those programs don't allow for the messy, on-the-ground work of educating kids. That's what has to happen and it looks different in different schools and communities."

When legislators criminalize bullying and require schools to implement antibullying programs, they take the kind of top-down approach that Mikel Brown believes doesn't go far enough. The researchers who conducted the comprehensive "Overview of State

13

Anti-Bullying Legislation" agree: "legal responses and mandates can at their best only facilitate the harder non-legal work that schools must undertake to create a kinder, braver world" (Sacco 22).

14 One-sentence paragraph (a question) points readers to last section of paper—local solutions.

14   What might this "harder non-legal" work look like?

15   In Sticks and Stones, Bazelon advises an approach that involves children, parents, and educators working in local school- and child-specific settings. She advises bullied kids to confide in a sympathetic adult or a trusted group. Those being harassed online should contact Web sites to remove offensive content. To those who witness bullying, she suggests that dramatic action (stepping in to break up a fight) isn't necessary—though private, low-key action, like sending a supportive note, may be. Bazelon advises educators to conduct surveys to clearly define the problem of bullying at their school (309–19) and make "an ongoing annual, monthly, weekly, even daily commitment" to reducing bullying (317).

15–18 An argument for local, grassroots solutions to bullying. A clear difference from top-down statewide solutions.

Writer relies on expert opinions.

16   In their companion book to the widely praised documentary film *Bully* (2011), Lee Hirsch and Cynthia Lowen offer an action plan for fostering an inclusive and safe school environment. Their guidelines help parents to distinguish between appropriate and inappropriate use of the Internet and urge parents to discuss bullying openly, along with strategies for reporting bullying to school authorities and promoting responsible behavior. Hirsch and Lowen provide educators with checklists to help determine whether or not effective anti-cyberbullying policies are in place. They also encourage explicit conversations among teachers about the nature and extent of the bullying problem in their school, and they suggest specific prevention and intervention strategies (159–70).

17   Like Bazelon, Rodkin recommends surveying students about bullying to gain a clear sense of the problem. He also recommends identifying students with no friends and finding ways to involve them in student life, encouraging peer groups to reject bullying, evaluating antibullying programs, and promoting character education that teaches students to be "assertive rather than aggressive" (White House).

18   All of these approaches involve "messy, on-the-ground work" that employs local experts to respond to local problems. Until researchers determine that one or another top-down approach to the problem of bullying will succeed in a wide variety of school environments, it seems best to develop a school-by-school, grassroots approach. This kind of grassroots strategy could help integrate both bullied children and bullies into the broader school culture. Of course, there's no guarantee that the grassroots approach to combating bullying will work any better than top-down, comprehensive programs like OBPP. Leaving large social problems like bullying for locals to resolve may result in uneven and unacceptable solutions. A parallel case: Challenged by President Kennedy to rid this country of racist Jim Crow laws, many advocates of local "solutions" who had no interest in changing the status quo argued that people on the ground, in the local communities, know best. "Leave the problem to us," they said. "We'll fix it." They didn't, of course, and it took courageous action by people like Martin Luther King, Jr., and President Lyndon Johnson to force a comprehensive solution.

19 Counterargument raised and a concession made: We should continue checking effectiveness of local antibullying efforts.

19   It's clear that local approaches to bullying can be inept. To take one example from the movie *Bully*, a principal tries making a victim shake hands with his tormentor as if that, alone, would end the problem. It didn't. So researchers must evaluate the effectiveness of local

solutions as rigorously as they do top-down solutions. If evaluations show that local solutions aren't effective, we should expect that community leaders, parents, and teachers will search for solutions that work. To the extent that they don't and bullying persists, state and federal authorities should step in with their own solutions, but only after their top-down, one-size-fits-all programs can be shown to work.

We should be pushing for antibullying programs that blend the top-down approach of state-mandated programs and the grassroots approach that tailors programs to the needs of specific communities. The state has the right to insist that every child be safe in a school environment and be free from the threat of bullying. At the same time, local teachers, parents, and administrators are often in the best position to know what approaches will show the greatest benefits in their own communities. Such a blended approach could well yield the best set of solutions to the complex and pervasive problem of bullying. And then, perhaps, the nerdy kid could ride the school bus in peace—or even in friendly conversation with his former tormentors.

20 20 Conclusion— leaves room for blended approach— bottom-up plus top-down.

Works Cited

Bauer, N. S., P. Lozano, and F. P. Rivara. "The Effectiveness of the Olweus Bullying Prevention Program in Public Middle Schools: A Controlled Trial." *Journal of Adolescent Health,* vol. 40, no. 3, 2007, pp. 266–74. *PubMed,* www.ncbi.nlm.nih.gov/pubmed/?term=Bauer%2C+N.+S.%2C+P.+Lozano%2C+and+F.+P.+Rivara.+"The+Effectiveness+of+the+Olweus+Bullying+Prevention+Program+In+Public+Middle+Schools%3A+A+Controlled+Trial."+Journal+of+Adolescent+Health%2C+vol.+40%2C+no.+3%2C+2007.

Bazelon, Emily. "Anti-Bully Laws Get Tough with Schools." Interviewed by Scott Simon. *National Public Radio*, 17 Sept. 2011, www.npr.org/2011/09/17/140557573/anti-bullying-laws-get-tough-with-schools.

---. "Defining Bullying Down." *New York Times*, 11 Mar. 2013, www.nytimes.com/2013/03/12/opinion/defining-bullying-down.html?_r=0.

---. *Sticks and Stones: Defeating the Culture of Bullying and Rediscovering the Power of Character and Empathy*. Random House, 2013.

Boyd, Danah, and Alice Marwick. "Bullying as True Drama." *New York Times*, 22 Sept. 2011, www.nytimes.com/2011/09/23/opinion/why-cyberbullying-rhetoric-misses-the-mark.html.

Bully. Directed by Lee Hirsch, The Weinstein Company, 2011, www.thebullyproject.com/.

"Bullying Definition." *Stopbully.gov*, U.S. Department of Health & Human Services, www.stopbullying.gov/what-is-bullying/definition/.

Copeland, William E., et al. "Adult Psychiatric Outcomes of Bullying and Being Bullied by Peers in Childhood and Adolescence." *JAMA Psychiatry,* vol. 70, no. 4, 2013, http://archpsyc.jamanetwork.com/article.aspx?articleid=1654916.

Ferguson, Christopher J., et al. "The Effectiveness of School-Based Anti-Bullying Programs: A Meta-Analytic Review." *Criminal Justice Review,* vol. 32, no. 4, 2007, pp. 401–14. *Sage Publications*, http://cjr.sagepub.com/content/32/4/401.short?rss=1&ssource=mfc.

Flannery, Mary Ellen. "Bullying: Does It Get Better?" *National Education Association*, Jan.-Feb. 2011, www.nea.org/home/41620.htm.

Fox, James Alan, et al. "Bullying Prevention Is Crime Prevention." *Fightcrime.org*, Fight Crime/ Invest in Kids, 2003, www.co.dakota.mn.us/. . ./BullyingPreventionCrimePrevention.pdf.

Gay-Straight Alliance Project. "Make It Better." *GSANetwork*, 26 Sept. 2011, https://gsanetwork.org/news/spotlight/make-it-better-project.

Hazelden Foundation. "Olweus Bullying Prevention Program: Scope and Sequence." Hazelden.org, 2007, www.violencepreventionworks.org/public/olweus_scope.page.

Hirsch, Lee, et al., editors. *Bully: An Action Plan for Teachers and Parents to Combat the Bullying Crisis.* Weinstein Books, 2012.

Hu, Winnie. "Bullying Law Puts New Jersey Schools on Spot." *New York Times,* 20 Aug. 2011, www.nytimes.com/2011/08/31/nyregion/bullying-law-puts-new-jersey-schools-on-spot.html.

Kosciw, Joseph G., et al. *The 2015 National School Climate Survey: The Experiences of Lesbian, Gay, Bisexual, Transgender, and Queer Youth in Our Nation's Schools.* Gay, Lesbian and Straight Education Network, 2016.

Merrell, Kenneth W., et al. "How Effective Are School Bullying Intervention Programs? A Meta-analysis of Intervention Research." *School Psychology Quarterly,* vol. 23, no. 1, 2008, pp. 26–42.

"Mo. High Court Strikes down Part of Harassment Law." *Associated Press*, 30 May 2012, www.firstamendmentcenter.org/mo-high-court-strikes-down-part-of-harassment-law.

National Education Association. "Nation's Educators Continue Push for Safe, Bully-free Environments." *National Education Association*, 8 Oct. 2012, www.nea.org/home/53298.htm.

Olweus, Dan. *Bullying at School: What We Know and What We Can Do.* Blackwell, 1993.

Patchin, Justin W. "Most Cases Aren't Criminal/Room for Debate: Cyberbullying and a Student's Suicide." *New York Times*, 30 Sept. 2010, www.nytimes.com/roomfordebate/2010/09/30/cyberbullying-and-a-students-suicide.

Porter, Susan Eva. "Overusing the Bully Label: Unfriendliness, Exclusion, and Unkind Remarks Aren't Necessarily Bullying." *Los Angeles Times*, Tribune Company, 15 Mar. 2013, http://articles.latimes.com/2013/mar/15/opinion/la-oe-porter-bullying-20130315.

Rodkin, Philip C. Interviewed by author. 15 Oct. 2016.

---. "White House Report/Bullying—and the Power of Peers." *Educational Leadership: Promoting Respectful Schools*, vol. 69, no. 1, 2011, pp. 10–16. *ASCD*, www.ascd.org/publications/educational-leadership/sept11/vol69/num01/Bullying%E2%80%94And-the-Power-of-Peers.aspx.

Sacco, Dena, Katharine Silbaugh, Felipe Corredor, June Casey, and Davis Doherty. *An Overview of State Anti-Bullying Legislation and Other Related Laws.* Berkman Center for Internet and Society, 2012.

"School Bullying Laws Exist in Most States, U.S. Department of Education Reports Analysis of Policies." TheHuffingtonPost.com, 10 Aug. 2012, www.huffingtonpost.com/2011/12/06/school-bullying-laws-exis_n_1132634.html.

Smith, David, et al. "The Effectiveness of Whole-School Antibullying Programs: A Synthesis of Evaluation Research." *School Psychology Review*, vol. 33, no. 4, 2004, pp. 547–60.

Swearer, Susan M., et al. "What Can Be Done About School Bullying? Linking Research to Educational Practice." *Educational Researcher*, vol. 39, no. 1, 2010, pp. 38–47. *Sage Publications*, http://edr.sagepub.com/content/39/1/38.abstract.

Villarreal, Daniel. "Jamey Rodemeyer's Bullies Are Happy He's Dead, but Is It a Bad Idea to Prosecute Them?" *Queerty,* 27 Sept. 2011, www.queerty.com/jamey-rodemeyers-bullies-are-happy-hes-dead-but-is-it-a-bad-idea-to-prosecute-them-20110927.

The Strategy of the Argument Synthesis

In his argument synthesis, Peter Simmons attempts to support a *claim*—one that favors blending local and statewide solutions to combat the problem of bullying—by offering *support* in the form of facts: statistics establishing bullying as an ongoing problem despite antibullying laws, news of a court's rejecting elements of an antibullying law, and studies concluding that antibullying programs are largely ineffective. Simmons also supports his claim with expert opinions like those of Bazelon, Rodkin, and the authors of a Harvard study who state that antibullying laws can "only facilitate the harder non-legal work" of reducing bullying. However, recall that Simmons's claim rests on an *assumption* about the value of local solutions to broad problems when systemwide solutions (that is, laws) aren't working. His ability to change our minds about bullying depends partially on the extent to which we, as readers, share his assumption. Readers who distrust local solutions may not be swayed. (See our discussion of assumptions in Chapter 2.)

Recall that an assumption, sometimes called a warrant, is a generalization or principle about how the world works or should work—a fundamental statement of belief about facts or values. Assumptions are often deeply rooted in people's psyches, sometimes derived from lifelong experiences and observations and, yes, prejudices. Assumptions are not easily changed, even by the most logical of arguments. Simmons makes explicit his assumption about the limitations of laws and the usefulness of local solutions. Though you are under no obligation to do so, stating assumptions explicitly will clarify your arguments to readers.

Another approach to an argument synthesis based on the same and additional sources could argue that antibullying laws are not yet working in the intended manner and should be changed. Such a position could draw on exactly the same support, both facts and expert opinion, that Simmons uses to demonstrate the inadequacies of current laws. But instead of making a move to local solutions, the writer could assert that a problem as widespread and significant as bullying must be addressed at the state and federal levels. Whatever your approach to a subject, in first *critically examining* the various sources and then *synthesizing* them to support a position about which you feel strongly, you are engaging in the kind of critical thinking that is essential to success in a good deal of academic and professional work.

Developing and Organizing the Support for Your Arguments

5.3   Use various strategies to develop and support your arguments.

Experienced writers seem to have an intuitive sense of how to develop and present supporting evidence for their claims; this sense is developed through much hard work and practice. Less experienced writers wonder what to say first and, having decided on that, wonder what to say next. There is no single method of presentation, but the techniques of even the most experienced writers often boil down to a few tried and tested arrangements.

As we've seen in the model synthesis in this chapter, the key to devising effective arguments is to find and use those kinds of support that strengthen your claim most persuasively. Some writers categorize support into two broad types: *evidence* and *motivational appeals*. Evidence, in the form of facts, statistics, and expert testimony, helps make the appeal to reason. Motivational appeals—appeals grounded in emotion and based on the authority of the speaker—are employed to get people to change their minds, to agree with the writer or speaker, or to decide on a plan of activity.

Following are the most common strategies for using and organizing support for your claims.

Summarize, Paraphrase, and Quote Supporting Evidence

In most of the papers and reports you will write in college and in the professional world, evidence and motivational appeals derive from your summarizing, paraphrasing, and quoting of material in sources that either have been provided to you or that you have independently researched. For example, in paragraph 12 of the model argument synthesis, Simmons uses a long quotation from a writer at the National Education Association (NEA) to introduce three key terms into the synthesis: "one-size-fits-all," "top-down," and "on-the-ground." You will find a number of brief quotations woven into sentences throughout. In addition, you will find summaries and paraphrases. In each case, Simmons is careful to cite the source.

Provide Various Types of Evidence and Motivational Appeals

Keep in mind that you can use appeals to both reason and emotion. The appeal to reason is based on evidence that consists of a combination of *facts* and *expert testimony*. For example, the sources by the Pacer organization and Kosciw (in paragraph 2) and by Fox and the NEA (in paragraph 11) factually establish the extent of bullying in America. Simmons draws on expert testimony by incorporating the opinions of Bazelon and others who argue that current antibullying programs are not working as intended.

Use Climactic Order

Climactic order is the arrangement of examples or evidence in order of anticipated impact on the reader, least to greatest. Organize by climactic order when you plan to offer a number of categories or elements of support for your claim. Recognize that some elements will be more important—and likely more persuasive—than others. The basic principle here is that you should *save the most important evidence for the end* because whatever you say last is what readers are likely to remember best. A secondary principle is that whatever you say first is what they are *next* most likely to remember. Therefore, when you have several reasons to offer in support of your claim, an effective argument strategy is to present the second most important, then one or more additional reasons, and finally the most important reason. Paragraphs 6–10 of the model synthesis do exactly this.

Use Logical or Conventional Order

Using a logical or conventional order involves using as a template a preestablished pattern or plan for arguing your case.

- One common pattern is describing or arguing a *problem/solution.* The model synthesis uses this pattern: You begin with an introduction in which you typically define the problem (perhaps explaining its origins), offer one or more solutions, then conclude. In the case of the model synthesis, paragraphs 1–3 introduce the problem, paragraphs 4–10 establish shortcomings of current solutions, and (after a transition) paragraphs 12–19 suggest solutions.
- Another common pattern presents *two sides of a controversy.* Using this pattern, you introduce the controversy and (in an argument synthesis) your own point of view or claim; then you explain the other side's arguments, providing reasons why your point of view should prevail.
- A third common pattern is *comparison and contrast.* This pattern—involving your close consideration of similarities and differences—is so important that we will discuss it separately in the next section.

The order in which you present elements of an argument is sometimes dictated by the conventions of the discipline in which you are writing. For example, lab reports and experiments in the sciences and social sciences often follow this pattern: *opening* or *introduction, methods and materials* (of the experiment or study), *results, discussion.* Legal arguments often follow the so-called IRAC format: *issue, rule, application, conclusion.*

Present and Respond to Counterarguments

When developing arguments on a controversial topic, you can effectively use *counterargument* to help support your claims. When you use counterargument, you present an argument *against* your claim and then show that this argument is weak or flawed. The advantage of this technique is that you demonstrate that you are aware of the other side of the argument and that you are prepared to answer it.

Here is how a counterargument is often developed:

I. Introduction and claim
II. Main opposing argument
III. Refutation of opposing argument
IV. Main positive argument

Use Concession

Concession is a variation of counterargument. As in counterargument, you present an opposing viewpoint, but instead of dismissing that position, you *concede* that it has some validity and even some appeal, although your own position is the more reasonable one. This concession shows that you are fair-minded and not blind to the virtues of opposing arguments. In the model synthesis, Simmons acknowledges that local solutions to the problem of bullying may rely too heavily on folk wisdom that may be inept or just plain wrong. Bullies and victims, for instance, cannot just shake hands and make the problem go away. Simmons recommends evaluating local solutions rigorously; he also acknowledges that state and federal, top-down solutions may have a role to play—but only after these programs have been proven effective. In his conclusion, he moves to a compromise position that "blends" top-down and grassroots, local solutions.

Given the structure of his argument, Simmons held off making his concession until the end of his paper. Here is an outline for a more typical concession argument:

   I. Introduction and claim

  II. Important opposing argument

 III. Concession that this argument has some validity

 IV. Positive argument(s) that acknowledge the counterargument and (possibly) incorporate some elements of it

Sometimes, when you are developing a counterargument or concession argument, you may become convinced of the validity of the opposing point of view and change your own views. Don't be afraid of this happening. Writing is a tool for learning. To change your mind because of new evidence is a sign of flexibility and maturity, and your writing can only be the better for it.

Developing and Organizing Support for Your Arguments

- *Summarize, paraphrase, and quote supporting evidence.* Draw on the facts, ideas, and language in your sources.

- *Provide various types of evidence and motivational appeal.*

- *Use climactic order.* Save the most important evidence in support of your argument for the *end*, where it will have the most impact. Use the next most important evidence *first*.

- *Use logical or conventional order.* Use a form of organization appropriate to the topic, such as

  problem/solution; sides of a controversy; comparison/contrast; or a form of organization appropriate to the academic or professional discipline, such as a report of an experiment or a business plan.

- *Present and respond to counterarguments.* Anticipate and evaluate arguments against your position.

- *Use concession.* Concede that one or more arguments against your position have some validity; reassert, nonetheless, that your argument is the stronger one.

Avoid Common Fallacies in Developing and Using Support

In Chapter 2, in the section on critical reading, we considered criteria that, as a reader, you may use for evaluating informative and persuasive writing (see pp. 75–78). We discussed how you can assess the accuracy, the significance, and the author's interpretation of the information presented. We also considered the importance in good argument of clearly defined key terms and the pitfalls of emotionally loaded language. Finally, we saw how to recognize such logical fallacies as either/or reasoning, faulty cause-and-effect reasoning, and hasty generalization. As a writer, no less than as a critical reader, you need to be aware of these common problems and how to avoid them.

Be aware, also, of your responsibility to cite source materials appropriately. When you quote a source, double- and triple-check that you have done so accurately. When you summarize or paraphrase, take care to use your own language and sentence structures (though you can, of course, also quote within these forms). When you refer to someone else's idea—even if you are not quoting, summarizing, or paraphrasing it—give the source credit. By being ethical about the use of sources, you uphold the highest standards of the academic community.

The Comparison-and-Contrast Synthesis

5.4   Use comparison and contrast, where appropriate, to develop your argument synthesis.

A particularly important type of argument synthesis is built on patterns of comparison and contrast. Techniques of comparison and contrast enable you to examine two subjects (or sources) in terms of each other. When you compare, you consider *similarities*. When you contrast, you consider *differences*. By comparing and contrasting, you perform a close, multipart analysis that often suggests subtleties that otherwise might not have come to your (or your reader's) attention.

To organize a comparison-and-contrast argument, you must carefully read sources in order to discover *significant criteria for analysis*. A *criterion* is a specific point to which both of your authors refer and about which they may agree or disagree. For example, in a comparative report on compact cars, criteria for *comparison and contrast* might be road handling, fuel economy, and comfort of ride. The best criteria are those that allow you not only to account for obvious similarities and differences—those concerning the main aspects of your sources or subjects—but also to plumb deeper, exploring subtle yet significant comparisons and contrasts among details or subcomponents, which you can then relate to your overall thesis.

Note that comparison and contrast is frequently not an end in itself but serves some larger purpose. Thus, a comparison-and-contrast synthesis may be a component of a paper that is essentially a critique, an explanatory synthesis, an argument synthesis, or an analysis.

Organizing Comparison-and-Contrast Syntheses

Two basic approaches to organizing a comparison-and-contrast synthesis are organization by *source or subject* and organization by *criteria.*

ORGANIZING BY SOURCE OR SUBJECT   You can organize a comparative synthesis by first summarizing each of your sources or subjects and then discussing the significant similarities and differences between them. Having read the summaries and become familiar with the distinguishing features of each source, your readers will most likely be able to appreciate the more obvious similarities and differences. In the discussion, your task is to consider both the obvious and the subtle comparisons and contrasts, focusing on the most significant—that is, on those that most clearly support your thesis.

Organization by source or subject works best with passages that can be briefly summarized. If the summary of your source or subject becomes too long, your readers might have forgotten the points you made in the first summary when they are reading the second. A comparison-and-contrast synthesis organized by source or subject might proceed like this:

I. Introduce the paper; lead to thesis.

II. Summarize the source or subject A by discussing its significant features.

III. Summarize the source or subject B by discussing its significant features.

IV. Discuss in a paragraph (or two) the significant points of comparison and contrast between sources or subjects A and B. Alternatively, begin the comparison and contrast in Section III as you introduce source or subject B.

V. Conclude with a paragraph in which you summarize your points and perhaps raise and respond to pertinent questions.

ORGANIZING BY CRITERIA   Instead of summarizing entire sources one at a time with the intention of comparing them later, you could discuss two sources simultaneously, examining the views of each author point by point (criterion by criterion), comparing and contrasting these views in the process. The criterion approach is best used when you have a number of points to discuss or when passages or subjects are long and/or complex. A comparison-and-contrast synthesis organized by criteria might look like this:

I. Introduce the paper; lead to thesis.

II. Criterion 1

  A. Discuss what author 1 says about this point.

  B. Discuss what author 2 says about this point, comparing and contrasting author 2's treatment of the point with that of author 1.

III. Criterion 2

    A. Discuss what author 1 says about this point.

    B. Discuss what author 2 says about this point, comparing and contrasting author 2's treatment of the point with that of author 1.

And so on, proceeding criterion by criterion until you have completed your discussion. Be sure to arrange criteria with a clear method. Knowing how the discussion of one criterion leads to the next ensures smooth transitions throughout your paper. End by summarizing your key points and perhaps raising and responding to pertinent questions.

However you organize your comparison-and-contrast synthesis, keep in mind that comparing and contrasting are not ends in themselves. Your discussion should point to a conclusion, an answer to the question "So what—why bother to compare and contrast in the first place?" If your discussion is part of a larger synthesis, point to and support the larger claim. If you write a stand-alone comparison-and-contrast synthesis, though, you must, by the final paragraph, answer the "Why bother?" question. The model comparison-and-contrast synthesis below does exactly this.

Exercise 5.6
Comparing and Contrasting

Over the course of two days, go online to the Web sites of three daily news outlets and follow how each, in its news pages, treats a particular story of national or international significance. One news outlet should be a local city outlet—perhaps the Web site of your home-town newspaper. (*Note:* The reporting should originate not with a syndicated newswire, like the Associated Press, but with the outlet's own staff writer.) One news outlet should have a national readership, like the *Wall Street Journal* or the *New York Times*. The third outlet should be any news source of your choice (and it needn't exist in print).

    Develop a comparison-and-contrast synthesis that leads to an argument about the news coverage. In making notes toward such a synthesis, you'll want to do the following:

- Define the news story: the who, what, when, where, and how of the issue.
- Develop at least three criteria with which to compare and contrast news coverage. Possible criteria: Do the outlets report the same facts? Do the outlets color these facts with an editorial slant? Do the outlets agree on the significance of the issue?
- As you take notes, point to specific passages.
- Review your notes. What patterns emerge? Can you draw any conclusions? Write a thesis that reflects your assessment.
- Using your notes and guided by your thesis, write a comparison-and-contrast-paper.
- Be sure that your paper answers the "So what?" question. What is the point of your synthesis?

A Case for Comparison and Contrast: World War I and World War II

Let's see how the principles of comparison and contrast can be applied to a response to a final examination question in a course on modern history. Imagine that, having attended classes involving lecture and discussion and having read excerpts from John Keegan's *The First World War* and Tony Judt's *Postwar: A History of Europe Since 1945,* you were presented with this examination question:

> Based on your reading to date, compare and contrast the two world wars in light of any three or four criteria you think significant. Once you have called careful attention to both similarities and differences, conclude with an observation. What have you learned? What can your comparative analysis teach us?

COMPARISON AND CONTRAST ORGANIZED BY CRITERIA   Here is a plan for a response, essentially a comparison-and-contrast synthesis, organized by *criteria* and beginning with the thesis—and the *claim.*

> *Thesis:* In terms of the impact on cities and civilian populations, the military aspects of the two wars in Europe, and their aftermaths, the differences between World War I and World War II considerably outweigh the similarities.
>
> **I.** Introduction. World Wars I and II were the most devastating conflicts in history. *Thesis*
>
> **II.** Summary of main similarities: causes, countries involved, battlegrounds, global scope
>
> **III.** First major difference: Physical impact of war
>   - **A.** WWI was fought mainly in rural battlegrounds.
>   - **B.** In WWII cities were destroyed.
>
> **IV.** Second major difference: effect on civilians
>   - **A.** WWI fighting primarily involved soldiers.
>   - **B.** WWII involved not only military but also massive noncombatant casualties: Civilian populations were displaced, forced into slave labor, and exterminated.
>
> **V.** Third major difference: combat operations
>   - **A.** WWI, in its long middle phase, was characterized by trench warfare.
>   - **B.** During the middle phase of WWII, there was no major military action in Nazi-occupied Western Europe.
>
> **VI.** Fourth major difference: aftermath
>   - **A.** Harsh war terms imposed on defeated Germany contributed significantly to the rise of Hitler and WWII.
>   - **B.** Victorious allies helped rebuild West Germany after WWII but allowed Soviets to take over Eastern Europe.
>
> **VII.** Conclusion. Since the end of World War II, wars have been far smaller in scope and destructiveness, and warfare has expanded to involve stateless combatants committed to acts of terror.

The following model exam response, a comparison-and-contrast synthesis organized by criteria, is written according to the preceding plan. (Thesis and topic sentences are highlighted.)

Model Exam Response

World War I (1914–1918) and World War II (1939–1945) were the most catastrophic and destructive conflicts in human history. For those who believed in the steady but inevitable progress of civilization, it was impossible to imagine that two wars in the first half of the twentieth century could reach levels of barbarity and horror that would outstrip those of any previous era. Historians estimate that more than 22 million people, soldiers and civilians, died in World War I; they estimate that between 40 and 50 million died in World War II. In many ways, these two conflicts were similar: They were fought on many of the same European and Russian battlegrounds, with more or less the same countries on opposing sides. Even many of the same people were involved: Winston Churchill and Adolf Hitler figured in both wars. And the main outcome in each case was the same: total defeat for Germany. However, in terms of the impact on cities and civilian populations, the military aspects of the two wars in Europe, and their aftermaths, the differences between World Wars I and II considerably outweigh the similarities.

1

1: Opens with comment on unprecedented level of destruction in both wars. Similarities between wars.

Thesis, last sentence of the paragraph, summarizes key differences and suggests structure of paper to follow.

The similarities are clear enough. In fact, many historians regard World War II as a continuation—after an intermission of about twenty years—of World War I. One of the main causes of each war was Germany's dissatisfaction and frustration with what it perceived as its diminished place in the world. Hitler launched World War II partly out of revenge for Germany's humiliating defeat in World War I. In each conflict Germany and its allies (the Central Powers in WWI, the Axis in WWII) went to war against France, Great Britain, Russia (the Soviet Union in WWII), and, eventually, the United States. Though neither conflict included literally the entire world, the participation of countries not only in Europe but also in the Middle East, the Far East, and the Western hemisphere made both conflicts global in scope. And, as indicated earlier, the number of casualties in each war was unprecedented in history, partly because modern technology had enabled the creation of deadlier weapons—including tanks, heavy artillery, and aircraft—than had ever been used in warfare.

2

2: Key similarities between world wars.

Despite these similarities, the differences between the two world wars are considerably more significant. One of the most noticeable differences was the physical impact of each war in Europe and in Russia—the western and eastern fronts. The physical destruction of World War I was confined largely to the battlefield. The combat took place almost entirely in the rural areas of Europe and Russia. No major cities were destroyed in the first war; cathedrals, museums, government buildings, urban houses, and apartments were left untouched. During the second war, in contrast, almost no city or town of any size emerged unscathed. Rotterdam, Warsaw, London, Minsk, and—when the Allies began their counterattack—almost every major city in Germany and Japan, including Berlin and Tokyo, were flattened. Of course, the physical devastation of the cities created millions of refugees, a phenomenon never experienced in World War I.

3

3: First criterion for contrast—both wars discussed. Difference.

The fact that World War II was fought in the cities as well as on the battlefields meant that the second war had a much greater impact on civilians than did the first war. With few exceptions, the civilians in Europe during WWI were not driven from their homes, forced into slave labor, starved, tortured, or systematically exterminated. But all of these crimes happened routinely during WWII. The Nazi occupation of Europe meant that the civilian populations of France, Belgium, Norway, the Netherlands, and other conquered lands, along with the industries, railroads, and farms of these countries, were put into the service of the Third Reich.

4

4: Second criterion for contrast—both wars discussed. Differences.

Millions of people from conquered Europe—those who were not sent directly to the death camps—were forcibly transported to Germany and put to work in support of the war effort.

5: Third criterion for contrast— both wars discussed. Differences.

5   During both wars, the Germans were fighting on two fronts—the western front in Europe and the eastern front in Russia. But while both wars were characterized by intense military activity during their initial and final phases, the middle and longest phases—at least in Europe—differed considerably. The middle phase of the First World War was characterized by trench warfare, a relatively static form of military activity in which fronts seldom moved, or moved only a few hundred yards at a time, even after major battles. By contrast, in the years between the German conquest of most of Europe by early 1941 and the Allied invasion of Normandy in mid-1944, there was no major fighting in Nazi-occupied Western Europe. (The land battles then shifted to North Africa and the Soviet Union.)

6: Fourth and final criterion for contrast—both wars discussed. Difference.

6   And, of course, the two world wars differed in their aftermaths. The most significant consequence of World War I was that the humiliating and costly war reparations imposed on the defeated Germany by the terms of the 1919 Treaty of Versailles made possible the rise of Hitler and thus led directly to World War II. In contrast, after the end of the Second World War in 1945, the Allies helped rebuild West Germany (the portion of a divided Germany that it controlled), transformed the new country into a democracy, and helped make it one of the most thriving economies of the world. But perhaps the most significant difference in the aftermath of each war involved Russia. That country, in a considerably weakened state, pulled out of World War I a year before hostilities ended so that it could consolidate its 1917 Revolution. Russia then withdrew into itself and took no significant part in European affairs until the Nazi invasion of the Soviet Union in 1941. In contrast, it was the Red Army in World War II that was most responsible for the crushing defeat of Germany. In recognition of its efforts and of its enormous sacrifices, the Allies allowed the Soviet Union to take control of the countries of Eastern Europe after the war, leading to fifty years of totalitarian rule—and the Cold War.

7: Summary of key similarities and differences. Ends with lessons learned and applied to more recent wars.

Conclusion answers the "So what?" question.

7   While the two world wars that devastated much of Europe were similar in that, at least according to some historians, they were the same war interrupted by two decades and similar in that combatants killed more efficiently than armies throughout history ever had, the differences between the wars were significant. In terms of the physical impact of the fighting, the impact on civilians, the action on the battlefield at mid-war, and the aftermaths, World Wars I and II differed in ways that matter to us decades later. The wars in Iraq, Afghanistan, and Bosnia have involved an alliance of nations pitted against single nations, but we have not seen, since the two world wars, grand alliances moving vast armies across continents. The destruction implied by such action is almost unthinkable today. Warfare is changing, and "stateless" combatants like Hamas and Al Qaeda wreak destruction of their own. But we may never again see, one hopes, the devastation that follows when multiple nations on opposing sides of a conflict throw millions of soldiers—and civilians—into harm's way.

The Strategy of the Exam Response

The general strategy of this argument is an organization by *criteria*. The writer argues that although the two world wars exhibited some similarities, the differences between the two conflicts were more significant. Note that the writer's thesis doesn't merely state these significant differences; it also presents them in a way that anticipates both the content and the structure of the paper to follow.

In argument terms, the *claim* the writer makes is the conclusion that the two global conflicts were significantly different, if superficially similar. The *assumption* is that key differences and similarities are clarified by employing specific criteria that make possible a careful study of both wars. The *support* comes in the form of historical facts regarding the levels of casualties, the scope of destruction, the theaters of conflict, and the events following the conclusions of the wars.

Summary of Synthesis Chapters

5.5   Use your purpose to guide your choice of writing an explanatory synthesis, argument synthesis, or comparison-and-contrast synthesis.

In this chapter and in Chapter 4, we've considered three main types of synthesis: the *explanatory synthesis,* the *argument synthesis,* and the *comparison-and-contrast synthesis.* Although for ease of comprehension we've placed these in separate categories, the types are not mutually exclusive. Argument syntheses often include extended sections of explanation and/or comparison and contrast. Explanations commonly include sections of comparison and contrast. Which type of synthesis you choose depends on your *purpose* and the method that you decide is best suited to achieve this purpose.

If your main purpose is to help your audience understand a particular subject, and in particular to help them understand the essential elements or significance of this subject, then you will be composing an explanatory synthesis. If your main purpose, on the other hand, is to persuade your audience to agree with your viewpoint on a subject, to change their minds, or to decide on a particular course of action, then you will be composing an argument synthesis. If your purpose is to clarify similarities or differences, you will compose a comparison-and-contrast synthesis—which may be a paper in itself (either an argument or an explanation) or part of a larger paper (again, either an argument or explanation).

In planning and drafting these syntheses, you can draw on a variety of strategies: supporting your claims by summarizing, paraphrasing, and quoting from your sources; using appeals to *logos, pathos,* and *ethos;* and choosing from among strategies such as climactic or conventional order, counterargument, and concession. Choose the approach that will best help you to achieve your purpose.

Chapter 6
Analysis

Learning Objectives

After completing this chapter, you will be able to:

6.1 Understand analysis as the study of something using an analytical tool.

6.2 Establish a principle or definition as the basis for an analysis.

6.3 Write an analysis.

What Is an Analysis?

6.1 Understand analysis as the study of something using an analytical tool.

An *analysis* is a type of argument in which you study the parts of something—a work of art, a group of people, a virus, bird migrations, a political rally, a star, *anything*—in order to deepen your understanding. An analysis can form part of a larger paper or be a paper entirely to itself. Aside from choosing a specific topic to study in an analysis, you'll choose a tool to help examine parts of that topic.

Your choice of tool depends on what you want to learn. Say you want to study the human hand. If you are an orthopedic surgeon, you might use an X-ray that enabled you to see the bones of a patient. If you are a choreographer and want to study the expressive quality of a ballerina's hands, you might use a camera to capture a dancer's hands in motion. When you change the tool for analysis, you change—and simultaneously limit—what you see.

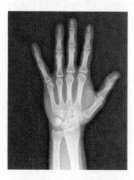

Ideas—principles and definitions—can serve as analytical tools equally as well as physical tools like X-ray machines. Consider two analyses of *The Wizard of Oz*, each using a different idea as an analytical tool:

> At the dawn of adolescence, the very time she should start to distance herself from Aunt Em and Uncle Henry, the surrogate parents who raised her on their Kansas farm, Dorothy Gale experiences a hurtful reawakening of her fear that these loved ones will be rudely ripped from her, especially her Aunt (Em—M for Mother!).[1]

> [*The Wizard of Oz*] was originally written as a political allegory about grass-roots protest. It may seem harder to believe than Emerald City, but the Tin Woodsman is the industrial worker, the Scarecrow [is] the struggling farmer, and the Wizard is the president, who is powerful only as long as he succeeds in deceiving the people.[2]

Is *The Wizard of Oz* the story of a girl's psychological development, or is it a story about politics? The answer is *both*. In the first example, the psychiatrist Harvey Greenberg applies the principles of his profession as his analytical tool and, not surprisingly, sees *The Wizard of Oz* in psychological terms. In the second example, a newspaper reporter uses the political theories of Karl Marx as an analytical tool and, again not surprisingly, discovers a story about politics.

Your choice of an analytical tool both creates and limits what you can see in an analysis. An X-ray machine is very good at helping you to study bones. It wouldn't help you to identify skin rashes, however. The same is true of analytical ideas, definitions, or theories. The psychological theories of Sigmund Freud would help you understand psychological relationships among characters in books and movies but would do little to help you appreciate economic relationships among these same characters. Those conducting analyses, therefore, choose tools appropriate to their topic of study, aware that however powerful any one tool may be, it will limit what can be seen.

---

[1]Harvey Greenberg, *The Movies on Your Mind* (New York: Dutton, 1975).
[2]Peter Dreier, "Oz Was Almost Reality." *Cleveland Plain Dealer*, 3 Sept. 1989.

Whatever tool you choose, the successful analysis should illuminate—both for yourself and your readers—the object being studied. A successful analysis will yield fresh, even surprising insights. Without Greenberg's analysis, for instance, we might never have considered Dorothy's adventures in Oz as a psychological journey. This is precisely the power of an analysis: its ability to reveal objects or events in ways we would not otherwise have considered.

Where Do We Find Written Analyses?

Here are just a few of the types of writing that involve analysis:

Academic Writing

- **Experimental and lab reports** analyze the meaning or implications of the study results in the Discussion section.
- **Research papers** analyze information in sources or apply theories to material being reported.
- **Process analyses** break down the steps or stages involved in completing a process.
- **Literary analyses** examine characterization, plot, imagery, or other elements in works of literature.
- **Essay exams** demonstrate understanding of course material by analyzing data using course concepts.

Workplace Writing

- **Grant proposals** analyze the issues you seek funding for in order to address them.
- **Reviews of the arts** employ dramatic or literary analysis to assess artistic works.
- **Business plans** break down and analyze capital outlays, expenditures, profits, materials, and the like.
- **Medical charts** record analytic thinking and writing in relation to patient symptoms and possible options.
- **Legal briefs** break down and analyze facts of cases and elements of legal precedents and apply legal rulings and precedents to new situations.
- **Case studies** describe and analyze the particulars of a specific medical, social service, advertising, or business case.

Let's consider a more extended example of analysis from the *Journal of Behavioral Addiction*. In this case, the authors use a psychological principle to examine cell-phone use.

from The Invisible Addiction: Cell-Phone Activities and Addiction among Male and Female College Students

—James A. Roberts, Luc Honore Petnji Yaya, and Chris Manolis

Establishes a broad definition for use as an analytical tool. Definition is referenced, giving readers confidence that the tool is a reasonable one.

Although the concept of addiction has multiple definitions, traditionally it has been described as the repeated use of a substance despite the negative consequences suffered by the addicted individual (Alavi et al., 2012). More recently, the notion of addiction has been generalized to include behaviors like gambling, sex, exercise, eating, Internet, and cell-phone use (Griffiths, 1995; Roberts & Pirog, 2012). Any entity that can produce a pleasurable sensation has the potential of becoming addictive (Alavi et al., 2012). Similar to substance addiction, behavioral addiction is best understood as a habitual drive or compulsion to continue to repeat a behavior despite its negative impact on one's well-being (Roberts & Pirog, 2012). Any oft-repeated behaviors that trigger "specific reward effects through biochemical processes in the body do have an addictive potential" (Alavi et al., 2012, p. 292). Loss of control over the behavior is an essential element of any addiction.

Griffiths (1999, 2000) sees technological addictions as a subset of behavioral addiction and defines them as "non-chemical (behavioral) addictions that involve human-machine interaction" (Griffiths, 2000, p. 211). As alluded to above, cell-phone addiction appears to be the latest technological addiction to emerge. As the cost of cell-phone use drops and the functionality of these devices expands, cell phones have ensconced themselves into the everyday lives of consumers around the globe. . . .

In the case of cell phones, . . . an addiction may begin when an initially benign behavior with little or no harmful consequences—such as owning a cell phone for safety purposes—begins to evoke negative consequences and the user becomes increasingly dependent upon its use. Owning a cell phone for purposes of safety, for instance, eventually becomes secondary to sending and receiving text messages or visiting online social networking sites; eventually, the cell-phone user may engage in increasingly dangerous behaviors such as texting while driving. Ultimately, the cell-phone user reaches a "tipping point" where he [or] she can no longer control [his or her] cell-phone use or the negative consequences from its overuse. The process of addiction suggests a distinction between liking and wanting. In other words, the cell-phone user goes from liking his [or] her cell phone to wanting it. This switch from liking to wanting is referred to by Grover et al. (2011) as the "inflection point." This tipping point signals a shift from a previously benign everyday behavior that may have been pleasurable with few harmful consequences to an addictive behavior where wanting (physically and/or psychologically) has replaced liking as the motivating factor behind the behavior.

Narrows analytical tool by defining "behavioral addiction."

Further narrows the analytical tool to "technological addiction."

Applies analytical tool, a definition of "technological addiction," to illuminate the process by which cell-phone use can turn addictive.

Before characterizing cell-phone use as a "technological" addiction, James Roberts and his co-authors define both "addiction" and, more specifically, "behavioral addiction." This definition is a well-suited tool for studying cell-phone use because it gives us a glimpse of the process by which a behavior can turn addictive.

Now consider a different analytical tool equally well suited to studying cell phones. In this next example, the tool is a principle, an idea stated directly in the first line. Again, notice how a change in analytical tool changes what can be seen and studied. In this case, the writer is a professor of science and technology interested in what the spread of a technology through a culture can teach us about that culture.

What's in a Phone?

Jon Agar

You can tell what a culture values by what it has in its bags and pockets. Keys, combs and money tell us that property, personal appearance or trade matter. But when the object is expensive, a more significant investment has been made. In our day the mobile or cell phone is just such an object. But what of the past? In the seventeenth century, the pocketwatch

Defines analytical tool: a principle. Implied question: "How does content of pockets reveal cultural priorities?" Analysis will answer.

Applies principle to examine an earlier technology, the pocketwatch.

was a rarity, so much so that only the best horological collections of today can boast an example. But if, in the following century, you had entered a bustling London coffee shop or Parisian salon, then you might well have spied a pocketwatch amongst the breeches and frock-coats. The personal watch was baroque high technology, a compact complex device that only the most skillful artisans could design and build. Their proud owners bought not only the ability to tell the time, but also bought into particular values: Telling the time mattered to the entrepreneurs and factory owners who were busy. As commercial and industrial economies began to roar, busy-ness conveyed business—and its symbol was the pocketwatch.

Extended example establishes power of analytical tool.

At first sight it might seem as if owning a pocketwatch gave freedom from the town clock and the church bell: making the individual independent of political and religious authorities. Certainly, possession granted the owner powers over the watchless: power to say when the working day might begin and finish, for example. While it might have felt like liberation from tradition, the owner was caught anew in a more modern rationality, for, despite the fact that the pocketwatch gave the owner personal access to exact time, accuracy depended on being part of a system. If the owner was unwilling personally to make regular astronomical observations, the pocketwatch would still have to be reset every now and then from the town clock. With the establishment of time zones, the system within which a pocketwatch displayed the "right" time spread over the entire globe. Seven o'clock in the morning in New York was exactly twelve noon in London, which was exactly eight o'clock in the evening in Shanghai. What is more, the owner of a pocketwatch could travel all day—could be mobile—and still always know what time it was. Such certainty was only possible because an immense amount of effort had put an infrastructure in place, and agreements had been hammered out about how the system should work. Only in societies where time meant money would this effort have been worth it.

Analysis turns from pocketwatches to newer technology, cell phones.

Pocketwatches provide the closest historical parallel to the remarkable rise of the mobile cellular phone in our own times. Pocketwatches, for example, started as expensive status symbols, but by the twentieth century most people in the West possessed one. When cellular phones were first marketed they cost the equivalent of a small car—and you needed the car to transport them since they were so bulky. But in 2002, global subscriptions to cellular phone services passed one billion. In countries such as Iceland, Finland, Italy, and the UK, over three-quarters of the population owned a phone, with other countries in Western Europe, the Americas, and the Pacific Rim not far behind. Like the pocketwatch, the phone had made the leap from being a technology of the home or street to being a much rarer creature indeed: something carried everywhere, on the person, by anybody. So, if pocketwatches resonated to the rhythm of industrial capitalism, what values do the ringtones of the mobile phone signify? What is it about humanity in the twenty-first-century world that has created a desire to be in constant touch?

Turns the principle into questions: Each question will guide part of the analysis that follows.

Selecting and Using an Analytical Tool

6.2   Establish a principle or definition as the basis for an analysis.

Your challenge in analysis is to convince readers that (1) the analytical tool you have chosen is legitimate and well matched to the topic at hand, and (2) you will use the analytical tool systematically to divide the topic into parts and make coherent, meaningful statements about these parts and their relation to the whole.

Planning and writing an analysis requires defining the object, behavior, or event to be studied and understanding your analytical tool. The tools examined here are ideas (as opposed to physical tools like X-ray machines). These ideas generally take the form of definitions and principles, as in these assignments calling for analysis.

Literature	Apply principles of Jungian psychology to Nathaniel Hawthorne's "Young Goodman Brown." In your analysis of the story, apply Jung's theories of the *shadow, persona,* and *anima*.
Physics	Use Newton's Second Law ($F = ma$) to analyze the acceleration of a fixed pulley from which two weights hang: m_1 (.45 kg) and m_2 (.90 kg).
Economics	Use Schumpeter's principle of creative destruction to analyze job loss and creation in the manufacturing sector of the American economy from 1975 to 2000.

Selecting the Analytical Tool

The three assignments illustrate how instructors sometimes choose for you the analytical tool to be used in an investigation. Just as often you will be asked to choose the tool yourself. When this is the case, consider two strategies.

- Look for a statement that expresses a rule or a law, as in this statement Jon Agar uses to open his paper on the cultural value of cell phones:

  > You can tell what a culture values by what it has in its bags and pockets.

  Statements of rules or laws tend to be conclusions drawn from extensive arguments. If you find an argument sound, its author reputable, and the source respected, consider using that conclusion as your analytical tool.

- Look for definitions that take the form *X can be defined as (or X consists of) the following: A, B, C, and so on.* For example, in the example of the psychological analysis of cell-phone use, James Roberts and his co-authors cite a source defining *behavior addiction*:

  > Similar to substance addiction, behavioral addiction is best understood as a habitual drive or compulsion to continue to repeat a behavior despite its negative impact on one's well-being.

Using this definition as his analytical tool, Roberts and his co-authors analyze cell-phone use as a potentially addictive behavior. If you read Roberts and his co-authors' paper and find their definition sound, you can use their same definition as your tool to study some other behavior—perhaps television viewing—and argue that it, too, is potentially addictive. Definitions that you find in dictionaries and encyclopedias can also be used as analytical tools.

Using the Analytical Tool

Once you have settled on a tool, identify its parts and turn them into questions. In the definition of behavioral addiction, we can isolate three parts of addictive behavior:

- Habitual drive/compulsion
- Repetition
- Negative impact

The next step in analysis is to turn each element of an analytical tool into a question and to direct these questions, one at a time, to the object, behavior, or event you are examining. Each question enables you to analyze a part of the whole. Frame your questions neutrally so that you can find both positive and negative examples. Here are analytical questions based on two elements of addictive behavior.

In what ways can smartphone use have negative impacts on users?
Is there any sense in which smartphone users feel compelled to use them?

Use your questions to examine the object, behavior, or event of interest and to generate notes. Pose one question, conduct your analysis, take notes—then move to the next question. Your notes become the raw material for your written analysis, in the case of smartphone dependence, evidence for or against the claim

Exercise 6.1

Using a Principle or Definition as a Tool for Analysis

James Roberts and co-authors introduce a definition of addiction to analyze cell-phone use from a behavioral point of view:

> Although the concept of addiction has multiple definitions, traditionally it has been described as the repeated use of a substance despite the negative consequences suffered by the addicted individual.

Jon Agar introduces a definition of value to analyze cell-phone use from a historical point of view:

> You can tell what a culture values by what it has in its bags and pockets.

Choose one of these statements as a principle by which to begin analyzing some behavior or object

unrelated to cell phones. (If you are using Roberts and co-authors, do *not* analyze behaviors already considered addictive, for instance, drug or alcohol abuse.) Your goal here is to generate notes:

1. Select either of the two statements as your analytical principle.

2. Identify a behavior or object to analyze.

3. Use the selected principle to generate questions for analysis.

4. Use your questions to identify parts of the behavior or object. List these parts and make notes as you apply your questions.

that it can become an addictive behavior. At this stage of the process, you will not yet have reached a conclusion or thesis.

Planning and Writing the Analysis Paper

6.3   Write an analysis.

You've conducted your analysis and made notes. You have in hand the materials from which you will devise a thesis, develop the paragraph-by-paragraph logic of your paper, write your paper, and review your analysis to make sure it passes key tests.

Devising a Thesis

Select from among your notes a subset about which you can make a clear generalization—your thesis—that answers one of these questions:

- What is this object, behavior, or event?
- What are its component parts?
- What happened?
- How does it work?
- What are its strengths and weaknesses?
- What does it mean?
- What is its significance?

Your one-sentence answer to one (or more) of these questions for analysis will become the thesis of your paper. It is also your conclusion. However you phrase your thesis in your final paper, clarify your thinking in an early working draft by rewriting the thesis in the following form (this exercise will establish that you are, in fact, conducting an analysis):

> By applying _analytical tool X_, we can understand _(subject)_ as _(conclusion based on analysis)_.

Here is the thesis (with slight modification) that appears in the model analysis at the end of this chapter:

> Robert Knapp's "A Psychology of Rumor" can help us understand why some contemporary rumors, like the "missing kidney," have been so frightening yet so effective.

Here is the claim rewritten to emphasize parts of the analysis:

> By applying Robert Knapp's theory of rumors, we can understand "the missing kidney" as a classic bogie rumor that, with its striking details, feeds on our fears of organ transplantation.

Developing the Paragraph-by-Paragraph Logic of Your Paper

The following paragraph illustrates the typical logic of a paragraph in an analytical paper. The paragraph appears in the model analysis of the missing kidney rumor (in which a traveling businessman is drugged and wakes to discover one of his kidneys has been surgically removed):

Introduction of
analytical tool.

Application of tool to
object under study:
kidney rumor.

The kidney rumor is first and foremost the perfect example of Knapp's bogie rumor, the rumor that draws its power from our fears and anxieties. Recall the scary folk tales about children lost in the forest, soon to encounter a witch? One classic anxiety of a bogie rumor similarly involves being alone in a strange place. In the case of the missing kidney, organ removals almost always occur when the victim is away from home, out of town or even out of the country. Most of us enjoy traveling, but we may also feel somewhat uneasy in unfamiliar cities. We're not comfortably on our own turf, so we don't quite know our way around; we don't know what to expect of the local population; we don't feel entirely safe, or at least, we feel that some of the locals may resent us and take advantage of us. Of course, our worry about being alone in an unfamiliar city is nothing compared to our anxiety about being cut open. Even under the best of circumstances (such as to save our lives), no one looks forward to surgery. The prospect of being drugged, taken to an unknown facility, and having members of a crime ring remove one of our organs without our knowledge or consent—as apparently happened to the various subjects of this rumor—would be our worst nightmare. It's little wonder that this particular "bogie" man has such a powerful grip on our hearts.

With analytical tool
applied, assessment
follows.

An analysis paper takes shape when you create a series of such paragraphs, link them with an overall logic and organization, and draw a general conclusion concerning what was learned through the analysis. You'll find an effective, paper-length example of analysis in the model student paper later in this chapter. Margin notes highlight key elements of the analysis.

Writing the Analysis Paper

Following are guidelines to help you prepare for and structure your analysis.

Guidelines for Writing Analyses

Before writing, conduct your analysis: Apply an analytical tool—and make notes.

- **Identify the object, behavior, or event to be studied.**

- **Identify the analytical tool:** a principle, rule, or definition that will organize your inquiry. The tool will be assigned, or you will select it.

- **Conduct the analysis.** Turn key elements of the analytical principle, rule, or definition into questions. Use those questions systematically to examine parts of the object, behavior, or event of interest.

- **Make notes.** Record your insights using the analytical tool.

- **Devise a thesis.** Review your notes and write an organizing, debatable statement based on insights gained through your analysis.

Write the analysis: Organize and present the information you have gathered.

- **Create a context for your analysis.** Introduce the object, behavior, or event to be studied. Why is this object or behavior of interest? Why should we learn more about it?

- **State your thesis.**

- **Explain, if necessary, the tool that has guided your analysis.** If readers will not likely understand the tool (or might think it inappropriate for the task), explain why the tool is useful.

- **Explain in detail, if necessary, the object, behavior, or event to be analyzed.**

- **Present key points of analysis, one point at a time.** Organize your paper around the questions of analysis that produced your most compelling insights. Each question should lead to a paragraph or section (a grouping of related paragraphs) that presents these analytical insights and, in so doing, supports your thesis.

- **Remember that you are making an argument.** You must *prove* to readers that what you have learned through your analysis is meaningful.

- **Conclude by stating the significance of your analysis.** Review what you have learned. What new or interesting insights have you discovered?

Reviewing Your Analysis: Does It Pass Key Tests?

HAVE YOU WRITTEN A SUMMARY RATHER THAN AN ANALYSIS?   The most common error made in writing analyses—an error that is *fatal* to the form—is to present readers with a summary only. For analyses to succeed, you must *apply* a principle or definition and reach a conclusion about the object, event, or behavior you are examining. By definition, a summary (see Chapter 1) includes none of your own conclusions. Summary is naturally part of analysis; you will need to summarize the object or activity being examined and, depending on the audience's needs, summarize the principle or definition being applied. But an analysis should take the next step and share insights that suggest the meaning or significance of some object, event, or behavior.

IS YOUR ANALYSIS SYSTEMATIC?   Analyses should give the reader the sense of a systematic, purposeful examination. Note that in the model analysis later in this chapter, Linda Shanker sets out specific elements of addictive behavior in separate paragraphs and then uses each, within its paragraph, to analyze a rumor. Shanker is systematic in her method, and we are never in doubt about her purpose.

   Imagine another analysis in which a writer lays out four elements of a definition and then applies only two, without explaining the logic for omitting the others. Or imagine an analysis in which the writer offers a principle for analysis but directs it to only a half or a third of the object being discussed, without providing a reason for doing so. In both cases, the writer fails to deliver on a promise basic to analyses: Once you introduce a principle or definition, you should apply it thoroughly and systematically.

HAVE YOU ANSWERED THE "SO WHAT?" QUESTION?   An analysis should make readers *want* to read it. It should give readers a sense of getting to the heart of the matter, that what is important in the object or activity under analysis is being laid bare and discussed in revealing ways. If, when rereading the first draft of your analysis, you cannot imagine readers saying, "I never thought of _____ this way," then something may be wrong.

HAVE YOU ATTRIBUTED SOURCES?   In an analysis, you often work with just a few sources and apply insights from them to some object or phenomenon you want to understand more thoroughly. Because you are not synthesizing large quantities of data and because the strength of an analysis derives mostly from *your* application of a principle or definition, you will have less need to cite sources. However, take special care to cite those sources you do draw on throughout the analysis.

Critical Reading for Analysis

- **Read to get a sense of the whole in relation to its parts.** Whether you are clarifying for yourself a principle or a definition to be used in an analysis or you are reading a text that you will analyze, understand how parts function to create the whole. If a definition or principle consists of parts, use them to organize sections of your analysis. If your goal is to analyze a text, be aware of its structure: Note the title and subtitle; identify the main point and subordinate points and where they are located; break the material into sections.

- **Read to discover relationships within the object being analyzed.** Watch for patterns. When you find them, be alert—for they create an occasion to analyze, to use a principle or

definition as a guide in discussing what the patterns may mean.

In fiction, a pattern might involve responses of characters to events or to each other, the recurrence of certain words or phrasings, images, themes, or turns of plot (to name a few).

In poetry, a pattern might involve rhyme schemes, rhythm, imagery, figurative or literal language, and more.

The challenge to you as a reader is first to see a pattern (perhaps using a guiding principle or definition to do so) and then to locate other instances of that pattern. Reading carefully in this way prepares you to conduct an analysis.

When *Your* Perspective Guides the Analysis

In some cases a writer's analysis of a phenomenon or a work of art may not result from anything as structured as a principle or a definition. It may instead follow from the writer's cultural or personal outlook, perspective, or interests. Imagine reading a story or observing the lines of a new building and being asked to analyze it—based not on someone else's definition or principle, but on your own. Your analysis of the story might largely be determined by your preference for fast pacing; intrepid, resourceful heroes; and pitiless, black-hearted villains. Among the principles you might use in analyzing the building are your admiration for curved exterior surfaces and the imaginative use of glass.

Analyses in this case continue to probe the parts of things to understand how they work and what they mean. And they continue to be carefully structured, examining one part of a phenomenon at a time. The essential purpose of the analysis, to *reveal*, remains unchanged. This goal distinguishes the analysis from the critique, whose main purpose is to *evaluate* and *assess validity.*

If you find yourself writing an analysis guided by your own insights, not by someone else's, then you owe your reader a clear explanation of your guiding principles and the definitions by which you will probe the subject under study. Continue using the Guidelines for Writing Analyses (see p. 168), modifying this advice as you think fit to accommodate your own personal outlook, perspective, or interests. Above all, remember to structure your analysis with care. Proceed systematically and emerge with a clear statement about what the subject means, how it works, or why it might be significant.

Exercise 6.2
Planning an Analysis

Create an outline of an analysis based on the principle and the behavior or object you selected in Exercise 6.1. Working with the notes you generated, formulate a thesis and develop an organizational plan. In completing this exercise, you may find the Guidelines for Writing Analyses useful.

Demonstration: Analysis

Linda Shanker wrote the following paper when she was a sophomore in response to this assignment from her sociology professor:

Read Robert H. Knapp's "A Psychology of Rumor" in your course anthology. Use some of Knapp's observations about rumor to examine a particular rumor that you have read about during the first few weeks of this course. Write for readers much like yourself: freshmen or sophomores who have taken one course in sociology. Your object in this paper is to draw upon Knapp to shed light on how the particular rumor you select spread so widely and so rapidly.

Model Analysis

Linda Shanker
Social Psychology 1
UCLA
17 November 2016

The Case of the Missing Kidney: An Analysis of Rumor

> Rumor! What evil can surpass her speed?
> In movement she grows mighty, and achieves
> strength and dominion as she swifter flies . . .
> [F]oul, whispering lips, and ears, that catch at all . . .
> She can cling
> to vile invention and malignant wrong,
> or mingle with her word some tidings true.

> —Virgil, *The Aeneid (Book IV, Ch. 8)*

1 Creates a context for the analysis by introducing the phenomenon of rumor.

1   The phenomenon of rumor has been an object of fascination since ancient times. In his epic poem *The Aeneid*, Virgil noted some insidious truths about rumors: they spread quickly (all the more so in our own day, by means of phones, TV, e-mail, Facebook, and Twitter); they can grow in strength and come to dominate conversation with vicious lies; and they are often mixed with a small portion of truth, a toxic combination that provides the rumor with some degree of credibility. In more recent years, sociologists and psychologists have studied various aspects of rumors: why they are such a common feature of any society, how they tie in to our individual and group views of the world, how and why they spread, why people believe them, and finally how they can be prevented and contained.

2 Introduces definition/tool to be used in analyzing the kidney rumor.

Citation lets readers decide if definition is substantial enough to be used in analysis.

2   One of the most important studies is Robert H. Knapp's "A Psychology of Rumor," published in 1944. Knapp's article appeared during World War II (during which he was in charge of rumor control for the Massachusetts Committee of Public Safety). Many of his examples are drawn from rumors that sprang up during that conflict, but his analysis of why rumors form and how they work remains just as relevant today. First, Knapp defines rumor as an unverified statement offered about some topic in the hope that others will believe it (22). He proceeds to classify rumors into three basic types: the *pipe-dream or wish rumor*, based on what we would like to happen; the *bogie rumor*, based on our fears and anxieties; and the *wedge-driving or aggression rumor*, based on "dividing groups and destroying loyalties" (23–24). He notes that rumors do not spread randomly through the population but rather through certain "sub-groups and factions" who are most susceptible to believing them. Rumors spread particularly fast, he notes, when these groups do not trust officials to tell them the truth. Most important, he maintains, "rumors express the underlying hopes, fears, and hostilities of the group" (27).

3 Introduces another part of definition to be used in analyzing the kidney rumor.

3   Not all rumors gain traction, of course, and Knapp goes on to outline the qualities that make for successful rumors. For example, a good rumor must be "short, simple, and salient." It must be a good story. Qualities that make for a good story include "a humorous twist . . . striking and aesthetic detail . . . simplification of plot and circumstances . . . [and] exaggeration" (29). Knapp explains how the same rumor can take various forms, each individually suited to the groups among which it is circulating: "[n]ames, numbers, and places are typically the most unstable components of any rumor." Successful rumors adapt themselves to the particular circumstances, anxieties, [and] prejudices of the group, and the details change according to the "tide of current swings in public opinion and interest" (30).

Knapp's insights are valuable in helping us to understand why some rumors have been so frightening and yet so effective—for instance, the missing kidney rumor. One version of the rumor, current in 1992, is recounted by Robert Dingwall, a sociologist at the University of Nottingham in England:

> A woman friend of another customer had a 17-year-old son who went to a nightclub in Nottingham, called the Black Orchid, one Friday evening. He did not come home, so she called the police, who were not very interested because they thought that he had probably picked up a girl and gone home with her. He did not come back all weekend, but rang his mother from a call box on Monday, saying he was unwell. She drove out to pick him up and found him slumped on the floor of the call box. He said that he had passed out after a drink in the club and remembered nothing of the weekend. There was a neat, fresh scar on his abdomen. She took him to the Queen's Medical Centre, the main emergency hospital in the city, where the doctors found that he had had a kidney removed. The police were called again and showed much more interest. A senior officer spoke to the mother and said that there was a secret surveillance operation going on in this club and others in the same regional chain in other East Midlands cities because they had had several cases of the same kind and they thought that the organs were being removed for sale by an Asian surgeon. (181)

It is not clear where this rumor originated, though at around this time the missing kidney story had served as the basis of a *Law and Order* episode in 1992 and a Hollywood movie, *The Harvest*, released in 1992. In any event, within a few months the rumor had spread throughout Britain, with the name of the nightclub and other details varying according to the city where it was circulating. The following year, the story was transplanted to Mexico; a year later it was set in India. In the Indian version, the operation was performed on an English woman traveling alone who went to a New Delhi hospital to have an appendectomy. Upon returning to England, she still felt ill, and after she was hospitalized, it was discovered that her appendix was still there but that her kidney had been removed. In subsequent years the rumor spread to the United States, with versions of the story set in Philadelphia, New Orleans, Houston, and Las Vegas. In 1997, the following message, addressed "Dear Friends," was posted on an Internet message board:

> I wish to warn you about a new crime ring that is targeting business travelers. This ring is well organized, well funded, has very skilled personnel, and is currently in most major cities and recently very active in New Orleans. The crime begins when a business traveler goes to a lounge for a drink at the end of the work day. A person in the bar walks up as they sit alone and offers to buy them a drink. The last thing the traveler remembers until they wake up in a hotel room bath tub, their body submerged to their neck in ice, is sipping that drink. There is a note taped to the wall

4   4 Introduction of topic to be analyzed: the missing kidney rumor. Expectation is set. Knapp's definitions will be used to help understand how rumor works.

5   5 Topic further explained. Describes how the missing kidney rumor changed and spread.

instructing them not to move and to call 911. A phone is on a small table next to the bathtub for them to call. The business traveler calls 911 who have become quite familiar with this crime. The business traveler is instructed by the 911 operator to very slowly and carefully reach behind them and feel if there is a tube protruding from their lower back. The business traveler finds the tube and answers, "Yes." The 911 operator tells them to remain still, having already sent paramedics to help. The operator knows that both of the business traveler's kidneys have been harvested. This is not a scam or out of a science fiction novel, it is real. It is documented and confirmable. If you travel or someone close to you travels, please be careful. ("You've Got to Be")

Subsequent posts on this message board supposedly confirmed this story ("Sadly, this is very true"), adding different details.

6 Topic further explained. Missing kidney rumor has no factual basis.

Thesis. Sets out the plan of the analysis to follow: persistence and power of the kidney rumor will be explained by applying Knapp's four-part definition.

6   Is there any truth to this rumor? None, whatsoever—not in any of its forms. Police and other authorities in various cities have posted strenuous denials of the story in the newspapers, on official Web sites, and in internal correspondence, as have the National Business Travel Association, the American Gem Trade Association, and the Sherwin Williams Co. ("'Stolen'"). As reported in the rumor-reporting website Snopes.com, "the National Kidney Foundation has asked any individual who claims to have had his or her kidneys illegally removed to step forward and contact them. So far no one's showed up." The persistence and power of the missing kidney rumor can be more fully understood if we apply four elements of Knapp's definition of rumor formation and circulation to this particular urban legend: his notion of the "bogie," the "striking" details that help authenticate a "good story" and that change as the rumor migrates to different populations, the ways a rumor can ride swings of public opinion, and the mingling of falsehood with truth.

7 Analysis begins. Writer applies the first of Knapp's definitions—the "bogie rumor"— to the missing kidney rumor.

7   The kidney rumor is first and foremost the perfect example of Knapp's bogie rumor, the rumor that draws its power from our fears and anxieties. One source of anxiety is being alone in a strange place. (Recall the scary folk tales about children lost in the forest, soon to encounter a witch.) These dreaded kidney removals almost always occur when the victim is away from home, out of town or even out of the country. Most of us enjoy traveling, but we may also feel somewhat uneasy in unfamiliar cities. We're not comfortably on our own turf, so we don't quite know our way around; we don't know what to expect of the local population; we don't feel entirely safe, or at least, we feel that some of the locals may resent us and take advantage of us. We can relate to the 17-year-old in the Nottingham nightclub, to the young English woman alone in New Delhi, to the business traveler having a drink in a New Orleans lounge.

8 Continues to apply Knapp's principle of the bogie rumor.

8   Of course, our worry about being alone in an unfamiliar city is nothing compared to our anxiety about being cut open. Even under the best of circumstances (such as to save our lives), no one looks forward to surgery. The prospect of being drugged, taken to an unknown facility, and having members of a crime ring remove one of our organs without our knowledge or consent—as apparently happened to the various subjects of this rumor—would be our worst nightmare. It's little wonder that this particular "bogie" man has such a powerful grip on our hearts.

9 Applies another aspect of the bogie rumor: fear that we deserve punishment for our poor choices or immoral actions.

9   Our anxiety about the terrible things that may happen to us in a strange place may be heightened because of the fear that our fate is just punishment for the bad things that we have done. In the Nottingham version of the rumor, the victim "had probably picked up a girl and gone home with her" (Dingwall 181). Another version of the story features "an older man picked up by an attractive woman" (Dingwall 182). Still another version of the story is set in Las Vegas, "Sin City, the place where Bad Things Happen to the Unwary (especially the 'unwary' who were seen as deservedly having brought it upon themselves, married men intent upon getting up to some play-for-pay hanky panky)" ("You've Got to Be"). As Dingwall notes of this anxiety about a deserved fate, "[t]he moral is obvious: young people ought to be careful about nightclubs, or more generally, about any activity which takes them out of a circle of family and friends" (183).

In addition to its being a classic bogie rumor, Knapp would suggest that the missing kidney rumor persists because its "striking and aesthetic detail[s]," while false, have the ring of truth and vary from one version to another, making for a "good story" wherever the rumor spreads. Notice that the story includes the particular names of the bar or nightclub and the medical facility; it also summarizes the instructions of the 911 operator to see if there is a tube protruding from the victim's back. (The detail about the bathtub full of ice and the advice to "call 911" was added to the story around 1995.) As Knapp observes, "[n]ames, numbers, and places are typically the most unstable components of any rumor" (30), and so the particular cities in which the kidney operations are alleged to have been performed, as well as the particular locations within those cities, changed as the rumor spread. Another changing detail concerns the chief villains of this story. Knapp notes that rumors adapt themselves to the particular anxieties and prejudices of the group. Many groups hate or distrust foreigners, and so we find different ethnic or racial "villains" named in different cities. In the Nottingham version of the story, the operation is performed by an "Asian surgeon." The English woman's kidney was removed by an Indian doctor. In another version of the story, a Kurdish victim of the kidney operation was lured to Britain "with the promise of a job by a Turkish businessman" ("You've Got to Be").

10 10 Applies second part of Knapp's definition: The "facts" in rumors are constantly changing to make for a "good story."

Third, Knapp observes that successful rumors "ride the tide of current swings in public opinion and interest" (30). From news reports as well as medical and police TV dramas, many people are aware that there is a great demand for organ transplants and that such demand, combined with a short supply, has given rise to a black market for illegally obtained organs. When we combine this awareness with stories that appear to provide convincing detail about the medical procedure involved (the "neat fresh scar," the tube, the name of the hospital), it is not surprising that many people accept this rumor as truth without question. One Internet correspondent, who affirmed that "Yes, this does happen" (her sister-in-law supposedly worked with a woman whose son's neighbor was a victim of the operation), noted that the only "good" thing about this situation was that those who performed the procedure were medically trained, used sterile equipment, made "exact and clean" incisions ("You've Got to Be"), and in general took measures to avoid complications that might lead to the death of the patient.

11 11 Applies the third part of Knapp's definition: Successful rumors are often based on topics of current public interest.

Finally, this rumor gains credibility because, as Virgil noted, rumor "mingle[s] with her word some tidings true." Although no documented case has turned up of a kidney being removed without the victim's knowledge and consent, there have been cases of people lured into selling their kidneys and later filing charges because they came to regret their decisions or were unhappy with the size of their payment ("You've Got to Be").

12 In applying the fourth part of Knapp's definition, writer returns to Virgil (see 1). Knapp and Virgil agree: Rumors may appear credible because they mix truth with fiction.

12

13 Conclusion
establishes
significance of
analysis: Knapp's
theory of rumors
illuminates "the
deeper structure
of rumors."

13   Rumors can destroy reputations, foster distrust of government and other social institutions, and create fear and anxiety about perceived threats from particular groups of outsiders.
Writing in the 1940s about rumors hatched during the war years, Knapp developed a powerful theory that helps us understand the persistence of rumors sixty years later. The rumor of
the missing kidney, like any rumor, functions much like a mirror held up to society: It reveals
anxiety and susceptibility to made-up but seemingly plausible "facts" related to contemporary
social concerns. By helping us to understand the deeper structure of rumors, Knapp's theories can help free us from the "domination" and the "Foul, whispering lips" that Virgil observed
so accurately 2,000 years ago.

Works Cited

Dingwall, Robert. "Contemporary Legends, Rumors, and Collective Behavior: Some
Neglected Resources for Medical Technology." *Sociology of Health and Illness*, vol. 23,
no. 2, 2001, pp. 180–202.

Knapp, Robert H. "A Psychology of Rumor." *Public Opinion Quarterly*, vol. 8, no. 1, 1944,
pp. 22–37.

Virgil. *The Aeneid*. Translated by Theodore C. Williams. *Perseus Digital Library*, www.perseus.
tufts.edu/hopper/text?doc=Perseus:text:1999.02.0054.

"You've Got to Be Kidneying." Snopes.com, 12 Mar. 2008, www.snopes.com/horrors/
robbery/kidney.asp.

Chapter 7
Locating, Mining, and Citing Sources

Source-Based Papers

7.1 Understand the importance of using sources and how to integrate research into the writing process.

Research extends the boundaries of your knowledge and enables you to share your findings with others. The process of locating and working with multiple sources draws on many of the skills we have discussed in this text:

1. Taking notes.
2. Organizing your findings.

3. Summarizing, paraphrasing, and quoting sources accurately and ethically.

4. Critically evaluating sources for their value and relevance to your topic.

5. Synthesizing information and ideas from several sources that best support your own critical viewpoint.

6. Analyzing topics for meaning and significance.

The model explanatory synthesis in Chapter 4, "The 'Idea' of Money" (pp. 117–19), and the model argument synthesis in Chapter 5, "Responding to Bullies" (pp. 142–48), are examples of research papers that fulfill these requirements. The quality of your research and the success of any paper on which it is based are directly related to your success in locating relevant, significant, reliable, and current sources. This chapter will help you in that process.

Where Do We Find Written Research?

Here are just a few of the types of writing that involve research:

Academic Writing

- **Research papers** investigate an issue and incorporate results in a written or oral presentation.

- **Literature reviews** research and review relevant studies and approaches to a particular science, social science, or humanities topic.

- **Experimental reports** describe primary research and often draw on previous studies.

- **Case studies** draw on primary and sometimes secondary research to report on or analyze an individual, a group, or a set of events.

- **Position papers** research approaches to an issue or solutions to a problem in order to formulate and advocate a new approach.

Workplace Writing

- **Reports** in business, science, engineering, social services, medicine

- **Market analyses**

- **Business plans**

- **Environmental impact reports**

- **Legal research:** memoranda of points and authorities

Writing the Research Paper

Here is an overview of the main steps involved in writing research papers. Keep in mind that you will likely return to many of these steps, such as refining your question and your thesis and finding new sources, throughout the process.

Brainstorming a Topic

- **Investigate topics that interest you.**

- **Narrow your topic.** Creating a concept map is one great way to help you narrow your topic down to something manageable.

Developing the Research Question

- **Develop a research question.** Formulate an important open-ended question that you propose to answer through your research.

Locating Sources

- **Conduct preliminary research.** Consult knowledgeable faculty members and friends, academic librarians, reputable Web sites, academic search engines called databases and discovery services at your library, and overviews in recent books and articles. Begin your search with well-chosen keywords and pay attention to other words and phrases that appear often in the titles, abstracts, and records of your results. Some of these words and phrases may give you new leads in expanding or refining your search.

- **Refine your research question.** Based on your preliminary research, brainstorm about your topic and ways to answer your research question. Sharpen your focus, refine your question, and plan the sources you'll need to consult.

- **Conduct focused research.** Consult books and general and discipline-specific databases for articles in periodicals and other material. Conduct interviews and surveys, as necessary.

Mining Sources

- **Develop a working thesis.** Based on your initial research, formulate a working thesis that responds to your research question. This thesis may change over time as you learn more about your topic.

- **Develop a working bibliography.** Keep track of your sources, either on paper or digitally. Include bibliographic information as well as key points about each source, and make it easy to sort and rearrange. Investigate bibliographic management tools like Mendeley, Zotero, and EndNote.

- **Evaluate sources.** Determine the reliability of your sources by comparing the source to similar works on the subject, finding out information about the author, looking up reviews, and using your own critical reading skills. Reviews are especially helpful and can be found in library databases and Amazon.com, among other places. Find out about the author by searching for her or his name or reading the "About the author" statements that often accompany scholarly articles.

- **Take notes from sources.** Paraphrase and summarize important information and ideas from your sources. Copy down important quotations. Note page numbers from sources of this quoted and summarized material. PDF annotation tools can be extremely useful for sources in this format.

- **Develop a working outline and arrange your notes according to your outline.**

Drafting; Citing Sources

- **Write your draft.** Write the preliminary draft of your paper, working from your notes and outline.

- **Avoid plagiarism.** Take care to cite all quoted, paraphrased, and summarized source material. Make sure that your own wording and sentence structure differ from those of your sources.

- **Cite sources.** Use in-text citations and a Works Cited or References list, according to the style you've been assigned to use (e.g., MLA, APA, CSE).

Revising (Global and Local Changes)

- **Revise your draft.** Consider global and local revisions. Check that your thesis still reflects your paper's focus and that you clearly answer your research question. Review topic sentences and paragraph development and logic. Use transitional words and phrases to ensure coherence. Make sure that the paper reads smoothly and clearly from beginning to end.

Editing (Surface Changes)

- **Edit your draft.** Check for style, combining short, choppy sentences and ensuring variety in your sentence structures. Check for grammatical correctness, punctuation, and spelling.

Developing a Topic into a Research Question

7.2   Brainstorm to identify fruitful topics and shape them into a useful research question.

Brainstorming a Topic

Coming up with a workable topic is one of the most challenging parts of research. The possibilities can seem endless and overwhelming, or it may be frustratingly difficult to think of a single one that interests you.

To get started with brainstorming, try creating a concept map of your ideas (see Figure 7.1). The concept map is a helpful way to organize your thinking, and allows you to explore all the different aspects of a topic. Your map doesn't have to look like the example in the figure; it can be a list or arranged in some other fashion that makes sense to you as long as it helps you break down and investigate your topic.

Figure 7.1 Concept Map

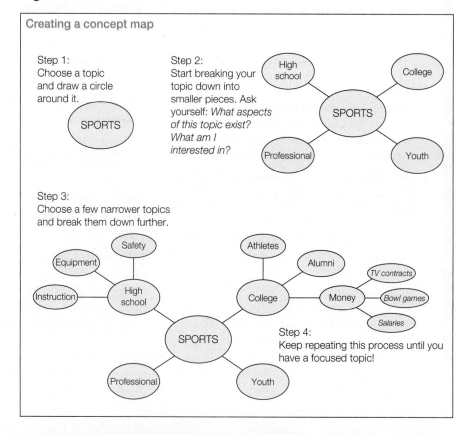

Narrowing Your Topic

If you need help narrowing a broad subject, try one or all of the following strategies:

- Brainstorm different aspects of your topic. Ask yourself, "What pieces of this topic exist?" "How can I break it down into smaller chunks?" "What am I really interested in about this topic?" Using a visual tool like a concept map or a mind map can be very helpful here.

- Do a quick keyword search for your topic in a library search engine or a general search engine like Google. Read a few articles about your topic and see how the authors approach it. You can get a lot of good ideas from other people's work.

- Consult with a reference librarian, your professor, and other members of your class. They may have ideas you haven't considered.

The Research Question

Once you have chosen a focused topic, create a *research question*. A research question is just that: a question that you can answer by doing research. A well-crafted research question helps you focus both your searching process and your paper writing because every source you find and every sentence you write should help you answer your question. In time, the answer you develop to your research question will become the thesis of your paper.

Some research questions are more effective and useful than others. A good research question is **unbiased**, **open-ended**, and **focused**.

Here are three suggestions for devising successful questions.

Unbiased: Pose neutral, unbiased questions that don't already assume a specific answer. Be open to whatever answer the research leads you to.

> **EFFECTIVE** How does the use of computers to compose and produce music influence the creative process?
> **LESS EFFECTIVE** Are musicians who rely on computers to compose and produce music cheating the creative process? [The use of "cheating" suggests that the researcher has already answered the question.]

Open-Ended: Emphasize how, why, and what questions that invite discussion and discovery. Avoid yes-or-no questions or questions that can be answered by a simple phrase or list. A good research question has many possible answers.

> **EFFECTIVE** How do software engineers create algorithms that map patterns in music?
> **LESS EFFECTIVE** Can music be analyzed with mathematics? [The yes-or-no question yields less information and leads to less understanding than the *how* question.]

Focused: Craft specific questions; a broad question can lead to frustration. Starting out somewhat broad and narrowing to something more specific as you learn more is a great strategy.

EFFECTIVE How has the use of computers affected the marketing of popular music in the United States?

LESS EFFECTIVE How has the use of computers affected American popular culture? [Assuming a brief paper, the topic is too broad.]

Exercise 7.1

Constructing Research Questions

Moving from a broad topic or idea to the formulation of **unbiased**, **open-ended**, and **focused** research questions can be challenging. Practice this skill by working with a small group of your classmates to construct research questions about the following topics (or come up with topics of your own). Use the methods above and the concept map in Figure 7.1 to narrow your topics. Write at least one research question that narrows each topic listed; then discuss these topics and questions with the other groups in class.

> Racial or gender stereotypes in television shows
>
> Drug addiction in the U.S. adult population
>
> Global environmental policies
>
> Employment trends in high-technology industries
>
> U.S. energy policy

Getting Started with Research

7.3 Use the resources that can help you in the research process.

Once you have a research question, find out what resources are available to help you answer it. Almost all of your research will be done online. To do an effective search online, it's important to know how search engines work.

Search engines can search all kinds of things. Google searches pages on the Web, for example, while library search engines search databases full of articles, books, and other records. There are many other kinds of search engines, but they all do basically the same thing (see Figure 7.2). For you as a researcher, this means that you must be careful in developing keywords. Always ask what words and phrases you think someone writing on your topic might use.

Consult Knowledgeable People

When you think of research, you may immediately think of search engines and libraries. But don't neglect a key reference: other people. Your *instructor* can probably suggest fruitful areas of research and some useful sources. Try to see your instructor during office hours, however, rather than immediately before or after class, so that you'll have enough time for a productive discussion.

Figure 7.2 How a Search Engine Works

How a search engine works

Search engines seem complicated, but they're actually very simple at their core. Here's what they do:

| cats | Search |

⬇

Displays all matching results with the word "cats" somewhere in them.

| cats Siamese | Search |

⬇

Displays all matching results with both the word "cats" and the word "Siamese" somewhere in them. Both words must be there for the result to be displayed.

| cats OR dogs | Search |

⬇

Displays all matching results with either the word "cats" or "dogs" somewhere in them. Only one of the words must be present in order for the result to be displayed.

| "cat food" | Search |

⬇

Displays all results with the exact phrase "cat food" somewhere in them. The words must be next to one another and in this order.

There are other ways search engines can limit results, but these are the basic ones. Search engines also present their results in varying orders, and many search engines have exclusive ways of showing you results in an order they think will be relevant to you. At the core, though, all search engines simply match words you type in with words that appear in whatever is being searched.

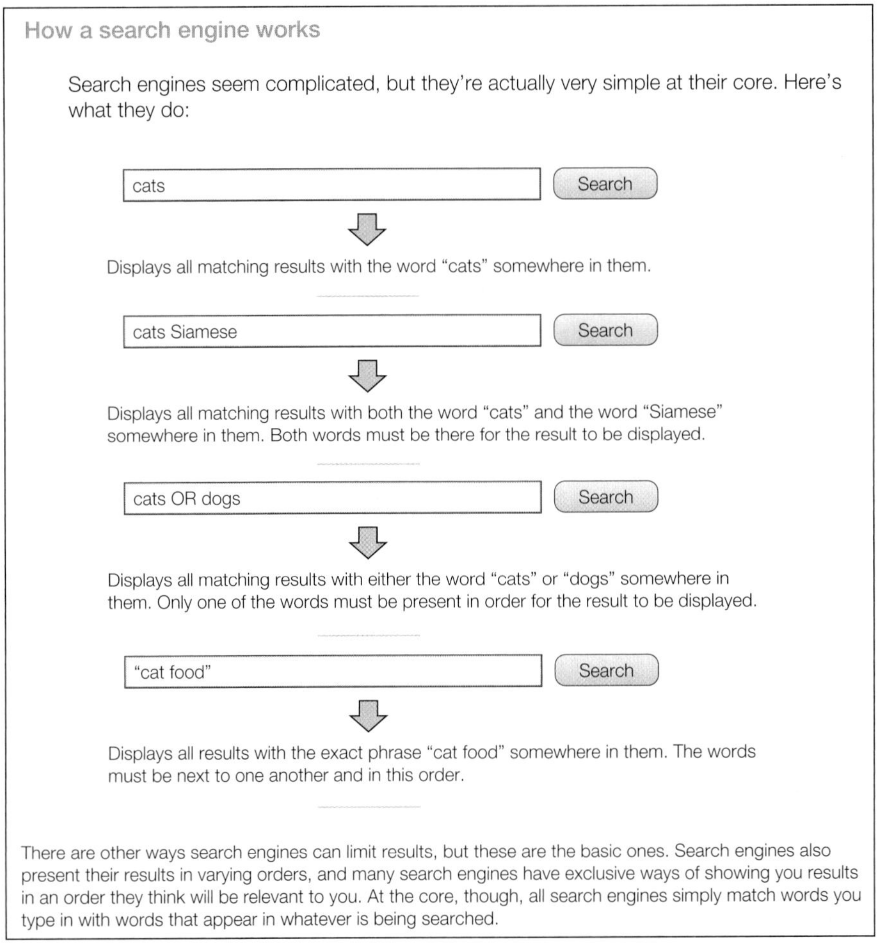

In addition to your instructor, *academic librarians* are among the most helpful people you can find in guiding you through the research process. Your librarian can suggest the following:

- Which reference sources (e.g., databases, specialized encyclopedias, dictionaries, and Web sites) might be fruitful for your particular area of research.
- Search strategies.
- Effective keywords to describe the various facets of your topic.
- Effective Boolean operators, truncation, and string (or phrase) searching (see the section Advanced Searching with Boolean Logic and Truncation in this chapter, pp. 196–97).
- Database results and bibliographies to find ways to extend your search.
- Searches using the library's databases.

Figure 7.3 A Sample Research Guide Page

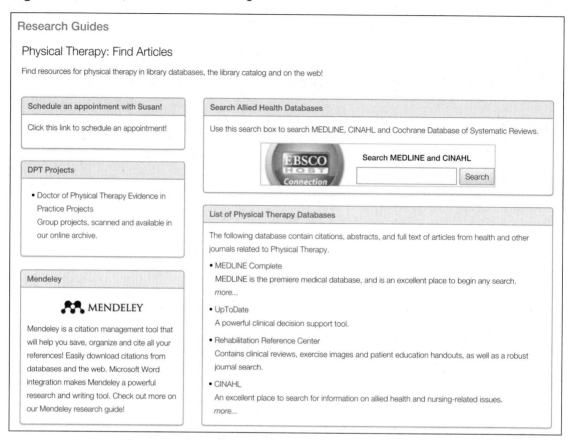

Familiarize Yourself with Your Library's Resources

Knowing how to use the resources of your library is an important part of your research. Among the most helpful guides to these resources are research guides, also known as subject guides or sometimes as libguides. These lists of your library's resources are focused around specific topics. Figure 7.3 shows an example of a library subject guide to physical therapy.

Look for subject guides or research guides on your own academic library's homepage.

Locating Preliminary Sources

7.4   Find and use general sources for preliminary research on a topic.

General sources, also known as reference sources, are a good way to get background information quickly. It's a good idea to use these sources to gather basic information on your topic so that you will be better prepared to do more focused research.

- Ask your instructor or librarian to recommend sources on the subject.
- Use an online database or search engine to explore your topic. (See Figure 7.2, How a Search Engine Works.) Type in different keyword or search term combinations and browse the sites you find for ideas and references to sources you can look up later.
- Scan the Suggestions for Further Reading sections of your textbooks. Ask your librarian for useful reference tools in your subject area.
- Read an encyclopedia or other general article on the subject and use the bibliography following the article to identify other sources.
- Read the introduction to a recent book on the subject and review that book's bibliography to identify more sources.

Encyclopedias

Reading an encyclopedia entry about your subject will give you a basic understanding of the most significant facts and issues. Encyclopedia articles—written by specialists in the respective fields—offer a broad overview that may serve as a launching point to more specialized research in a particular area. An encyclopedia article frequently concludes with a brief *bibliography* describing important books and articles on the subject, which can be another important resource. Encyclopedias have limitations, however:

1. Most professors don't accept encyclopedia articles—and particularly Wikipedia articles (see below)—as legitimate sources for academic papers. Use encyclopedias to familiarize yourself with the subject area and as a springboard for further research.
2. Not all encyclopedias, even ones that appear online, are kept up to date. Check to see if any article you're reading is still current.

Look for encyclopedias in your library's online holdings. They are part of collections like Credo Reference and Gale Virtual Reference Library, or they exist by themselves.

Wikipedia: Let the Buyer Beware

Perhaps the Web's most widely used site for general information is Wikipedia (http://www.wikipedia.org). According to Wikipedia itself, the site contains 30 million articles in 287 languages, 4.3 million of them in the English edition. Wikipedia bills itself as "the free encyclopedia that anyone can edit." This site is thoroughly democratic: Not only can anyone write articles for Wikipedia, anyone can edit most articles others have written.

At the same time and for the same reasons, these articles can be of doubtful accuracy and reliability. Authors of Wikipedia articles need no qualifications to write on their chosen subject, and their entries are subject to no peer review or fact checking. (On numerous occasions, vandals have written or rewritten defamatory articles.)

The bottom line on Wikipedia is that it can be a source of useful information not readily available elsewhere, but *caveat emptor*, or "let the buyer beware." Even if researchers can't always be sure of the reliability of Wikipedia entries, many articles conclude with a section of footnote references and external links that can be very useful for further research.

You will likely find it helpful to consult both *general* and *specialized* encyclopedias, such as the *Grove* encyclopedias of art and architecture, the *McGraw-Hill Encyclopedia of Science and Technology, Digital World Biology,* and Corsini's *Encyclopedia of Psychology.* Specialized encyclopedias restrict themselves to a particular disciplinary area, such as chemistry, law, or film, and are considerably more detailed in their treatment of a subject than are general encyclopedias.

Some library tools, such as Credo Reference and Gale Virtual Reference Library, are collections of online general and specialized encyclopedias.

Exercise 7.2

Exploring Encyclopedias

Locate several specialized encyclopedias within your major or area of interest either in print or online. If your library has an online list of reference sources, look through it. Otherwise, search your library's catalog using a word that describes the broader discipline encompassing the topic (e.g., "film," "chemistry," or "law") along with the word *encyclopedia.*

Search through the encyclopedias and read entries on topics that interest you. Jot down notes describing the kinds of information you find. You might look for important concepts, terms, or the names of important people related to your topic or for events, dates, or definitions. These can make up the sets of words (keywords) that you subsequently take to library search engines.

In addition, if you are in the library building instead of online, browse around the area where you found a particularly useful encyclopedia or book. Because of the way that books are arranged in the library, you'll be able to find books on similar topics near each other. For example, the books on drug abuse should be clustered near each other. Browsing a physical location can be a powerful tool for finding unexpectedly useful material.

Biographical Sources

Your preliminary research may prompt you to look up information on particular people. In these cases, consult biographical sources, which can be classified in several ways: by person (living or dead), geography, subject area, gender, race, or historical period.

Here are examples of biographical sources, almost all of which are available online for free or through your library's collections:

American National Biography Online
Biography and Genealogy Master Index

Biography in Context (a general biographical reference that incorporates numerous, previously separate specialized biographical guides)

Biology Reference Bank

Black Americans in Congress, 1870–2007 (freely available online at history.house.gov)

Contemporary Authors

Current Biography

Dictionary of Literary Biography

Notable American Women: A Biographical Dictionary

Oxford Dictionary of National Biography

Who's Who in America

Who's Who in the Arab World

Statistical Sources

You may want to consult sources with statistics and demographics. One useful source is USA.gov. This site is the federal government's homepage, but it has a search engine that searches government information at the federal, state, and local level in the United States. By searching for your topic and the word *statistics,* you will often be able to find some of the figures the government keeps. Here are a few other statistical sources:

CQ Almanac (formerly Congressional Quarterly Almanac) is available both in print and online versions.

State of the World's Children (published by UNICEF).

The U.S. Census Web site (http://factfinder.census.gov) has detailed information about the people who live in locations all around the country (see Figure 7.4).

In Figure 7.4, note the two columns comparing the city of Hartford to the rest of the state, as well as the link to more detailed information.

Figure 7.4 A Sample Page from the U.S. Census Web Site

Connecticut counties— selection map	Connecticut cities— place search	▶ More Connecticut data sets
Select a county ▾ Go	Select a city ▾ Go	

Hartford (city), Connecticut

Want more? Browse data sets for Hartford (city)

People QuickFacts	Hartford	Connecticut
ⓘ Population, 2014 estimate	124,705	3,596,677
ⓘ Population, 2010 (April 1) estimates base	124,775	3,574,096
ⓘ Population, percent change — April 1, 2010 to July 1, 2014	–0.1%	0.6%
ⓘ Population, 2010	124,775	3,574,097
ⓘ Persons under 5 years, percent, 2010	7.6%	5.7%
ⓘ Persons under 18 years, percent, 2010	25.8%	22.9%
ⓘ Persons 65 years and over, percent, 2010	8.9%	14.2%

Overviews and Bibliographies

If your professor or a bibliographic source directs you to an important recent book on your topic, skim the introductory (and possibly concluding) material, along with the table of contents, for an overview of key issues.

Check also for a bibliography, also known as Works Cited or a References list. These lists are extremely valuable resources for locating material for research. For example, Robert Dallek's 2003 book *An Unfinished Life: John Fitzgerald Kennedy, 1917–1963,* includes a seven-page bibliography of sources on President Kennedy's life and times.

Conducting Focused Research

7.5   Conduct focused research on a topic and evaluate your sources.

Once you have completed preliminary research, your objective becomes learning as much as you can about your topic so that you can provide the best possible answer to your research question.

Types of Sources

Sources for focused research often fall into two broad categories: *primary* and *secondary*.

Primary Sources
- Original materials such as experiments, observations, surveys, interviews, diaries, first-person accounts, and so on.

Secondary Sources
- Sources that analyze, synthesize, and/or collect other primary or secondary sources. Much of the work you'll create in college is secondary.

All primary and secondary work appears in one of several different kinds of format. These formats are becoming less and less defined as information migrates online, but we can still identify some basic types of sources that you might encounter. The chart in Figure 7.5 will help you determine which types you might want to use.

BOOKS   Books, both popular and academic, are useful for providing both breadth and depth of coverage of a subject. Because they are generally published at least a year or two after the events treated, they also tend to provide the critical distance that is sometimes missing from articles. Conversely, this delay in coverage means that the information in books won't be as current as the information you find in periodicals. Any piece of writing, books included, may be inaccurate, outdated, or biased.

Book Reviews   One way to determine the reliability and credibility of a book you may want to use is to look up the reviews published in resources such as

Figure 7.5 Types of Sources Used for Focused Research

Type	Books	Academic/Scholarly material (journals)	News/Magazine sources	General Web sources
Length	Long, covers material in depth	Medium length	Short	Varied, mostly short
Editing	Usually goes through a thorough editing process	Reviewed by other scholars and experts for methodology and accuracy	Usually given a quick edit and fact-checked	Varied, but often not edited or reviewed at all
Authors	Usually an expert, but this can vary depending on the book	An expert with detailed specialized knowledge, often either a university professor or someone working at a high level in the field	Journalists	Anyone
Currency	Books can take many years to write, edit, develop, and publish	Takes around a year and a half between when a study is performed and when the article is published	Articles can appear within an hour of an event happening	Varied, often immediate
Subject	Often broad	Usually very specific, often having to do with an experiment or study	Can be either broad or somewhat specific	Varied
Audience	Depends on the book	Other experts, people who work in the field, and students	General public	General public
Bias	Varied	Should be objective	Often objective, with the exception of opinion pieces	Varied, often biased

Publishers Weekly, Library Journal, or the *New York Times Book Review.* You can also look at book reviews either in the online *Book Review Digest* or on Amazon. com.

If a book receives bad reviews, you don't necessarily have to avoid it. The book may still have something useful to offer, and the review itself may be unreliable. But you should take negative reactions into account when using that book as a source.

NEWSPAPERS, MAGAZINES, AND JOURNALS Because many more news and magazine articles than books are published every year, you are likely, depending on the subject, to find more information in periodicals than in books. By their nature, recent news and magazine articles are more current than books. For example, the best way to find out about a political party's position on Social Security reform is to look for current articles in magazines and newspapers. But these articles may have less critical distance than books and, like books, they may become dated, to be superseded by more recent articles.

Newspapers News stories, feature stories, and editorials (even letters to the editor) may be important sources of information. Your college library may have online access to the *New York Times* and other important newspapers such as the *Washington Post,* the *Los Angeles Times,* the *Chicago Tribune,* the *Wall Street Journal,* and the *Christian Science Monitor,* as well as collections of newspapers like those in Lexis-Nexis and EBSCO Newspaper Source.

Magazines General magazines such as *The Atlantic,* the *New Republic,* and the *Nation* are intended for nonspecialists. Their articles, which tend to be highly readable, may be written by staff writers, freelancers, or specialists. But they usually don't provide citations or other indications of sources, so they're of limited usefulness for scholarly research. Some magazines are very specialized and have specific themes, like politics, cars, sports, and more.

academic journal articles

Specialized, highly specific scholarly articles written by experts in a certain field.

Journals (Scholarly Material)   Some professors expect at least some of your research to be based on articles in specialized sources called scholarly or academic journals. So instead of (or in addition to) relying on an article from *Psychology Today* (considered a magazine even though its subject is somewhat specialized) for an account of the effects of crack cocaine on mental functioning, you might also rely on an article from the *Journal of Abnormal Psychology*. If you are writing a paper on the satirist Jonathan Swift, in addition to a recent reference to him that may have appeared in *The New Yorker*, you may need to locate a relevant article in *Eighteenth-Century Studies*.

Articles in such journals are normally written by specialists and professionals in the field rather than by staff writers or freelancers, and the authors will assume that their readers already understand the basic facts and issues concerning the subject. Other characteristics of scholarly journals:

- They tend to be heavily researched, as indicated by their numerous notes and references.
- They are generally published by university presses or large academic publishers.
- Most of the authors are university professors or experts working in the field.
- The articles, which have a serious, formal, and scholarly tone (and so are less reader-friendly than those in general magazines), are generally peer-reviewed by other scholars in the field.

Most library databases such as Academic Search Premier or JSTOR have some academic journal articles in them. To be sure that you are finding these articles, look for a checkbox or option that says "peer-reviewed" or "academic

Figure 7.6 Reading Journal Articles

Reading and Understanding an Academic Journal Article	
Journal articles often are broken down into specific pieces. Understanding what these pieces do will help you understand the article.	
Abstract	A basic summary of the article that appears right at the beginning. Explains the major points.
Introduction	Provides context for what the authors want to do, and often includes a review of other work that has been done on this topic in the past.
Methods	Describes what the authors plan to do to investigate their topic. This could be an experiment, thorough research into others' work, interviews, or something else.
Results	A report on what happened when the authors investigated their topic.
Discussion	This section describes what the authors think their results mean. This is usually the most important section of the article.
References	A list of all the other works the authors used to help them write this article.

journals." *A cautionary note:* Students too often think that they can simply browse their way to enough sources to write their papers. But this would be a hit-or-miss approach. To be a successful (more purposeful and systematic) browser, try instead to use the article databases in your discipline to identify one or two or twelve potentially interesting sources; then search within those issues of journals to see if anything else seems interesting.

Exercise 7.3

Exploring Academic Journals

Search online for academic journal articles. Go to your library's online resources and access a database in your area of study. Enter a simple keyword and then limit your search to academic journal articles by checking "peer reviewed" or "academic journals." If you aren't sure how to do this, ask a librarian or someone you may know who has done this sort of research before.

Look at an academic article and try to figure out what the main idea is. (See Figure 7.6.) What is the researcher studying? Why? Did she or he do an experiment? What was it? What did the researcher find out? Answering these questions will help you begin to understand how advanced academic research is done.

For Best Results, Plan Your Searches

You'll find more—and more relevant—sources on Internet search engines and library databases if you plan your search strategies carefully. Here are some suggestions:

1. **Identify multiple keywords:** Write down your topic and/or your research question, and then brainstorm synonyms and related terms for the words in that topic or research question.
   Sample topic: Political activism on college campuses
   Sample research question: What kinds of political activism are college students involved in today?

Keywords: Political activism, college students
Synonyms and related terms: politics, voting, political organizations, protests, political issues, universities, colleges, campus politics

2. **Conduct searches using different combinations of synonyms and related terms.**

3. **Find new terms in the sources you locate and search with them.**

4. **Use quotation marks around words you want to search as a phrase: "political activism"**

5. **Conduct advanced searches using Boolean operators and truncation.**

Finding Material for Focused Research

Much of the material you will need for focused research is hidden from general search engines like Google. You will need to use library search engines, databases, and other specialized tools in order to find the most useful sources.

database

An organized, searchable collection of information, often containing academic articles and records.

DATABASES   One of the major ways to do focused research online is through a database. Databases are massive, searchable collections of all kinds of material in all kinds of formats. A database may contain academic articles, magazine and newspaper articles, streaming videos, music files, online books, and more. Databases also contain detailed records that describe the material they contain.

Some databases are available online for free. One example is Google Scholar, which is a huge repository of citations of academic, scholarly articles and books. Google Scholar also sometimes contains links to the full text of articles and sometimes can be set up to work with your library's holdings.

However, most databases are available only through your college or university library. They usually contain information and material that are not available to the general public—you usually must be a student at a college to gain access to its resources online.

There are quite a few types of databases to search through. Your library may offer access to dozens or even hundreds of general and subject-specific databases. A few examples are described below.

General Databases   Some databases have a wide variety of material on all different subjects. These are often good places to begin your research.

Academic Search Complete (also Academic Search Elite or Academic Search Premier)

Academic OneFile

JSTOR (digital library of academic journals, books, and primary sources)

Opposing Viewpoints in Context (current events)

Periodicals Index Online

Project Muse (humanities and social science articles from nonprofit publishers)

ProQuest Research Library

Reader's Guide Retrospective (covers 1890–1982)

Subject-Specific Databases   Many other databases are focused on specific subject areas. In addition to this list, you can ask your librarians which databases might be the best to search, or explore research guides and subject guides.

Anthropology: Anthropology Plus

Art: Art Full Text

Art Index Retrospective

Athletics: SportDiscus

Biography: Biography in Context

Biology: Biosis

Biological Science Database

Business: ABI/Inform

Business Source Complete

EconLit

Classics: Le Année Philologique

Education: ERIC

English and Other Literatures: MLA International Bibliography

History: America: History and Life

Historical Abstracts

Law: LexisNexis

WestLaw

Medicine: MEDLINE

PubMed

Music: Music Index Online

RILM Abstracts of Music Literature

News: LexisNexis

Access World News

New York Times

Political Science: PAIS International

Worldwide Political Science Abstracts (political science, international relations, law, public administration/policy)

ProQuest Congressional (public policy, law, social, economic issues)

Psychology: PsycINFO and PsycARTICLES (psychology, behavioral sciences, and mental health)

Religion: ATLA

Sciences (General): ScienceDirect

Sociology: Sociological Abstracts

DISCOVERY SERVICES   More and more libraries are now using discovery services. These tools may have a brand name like Primo or Encore, a catchy name like the University of Iowa's Smart Search, or simply be a search box inviting you to search "everything." Discovery services operate by searching several databases at the same time. The search usually also includes the library's online catalog, online journals, and any e-books that the library may have.

> **discovery service**
>
> A library search engine that searches many databases and the library catalog at once.

A discovery service can be a powerful tool because it can locate a vast number of resources quickly and highlight the variety of tools at your fingertips. In addition, it offers a friendly interface that you are probably used to seeing in other contexts.

As with all tools, however, using a discovery service has its pros and cons. (See Figure 7.7.) In some cases, you may find exactly what you are looking for via a discovery service. In other instances, the discovery tool may serve as a gateway, giving you ideas for terms to use for effective searching and steering you toward databases where you can do more targeted searches.

THE OPEN WEB   While a great deal of content is available only through library sources, enormous amounts of content can still be found on the open, freely

Figure 7.7 Discovery Services

Pros and Cons of Discovery Services	
Pros	**Cons**
Searches many different resources at the same time	Search can be slow sometimes
Includes books, journal articles, e-books, films, and more	The amount and variety of information can sometimes be confusing and overwhelming
Simple, unified interface that makes searching and finding easy	Individual databases often have specific search options like "age" and "type of study" that the discovery service lacks
Great for beginning research	Not so great for more advanced, in-depth research

available Web. The open Web offers print, graphic, and video content that can be enormously helpful to your research. Keep in mind, however, that search engines like Google and Bing are only tools and that your own judgment in devising a precise search query determines how useful these tools will be to your inquiries.

Two free online tools can help you conduct focused research: Google Scholar and USA.gov.

Google Scholar   Google Scholar is a massive collection of citations, or basic descriptive information, to academic articles and books.

Google Scholar is easy to search and to understand, and contains large amounts of information. Using Google Scholar can make academic research feel a lot less intimidating and much more familiar.

A cautionary note: The links on Google Scholar often go to publishers' sites, where you will be asked to pay for the article you want. However, your college library may have this material available in its collection—try doing a search for it there. If the library doesn't have it, a librarian will likely be able to order it through a service called interlibrary loan. Ask librarians at your institution how this works.

Many libraries also now put tools in place to associate Google Scholar with library holdings. To find out if your library offers this service, go to the settings and then click on Library Links. (See Figure 7.8.) Search for your institution, and add it if it's there. Full text links to articles that your library holds will now appear.

USA.gov   The federal government's homepage features a powerful search engine. Search this site for information from government agencies at the federal, state, and local level.

You will find statistics, in-depth government reports, useful background information, and much more by searching this site.

Figure 7.8 Adding Library Links to Google Scholar

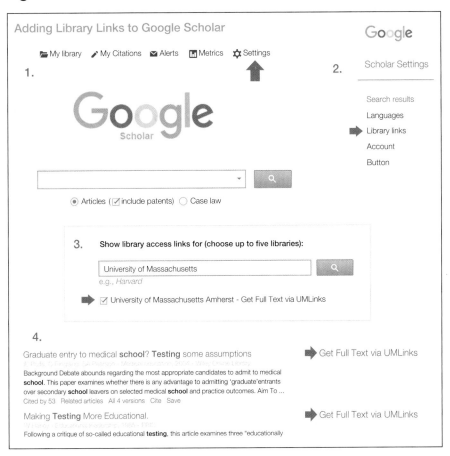

Focused Research: Constructing Effective Search Queries

Search strategies for focused research database systems in use today are still pretty dumb—that is, they are literal. They will return only the specific information requested and nothing more, however closely related. If we search for sources on AIDS, we will get lots on AIDS, but we will miss those items in the database that specify, instead, HIV or "acquired immune deficiency syndrome" or other ways of saying, basically, AIDS.

So you need to start the research process by thinking of the variety of ways an experienced researcher writing on your topic might refer to the different facets of your topic. You may be looking for articles on *college* students, but a scholar might write about *university* students. We may be looking for articles on *children*, but a scholar might write about *boys* OR *girls* OR *adolescents*.

A well-constructed query will return a list of useful results. Refer again to Figure 7.2 (How a Search Engine Works) to start thinking about how to craft good keywords, then try the following tips.

1. **Focus on a noun: a person, place, or item.** The most important terms in your query should be *objects*—that is, tangible items. The item (or person

or place) you want to learn more about is the center of your search, your subject.

2. **Narrow the search with another noun or a modifier.** When you qualify your search terms by combining them in meaningful ways, searches become more pointed and useful because the search engine will be trying to match all the words you type in. You could create a more productive search by narrowing the keyword "computers" to "computers music" or "computers music culture." See the section about searching with Boolean logic (pp. 196–97) for more information on this topic.

3. **Try substituting words if the search is not working.** When a search does not yield useful information, change your search terms. Think of synonyms for keywords in your query. For non-academic topics, you might use a thesaurus to locate synonyms. For example, you might substitute "cardiac" for "heart" and "aircraft" for "plane."

4. ***Re-search.*** Librarians sometimes describe the process of library research as one of re-search. When reading material on your topic, note any unique vocabulary and particular events, people, or results associated with your topic. Try your search again using these topics.

5. **Use "advanced" features to refine your search.** Search engines typically provide a "re-fine" function—sometimes called an "advanced" or "power" search tool—that allows you to narrow a search by date, type of publication, and type of Web site. You might instruct the engine to search only a specific site, for instance. You can also search in fields such as title, author, industry code, reviews, and so on.

Advanced Searching with Boolean Logic and Truncation

If you really want to make the most of your search, it's useful to understand Boolean logic and truncation. All search engines work according to Boolean logic, which tells the search engine what to do with the terms you enter.

The words AND, OR, and NOT are used in Boolean logic to combine search terms and get more precise results than using keywords alone.

AND: Connecting keywords with AND narrows a search by retrieving only those sources that contain *both* keywords:

activism AND students

Note: Almost all search engines automatically add an invisible AND between terms.

OR: Connecting keywords with OR broadens a search by retrieving all sources that contain at least one of the search terms. This operator is useful when you have a topic or a keyword that has a number of synonyms. Linking synonyms with OR will lead you to the widest array of sources:

activism OR protests OR voting OR campus politics OR college OR university OR campus OR students

AND and **OR:** You can use these terms in combination, by putting the OR phrase in parentheses:

(political activism OR protests) AND (college OR university)

NOT: Connecting keywords with NOT (or, in some cases, AND NOT) narrows a search by excluding certain terms. If you want to focus on a very specific topic, NOT can be used to limit what the search engine retrieves; however, this operator should be used carefully because it can cause you to miss sources that may actually be relevant:

> college students NOT high school
> political activism NOT voting

In addition to Boolean operators, researchers use truncation—often an asterisk (*), sometimes a question mark (?)—immediately following the search term (no space) as a so-called wild card. A search for the word *children* will identify items in which the title or abstract or subject tags include the word *children*, but you will not see items that instead refer to *childhood* or to the *child*. A truncated search for "child*" will yield results in which any variation of *child* appears: *child, childhood, childish, childlike, children,* and so on.

Exercise 7.4

Exploring Online Sources

Go online and access one of the search engines or academic or professional databases discussed in this chapter. Select a topic or research question that interests you. Review the section Advanced Searching with Boolean Logic and Truncation, and try different combinations of keywords and Boolean operators to see what sources you can find for your topic. Jot down notes describing the kinds of sources you find and which terms seem to yield the best results.

Interviews and Surveys

Depending on the subject of your paper, you may want to *interview* your professors, your fellow students, or other individuals knowledgeable about your subject. In addition, or as an alternative, you may wish to conduct *surveys* via

---

Guidelines for Conducting Interviews

- Become knowledgeable about the subject before the interview so that you can ask intelligent questions. Prepare most of your questions beforehand.

- Ask open-ended questions designed to elicit meaningful responses rather than forced-choice questions that can be answered with a word or two. Avoid leading questions that presume a particular answer. For example, instead of asking, "Do you think that male managers should be more sensitive to women's concerns for equal pay in the workplace?" ask, "To what extent do you see evidence that male managers are insufficiently sensitive to women's concerns for equal pay in the workplace?"

- Ask follow-up questions to elicit additional insights or details.

- If you record the interview, get your subject's permission, preferably in writing.

questionnaires. When well prepared and insightfully interpreted, such tools can produce valuable information about the ideas or preferences of a group of people.

Guidelines for Conducting Surveys and Designing Questionnaires

- Determine your *purpose* in conducting the survey: what kind of *information* you seek and *whom* (i.e., what subgroup of the population) you intend to survey.

- Decide whether you want to collect information on the spot or have people send their responses back to you. (You will get fewer responses if they are sent back to you, but those you do get will likely be more complete than surveys conducted on the spot.)

- Devise and word questions carefully so that they (1) are understandable and (2) don't reflect your own biases. For example, for a survey on attitudes toward capital punishment, if you ask, "Do you believe that the state should endorse legalized murder?" you've loaded the question to influence people to answer in the negative.

- Devise short-answer or multiple-choice questions; open-ended questions encourage responses that are difficult to quantify. (You may want to leave space, however, for additional comments.) Conversely, yes-or-no responses or rankings on a five-point scale are easy to quantify.

- It may be useful to break out the responses by as many meaningful categories as possible—for example, gender, age, ethnicity, religion, education, geographic locality, profession, and income.

Evaluating Sources

Few sources are perfect. Many have significant flaws that make them unusable for your research. Some might be biased or have incorrect information, while others may be outdated or incomplete. To write the best possible paper, you'll need to use reliable sources—so always make sure to evaluate every source you find.

Guidelines for Evaluating Sources

- **Skim the source.** With a book, look over the table of contents, the introduction and conclusion, and the index; zero in on passages that your initial survey suggests are important. With an article, skim the introduction, headings, and conclusion.

- **Be alert for references** in your sources to other important sources, particularly to sources that several authors treat as important.

- **Find recent sources.** Other things being equal, the *more recent* the source, the better. Recent work usually incorporates or refers to important earlier work.

- **Look for reviews.** If you're considering making multiple references to a book, look up the reviews in the *Book Review Digest* or via articles found using online databases. Also, check the author's credentials in a source such as *Contemporary Authors* or *Current Biography Illustrated*. If an author is not listed in either of these sources, you may choose to do a Web search for the author and look for online résumés, online portfolios, or references to the author's work.

EVALUATING WEB SOURCES   The Web makes it possible for people at home, work, or school to gain access to corporate, government, and personal Web sites. Academic researchers are obligated to read Web-based material just as critically as they read print-based material. Chapter 2, "Critical Reading and Critique," offers criteria for evaluating the quality and reliability of information and ideas in *any* source (pp. 65–81). Web sources are no exception, particularly self-published pages that are not subject to editorial review.

Reference librarians Jan Alexander and Marsha Tate have offered useful guidelines for helping researchers assess Web sources. First, they point out, it's important to determine what *type* of Web page you are dealing with. Web pages generally fall into one of five types, each with a different purpose:

1. Business/marketing
2. Reference/information
3. News
4. Advocacy of a particular point of view or program
5. Personal page

The purpose of a Web site—to sell, persuade, entertain—has a direct bearing on the objectivity and reliability of the information presented. When evaluating a site and determining its reliability for use in a research project, apply the same general criteria that you apply to print sources: (1) accuracy, (2) authority, (3) objectivity, (4) currency, (5) coverage. You might pose the following questions in an effort to assess reliability:

- What is the likelihood that the information has been checked by anyone other than the author?
- What are the author's qualifications to write on the subject?
- What is the reputation of the publisher?
- Who is the author?
- What are the biases—stated or unstated—of the site?

Exercise 7.5

Practice Evaluating Web Sources

To practice applying the evaluation criteria discussed in the section on Web sources, go to an open Web search engine like Google and look for sources addressing a topic of interest to you (perhaps after completing Exercise 7.1). Regarding that topic, try to locate one source representing each of the five types of Web pages (business/marketing, reference/information, news, advocacy, and personal). Print the homepage of each source and bring the copies to class. In small groups, look over the sites each student found and make notes on each example's (1) accuracy, (2) authority, (3) objectivity, (4) currency, and (5) coverage.

- How current is the site?

- Which topics are included (and not included) in the site? To what extent are the topics covered in depth?

Pose these questions and determine, as you would for any non-Web source, the Web site's reliability and suitability for your research project.

Mining Sources

7.6 Compile a working bibliography and arrange your notes in an outline.

Having located your sources (or at least having begun the process), proceed to mining them—that is, extracting from them information and ideas that you can use in your paper. Mining sources involves three important tasks:

- Taking notes on your sources and evaluating them for reliability and relevance.

- Compiling a working bibliography to keep track of what information you have and how it relates to your research question.

- Developing some kind of outline—formal or informal—that allows you to see how you might subdivide and organize your discussion and at which points you might draw on relevant sources.

Critical Reading for Research

- **Use all the critical reading tips we've suggested** in Chapters 1 and 2.

- **Read for relationships to your research question.** How does the source help you formulate, clarify, and answer your research question?

- **Read for relationships among sources.** How does each source illustrate, support, expand upon, contradict, or offer an alternative perspective to those of your other sources?

- **Consider the relationship between your source's form and content.** How does the form of the source—specialized encyclopedia, book, article in a popular magazine, article in a professional journal—affect its content, the manner in which that content is presented, and its relationship to other sources?

- **Pay special attention to the legitimacy of Internet sources.** Consider how the content and validity of the information on the Web page may be affected by the purpose of the site. Assess Web-based information for its (1) accuracy, (2) authority, (3) objectivity, (4) currency, and (5) coverage.

The Working Bibliography

As you conduct your research, keep a working bibliography, a record of bibliographic information on all the sources you're likely to use in preparing the paper. If you are careful to record *full* bibliographic information—author(s), title, publisher, and so on—you'll spare yourself the frustration of hunting for it during the composition of your paper.

In addition to a working bibliography, it's a good idea to keep a research log. As you search, note which database you are searching and which words you use in each search. Note significant sources that you find (your working bibliography), but also note new words or phrases or concepts that you might use on subsequent searches. By keeping a running research log, you can go back to previously searched databases with new search strategies—without risking running the same search over and over again.

Online catalogs and databases make it easy to copy and paste your sources' (or potential sources') bibliographic information into a document or to e-mail citations to yourself for cutting and pasting later. Note, also, that certain software programs allow you to create sortable, searchable digital records. A more traditional but still very efficient way to compile bibliographic information is on 3″ × 5″ cards. Using any of these methods, you can easily add, delete, and rearrange individual bibliographic records as your research progresses. No matter how you keep your information, be sure to record the following:

- Author or editor (last name first) and, if relevant, the translator
- Title (and subtitle) of the book or article
- Publisher and place of publication (if a book) or the title of the periodical
- Date and/or year of publication; if a periodical, volume and issue number
- Date you accessed the source (if you are working with a Web site)
- Edition number of a book beyond its first edition
- Inclusive page numbers (if an article)
- Specific page number of a quotation or other special material you might paraphrase

You'll also find it helpful to include this additional information:

- Brief description of the source to help you recall it later in the research process
- Library call number or the URL so that you can readily return to the source
- Code number, which you can use as a shorthand reference to the source in your notes (see the sample note records below)

Here's an example of a working bibliography record:

> Gorham, Eric B. *National Service, Political Socialization, and Political Education*. SUNY P, 1992.
>
> Argues that the language government uses to promote national service programs betrays an effort to "reproduce a postindustrial, capitalist economy in the name of good citizenship." Chap. 1 provides a historical survey of national service.

Here's an example of a working bibliography record for an article:

> Gergen, David. "A Time to Heed the Call." *U.S. News & World Report*, 24 Dec. 2001, pp. 60–61.
>
> Argues that, in the wake of the surge of patriotism that followed the September 11 terrorist attacks, the government should encourage citizens to participate in community and national service. Supports the McCain-Bayh bill.

Here's an example of a working bibliography record for an online source:

> Bureau of Labor Statistics. "Table 1: Volunteers by Selected Characteristics, September 2009." 27 Jan. 2010, www.bls.gov/news.release/volun.t01.htm.
>
> Provides statistical data on volunteerism in the United States.

Some instructors may ask you to prepare—either in addition to or instead of a research paper—an annotated bibliography, which is a list of relevant works on a subject, with the contents of each work briefly described or assessed. The sample bibliography records above could become the basis for three entries in an annotated bibliography on national service. Annotations differ from abstracts because annotations aren't comprehensive summaries; rather, they indicate how the items may be useful to the researcher.

Note Taking

People have their favorite ways of note taking. Some use legal pads, note cards, or spiral notebooks; others type notes into a laptop or tablet computer, perhaps using a notes app, bibliographic management software, or an article annotation tool. Whatever your preferred approach, consider including the following information along with the note:

- Topic or subtopic label corresponding to your outline (see below)
- Code number corresponding to the number assigned to the source in the working bibliography
- Page reference at the end of the note

Here's a sample note record for the table "Volunteers by Selected Characteristics, September 2009" from the Bureau of Labor Statistics (see the bibliographic record above):

> Pervasiveness of Volunteerism (I)   7
>
> Shows that 26.8 percent of Americans age 16 and older, 63.3 million in all, devote time to community service.

Here's a note record for the periodical article by Gergen (see the bibliography note above):

> Beneficial Paid Volunteer Programs (II)   12
>
> Says that both the community and the individual benefit from voluntary service programs. Cites Teach for America, Alumni of City Year, Peace Corps as programs in which participants receive small stipends and important benefits (60). "Voluntary service when young often changes people for life. They learn to give their fair share." (60)

Both note records are headed by a topic label followed by the tentative location (indicated by a Roman numeral) in the paper outline where the information may be used. The number at the upper right corresponds to the number you assigned to the source in your bibliography note. The note in the first record uses *summary.* The note in the second record uses *summary* (sentence 1), *paraphrase* (sentence 2), and *quotation* (sentence 3). Notice the inclusion of page references, which the writer will reference in the paper itself if the note is used. For hints on when to choose summary, paraphrase, and quotation, see Chapter 1.

Remember: Use quotation marks to distinguish between your language and the source author's language. Cite page references when you note an author's exact language *or* ideas. If you're careful to keep the distinctions between your language and that of authors clear, you'll avoid plagiarizing your sources. See the discussion of plagiarism in Chapter 1 on pages 63–64 and later in this chapter for more details.

BIBLIOGRAPHIC MANAGEMENT TOOLS   One great way to keep a working bibliography is by using bibliographic management software. Your college or university may subscribe to products like RefWorks or EndNote, or you may decide to use free tools like Mendeley or Zotero. These tools can help you save basic information about material you're working with, save and annotate (i.e., take notes on) PDFs of articles, and even insert citations into your work.

Check with your library or academic support services to see what tools are available for you. Or you can start by going to Mendeley's or Zotero's Web sites and downloading these free programs.

Arranging Your Notes: The Outline

You won't use all the notes you take during the research process. Instead, you'll need to do some selecting, which requires you to distinguish more important from less important (and unimportant) material. Use your original working thesis (see Chapter 3, pp. 88–92 on writing thesis statements) or use a new thesis that you have developed during the course of data gathering and invention. Working with your thesis, begin constructing a preliminary outline of your paper. This outline will indicate which elements of the topic you intend to discuss and in what order. You can then arrange relevant notes accordingly and remove or flag notes that will not likely find their way into the paper.

Some people prefer not to develop an outline until they have more or less completed their research. At that point they look over their notes, consider the relationships among the various pieces of evidence, possibly arrange notes or cards into separate piles, and then develop an outline based on their perceptions and insights about the material. Subsequently, they rearrange and code the notes to conform to their outline—an informal outline indicating just the main sections of the paper and possibly one level below that.

The model paper on responding to bullies (see Chapter 5, pp. 142–48) could be informally outlined as follows:

> **Introduction:** Examples of bullying (physical and cyber), who is bullied, anti-bullying laws
>
> **Thesis:** A blend of local, ground-up strategies and state-mandated programs and laws promises to be the best approach to dealing with bullying in American schools.
>
> **Problems with antibullying laws:** Rushed, some elements unconstitutional, some laws ignore standard definitions, often ineffective
>
> **Alternate solution needed:** Think local
>
> **Limits of local solutions:** Flaws, difficulty evaluating
>
> **Conclusion**

Such an outline will help you organize your research and should not be an unduly restrictive guide for your writing.

The formal outline is a multilevel plan with Roman and Arabic numerals and uppercase and lowercase lettered subheadings that can provide a useful blueprint for composition as well as a guide to revision. See page 141 in Chapter 5 for a formal outline of the paper on bullying. Here is one section of that outline. Compare its level of detail with the level of detail in the informal outline immediately above:

> **III.** An alternate solution to the problem of bullying
> **A.** Rationale and blueprint for alternate approach
> **B.** A local from-the-ground-up solution
>   **1.** Emily Bazelon
>   **2.** Lee Hirsch and Cynthia Lowen
>   **3.** Philip Rodkin

Outlining your draft after you have written it may help you discern structural problems: illogical sequences of material, confusing relationships between ideas, poor unity or coherence, or unevenly developed content.

Instructors may require that a formal outline accompany the finished research paper. Formal outlines are generally of two types: topic outlines and sentence outlines. In the topic outline, headings and subheadings are words or phrases. In the sentence outline, each heading and subheading is a complete sentence. Both topic and sentence outlines are typically preceded by the thesis.

Research and Plagiarism

7.7 Employ strategies to avoid the pressures that can lead to plagiarism.

All too easily, research can lead to plagiarism. See pages 63–64 in Chapter 1 for a definition and examples of plagiarism. The discussion here will suggest ways of avoiding plagiarism.

None of the situations that lead to plagiarism discussed below assumes that the plagiarist is a bad person. All kinds of pressures can cause someone to plagiarize. By understanding those pressures, you may come to recognize them and take corrective action before plagiarism seems like a reasonable option.

Time Management and Plagiarism

The problem: You do not allocate time well and face crushing deadlines. Work, sports, and family responsibilities are the kinds of commitments that can squeeze the time needed to conduct research and write.

A solution: Improve your time management skills. Consider taking four steps:

1. Begin the paper on the day it is assigned. Work on the paper for a set amount of time each day.
2. Visit the on-campus learning skills center and enroll in a time management class. Most schools offer this on a noncredit basis. If your school has no such class, you can readily find one online.
3. Use technology like reminder apps for your phone, online calendars, and alarms that remind you to work on your paper for a set amount of time.
4. When (despite your best efforts) you discover that you will not make a deadline, explain the situation to your instructor and seek an extension *before* the paper is due. State that you are seeking help and do not expect the problem to recur. Do not ask for a second extension.

Note Taking and Plagiarism

The problem: Inaccurate note taking results in inadvertent plagiarism: You neglect to place quotation marks around quoted language and later copy the note into the paper without using quotation marks.

A solution: Develop careful note-taking skills. Here are some useful approaches and techniques:

1. Enroll in a study skills class on working with sources, in which you will learn techniques for improving the accuracy and efficiency of note taking.
2. Make certain to gather bibliographic information for every source and to link every note with a source. Then you can go back and double-check quotes you aren't sure about.
3. Save sources onto your own device when possible, and make sure to include publication information. When you use a source in a paper, check your language against the original language. Make corrections and add quotation marks as needed.
4. Learn the difference between quotation, summary, and paraphrase (see Chapter 1).

Digital Life and Plagiarism

The problem: Plagiarism has never been easier, given the volume of information on the Internet and the ease of digital copying and pasting.

A solution: Recall some of the reasons you are in college:

1. To improve your ability to think critically
2. To learn how to think independently
3. To discover your own voice as a thinker and writer

Borrowing the work of others without giving due credit robs you of an opportunity to pursue these goals. Don't allow the ease of plagiarism in the digital age to compromise your ethics. Plagiarism is cheating.

Determining Common Knowledge

Note one exception to the rule that you must credit sources: when ideas and information are considered common knowledge. This can be a tricky thing to determine. You can best understand common knowledge through examples:

General Eisenhower commanded American forces during World War II.

Mars is the fourth planet from the sun.

Ernest Hemingway wrote *The Sun Also Rises.*

These statements represent shared, collective information. When an idea or item of information is thus shared, or commonly known, you do not need to cite it even though you may have learned of that information in a source. What is considered common knowledge changes from subject area to subject area. When in doubt, ask your instructor.

The key issue underlying the question of common knowledge is the likelihood of readers' mistakenly thinking that a certain idea or item of information originated with you when, in fact, it did not. If there is *any* chance of such a mistake occurring, *cite the source.*

A GUIDELINE FOR DETERMINING COMMON KNOWLEDGE   If the idea or information you intend to use can be found unattributed (that is, *not* credited to a specific author) in three or more sources, then you can consider that material common knowledge. *Remember:* If you quote a source, even if the material could be considered common knowledge, you must use quotation marks and give credit.

Figure 7.9 shows an example of a paragraph in which the writer summarizes one source, quotes another, and draws on common knowledge. Only the summary and the quotation need to be cited. Where the writer draws on common knowledge, sources that could have been cited were not because evidence for the statement appeared in at least three sources.

Figure 7.9 Determining Common Knowledge

Summary	Very soon, half of America will communicate via e-mail, according to analysts (Singh 283). We can only assume that figure will grow-rapidly-as children who have matured in the Internet era move to college and into careers. With e-mail becoming an increasingly common form of communication, people are discovering and conversing with one another in a variety of ways that bring a new twist to old, familiar patterns. Using e-mail, people meet "to exchange pleasantries and argue, engage in intellectual discourse, conduct commerce, exchange knowledge, share emotional support, make plans, brainstorm, gossip, feud, [and] fall in love" (Chenault). That is, through e-mail, people do what they have always done: communicate. But the medium of that communication has changed, which excites some people and concerns others.
Common Knowledge	
Quotation	

Plagiarism, the Internet, and Fair Use

The Internet is a medium just like paper, television, or radio. Intellectual property (stories, articles, pictures) is transmitted through the medium. This means that *the same rules that apply to not plagiarizing print sources also apply to not plagiarizing Internet sources.* Any content posted on the Internet that is not your original work is the intellectual property of others. Doing either of the following constitutes plagiarism:

- Copying and pasting digital content from the Internet into your document without citing the source.
- Buying a prewritten or custom-written paper from the Internet.[1]

INTERNET PAPER MILLS   Online paper mills merit special attention because they make available prewritten papers on almost any topic. Remember that instructors know how to use search engines to find the same papers and identify cases of plagiarism.

FAIR USE AND DIGITAL MEDIA   U.S. copyright law permits "fair use" of copyrighted materials—including print (paper- and digital-based), images, video, and sound—for academic purposes. As long as you fully credit your sources, you may quote "excerpts in a review or criticism for purposes of illustration or comment; [and] . . . short passages in a scholarly or technical work."[2]

---

[1]Buying or using any part(s) of a paper written by another person is considered plagiarism—regardless of its source.

[2]"Fair Use." U.S. Copyright Office. May 2009. Web. 23 Mar. 2010.

The key to fair use of any material relies on the extent to which you have "transformed" the original work for your purposes. Thus:

- It is *illegal* for a student to copy a song from a CD and place it on a peer-to-peer file-sharing network.
- It is *legal* to "transform" that same song by including it as the background track to a digital movie or podcast that includes other media elements created by the student as long as it is created for educational purposes and cited on a bibliography page.

Citing Sources

7.8   Cite sources using APA format and MLA format.

When you refer to or quote the work of another, you are obligated to credit or cite your source properly. Citations both give credit where credit is due and allow others to find the work you cited. There are two types of citations—*in-text citations* in the body of a paper and *full citations* (Works Cited or References) at the end of the paper—and they work in tandem.

Many academic libraries (and writing centers) maintain brief guides to American Psychological Association (APA), Modern Language Association (MLA), and other format styles. Students can find these easily with an online search. The Purdue Online Writing Lab (OWL) maintains an excellent online guide to APA, *Chicago Manual of Style* (CMS), and MLA.

Types of Citations

- In-text citations indicate the source of quotations, paraphrases, and summarized information and ideas. These citations, generally limited to the author's last name, relevant page number, and the publication date of the source, appear *in the text of your paper*, within parentheses.
- Full citations appear in an alphabetical list of "Works Cited" (MLA) or "References" (APA) at the end of the paper, always starting on a new page. These citations provide full bibliographical information on the source.

If you are writing a paper in the humanities, you will probably be expected to use the Modern Language Association (MLA) format for citation. This format is fully described in the *MLA Handbook for Writers of Research Papers*, 8th ed. (Modern Language Association of America, 2016), or go to https://style.mla.org/. A paper in the social sciences will probably use the American Psychological Association (APA) format. This format is fully described in the *Publication Manual of the American Psychological Association*, 6th ed. (American Psychological Association, 2010). These are two of the most common citation styles. Always ask your professor which style he or she expects of you if you're not sure.

In the following section, we provide a brief guide to the major MLA and APA citation types you will use when researching and writing a paper. Look online for format guidance when citing sources not listed here. And bear in mind that instructors often have their own preferences. Check with your instructor for the preferred documentation format if this is not specified in the assignment.[3]

APA Documentation Basics

APA IN-TEXT CITATIONS IN BRIEF   When quoting or paraphrasing, place a parenthetical citation in your sentence that includes the author, publication year, and page or paragraph number.

> **Direct quotation, author and publication year not mentioned in sentence**
>
> > Research suggests that punishing a child "promotes only momentary compliance" (Berk & Ellis, 2002, p. 383).
>
> **Paraphrase, author and year mentioned in the sentence**
>
> > Berk and Ellis (2002) suggest that punishment may be ineffective (p. 383).
>
> **Direct quotation from Internet source**
>
> > Others have noted a rise in "problems that mimic dysfunctional behaviors" (Spivek, Jones, & Connelly, 2006, Introduction section, para. 3).

APA REFERENCES LIST IN BRIEF   On a separate, concluding page titled "References," alphabetize sources by author, providing full bibliographic information for each.

Article from a Journal   Conclude your entry with the digital object identifier (DOI)—the article's unique reference number. Note that the letters *doi* are roman and lowercase in the References list. When a DOI is not available and you have located the article on the Web, conclude with *Retrieved from* and the URL of the homepage. For articles located through a database such as LexisNexis, do not list the database in your entry.

> ARTICLE (WITH VOLUME AND ISSUE NUMBERS) LOCATED VIA PRINT OR DATABASE
>
> > Ivanenko, A., & Massie, C. (2006). Assessment and management of sleep disorders in children. *Psychiatric Times, 23*(11), 90–95.
>
> ARTICLE (WITH DOI AND VOLUME NUMBER) LOCATED VIA PRINT OR DATABASE
>
> > Jones, K. L. (1986). Fetal alcohol syndrome. *Pediatrics in Review, 8,* 122–126. doi:10.1542/10.1542/pir.8-4-122

---

[3]Some instructors require the documentation style specified in the *Chicago Manual of Style,* 16th ed. (Chicago: University of Chicago Press, 2010). This style is similar to the American Psychological Association style except that publication dates are not placed within parentheses. Instructors in the sciences often follow the Council of Science Editors (CSE) formats, one of which is a number format: Each source listed on the bibliography page is assigned a number, and all text references to the source are followed by the appropriate number within parentheses. Some instructors prefer the old MLA style, which called for footnotes and endnotes.

Article located via Web

> Ivanenko, A., & Massie, C. (2006). Assessment and management of sleep disorders in children. *Psychiatric Times, 23*(11), 90–95. Retrieved from http://www.psychiatrictimes.com

Article from a Magazine

Article (with volume and issue numbers) located via print or database

> Landi, A. (2010, January). Is beauty in the brain of the beholder? *ARTnews, 109*(1), 19–21.

Article located via Web

> Landi, A. (2010, January). Is beauty in the brain of the beholder? *ARTnews, 109*(1). Retrieved from http://www.artnews.com

Article from a Newspaper

Article located via print or database

> Wakabayashi, D. (2010, January 7). Sony pins future on a 3-D revival. *The Wall Street Journal*, pp. A1, A14.

Article located via Web

> Wakabayashi, D. (2010, January 7). Sony pins future on a 3-D revival. *The Wall Street Journal*. Retrieved from http://www.wsj.com

Book

Book located via print

> Mansfield, R. S., & Busse, T. V. (1981). *The psychology of creativity and discovery: Scientists and their work*. Chicago, IL: Nelson-Hall.

Book located via Web

> Freud, S. (1920). *Dream psychology: Psychoanalysis for beginners* (M. D. Elder, Trans.). Retrieved from http://www.gutenberg.org

Selection from an edited book

> Halberstam, D. (2002). Who we are. In S. J. Gould (Ed.), *The best American essays 2002* (pp. 124–136). New York, NY: Houghton Mifflin.

Later edition

> Samuelson, P., & Nordhaus, W. D. (2005). *Economics* (18th ed.). Boston, MA: McGraw-Hill Irwin.

MLA Documentation Basics

When writers document sources clearly and consistently, readers can access those sources and draw their own conclusions about them. Different discipline areas—the sciences, social sciences, and humanities—use different guidelines for capturing key information about sources. In the humanities, MLA citation guidelines are used most often. Designed for simplicity, they consist of two steps: brief in-text citations, and a complete list of works cited.[4]

MLA CITATIONS IN BRIEF When referring to a source in the text of your papers, use parentheses to enclose a page number reference. Include the author's name if you do not mention it in your sentence.

> From the beginning, the AIDS test has been "mired in controversy" (Bayer 101).

Or if you name the author in the sentence:

> Bayer claims the AIDS test has been "mired in controversy" (101).

For sources with no pagination (Web sites, for instance), cite the author's name only:

> From the beginning, the AIDS test has been "mired in controversy" (Bayer).

MLA WORKS CITED LIST IN BRIEF In MLA documentation style, every brief citation in your paper points to a detailed citation at the end of the paper, in a Works Cited list. Every detailed entry in that list consists of what MLA terms "core elements," arranged in a set order and separated by either a comma or a period:

- Author.
- Title of source.
- Title of container,
- Other contributors,
- Version,
- Number,
- Publisher,
- Publication date,
- Location.

To clarify two terms in this list: A *container,* according to MLA, is the italicized name of the newspaper, magazine, journal, book, Web site, database, or any larger entity that "holds" a source. *Location* identifies where a source can be found. For printed sources such as anthologies or periodicals (articles in newspapers or magazines), *location* is expressed as a page number (p.) or page range (pp.); for a Web site, as a URL or digital object identifier (DOI)—a unique identification number; for an online database such as *JSTOR,* as a page range (if the source is a periodical), and also a digital address—either a DOI or some other digital identifier marking the source's location in the database.

---

[4]This overview addresses the basics of Modern Language Association citation format. For complete coverage, see *MLA Handbook*, 8th Edition (2016), or go to https://style.mla.org/.

Note especially the punctuation after each core element. Information that follows a period should begin with an uppercase letter. Information that follows a comma (after the title of a container, for instance) should begin with a lowercase letter. Thus, below, you'll find that the capitalization of "edited by" is treated differently in the example entries listed under "Selection from an Anthology, Print" and "Book, Print."

Review these examples of common Works Cited entries. For additional examples, see (in this text) the Works Cited pages for the model papers in Chapter 2, page 86; Chapter 4, page 124; Chapter 5, pages 147–48; and Chapter 6, page 176. For complete coverage, refer to the *MLA Handbook*, 8th Edition, or go to https://style.mla.org/.

MAGAZINE OR NEWSPAPER ARTICLE, PRINT

Collins, Gail. "Behind Hillary's Mask." *The New York Times Sunday Review*, 24 July 2016, pp. 1+.

Packer, George. "The Choice." *The New Yorker*, 28 Jan. 2008, pp. 28–35.

MAGAZINE OR NEWSPAPER ARTICLE, WEB

Bower, Bruce. "Birth of the Beat: Music's Roots May Lie in Melodic Exchanges Between Mothers and Babies." *Science News*, 14 Aug. 2010, www.sciencenews.org/sites/default/files/birth_of_beat.pdf.

Collins, Gail. "Behind Hillary's Mask." *The New York Times Sunday Review*, 24 July 2016, www.nytimes.com/2016/07/24/opinion/campaign-stops/behind-hillarys-mask.html.

Packer, George. "The Choice." *The New Yorker*, 28 Jan. 2008, www.newyorker.com/magazine/2008/01/28/the-choice-6.

MAGAZINE OR NEWSPAPER ARTICLE, DATABASE

Petrou, Michael. "A Plan to Save the World." *Maclean's*, 29 Dec. 2014, p. 46. *Gale General OneFile*, www.go.galegroup.com/ps/retrieve.do?sor/CA394515226.

SELECTION FROM AN ANTHOLOGY, PRINT

Cott, Nancy F. "Early Twentieth-Century Feminism in Political Context: A Comparative Look at Germany and the United States." *Suffrage and Beyond: International Feminist Perspectives*, edited by Caroline Daly et al., New York UP, 1994, pp. 234–51.

SCHOLARLY ARTICLE, PRINT [TWO AUTHORS]

Ivanenko, Anna, and Clifford Massie. "Assessment and Management of Sleep Disorders in Children." *Psychiatric Times*, vol. 23, no. 11, 1 Oct. 2006, pp. 90–95.

SCHOLARLY ARTICLE, WEB [THREE OR MORE AUTHORS]

Ivanenko, Anna, et al. "Sleep in Children with Psychiatric Disorders." *Pediatric Clinics of North America*, vol. 51, no. 1, Feb. 2004, www.pediatric.theclinics.com/article/S0031-3955(03)00181-0/abstract.

Ivanenko, Anna, et al. "Sleep in Children with Psychiatric Disorders." *Pediatric Clinics of North America,* vol. 51, no. 1, Feb. 2004, doi:10.1016/S0031-3955(03)00181-0.

SCHOLARLY ARTICLE, DATABASE

Bodenheimer, Rosemarie. "Looking at the Landscape in Jane Austen." *Studies in English Literature,* vol. 21, no. 4, Autumn 1981, pp. 603–623. *JSTOR,* www.jstor.org/stable/450229.

BOOK, PRINT

De Beauvoir, Simone. *The Second Sex.* Translated by H. M. Parshly, Penguin Press, 1972.

Gleick, James. *Chaos: Making a New Science.* Penguin Press, 1987.

Twain, Mark. *Adventures of Huckleberry Finn.* Edited by Stephen Railton, Broadview Press, 2011.

BOOK [TWO OR MORE EDITORS], DATABASE

Daly, Caroline, et al., editors. *Suffrage and Beyond: International Feminist Perspectives.* New York UP, 1994. *ACLS Humanities E-book,* http://quod.lib.umich.edu/cgi/t/text/text-idx?c=acls;idno=heb02496.

UP is an abbreviation for *University Press.* Compare this entry with the example citation listed under "Selection from an Anthology, Print," which emphasizes a work *in* an anthology. When citing the anthology itself, begin with the name(s) of the editor(s) and treat as shown. Note also the difference between this entry and the example citation listed under "Book, Print," which emphasizes the author of a work, *not* the editor.

ARTICLE/POST, WEB SITE

Spring, Jake. "Now Legal in China: Uber." *HuffingtonPost,* 28 July 2016, www.huffingtonpost.com/entry/uber-china-legal-ride-hailing_us_5 79a38fae4b02d5d5ed4be34.

Part II
Brief Takes

In this section, you'll practice the skills you've learned in summary, critique, synthesis, and analysis. These three "brief take" chapters are—as their name suggests—shorter than the five chapters that make up the main part of the anthology (Part III of this book) and feature a more limited number of writing assignments. In two of these chapters, assignments are sequenced so that the early ones, such as summary and critique, can be incorporated into the more complex later ones, such as analysis and argument synthesis.

The subject matters of these short chapters—musical covers, the obedience we owe those in authority, and "tiger moms"—span the academic disciplines. Each chapter includes six to nine articles. After reading them, you'll be asked to create various kinds of papers that draw upon the skills you have learned in Part I of this book.

Your reading and writing will help firm up the skills you've learned earlier in the course and will prepare you both for the lengthier reading and writing assignments of Part III and for the assignments of your other courses. Beyond the value of that preparation, we hope that you'll find yourself pleasantly absorbed by the subject matter. The "conversations" you are about to enter are fascinating.

Chapter 8

"Over the Rainbow" and the Art of the Musical Cover

The earliest man-made musical instrument—a flute constructed out of mammoth ivory and bird bone—dates back more than 40,000 years. But long before there were flutes, there were other instruments: Our feet stomping the ground. Our hands clapping. Our own voices. It's quite likely that human beings have been making music for as long as there have been human beings.

Today, music remains part of many of our most important rites and ceremonies—such as weddings and religious events—but music also accompanies our road trips, our runs, our meals in restaurants, our movies and video games and TV shows. We put on music during the highest and lowest points in our days. We listen to music that matches our mood, and we listen to music in order to *change* our mood. We stream and download tunes, we share YouTube clips with friends, we hang out with music on and dance to it. For many of us, our musical lives are inseparable from our social lives. In fact, *who we are* is to some degree defined by the music we listen to.

And yet for something so ubiquitous, music can be difficult to write about. Unlike poetry or fiction, for example, music is a nonverbal art form. (Even when a song has lyrics, those lyrics tell only part of the story.) When we love a song, we often do so not for any intellectual reason, but rather because of the way the song somehow finds an express route to our deepest emotional selves. It hits us in the gut. It makes us feel.

Now, the same can be said of poetry or fiction—they can hit us in the gut, too—but poetry and fiction are based in language. The challenge of writing about music, then, is to take an art form that isn't language-based and to describe it using language. Yet it's a challenge well worth embarking on, because if you can learn to describe *how* something goes about producing an emotional effect, then you are demonstrating a very high degree of thought and understanding.

This chapter focuses attention on the "cover song," a new version of a previously recorded song, redone by a singer or a band. Cover songs are nothing new, though they aren't all that old, either. In the early days of sound recording, most performers didn't write their own songs, and there was far less of a sense that a song "belonged" to any particular singer. Then, at the beginning of the rock-and-roll era, cover songs were mainly the product of white musicians re-recording songs first recorded by black musicians and releasing them to a larger white audience in order to eclipse the market—an insidious practice that critics have called "hijacking hits."

Today, the term "cover song" no longer has a negative connotation. It refers more generally to a recording artist creating a new version of someone else's previously recorded song. When we hear Tori Amos's version of Nirvana's biggest hit song, "Smells Like Teen Spirit," no one is thinking that Amos is trying to pass off Nirvana's song as her own, or trying to eclipse their record sales. Rather, we are interested in seeing how Amos, an artsy pianist/vocalist, is able to put her unique spin on the classic grunge song.

This notion of originality and interpretation lies at the heart of why songs get covered—an artist bringing his or her own talents and imagination to an older song and making it new. One song that has been "covered" again and again through the years is "Over the Rainbow," written by Harold Arlen (music) and E. Y. Harburg (lyrics) for the 1939 film *The Wizard of Oz*. We begin by listing numerous versions of "Over the Rainbow" available on YouTube, which will give you a clearer sense of the astounding range of musical styles in which artists have presented this classic. We move next to an account of the circumstances surrounding the song's creation and then to a PBS Newshour interview with musician Rob Kapilow, who illustrates (while seated at a piano, if you follow the online link) how "Over the Rainbow" succeeds as a song of leaps, circling, and yearning. To help you become familiar with the specialized language of musical description, we offer a glossary of key musical terms that you'll find useful in developing your own analyses. In the online version of the glossary, musician Greg Blair explains and demonstrates each of the fifteen musical terms defined in the text. And as a model of the comparison and contrast you'll be asked to write at the end of the chapter, we present a paper by Blair examining three covers of another classic, "Stormy Weather."

To increase the chances you'll analyze a song you especially enjoy, we conclude by pointing you to other covers: Leonard Cohen's celebrated "Hallelujah," the much-loved classic, "Stormy Weather," and a *Rolling Stone* listing of "The Greatest Covers of All Time." Of course, no such list is definitive, and you'll be free to select some other song and its covers as the basis of your comparative analysis.

The Art of "Over the Rainbow"

Harold Arlen and E. Y. (Yip) Harburg

Written by Harold Arlen and E. Y. (Yip) Harburg to anchor MGM's 1939 musical-drama *The Wizard of Oz*, "Over the Rainbow" is widely acknowledged as one of the great American ballads. Sixteen-year-old Judy Garland played the role of Dorothy Gale, a Kansas farm girl yearning to find her place in the world—a place where her dreams might come true and her troubles "melt like lemon drops." "Over the Rainbow" won

that year's Academy Award for Best Original Song; (much) later, both the Recording Industry Association of America/National Endowment of the Arts and the American Film Institute honored "Rainbow" as the number one song of the twentieth century. Arlen and Harburg's classic has served as a continuing source of inspiration for musical interpretations by artists as varied as big-band leader Glenn Miller, pop icon Lady Gaga, and the famed Hawaiian ukulele player and singer Israel Kamakawiwo'ole (Iz). Miller recorded what is likely the first cover, which became a number-one hit the same year the movie was released. In 2016, former American Idol runner-up Katharine McPhee covered the song for her final performance on the show. In that seventy-seven-year span, "Over the Rainbow" has been covered almost continuously.

You will readily find the lyrics online, searching on "over the rainbow lyrics harburg."

To get some idea of the wide range of moods the same song can convey when performed by musicians with their own very personal interpretations, listen to the following three distinctive covers of "Over the Rainbow": Go to YouTube and search for "over the rainbow judy garland." Play this version, and you'll hear the classic, initial performance, the source from which all subsequent covers have sprung. Next, search for "over the rainbow iz" and you'll be treated to Israel Kamakawiwo'ole's compelling voice and ukulele version, which has been viewed an astonishing 276 *million* times. (Choose the "official" version. Length: 3:48.) Finally, for a jazzy-Latin interpretation (in which a viola is played like a guitar), search for "over the rainbow melody gardot."

This kind of exhilaratingly creative reinterpretation of song is the phenomenon we will be exploring in this chapter.

"Over the Rainbow" has a standard AABA form, which simply means that it begins with a verse (the first A section) that gets repeated (the second A section). The song continues with a "bridge"—the B section—which has a different melody than the A section, followed by a return to the final A section. (For more on this topic, search on YouTube, "aba song form.) "Rainbow" deviates slightly from this classic form by ending with a brief echo of the B section. Strictly speaking, its form is AABA(B).[1]

Thousands of popular songs follow the AABA structure. Think of "Rudolph, the Red-Nosed Reindeer," for example, or Paul McCartney's "Yesterday," and sing or hum the verses to yourself, one at a time, with this structure in mind. When you listen to the various versions of "Over the Rainbow," you'll notice that many artists take liberties with this basic form that become part of their own interpretations.

For example, go to YouTube and search for "over the rainbow glenn miller instrumental." As you listen to this rendition (the 2:13 version), its tempo quickened to give the song a rolling, big-band sound, identify each section as Glenn Miller's band plays it:

```
0:00–0:19 A
0:19–0:39 A
0:40–0:59 B
1:00–1:18 A
1:19–1:39 B
1:40–1:58 A
1:59–2:12 B
```

---

[1] For a better understanding of musical concepts and terminology, see the glossary later in this chapter—and the accompanying videos—by Greg Blair.

Miller extends Arlen/Harburg's original AABA(B) structure by repeating the last two sections—one (likely) reason being to lengthen his up-tempo version, which would otherwise have ended at 1:40, too brief for a dance tune. Notice that even though the basic melody remains the same from one A or B section to another, there are subtle differences in instrumentation and dynamics (volume), providing variety and a sense of forward movement as the song progresses.

In this first section, we'd like you to listen to (and in some cases watch) some of the numerous covers of "Over the Rainbow" online. We promise that no matter how many times you hear this remarkable song, you'll never grow tired of it. And if you do, you must be in a bad mood!

Listening Suggestions

Go to YouTube and type in "over the rainbow" followed by the name of the lead artist listed below. (Remember that YouTube search boxes are not case sensitive, so using lowercase letters is fine.) We have specified videos of particular lengths to differentiate between two or more covers of the song by the same artist.

Note: For the moment, simply listen and respond informally to Judy Garland's "Over the Rainbow" and the various covers, noting your reactions. What differences do you observe? Which version(s) do you prefer? Do you know why? Later in the chapter, and accompanying in online videos, you'll gain a better grounding in the elements of music so that you can listen again with a more formal awareness. To begin, listen to some of the most well-known versions of "Over the Rainbow."

> **Judy Garland** [*2:58*]
> **Iz** [*3:48 "official"*]
> **Melody Gardot** [*6:04*]
> **Jake Shimabukuro** [*4:36*]
> **Eva Cassidy** [*5:37*]
> **Ray Charles** [*4:10*]

Next, sample some of these additional covers.

> **Ben Webster** [*4:53*]
> **The Ramones** [*1:32*]
> **Ella Fitzgerald** [*4:22*]
> **Keith Jarrett** [*5:51*]
> **Dimensions** [*3:18*]
> **Glenn Miller** [*2:13*]
> **Eric Clapton** [*4:48*]
> **Tony Bennett** [*2:54*]
> **Chet Atkins** [*3:05*]
> **James Galway** [*4:16*]
> **Frank Sinatra** [*3:20*]
> **Train passengers** [*4:38*]
> **40 Singers** [*5:59*]

"40 Singers" includes Beyoncé, Barbra Streisand, Mariah Carey, Celine Dion, Katharine McPhee, Aretha Franklin, Susan Boyle, Jennifer Hudson, Connie Talbot, Patty LaBelle, Tori Amos, Lady Gaga (in Dorothy costume), Faith Hill, and Doris Day.

Finally, you may find it interesting to sample covers of "Over the Rainbow" by other artists. (There are many.) Just type in "over the rainbow covers," scroll through the results list, and follow your instincts.

Discussion and Writing Suggestions

1. Which of these versions do you like the best? Which the least? Explain the reasons for your preferences.

2. Listen to three of the six instrumental covers of "Over the Rainbow" included in our suggested list: Jake Shimabukuro, Ben Webster, Keith Jarrett, Glenn Miller, Chet Atkins, and James Galway. What makes them sound different? How do these different performances affect the mood of the song?

3. Over 272 million people have listened to Israel Kamakawiwo'ole's version of "Over the Rainbow." What explains its popularity?

4. What qualities distinguish the "punk" version of "Over the Rainbow" by the Ramones? How do they change the Judy Garland version? In what ways can you hear Judy Garland's version in theirs?

5. Which of these covers of "Over the Rainbow" is the most surprising to you? Why? Note that "surprising" does not mean "likeable."

6. Glenn Miller turned "Over the Rainbow" into an up-tempo, danceable big-band song. The Dimensions turned it into a doo-wop slow dance. Listen to these covers and make some observations about the musical arrangement of each—especially the tempo. Which version do you prefer? Why?

7. Do you find yourself more interested in the versions that stick closer to the original song and its mood or to versions that depart significantly from the original?

8. Melody Gardot introduces her cover with these words: "If you try to duplicate, you do no justice. I think the only reason to interpret a song is to truly do just that. You put your mark and your stamp on it, and you make your own." Has she succeeded with her version? Which of the other artists covering "Over the Rainbow" have claimed the song as "their own"? Why do you think so? What elements of a cover are essential to making a song one's own?

Who Put the Rainbow in The Wizard of Oz?

Harold Meyerson and Ernie Harburg

Writing duties for songs in movies and Broadway shows often pair a composer, who creates the tunes, and a lyricist, who writes the words. In *The Wizard of Oz*, those duties fell to the seasoned Harold Arlen (composer) and E. Y. Harburg (lyricist). Together and separately, working with other collaborators, they wrote hundreds of songs, many, like "Over the Rainbow," among the most famous of the twentieth century. The movie studio MGM hired Arlen (1905–1986) and Harburg (1896–1981) to write every song for *The Wizard of Oz*—a task they completed in just over fourteen weeks.

In their 1993 biography of Harburg (an excerpt of which follows), Harold Meyerson and Ernie Harburg (Yip's son) offer a fascinating account of how "Over the Rainbow" came to be written—an account replete with creative tensions, bursts of insight, setbacks, and success. **Perhaps most surprising is the revelation that the word** *rainbow* **never appears in L. Frank Baum's book,** *The Wizard of Oz.* **It was the lyricist Yip Harburg who put it in the film.**

When they wrote *Who Put the Rainbow in the Wizard of Oz,* **Ernie Harburg was an emeritus research scientist in the University of Michigan Departments of Epidemiology and Psychology and also president of the Yip Harburg Foundation. Harold Meyerson was an editor-at-large for** *The American Prospect* **and a columnist for the Washington Post.**

> The magic in song only happens when the words give destination and meaning to the music and the music gives wings to the words. Together as a song they go places you've never been before.
>
> The reason is obvious: *words make you think thoughts. Music makes you feel a feeling. But a song makes you feel a thought.* That's the great advantage. To feel the thought. . . . And that's why . . . you can teach more through song and you can rouse more through song than all the prose in the world or all the poems. . . .
>
> Songs have been the not-so-secret weapon behind every fight for freedom, every struggle against injustice and bigotry: "The Marseillaise," "The Battle Hymn of the Republic," "We Shall Overcome," and many more. . . .
>
> Songs are the pulse of a nation's heart. A fever chart of its health. Are we at peace? Are we in trouble? Are we floundering? Do we feel beautiful? Do we feel ugly? . . . Listen to our songs. . . . The lyricist, like any artist, cannot be neutral. He should be committed to the side of humanity.
>
> —Yip Harburg

The Signature Song

Oz begins, of course, with the one song not set in *Oz,* surely, the most widely known song Yip and Harold together or with others ever wrote. Though "Over the Rainbow" was the first song in the picture, it was actually the last to be written and the last to be filmed. Nothing on "Over the Rainbow" came easy, Yip told the audience during one of the Ninety-second Street Y[2] lyricists' evenings:

> You always have trouble writing a ballad. Of course, I was writing for a situation of a little girl who was desperate, had never seen anything beyond an arid Kansas where there was no color in her life; there were no flowers [according to Baum]. It was all brown and sepia and at a moment when she was troubled in a childish way, she wanted to escape in a song of escape—where could she go? The only thing colorful that she's ever seen in her life was the rainbow.
>
> *The book had no reference to a rainbow.* In fact, it gave the makers of the picture, the producers, the director, the idea of having the first part done in routine everyday black and white, so that when she got over the rainbow, she got into a colorful Munchkinland. So I had that idea in mind: of a little girl wanting something, a place somewhere that was over that rainbow and I told Harold about it and we went to work on a tune.

Arlen and Harburg agreed that the ballad should be "a song of yearning," Yip told Harmetz. "Its object would be to delineate Dorothy and to give an emotional touch to the scene where she is frustrated and in trouble." Only, Arlen could not get the music for that emotion, that situation. "I can't tell you the misery that a composer goes through when the whole

---

[2] Founded in 1874 in New York City, the Ninety-second Street Y is a cultural, literary, and recreational center well known for its public conversations with people in the arts.

score is written but he hasn't got that big theme song that Louis B. Mayer[3] is waiting for," Yip told the Y audience. "The contract was for fourteen weeks and we were on our fourteenth week. We didn't get paid after the fourteenth. He surely sweated it out, but he couldn't get a tune."

The melody finally carne to Arlen as he was out driving with his wife. As Arlen biographer Edward Jablonski recounts it,

> He and Anya had decided to drive to a movie at Grauman's Chinese Theater[4]—that is, Anya drove, the composer was too nervous with anxiety about the ballad he hoped to find. They had reached the spot where the original Schwab's drugstore[5] was located, on Sunset Boulevard, when the "broad, long-lined, melody" came to Arlen; he jotted it down in the car. "It was as if the Lord said, 'Well, here it is, now stop worrying about it!'"

"He called me," Yip told the Y. "It was twelve o'clock at night and he said, 'Please, please, come right over. I've got the tune.'" (This was not so exceptional as it may sound: Yip and Harold generally worked at night on *Oz* so that Yip could play tennis and Harold golf during the daytime. Writing the score may have been fraught with anxiety, but the working conditions were nothing to complain about.)

"I ran to meet him at home," Yip wrote in 1973.

> He approached the piano with the usual blue-eyes-toward-heaven ritual and played the first eight bars of "Over the Rainbow." My heart fell. He played it with such symphonic sweep and bravura that my first reaction was: "Oh, no, not for little Dorothy! That's for Nelson Eddy."[6] Harold, always sensitive, never aggressive or defensive, was shattered. His Hillcrest [Country Club] suntan suddenly took flight. I was miserable. I confess with head bowed low: the song almost suffered extinction by me while it was still aborning.

5   "For two weeks after," Yip told the Y audience,

> without money from Metro, he was still working on that tune. Finally, he called me over and said, "I *feel* this tune; this is a great tune. Now you must write it." When a composer like Harold says that, then you've got to, as Willy Loman's[7] wife says, pay attention.
>
> When Ira and George[8] were working on a thing, and they met an impasse, they'd always call me or call Harold. So I called in Ira. I said, "Ira, Harold's got a tune here and here's the situation," and I told him. I was too involved emotionally to analyze the thing, to put my finger on it to communicate it to Harold. But Ira, being a third person, was more clearheaded and less involved. He said, "Harold, play that tune with a little more rhythm." Harold sat down and said, "What do you mean? This way?" [When] he played, the thing cleared itself up for me, and Ira said, "See, it's the way Harold's playing it." Harold and I were both too intense to have figured that thing out. I said, "Ira, you're right, that's fine."

---

[3] Louis B. Mayer (1884–1957) was a film producer and the co-founder of Metro-Goldwyn-Mayer (MGM) studios.

[4] Grauman's Chinese Theatre is a famed movie theater in Hollywood.

[5] In the 1930s and 1940s, the ice cream counter at Schwab's Pharmacy (in Hollywood) was a famous gathering spot for movie producers, actors, and would-be actors hoping to be discovered.

[6] Nelson Eddy (1901–1967) was a veteran Hollywood actor and singer in Hollywood musicals.

[7] Willy Loman is the main character, a tragic figure, in Arthur Miller's *Death of a Salesman*. At a pivotal moment in the play, his wife (Linda) tells their son (Biff) that "attention must be . . . paid" to Willy, a flawed man whose fortunes are deteriorating.

[8] Brothers Ira (1896–1983) and George (1898–1937) Gershwin were a famed composer-lyricist team in the 1920s–1930s.

> Next Harold couldn't get a middle. Well, Harold had a little dog, Pan, a silly little dog, who ran away. Harold had a little whistle for him that went like this [whistles middle tune—"Someday I'll wish upon a star"]. I said, "Harold . . . This is the crazy life we lead. This is the way songs are written."

It was an almost automatic thing for Arlen to do. "We'd instinctively give each other clues about what we were thinking," Yip recalled nearly forty years later. "I'd incorporate his ideas into my lyrics. He'd incorporate my ideas into his music."

Yip remembered bits and pieces of what had happened when Arlen then left the ballad in his hands. "The girl was in trouble," he told Harmetz,

> but it was the trouble of a child. In *Oliver,* the little boy was in a similar situation, was running away. Someone thought up a song for him, "Where Is Love?" How can a little boy sing about an adult emotion? I would never write "Where Is Love?" for a child. That's analytical adult thinking, not childish thinking. This little girl thinks: *My life is messed up. Where do I run?* The song has to be full of childish pleasures. Of lemon drops. The book had said Kansas was [an] arid place where not even flowers grew. The only colorful thing Dorothy saw, occasionally, would be the rainbow.
>
> "Over the Rainbow Is Where I [Want] to Be" was my title, the title I gave Harold. A title has to ring a bell, has to blow a couple of Roman candles off. But he gave me a tune with those first two notes [an octave apart]. I tried *I'll go over the rainbow, Someday over the rainbow* or *the other side of the rainbow.* I had difficulty coming to the idea of *Somewhere.* For a while I thought I would just leave those first two notes out! It was a long time before I came to *Somewhere over the rainbow.*

● ● ●

In *Oz,* . . . the rainbow is Yip's invention—his metaphor for dreaming, his device to propel a black-and-white consciousness into color, the most colorful thing, he realized, that Dorothy had ever seen. After *Oz,* the rainbow was no mere rhetorical device for Yip, but a complex symbol of human aspiration.

Discussion and Writing Suggestions

1. What surprises you the most in this behind-the-scenes look at the creation of "Over the Rainbow"? Why?

2. In the epigraph, Yip Harburg is quoted as saying *"a song makes you feel a thought."* What does this mean in the context of Harburg's lyrics and Arlen's music? What *thought* do you feel is being expressed in "Over the Rainbow"?

3. The authors write: "Arlen and Harburg agreed that the ballad should be 'a song of yearning.'" Listen to Judy Garland sing "Over the Rainbow" in the film. Do you feel this "yearning" in her rendition? What is Dorothy yearning *for*? If you've listened to covers of "Over the Rainbow," are you convinced that the cover artists have retained this yearning quality?

4. Harburg writes how, when they reached an "impasse" in the writing of a song, the famous composing team of Ira and George Gershwin ("Summertime")

would call him or Harold Arlen for help. Harburg did the same in the writing of "Over the Rainbow" and called Ira Gershwin for advice. What observations can you make here about creativity and collaboration?

5. Though "Over the Rainbow" appears to be a simple song written for a farm girl, Harburg thinks deeply about his lyrics for Dorothy Gale. He writes: "The girl was in trouble . . . but it was the trouble of a child. In *Oliver*, the little boy was in a similar situation, was running away. Someone thought up a song for him, 'Where Is Love?' How can a little boy sing about an adult emotion? I would never write 'Where Is Love?' for a child. That's analytical adult thinking, not childish thinking. This little girl thinks: *My life is messed up. Where do I run?* The song has to be full of childish pleasures. Of lemon drops." Re-read the lyrics of "Over the Rainbow." Did Harburg achieve his goal of matching lyrics to the character? Explain.

On the Web: *Why "Over the Rainbow" Takes Us to a Magical, Musical Place*

PBS Newshour interview with composer Rob Kapilow

Go online to listen to and watch a remarkably enjoyable and informative PBS Newshour interview with composer and musical guide Rob Kapilow. Kapilow has made an art of explaining (while seated at a piano, slowing down and replaying key passages) why great songs succeed. In this segment with PBS reporter Jeffrey Brown, "Over the Rainbow" receives his expert treatment. The interview aired on October 6, 2015. (Running time: 5:59.)

Open any browser.
Search terms: "pbs kapilow rainbow"

Discussion and Writing Suggestions

1. Quoting Yip Harburg, Kapilow says that "a song makes you feel a thought." To what extent did you feel thoughts concerning "Over the Rainbow" *before* reading Kapilow's analysis? (What were these thoughts?) To the extent the music did "speak" and you found yourself deeply appreciating "Over the Rainbow," why are analyses like Kapilow's nonetheless useful?

2. Kapilow connects musical states to emotional states in "Over the Rainbow." For instance, he speaks of *leaps*: "Now, this leap isn't just a big leap musically. It's a leap between two different worlds and two parts of the voice. The first note is kind of low down there in [the] chest voice. It's

Dorothy's troubled reality. It's Kansas, aridity, no flowers. It's the black and white of the beginning of the film." According to Kapilow, the logic of the notes and the logic of the words align in "Over the Rainbow." To what extent do you detect such an alignment—the perfect matching of music and emotions—in other songs? What other songs have enabled you to "feel a thought"?

3. Emotionally, what does *yearning* mean? Kapilow makes much of this word with respect to "Over the Rainbow." When you listen to the song, do you hear the yearning both in the music *and* the lyrics? Explain.

4. According to Kapilow, the song "Over the Rainbow" summarizes the story of *The Wizard of Oz.* The words *yearning, home,* and *transformation* figure importantly in this summary. How so—and do you agree? Explain.

Why Cover a Song?

George Plasketes and Tom Bligh

Excerpts from two selections follow, grouped under the title "Why Cover a Song?" The first, "The Sincerest Form of Flattery," by George Plasketes, appeared originally as "Reflections on the Cover Age: A Collage of Continuous Coverage in Popular Music" in *Popular Music and Society* **(2005). Tom Bligh's "A Treatise on Cover Songs" appeared originally in** *Oxford American*: *The Music Issue* **(2006). Plasketes is the director of media studies at Auburn University. Bligh is a fiction writer and director of creative writing at Mount St. Mary's University.**

The Sincerest Form of Flattery
by George Plasketes

> Re-creation is the sincerest form of flattery. (advertisement for Duran Duran's *Thank You*, 1995)

> [Covering is] the highest compliment to a songwriter. Even [William] Shatner's "Rocket Man" sounds good to me. (Sir Elton John, *Today Show*)

> One of the pleasures of life is to sing great lyrics. (Lucy Kaplansky, on contributing a song to A Nod to Bob (2001) *All Things Considered* (National Public Radio, 2001))

A scene in the film *Love Actually* (2003) depicts a recording studio session with a waning star struggling to convert the Troggs' "Love Is All Around" into a commercial "Christmas Is All Around." "I'm afraid you did it again, Bill," says the producer to the singer, who repeatedly fails to make the desired seasonal substitution in the lyrics. "It's just that I know the old version so well, you know," apologizes the singer. Not missing a beat, the producer unsympathetically responds, "Well, we all did, that's why we're making the new version." Though artists and audience alike comfortably cling to the original, and commonly question the necessity of a cover version, there are many legitimate reasons for "making a new version." . . . Proponents recognize redeeming qualities in recycling songs such as the historical context, apprenticeship, homage, empathy, adaptation, translation, interpretation, preservation, revitalization and the value of exposing songwriters, their songs and styles, old and new, to an audience.

As a musical tradition, covering has always provided a practical point in the apprenticeship process. By employing the "playing songs we like" or "what we grew up listening to" method, bands learn form, structure, and style. "You've got to [play covers] if you're going to learn anything [about songwriting]. It's the only way to really figure it out. I can't imagine not starting that way," explains Tom Petty.

Canadian songwriter Ron Sexsmith characterized his dues paying as being "a Human Jukebox" playing familiar songs. He echoes Petty's point. "Covers are about learning structure and the importance of the song." Sexsmith also recognizes a sense of redemption in covering, that is, being drawn to "a song I'd aspire to write or wish I could have written." (For Sexsmith, Anne Murray's "Snowbird" is his "redemption song.")

The arts have always borrowed from their past. The imitation intrinsic in the act of covering in music, even with the honorable intent of homage from a disciple, is incongruent with authenticity. Critics frequently cite the absence of originality and pointless duplicity of covering. After all, as Rolling Stone Mick Jagger wondered circa 1968, "What's the point [of] listening to us doing 'I'm a King Bee' when you can listen to Slim Harpo doing it?" Yet there are points beyond the popular premise expressed by Jagger and playfully proclaimed in a Dr. Pepper ad that "Nothing is as good as the original." The adage "never expect anything original from an echo" does not necessarily ring true with covers.

5 The process of covering a song is essentially an adaptation, in which much of the value lies in the artists' interpretation. A song travels a slightly different course than a piece which evolves from page to stage to screen, whether silver or small. With music, the song undergoes a recontextualization, remaining in the same medium, with the artists translating the material into a particular style. Measuring the interpreter's skill, in part, lies in how well the artist uncovers and conveys the spirit of the original, enhances the nuances of its melody, rhythm, phrasing, or structure, maybe adding a new arrangement, sense of occasion or thread of irony.

Musical mirroring may not be as simple as it seems on the surface. "In the best tributes the covering artist steals a song from the original and makes it their own, while they keep, even exaggerate, its original spirit. It's a tough trick, demanding authenticity and empathy," writes D. Dasein. In the process, the interpretation might offer a fresh insight into the song, its composer or a particular period. The imitative method allows artists to explore and expose their musical roots, perhaps broaden their own oeuvre with uncharacteristic materials, and pay homage not only to songs but to influential artists, composers, styles and eras. "When you do this, it's like being in the studio with a few great collaborators," explains Bryan Ferry, whose cover compilations include *Taxi* (1993), *As Time Goes By* (2001) and *Frantic* (2002). "Goffin and King[9] are there, saying: 'This is the tune. This is the lyric. Have a go?'"

---

[9] In the 1960s, husband-and-wife (for a time) songwriting team Gerry Goffin and Carol King wrote dozens of chart-topping songs for other artists [e.g., "Up on the Roof" for the Drifters and "(You Make Me Feel Like) A Natural Woman" for Aretha Franklin]. Their work has been covered many times. In 1971, King broke through as a solo artist with her album *Tapestry*.

A Treatise on Covers

by Tom Bligh

In a pub in Ireland, I heard an entertainer perform "I Just Called to Say I Love You" with only an acoustic guitar. He played slowly, drawing out the words through a brogue. Until that moment, I had no love for Stevie Wonder's song—his gleeful singing and the "from the bottom of my heart" line were too much. The plinky synthesizer sounded like an Atari game. I'd long since forgotten it until hearing the bare-bones performance in the pub. The cover version rescued it for me.

Movies get remade, songs get covered. A cover song comes with history attached. The song's past blends with its present to create something surprising yet recognizable: two stories in one, two contexts, two visions. Covers are familiar enough that we know what to expect, plus there's opportunity for the unexpected, an appealing combination of same/different. Our favorite songs slip away from us when overplayed. The familiarity does breed contempt. They become routine. We hardly notice what makes them special. A friend of mine says these songs don't register again unless you're drunk. Then they come through, fresh and strange; you appreciate them all over again. I propose another way to make old songs new: the cover version. The best covers show both artists in a new light. Sheryl Crow's "The First Cut Is the Deepest," however, doesn't stray much from Cat Stevens's original, other than flipping the pronouns for gender agreement and doing away with the George Harrisonesque guitar. Sometimes you just want to sing somebody else's song. I do. Why shouldn't Sheryl Crow? Covers needn't have a point. There's no point to singing in the shower.

• • •

Covers introduce us to artists we might otherwise miss. If A covers B, maybe B is worth looking into. Think of covers as gateway drugs that lead to strong musical addictions. On his latest release, *We Shall Overcome: The Seeger Sessions*, Bruce Springsteen performs a mix of traditionals and protest songs previously recorded by Pete Seeger. Through this romp of accordion, banjo, horns, and fiddles, Springsteen and his band tackle interpretations of "John Henry," "Froggie Went A-Courtin'," and others that lend themselves to washboard and moonshine jug. On "Pay Me My Money Down," Springsteen improvises, "I wish I was Mr. Gates / Pay me my money down / They'd haul my money in in crates."

• • •

When people like a cover, the common saying is that the artist "made it his/her own." That's never entirely true. Bits of associative residue cling to even the best covers. The relationship of cover to original is not wax-museum dummy to real person. We don't listen to a cover song because we can't find the original—we listen to experience the pleasures of a familiar song in a different way.

• • •

Covers aren't substitutes. Songs can supersede their creators just as children can grow   **5**
up to outshine their parents, but nobody really usurps ownership of a song by covering it. John Hiatt's "Thing Called Love" is in capable hands when Bonnie Raitt sings it on her 1989 album, *Nick of Time*, but listen to his version from 1987's *Bring the Family* and the catchy bass line might make you swear off Raitt's version.

• • •

The original artist doesn't refer to the person who wrote the song. The original refers to the first public recording. Frank Sinatra was a performer, not a composer. Yet it's accurate to say that other artists have covered Sinatra. "My Way" is Sinatra's song because it's become associated with him. Elvis Presley is another good example. He covered "Hound Dog" in 1956, three years after it had been a hit for Big Mama Thornton. But "Heartbreak Hotel" is an Elvis original, though Mae Boren Axton and Tommy Durden wrote it. (Elvis received songwriting credit through a scheme by Colonel Parker.)

A song written for one artist by another isn't a cover unless the song's composer recorded it and released it first. Patsy Cline's "Crazy" isn't really a Willie Nelson cover, though Nelson wrote the song. Technically, his version is the cover. The operative word is technically—it doesn't make any sense to think of it that way.

Although disadvantaged in many respects, the cover artist has the benefit of evaluating the original and formulating a strategy to take it in a different direction. The cover artist can play softer, louder, stranger, sadder, or add string orchestrations. Some covers succeed merely by removing distractions. The overproduction and pyrotechnics ubiquitous on Britney Spears records often obscure the lyrics. On "Oops! . . . I Did It Again," Britney changes her voice from crackling-baby-doll to sex-robot to teenybopper-sex-robot-with-crackling-voice. Richard Thompson's live version of "Oops!" strips away these studio effects to unearth a song about making mistakes and not feeling particularly sorry. Thompson even allows for a singalong, trusting his audience to know the words. (He isn't disappointed.)

Covering another artist's song should be a creative endeavor, just like recording a new song would be.

Discussion and Writing Suggestions

1. Plasketes finds a great deal of potential merit in covers. Still, he does present common arguments against: one, that we should "never expect anything original from an echo"; another, that imitation "is incongruent with authenticity." How important are originality and authenticity in popular music? To the extent a cover lacks either or both, can it succeed in your view? Explain.

2. Plasketes writes that "[m]easuring the interpreter's skill, in part, lies in how well the artist uncovers and conveys the spirit of the original, enhances the nuances of its melody, rhythm, phrasing, or structure, maybe adding a new arrangement, sense of occasion or thread of irony." Following these criteria, take the "measure" of one of the covers of "Over the Rainbow." How well has the interpreting artist done when judged by these criteria?

3. Plasketes writes: "In the best tributes the covering artist steals a song from the original and makes it their own, while they keep, even exaggerate, its original spirit." Use this observation to analyze one cover of "Over the Rainbow."

4. Bligh writes that hearing a cover once "rescued the song" for him. In what sense *rescued*? Do you think it possible that a songwriter can misinterpret or wrongly produce her or his own music? In this respect, can a cover be *better* than the original? Can you think of examples?

5. Bligh writes: "We don't listen to a cover song because we can't find the original—we listen to experience the pleasures of a familiar song in a different way." *Familiar* yet *different*: Use these terms to analyze one cover of "Over the Rainbow." Is there a point at which covers can become so different they become something new entirely? To what extent are you *drawn* to radical reinterpretations of songs? How important is familiarity? Discuss.

6. Do you agree with Bligh that the "best covers show both artists in a new light"? Why or why not? How can a cover show the *original* artist in a new light?

How to Talk—And Write—About Popular Music

Greg Blair

People in any profession talk shop, and when they do they often use "in-house" language. By this we mean the specialized vocabulary of a trade. Carpenters use the words "plumb" and "square." Software designers use the acronym "GUI" (for graphical user interface). Musicians also have their specialized language, and in the glossary that follows we'll introduce you to several key terms that should help you identify and then compare and contrast notable elements of songs and their covers. This glossary, written in nontechnical language, isn't meant to be exhaustive. Rather, it's limited to fundamental musical concepts that will help you consider the songs you hear and write about them with greater nuance and precision.

Musician Greg Blair has created companion YouTube videos that demonstrate (on musical instruments) each of the glossary terms. You'll find directions for locating these videos after the glossary.

Glossary

Accompaniment refers to everything that happens musically in support of the melody, or main tune. In many types of Western music (rock, country, jazz, pop, etc.), it is typical for an accompaniment to consist of a percussive beat, perhaps from drums, bass guitar, and chords being played on the guitar or piano. However, any instrument playing anything at all besides the melody can contribute to a song's accompaniment.

Dynamics means, quite simply, volume—specifically, it refers to the use of volume as an expressive performance element. When a musician or group of musicians play their instruments at a low or soft dynamic level, they are playing quietly. An elevated dynamic level means that the musicians are playing their instruments loudly. A piece of music can be described as having a narrow or wide "dynamic range," depending on how big the changes in dynamics are.

Note that "dynamics" refers only to the music as it is performed, and not how the listener plays the music on his or her speakers. If you were to crank up your speakers to make a soft part loud, you haven't changed the dynamics of the work itself.

Harmony is the result of multiple notes being played or sung simultaneously to form chords. Unless we are listening to a solo performer, we are typically hearing harmony in music all the time. Harmony is an essential element of musical accompaniment, the function of which is to support the melody. Harmony is used to evoke various moods throughout a piece, and different harmonies can radically change the way a melody sounds and the mood it evokes.

Over time, musicians have codified various types of harmonies and the ways in which one moment of harmony moves to the next; these are called "chord progressions." The "twelve-bar blues" is a popular progression of one set of harmonies—or chords—to the next, meaning that many different blues songs have the same underlying harmonies.

Instrumentation refers both to the number and type of instruments chosen for a performance of a piece of music. Music can have a large instrumentation (symphony orchestra), small (string quartet), or anywhere in between. A diverse instrumentation would be one with many different instruments, and a uniform instrumentation would feature multiple musicians playing the same instrument. In a choral piece for which the only musicians are the singers, there is only one "instrument," but there can be many or few of them. In this way, an instrumentation can be diverse or uniform regardless of the size of the group.

Typical Instrumentations:

Rock/Pop/Blues Band: Lead vocals, backup vocals, guitar(s), electric bass, keyboard, drums, and sometimes other instruments such as saxophone, trumpet, violin, or synthesizer.

Big Band: Clarinet(s), 5 saxes, 5 trumpets, 5 trombones, and piano, bass, and drums. Sometimes a lead singer is added to this instrumentation.

Orchestra: Large instrumentation typically comprised of strings (violins, violas, cellos, double bass), woodwinds (flutes, clarinets, oboes, bassoons), brass (trumpet, trombone, French horn, tuba), and percussion (timpani, cymbals, etc.).

Jazz Combo: Trumpet or saxophone (or both), piano, upright bass, and drums.

Bluegrass: Mandolin, fiddle, acoustic guitar, upright bass, and singers.

There are, of course, as many options for instrumentation as there are instruments and musicians who play them. This list is only a selection of some common instrumentations used in American music.

Improvisation occurs when a performer creates music—either a new melody or, for an instrument like piano, both melody and accompaniment—that has not previously been written down or planned ahead of time. This can take the form of embellishments to a melody or a departure altogether from the melody. The essential ingredient of improvisation is its spontaneity, though such spontaneity is typically rooted in a high degree of musical knowledge and practice.

Not every genre of music has improvisation as an element. For instance, in most classical music, the musicians perform a precisely written part. However, other musical genres, especially jazz, feature the heavy use of improvisation. In fact, the quality of a jazz musician is partly based on how well he or she improvises.

Usually, only one musician improvises at a time, while the others play an accompaniment to the improvised melody.

Legato notes are held for maximum duration and connected to one another without a noticeable break between them. They thicken and smooth out the texture of the music being played. (The opposite of "legato" is "staccato," defined below.)

"Legato" and "staccato" are terms that are independent of dynamic level—that is, one can play legato/staccato notes loudly or softly. Additionally, legato and staccato do not refer to the number of notes being played, or the speed at which they are played. A musician can play one note by itself or many fast ones in a row. As long as the note or notes sound long and connected, then they are being played legato. If they sound short and separated, then they are being played staccato.

A **melody** is a collection of notes played in a certain order and is typically the most recognizable part of a song. When many notes are being played at once, the melody is the lead or most prominent line. The melody is particularly easy to identify in music with a vocalist, because it is often the part of the music to which the principle lyrics are set—and the part that the lead singer sings.

Pitch refers to how "high" or "low" a note is and is sometimes used synonymously with "note." A piccolo plays high pitches, while a tuba plays low ones, and every instrument (except for some percussion instruments) play a range of pitches. Technically, the pitch of a note has a frequency that can be measured as the number of vibrations or "beats" per second. For instance, when an orchestra tunes to "Concert A," that pitch corresponds precisely to 440 beats per second. When a guitar gets tuned, the musician is adjusting the instrument so that each string corresponds to a specific pitch. When musicians are imprecise with their pitches, the result is an unpleasant, muddy sound—though some musicians intentionally adjust or "bend" their pitch to create a bluesy, gritty effect.

Rhythm Generally speaking, musical notes are comprised of two main elements: "pitch," which corresponds to how high or low the notes are, and "rhythm," which corresponds to their duration, emphasis, and the time between one note and the next. For example, if you were to tap out the melody of "Happy Birthday" on your tabletop, you would be playing the song's rhythm. In fact, it's possible that somebody walking by and hearing you would *recognize* the song as "Happy Birthday" even though you aren't playing any pitches at all.

If a flute and a tuba were to play the same melody, the pitches would be quite different—the flute's pitch would be much higher than the tuba's—but the rhythms played by the two instruments would be the same.

"Rhythm" is also used to describe a song's metrical sound more generally and is frequently used synonymously with "beat," "meter," and "tempo."

A band's "rhythm section" is comprised of instruments whose primary purpose is to create and sustain the song's beat—typically, drums and bass guitar.

Riffs are brief, memorable melodies that often recur throughout a piece of music. They can either be part of the main melody or part of the accompaniment that momentarily jumps out to the forefront. In pop music, riffs are often called "hooks," as they "hook" the listener's ear and help the song stick in the listener's head.

A **rubato** section is a part of a piece of music that temporarily breaks from the established beat or tempo. Rubato sections allow the instrumentalist or singer to add a personal, often dramatic touch to a piece of music. These sections are often found at the very beginning or end of a piece, or at the end of a particularly dramatic section of music, though they can occur anywhere.

A **staccato** note is one that is played in a short, punctuated manner. Staccato notes have the effect of sounding clipped and succinct, and often thin the texture of the music being played. The opposite of "staccato" is "legato." (See definition above.)

Tempo is the Italian word for "time." It is fitting, then, that the tempo of a piece of music has to do with how fast it moves through time—specifically, its "speed" or "pace." A fast tempo (or "up-tempo") song is one with a fast beat, and a slow tempo song has a slow beat. The exact tempo of a piece of music can be described by its "beats per minute" (bpm). The higher the bpm, the faster the tempo.

Timbre (pronounced TAM-ber) most closely translates to "tone color." Any individual instrument or sound has a timbre, and a collection of instruments or sounds playing together also has a timbre.

Think of the difference between an electric guitar and a violin, or between an opera singer and the lead singer of a rock band. Even when they all play the same notes, all of these instruments or voices produce sounds with distinct tone qualities, or timbres.

Words often used to describe timbre include: warm, harsh, dark, bright, thin, velvety.

Note that "loud" and "soft" are not descriptions of timbre. Rather, they are dynamics. (See "dynamics," defined above.)

Vibrato, loosely translated as "vibration," is a technique that musicians use to make a note seem to waver or vibrate. It involves changing the dynamic of the note very quickly between soft and loud. This is often accompanied by a subtle upward and downward bending of a pitch. Many, though not all, singers use vibrato to some degree. While most instruments can be played with vibrato, several of them (violin, cello, flute) are almost always played with vibrato by expert musicians, while others (clarinet and most brass instruments) are less often played with vibrato. It is not possible to achieve vibrato on most percussion instruments (except, notably, on the vibraphone, named for its characteristic vibrato).

A vibrato can be wide—sometimes called "fat"—and dramatic, with a noticeable bending of a note and large dynamic changes (something more common in older instrumental and operatic music), or it can be narrow and subtle, or even nonexistent.

Music Glossary Videos

Visit the Revel version of the text or go to YouTube and search for "WRAC Music Glossary Videos." Select from this group those individual videos you wish to see. Individual videos may also be found by typing key search terms in YouTube's search box; for example, "rhythm greg blair"

Comparing and Contrasting Three Covers of "Stormy Weather"

Greg Blair

The following paper compares and contrasts three very different versions of the song "Stormy Weather," written in 1933 by Harold Arlen (who also wrote the music to "Over the Rainbow") and Ted Koehler. "Stormy Weather" is a classic "torch song"—one in which the artist sings longingly and with disappointment about her (or his) lost or unrequited love. Like many popular songs from the thirties written for the musical theater or musical films, "Stormy Weather" has been covered hundreds of times. In the paper that follows, Greg Blair compares three of these covers using terms from the glossary immediately preceding. His paper demonstrates how to write about music in a way that's descriptive, analytical, and comparative.

You can find two of the three versions of the song on YouTube by searching on the following terms:

Lena Horne: "lena horne stormy weather 1943"

Royal Crown Revue: "stormy weather royal crown revue" (3:31 version)

Although you don't need to be a musician to read and understand this paper, it contains certain musical terms that might be unfamiliar to you. When reading the paper—and later, when writing your own musical analyses—you'll probably find it helpful to refer to the musical glossary created especially for this chapter. The text version begins on page 229, and the online version, featuring videos that demonstrate each term, is available in the Revel version of the text or on the "WRAC Music Glossary Videos" YouTube channel.

Greg Blair is a saxophonist, arranger, and composer—and licensed sailing instructor—living in Amherst, MA. He has a degree in music from the University of Massachusetts, Amherst.

One of the more enduring songs of the last eighty years is Harold Arlen and Ted Koehler's now-classic "Stormy Weather." It is a narrative about lost love in which the singer explains that she and her "man ain't together" and, because of that, it "keeps raining all the time." The singer Ethel Waters debuted "Stormy Weather" at New York's famous Cotton Club in 1933, and both she and Frances Langford recorded it that year—as did composer and bandleader Duke Ellington in a purely instrumental arrangement. Vocalists and instrumentalists, hundreds by this point, have been reinterpreting the song ever since. We get a sense of the variety of these covers by examining three very different approaches: recordings by singer Lena Horne and by the bands Royal Crown Revue and the Kooks.

Lena Horne's version of "Stormy Weather" appears in the 1943 movie of the same name. This early performance, set in a nightclub, includes trumpets, trombones, saxophones, and clarinet in addition to the usual rhythm section of piano, upright bass, and drums—a classic "big band" accompaniment. From the outset, the sound of this iconic instrumentation transports the listener back in time to the jazz age of the thirties and forties. This was a time when hundreds of couples in ballrooms danced to the swing rhythms of the big bands led by bandleaders like Benny Goodman, Paul Whiteman, and Ted Lewis. Following the intro, Ms. Horne launches into the melody of the song at 0:30, at a gentle yet steady tempo in which she mourns the breakup with her man in a performance that is dramatic and sincere. The band's accompaniment—warm and lush, with legato playing from all instruments—gracefully sustains this musical lament. It isn't until almost halfway through the song (2:49) that we finally hear some short, punctuated staccato hits from the band that change the texture of the accompaniment and create a sense of emotional urgency, as if the singer has reached a point of crisis in this tale of broken love. At 2:58, the group enters a rubato section in which the band breaks from a steady tempo to achieve a moment of reflection before the main melody returns for the last time. At 3:13, the original tempo returns and the song ends at 3:48, when the orchestra abruptly transitions to the next piece of music in their program. Throughout, Ms. Horne's vocal timbre is slightly nasal but warm, velvety, and rich in vibrato. This is characteristic of much of the popular music of the time and contributes to the song's mournful mood.

One might think that a tale of broken love can only be mournful, but Royal Crown Revue's 1998 cover of "Stormy Weather" proves otherwise. Royal Crown Revue is a band from Los Angeles, formed in 1989. Improbably, their performance of the song is an up-tempo, finger-snapping version. It opens with a sharp, gun-like burst of drums that gives way to swinging saxophone riffs, announcing a peppy, sassy take on the song. This version is borne out with the condensed, modern instrumentation of electric guitar and bass, drums, trumpet, saxophone, and vocals, further differentiating it from the expansive instrumentation of Ms. Horne's version. At 0:08 the lead singer enters with the melody, with a warm vocal timbre and just a touch of vibrato. This is not the mournful, soul-searching vocal we hear from Horne. Rather, lead singer Eddie Nichols sounds slightly amused as he sings ". . . can't get my poor self together," as if he knows that this spell of stormy weather is precisely what he deserves and that he might as well enjoy it. At 0:34, the melody repeats with the addition of background vocals, which support the lead singer and add a new texture to the musical and emotional landscape. We hear a new riff from the trumpet, sax, and guitar at 0:57, and at 1:23 there is a return to both the main melody and the riff that we've heard previously. A unique feature of this version of the song is the sax solo at 1:49. The saxophonist plays with a rough, thick, growling tone, which is typical of the upbeat and sassy swing style of music the group is playing. At 2:57, the band uses a common tactic of repeating the last phrase of the melody ("rainin' all the time") several times. This is known as "tagging" the ending. Following the tag, the band plays a few rubato hits to end the song.

The Kooks, a British band formed in 2004, have yet another distinctive take on "Stormy Weather." The overall feel of their recording is swampy and earthy, certainly more raw sounding than the other two versions. It features only acoustic guitar, harmonica (heard at 0:16 in the intro and for a solo at 2:47), and a singer, with his raspy, rock-and-roll vocal timbre. The tempo of this version is on the slow side, similar to Ms. Horne's version, and as such it shares with the Horne version an earnestness that contrasts with Royal Crown Revue's slicker, more ironic version. The Kooks add some simple but pleasing vocal harmonies beginning at 1:33. These harmonies add a welcome yet brief change in texture, breathing fresh air into the arrangement. At 1:57, drums enter softly, lending more forward drive without changing the overall melancholy mood. The drums become louder at 2:24, then softer again for the harmonica solo at 2:47. These small changes in instrumentation and dynamics provide just enough variation in this stripped-down version to keep it from becoming predictable. The ending is simple but effective—the singer and guitarist slow down a bit on the last phrase of the song, and the guitarist strums the final chord.

5   From the number and types of instruments, to decisions about tempo and dynamics, to the singer's distinctive approach to the melody, these three versions of "Stormy Weather"

demonstrate the wide range of options musicians have when covering a song. Whether it's Royal Crown Revue upping the tempo and adding recurring riffs, the Kooks paying special attention to dynamics, or Horne employing a thick vibrato that soars above the lush big band accompaniment, each version finds unique ways to interpret Harold Arlen and Ted Koehler's song. In fact, these versions, taken together, pay tribute to Arlen and Koehler's classic song by revealing just how rich in potential it remains even after eight decades.

Covers of "Stormy Weather"

Harold Arlen and Ted Koehler

"Stormy Weather," written in 1933 by Harold Arlen and Ted Koehler, is one of the most enduring songs in "The Great American Songbook."[10] It is a classic "torch song"—one in which the artist sings longingly and disappointedly about her (or his) lost or unrequited love. The song was first sung in public by Ethel Waters at Harlem's Cotton Club, to the accompaniment of Duke Ellington and his orchestra. Waters's version of "Stormy Weather" became famous, but the song has been recorded by many other artists, including Lena Horne, Billie Holliday, Francis Langford, Glenn Miller (an orchestral version), Frank Sinatra, Sarah Vaughan, Etta James, Shirley Bassey, Joni Mitchell, the Muppets, and at least two finalists on *American Idol*.

The best-known covers of "Stormy Weather":

> **Ethel Waters**
> **Ella Fitzgerald**
> **Lena Horne**
> **Billie Holiday**
> **Judy Garland**
> **Frank Sinatra** [*4:15 and 3:38 versions*]
> **Louis Armstrong**

Additional covers of "Stormy Weather":

> **Ted Lewis**
> **Coleman Hawkins**
> **Glenn Miller**
> **Frances Langford**
> **Charlie and His Orchestra** [*Nazi propaganda version!*]
> **Art Tatum**
> **Peggy Lee**
> **Liberace** [*"Mr. Showmanship"*]
> **Carmen Cavallaro**

---

[10] "The Great American Songbook" is a term used to indicate popular songs, mainly from musical theater and musical films, that were written and performed from the 1920s to the 1950s. Among the most popular composers of such songs were Irving Berlin, Sigmund Romberg, George Gershwin, Cole Porter, Jerome Kern, Harold Arlen, Richard Rodgers, Hoagy Carmichael, Johnny Green, Johnny Mercer, Herman Hupfield, Billy Strayhorn, Duke Ellington, Sammy Fain, Frank Loesser, Henry Mancini, Harry Ruby, Arthur Schwartz, Jule Styne, Frederick Lowe, Jimmy van Heusen, Harry Warren, Dorothy Fields, Naio Herb Brown, and Victor Young.

Etta James
Sarah Reid and Alex Serra
Amos Milburn
Charles Mingus [*3:19*]
Kay Starr
Eydie Gormé
Keely Smith
Willie Nelson and Shelby Lynne
The Spaniels
Elizabeth Welch
The Muppets
Reigning Sound [*punk version*]
Royal Crown Revue [*L.A. band: 3:31 and 3:49*]
Barbara Dennerlein
Oscar Peterson and Itzhak Perlman
Liza Minnelli
Joni Mitchell
Shirley Bassey
George Benson
Fantasia [*5:40 and 3:30*]

We have not nearly listed all of the covers of "Stormy Weather," and you may find it interesting to sample others. Go to YouTube, type "stormy weather covers" into the search box, and scroll through some of the results. For example, try the version by Vanessa Williams, Sal Grippaldi's 2013 trumpet solo, or the duet by Tony Bennett and Natalie Cole.

Discussion and Writing Suggestions

1. Which of these versions do you like the best? Which the least? Explain the reasons for your preferences.

2. Compare Judy Garland's cover of "Stormy Weather" to that of her daughter, Liza Minnelli. What similarities and differences in style and sound do you find between these two versions of the song?

3. Listen to the three piano versions of "Stormy Weather": those by Art Tatum, Liberace, and Carmen Cavallaro. (Add Barbara Dennerlein's organ version to the mix, if you wish.) What makes them sound different? How do these different performances affect the mood of the song?

4. Both Lena Horne's and Elisabeth Welch's covers of "Stormy Weather" are staged versions, involving a set and other characters who interact with the performer. Compare and contrast these performances in style and mood.

5. How well, in your view, does the "punk" sound of Reigning Sound's 2002 performance of "Stormy Weather" fit with the music and lyrics of the song? Why do you think the band might have chosen to record this particular song? How does their interpretation compare with that of the Spaniels's 1957 performance?

6. How do the gravelly voice of Louis Armstrong and the smooth voice of Frank Sinatra bring out different qualities of "Stormy Weather"?

7. Compare and contrast Ethel Waters and Fantasia (or two other singers of your choice) as interpreters of "Stormy Weather." Note: This is less a matter of determining which singer is "better," but rather, how the singers convey different moods and interpretations.

8. Shirley Bassey's cover of "Stormy Weather" is offered as a "tribute" to Lena Horne's. Compare and contrast the two performances.

9. From your review of these covers, can you draw some preliminary conclusions about which qualities make for the most successful covers? Do you find yourself being more interested in the versions that stick closer to the original song and its mood, or to versions that depart significantly from the original?

Covers of "Hallelujah"

Leonard Cohen

Nearly half a century after the release of "Over the Rainbow," songwriter Leonard Cohen wrote "Hallelujah" (1984), widely regarded as a modern classic. With its haunting melody and compelling lyrics, "Hallelujah" has attracted many cover artists. Give the song and a few of its covers a listen. If your musical preferences lead you away from writing about "Over the Rainbow" or "Stormy Weather" (see pages 235–236), consider comparing and contrasting different covers of "Hallelujah." You'll find most of the versions listed here on YouTube. Type "cohen hallelujah" and the cover artist's name into the search box.

The four most influential covers are those by the following artists:

Leonard Cohen
John Cale
Jeff Buckley
Rufus Wainwright

Other noteworthy covers have been produced by these artists or groups:

K. D. Lang
Bono *(a highly idiosyncratic treatment)*
Bob Dylan
Willie Nelson
Over the Rhine
Ari Hest
Brandi Carlile
Justin Timberlake
Regina Spektor
Alendra Burke with Elton John
Casey Pitel

Beirut

Amanda Palmer

Imogen Heap

Kathryn Williams

Damien Rice

Keren Ann

Jake Shimabukuro *(ukulele version)*

The various covers of "Hallelujah" have been given insightful book-length treatment by Alan Light in *The Holy or the Broken: Leonard Cohen, Jeff Buckley, and the Unlikely Ascent of "Hallelujah"* (2012). We have drawn upon Light's remarks about the various "Hallelujah" covers in several of the following questions.

Discussion and Writing Suggestions

1. Which of these versions do you like best? Why?

2. From your review of two or more versions of "Hallelujah," can you draw some preliminary conclusions about which qualities make for the most successful covers? Do you find yourself being more interested in the versions that stick closer to the original song and its mood, or to versions that depart significantly from the original?"

3. Write a comparative analysis of any three versions of "Hallelujah," using Greg Blair's comparative analysis of "Stormy Weather" covers as a model.

4. In Alan Light's interviews with the producer John Lissauer and others concerning the recording of and reactions to Cohen's "Hallelujah," we find emotionally loaded expressions like "makes me feel good"; "uplifting"; "blessed"; "sincerity"; and "struggle, conflict, and resignation." What has emotion to do with music? Discuss one of your favorite songs—or one of its covers—in terms of your emotional responses to the particular performance. How does emotion attach itself to, and in what sense is it *in*, the song?

5. Light writes about John Cale's editing of Cohen's "Hallelujah": "Despite his implication that he avoided the spiritual dimension of the song, Cale sensed the elemental power of the biblical stories and languages, and returned them to the position of the song's entry point, but then undercut them with the lyrics focused on . . . longing and tragic romance." Light is saying that in interpreting Cohen's song, Cale in some sense re- or co-created it. How is this possible? Again selecting one of your favorite songs, explain how a cover artist brings a song that is already in existence into existence (again).

6. Light writes that in recording many takes of "Hallelujah," Jeff Buckley searched "for the subtleties and nuances he wanted, for a precise shading in the ultimate delivery of this song that he had come to inhabit so fully." Think of a particular song that you love. In what sense do you "inhabit" it? In what sense does the song, which someone else has written, become "yours"? If you were, or are, a musician, how might your answers to these questions

influence the cover you might do of this song? That is, on what basis, or by what right, do you have to sing someone else's song *your* way?

7. Consider Light's description of Jeff Buckley's "Hallelujah" cover: "Where the older Cohen and Cale sang the words with a sense of experience and perseverance, of hard lessons won, this rising star delivered the lyrics with swooning emotion, both fragile and indomitable." In drawing upon such subjective vocabulary, Light does not use objective or technical terms of music (like the ones you'll find in this chapter's glossary) to describe Buckley's cover. Still, his description is effective in helping you understand the distinctive flavor and power of a particular cover. How so?

The Greatest Covers of All Time

Ranking artistic works is a very subjective, and controversial, matter. For example, in 2012, Alfred Hitchcock's 1958 thriller *Vertigo* was ranked first in *Sight and Sound*'s once-in-a-decade list of the greatest films of all time. But in the American Film Institute's comparable listing, this same film was ranked sixty-first. So much for critical consensus on the greatest films of all time.

Despite—or perhaps because of—such disagreements, ranking artistic efforts is both a pleasurable and useful exercise. It's pleasurable because in the process of such ranking we enjoy the work again and therefore reexperience those qualities that so appealed to us in the first place. And it's useful because it requires us to exercise our judgment and to justify our choices to others, thereby sharpening our critical faculties.

So let's take the phrase "the greatest covers of all time" with a grain of salt and admit, first, that all such listings represent the personal preferences of individuals or groups of individuals and, second, that we may assemble a very different list based on differences of taste. But let's also agree that such listings are a starting point for some great listening and some interesting conversations/arguments. As a practical matter for the assignments in this chapter, they provide an extensive set of resources from which you can select and discuss your own favorite covers.

We begin with a *Rolling Stone* listing (compiled by Andy Greene) of reader-selected best cover songs:[11]

1. Jimi Hendrix—"All Along the Watchtower"

Last weekend we asked our readers to pick their favorite cover song of all time. Unlike previous readers' polls, the top vote getter won by a gigantic margin. Your favorite cover (with no close second) is Jimi Hendrix's take on Bob Dylan's "All Along the Watchtower." Released six months after Dylan's original appeared on *John Wesley Harding* in December 1967, Hendrix's version radically rearranged Dylan's acoustic original. Dylan didn't play the song live until 1974, and said Hendrix's rendition made him reconsider how to approach the song.

---

[11] "Rolling Stone Readers Pick the Top 10 Greatest Covers," by Andy Greene, RollingStone.com, March 2, 2011. Copyright © Rolling Stone LLC 2011. All Rights Reserved. Used by Permission.

"[Hendrix] could find things inside a song and vigorously develop them," Dylan told the *Fort Lauderdale Sun Sentinel* in 1995. "He found things that other people wouldn't think of finding in there. He probably improved upon it by the spaces he was using. I took license with the song from his version, actually, and continue to do it to this day."

2. Johnny Cash—"Hurt"

Trent Reznor remembers the first time he saw the video for Johnny Cash's cover of his 1994 song "Hurt." "Tears started welling up," he said. "I realized it wasn't really my song anymore. It just gave me goose bumps up and down my spine. It's an unbelievably powerful piece of work. After he passed away I remember feeling saddened, but being honored to have framed the end of his life in something that is very tasteful."

3. Jeff Buckley—"Hallelujah"

Leonard Cohen's career was at a low point when he wrote "Hallelujah" in the early eighties, and his record label had no interest in even releasing the track or the rest of the songs that eventually came out on 1984's *Various Positions*. The track was a fan favorite, but it didn't receive much love until the Velvet Underground's John Cale created a stripped-down piano version for a 1991 Leonard Cohen tribute album.

Jeff Buckley used Cale's version as the basis for his stunningly beautiful version of the song on his 1994 LP *Grace*. The track wasn't a single, but after Buckley's tragic death in 1997 the song slowly started to become recognized as a classic.

4. Joe Cocker—"With a Little Help from My Friends"

It's one of the most indelible images from Woodstock: Joe Cocker, looking so stoned he can barely stand upright, belting out the Beatles classic "With a Little Help from My Friends" like it was an old soul standard. The performance became a key part of 1971's Woodstock documentary, instantly turning the radical reimagining of the tune into Cocker's signature song. In the late eighties, when the producers of *The Wonder Years* needed a single song to represent the sixties, they went with this.

5. Nirvana—"The Man Who Sold the World"

Until Nirvana taped their *MTV Unplugged* special in late 1993, "The Man Who Sold the World" was known only as one of David Bowie's earliest hits. After Kurt Cobain's suicide the song became his, and the tale of a man who had the world and gave it away seemed eerily prophetic. When Bowie revived the song on his 1995 tour with Nine Inch Nails many of the young fans in the audience had no idea it was his song, assuming he was doing a special Nirvana tribute.

6. The Beatles—"Twist and Shout"

The Beatles cut their 1963 LP *Please Please Me* in a single day, so when it came time for John Lennon to sing a cover of the Isley Brothers' "Twist and Shout" near the end of the session his voice was shredded. He rallied by gargling milk and swallowing cough drops before nailing the song in just two takes. He was unhappy with how his voice sounded, but the raw sound is part of what makes the track so memorable.

7. The White Stripes—"Jolene"

Dolly Parton's 1973 classic song "Jolene" is hardly a feminist anthem. Inspired by a true story, the song is in the voice of a desperate woman begging a more attractive woman to not steal her man. Not a single word is reserved for the man in the love triangle. The White Stripes recorded a snarling, feedback-laden cover of it in 2000, and it was a highlight of their live show through their last tour in 2007.

8. Nirvana—"Where Did You Sleep Last Night"

Unlike most *Unplugged* specials, Nirvana did very few of their hits at the TV taping. They opted mainly for deep cuts and covers of songs by the Vaselines, David Bowie, and the Meat Puppets—as well as this 19th-century folk standard that was popularized by folk legend Lead Belly. A 1990 home demo of the song appears on Nirvana's 2004 box set *With the Lights Out*, but the definitive version (with the screaming final verse) is on *Unplugged*.

9. Guns N' Roses—"Knockin' on Heaven's Door"

Originally written for the soundtrack to *Pat Garrett and Billy the Kid*, "Knockin' on Heaven's Door" gave Bob Dylan a much-needed hit after years of being written off as a washed-up sixties relic. The song was covered by everybody from Eric Clapton to U2, but in 1990 Guns N' Roses recorded it for the *Days of Thunder* soundtrack and introduced it to an entirely new generation. [It became a staple of their live show.]

10. Muse—"Feeling Good"

Written for the widely forgotten 1965 Broadway musical *The Roar of the Greasepaint—The Smell of the Crowd*, "Feeling Good" has been covered by Nina Simone, Bobby Darin, Frank Sinatra, George Michael, and countless others. Muse recorded a popular version for their 2001 LP *Origin of Symmetry*, which has recently gotten a lot of play in America in a commercial for Virgin Airlines.

Here are some additional best cover lists you may enjoy browsing through. YouTube provides links to many of the songs listed:

Search for:
"100 best songs of the past twenty-five years"
"15 best song covers ever"
"10 most covered songs"
"jack whites best classic rock cover songs"
"rolling stones top greatest cover songs"
"24 greatest cover versions of all time"
"top ten cover songs that are better than the original"
"top forty cover songs from the movies"
"top 21 cover songs that make you realize how amazing the originals were"
"unexpected cover songs 20 unique renditions of famous tunes"
"elvis hound dog among best 11 cover songs of all time"
"20 bob dylan songs deserve a listen"

Assignment: Comparative Analysis

Working with your favorite song from among those cited in the *Rolling Stone* list or the list of covers we've provided for "Over the Rainbow," "Stormy Weather," and "Hallelujah," write a comparative analysis. Open your analysis with the best-known version of the song (Judy Garland for "Rainbow," Lena Horne for "Stormy Weather," and Leonard Cohen for "Hallelujah"). Choose at least two covers and write an analysis in which you compare and contrast covers with the original/signature version. Use Greg Blair's comparative analysis of "Stormy Weather" (pages 233–235) as a model.

In this chapter, you have several sources to draw from in choosing criteria for analysis. Following Blair, you could use terms from the musical glossary and discuss, for instance, different tempos or instrumentation. George Plasketes suggests potentially useful criteria when he discusses "the spirit of the original," the "rhythm, phrasing, or structure." Tom Bligh uses the terms "familiar" and "different" to discuss covers.

We suggest opening the paper as follows:

- In a few paragraphs, discuss the original artist's performance of the song you've selected. For a model of such a discussion, review Greg Blair's discussion of "Stormy Weather."

- For criteria, you can draw on terms discussed by Greg Blair in his glossary— or terms offered by Plasketes or Bligh—to indicate what is happening musically as the song progresses. (You may wish to rewatch one or more of Blair's videos on YouTube.)

- At the end of this section of your paper, draw conclusions about the overall impact of the original song and how it achieves its distinctive mood and voice and its emotional power.

Next, select at least two covers of this song performed by other artists. In the same manner as you described the song performed by the original artist(s), explain how the cover artists reinterpret this song in a way that retains (to some extent) the identity of the original while transmuting it into a different form. Draw comparisons and contrasts.

As you work toward a conclusion, discuss which version of the song you like best and/or least, offering reasons for your preferences. How did the musical artist(s) get it just right for you? How did other versions fall short? Finally, what do you conclude about the qualities that make for successful musical covers?

Chapter 9
Obedience to Authority

Would you obey an order to inflict pain on another person? Most of us, if confronted with this question, would probably be quick to answer, "Never!" Yet if the conclusions of researchers are to be trusted, it is not psychopaths who kill noncombatant civilians in wartime and torture victims in prisons around the world, but rather ordinary people following orders—or caught up in the singularly *un*ordinary circumstances of the moment. People obey. This is a basic, necessary fact of human society. As psychologist Stanley Milgram has written, "Obedience is as basic an element in the structure of social life as one can point to. Some system of authority is a requirement of all communal living."

Setting aside the dramatic cases where people have acted badly, or worse, in following immoral orders of authority figures, the more realistic challenge may be this: Would you follow a manager's order and not report an act of theft at your workplace? Or this: Backed by years of tradition and the urging of your teammates or fraternity/sorority brothers and sisters, would you physically or emotionally abuse a junior member of a sports team or a "pledge" as part of an induction ceremony? These are not hypothetical questions. Hazing rituals are common and recipients suffer. In an extreme case, in 2011 a band member from Florida A&M's famous marching band was beaten to death in a hazing ritual.

The selections that follow will explore the question of when, and to what extent, one should obey the orders of an authority figure. The chapter opens with Christopher Wellman and John Simmons making the classic case for obedience: without it, according to seventeenth-century political philosopher Thomas Hobbes, "the life of man [would be] solitary, poore, nasty, brutish, and short." Next, psychoanalyst and philosopher Erich Fromm discusses the comforts—and dangers—of obedience in "Disobedience as a Psychological and Moral Problem." In "The Power of Situations," social psychologists Lee Ross and Richard Nisbett provide an overview of the situational forces that can strongly influence behavior. Saul McLeod then reports on the landmark Milgram experiments, which revealed the extent to which ordinary individuals will obey the clearly immoral orders of an authority figure. Pointers to two online videos follow, both concerning famous experiments in social psychology. In the Stanford Prison Experiment, college students role-played becoming guards and prisoners in a mock prison—with disturbing results. In the Asch Line-Length experiment, subjects denied the evidence of their own eyes in order to fit into a group. Columnist David Brooks of the *New York Times* reviews some of the paradoxes of power—of both leadership and what he calls "followership."

Obedience is fundamental to any civil society. To what extent and under what circumstances we should obey is the challenging question you will explore in this Brief Takes chapter.

Read; Prepare to Write

As you read these selections, prepare for the assignments by marking up the texts: Write notes to yourself in the margins, and comment on what the authors have said.

To prepare for the more ambitious of the assignments that follow—the explanatory and argument syntheses—consider drawing up a topic list of your sources as you read. For each topic about which two or more authors have something to say, jot down notes and page (or paragraph) references. Here's an example:

Topic: *Obedience is a given in human society.*

- Wellman and Simmons quote Thomas Hobbes on the necessity of obedience, without which humans would be in a continual state of war. (¶s 1–2 , p. 245)
- Fromm: Obedience and disobedience exist in a balance. (¶7, p. 248)
- McLeod: Obedience "to legitimate authority is learned in a variety of situations, for example in the family, school and workplace." (¶18, p. 256)

A robust topic list, keyed to your sources, will spare you the frustration of reading these three sources and flipping through them later, saying, "Now where did I read that?" At this early point, you don't need to know how you might write a paper using this or any other topic. But a list with multiple topics and accurate notes for each lays the groundwork for your own discussion later and puts you in a good position to write a synthesis.

Group Assignment: Make a Topic List

Working in groups of three or four, create a topic list for the selections in this chapter, jotting down notes and page (or paragraph) references. Try making notes for one or two of the following topics to get you started. Find and take notes on other topics common to two or more sources. When you're done, share your topic lists with fellow group members.

- Obedience and progress
- Disobedience and progress

- Misguided disobedience
- Just vs. unjust authority
- Examples of disobedience
- The role of conscience
- The tension between obedience and disobedience

The Readings and Videos

Why I Am Not an Anarchist

Christopher Wellman and John Simmons

This selection makes the classic case for obedience: that without it, "the life of man [would be] solitary, poore, nasty, brutish, and short." Quoting the seventeenth-century political philosopher Thomas Hobbes, Wellman and Simmons define one pole of the debate you'll be reading about in this chapter. As you read, bear in mind the crucial question on which you'll be writing: under what circumstances, if ever, should one disobey a law or the direct order of an authority figure? Christopher Heath Wellman teaches philosophy and education at Washington University (St. Louis). A. John Simmons teaches ethics, political philosophy, and philosophy of law at the University of Virginia. The following first appeared in Chapter 1 of their *Is There a Duty to Obey the Law*? (2005).

[I]n the absence of a political state, one should expect three especially glaring problems to emerge. Without an authoritative legislative body to establish a definitive set of rules that everyone must follow, there will be conflicts even among well-intentioned people who genuinely seek to treat each other according to the demands of morality. Without an effective executive body to ensure that a reasonable percentage of rule breakers are caught and punished, those disinclined to respect the moral rights of others will not be sufficiently deterred and, ultimately, everyone's incentives to pursue productive projects and meaningful relationships will diminish markedly. Finally, without a standing judicial body to impartially adjudicate conflicts and assign criminal punishments, attempts to exact revenge and mete out justice will lead to increasingly bloody conflicts. Moreover, it is important to recognize that the cumulative effect of these three factors is more than additive; these elements will combine to create a vicious cycle in which each consideration presents an aggravating factor that exacerbates the others.

It is hard to exaggerate how horrible life would be in the absence of political security, but one theorist who has been accused of doing so is Thomas Hobbes. He famously describes life without political order (often referred to as the "state of nature") as follows:

> Hereby it is manifest, that during the time men live without a common Power to keep them all in awe, they are in that condition which is called Warre; and such a warre, as is of every man, against every man. . . . Whatsoever therefore is consequent to a time of Warre, where every man is Enemy to every man; the same is consequent to the time, wherein men live without other security, than what their own strength, and their own invention shall furnish them withall. In such condition, there is no place for Industry; because the fruit thereof is uncertain: and consequently no Culture of the Earth; no Navigation, nor use of the commodities that may be imported by Sea; no commodious Building; no Instruments of moving, and removing such things as require much force; no Knowledge of the face of the Earth; no account of Time; no Arts; no Letters; no Society; and which is worst of all, continuall feare, and danger of violent death; And the life of man, solitary, poore, nasty, brutish, and short.

Certainly there is reason to quibble with various details of Hobbes's description of the state of nature as well as his elaborate argument in support of that description, but it strikes me as difficult to deny the general picture. Put plainly, for the vast majority of us, life without political order would be a horribly perilous environment.

Part of the explanation for why I am not an anarchist, then, is that states perform incredibly important legislative, executive, and judicial functions.

Discussion and Writing Suggestions

1. Have you any evidence from your own life, from both informal groups and more formal ones like clubs or teams, of what happens when there are no clear rules? Does behavior inevitably turn bad?

2. Wellman and Simmons make the classic case for obedience as a relinquishing of some rights in exchange for civil order, safety, and productivity. Consider the individual rights being exchanged. What are they? Why are they to be valued? Were you, are you, conscious of giving over your rights in exchange for the opportunity to live in a community?

3. Paraphrase the famous passage that Wellman and Simmons quote from Thomas Hobbes. Once you have rendered Hobbes's language in your own words, comment on it. Do you agree with him?

4. Prior to reading this selection, to what extent did you think through the logic of a state's having separate legislative, executive, and judicial functions? What is the importance of each function, according to the authors?

Disobedience as a Psychological and Moral Problem

Erich Fromm

Erich Fromm (1900–1980) was one of the twentieth century's distinguished writers and thinkers. Psychoanalyst and philosopher, historian and sociologist, he ranged widely in his interests and defied easy characterization. Fromm studied the works of Freud and Marx closely, and published on them both, but he was not aligned strictly with either. In much of his voluminous writing, he struggled to articulate a view that could help bridge ideological and personal conflicts and bring dignity to those who struggled with isolation in the industrial world. Author of more than thirty books and contributor to numerous edited collections and journals, Fromm is best known for *Escape from Freedom* (1941), *The Art of Loving* (1956), and *To Have or to Be?* (1976).

In the essay that follows, first published in 1963, Fromm discusses the seductive comforts of obedience, and he makes distinctions among varieties of obedience, some of which he believes are destructive, and others, life affirming. His thoughts on nuclear annihilation may seem dated in these days of post–Cold War cooperation, but it is worth remembering that Fromm wrote his essay just after the Cuban missile crisis, when fears of a third world war ran high. We might note that today, despite the welcome reductions of nuclear stockpiles, the United States and Russia still possess—and retain battle plans for—thousands of warheads. And

North Korea, a recent member of the nuclear club, has tested both nuclear devices and long-range missile systems capable of threatening its neighbors. On the major points of his essay, concerning the psychological and moral problems of obedience, Fromm remains as pertinent today as when he wrote more than fifty years ago.

For centuries kings, priests, feudal lords, industrial bosses, and parents have insisted that *obedience is a virtue* and that *disobedience is a vice.* In order to introduce another point of view, let us set against this position the following statement: *human history began with an act of disobedience, and it is not unlikely that it will be terminated by an act of obedience.*

Human history was ushered in by an act of disobedience according to the Hebrew and Greek myths. Adam and Eve, living in the Garden of Eden, were part of nature; they were in harmony with it, yet did not transcend it. They were in nature as the fetus is in the womb of the mother. They were human, and at the same time not yet human. All this changed when they disobeyed an order. By breaking the ties with earth and mother, by cutting the umbilical cord, man emerged from a prehuman harmony and was able to take the first step into independence and freedom. The act of disobedience set Adam and Eve free and opened their eyes. They recognized each other as strangers and the world outside them as strange and even hostile. Their act of disobedience broke the primary bond with nature and made them individuals. "Original sin," far from corrupting man, set him free; it was the beginning of history. Man had to leave the Garden of Eden in order to learn to rely on his own powers and to become fully human.

The prophets, in their messianic concept, confirmed the idea that man had been right in disobeying; that he had not been corrupted by his "sin," but freed from the fetters of prehuman harmony. For the prophets, *history* is the place where man becomes human; during its unfolding he develops his powers of reason and of love until he creates a new harmony between himself, his fellow man, and nature. This new harmony is described as "the end of days," that period of history in which there is peace between man and man, between man and nature. It is a "new" paradise created by man himself, and one which he alone could create because he was forced to leave the "old" paradise as a result of his disobedience.

Just as the Hebrew myth of Adam and Eve, so the Greek myth of Prometheus sees all human civilization based on an act of disobedience. Prometheus, in stealing the fire from the gods, lays the foundation for the evolution of man. There would be no human history were it not for Prometheus' "crime." He, like Adam and Eve, is punished for his disobedience. But he does not repent and ask for forgiveness. On the contrary, he proudly says: "I would rather be chained to this rock than be the obedient servant of the gods."

Man has continued to evolve by acts of disobedience. Not only was his spiritual development possible only because there were men who dared to say no to the powers that be in the name of their conscience or their faith, but also his intellectual development was dependent on the capacity for being disobedient—disobedient to authorities who tried to muzzle new thoughts and to the authority of long-established opinions which declared a change to be nonsense.

5

If the capacity for disobedience constituted the beginning of human history, obedience might very well, as I have said, cause the end of human history. I am not speaking symbolically or poetically. There is the possibility, or even the probability, that the human race will destroy civilization and even all life upon earth within the next five to ten years. There is no rationality or sense in it. But the fact is that, while we are living technically in the Atomic Age, the majority of men—including most of those who are in power—still live emotionally in the Stone Age; that while our mathematics, astronomy, and the natural sciences are of the twentieth century, most of our ideas about politics, the state, and society lag far behind the age of science. If mankind commits suicide it will be because people will obey those who command them to push the deadly buttons; because they will obey the archaic passions of fear, hate, and greed; because they will obey obsolete clichés of State sovereignty and national honor. The Soviet leaders talk much about revolutions, and we in the "free world" talk much about freedom. Yet they and we discourage disobedience—in the Soviet Union explicitly and by force, in the free world implicitly and by the more subtle methods of persuasion.

But I do not mean to say that all disobedience is a virtue and all obedience is a vice. Such a view would ignore the dialectical relationship between obedience and disobedience. Whenever the principles which are obeyed and those which are disobeyed are irreconcilable, an act of obedience to one principle is necessarily an act of disobedience to its counterpart and vice versa. Antigone is the classic example of this dichotomy. By obeying the inhuman laws of the State, Antigone necessarily would disobey the laws of humanity. By obeying the latter, she must disobey the former. All martyrs of religious faiths, of freedom, and of science have had to disobey those who wanted to muzzle them in order to obey their own consciences, the laws of humanity, and of reason. If a man can only obey and not disobey, he is a slave; if he can only disobey and not obey, he is a rebel (not a revolutionary); he acts out of anger, disappointment, resentment, yet not in the name of a conviction or a principle.

· · ·

The word *conscience* is used to express two phenomena which are quite distinct from each other. One is the "authoritarian conscience" which is the internalized voice of an authority whom we are eager to please and afraid of displeasing. This authoritarian conscience is what most people experience when they obey their conscience. It is also the conscience which Freud speaks of, and which he called "Super-Ego." This Super-Ego represents the internalized commands and prohibitions of [the] father, accepted by the son out of fear. Different from the authoritarian conscience is the "humanistic conscience"; this is the voice present in every human being and independent from external sanctions and rewards. Humanistic conscience is based on the fact that as human beings we have an intuitive knowledge of what is human and inhuman, what is conducive of life and what is destructive of life. This conscience serves our functioning as human beings. It is the voice which calls us back to ourselves, to our humanity.

Authoritarian conscience (Super-Ego) is still obedience to a power outside of myself, even though this power has been internalized. Consciously I believe that I am following *my* conscience; in effect, however, I have swallowed the principles of *power*; just because of the illusion that humanistic conscience and Super-Ego are identical, internalized authority is so much more effective than the authority which is clearly experienced as not being part of me. Obedience to the "authoritarian conscience," like all obedience to outside thoughts and power, tends to debilitate "humanistic conscience," the ability to be and to judge oneself. . . .

10 An example of rational authority is to be found in the relationship between student and teacher; one of irrational authority in the relationship between slave and master. Both relationships are based on the fact that the authority of the person in command is accepted. Dynamically, however, they are of a different nature. The interests of the teacher and the student, in the ideal case, lie in the same direction. The teacher is satisfied if he succeeds in furthering the student; if he has failed to do so, the failure is his and the student's. The slave owner, on the other hand, wants to exploit the slave as much as possible. The more he gets out of him the more satisfied he is. At the same time, the slave tries to defend as best he can his claims for a minimum of happiness. The interests of slave and master are antagonistic, because what is advantageous to the one is detrimental to the other. The superiority of the one over the other has a different function in each case; in the first it is the condition for the furtherance of the person subjected to the authority, and in the second it is the condition for

his exploitation. Another distinction runs parallel to this: rational authority is rational because the authority, whether it is held by a teacher or a captain of a ship giving orders in an emergency, acts in the name of reason which, being universal, I can accept without submitting. Irrational authority has to use force or suggestion, because no one would let himself be exploited if he were free to prevent it.

Why is man so prone to obey and why is it so difficult for him to disobey? As long as I am obedient to the power of the State, the Church, or public opinion, I feel safe and protected. In fact it makes little difference what power it is that I am obedient to. It is always an institution, or men, who use force in one form or another and who fraudulently claim omniscience and omnipotence. My obedience makes me part of the power I worship, and hence I feel strong. I can make no error, since it decides for me; I cannot be alone, because it watches over me; I cannot commit a sin, because it does not let me do so, and even if I do sin, the punishment is only the way of returning to the almighty power.

In order to disobey, one must have the courage to be alone, to err, and to sin. But courage is not enough. The capacity for courage depends on a person's state of development. Only if a person has emerged from mother's lap and father's commands, only if he has emerged as a fully developed individual and thus has acquired the capacity to think and feel for himself, only then can he have the courage to say "no" to power, to disobey.

Discussion and Writing Suggestions

1. Fromm suggests that scientifically we live in the modern world but that politically and emotionally we live in the Stone Age. Based on your observation of events, do you agree? Why?

2. Fromm writes: "If a man can only obey and not disobey, he is a slave; if he can only disobey and not obey, he is a rebel (not a revolutionary)." Explain Fromm's meaning here. Explain, as well, the implication that to be fully human one must have the freedom to both obey and disobey.

3. Fromm writes that "obedience makes me part of the power I worship, and hence I feel strong." Does this statement ring true for you? Discuss an occasion in which you felt powerful because you obeyed a group norm. You may want to take your answer in a different direction: Have you ever felt powerful because you *dis*obeyed a group norm?

*The Power of Situations**

Lee Ross and Richard E. Nisbett

Erich Fromm conceives of obedience and disobedience as products of one's character or of one's moral choices. Following the philosopher Thomas Hobbes, Wellman and Simmons conceive of obedience as a political necessity. In the selection that follows, Lee Ross and Richard E. Nisbett present findings from experiments in social psychology that suggest that situations, rather than some essential personal quality

or the dictates of one's conscience, tend to determine behavior. From this vantage point, a "helpful" person may not be consistently helpful nor a "kind" person consistently kind. In each new situation, subtle and profound social cues influence our ultimate behavior—which is why, as we all know, people behave inconsistently.

According to philosopher Gilbert Harman, "It seems that ordinary attributions of character traits to people are often deeply misguided, and it may even be the case that there is no such thing as character, no ordinary character traits of the sort people think there are, none of the usual moral virtues and vices." Harmon reached this radical notion after reading accounts of the same experiments in social psychology that you are about to read in this chapter. You may not draw the same conclusions, but Ross and Nisbett mount a persuasive case that the situation in which we act can powerfully influence our behavior—including our choice to obey or disobey a questionable order.

Lee Ross is a professor of psychology at Stanford University. Richard E. Nisbett is a professor of psychology at the University of Michigan. This selection is excerpted from their text *The Person and the Situation: Perspectives of Social Psychology* (1991).

Undergraduates taking their first course in social psychology generally are in search of an interesting and enjoyable experience, and they rarely are disappointed. They find out many fascinating things about human behavior, some of which validate common sense and some of which contradict it. The inherent interest value of the material, amounting to high-level gossip about people and social situations, usually ensures that the students are satisfied consumers.

The experience of serious graduate students, who, over the course of four or five years, are immersed in the problems and the orientation of the field, is rather different. For them, the experience is an intellectually wrenching one. Their most basic assumptions about the nature and the causes of human behavior, and about the very predictability of the social world, are challenged. At the end of the process, their views of human behavior and society will differ profoundly from the views held by most other people in their culture. Some of their new insights and beliefs will be held rather tentatively and applied inconsistently to the social events that unfold around them. Others will be held with great conviction, and will be applied confidently. But ironically, even the new insights that they are most confident about will tend to have the effect of making them less certain than their peers about predicting social behavior and making inferences about particular individuals or groups. Social psychology rivals philosophy in its ability to teach people that they do not truly understand the nature of the world. This book is about that hard-won ignorance and what it tells us about the human condition.

•   •   •

Consider the following scenario: While walking briskly to a meeting some distance across a college campus, John comes across a man slumped in a doorway, asking him for help. Will John offer it, or will he continue on his way? Before answering such a question, most people would want to know more about John. Is he someone known to be callous and unfeeling, or is he renowned for his kindness and concern? Is he a stalwart member of the Campus Outreach Organization, or a mainstay of the Conservative Coalition Against Welfare Abuse? In short, what kind of person is John and how has he behaved when his altruism has been tested in the past? Only with such information in hand, most people would agree, could one make a sensible and confident prediction.

In fact, however, nothing one is likely to know or learn about John would be of much use in helping predict John's behavior in the situation we've described. In particular, the type of information about personality that most laypeople would want to have before making a prediction would prove to be of relatively little value. A half century of research has taught us that in this situation, and in most other novel situations, one cannot predict with any accuracy how particular people will respond. At least one cannot do so using information about an individual's personal dispositions or even about that individual's past behavior.

• • •

While knowledge about John is of surprisingly little value in predicting whether he will **5** help the person slumped in the doorway, details concerning the specifics of the situation would be invaluable. For example, what was the appearance of the person in the doorway? Was he clearly ill, or might he have been a drunk or, even worse, a nodding dope addict? Did his clothing make him look respectably middle class or decently working class, or did he look like a homeless derelict?

Such considerations are fairly obvious once they are mentioned, and the layperson, upon reflection, will generally concede their importance. But few laypeople would concede, much less anticipate, the relevance of some other, subtler, contextual details that empirical research has shown to be important factors influencing bystander intervention. Darley and Batson (1973) actually confronted people with a version of the situation we've described and found what some of these factors are. Their subjects were students in a religious seminary who were on their way to deliver a practice sermon. If the subjects were in a hurry (because they thought they were late to give a practice sermon), only about 10 percent helped. By contrast, if they were not in a hurry (because they had plenty of time before giving their sermon), about 63 percent of them helped.

Social psychology has by now amassed a vast store of such empirical parables. The tradition here is simple. Pick a generic situation; then identify and manipulate a situational or contextual variable that intuition or past research leads you to believe will make a difference (ideally, a variable whose impact you think most laypeople, or even most of your peers, somehow fail to appreciate), and see what happens. Sometimes, of course, you will be wrong and your manipulation won't "work." But often the situational variable makes quite a bit of difference. Occasionally, in fact, it makes nearly all the difference, and information about traits and individual differences that other people thought all-important proves all but trivial. If so, you have contributed a situationist classic destined to become part of our field's intellectual legacy. Such empirical parables are important because they illustrate the degree to which ordinary men and women are apt to be mistaken about the power of the situation—the power of particular situational features, and the power of situations in general.

People's inflated belief in the importance of personality traits and dispositions, together with their failure to recognize the importance of situational factors in affecting behavior, has been termed the "fundamental attribution error" (Ross, 1977; Nisbett & Ross, 1980; see also Jones, 1979; Gilbert & Jones, 1986). Together with many other social psychologists, we have directed our attention to documenting this . . . error and attempting to track down its origins.

References

Darley, J. M., & Batson, C. D. (1973). From Jerusalem to Jericho: A study of situational and dispositional variables in helping behavior. *Journal of Personality and Social Psychology, 27,* 100–119.

Gilbert, D. T., & Jones, E. E. (1986). Perceiver-induced constraints: Interpretation of self-generated reality. *Journal of Personality and Social Psychology, 50,* 269–280.

Jones, E. E. (1979). The rocky road from acts to dispositions. *American Psychologist, 34,* 107–117.

Nisbett, R. E., & Ross, L. (1980). *Human inference: Strategies and shortcomings of social judgment.* Englewood Cliffs, NJ: Prentice-Hall.

Ross, L. (1977). The intuitive psychologist and his shortcomings. In L. Berkowitz (Ed.), *Advances in experimental social psychology* (Vol. 10). New York: Academic.

Discussion and Writing Suggestions

1. Conceive of another scenario, analogous to John's encountering the man slumped in the doorway. What kinds of situational factors might determine how one behaves when faced with this scenario?

2. How did you react to what is known as the "Good Samaritan" experiment (involving John and the person slumped in the doorway)? Most people would like to think they would behave differently, but the experiments suggest otherwise. Your comments? Can you see yourself responding differently in a variety of circumstances?

3. "Social psychology," write Ross and Nisbett, "rivals philosophy in its ability to teach people that they do not truly understand the nature of the world." How solid do you feel your understanding is of "the world"? If you guessed incorrectly about John and how he would react to the person slumped in the doorway, are you prepared to see your commonsense understanding of how people behave undermined?

4. Reconsider the radical proposition mentioned in the headnote: that based on experiments such as the "Good Samaritan" described in this selection, one might conclude, "It seems that ordinary attributions of character traits to people are often deeply misguided, and it may even be the case that there is no such thing as character, no ordinary character traits of the sort people think there are, none of the usual moral virtues and vices." Even assuming you do not accept this extreme view, are you troubled by the assertion that "character" might be a fiction—that we do not possess some inner qualities called "honor" and "loyalty" that are impervious to all situational pressures? Discuss.

The Milgram Experiment

Saul McLeod

In 1963, a Yale psychologist conducted one of the classic studies on obedience. Stanley Milgram designed an experiment that forced participants either to violate their conscience by obeying the immoral demands of an authority figure or to refuse those demands. Surprisingly, Milgram found that few participants could resist the authority figure's orders, even when the participants knew that following these orders would result in another person's pain. Were the participants in these experiments incipient mass murderers? No, said Milgram. They were "ordinary

people, simply doing their jobs." The implications of Milgram's conclusions are immense.

Consider these questions: Where does evil reside? What sort of people were responsible for the Holocaust, and for the long list of other atrocities that seem to blight the human record in every generation? Is it a lunatic fringe, a few sick people who are responsible for atrocities? If so, then we decent folk needn't ever look inside ourselves to understand evil since (by our definition) evil lurks out there, in "those sick ones." Milgram's study suggested otherwise: that under a special set of circumstances the obedience we naturally show authority figures can transform us into agents of terror.

Stanley Milgram (1933–1984) taught and conducted research at Yale and Harvard Universities and at the Graduate Center, City University of New York. He was named Guggenheim Fellow in 1972–1973 and a year later was nominated for the National Book Award for *Obedience to Authority*. His other books include *Television and Antisocial Behavior* (1973), *The City and the Self* (1974), *Human Aggression* (1976), and *The Individual in the Social World* (1977).

This account of Milgram's experiments was written by Saul McLeod in 2007 for the Web site *Simply Psychology*.[1] McLeod is a psychology tutor at the University of Manchester in the United Kingdom.

One of the most famous studies of obedience in psychology was carried out by Stanley Milgram (1963).

Stanley Milgram, a psychologist at Yale University, conducted an experiment focusing on the conflict between obedience to authority and personal conscience.

He examined justifications for acts of genocide offered by those accused at the World War II, Nuremberg War Criminal trials. Their defense often was based on "obedience"—that they were just following orders of their superiors.

The experiments began in July 1961, a year after the trial of Adolf Eichmann in Jerusalem.[2] Milgram devised the experiment to answer the question "Could it be that Eichmann and his million accomplices in the Holocaust were just following orders? Could we call them all accomplices?" (Milgram, 1974).

Milgram (1963) wanted to investigate whether Germans were particularly obedient to   **5** authority figures as this was a common explanation for the Nazi killings in World War II.

Milgram selected participants for his experiment by newspaper advertising for male participants to take part in a study of learning at Yale University. The procedure was that the participant was paired with another person and they drew lots to find out who would be the "learner" and who would be the "teacher." The draw was fixed so that the participant was always the teacher, and the learner was one of Milgram's confederates (pretending to be a real participant).

The learner (a confederate called Mr. Wallace) was taken into a room and had electrodes attached to his arms, and the teacher and researcher went into a room next door that

---

[1]https://www.simplypsychology.org/milgram.html
[2]*Adolf Eichmann* (1906–1962), the Nazi official responsible for implementing Hitler's "Final Solution" to exterminate the Jews, escaped to Argentina after World War II. In 1960, Israeli agents captured him and brought him to Israel, where he was tried as a war criminal and sentenced to death. At his trial, Eichmann maintained that he was merely following orders in arranging the murders of his victims.

contained an electric shock generator and a row of switches marked from 15 volts (Slight Shock) to 375 volts (Danger: Severe Shock) to 450 volts (XXX).

Aim

Milgram (1963) was interested in researching how far people would go in obeying an instruction if it involved harming another person. Stanley Milgram was interested in how easily ordinary people could be influenced into committing atrocities, for example, Germans in WWII.

Procedure

Volunteers were recruited for a lab experiment investigating "learning" (re: ethics: deception). Participants were 40 males, aged between 20 and 50, whose jobs ranged from unskilled to professional, from the New Haven area. They were paid $4.50 for just turning up.

At the beginning of the experiment they were introduced to another participant, who was actually a confederate of the experimenter (Milgram). They drew straws to determine their roles—learner or teacher—although this was fixed and the confederate always ended [up being] the learner. There was also an "experimenter" dressed in a grey lab coat, played by an actor (not Milgram).

Two rooms in the Yale Interaction Laboratory were used—one for the learner (with an electric chair) and another for the teacher and experimenter with an electric shock generator.

The "learner" (Mr. Wallace) was strapped to a chair with electrodes. After he has learned a list of word pairs given him to learn, the "teacher" tests him by naming a word and asking the learner to recall its partner/pair from a list of four possible choices.

The teacher is told to administer an electric shock every time the learner makes a mistake, increasing the level of shock each time. There were 30 switches on the shock generator marked from 15 volts (slight shock) to 450 (danger—severe shock).

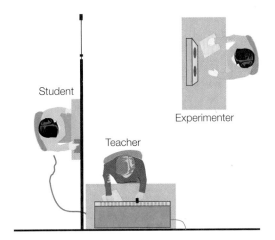

The learner gave mainly wrong answers (on purpose) and for each of these the teacher gave him an electric shock. When the teacher refused to administer a shock and turned to the experimenter for guidance, he was given the standard instruction/order (consisting of 4 prods):

Prod 1: Please continue.

Prod 2: The experiment requires you to continue.

Prod 3: It is absolutely essential that you continue.

Prod 4: You have no other choice but to continue.

Results

65% (two-thirds) of participants (i.e. teachers) continued to the highest level of 450 volts. All **15** the participants continued to 300 volts.

Milgram did more than one experiment—he carried out 18 variations of his study. All he did was alter the situation to see how this affected obedience.

Conclusion

Ordinary people are likely to follow orders given by an authority figure, even to the extent of killing an innocent human being. Obedience to authority is ingrained in us all from the way we are brought up.

People tend to obey orders from other people if they recognize their authority as morally right and/or legally based. This response to legitimate authority is learned in a variety of situations, for example in the family, school and workplace.

Milgram summed up in the article "The Perils of Obedience" (Milgram 1974), writing:

> The legal and philosophic aspects of obedience are of enormous import, but they say very little about how most people behave in concrete situations. I set up a simple experiment at Yale University to test how much pain an ordinary citizen would inflict on another person simply because he was ordered to by an experimental scientist. Stark authority was pitted against the subjects' [participants'] strongest moral imperatives against hurting others, and, with the subjects' [participants'] ears ringing with the screams of the victims, authority won more often than not. The extreme willingness of adults to go to almost any lengths on the command of an authority constitutes the chief finding of the study and the fact most urgently demanding explanation.

Milgram's Agency Theory

20 Milgram (1974) explained the behavior of his participants by suggesting that people actually have two states of behavior when they are in a social situation:

- The **autonomous state**—people direct their own actions, and they take responsibility for the results of those actions.
- The **agentic state**—people allow others to direct their actions, and they pass off the responsibility for the consequences to the person giving the orders. In other words, they act as agents for another person's will.

Milgram suggested that two things must be in place in order for a person to enter the agentic state:

1. The person giving the orders is perceived as being qualified to direct other people's behavior. That is, they are seen as legitimate.
2. The person being ordered about is able to believe that the authority will accept responsibility for what happens.

Agency theory says that people will obey an authority when they believe that the authority will take responsibility for the consequences of their actions. This is supported by some aspects of Milgram's evidence. For example, when participants were reminded that they had responsibility for their own actions, almost none of them were prepared to obey. In contrast, many participants who were refusing to go on did so if the experimenter said that he would take responsibility.

Milgram Experiment Variations

The Milgram experiment was carried out many times whereby Milgram varied the basic procedure. By doing this Milgram could identify which factors affected obedience. Obedience was measured by how many participants shocked to the maximum 450 volts (65% in the original study).

In total 636 participants have been tested in 18 different variation studies.

Change of Location Condition
- The experiment was moved to a set of run-down offices rather than the impressive Yale University.
- Obedience dropped to 47.5%.
- This suggests that status of location affects obedience.

Two Teacher Condition
- When there is less personal responsibility obedience increases.
- When participants could instruct an assistant (confederate) to press the switches, 92.5% shocked to the maximum 450 volts.
- This relates to Milgram's Agency Theory.

Touch Proximity Condition
- The teacher had to force the learner's hand down onto a shock plate when they refuse to participate after 150 volts.
- Obedience fell to 30%.
- The participant is no longer buffered/protected from seeing the consequences of their actions.

Uniform Condition
- Milgram's experimenter wore a laboratory coat (a symbol of scientific expertise) [that] gave him a high status.
- But when the experimenter dressed in everyday clothes obedience was very low.
- The uniform of the authority figure can give them status.

Social Support Condition
- Two other participants (confederates) were also teachers but refused to obey.
- Confederate 1 stopped at 150 volts and confederate 2 stopped at 210 volts.
- The presence of others who are seen to disobey the authority figure reduces the level of obedience to 10%.

Absent Experimenter Condition
- Authority figure distant.
- It is easier to resist the orders from an authority figure if they are not close by.
- When the experimenter instructed and prompted the teacher by telephone from another room, obedience fell to 20.5%.
- Many participants cheated and missed giving out shocks or gave less voltage than ordered by the experimenter.
- Proximity of authority figure affects obedience.

Criticisms

The Milgram studies were conducted in laboratory type conditions and we must ask if this tells us much about real-life situations. We obey in a variety of real-life situations that are far more subtle than instructions to give people electric shocks, and it would be interesting to see what factors operate in everyday obedience. The sort of situation Milgram investigated would be more suited to a military context.

25

Orne & Holland (1968) accused Milgram's study of lacking "experimental realism," i.e. participants might not have believed the experimental set-up they found themselves in and knew the learner wasn't really receiving electric shocks.

Milgram's sample was biased:

- The participants in Milgram's study were all male. Do the findings transfer to females?
- Milgram's study cannot be seen as representative of the American population as his sample was self-selected. This is because they became participants only by electing to respond to a newspaper advertisement (selecting themselves). They may also have a typical "volunteer personality"—not all the newspaper readers responded so perhaps it takes this personality type to do so.

Yet a total of 636 participants were tested in 18 separate experiments across the New Haven area, which was seen as being reasonably representative of a typical American town.

Milgram's findings have been replicated in a variety of cultures and most lead to the same conclusions as Milgram's original study and in some cases see higher obedience rates.

However, Smith & Bond (1998) point out that with the exception of Jordan (Shanab & Yahya, 1978), the majority of these studies have been conducted in industrialized Western cultures and we should be cautious before we conclude that a universal trait of social behavior has been identified.

Ethical Issues

- **Deception**—the participants actually believed they were shocking a real person, and were unaware the learner was a confederate of Milgram's.

  However, Milgram argued that "illusion is used when necessary in order to set the stage for the revelation of certain difficult-to-get-at-truths." Milgram also interviewed participants afterwards to find out the effect of the deception. Apparently 83.7% said that they were "glad to be in the experiment," and 1.3% said that they wished they had not been involved.

- **Protection of participants**—Participants were exposed to extremely stressful situations that may have the potential to cause psychological harm. Many of the participants were visibly distressed.

  Signs of tension included trembling, sweating, stuttering, laughing nervously, biting lips and digging fingernails into palms of hands. Three participants had uncontrollable seizures, and many pleaded to be allowed to stop the experiment.

  Full blown seizures were observed for 3 participants; one so violent that the experiment was stopped.

  In his defense, Milgram argued that these effects were only short term. Once the participants were debriefed (and could see the confederate was OK) their stress levels decreased. Milgram also interviewed the participants one year after the event and concluded that most were happy that they had taken part.

- However, Milgram did debrief the participants fully after the experiment and also followed up after a period of time to ensure that they came to no harm.

References

Milgram, S. (1963). Behavioral study of obedience. *Journal of Abnormal and Social Psychology*, 67, 371–378.

Milgram, S. (1974). *Obedience to authority: An experimental view*. HarperCollins.

Orne, M. T., & Holland, C. H. (1968). On the ecological validity of laboratory deceptions. *International Journal of Psychiatry,* 6(4), 282–293.

Shanab, M. E., & Yahya, K. A. (1978). A cross-cultural study of obedience. *Bulletin of the Psychonomic Society*.

Smith, P. B., & Bond, M. H. (1998). *Social Psychology Across Cultures* (2nd Edition). Prentice Hall.

Discussion and Writing Suggestions

1. Milgram has written: "Conservative philosophers argue that the very fabric of society is threatened by disobedience, while humanists stress the primacy of the individual conscience." Develop the arguments of both the conservative and the humanist regarding obedience to authority. Be prepared to debate the ethics of obedience by defending one position or the other.

2. Would you have been glad to have participated in the Milgram experiments? Why or why not?

3. McLeod summarizes some of the chief criticisms, both procedural and ethical, of the Milgram experiment. To what extent do you agree with some of these criticisms? How might you counter some of these criticisms?

4. Does the outcome of the experiment upset you in any way? Do you feel the experiment teaches us anything new about human nature?

5. The wife of one of the experimental subjects said to him after he described what he had done: "You can call yourself Eichmann." [See the footnote on p. 253.] Do you agree with her? Explain.

6. Milgram concluded: "ordinary people . . . without any particular hostility on their part, can become agents in a terrible destructive process." What present-day situations occur to you that suggest Milgram's findings are just as valid as they were in the 1960s when he conducted his experiments? Consider events of both national and international scope that you have read about or seen on television or situations closer to home.

On the Web: *Opinions and Social Pressure*

In the early 1950s, Solomon Asch (1907–1996), a social psychologist at Rutgers University, conducted a series of simple but ingenious experiments on the influence of group pressure upon the individual. Essentially, he discovered, individuals can be influenced by groups to deny the evidence of their own senses. Together with the Milgram experiments of the next decade (see the preceding selection), these studies provide powerful evidence of the degree to which individuals can surrender their own judgment to others, even when those others are clearly in the wrong. The results of these experiments have implications far beyond the laboratory: They can explain a good deal of the normal human behavior we see every day—at school, at work, at home.

Go to: YouTube

Search terms: *"asch conformity experiment"*

On the Web: *The Stanford Prison Experiment*

As well known—and as controversial—as the Milgram obedience experiments, the Stanford Prison Experiment (1973) raises troubling questions about the ability of individuals to resist authoritarian or obedient roles, if the social setting requires these roles. Philip G. Zimbardo, professor of psychology at Stanford University, set out to study the process by which prisoners and guards "learn" to become compliant and authoritarian, respectively. To find subjects for the experiment, Zimbardo placed an advertisement in a local newspaper:

> Male college students needed for psychological study of prison life. $15 per day for 1–2 weeks beginning Aug. 14. For further information & applications, come to Room 248, Jordan Hall, Stanford U.

The ad drew 75 responses. From these, Zimbardo and his colleagues selected 21 college-age men, half of whom would become "prisoners" in the experiment, the other half "guards." The elaborate role-playing scenario, planned for two weeks, had to be cut short due to the intensity of subjects' responses. You will find numerous video accounts of the experiment online. View one or more lasting longer than twenty minutes to gain a clear (and perhaps uncomfortable) sense of how intensely students responded to playacting at being prisoners and guards:

Go to: YouTube

Search terms: *"zimbardo prison experiment documentary"*

The Follower Problem*

David Brooks

In the following op-ed, first published in the _New York Times_ on June 12, 2012, columnist David Brooks argues that partly because of a legacy of antiauthoritarianism, America may not have a leadership problem, but "it certainly has a followership problem." In the course of his article, Brooks refers to a number of monuments in and around the National Mall in Washington, D.C. You can readily find images and videos of these monuments online. For additional background on David Brooks, see the headnote to "Amy Chua Is a Wimp" in Chapter 10.

If you go to the Lincoln or Jefferson memorials in Washington, you are invited to look up in admiration. Lincoln and Jefferson are presented as the embodiments of just authority. They are strong and powerful but also humanized. Jefferson is a graceful aristocratic democrat. Lincoln is sober and enduring. Both used power in the service of higher ideas, which are engraved nearby on the walls.

The monuments that get built these days are mostly duds. That's because they say nothing about just authority. The World War II memorial is a nullity. It tells you nothing about the war or why American power was mobilized to fight it. The Rev. Dr. Martin Luther King Jr. memorial brutally simplifies its subject's nuanced and biblical understanding of power. It gives him an imperious and self-enclosed character completely out of keeping with his complex nature.

As Michael J. Lewis of Williams College has noted, the Franklin Delano Roosevelt Memorial transforms a jaunty cavalier into a "differently abled and rather prim nonsmoker." Instead of a crafty wielder of supreme power, Roosevelt is a kindly grandpa you would want to put your arm around for a vacation photo.

The proposed Eisenhower memorial shifts attention from his moments of power to his moments of innocent boyhood. The design has been widely criticized, and last week the commission in charge agreed to push back the approval hearing until September.

Even the more successful recent monuments evade the thorny subjects of strength   **5** and power. The Vietnam memorial is about tragedy. The Korean memorial is about vulnerability.

Why can't today's memorial designers think straight about just authority?

Some of the reasons are well-known. We live in a culture that finds it easier to assign moral status to victims of power than to those who wield power. Most of the stories we tell ourselves are about victims who have endured oppression, racism and cruelty.

Then there is our fervent devotion to equality, to the notion that all people are equal and deserve equal recognition and respect. It's hard in this frame of mind to define and celebrate greatness, to hold up others who are immeasurably superior to ourselves.

But the main problem is our inability to think properly about how power should be used to bind and build. Legitimate power is built on a series of paradoxes: that leaders have to wield power while knowing they are corrupted by it; that great leaders are superior to their followers while also being of them; that the higher they rise, the more they feel like instruments in larger designs. The Lincoln and Jefferson memorials are about how to navigate those paradoxes.

These days many Americans seem incapable of thinking about these paradoxes. Those   **10** "Question Authority" bumper stickers no longer symbolize an attempt to distinguish just and unjust authority. They symbolize an attitude of opposing authority.

The old adversary culture of the intellectuals has turned into a mass adversarial cynicism. The common assumption is that elites are always hiding something. Public servants are in it for themselves. Those people at the top are nowhere near as smart or as wonderful as pure and all-knowing Me.

You end up with movements like Occupy Wall Street and the Tea Parties that try to dispense with authority altogether. They reject hierarchies and leaders because they don't believe in the concepts. The whole world should be like the Internet—a disbursed semianarchy in which authority is suspect and each individual is king.

Maybe before we can build great monuments to leaders we have to relearn the art of following. Democratic followership is also built on a series of paradoxes: that we are all created equal but that we also elevate those who are extraordinary; that we choose our leaders but also have to defer to them and trust their discretion; that we're proud individuals but only really thrive as a group, organized and led by just authority.

I don't know if America has a leadership problem; it certainly has a followership problem. Vast majorities of Americans don't trust their institutions. That's not mostly because our institutions perform much worse than they did in 1925 and 1955, when they were widely trusted. It's mostly because more people are cynical and like to pretend that they are better than everything else around them. Vanity has more to do with rising distrust than anything else.

In his memoir, *At Ease*, Eisenhower delivered the following advice: "Always try to associ-   **15** ate yourself with and learn as much as you can from those who know more than you do, who do better than you, who see more clearly than you." Ike slowly mastered the art of leadership by becoming a superb apprentice.

To have good leaders you have to have good followers—able to recognize just authority, admire it, be grateful for it and emulate it. Those skills are required for good monument building, too.

Discussion and Writing Suggestions

1. In Brooks's view, what is a "just" authority? What are its key elements? Cite present-day examples of such authority that in your view we should admire, emulate, and be proud to follow.

2. Brooks asserts: "We live in a culture that finds it easier to assign moral status to victims of power than to those who wield power." Comment on this assertion, using examples from your reading and your own observations and experience to support or rebut Brooks's contention.

3. Brooks writes that we may need to "relearn the art of following." What does he mean? Why use the word *art*?

4. Brooks writes that there are paradoxes both of leading and following. Review these paradoxes and choose one to explore in a freewheeling journal entry. Don't try to shape your thoughts into an essay. A few hours or a day later, read what you wrote. What statements stand out to you? Why?

The Assignments

Summary & Paraphrase

Summarize "The Follower Problem" by David Brooks. In preparing your summary, consult the Guidelines for Writing Summaries on page 27.

Paraphrase the paragraph by Thomas Hobbes quoted by Wellman and Simmons. You can find guidance on writing paraphrases on pages 25–26.

Critique

Write a critique of David Brooks's "The Follower Problem." Draw on "Why I Am Not an Anarchist" by Wellman and Simmons. Be sure to develop both an introduction and a conclusion as well as the main body of the critique. See Chapter 2 for advice on critical reading. See particularly the Guidelines for Writing Critiques box on pages 82–83, along with the hints on incorporating quoted material into your own writing on page 62. Organize and develop the body of your evaluation around specific points that Brooks makes in support of positive disobedience.

- Restate and discuss each of Brooks's main points. Develop each into a paragraph.

- For each of Brooks's points that you summarize, devote two paragraphs or more to evaluation, drawing to the extent you can on arguments made by Wellman and Simmons (including those of Thomas Hobbes, whom they quote) and also on your own arguments.

In preparing to write, consider a pair of questions. Your responses may help you formulate elements of your critique:

- What assumptions does Brooks make about greatness? power? the willingness to follow?
- Do you agree with Brooks that "To have good leaders you have to have good followers"?

Explanatory Synthesis

Explain—in no more than two pages—a situation in which you or others you observed were disobedient, whether positively or negatively. Use vivid details to re-create the scene for your readers, giving attention to the actors involved, the stakes, the actions taken, and the outcome.

If you prefer, explain an occasion on which you or others were obedient. Choose an occasion on which this act of obedience had important consequences, whether positive or negative.

This assignment requires that you understand the terms *obedience* and *disobedience*. Several sources in the chapter will help with definitions: Wellman and Simmons, Fromm, Brooks, and Ross and Nisbett. In developing your explanation, consult the Guidelines for Writing Syntheses on pages 110–111. More specifically, consider the following:

Suggestions for Developing the Assignment

Develop your explanation systematically, remembering throughout that you're a *storyteller*. Disobedience involves conflict; conflict creates tension. How do you plan to create tension for readers so that they'll want to keep reading and learn what you did (or did not do)?

- Provide the who, when, and where of the situation.
- What was the disobedient action?
- Why was it consequential? What were the stakes to all involved? To answer these questions, begin with a definition of *obedience*.
- How did this action unfold? What were the consequences of this action?
- To what extent was this action a choice? Did you act instinctively, or were you more deliberative?
- What forces favoring obedience were in play—for instance, religious or parental training/rules, the advice of friends or teachers, the expectations of coaches?

Keep in mind that this brief paper is an explanation—not, at this point, an analysis of your decision. Be sure to cite the sources you use to define *obedience* and *disobedience*. See pages 208–213 for a review of proper citation format.

Analysis

Use the views of Thomas Hobbes on the conditions of life without a "common Power" to analyze the actions you described in the preceding assignment (the explanatory synthesis). Break that account down into parts, and analyze each according to the analytical tool you've selected (from Hobbes). In your conclusion, consider the positive and negative consequences of your actions and reflect on the likelihood that you would act the same way in the future.

Suggestions for Developing the Assignment

Before beginning, you may find it useful to review the discussion of analysis on pages 160–176. We recommend the following structure for your paper:

- Paragraph 1: Open with a general introduction to the topic of obedience and disobedience. Introduce your particular act of obedience or disobedience—the events you explained in the assignment above. State that you'll be analyzing this action.

- Paragraph 2: More fully summarize the event in which you were obedient or disobedient. Conclude with your thesis: that you would or would not act the same way in the future.

- Paragraph 3: Introduce the analytic tool from Hobbes you will use to analyze the event.

- Paragraphs 4–7: Divide a more detailed account of the event into distinct parts. Analyze each part, using your analytical tool. Remember: your goal is to reveal interesting, nonobvious insights into your action.

- Paragraphs 8–9: Conclude. Reconsider key points of your analysis, both the positive and negative consequences of your action. Based on your analytical insights, reflect on the likelihood of your taking a similar action in the future.

Argument Synthesis

A certain amount of obedience is a given in society. Stanley Milgram, Fromm, and Wellman and Simmons (quoting Hobbes) observe that social order—civilization itself—would collapse unless individuals were willing to surrender a portion of their autonomy to the state. David Brooks emphasizes the importance, and the paradoxes, of what he calls "followership." Allowing that we all are obedient (to some extent we must be), define the point at which obedience to a figure of authority becomes dangerous. That is, when, in your view, must a person disobey? Why?

To make this argument more personal, use a running example of a moment in your life when you chose to obey or disobey. Discuss the consequences of your action and use your example to illustrate your argument concerning where to draw the line between obedience and disobedience. Use either the example you developed for your explanatory synthesis or search the Internet for examples of obedience gone to extremes: say, in hazing rituals among collegiate fraternities, sororities, or sports teams.

As you argue for your definition, consider the ways you might use the work of authors in this chapter. For guidance on citing sources, see pages 208–213.

Suggestions for Developing the Assignment

Review the guidelines in Chapter 5 on writing an argument synthesis, pages 134–142. Remember you are making an argument: You are using logic and evidence in support of a statement (a claim) about which reasonable people may disagree.

This will be an argument about definitions. In devising your claim, your definition of when to (dis)obey, look to the sources in this chapter for inspiration and support. Multiple authors define obedience and disobedience and either implicitly or explicitly suggest the limits at which one must give way to the other. As you think about your claim, use a running example to ground the discussion. Tell a story that both engages readers and gives you an opportunity to develop your argument.

Your paper might take the following form:

- Paragraph 1: Begin with your scenario (either the account in your explanatory synthesis or some other example) and related questions concerning obedience and disobedience. Create tension in this account. Draw readers into your scenario, which you will use as a running example both to make your points in the argument and to maintain the reader's interest.

- Paragraphs 2–3: Provide background on the questions regarding obedience and disobedience. Demonstrate your grasp of large questions of political philosophy: that some amount of obedience in a society is a given—and that drawing the line of how much obedience is too much can be difficult. Then move readers to your claim: your argument regarding where to draw the line.

- Paragraphs 4–9: This is the body of your argument where you will support your claim, establishing it as reasonable. These six paragraphs (more or less) should work together. Plan them carefully.

  - One strategy would be to divide your running example across these body paragraphs—in each, telling a bit of the story and then discussing its significance relative to your argument. Use each body paragraph to support your claim.

- Draw on sources for help. Cite your sources.

- You might borrow from your analysis paper—but understand the differences between that paper and this one. In the analysis you were determining whether or not you obeyed (or disobeyed) appropriately and would act the same way in the future. Your argument paper is making a broader claim about society in general and about the limits of obedience.

- Paragraph 10: Concession or rebuttal. Examine your argument's weak points. Perhaps you've assumed people behave consistently and, once defined, a principle about when to (dis)obey would hold up across all situations. Yet Ross and Nisbett argue that we can draw no such generalizations about human behavior because behavior changes from one situation to the next. Respond to the criticism. Dismiss (rebut) it—and explain yourself. Or accept it, at least in part, and adjust your claim accordingly.

- Paragraphs 11–12: Take stock of what you've accomplished and conclude. Bring your running example, and lessons learned, to an end. Restate your claim and return readers to their world, wiser (you hope!) for having read your paper.

Chapter 10
The Roar of the Tiger Mom

Writing and Reading in Sociology

In January 2011, an op-ed adapted from Yale Law School professor Amy Chua's book *Battle Hymn of the Tiger Mother* ignited a furious national debate over parenting methods. The online edition of the newspaper in which the excerpt appeared records over 8,800 responses to the initial op-ed in which Chua lists the activities she does not allow her children to do (including attend a sleepover, watch TV or play computer games, or get any grade less than A). In the piece, Chua also describes her efforts to motivate her children to excellence (by calling one child "garbage," rejecting an amateurish birthday card as unworthy, and driving her 7-year-old to tears after she is unable, after hours of practice, to perfectly execute a complex piano piece). A cover story in *Time* magazine reports that when Chua appeared on the *Today* show, "the usually sunny host Meredith Viera could hardly contain her contempt as she read aloud a sample of viewer comments: 'She's a monster'; 'The way she raised her kids is outrageous'; 'Where is the love, the acceptance?'"

But Chua's ideas and methods resonated with many readers. At a time when American students are ranked seventeenth in the world in reading, twenty-third in science, and thirty-first in math, can the country settle for anything less than excellence? Can American citizens hope to compete with China and other rising economies in the global marketplace if they find academic mediocrity acceptable? And on the personal level, are parents helping their children if they accept anything less than the best, if they strive, in "Western" manner, not to damage their children's unearned self-esteem and to protect them from the consequences of failure?

And yet—what are the psychological consequences of the "Chinese" parenting methods advocated by Chua? To what extent should we allow children a childhood that is filled with play and exploration, not rigid goals? What is Chua's goal beyond strictly defined academic excellence? Does academic excellence correspond with success in one's profession? With one's broader happiness in life? Does a relentless focus on academic excellence in any way limit developing social skills? (The final selection in this chapter, new to this edition, reports on recent studies that provide some answers to these questions.)

These issues are the subject of the readings that follow. You'll be asked to consider such questions as you prepare several writing assignments of the type discussed in the previous chapters. These assignments will culminate in an argument synthesis, a paper that will draw upon what you have already written for the summary, the critique, the explanatory synthesis, and the analysis.

Preceding the reading selections is a group of activities that will help prepare you for the writing assignments to come. The writing assignments themselves follow the readings.

Read; Prepare to Write

As you read these selections, prepare for the assignments by marking up the texts: Write notes to yourself in the margins and comment on what the authors have said.

And to prepare for the more ambitious of the assignments that follow—the explanatory and argument syntheses—consider drawing up a topic list of your sources as you read. For each topic about which two or more authors have something to say, jot down notes and page references. Here's an example entry:

Shaming/threatening children who underperform

Amy Chua: Sophia incident ("garbage") (p. 5); Lulu incidents ("Little White Donkey") (p. 7)

Elizabeth Kolbert: Kolbert's sons' reaction to the Sophia episode (p. 17)

Such a topic list, keyed to your sources, will spare you the frustration of reading eight or nine sources and flipping through them later, saying, "Now where did I read that?" In the sample entry, we see two authors speaking to the wisdom of shaming or threatening underperforming children. At this early point, you don't need to know how you might write a paper based on this or any other topic. But a robust list with multiple topics and accurate notes for each lays the groundwork for your own discussion later and puts you in a good position to write a synthesis.

As it happens, the sample entry above should come in handy when you're preparing to write your own explanatory and argument syntheses on the subject of tiger moms. Creating a topic list with multiple entries will take you a bit more time as you read, but it will save you time as you write.

Group Assignment #1: Make a Topic List

Working in groups of three or four, create a topic list for the selections in this chapter, making sure to jot down notes and page references for each. Here are some entries to get you started; find other topics common to two or more sources.

- academic and musical excellence

- "wasting" time—meaning?

- hard work and self-esteem

- effects of relentless academics on child's creativity and/or social skills

- American competitiveness (or decline) in a global economy

Group Assignment #2: Create a Topic Web

Working in groups of three or four, create a network, or web, of connections among selected topics. That is, determine which topics relate or "speak" to other topics.

Articulate these connections in a series of different webs, understanding that not all topics will be connected to each web. For example, draw a line from one topic (say, the overriding importance of children excelling academically) to another (say, factors contributing to American competitiveness in a global economy). How are these topics related? As a group, generate as many topic webs as possible and, for each, as many connections as possible. At the conclusion of the session, you'll have in hand not only the fruits of Assignment #1, multiple authors discussing common topics, but you'll also have a potential connection *among* topics—basically, the necessary raw material for writing your synthesis.

Note that one synthesis—a single paper—couldn't possibly refer to every topic, or every connection among topics, that you have found. Your skill in preparing and writing a synthesis depends on your ability to *identify* closely related topics and to make and develop a claim that links and is supported by these topics.

The readings on "tiger moms" follow. After the readings, you will find a series of linked assignments that will lead you to write some combination of summary, critique, analysis, explanatory synthesis, and argument synthesis.

The Readings

Adapted from Battle Hymn of the Tiger Mother

Amy Chua

Amy Chua, a professor at Yale Law School, is the author of *The World on Fire: How Exporting Free Market Democracy Breeds Ethnic Hatred and Global Instability* (2002), *Day of Empire: How Hyperpowers Rise to Global Dominance—and Why They Fall* (2007), and *Battle Hymn of the Tiger Mother* (2011), from which the following selection was excerpted as a newspaper op-ed on January 8, 2011. The editors of the newspaper gave the excerpt a controversial title, referenced in the responses that follow Chua's piece, most likely in an attempt (a successful one) to attract attention and encourage controversy.

A lot of people wonder how Chinese parents raise such stereotypically successful kids. They wonder what these parents do to produce so many math whizzes and music prodigies, what it's like inside the family, and whether they could do it too. Well, I can tell them, because I've done it. Here are some things my daughters, Sophia and Louisa, were never allowed to do:

- attend a sleepover
- have a playdate
- be in a school play
- complain about not being in a school play
- watch TV or play computer games
- choose their own extracurricular activities
- get any grade less than an A
- not be the No. 1 student in every subject except gym and drama
- play any instrument other than the piano or violin
- not play the piano or violin.

I'm using the term "Chinese mother" loosely. I know some Korean, Indian, Jamaican, Irish and Ghanaian parents who qualify too. Conversely, I know some mothers of Chinese heritage, almost always born in the West, who are not Chinese mothers, by choice or otherwise. I'm also using the term "Western parents" loosely. Western parents come in all varieties.

All the same, even when Western parents think they're being strict, they usually don't come close to being Chinese mothers. For example, my Western friends who consider themselves strict make their children practice their instruments 30 minutes every day. An hour at most. For a Chinese mother, the first hour is the easy part. It's hours two and three that get tough.

Despite our squeamishness about cultural stereotypes, there are tons of studies out there showing marked and quantifiable differences between Chinese and Westerners when it comes to parenting. In one study of 50 Western American mothers and 48 Chinese immigrant mothers, almost 70% of the Western mothers said either that "stressing academic success is not good for children" or that "parents need to foster the idea that learning is fun." By contrast, roughly 0% of the Chinese mothers felt the same way. Instead, the vast majority of the Chinese mothers said that they believe their children can be "the best" students, that "academic achievement reflects successful parenting," and that if children did not excel at school then there was "a problem" and parents "were not doing their job." Other studies indicate that compared to Western parents, Chinese parents spend approximately 10 times as long every day drilling academic activities with their children. By contrast, Western kids are more likely to participate in sports teams.

5   What Chinese parents understand is that nothing is fun until you're good at it. To get good at anything you have to work, and children on their own never want to work, which is why it is crucial to override their preferences. This often requires fortitude on the part of the parents because the child will resist; things are always hardest at the beginning, which is where Western parents tend to give up. But if done properly, the Chinese strategy produces a virtuous circle. Tenacious practice, practice, practice is crucial for excellence; rote repetition is underrated in America. Once a child starts to excel at something—whether it's math, piano, pitching or ballet—he or she gets praise, admiration and satisfaction. This builds confidence and makes the once not-fun activity fun. This in turn makes it easier for the parent to get the child to work even more.

Chinese parents can get away with things that Western parents can't. Once when I was young—maybe more than once—when I was extremely disrespectful to my mother, my father angrily called me "garbage" in our native Hokkien dialect. It worked really well. I felt terrible and deeply ashamed of what I had done. But it didn't damage my self-esteem or anything like that. I knew exactly how highly he thought of me. I didn't actually think I was worthless or feel like a piece of garbage.

As an adult, I once did the same thing to Sophia, calling her garbage in English when she acted extremely disrespectfully toward me. When I mentioned that I had done this at a dinner party, I was immediately ostracized. One guest named Marcy got so upset she broke down in tears and had to leave early. My friend Susan, the host, tried to rehabilitate me with the remaining guests.

The fact is that Chinese parents can do things that would seem unimaginable—even legally actionable—to Westerners. Chinese mothers can say to their daughters, "Hey fatty—lose some weight." By contrast, Western parents have to tiptoe around the issue, talking in terms of "health" and never ever mentioning the f-word, and their kids still end up in therapy for eating disorders and negative self-image. (I also once heard a Western father toast his adult daughter by calling her "beautiful and incredibly competent." She later told me that made her feel like garbage.)

Chinese parents can order their kids to get straight As. Western parents can only ask their kids to try their best. Chinese parents can say, "You're lazy. All your classmates are getting ahead of you." By contrast, Western parents have to struggle with their own conflicted feelings about achievement, and try to persuade themselves that they're not disappointed about how their kids turned out.

I've thought long and hard about how Chinese parents can get away with what they do. **10** I think there are three big differences between the Chinese and Western parental mindsets.

First, I've noticed that Western parents are extremely anxious about their children's self-esteem. They worry about how their children will feel if they fail at something, and they constantly try to reassure their children about how good they are notwithstanding a mediocre performance on a test or at a recital. In other words, Western parents are concerned about their children's psyches. Chinese parents aren't. They assume strength, not fragility, and as a result they behave very differently.

For example, if a child comes home with an A-minus on a test, a Western parent will most likely praise the child. The Chinese mother will gasp in horror and ask what went wrong. If the child comes home with a B on the test, some Western parents will still praise the child. Other Western parents will sit their child down and express disapproval, but they will be careful not to make their child feel inadequate or insecure, and they will not call their child "stupid," "worthless" or "a disgrace." Privately, the Western parents may worry that their child does not test well or have aptitude in the subject or that there is something wrong with the curriculum and possibly the whole school. If the child's grades do not improve, they may eventually schedule a meeting with the school principal to challenge the way the subject is being taught or to call into question the teacher's credentials.

If a Chinese child gets a B—which would never happen—there would first be a screaming, hair-tearing explosion. The devastated Chinese mother would then get dozens, maybe hundreds of practice tests and work through them with her child for as long as it takes to get the grade up to an A.

Chinese parents demand perfect grades because they believe that their child can get them. If their child doesn't get them, the Chinese parent assumes it's because the child didn't work hard enough. That's why the solution to substandard performance is always to excoriate, punish and shame the child. The Chinese parent believes that their child will be strong enough to take the shaming and to improve from it. (And when Chinese kids do excel, there is plenty of ego-inflating parental praise lavished in the privacy of the home.)

15   Second, Chinese parents believe that their kids owe them everything. The reason for this is a little unclear, but it's probably a combination of Confucian filial piety and the fact that the parents have sacrificed and done so much for their children. (And it's true that Chinese mothers get in the trenches, putting in long grueling hours personally tutoring, training, interrogating and spying on their kids.) Anyway, the understanding is that Chinese children must spend their lives repaying their parents by obeying them and making them proud.

By contrast, I don't think most Westerners have the same view of children being permanently indebted to their parents. My husband, Jed, actually has the opposite view. "Children don't choose their parents," he once said to me. "They don't even choose to be born. It's parents who foist life on their kids, so it's the parents' responsibility to provide for them. Kids don't owe their parents anything. Their duty will be to their own kids." This strikes me as a terrible deal for the Western parent.

Third, Chinese parents believe that they know what is best for their children and therefore override all of their children's own desires and preferences. That's why Chinese daughters can't have boyfriends in high school and why Chinese kids can't go to sleepaway camp. It's also why no Chinese kid would ever dare say to their mother, "I got a part in the school play! I'm Villager Number Six. I'll have to stay after school for rehearsal every day from 3:00 to 7:00, and I'll also need a ride on weekends." God help any Chinese kid who tried that one.

Don't get me wrong: It's not that Chinese parents don't care about their children. Just the opposite. They would give up anything for their children. It's just an entirely different parenting model.

Here's a story in favor of coercion, Chinese-style. Lulu was about 7, still playing two instruments, and working on a piano piece called "The Little White Donkey" by the French composer Jacques Ibert. The piece is really cute—you can just imagine a little donkey ambling along a country road with its master—but it's also incredibly difficult for young players because the two hands have to keep schizophrenically different rhythms.

20   Lulu couldn't do it. We worked on it nonstop for a week, drilling each of her hands separately, over and over. But whenever we tried putting the hands together, one always morphed into the other, and everything fell apart. Finally, the day before her lesson, Lulu announced in exasperation that she was giving up and stomped off.

"Get back to the piano now," I ordered.

"You can't make me."

"Oh yes, I can."

Back at the piano, Lulu made me pay. She punched, thrashed and kicked. She grabbed the music score and tore it to shreds. I taped the score back together and encased it in a plastic shield so that it could never be destroyed again. Then I hauled Lulu's dollhouse to the car and told her I'd donate it to the Salvation Army piece by piece if she didn't have "The Little White Donkey" perfect by the next day. When Lulu said, "I thought you were going to the Salvation Army, why are you still here?" I threatened her with no lunch, no dinner, no Christmas or Hanukkah presents, no birthday parties for two, three, four years. When she still kept playing it wrong, I told her she was purposely working herself into a frenzy because she was secretly afraid she couldn't do it. I told her to stop being lazy, cowardly, self-indulgent and pathetic.

25   Jed took me aside. He told me to stop insulting Lulu—which I wasn't even doing, I was just motivating her—and that he didn't think threatening Lulu was helpful. Also, he said, maybe Lulu really just couldn't do the technique—perhaps she didn't have the coordination yet—had I considered that possibility?

"You just don't believe in her," I accused.

"That's ridiculous," Jed said scornfully. "Of course I do."

"Sophia could play the piece when she was this age."

"But Lulu and Sophia are different people," Jed pointed out.

"Oh no, not this," I said, rolling my eyes. "Everyone is special in their special own way," I **30** mimicked sarcastically. "Even losers are special in their own special way. Well don't worry, you don't have to lift a finger. I'm willing to put in as long as it takes, and I'm happy to be the one hated. And you can be the one they adore because you make them pancakes and take them to Yankees games."

I rolled up my sleeves and went back to Lulu. I used every weapon and tactic I could think of. We worked right through dinner into the night, and I wouldn't let Lulu get up, not for water, not even to go to the bathroom. The house became a war zone, and I lost my voice yelling, but still there seemed to be only negative progress, and even I began to have doubts.

Then, out of the blue, Lulu did it. Her hands suddenly came together—her right and left hands each doing their own imperturbable thing—just like that.

Lulu realized it the same time I did. I held my breath. She tried it tentatively again. Then she played it more confidently and faster, and still the rhythm held. A moment later, she was beaming.

"Mommy, look—it's easy!" After that, she wanted to play the piece over and over and wouldn't leave the piano. That night, she came to sleep in my bed, and we snuggled and hugged, cracking each other up. When she performed "The Little White Donkey" at a recital a few weeks later, parents came up to me and said, "What a perfect piece for Lulu—it's so spunky and so *her*."

Even Jed gave me credit for that one. Western parents worry a lot about their children's **35** self-esteem. But as a parent, one of the worst things you can do for your child's self-esteem is to let them give up. On the flip side, there's nothing better for building confidence than learning you can do something you thought you couldn't.

There are all these new books out there portraying Asian mothers as scheming, callous, overdriven people indifferent to their kids' true interests. For their part, many Chinese secretly believe that they care more about their children and are willing to sacrifice much more for them than Westerners, who seem perfectly content to let their children turn out badly. I think it's a misunderstanding on both sides. All decent parents want to do what's best for their children. The Chinese just have a totally different idea of how to do that.

Western parents try to respect their children's individuality, encouraging them to pursue their true passions, supporting their choices, and providing positive reinforcement and a nurturing environment. By contrast, the Chinese believe that the best way to protect their children is by preparing them for the future, letting them see what they're capable of, and arming them with skills, work habits and inner confidence that no one can ever take away.

Discussion and Writing Suggestions

1. To get the benefits of raising "math whizzes and music prodigies," Chua writes, a parent must pay the costs, which she lists in a series of bullet points. Reread her list. In your view, are the costs worth the benefits? Explain.

2. Chua clearly states why she's so vigilant as a parent: "Chinese parents understand . . . that nothing is fun until you're good at it. To get good at anything you have to work, and children on their own never want to work, which is why it is crucial to override their preferences." The key element of this argument is the

assumption that "children on their own never want to work." Do you agree? Discuss your own motivation to work hard. To what extent does your motivation come from within? To what extent have others pushed you to achieve?

On the Web: *Tale of a Tiger Mom*

On January 12, 2012, Amy Chua spoke before the Commonwealth Club of California, "the nation's oldest and largest public affairs forum." At this event, Chua shares her motivations for writing her controversial book and is quick to establish (a point often overlooked by her critics) that she does *not* believe the Chinese approach to child rearing is superior to Western methods. You may find Chua, as a speaker, more sympathetic than you do as author of *Battle Hymn of the Tiger Mother*. Including the question/answer period, this presentation lasts for an hour and ten minutes. You need listen only to the segment between time markers 2:54 and 25:12.

Go to YouTube.
Search terms: *chua tiger commonwealth club 1/12/12*

Amy Chua Is a Wimp*
David Brooks

David Brooks is a columnist for the *New York Times* and a commentator on the PBS News Hour and National Public Radio. He has written for the *Wall Street Journal* and the *Washington Times* and has been an editor for the *Weekly Standard,* the *Atlantic*, and *Newsweek*. His books include the anthology *Backward and Upward: The New Conservative Writing* (1996), a book of cultural commentary; *Bobos in Paradise: The New Upper Class and How They Got There* (2000); *On Paradise Drive: How We Live Now (And Always Have) in the Future Tense* (2004); and *The Social Animal* (2011). This article appeared in the *New York Times* on January 17, 2011.

Sometime early last week, a large slice of educated America decided that Amy Chua is a menace to society. Chua, as you probably know, is the Yale professor who has written a bracing critique of what she considers the weak, cuddling American parenting style.

Chua didn't let her own girls go out on play dates or sleepovers. She didn't let them watch TV or play video games or take part in garbage activities like crafts. Once, one of her daughters came in second to a Korean kid in a math competition, so Chua made the girl do 2,000 math problems a night until she regained her supremacy. Once, her daughters gave her birthday cards of insufficient quality. Chua rejected them and demanded new cards. Once, she threatened to burn all of one of her daughter's stuffed animals unless she played a piece of music perfectly.

As a result, Chua's daughters get straight As and have won a series of musical competitions.

In her book, *Battle Hymn of the Tiger Mother*, Chua delivers a broadside against American parenting even as she mocks herself for her own extreme "Chinese" style. She says American parents lack authority and produce entitled children who aren't forced to live up to their abilities.

The furious denunciations began flooding my in-box a week ago. Chua plays into **5** America's fear of national decline. Here's a Chinese parent working really hard (and, by the way, there are a billion more of her) and her kids are going to crush ours. Furthermore (and this Chua doesn't appreciate), she is not really rebelling against American-style parenting; she is the logical extension of the prevailing elite practices. She does everything over-pressuring upper-middle-class parents are doing. She's just hard core.

Her critics echoed the familiar themes. Her kids can't possibly be happy or truly creative. They'll grow up skilled and compliant but without the audacity to be great. She's destroying their love for music. There's a reason Asian-American women between the ages of 15 and 24 have such high suicide rates.

I have the opposite problem with Chua. I believe she's coddling her children. She's protecting them from the most intellectually demanding activities because she doesn't understand what's cognitively difficult and what isn't.

Practicing a piece of music for four hours requires focused attention, but it is nowhere near as cognitively demanding as a sleepover with 14-year-old girls. Managing status rivalries, negotiating group dynamics, understanding social norms, navigating the distinction between self and group—these and other social tests impose cognitive demands that blow away any intense tutoring session or a class at Yale.

Yet mastering these arduous skills is at the very essence of achievement. Most people work in groups. We do this because groups are much more efficient at solving problems than individuals (swimmers are often motivated to have their best times as part of relay teams, not in individual events). Moreover, the performance of a group does not correlate well with the average I.Q. of the group or even with the I.Q.'s of the smartest members.

Researchers at the Massachusetts Institute of Technology and Carnegie Mellon have **10** found that groups have a high collective intelligence when members of a group are good at reading each others' emotions—when they take turns speaking, when the inputs from each member are managed fluidly, when they detect each others' inclinations and strengths.

Participating in a well-functioning group is really hard. It requires the ability to trust people outside your kinship circle, read intonations and moods, understand how the psychological pieces each person brings to the room can and cannot fit together.

This skill set is not taught formally, but it is imparted through arduous experiences. These are exactly the kinds of difficult experiences Chua shelters her children from by making them rush home to hit the homework table.

Chua would do better to see the classroom as a cognitive break from the truly arduous tests of childhood. Where do they learn how to manage people? Where do they learn to construct and manipulate metaphors? Where do they learn to perceive details of a scene the way a hunter reads a landscape? Where do they learn how to detect their own shortcomings? Where do they learn how to put themselves in others' minds and anticipate others' reactions?

These and a million other skills are imparted by the informal maturity process and are not developed if formal learning monopolizes a child's time.

So I'm not against the way Chua pushes her daughters. And I loved her book as a cou- **15** rageous and thought-provoking read. It's also more supple than her critics let on. I just wish she wasn't so soft and indulgent. I wish she recognized that in some important ways the school cafeteria is more intellectually demanding than the library. And I hope her daughters grow up to write their own books, and maybe learn the skills to better anticipate how theirs will be received.

Discussion and Writing Suggestions

1. Brooks writes: "Practicing a piece of music for four hours requires focused attention, but it is nowhere near as cognitively demanding as a sleepover with 14-year-old girls. Managing status rivalries, negotiating group dynamics, understanding social norms, navigating the distinction between self and group—these and other social tests impose cognitive demands that blow away any intense tutoring session or a class at Yale." What do you think? You're in school, learning challenging subjects. You also (presumably) find yourself in groups and must negotiate complex group dynamics. Observe and comment on some of the difficulties of each.

2. Do you agree that Chua is, in effect, short-changing her daughters by denying them play dates and sleepovers (that is, socially complex activities) in favor of intense, solitary study?

Whatever Happened to the Original Tiger Mum's Children?

Tanith Carey

It's hardly possible to read an account of tiger parenting and not wonder how Amy Chua's daughters "turned out." Did the experience of having so vigilant a parent with such high expectations somehow harm the children, as critics predicted? Not at all. Writing for *The Telegraph* (UK, January 17, 2016), Tanith Carey caught up with Amy Chua and her daughters Lulu and Sophia—and the story is, well, the profile of a regular, if high-achieving, family. Carey is an opinion and feature writer for the *Guardian*, the *Daily Mail*, and other publications. Her most recent book is *Taming the Tiger Parent: How to Put Your Child's Well-Being First in a Competitive World* (2014).

For any [freshman], the first term at university is an important time to find friends and forge an identity away from home and parents. So what must it be like to turn up and find the psychology course includes lectures on your childhood and the lessons that can be learned from it?

Such was the plight of Lulu Chua-Rubenfeld when she fulfilled the destiny her mother Amy had mapped out for her and took up her place at Harvard 18 months ago. Now in her second year studying Art History, Lulu, 19, says: "I was in the library when my friend called me over to her computer to show me that her upcoming lecture was on the subject of my childhood. They were holding an entire seminar on how my personality had responded to my mother's parenting style—and the professor had never even met me!"

But that is what happens when your mother is Amy Chua, a Yale law professor whose book on her philosophy of child-rearing, *Battle Hymn of the Tiger Mother*, became a global best seller. It's a philosophy that can be summarised as no grade below an A, no play dates and no life outside school except violin and piano practice. When the book was published in 2011, Chua's approach was met with a global firestorm. Overnight she became a household name, and despite their background of incredible privilege, Lulu, and her older sister Sophia, 23, became known as two of the world's most abused children.

Yet four years on, it seems the opposition has died down to such an extent that Amy's philosophies have won a fan in no less than David Cameron.[1]

"Character—persistence—is core to success," said the Prime Minister in his rallying cry **5** for improving Britain last week. "No matter how clever you are, if you do not believe in continued hard work and concentration, and if you do not believe that you can return from failure, you will not fulfill your potential. It is what the Tiger Mothers' battle hymn is all about: work, try hard, believe you can succeed, get up and try again."

Considering Chua's older daughter Sophia has also recently graduated from Harvard to start a postgraduate law degree at Yale, you can see why Cameron might like to see more UK parents put toddlers out in sub-zero temperatures when they refuse to do as they are told, as Chua famously did.

Both her daughters are so polite, modest and thoughtful, it seems Amy has had the last laugh at the critics who predicted they would grow up into mentally ill, friendless robots. However, before too many parents start ripping up their offsprings' underwhelming birthday cards, it's probably safe to say Mr. Cameron is unlikely to have actually read the book. Although touted in his speech as a child-care manual, *Battle Hymn of the Tiger Mother* never has been a how-to guide on getting your children into the world's most elite institutions. Instead, it is a complex account of how children can become rebellious and alienated when one-size-fits-all education philosophies are applied, regardless of their personality or aptitudes.

So with more parents being encouraged to adopt hard-line methods, who better than Sophia and Lulu to say whether it will work here? Does their mother's magic formula of Maths tutoring plus six hours of music practice, minus a social life, always equal success? The Chua-Rubenfeld sisters may have sought-after Ivy League places, but even they have reservations. As students at two of the most prestigious colleges in the world, they have met plenty of casualties of some of the high pressure parenting techniques they experienced themselves—and are the first to say not everyone survives unscathed.

"I have come across Harvard students who tell me, 'My grade wasn't good enough. I can't go home for Thanksgiving,'" says Sophia, noting that her parents cut her much more slack.

In fact, far from the bootcamp described in the book, both sisters paint a far rosier pic- **10** ture of their upbringing and say the strict regimentation was always balanced with plenty of support.

"We are a close family," says Lulu. "Even when there was a lot of screaming, that was work. When it was over, that was family time and we'd go upstairs and watch movies together."

For Sophia, the main lesson of her childhood is that hard work pays off. She may have come home at break-times to practise the piano (something she concedes was not normal for a child of that age), but when she did, it was she who was pleased when her concert recitals went better.

"Everyone talks about my mother threatening to throw my toys on the fire, but the funny thing is that was not a major memory. I remember my childhood as happy," she says. "I am not scared of my mom and never have been. It was my dad [law professor Jed Rubenfeld, who makes only a shadowy appearance in the book] who I was much more afraid of

---

[1] David Cameron: Prime Minister of the United Kingdom, 2010–2016.

disappointing. It was always unequivocally clear in my mind that my parents were on my side, no matter what. They did have high expectations of me, but because they had the confidence that I could do amazing things."

Lulu, who kicked back against her mother's child-rearing methods, has a more circumspect response.

15 "I think I had a tough childhood, but a happy one," she says after a long pause. "I was playing up to six hours of violin a day and it was too much. However, when I rebelled because it was putting too much of a strain on me, my mom could easily have given up on me. If I did poorly in a test, she did not let me lie in bed and wallow. She'd tell me I needed to get up and study to get a better mark so I would feel better. She pushed me when I needed it."

Perhaps the ultimate test has to be whether they would raise their own children the same way. Both girls say yes, albeit with tweaks to make allowances for a child's individuality. Rather than just stick to the usual array of extra-curriculars prized by Asian parents, Sophia would want to guide them towards activities "they are naturally drawn to."

Amy, ironically, is now one of the most hands-off mothers they know. "My mom feels she has done her job, so she does not hover over my life in the way some of my friends' parents do," says Lulu.

In her most recent book, *The Triple Package*, it is Amy herself who points out that hot-housed Asian-American children often feel like miserable instruments of their parents' ambition.

So is such an approach really going to help the UK, where children are already the most tested on earth and also rank among the unhappiest globally?

20 "No, assuming every kid can do this is dangerous," says Lulu. "I know too many kids who have cracked."

For her older sister, it is a question of degree. "I don't think what we should take from tiger parenting that every kid needs to become a violin prodigy or get into Harvard," she says. "But when it comes to smaller issues like, 'You won't get every toy you want until your grades improve,' or 'You can't quit the team because you lost two games in a row,' then I believe tiger parenting does have its place."

Discussion and Writing Suggestions

1. Carey writes: "Both [Lulu and Sophia] are so polite, modest and thoughtful, it seems Amy [Chua] has had the last laugh at the critics who predicted they would grow up into mentally ill, friendless robots." Given what you've read of the girls' upbringing, are you surprised? Discuss.

2. "[A]ssuming every kid can [flourish in a Chua-like home with exceedingly high expectations] is dangerous. . . . I [Lulu] know too many kids who have cracked." How are parents to distinguish between pushing children who will flourish under such pressures and laying off children who will "crack"— especially when the one obvious way to differentiate is to push the kids hard? Isn't it true that some (many?) children don't know the heights they can reach because they've never been pushed hard enough to reach a lofty goal? How is a parent to calibrate how hard to push?

Tiger Mother Stirs Reflections on Parenthood

Tina Griego

Tina Griego reports for the *Denver Post*, where this article first appeared on January 20, 2011.

Yes, of course, I read the Tiger Mother in *The Wall Street Journal*. I'm a modern-day mother of two children, one in middle school, one in third grade. By definition, this makes me neurotic.

Naturally, I'm compelled to read a newspaper article called 'Why Chinese Mothers Are Superior'—a headline that author and Tiger Mother Amy Chua complained about, but for which she should be giving an unknown copy editor a cut of her book profits.

The modern-day neurotic parent gravitates toward that which is guaranteed to shake confidence in his or her parenting ability. We are expert self-flagellators. Typically, this is offset by a similar pull toward that which makes us feel superior in our parenting skills, the cool balm of sanctimony. Chua offered one-stop shopping. Self-doubt undone by horror. Her teenage daughter played Carnegie Hall! She called her daughter garbage!

A million words have been written in response to the *Journal* excerpt, most amounting to what we all already know: Balance in all things. Which is boring.

I have to wonder, not for the first time, what my grandmothers would make of all this   5
churning of the parental waters. I figure they'd understand Chua, or, at the very least, share her confidence. Grandmas Jacquez and Griego were not, as Chua is, born of immigrants, but they were children of the Depression, children of laborers, and parental doubt was a self-indulgence. You work hard. Your children obey, and if, with the imposition of the values of obedience and duty to family, childhood is fleeting, so it must be. When the children are old enough, they will work hard. If you've taught them well, they will succeed and, in turn, take care of you.

In fact, my grandmothers' view was not long ago expressed to me by a 20-something refugee from Bhutan, Deg Adhikari. 'My parents, they do not have school. They just work and work for us. Now it is our job to make them happy and to work for the coming generations.'

How long do you think it will be before the Adhikari family and its descendants succumb to the lure of the more individualistic, more hedonistic culture that will surround them here? If you think you detect a strain of lament in the question, you would not be mistaken. Yeah, your kids are obedient and respectful now, a Chicano friend once teased a Mexican immigrant friend, but just wait until the U.S. gets ahold of them.

What's been most interesting about the discussion Chua provoked is not whether she's a good parent or bad parent. No, I'm more intrigued by how she has chosen to operate within the currents of her culture, economic class and generational expectation, in the way she negotiated the sometimes-competing values of the three. Most parents engage in this negotiation. It's inevitable. People are shaped, though not bound, by their culture, class and time, and the influences of each rise and fall.

A small example: I come from small-town, Catholic, been-here-forever Latino New Mexico. I grew up and away from the communal values of my family. The times holding sway over culture. I moved, only for a year, to a village in Japan and a culture much like my grandparents': patriarchal, disciplined, consensus-oriented, shame-conscious and so averse to risk.

10   We went out for pancakes when I returned. But this was the conversation in the car as we left the airport. Dad: 'Let's go get huevos rancheros.' Sisters and brothers in the back seat, drowning out Dad: 'No-o-o-o.' Tina sitting next to siblings, shaken by their lack of respect: 'What are you doing? Let Dad decide.' Culture holding sway over time.

And no, it didn't last. Nothing is that neat, and the currents move fast. They inform and hinder and bless me, and as aware, ridiculously so, as I am of what influences me as a parent, my kids are not. Why should they be? My job is to keep the boat straight, give them safe harbor, to love and guide and prepare them as best as I know how for the day they take the oars.

Discussion and Writing Suggestions

1. Griego writes that she's "intrigued by how [Chua] has chosen to operate within the currents of her culture, economic class and generational expectation, in the way she negotiated the sometimes-competing values of the three." What might some of these "competing values" be?

2. Griego suspects her grandmothers would have been comfortable with Chua's self-assurance in raising her children. Griego, on the other hand, is a less-assured parent. Why?

3. "Yeah, your kids are obedient and respectful now, a Chicano friend once teased a Mexican immigrant friend, but just wait until the U.S. gets ahold of them." What does the friend mean? What is it about American culture that might undermine a child's obedience at home?

4. In paragraph 9, Griego writes: "The times holding sway over culture." In paragraph 10 she writes, "Culture holding sway over time." What does she mean?

Tiger Mom vs. Tiger Mailroom

Patrick Goldstein

Patrick Goldstein writes "The Big Picture," a *Los Angeles Times* column dealing with the film industry. This article first appeared in the *Times* on February 6, 2011.

It's hard to go anywhere these days, especially if you're a parent with young kids, where the conversation doesn't eventually turn to Amy Chua's red-hot child-rearing memoir, *Battle Hymn of the Tiger Mother*. It offers a provocative depiction of Chinese-style extreme parenting—her daughters are not allowed to watch TV, have playdates or get any grade below an A, all as preparation for success in life, beginning with getting into an Ivy League school, like their Tiger Mom, who went to Harvard and now teaches at Yale Law School.

But of all the heated reaction to Chua's parenting strategy, none was as compelling as what former Harvard President Larry Summers had to say when he discussed parenting with Chua at the recent World Economic Forum in Davos, Switzerland. Summers made a striking point, arguing that the two Harvard students who'd had the most transformative impact on the world in the past 25 years were Bill Gates and Mark Zuckerberg, yet neither had, ahem, graduated from college. If they had been brought up by a Tiger Mom, Summers imagined, she would've been bitterly disappointed.

I have no beef with Chua's parenting code, which hardly seems any more extreme than the neurotic ambitions of mothers and fathers I'm exposed to living on the Westside of Los Angeles. But if Chua wants a radically different perspective on the relationship between higher education and career achievement, she should spend some time in Hollywood, a place that's been run for nearly a century by men who never made it through or even to college. The original moguls were famously uneducated, often having started as peddlers and furriers before finding their perches atop the studio dream factories. But even today, the industry is still dominated by titanic figures, both on the creative and on the business side, who never got anywhere near Harvard Yard.

A short list of the industry leaders who never finished or even attended college would include Steve Jobs, David Geffen, Steven Spielberg, Jeffrey Katzenberg, James Cameron, Clint Eastwood, Barry Diller, Ron Meyer, Peter Jackson, Harvey Weinstein, Scott Rudin and Quentin Tarantino. Some of this is clearly a generational thing, since everyone on that list is over 40. On the other hand, the younger new-media icons seem as likely to be degree-free as their Hollywood brethren, whether it's Zuckerberg or the founders of Twitter, who didn't graduate from college either. (Though it's true that Zuckerberg might not have even thought of Facebook if he hadn't been in the sexually charged freshman swirl at Harvard.)

Common Thread

But in showbiz, you learn by doing. If there is a common denominator to all of those success   5
stories, it's that they were all men in a hurry, impatient with book learning, which could only take them so far in the rough-and-tumble world of Hollywood. Ron Meyer, a founder of Creative Artists Agency and now president of Universal Studios, dropped out of high school, served in the Marines and proudly notes on his résumé that his first job was as a messenger boy for the Paul Kohner Agency.

"The truth is that if you have a particular talent and the will to succeed, you don't really need a great education," Meyer told me last week. "In showbiz, your real college experience is working in a talent agency mail-room. That's the one place where you can get the most complete understanding of the arena you're playing in and how to deal with the complicated situations you'll come across in your career."

There are plenty of successful lawyers and MBAs in Hollywood, but the raw spirit of can-do invention and inspiration will take people further than the ability to read a complex profit and loss statement. Years ago, Geffen, who dropped out of night school at Brooklyn College before eventually landing a job in the William Morris mail-room, once told me that his early success was rooted in the ability to develop relationships. "It's not about where you went to college or how good-looking you are or whether you could play football—it's about whether you can create a relationship."

To produce a film or create a TV show or found a company requires the same kind of raw entrepreneurial zeal that it must have taken the '49ers who came west in search of gold. "You often feel like you're surrounded by a do-it-yourself ethic, almost a pioneer spirit," says Michael De Luca, producer of *The Social Network*, who dropped out of NYU four credits short of graduation to take a job at New Line Cinema, where he rose to become head of production. "All those successful guys you're talking about—they had an intense desire to create something big, new and different. They didn't need to wait around for the instruction manual."

In David Rensin's wonderful oral history *The Mailroom: Hollywood History From the Bottom Up*, survivors of the Mike Ovitz-era CAA experience tell war stories about how, as mail-room flunkies, they had to replenish Ovitz's candy dishes, stock his jars with raw cashews and fill his water jar with Evian. It seemed like hellish drudgery but, as the agents recalled, it prepared you for all the craziness of later Hollywood life, where multimillion-dollar movie star deals could fall apart if someone's exercise trainer or makeup specialist wasn't provided.

Do the Hustle

10   Even today, people in Hollywood are far more impressed by, say, your knack for finding new talent than by what your grades were like. "Show business is all about instinct and intuition," says Sam Gores, head of the Paradigm Agency, who went to acting school but never to college, having joined a meat-cutters' union by the time he was 18. "To succeed, you need to have a strong point of view and a lot of confidence. Sometimes being the most well-informed person in your circle can almost get in your way."

In show business, charm, hustle and guile are the aces in the deck. When *New York Times* columnist David Brooks was dissecting Chua's book recently, he argued that "managing status rivalries, negotiating group dynamics, understanding social norms, navigating the distinction between self and group" imposed the kind of cognitive demands that far exceed what's required of students in a class at Yale. He probably picked that up reading a fancy sociology text, but it was a letter-perfect description of the skill set for a gifted filmmaker, agent or producer.

In Hollywood, whether you were a C student or *summa cum laude*, it's a level playing field. "When you're working on a movie set, you've got 50 film professors to learn from, from the sound man to the cinematographer," says producer David Permut, who dropped out of UCLA to work for Roger Corman. "I've never needed a résumé in my whole career. All you need is a 110-page script that someone is dying to make and you're in business."

Discussion and Writing Suggestions

1. Goldstein points to many ambitious self-starters in the movie industry. Some never finished college; others never attended. Yet these people succeeded on a grand scale, working from the bottom of the industry, up. What would *you* say to a friend or son or daughter who quit college just four credits shy of a degree (as one of these self-starters did) to take a job in the movie industry?

2. Goldstein offers "a radically different perspective [than Chua's] on the relationship between higher education and career achievement." Which perspective on this relationship appeals to you more, the Hollywood perspective or Chua's? Why?

3. Are you relieved to learn of successful people "who never got anywhere near Harvard Yard"? Chua likely wouldn't be impressed enough by these people to push her daughters any less hard for conventional academic success. Why not?

America's Top Parent

Elizabeth Kolbert

Elizabeth Kolbert is a staff writer for the *New Yorker,* where this article first appeared on January 20, 2011. Kolbert has also written for the *New York Times* and is the author of *Field Notes from a Catastrophe: Man and Nature and Climate Change* (2006).

"Call me garbage."

The other day, I was having dinner with my family when the subject of Amy Chua's new book, *Battle Hymn of the Tiger Mother* (Penguin Press; $25.95), came up. My twelve-year-old twins had been read an excerpt from the book by their teacher, a well-known provocateur. He had been sent a link to the excerpt by another teacher, who had received it from her sister, who had been e-mailed it by a friend, and, well, you get the point. The excerpt, which had appeared in the *Wall Street Journal* under the headline "WHY CHINESE MOTHERS ARE SUPERIOR," was, and still is, an Internet sensation—as one blogger put it, the "Andromeda Strain of viral memes." Within days, more than five thousand comments had been posted, and "Tiger Mother" vaulted to No. 4 on Amazon's list of best-sellers. Chua appeared on NPR's "All Things Considered" and on NBC's "Nightly News" and "Today" show. Her book was the topic of two columns in last week's Sunday *Times*, and, under the racially neutral headline "IS EXTREME PARENTING EFFECTIVE?," the subject of a formal debate on the paper's Web site.

Thanks to this media blitz, the basic outlines of *Tiger Mother's* story are by now familiar. Chua, the daughter of Chinese immigrants, is a Yale Law School professor. She is married to another Yale law professor and has two daughters, whom she drives relentlessly. Chua's rules for the girls include: no sleepovers, no playdates, no grade lower than an A on report cards, no choosing your own extracurricular activities, and no ranking lower than No. 1 in any subject. (An exception to this last directive is made for gym and drama.)

In Chua's binary world, there are just two kinds of mother. There are "Chinese mothers," who, she allows, do not necessarily have to be Chinese. "I'm using the term 'Chinese mothers' loosely," she writes. Then, there are "Western" mothers. Western mothers think they are being strict when they insist that their children practice their instruments for half an hour a day. For Chinese mothers, "the first hour is the easy part." Chua chooses the instruments that her daughters will play—piano for the older one, Sophia; violin for the younger, Lulu—and stands over them as they practice for three, four, sometimes five hours at a stretch. The least the girls are expected to do is make it to Carnegie Hall. Amazingly enough, Sophia does. Chua's daughters are so successful—once, it's true, Sophia came in second on a multiplication test (to a Korean boy), but Chua made sure this never happened again—that they confirm her thesis: Western mothers are losers. I'm using the term "losers" loosely.

Chua has said that one of the points of the book is "making fun of myself," but plainly **5** what she was hoping for was to outrage. Whole chapters of "Tiger Mother"—admittedly, many chapters are only four or five pages long—are given over to incidents like that of the rejected smiley face.

"I don't want this," she tells Lulu, throwing back at her a handmade birthday card. "I want a better one."

In another chapter, Chua threatens to take Lulu's doll house to the Salvation Army and, when that doesn't work, to deny her lunch, dinner, and birthday parties for "two, three, four years" because she cannot master a piece called "The Little White Donkey." The kid is seven years old. In a third chapter, Chua tells Sophia she is "garbage." Chua's own father has called her "garbage," and she finds it a highly effective parenting technique. Chua relates this at a dinner party, and one of the guests supposedly gets so upset that she breaks down in tears. The hostess tries to patch things up by suggesting that Chua is speaking figuratively.

"You didn't actually call Sophia garbage," the hostess offers.

"Yes, I did," Chua says.

10   When the dinner-party episode was read in class, my sons found it hilarious, which is why they were taunting me. "Call me garbage," one of the twins said again. "I dare you."

"O.K.," I said, trying, for once, to be a good mother. "You're garbage."

If Chua's tale has any significance—and it may not—it is as an allegory. Chua refers to herself as a Tiger because according to the Chinese zodiac she was born in the Year of the Tiger. Tiger people are "powerful, authoritative, and magnetic," she informs us, just as tigers that walk on four legs inspire "fear and respect." The "tiger economies" of Asia aren't mentioned in the book, but they growl menacingly in the background.

It's just about impossible to pick up a newspaper these days—though who actually *picks up* a newspaper anymore?—without finding a story about the rise of the East. The headlines are variations on a theme: "SOLAR PANEL MAKER MOVES WORK TO CHINA"; "CHINA DRAWING HIGH-TECH RESEARCH FROM U.S."; "IBM CUTTING 5,000 SERVICE JOBS; MOVING WORK TO INDIA." What began as an outflow of manufacturing jobs has spread way beyond car parts and electronics to include information technology, legal advice, even journalism. (This piece could have been written much more cost-effectively by a team in Bangalore and, who knows, maybe next month it will be.)

On our good days, we tell ourselves that our kids will be all right. The new, global economy, we observe, puts a premium on flexibility and creativity. And who is better prepared for such a future than little Abby (or Zachary), downloading her wacky videos onto YouTube while she texts her friends, messes with Photoshop, and listens to her iPod?

15   "Yes, you can brute-force any kid to learn to play the piano—just precisely like his or her billion neighbors" is how one of the comments on the *Wall Street Journal's* Web site put it. "But you'll never get a Jimi Hendrix that way."

On our bad days, we wonder whether this way of thinking is, as Chua might say, garbage. Last month, the results of the most recent Programme for International Student Assessment, or PISA, tests were announced. It was the first time that Chinese students had participated, and children from Shanghai ranked first in every single area. Students from the United States, meanwhile, came in seventeenth in reading, twenty-third in science, and an especially demoralizing thirty-first in math. This last ranking put American kids not just behind the Chinese, the Koreans, and the Singaporeans but also after the French, the Austrians, the Hungarians, the Slovenians, the Estonians, and the Poles.

"I know skeptics will want to argue with the results, but we consider them to be accurate and reliable," Arne Duncan, the U.S. Secretary of Education, told the *Times*. "The United States came in twenty-third or twenty-fourth in most subjects. We can quibble, or we can face the brutal truth that we're being out-educated."

Why is this? How is it that the richest country in the world can't teach kids to read or to multiply fractions? Taken as a parable, Chua's cartoonish narrative about browbeating her daughters acquires a certain disquieting force. Americans have been told always to encourage their kids. This, the theory goes, will improve their self-esteem, and this, in turn, will help them learn.

After a generation or so of applying this theory, we have the results. Just about the only category in which American students outperform the competition is self-regard. Researchers at the Brookings Institution, in one of their frequent studies of education policy, compared students' assessments of their abilities in math with their scores on a standardized test. Nearly forty per cent of American eighth graders agreed "a lot" with the statement "I usually do well in mathematics," even though only seven per cent of American students actually got enough correct answers on the test to qualify as advanced. Among Singaporean students, eighteen per cent said they usually did well in math; forty-four per cent qualified as advanced. As the Brookings researchers pointed out, even the least self-confident Singaporean students, on average, outscored the most self-confident Americans. You can say it's sad that kids in Singapore are so beaten down that they can't appreciate their own accomplishments. But you've got to give them this: at least they get the math right.

Our problems as a country cannot, of course, be reduced to our problems as educators **20** or as parents. Nonetheless, there is an uncomfortable analogy. For some time now, the U.S. has, in effect, been drawing crappy, smiley-face birthday cards and calling them wonderful. It's made us feel a bit better about ourselves without improving the basic situation. As the cover story on China's ascent in this month's *Foreign Policy* sums things up: "American Decline: This Time It's Real."

It's hard to believe that Chua's book would be causing quite as much stir without the geopolitical subtext. (Picture the reaction to a similar tale told by a Hungarian or an Austrian über-mom.) At the same time, lots of people have clearly taken "Tiger Mother" personally.

Of the zillions of comments that have been posted on the Web, many of the most passionate are from scandalized "Western" mothers and fathers, or, as one blogger dubbed them, "Manatee dads." Some have gone as far as to suggest that Chua be arrested for child abuse. At least as emotional are the posts from Asians and Asian-Americans.

"Parents like Amy Chua are the reason why Asian-Americans like me are in therapy," Betty Ming Liu, who teaches journalism at N.Y.U., wrote on her blog.

"What's even more damning is her perpetuation of the media stereotypes of Asian-Americans," Frank Chi, a political consultant, wrote in the Boston *Globe*'s opinion blog.

"Having lived through a version of the Chinese Parenting Experience, and having been **25** surrounded since birth with hundreds of CPE graduates, I couldn't not say something," a contributor to the Web site Shanghaiist wrote after the *Wall Street Journal* excerpt appeared. "The article actually made me feel physically ill."

Chua's response to some of the unkind things said about her—she has reported getting death threats—has been to backpedal. "RETREAT OF THE 'TIGER MOTHER'" was the headline of one *Times* article. (It, too, quickly jumped to the top of the paper's "most e-mailed" list.) Chua has said that it was not her plan to write a parenting manual: "My actual book is not a how-to guide." Somehow or other, her publisher seems to be among those who missed this. The back cover spells out, in black and red type, "How to Be a Tiger Mother."

According to Chua, her "actual book" is a memoir. Memoir is, or at least is supposed to be, a demanding genre. It requires that the author not just narrate his or her life but reflect on it. By her own description, Chua is not a probing person. Of her years studying at Harvard Law School, she writes:

> I didn't care about the rights of criminals the way others did, and I froze whenever a professor called on me. I also wasn't naturally skeptical and questioning; I just wanted to write down everything the professor said and memorize it.

Battle Hymn of the Tiger Mother exhibits much the same lack of interest in critical thinking. It's breezily written, at times entertaining, and devoid of anything approaching introspection. Imagine your most self-congratulatory friend holding forth for two hours about her kids' triumphs, and you've more or less got the narrative. The only thing that keeps it together is Chua's cheerful faith that whatever happened to her or her daughters is interesting just because it happened to happen to them. In addition to all the schlepping back and forth to auditions, there are two chapters on Chua's dogs (Samoyeds named Coco and Pushkin), three pages of practice notes that she left behind for Lulu when she could not be there to berate her in person, and a complete list of the places that she had visited with her kids by the time they were twelve and nine:

> London, Paris, Nice, Rome, Venice, Milan, Amsterdam, The Hague, Barcelona, Madrid, Málaga, Liechtenstein, Monaco, Munich, Dublin, Brussels, Bruges, Strasbourg, Beijing, Shanghai, Tokyo, Hong Kong, Manila, Istanbul, Mexico City, Cancún, Buenos Aires, Santiago, Rio de Janeiro, São Paulo, La Paz, Sucre, Cochabamba, Jamaica, Tangier, Fez, Johannesburg, Cape Town, and the Rock of Gibraltar.

Chua's husband is not Chinese, in either sense of the word. He makes occasional appearances in the book to try—ineffectually, it seems—to shield the girls. Chua has said that she wrote more about their arguments, but her husband didn't like those passages, so they've been cut. Perhaps had more of his voice been included it would have provided some grit and at least the semblance of engagement. As it is, though, it's just her. "I'm happy to be the one hated," she tells her husband at one point, and apparently she means it.

30   Parenting is hard. As anyone who has gone through the process and had enough leisure (and still functioning brain cells) to reflect on it knows, a lot of it is a crapshoot. Things go wrong that you have no control over, and, on occasion, things also go right, and you have no control over those, either. The experience is scary and exhilarating and often humiliating, not because you're disappointed in your kids, necessarily, but because you're disappointed in yourself.

Some things do go wrong in Chua's memoir. Her mother-in-law dies; her younger sister develops leukemia. These events get roughly the same amount of space as Coco and Pushkin, and yet they are, on their own terms, moving. More central to the story line is a screaming fit in a Moscow restaurant during which a glass is thrown. The upshot of the crisis is that Lulu is allowed to take up tennis, which Chua then proceeds to micromanage.

Chua clearly wants to end her book by claiming that she has changed. She knows enough about the conventions of memoir-writing to understand that some kind of transformation is generally required. But she can't bring herself to do it. And so in the final pages she invokes the Founding Fathers. They, too, she tells her daughters, would not have approved of sleepovers.

Discussion and Writing Suggestions

1. Kolbert devotes the first ten paragraphs of her essay to summarizing Chua's *Battle Hymn of the Tiger Mother*. It is not a neutral summary. Point to the word choices and phrasings that reveal Kolbert's point of view. How would you describe this point of view? Point to other passages in the piece that confirm your answer. Consider, for instance, the last two paragraphs.

2. Kolbert uses Chua's book and the controversy it stirred as an "allegory" to make a larger point about the competitiveness of the U.S. economy. "Our problems as a country cannot, of course, be reduced to our problems as educators or as parents. Nonetheless, there is an uncomfortable analogy. For some time now, the U.S. has, in effect, been drawing crappy, smiley-face birthday cards and calling them wonderful. It's made us feel a bit better about ourselves without improving the basic situation." Your response? If

Kolbert is right, what's the solution? Is it time to begin recommending Chua's style of parenting?

3. Kolbert raises a common objection to Chua's style of parenting: that it promotes rote memorization at the expense of critical thinking and reflection. What do you think?

Your Perfectionist Parenting Style May Be Detrimental to Your Child*

Ariana Eunjung Cha

The previous selections argue particular positions on the subject of tiger mothers based on the writers' own viewpoints or experiences. These are opinion-based pieces. In contrast, the following article reports on empirical, fact-based studies in which researchers tested the thesis that the rigorous, demanding parenting advocated by Chua results in more highly accomplished children. Here you will find hard data, which can be very useful when writing arguments of your own. Ariana Eunjung Cha is a staff writer for the *Washington Post*. This article first appeared on June 27, 2016.

Even if you were horrified at the idea of hovering over your child as Amy Chua did in her polarizing 2011 bestseller "The Battle Hymn of the Tiger Mother," I'm betting there was a part of you that looked at her perfect children with at least a tinge of envy. As portrayed in the book, Chua's magic formula of no playdates, no TV and always being No. 1 in everything (except for gym and drama, of course) ended up producing two girls who were straight-A students and who also were wildly talented in music. Oh, and they both ended up going to Harvard University.

Critics predicted that daughters Sophia and Lulu would end up being "mentally ill, friendless robots," according to a recent "where are they now" profile in the *Telegraph*. Instead, they ended up being "polite, modest and thoughtful" as well as successful, the article says, and they remember their childhood as tough—but happy.

But are the sisters the norm or exception to this type of parenting?

A new study out of the notoriously high-pressure, high-performing Asian city-state of Singapore takes a stab at this question and comes to worrisome conclusions. The research, published in the *Journal of Personality*, involved 263 children in primary school who were 7 years old when it began and were followed for five years from 2010 to 2014.

The work looks at the dark side of perfectionism—maladaptive perfectionism, in   **5** research parlance—and how this develops in schoolchildren.

Scientists measured what they called "parental intrusiveness" in the first year of the study by asking the child to solve some puzzles while a parent—whichever one was more involved in care—was present. They told the parents that they should feel free to help the child whenever necessary and then secretly rated their behaviors. Their goal was to figure out whether the parents interfered with the child's problem-solving and whether that help was needed.

At the extreme end of the spectrum were parents with what they called highly intrusive behavior. These were the moms and dads who "took over the game to retract a move made by the child," the researchers said. Each of these attempts was logged and coded. Similar tests were repeated as the children aged—at 8, 9 and 11.

The researchers then assessed aspects of the child's mental health from talking to both the child and parent.

And here's the part where the study becomes alarming. The children with intrusive parents were more likely to be overly critical of themselves, and this tendency increased over the years. And that high or increased level of self-criticism was correlated to elevated levels of depression or anxiety.

10   "When parents become intrusive in their children's lives, it may signal to the children that what they do is never good enough. As a result, the child may become afraid of making the slightest mistake and will blame himself or herself for not being 'perfect.' Over time, such behaviour, known as maladaptive perfectionism, may be detrimental to the child's well-being as it increases the risk of the child developing symptoms of depression, anxiety and even suicide in very serious cases," study author Ryan Hong explained.

In the Singapore sample, it turned out that huge numbers exhibited some maladaptive thinking about themselves. Sixty percent were classified as high or increasing in "self-criticalness" and 78 percent of the children as high in "socially prescribed perfectionism." The majority—59 percent—had both. Self-criticalness is a measure of concern about one's own imperfections and mistakes. Socially prescribed perfectionism refers to a belief that one needs to meet unrealistically high expectations.

Previous studies have also been critical of overly intrusive parenting.

Earlier this year, one study by Erica Musser, an assistant professor of psychology at Florida International University, looked at why some children tend to lose a diagnosis of attention-deficit/hyperactivity disorder in their teenage years while it persists in others and were surprised to find that high levels of harsh, negative statements during interviews with researchers appeared to be associated with the continuance of ADHD symptoms. But this study did not find that parental over-involvement—as characterized by being very emotional about a child and doing things such as using references to "we" when talking about the child's activities or actions—had an impact on the continuation of ADHD symptoms. (Who hasn't met that annoying parent who says things like "we're doing baseball in the spring, and we don't have time for soccer"?)

In a paper on college students published in 2014 in the journal Education and Training, researchers emphasized that there's an important distinction between parental involvement and over-parenting. "While parental involvement might be the extra boost that students need to build their own confidence and abilities, over-parenting appears to do the converse in creating a sense that one cannot accomplish things socially or in general on one's own," the authors wrote.

15   As described by my colleague Amy Joyce, "the study showed that those college students with 'helicopter parents' had a hard time believing in their own ability to accomplish goals. They were more dependent on others, had poor coping strategies and didn't have soft skills, like responsibility and conscientiousness throughout college."

Hong, an assistant professor of psychology at the National University of Singapore, said that parental intrusiveness manifests itself in simple everyday ways: by parents having very high expectations of their children's academic performance and demonstrating this by urging the child to get good grades or overreacting when a child does something wrong.

He suggested that even small changes in how you talk to your children might help. Instead of asking whether your child got 100 percent or an A, you might ask more generally how they did on a test.

"The former question conveys a message to the child that he or she is expected to get full marks on the test while the second question does not convey such a message," he said.

Hong's advice boils down to: Cut down on the helicopter parenting. If you must be a Tiger Mom, encourage rather than pressure children. Let children make mistakes.

Discussion and Writing Suggestions

1. In one study that Cha reports on, researchers observed that overintrusive parenting resulted in children who were more prone to self-criticism, which "was correlated to elevated levels of depression or anxiety." When you haven't achieved an outcome that you, or a parent, desired, you're naturally disappointed. What's the difference between disappointment and depression?

2. We learn in this selection that "maladaptive perfectionism" can have pernicious effects on children and teens. If you are a perfectionist or know anyone who is, have you witnessed any of these pernicious effects? How can perfectionism be a positive quality? When does it shade into something darker?

3. You don't get to choose—but if you did choose a parent, would you prefer one who was overly intrusive or one who showed little or no interest in your work? Why?

4. A psychologist in Singapore advises parents to "[l]et children make mistakes." Is this sound advice, in your view? Discuss.

The Assignments

Summary

Following the guidelines in Chapter 1, particularly the Guidelines for Writing Summaries box (p. 27), summarize the excerpt adapted from *Battle Hymn of the Tiger Mother* by Amy Chua. In preparation for writing the summary, review the model summary (p. 30) and consult the advice on note taking (pp. 21–22).

As an alternative, summarize one of the other selections in this chapter. The article by Kolbert would also be a good subject for summary.

Critique

Following the guidelines in Chapter 2, particularly the Guidelines for Writing Critiques box (p. 82), write a critique of Chua's op-ed. The early part of the critique should draw upon the summary of Chua that you prepared for the previous assignment. In preparation for writing the critique, review the model critique (pp. 83–86).

You've probably already noticed that most of the articles following Chua are to some extent critiques of either the excerpt adapted from *Battle Hymn of the Tiger Mother* or the book as a whole. Some authors argue with her basic premise, some support it, though perhaps with reservations, and others discuss related issues such as the preparedness of America's youth to compete with their counterparts in China. In developing your own critique, you're free to draw upon these other authors; but you should also stake out your own position based upon your own observations and experience and your own understanding of the issues Chua discusses. Doing so will help ensure that your critique isn't merely a compendium of other authors' observations and arguments.

Begin preparing for the critique by reflecting on your own observations and experiences in relation to Chua's main assumption (expressed in the two sentences that open paragraph 5): "What Chinese parents understand is that nothing is fun until you're good at it. To get good at anything you have to work, and children on their own never want to work, which is why it is crucial to override their preferences." Ask yourself:

- To what extent do you agree that "nothing is fun until you're good at it"? Do your own experiences and the experiences of your friends and relatives bear out this assumption? What have you read that supports or refutes it?

- Do you agree that "children on their own never want to work"? Cite examples in support or to the contrary.

- Consider the proposition that it is crucial for parents to override children's natural disinclination to work, in light of your own experiences, observations, and reading.

Throughout Chua's op-ed, you'll encounter controversial statements such as those in the first two bullet points above, along with anecdotes about the ways she has driven her children, sometimes mercilessly, in pursuit of her standards of excellence and success. And you'll find numerous comparisons between "Chinese" and "Western" approaches to child rearing. Your assessment of these statements should provide a rich source of material for your own critique.

Here's a suggested organizational plan for your critique:

1. An introduction, setting the issue in context (see Chapter 3 for advice on creating introductions)

2. A summary of Chua's op-ed (a brief version of your response to the summary assignment above)

3. An evaluation of Chua's piece for clarity, logic, and/or fairness (the Question #1 topics in Chapter 2, p. 66)

4. An account of your own agreement or disagreement with Chua's argument (the Question #2 topics in Chapter 2, pp. 79–81)

5. A conclusion (see Chapter 3 for advice on creating conclusions)

In preparing your critique, follow the advice in Chapter 2; see particularly the Guidelines for Writing Critiques box (pp. 82–83), along with the hints in Chapter 1 on incorporating summaries, paraphrases, and quoted material into your own writing (pp. 14–64).

Explanatory Synthesis

Based on the readings in this chapter, write an explanatory synthesis that you might use in a broader argument on the subject of varying approaches to child rearing and preparing children to be competitive in the workplace of the future. The synthesis should consist of three or more well-developed paragraphs on each of the following topics: (1) an account of the controversy over Chua's op-ed and the book from which it was drawn; (2) an account of the two different approaches to parenting represented by the "Chinese" and "Western" models; and (3) an account of the different approaches to preparing children to be competitive in the current and future marketplace. Follow the guidelines in Chapter 4, particularly the Guidelines for Writing Syntheses box (pp. 110–11); review also the model explanatory synthesis (pp. 120–25), though your assignment here calls for a briefer paper. In your synthesis, take into account the results of the study in Singapore, as reported by Ariana Cha.

Key requirements for the explanatory synthesis:

- Craft a thesis for your paper, a single statement that will guide the writing of the paragraphs of explanation that follow.

- Begin each paragraph of explanation that follows the explanatory thesis with a clear topic sentence.

- Refer in each paragraph of explanation to *at least two* different sources. Set up the references carefully, using an appropriate citation format, most likely MLA (see Chapter 7).

- In developing your explanatory synthesis, draw on facts, examples, statistics, and expert opinions from your sources.

Analysis

Select a principle or definition discussed in one of the readings in "The Roar of the Tiger Mom" and apply this principle or definition to either (1) a particular situation of which you have personal knowledge or (2) a situation that you have learned about in the course of your reading. Follow the guidelines in Chapter 6, particularly the Guidelines for Writing Analyses box (p. 168); review also the model analysis (pp. 172–76).

First, review the topic list you created in Group Assignment #1 after reading the selections in this chapter. At least one of the items on the list may point the way to an analytic principle that resonates with you. If so, follow through by locating a particular quotation that articulates this principle. Here are some examples of such quotations from the readings:

- "But as a parent, one of the worst things you can do for your child's self-esteem is to let them give up. On the flip side, there's nothing better for building confidence than learning you can do something you thought you couldn't." (Chua, p. 8)

- "Managing status rivalries, negotiating group dynamics, understanding social norms, navigating the distinction between self and group—these and other social tests impose cognitive demands that blow away any intense tutoring session or a class at Yale." (Brooks, p. 10)

- "For some time now, the U.S. has, in effect, been drawing crappy, smiley-faced birthday cards and calling them wonderful." (Kolbert, p. 18)

- "You work hard. Your children obey, and if, with the imposition of the values of obedience and duty to family, childhood is fleeting, so it must be." (Griego, p. 14)

- "[T]he study showed that those college students with 'helicopter parents' had a hard time believing in their own ability to accomplish goals. They were more dependent on others, had poor coping strategies and didn't have soft skills, like responsibility and conscientiousness throughout college." (Cha, p. 23)

Consider using the following structure for your analysis:

1. An introductory paragraph that sets a context for the topic and presents the claim you intend to support in the analysis that follows. Your claim (your thesis) distills the conclusions you've drawn from your analysis. Your claim may appear at the end of the introductory paragraph (or introductory section).

2. A paragraph or two introducing the analytic tool or principle you intend to use and discussing its key components. Suppose you decided to use Brooks's

quotation as an analytic principle. You would need to explain what he means by one or more of these skills: "[m]anaging status rivalries," "negotiating group dynamics," "understanding social norms," and "navigating the distinction between self and group." You would also need to explain how successfully managing such social tests imposes "cognitive demands that blow away any intense tutoring session or a class at Yale." Note, however, that you're not required to establish that one set of tasks is *more* difficult or important than the other. It may be sufficient for your purpose to establish simply that the social skills are at least *as* important as the academic skills. Once you establish this analytic principle, you can proceed with the analysis.

3. A paragraph or two describing the situation that you will analyze—drawn from your own personal experience or observation or from your reading.

4. Several paragraphs (this is the heart of your analysis) in which you systematically apply the key components of the principle you have selected to the situation you have described. Staying with Brooks, you would apply such key components as managing status rivalries, negotiating group dynamics, and so on to the situation you have described. As you apply these key components in turn, in separate paragraphs or groupings of paragraphs, you would discuss why such skills are, if not *more* difficult than undergoing a demanding class or tutoring session, then at least *as valuable* for success in later life as academic skills.

5. A conclusion in which you argue that, based on the insights gained through your analysis, the experience or situation in question can now be understood more deeply. See Chapter 3 (pp. 98–104) for advice on concluding your paper.

Argument

Write an argument synthesis based upon the selections in "The Roar of the Tiger Mom." You may find it useful to draw upon the products of your earlier assignments in this section on summary, critique, explanatory synthesis, and analysis. In your synthesis, take into account the results of the study in Singapore, as reported by Ariana Cha.

Follow the guidelines in Chapter 5 and reference the Guidelines for Writing Synthesis box in Chapter 4 (pp. 110–11); review also the model argument synthesis (pp. 142–48).

In planning your synthesis, review the master list of topics and notes that you and your classmates generated for Group Assignment #1 above (p. 3), and draw upon what the authors of the passages have written about these topics in developing your outline. Devise a claim, a thesis that distills your argument to a sentence or two. Plan to support your claim with facts, opinions, and statistics from the passages.

Note that one synthesis—a single paper—could not possibly refer to every topic, or every connection among authors, that you have found. The craft of preparing and writing a synthesis depends on your ability to *select* closely related topics and then to make and develop a claim that links and can be supported by them. You don't have to refer to *all* of the selections in this chapter while developing your paper; but you will likely want to refer to most. You may even want to research additional sources.

In formulating arguments on a controversial issue—for example, immigration, abortion, the size of government, or capital punishment—the immediate temptation is to adopt one strong (and uncompromising) position or to adopt its counterpart on the opposite side. Many commentators on Chua's book or op-ed tend to divide themselves into pro-Chua or anti-Chua camps: she's either dead right about her approach to parenting or she's dead wrong. Arguments supporting such polarized positions may be forceful, even eloquent, but seldom persuade those predisposed to the opposite point of view. (See "The Limits of Argument" in Chapter 5, pp. 132–33.)

After considering all the facts and the assertions, strive for a more nuanced approach. This doesn't necessarily mean adopting a straight-down-the-middle/split-the-difference position, which is likely to persuade no one. It does mean acknowledging opposing arguments and dealing with them in good faith. (See "Present and Respond to Counterarguments" in Chapter 5, p. 151.) It also means considering the issue afresh, thinking about the implications of the problems and the possible solutions, and coming up with your own insights, your own distinctive take on the subject. Such thought, such nuance, should be reflected in your thesis. (See "Writing a Thesis" in Chapter 3, pp. 88–93.)

Without writing your thesis for you, we'll suppose for the sake of example that the subject of your argument synthesis concerns how the debate over Chua's ideas clarifies how parents can best help their children succeed as they prepare for adulthood. An arguable claim on the subject would likely state which approach to child rearing, in your opinion, would best prepare children. Here's one way of structuring such an argument synthesis:

- An introductory paragraph that sets a context for the topic—in the example above, the debate over Chua's op-ed and the best pathway to success—and presents the claim you intend to support in the argument that follows. Your claim (that is, your argumentative thesis) may appear at the end of this paragraph (or introductory section).

- A paragraph or two summarizing Chua's ideas. This section may be an abbreviated version of the summary you wrote earlier.

- One to three paragraphs discussing some of the commentary on Chua's ideas, organized by topic, rather than author. That is, identify two or three main categories of response to Chua—favorable, unfavorable, and neutral—and take up each category in turn. You may have created topic webs for these categories when preparing to write. See Group Assignments #1 and #2.

- Several paragraphs arguing for your own assessment of the best pathway (or pathways) to success, supported in part by the comments of some of the authors in this chapter. Relate this assessment to ideas contained within the articles by Chua and her critics. For this section you may want to draw upon your responses to the earlier analysis or critique assignments. You may even elect to consult additional sources on the subject.

- A counterargument section, in which you concede the validity of positions on the subject different from your own and acknowledge the ideas of authors in this section with whom you disagree.

- A "nevertheless" section, in which you respond to the counterarguments and reaffirm your own position.

- A paragraph or two of conclusion. See Chapter 3 (pp. 98–104) for advice on concluding your paper.

Where you place the various elements of this argument synthesis will be your decision as a writer. Which sources to use and what logic to present in defense of your claim is also yours to decide. See Chapter 5 for help in thinking about structuring and supporting your argument.

A Note on Incorporating Quotations and Paraphrases

Identify the sources you intend to use for your synthesis. Working with a phrase, sentence, or brief passage from each, use a variety of the techniques discussed in the section Incorporating Quotations into Your Sentences, Chapter 1 (pp. 59–62), to write sentences that you can use to advance your argument. Some of these sentences should demonstrate the use of ellipsis marks and brackets. See pages 55–57 in Chapter 1. Paraphrase passages, as needed, and incorporate these as well into your paper.

Part III
An Anthology of Readings

 Learning Objectives

Chapters 11–15 share a single set of Learning Objectives, which follow from instruction in Part I of this text. After completing reading- and writing-based assignments in Chapters 11–15, you will be able to:

1. Read and understand source materials.
2. Summarize source materials.
3. Critically evaluate and discuss source materials.
4. Formulate and express a definite point of view by writing a thesis statement.
5. Synthesize source materials by writing explanations and arguments, guided by a thesis.
6. Analyze phenomena by applying principles and definitions.

Chapter 11

First Impressions: The Art and Craft of Storytelling

> "So now, get up."
>
> Felled, dazed, silent, he has fallen; knocked full length on the cobbles of the yard. His head turns sideways; his eyes are turned toward the gate, as if someone might arrive to help him out. One blow, properly placed, could kill him now.

These are the first words of *Wolf Hall*, the first book of Hilary Mantel's trilogy about Thomas Cromwell, counselor to Henry VIII. Imagine you just bought the book based on a friend's recommendation.

Would you keep reading? Or would you keep reading a novel with this opening sentence:

> If you really want to hear about it, the first thing you'll probably want to know is where I was born, and what my lousy childhood was like, and how my parents were occupied and all before they had me, and all that David Copperfield kind of crap, but I don't feel like going into it, if you want to know the truth.
>
> —J. D. Salinger: *The Catcher in the Rye* (1951)

Who *is* this narrator? And if he isn't going into his "lousy childhood," then what *is* he going into?

Aspiring novelists are often told that they must grab readers by the end of the first chapter—ideally, by the end of the first scene or even the first page. That's putting a lot of weight on that first impression, but this is good advice. We readers are busy people, and even when we aren't busy, we're being bombarded constantly with potential distractions. A novelist who expects complete strangers to spend ten or fifteen or twenty hours reading her work has the formidable task of making us want to put aside everything else in our lives except for the book in front of us. In that first chapter, she must convince us to read the second one. She must convince us that our time spent reading her novel will be put to good use.

As you must already know, novels begin in strikingly different ways. From the writer's perspective, however, first chapters typically have a number of similar objectives. In relatively few pages, they must introduce the main characters, reveal the premise, get the plot moving, establish the time and place, set the tone and mood, and establish the voice or writing style. Perhaps the most important goal for the first chapter is to convince readers to keep reading. After all, unless the novel is a school assignment, readers always have the option of closing the book or shutting off the e-reader and finding some other way to spend their time.

So those opening pages of a novel, then, are crucial. And book publishers know it, which is why so many of them make the first chapters of novels available for free online: they need to hook the reader.

Effective opening "chapters" are just as important in movies as in novels, and for the same reasons. Consider the opening scene of *Vertigo*, directed by Alfred Hitchcock. A crook clutches a rail on an iron ladder attached to a building, pulls himself up onto the roof, and runs away. A second later, a uniformed cop climbs up after him and heads in the same direction as the crook. A moment after that, a plainclothes cop (James Stewart) also climbs onto the roof and runs in the same direction. From a distance, we see the three on the roof, the crook in the lead, the two cops following. The crook jumps across the opening between adjacent buildings, grabs onto a steeply banked roof, and keeps climbing until he reaches the top, then continues to run. The uniformed cop does the same. The plainclothes cop tries to follow but loses his grip and falls, hanging precariously from the sagging rain gutter. He looks down several stories and almost blanks out from vertigo. The uniformed cop abandons the pursuit and tries to help the other cop. But in reaching down to grab his arm, he loses his footing and falls to his death. The plainclothes cop looks on helplessly, still holding on to the gutter for dear life. The scene fades out.

Film openings can set "hooks" into an audience just as effectively as the openings to novels can. Recall the opening scene of *The Wizard of Oz*, showing Dorothy frantically running home after wicked Miss Gulch has threatened to sic the sheriff on Toto. Recall the opening scene of Stanley Kubrick's *2001: A Space Odyssey*, with three heavenly bodies—sun, moon, and earth—aligning vertically, to the accompaniment of the pounding chords of Richard Strauss's *Thus Spoke Zarathustra*. Watch the opening scene of *The Social Network*, showing Facebook founder-to-be Mark Zuckerberg managing to thoroughly alienate his date as he attempts to demonstrate his brilliance. As portrayed by Jesse Eisenberg, Zuckerberg is an obnoxious genius, but a character so compelling that he makes us want to see just how he came to create one of the most celebrated and influential companies of recent decades.

In this chapter, you'll read the first chapters of several novels and view the openings of several movies so that you can assess what qualities do—or don't—pique your interest and propel you into a story. As tools for your inquiry, we include two essays, the first by contemporary novelist K. M. Weiland, who introduces the concept of "the hook": the question the writer sets in the reader's mind to create a compelling need to continue reading. Scriptwriter Tim Long discusses how filmmakers blend *theme, tone, character,* and *backstory* to hook viewers in the opening scene.

You may well have it in you to write your own novel or shoot your own film one day. For the moment, though, you'll be working with the materials here to write analyses, not fiction. That is, you'll be applying the insights of Weiland and Long in order to understand how these openings achieve their effects. So happy reading—and viewing!

Here's the lineup of six Chapter Ones, each of which has been made into one or more films readily available online or through streaming services.

- *Pride and Prejudice* (1813) by Jane Austen (1775–1817). Austen's second published novel chronicles the life of Elizabeth Bennet and her four sisters, whom their mother intends on marrying well in early nineteenth-century England.
- *Jane Eyre* (1847) by Charlotte Brontë (1816–1855). This coming-of-age novel chronicles the life of its title character from unhappy childhood to marriage.
- *Great Expectations* (1860) by Charles Dickens (1812–1870). Often considered Dickens's finest novel, this is the coming-of-age story of an English orphan named Pip.
- *The Strange Case of Dr. Jekyll and Mr. Hyde* (1886) by Robert Louis Stevenson (1850–1894). This Scottish writer's novella explores the dual nature of the mind, with good and evil at war within us all.
- *The Wonderful Wizard of Oz* (1900) by L(yman) Frank Baum (1856–1919). The American author wrote the *Oz* books that gave the world Dorothy, the Tin Man, and the Great and Powerful Oz.
- *My Ántonia* (1918) by Willa Cather (1873–1947). This moving story of two children living on the Nebraska frontier is the third of Cather's "prairie trilogy."

Following is the lineup of twenty-four Scene Ones, arranged in two sections, the first a listing of six films based on the novels excerpted in this chapter.

You can readily find the films we discuss either online or through streaming services such as Amazon Video, Netflix, or iTunes. Your instructor may also make these films available to you, either by showing them in class or by placing them on reserve. Watch and enjoy. Use the questions following both the Chapter Ones and the introductions to the films to prompt discussions with classmates and to formulate your own thoughts on what makes for effective openings.

Part I: Scene Ones of films adapted from novels excerpted in this chapter

- *Pride and Prejudice* (1995) directed by Simon Langton; *Pride & Prejudice* (2005) directed by Joe Wright. Two interpretations: one for TV; one for the big screen.

- *Jane Eyre* (1943) directed by Robert Stevenson. One—but an influential one—of numerous film versions of Brontë's romantic novel.
- *Great Expectations* (1946) directed by David Lean. The classic, terrifying scene on an English marsh between young Pip and the escaped convict has never been surpassed.
- *The Strange Case of Dr. Jekyll and Mr. Hyde* (1931) directed by Rouben Mamoulian; (1941) directed by Victor Fleming. Two versions of a strange, ugly transformation.
- *The Wonderful World of Oz* (1939), directed by Victor Fleming. From Kansas to Munchkinland—and back.
- *My Ántonia* (1995) directed by Joseph Sargent. The frontier, two children, and an unforgettable story.

Part II: Scene Ones from other notable films

- *Dracula* (1931) directed by Tod Browning, and *Bram Stoker's Dracula* (1992) directed by Francis Ford Coppola. Here are two film versions of Bram Stoker's classic vampire story, created more than sixty years apart by directors with very different artistic visions.
- *Citizen Kane* (1941) directed by Orson Welles. This is the work most frequently cited as the greatest film of all time. Whether or not you agree, the opening scene of a newspaper magnate's final moments make for compelling viewing.
- *Brief Encounter* (1945) directed by David Lean. This is one of the greatest romantic dramas ever filmed—in typically restrained British fashion.
- *The Red Badge of Courage* (1951) directed by John Huston. Crane's novel of a Civil War soldier wondering how he will act in battle is faithfully filmed—and then heavily edited by the studio bosses.
- *Shane* (1953) directed by George Stevens. In many ways, this is the archetypal Western: Set against magnificent Wyoming scenery, the film depicts an epic battle between a reluctant gunfighter and a rancher trying to drive homesteaders off their land.
- *Rear Window* (1954) directed by Alfred Hitchcock. A feature film made entirely from the viewpoint of a man (James Stewart) confined to a wheelchair, his leg in a cast, who can look only around his own apartment and at his various neighbors in the courtyard outside his rear window.
- *The Godfather, Part One* (1972) directed by Francis Ford Coppola. The greatest gangster film ever made is also a family drama—which begins at a wedding celebration.
- *Do the Right Thing* (1989) directed by Spike Lee. A simmering racial conflict on the hottest day of the year in the Bedford-Stuyvesant neighborhood of Brooklyn is the focus of Spike Lee's controversial film.
- *Dead Again* (1991) directed by Kenneth Branagh. A reincarnation film that focuses on two young couples who live forty years apart.

- *Sleepless in Seattle* (1993) directed by Nora Ephron. In the tradition of classic romantic dramas, Ephron focuses on two people thousands of miles apart gravitating (haltingly) toward each other.
- *The Devil in a Blue Dress* (1995) directed by Carl Franklin. The classic private detective formula is reimagined along racial lines in Walter Mosley's story of an unemployed African American World War II veteran tasked with finding the missing girlfriend of a Los Angeles mayoral candidate.
- *Emma* (1996) directed by Robert McGrath, and *Clueless* (1995) directed by Amy Heckerling. Here are two versions of Austen's classic novel—the first a period piece, like Austen's novel, set in the county of Surrey, England; the second is set in Beverly Hills.
- *Chicago* (2002) directed by Rob Marshall. Kander and Ebb's scintillating musical about two female murderers begins with two knockout songs set partially in the characters' heads.
- *The Hurt Locker* (2008) directed by Kathryn Bigelow. This tense film chronicles the daily life-and-death struggles of a bomb disposal unit during the Iraq War.
- *Inception* (2010) directed by Christopher Nolan. One of the more recent films to focus on dreams—and more specifically, on deliberately leaving audiences uncertain about whether the action they are watching on screen is dream or "reality" (however one defines that).
- *Gravity* (2013) directed by Alfonso Cuarón. This visually stunning film about an astronaut trying to return to earth after a catastrophic accident keeps audiences on the edge of their seats.
- *12 Years a Slave* (2013) directed by Steve McQueen. A brutally intense drama about a free black man sold into slavery is unforgettably depicted in McQueen's film, which won the Academy Award for Best Picture of 2013.
- *Moonlight* (2016) directed by Barry Jenkins. A Best Picture coming-of-age story that focuses on the transition of the protagonist from one stage of life to the next—from childhood to adolescence and/or from adolescence to adulthood.

The Art and Craft of Starting Your Story

Like a lens you hold up to a leaf or to the back of your hand, revealing details invisible to the unaided eye, a good question or a carefully defined concept can help you read a book or watch a film and see things you might otherwise overlook. Exactly *how* does an opening scene of a film or chapter of a novel engage your interest and move you from living in your world to imaginatively inhabiting a fictional one? Writers and directors don't leave the answering of such important questions to chance. They employ time-tested techniques to grab your attention and prepare you for what is to come. Whether or not they succeed is for you to decide.

Two selections in this chapter provide questions and concepts you can use to read deeply and view deeply the Chapter Ones and Scene Ones we've gathered for your analysis. Novelist K. M. Weiland begins by defining "The Hook" and emphasizing the importance of questions. Scriptwriter Tim Long (see pages 330–333) regards the opening scene of a film as a snapshot that creates the all-important desire to learn more. Read these selections with care, and you'll have the tools to write with authority about what makes for an effective Chapter One or Scene One.

The Hook

K. M. Weiland

Among the numerous handbooks offering practical advice to aspiring novelists, K. M. Weiland's *Structuring Your Novel* (2013) stands out. Weiland is a prolific writer of books and audios on the craft of writing, including *Outlining Your Novel* (2011) and *Structuring Your Novel*, in which the present selection appears. She is also the author of a Western, *A Man Called Outlaw* (2007); a medieval epic, *Behold the Dawn* (2009); and the epic fantasy *Dreamlander* (2012). *Writer's Digest* has listed Weiland's Web site, "Helping Writers Become Authors," as one of the "101 Best Websites for Writers." She's a prolific blogger on matters of craft, and you may visit her site, www.helpingwritersbecomeauthors.com, to read posts like this one: "Why Protagonists Must Suffer to Be Interesting."

Readers are like fish. Smart fish. Fish who know authors are out to get them, reel them in, and capture them for the rest of their seagoing lives. Like all self-respecting fish, readers aren't caught easily. They aren't about to surrender themselves to the lure of your story unless you've presented them with an irresistible hook.

Our discussion of story structure very naturally begins at the beginning—and the beginning of any good story is its hook. Unless you hook readers into your story from the very first chapter, they won't swim in deep enough to experience the rest of your rousing adventure, no matter how amazing it is.

The hook comes in many forms, but stripped down to its lowest common denominator, it's nothing more or less than a question. If we can pique our readers' curiosity, we've got 'em. Simple as that.

The beginning of every story should present character, setting, and conflict. But, in themselves, none of these represent a hook. We've created a hook only when we've convinced readers to ask the general question, "What's going to happen?" because we've also convinced them to ask a more specific question—"What scary reptilian monster killed the worker?" (*Jurassic Park* by Michael Crichton) or "How does a city hunt?" (*Mortal Engines* by Philip Reeve).

Your opening question might be explicit: perhaps you open with the character wondering something, which will hopefully make readers wonder the same thing. But more often, the question is implicit, as it is, for example, in Elizabeth Gaskell's short story "Lizzie Leigh," which opens with a dying man's last words to his wife. All he says is, "I forgive her, Anne! May God forgive me." Readers have no idea whom the man is forgiving, or why he might need to beg God's forgiveness in turn. The very fact that we don't know what he's talking about makes us want to read on to find the answers.

5

The important thing to remember about presenting this opening question is that it cannot be vague. Readers have to understand enough about the situation to mentally form a specific question. *What the heck is going on here?* does not qualify as a good opening question.

It's not necessary for the question to remain unanswered all the way to the end of the story. It's perfectly all right to answer the question in the very next paragraph, so long as you introduce another question, and another and another, to give readers a reason to keep turning those pages in search of answers.

Beginnings are the sales pitch for your entire story. Doesn't matter how slam-bang your finish is, doesn't matter how fresh your dialogue is, doesn't matter if your characters are so real they tap dance their way off the pages. If your beginning doesn't fulfill all its requirements, readers won't get far enough to discover your story's hidden merits.

Although no surefire pattern exists for the perfect opening, most good beginnings share the following traits:

- **They don't open *before* the beginning.** Mystery author William G. Tapley points out, "Starting before the beginning . . . means loading up your readers with background information they have no reason to care about." Don't dump your backstory into your reader's lap right away, no matter how vital it is to the plot. How many of us want to hear someone's life story the moment after we meet him?
- **They open with characters, preferably the protagonist.** Even the most plot-driven tales inevitably boil down to characters. The personalities that inhabit your stories are what will connect with readers. If you fail to connect them with the characters right off the bat, you can cram all the action you want into your opening, but the intensity and the drama will still fall flat.
- **They open with conflict.** No conflict, no story. Conflict doesn't always mean nuclear warheads going off, but it does demand your characters be at odds with someone or something right from the get-go. Conflict keeps the pages turning, and turning pages are nowhere more important than in the beginning.
- **They open with movement.** Openings need more than action, they need motion. Motion gives readers a sense of progression and, when necessary, urgency. Whenever possible, open with a scene that allows your characters to keep moving, even if they're just checking the fridge.
- **They establish the setting.** Modern authors are often shy of opening with description, but a quick, incisive intro of the setting serves not only to ground readers in the physicality of the story, but also to hook their interest and set the stage. Opening lines "that hook you immediately into the hero's dilemma almost always follow the hook with a bit of stage setting," and vice versa.
- **They orient readers with an "establishing" shot.** Anchoring readers can often be done best by taking a cue from the movies and opening with an "establishing" shot. If done skillfully, you can present the setting and the characters' positions within it in as little as a sentence or two.
- **They set the tone.** Because your opening chapter sets the tone for your entire story, you need to give readers accurate presuppositions about the type of tale they're going to be reading. Your beginning needs to set the stage for the denouement—without, of course, giving it away.

10 If you can nail all these points in your opening chapter, your readers will keep the pages turning into the wee hours of the morning.

Five Elements of a Riveting First Line

Because your ability to convince readers to keep reading is dependent on your hook, you will need to present it as early as possible in your first scene. In fact, if you can get it into your first line, so much the better. However, the hook *must be organic*. Teasing readers with a killer opening line ("Mimi was dying again") only to reveal all is not as it seems (turns out Mimi is an actress performing her 187th death scene) both negates the power of your hook and betrays readers' trust. And readers don't like to be betrayed. Not one little bit.

The opening line of your book is your first (and, if you don't take advantage of it, *last*) opportunity to grab your readers' attention and give them a reason to read your story. That's a gargantuan job for a single sentence. But if we analyze opening lines, we discover a number of interesting things. One of the most surprising discoveries is that very few opening lines are memorable.

Say *what*?

Before you start quoting the likes of "Call me Ishmael" and "Happy families are all alike," take a moment to think about the last few books you read and loved. Can you remember the opening lines?

The very fact that these unremembered lines convinced us to keep reading until we **15** loved the books means they did their jobs to sparkly perfection. I looked up the first lines of five of my favorite reads from the last year:

> When I wake up, the other side of the bed is cold. (*The Hunger Games* by Suzanne Collins)
> When he woke in the woods in the dark and the cold of the night he'd reach out to touch the child sleeping beside him. (*The Road* by Cormac McCarthy)
> It was night again. The Waystone Inn lay in silence, and it was a silence of three parts. (*The Name of the Wind* by Patrick Rothfuss)
> They used to hang men at Four Turnings in the old days. (*My Cousin Rachel* by Daphne du Maurier)
> On the night he had appointed his last among the living, Dr. Ben Givens did not dream, for his sleep was restless and visited by phantoms who guarded the portal to the world of dreams by speaking relentlessly of this world. (*East of the Mountains* by David Guterson)

What makes these lines work? What about them makes us want to read on? Let's break them down into five parts.

1. **Inherent Question.** To begin with, they all end with an invisible question mark. Why is the other side of the bed cold? Why are these characters sleeping outside in bad weather? How can silence be divided into three separate parts? Whom did they hang in the old days—and why don't they hang them anymore? And why and how has Ben Givens appointed the time of his death? You can't just tell readers what's going on in your story; you have to give them enough information to make *them* ask the questions—so you can then answer them.

2. **Character.** Most of these opening lines give us a character (and the rest introduce their characters in the sentences that follow). The first line is the first opportunity readers have to meet and become interested in your main character. Guterson ramps this principle to the max by naming his character, which allows readers that many more degrees of connection.

3. **Setting.** Most of these lines also offer a sense of setting. In particular, McCarthy, du Maurier, and Rothfuss use their settings to impart a deep sense of foreboding

and to set the tone of the book. The opening line doesn't have to stand alone. It is supported by and leads into the scaffolding of all the sentences and paragraphs that follow.

4. **Sweeping Declaration.** Only one of our example books (du Maurier's) opens with a declaration. Some authors feel this is another technique that's fallen by the wayside, along with the omniscient narrators of Melville and Tolstoy. But the declaration is still alive and well, no matter what point of view you're operating from. The trick is using the declaration to make readers ask that all-important inherent question. "The sky is blue" or "a stitch in time saves nine" are the kind of yawn-infested declarations that lead nowhere. But if you dig a little deeper—something along the lines of William Gibson's "The sky above the port was the color of television, tuned to a dead channel"—you find not only a bit of poetry, but also a sense of tone and the question of *why?* that makes readers want to keep going.

5. **Tone.** Finally, in every one of our examples readers can find the introduction of tone. Your first line is your "hello." Don't waste it. Set the tone of your story right from the start. Is your book funny, snarky, wistful, sad, or poetic? Make sure we find that core element in your opening line. Don't hand them a joke at the beginning if your story is a lyrical tragedy.

Opening lines offer authors their first and best opportunity to make a statement about their stories. Play around until you find something that perfectly introduces your story's character, plot, setting, theme, and voice. Your opening line may be as short as Suzanne Collins's. It may be longer than David Guterson's. It may be flashy, or it may be straightforward. Whatever the case, it needs to be an appropriate starting line for the grand adventure that is your story.

Examples from Film and Literature

Now that we have a basic idea of what a hook is and where it belongs, let's consider a few examples. I've selected two movies and two novels (two classics and two recent), which we'll use as examples throughout the book, so you can follow the story arc as presented in popular and successful media. Let's take a look at how the professionals hook us so effectively we never realize we've swallowed the worm.

- *Pride and Prejudice* **by Jane Austen (1813):** Austen begins by masterfully hooking us with her famous opening line, "It is a truth universally acknowledged, that a single man in possession of a good fortune must be in want of a wife." The subtle irony gives us a sense of conflict from the very first and lets us know that neither the wife in search of the fortune nor the man in search of the wife will find their goals so easily. Austen deepens the pull of her hook in her opening paragraph by further highlighting the juxtaposition of her opening statement with the realities of her plot. She deepens it still further throughout the opening scene, which introduces readers to the Bennet family in such a way that we not only grow interested in the characters, but also realize both the thrust of the plot and the difficulties of the conflict.
- *It's a Wonderful Life* **directed by Frank Capra (1947):** Capra opens with a framing device that hooks viewers with a sneak peek of the Climax. The movie opens at the height of the main character's troubles and has us wondering why George Bailey is in such a fix that the whole town is praying for him. Next thing we know, we're staring at an unlikely trio of angels, manifested as blinking constellations. The

presentation not only fascinates us with its unexpectedness, it also succinctly expresses the coming conflict and stakes and engages readers with a number of specific need-to-know questions.

- ***Ender's Game* by Orson Scott Card (1977):** The opening line to Card's acclaimed science-fiction novel is packed with hooking questions: "I've watched through his eyes, I've listened through his ears, and I tell you he's the one. Or at least as close as we're going to get." Just like that, Card's got us wondering how the speaker is watching and listening through someone else's mind, who is "the one," what is "the one" supposed to do, and why are they settling for a "one" who is less than perfect? He then successfully builds his killer opening into a scene that introduces his unlikely hero, six-year-old Ender Wiggin, just as his life is about to be turned upside down.
- ***Master and Commander: The Far Side of the World* directed by Peter Weir (2004):** As a brilliant adaptation of Patrick O'Brian's beloved Aubrey/Maturin series, this movie is unusual in a number of areas, not least in its non-formulaic tone and plot. Nevertheless, it follows the requirements of structure to a T, beginning with the stark opening that shows the morning ritual aboard the man of war HMS *Surprise*. Aside from arousing our natural curiosity about the unique setting, the hook doesn't appear until a minute or so into the film when one of the midshipmen spots what might be an enemy ship. The film never slows to explain the situation to the viewers. It carries them through a few tense moments of uncertainty and indecision, then, almost without warning, plunges them into the midst of a horrific sea battle. We are hooked almost before we see the hook coming.

Takeaway Value

So what can we learn from these masterful hooks?

1. Hooks should be inherent to the plot.
2. Hooks don't always involve action, but they always set it up
3. Hooks never waste time.
4. Hooks almost always pull double or triple duty in introducing character, conflict, and plot—and even setting and theme.

Your hook is your first chance to impress readers, and like it or not, first impressions will **20** make you or break you. Plan your hook carefully and wow readers so thoroughly they won't ever forget your opening scene.

Review Questions

1. Weiland claims that questions play a central role in setting a narrative hook. How so?

2. In what ways does an explicit hook-related question differ from an implicit one?

3. What important elements do successful openings share?

4. Why is a novel's first line so important, and why *doesn't* it need to be memorable?

5. What kinds of information can first lines convey?

Discussion and Writing Suggestions

1. Reread Weiland's final section on "Takeaway Value." Choose one such value and discuss how it emerges from the opening to either of the two novels or two films she analyzes. For instance, how can Value #1 ("Hooks should be inherent to the plot") be observed at work in *Pride and Prejudice*?

2. Weiland compares readers to "smart fish." In your experience, how well does this image describe your situation as you settle down to read a book or view the opening of a film? For instance, when you read a book or view a film, do you feel hooked and "reeled" into the action? Do you sense that the writer or director has gone "fishing" for you? Suggest another image that could illuminate the relationship between a reader/viewer and an opening chapter/scene.

3. Weiland's lists concerning effective openings and first lines are descriptive. That is, she has read numerous books and seen numerous movies and distilled her observations into succinct lists. Imagine you're a novelist. How readily do you think the process could work in reverse? Guided by Weiland's lists, how readily could you write a successful opening to a novel? Give it a go! Write a great opening line or paragraph, try it out on your friends, and then analyze its effectiveness according to Weiland's criteria.

4. In her discussion of narrative openings, Weiland emphasizes questions and the corresponding need for answers. Consider this need to know about the lives of strangers on the page and on the screen. Why are we remotely interested? After all, there are plenty of *living, breathing* people surrounding us every day in our actual, lived lives. Why should fictional characters make any claim at all on our curiosity?

Chapter Ones: The Novels

Here we invite you to read the first chapter of six classic novels. As you read, consider how the authors go about creating their fictional worlds: What details do they give the reader about characters, plot, and setting? What information do the authors refrain from giving us? What do you find yourself thinking about—and feeling—as you read? Perhaps most importantly, how do these authors, in just a handful of pages, go about making us care about the lives of made-up people in made-up situations?

The Discussion and Writing Suggestions assume that you have only read the first chapters of these novels. That said, if a first chapter intrigues you, then by all means read the whole novel—they are all available on Project Gutenberg, a Web site that offers free versions of work that is in the public domain: http://www.gutenberg.org.

Pride and Prejudice

Jane Austen

In her own day, Jane Austen (1775–1817) was a little-known English novelist who published her best-known works—*Sense and Sensibility*, *Pride and Prejudice*, *Mansfield Park*, and *Emma* under a pen name. It was only after her death that her brother revealed her identity as a prolific author and her reputation grew. Austen is admired today both by critics and the general reading public for romances that explore manners, marriage, finances, and family in early nineteenth-century England. *Pride and Prejudice*, her second novel, chronicles the life of Elizabeth Bennet, one of five sisters intent on marrying well. Note well the playfully ironic, often-quoted first line of the novel. K. M. Weiland devotes a paragraph (see page 10) to analyzing strategies Austen uses to hook readers in her opening chapter.

Chapter 1

It is a truth universally acknowledged, that a single man in possession of a good fortune, must be in want of a wife.

However little known the feelings or views of such a man may be on his first entering a neighborhood, this truth is so well fixed in the minds of the surrounding families, that he is considered the rightful property of some one or other of their daughters.

"My dear Mr. Bennet," said his lady to him one day, "have you heard that Netherfield Park is let[1] at last?"

Mr. Bennet replied that he had not.

"But it is," returned she; "for Mrs. Long has just been here, and she told me all about it."   **5**

Mr. Bennet made no answer.

"Do you not want to know who has taken it?" cried his wife impatiently.

"*You* want to tell me, and I have no objection to hearing it."

This was invitation enough.

"Why, my dear, you must know, Mrs. Long says that Netherfield is taken by a young   **10**
man of large fortune from the north of England; that he came down on Monday in a chaise and four[2] to see the place, and was so much delighted with it, that he agreed with Mr. Morris immediately; that he is to take possession before Michaelmas,[3] and some of his servants are to be in the house by the end of next week."

"What is his name?"

"Bingley."

"Is he married or single?"

"Oh! Single, my dear, to be sure! A single man of large fortune; four or five thousand a year. What a fine thing for our girls!"

"How so? How can it affect them?"   **15**

"My dear Mr. Bennet," replied his wife, "how can you be so tiresome! You must know that I am thinking of his marrying one of them."

"Is that his design in settling here?"

---

[1] Leased; rented.

[2] A carriage pulled by four horses.

[3] A Christian festival—the Feast of St. Michael—observed on September 29.

"Design! Nonsense, how can you talk so! But it is very likely that he *may* fall in love with one of them, and therefore you must visit him as soon as he comes."

"I see no occasion for that. You and the girls may go, or you may send them by themselves, which perhaps will be still better, for as you are as handsome as any of them, Mr. Bingley may like you the best of the party."

20 "My dear, you flatter me. I certainly *have* had my share of beauty, but I do not pretend to be anything extraordinary now. When a woman has five grown-up daughters, she ought to give over thinking of her own beauty."

"In such cases, a woman has not often much beauty to think of."

"But, my dear, you must indeed go and see Mr. Bingley when he comes into the neighbourhood."

"It is more than I engage for, I assure you."

"But consider your daughters. Only think what an establishment it would be for one of them. Sir William and Lady Lucas are determined to go, merely on that account, for in general, you know, they visit no newcomers. Indeed you must go, for it will be impossible for *us* to visit him if you do not."

25 "You are over-scrupulous, surely. I dare say Mr. Bingley will be very glad to see you; and I will send a few lines by you to assure him of my hearty consent to his marrying whichever he chooses of the girls; though I must throw in a good word for my little Lizzy."

"I desire you will do no such thing. Lizzy is not a bit better than the others; and I am sure she is not half so handsome as Jane, nor half so good-humoured as Lydia. But you are always giving *her* the preference."

"They have none of them much to recommend them," replied he; "they are all silly and ignorant like other girls; but Lizzy has something more of quickness than her sisters."

"Mr. Bennet, how *can* you abuse your own children in such a way? You take delight in vexing me. You have no compassion for my poor nerves."

"You mistake me, my dear. I have a high respect for your nerves. They are my old friends. I have heard you mention them with consideration these last twenty years at least."

30 "Ah, you do not know what I suffer."

"But I hope you will get over it, and live to see many young men of four thousand a year come into the neighbourhood."

"It will be no use to us, if twenty such should come, since you will not visit them."

"Depend upon it, my dear, that when there are twenty, I will visit them all."

Mr. Bennet was so odd a mixture of quick parts, sarcastic humour, reserve, and caprice, that the experience of three-and-twenty years had been insufficient to make his wife understand his character. *Her* mind was less difficult to develop. She was a woman of mean understanding, little information, and uncertain temper. When she was discontented, she fancied herself nervous. The business of her life was to get her daughters married; its solace was visiting and news.

Discussion and Writing Suggestions

1. The first line of *Pride and Prejudice* is famous. Explain the playful irony of the line: "It is a truth universally acknowledged, that a single man in possession of a good fortune, must be in want of a wife." What evidence do you find in the rest of the chapter that the narrator accepts or does not accept this "universally acknowledged" truth?

2. How does the first line set up both the paragraph and the dialogue that immediately follow? What's the relationship between that line and Mrs. Bennet's assumptions regarding the new tenant at Netherfield Park?

3. How does the chapter establish that the novel will focus mainly on one of the five daughters, Lizzy Bennet?

4. Based on this opening chapter, what guesses can you make about the story about to unfold?

Jane Eyre

Charlotte Brontë

Charlotte Brontë (1816–1855) was the eldest of three novelist sisters, including *Wuthering Heights* author Emily Brontë. After the death of her mother, she and her sisters spent a great deal of time together inventing their own fictional worlds, which set the stage for a lifetime of imaginative writing. After leaving home and going to school, Charlotte Brontë worked as a teacher and governess, experiences that would find their way into her fiction. *Jane Eyre* (1847), Brontë's first published novel, chronicles the life of its title character from childhood to marriage. Upon publication, the novel was well received by critics and readers but was considered controversial because of its calling into question the traditional roles of gender and social class. It remains a classic of nineteenth-century English literature and has been adapted for film and television many times.

Charlotte Brontë went on to publish two subsequent novels during her lifetime: *Shirley* and *Villette*. Like her sisters, she published her work under a male pen name in order for the work to be taken seriously; the name she used was Currer Bell. She died tragically—pregnant and newly married—at age 38.

Chapter 1

There was no possibility of taking a walk that day. We had been wandering, indeed, in the leafless shrubbery an hour in the morning; but since dinner (Mrs. Reed, when there was no company, dined early) the cold winter wind had brought with it clouds so sombre, and a rain so penetrating, that further out-door exercise was now out of the question.

I was glad of it: I never liked long walks, especially on chilly afternoons: dreadful to me was the coming home in the raw twilight, with nipped fingers and toes, and a heart saddened by the chidings of Bessie, the nurse, and humbled by the consciousness of my physical inferiority to Eliza, John, and Georgiana Reed.

The said Eliza, John, and Georgiana were now clustered round their mama in the drawing-room: she lay reclined on a sofa by the fireside, and with her darlings about her (for the time neither quarrelling nor crying) looked perfectly happy. Me, she had dispensed from joining the group; saying, "She regretted to be under the necessity of keeping me at a distance; but that until she heard from Bessie, and could discover by her own observation, that I was endeavouring in good earnest to acquire a more sociable and childlike disposition, a more attractive and sprightly manner—something lighter, franker, more natural, as it were—she really must exclude me from privileges intended only for contented, happy, little children."

"What does Bessie say I have done?" I asked.

5   "Jane, I don't like cavillers or questioners; besides, there is something truly forbidding in a child taking up her elders in that manner. Be seated somewhere; and until you can speak pleasantly, remain silent."

A breakfast-room adjoined the drawing-room, I slipped in there. It contained a bookcase: I soon possessed myself of a volume, taking care that it should be one stored with pictures. I mounted into the window-seat: gathering up my feet, I sat cross-legged, like a Turk; and, having drawn the red moreen curtain nearly close, I was shrined in double retirement.

Folds of scarlet drapery shut in my view to the right hand; to the left were the clear panes of glass, protecting, but not separating me from the drear November day. At intervals, while turning over the leaves of my book, I studied the aspect of that winter afternoon. Afar, it offered a pale blank of mist and cloud; near a scene of wet lawn and storm-beat shrub, with ceaseless rain sweeping away wildly before a long and lamentable blast.

I returned to my book—Bewick's *History of British Birds:* the letterpress thereof I cared little for, generally speaking; and yet there were certain introductory pages that, child as I was, I could not pass quite as a blank. They were those which treat of the haunts of sea-fowl; of "the solitary rocks and promontories" by them only inhabited; of the coast of Norway, studded with isles from its southern extremity, the Lindeness, or Naze, to the North Cape—

Where the Northern Ocean, in vast whirls,

Boils round the naked, melancholy isles

Of farthest Thule; and the Atlantic surge

Pours in among the stormy Hebrides.

10   Nor could I pass unnoticed the suggestion of the bleak shores of Lapland, Siberia, Spitzbergen, Nova Zembla, Iceland, Greenland, with "the vast sweep of the Arctic Zone, and those forlorn regions of dreary space,—that reservoir of frost and snow, where firm fields of ice, the accumulation of centuries of winters, glazed in Alpine heights above heights, surround the pole, and concentre the multiplied rigours of extreme cold." Of these death-white realms I formed an idea of my own: shadowy, like all the half-comprehended notions that float dim through children's brains, but strangely impressive. The words in these introductory pages connected themselves with the succeeding vignettes, and gave significance to the rock standing up alone in a sea of billow and spray; to the broken boat stranded on a desolate coast; to the cold and ghastly moon glancing through bars of cloud at a wreck just sinking.

I cannot tell what sentiment haunted the quite solitary churchyard, with its inscribed headstone; its gate, its two trees, its low horizon, girdled by a broken wall, and its newly-risen crescent, attesting the hour of eventide.

The two ships becalmed on a torpid sea, I believed to be marine phantoms.

The fiend pinning down the thief's pack behind him, I passed over quickly: it was an object of terror.

So was the black horned thing seated aloof on a rock, surveying a distant crowd surrounding a gallows.

15   Each picture told a story; mysterious often to my undeveloped understanding and imperfect feelings, yet ever profoundly interesting: as interesting as the tales Bessie sometimes narrated on winter evenings, when she chanced to be in good humour; and when, having brought her ironing-table to the nursery hearth, she allowed us to sit about it, and while she got up Mrs. Reed's lace frills, and crimped her nightcap borders, fed our eager attention with passages of love and adventure taken from old fairy tales and other ballads; or (as at a later period I discovered) from the pages of Pamela, and Henry, Earl of Moreland.

With Bewick on my knee, I was then happy: happy at least in my way. I feared nothing but interruption, and that came too soon. The breakfast-room door opened.

"Boh! Madam Mope!" cried the voice of John Reed; then he paused: he found the room apparently empty.

"Where the dickens is she!" he continued. "Lizzy! Georgy! (calling to his sisters) Joan is not here: tell mama she is run out into the rain—bad animal!"

"It is well I drew the curtain," thought I; and I wished fervently he might not discover my hiding-place: nor would John Reed have found it out himself; he was not quick either of vision or conception; but Eliza just put her head in at the door, and said at once—

"She is in the window-seat, to be sure, Jack."   **20**

And I came out immediately, for I trembled at the idea of being dragged forth by the said Jack.

"What do you want?" I asked, with awkward diffidence.

"Say, 'What do you want, Master Reed?'" was the answer. "I want you to come here;" and seating himself in an arm-chair, he intimated by a gesture that I was to approach and stand before him.

John Reed was a schoolboy of fourteen years old; four years older than I, for I was but ten: large and stout for his age, with a dingy and unwholesome skin; thick lineaments in a spacious visage, heavy limbs and large extremities. He gorged himself habitually at table, which made him bilious, and gave him a dim and bleared eye and flabby cheeks. He ought now to have been at school; but his mama had taken him home for a month or two, "on account of his delicate health." Mr. Miles, the master, affirmed that he would do very well if he had fewer cakes and sweetmeats sent him from home; but the mother's heart turned from an opinion so harsh, and inclined rather to the more refined idea that John's sallowness was owing to over-application and, perhaps, to pining after home.

John had not much affection for his mother and sisters, and an antipathy to me. He   **25**
bullied and punished me; not two or three times in the week, nor once or twice in the day, but continually: every nerve I had feared him, and every morsel of flesh in my bones shrank when he came near. There were moments when I was bewildered by the terror he inspired, because I had no appeal whatever against either his menaces or his inflictions; the servants did not like to offend their young master by taking my part against him, and Mrs. Reed was blind and deaf on the subject: she never saw him strike or heard him abuse me, though he did both now and then in her very presence, more frequently, however, behind her back.

Habitually obedient to John, I came up to his chair: he spent some three minutes in thrusting out his tongue at me as far as he could without damaging the roots: I knew he would soon strike, and while dreading the blow, I mused on the disgusting and ugly appearance of him who would presently deal it. I wonder if he read that notion in my face; for, all at once, without speaking, he struck suddenly and strongly. I tottered, and on regaining my equilibrium retired back a step or two from his chair.

"That is for your impudence in answering mama awhile since," said he, "and for your sneaking way of getting behind curtains, and for the look you had in your eyes two minutes since, you rat!"

Accustomed to John Reed's abuse, I never had an idea of replying to it; my care was how to endure the blow which would certainly follow the insult.

"What were you doing behind the curtain?" he asked.

30   "I was reading."

"Show the book."

I returned to the window and fetched it thence.

"You have no business to take our books; you are a dependent, mama says; you have no money; your father left you none; you ought to beg, and not to live here with gentlemen's children like us, and eat the same meals we do, and wear clothes at our mama's expense. Now, I'll teach you to rummage my bookshelves: for they *are* mine; all the house belongs to me, or will do in a few years. Go and stand by the door, out of the way of the mirror and the windows."

I did so, not at first aware what was his intention; but when I saw him lift and poise the book and stand in act to hurl it, I instinctively started aside with a cry of alarm: not soon enough, however; the volume was flung, it hit me, and I fell, striking my head against the door and cutting it. The cut bled, the pain was sharp: my terror had passed its climax; other feelings succeeded.

35   "Wicked and cruel boy!" I said. "You are like a murderer—you are like a slave-driver— you are like the Roman emperors!"

I had read Goldsmith's *History of Rome*, and had formed my opinion of Nero, Caligula, etc. Also I had drawn parallels in silence, which I never thought thus to have declared aloud.

"What! what!" he cried. "Did she say that to me? Did you hear her, Eliza and Georgiana? Won't I tell mama? but first—"

He ran headlong at me: I felt him grasp my hair and my shoulder: he had closed with a desperate thing. I really saw in him a tyrant, a murderer. I felt a drop or two of blood from my head trickle down my neck, and was sensible of somewhat pungent suffering: these sensations for the time predominated over fear, and I received him in frantic sort. I don't very well know what I did with my hands, but he called me "Rat! Rat!" and bellowed out aloud. Aid was near him: Eliza and Georgiana had run for Mrs. Reed, who was gone upstairs: she now came upon the scene, followed by Bessie and her maid Abbot. We were parted: I heard the words—

"Dear! dear! What a fury to fly at Master John!"

40   "Did ever anybody see such a picture of passion!"

Then Mrs. Reed subjoined—

"Take her away to the red-room, and lock her in there." Four hands were immediately laid upon me, and I was borne upstairs.

Discussion and Writing Suggestions

1. How is the weather described at the beginning of the novel? What mood does it set up?

2. From the opening chapter, what can you infer about Jane's personality? In what ways is she different from the others living in the house?

3. While reading *The History of British Birds*, Jane "feared nothing but interruption." Why does reading and not being interrupted seem so important to her?

4. Why do you think this first chapter includes the fight between Jane and John Reed? What does the fight, and the family's reaction to it, suggest about Jane's status in the family? Why is she, rather than Master John, punished for fighting?

5. Do your own feelings about Jane differ from how the other characters in the novel (like Mrs. Reed and John Reed) feel about her? If so, in what ways?

6. We're told, at the end of the chapter, that Jane is being banished to the "red room." But we don't yet know what this room is. What other mysteries does this first chapter introduce? What do you most want to know more about in Chapter 2 and beyond?

Great Expectations

Charles Dickens

Charles Dickens was born on England's southern coast and at age ten moved with his family to London. He attended school until age twelve, at which point his father was imprisoned for bad debt, forcing Charles to take a job at a boot-polishing factory. He later worked as an office boy before beginning to write for several newspapers, which marked the beginning of an extremely prolific and successful literary career. By the time *Great Expectations* was published in 1860, Dickens had already published over a dozen novels, delivered lectures across America, and become on two continents what many consider to be the first modern celebrity. Like several of Dickens's novels, *Great Expectations* was originally published in serial form, with new chapters appearing every week in the magazine *All the Year Round*. Often considered Dickens's finest novel, *Great Expectations* is a classic "bildungsroman"—that is, a "novel of formation" or, more simply, a coming-of-age novel. Specifically, *Great Expectations* chronicles the life of a poor orphan named Pip who gradually matures to become a gentleman. In this opening chapter, Pip describes in his own words the first significant event that he can remember.

Chapter 1

My father's family name being Pirrip, and my Christian name Philip, my infant tongue could make of both names nothing longer or more explicit than Pip. So, I called myself Pip, and came to be called Pip.

I give Pirrip as my father's family name, on the authority of his tombstone and my sister,—Mrs. Joe Gargery, who married the blacksmith. As I never saw my father or my mother, and never saw any likeness of either of them (for their days were long before the days of photographs), my first fancies regarding what they were like were unreasonably derived from their tombstones. The shape of the letters on my father's, gave me an odd idea that he was a square, stout, dark man, with curly black hair. From the character and turn of the inscription, "Also Georgiana Wife of the Above," I drew a childish conclusion that my mother was freckled and sickly. To five little stone lozenges, each about a foot and a half long, which were arranged in a neat row beside their grave, and were sacred to the memory of five little brothers of mine,—who gave up trying to get a living, exceedingly early in that universal struggle,—I am indebted for a belief I religiously entertained that they had all been born on their backs with their hands in their trousers-pockets, and had never taken them out in this state of existence.

Ours was the marsh country, down by the river, within, as the river wound, twenty miles of the sea. My first most vivid and broad impression of the identity of things seems to me to have been gained on a memorable raw afternoon towards evening. At such a time I found out for certain that this bleak place overgrown with nettles was the churchyard; and that Philip Pirrip, late of this parish, and also Georgiana wife of the above, were dead and buried; and that Alexander, Bartholomew, Abraham, Tobias, and Roger, infant children of the aforesaid, were also dead and buried; and that the dark flat wilderness beyond the churchyard, intersected with dikes and mounds and gates, with scattered cattle feeding on it, was the marshes; and that the low leaden line beyond was the river; and that the distant savage lair from which the wind was rushing was the sea; and that the small bundle of shivers growing afraid of it all and beginning to cry, was Pip.

"Hold your noise!" cried a terrible voice, as a man started up from among the graves at the side of the church porch. "Keep still, you little devil, or I'll cut your throat!"

5   A fearful man, all in coarse gray, with a great iron on his leg. A man with no hat, and with broken shoes, and with an old rag tied round his head. A man who had been soaked in water, and smothered in mud, and lamed by stones, and cut by flints, and stung by nettles, and torn by briars; who limped, and shivered, and glared, and growled; and whose teeth chattered in his head as he seized me by the chin.

"Oh! Don't cut my throat, sir," I pleaded in terror. "Pray don't do it, sir."

"Tell us your name!" said the man. "Quick!"

"Pip, sir."

"Once more," said the man, staring at me. "Give it mouth!"

10   "Pip. Pip, sir."

"Show us where you live," said the man. "Point out the place!"

I pointed to where our village lay, on the flat in-shore among the alder-trees and pollards, a mile or more from the church.

The man, after looking at me for a moment, turned me upside down, and emptied my pockets. There was nothing in them but a piece of bread. When the church came to itself,—for he was so sudden and strong that he made it go head over heels before me, and I saw the steeple under my feet,—when the church came to itself, I say, I was seated on a high tombstone, trembling while he ate the bread ravenously.

"You young dog," said the man, licking his lips, "what fat cheeks you ha' got."

15   I believe they were fat, though I was at that time undersized for my years, and not strong.

"Darn me if I couldn't eat 'em," said the man, with a threatening shake of his head, "and if I han't half a mind to't!"

I earnestly expressed my hope that he wouldn't, and held tighter to the tombstone on which he had put me; partly, to keep myself upon it; partly, to keep myself from crying.

"Now lookee here!" said the man. "Where's your mother?"

"There, sir!" said I.

20   He started, made a short run, and stopped and looked over his shoulder.

"There, sir!" I timidly explained. "Also Georgiana. That's my mother."

"Oh!" said he, coming back. "And is that your father alonger your mother?"

"Yes, sir," said I; "him too; late of this parish."

"Ha!" he muttered then, considering. "Who d'ye live with,—supposin' you're kindly let to live, which I han't made up my mind about?"

25   "My sister, sir,—Mrs. Joe Gargery,—wife of Joe Gargery, the blacksmith, sir."

"Blacksmith, eh?" said he. And looked down at his leg.

After darkly looking at his leg and me several times, he came closer to my tombstone, took me by both arms, and tilted me back as far as he could hold me; so that his eyes looked most powerfully down into mine, and mine looked most helplessly up into his.

"Now lookee here," he said, "the question being whether you're to be let to live. You know what a file is?"

"Yes, sir."

"And you know what wittles is?"   **30**

"Yes, sir."

After each question he tilted me over a little more, so as to give me a greater sense of helplessness and danger.

"You get me a file." He tilted me again. "And you get me wittles." He tilted me again. "You bring 'em both to me." He tilted me again. "Or I'll have your heart and liver out." He tilted me again.

I was dreadfully frightened, and so giddy that I clung to him with both hands, and said, "If you would kindly please to let me keep upright, sir, perhaps I shouldn't be sick, and perhaps I could attend more."

He gave me a most tremendous dip and roll, so that the church jumped over its own   **35** weathercock. Then, he held me by the arms, in an upright position on the top of the stone, and went on in these fearful terms:—

"You bring me, to-morrow morning early, that file and them wittles. You bring the lot to me, at that old Battery over yonder. You do it, and you never dare to say a word or dare to make a sign concerning your having seen such a person as me, or any person sumever, and you shall be let to live. You fail, or you go from my words in any partickler, no matter how small it is, and your heart and your liver shall be tore out, roasted, and ate. Now, I ain't alone, as you may think I am. There's a young man hid with me, in comparison with which young man I am an angel. That young man hears the words I speak. That young man has a secret way pecooliar to himself, of getting at a boy, and at his heart, and at his liver. It is in wain for a boy to attempt to hide himself from that young man. A boy may lock his door, may be warm in bed, may tuck himself up, may draw the clothes over his head, may think himself comfortable and safe, but that young man will softly creep and creep his way to him and tear him open. I am a keeping that young man from harming of you at the present moment, with great difficulty. I find it wery hard to hold that young man off of your inside. Now, what do you say?"

I said that I would get him the file, and I would get him what broken bits of food I could, and I would come to him at the Battery, early in the morning.

"Say Lord strike you dead if you don't!" said the man.

I said so, and he took me down.

"Now," he pursued, "you remember what you've undertook, and you remember that   **40** young man, and you get home!"

"Goo-good night, sir," I faltered.

"Much of that!" said he, glancing about him over the cold wet flat. "I wish I was a frog. Or a eel!"

At the same time, he hugged his shuddering body in both his arms,—clasping himself, as if to hold himself together,—and limped towards the low church wall. As I saw him go, picking his way among the nettles, and among the brambles that bound the green mounds, he looked in my young eyes as if he were eluding the hands of the dead people, stretching up cautiously out of their graves, to get a twist upon his ankle and pull him in.

When he came to the low church wall, he got over it, like a man whose legs were numbed and stiff, and then turned round to look for me. When I saw him turning, I set my face towards home, and made the best use of my legs. But presently I looked over my shoulder, and saw him going on again towards the river, still hugging himself in both arms, and picking his way with his sore feet among the great stones dropped into the marshes here and there, for stepping-places when the rains were heavy or the tide was in.

45   The marshes were just a long black horizontal line then, as I stopped to look after him; and the river was just another horizontal line, not nearly so broad nor yet so black; and the sky was just a row of long angry red lines and dense black lines intermixed. On the edge of the river I could faintly make out the only two black things in all the prospect that seemed to be standing upright; one of these was the beacon by which the sailors steered—like an unhooped cask upon a pole—an ugly thing when you were near it; the other, a gibbet, with some chains hanging to it which had once held a pirate. The man was limping on towards this latter, as if he were the pirate come to life, and come down, and going back to hook himself up again. It gave me a terrible turn when I thought so; and as I saw the cattle lifting their heads to gaze after him, I wondered whether they thought so too. I looked all round for the horrible young man, and could see no signs of him. But now I was frightened again, and ran home without stopping.

Discussion and Writing Suggestions

1. From their tombstones, Pip determines that his father was "a square, stout, dark man, with curly black hair" and that his mother was "freckled and sickly." Do you suppose the descriptions are accurate? How do these supposed details about the family Pip never knew help characterize him?

2. What does this chapter's setting—specifically, the location and the weather—do for the chapter's overall mood?

3. This first chapter depicts Pip's "first most vivid and broad impression of the identity of things." If you were to narrate your own life story, what would your "first most vivid and broad impression" be?

4. Dickens describes the escaped convict as "a man who had been soaked in water, and smothered in mud, and lamed by stones, and cut by flints, and stung by nettles, and torn by briars." What does this description reveal about the man? What does it reveal about the way Dickens describes his characters?

5. The convict mentions a second man, far crueler than himself, who is presumably listening in on their conversation. Do you think this second man really exists? Why does the convict mention him?

6. What do we learn about Pip from the way he deals with the escaped convict?

7. Does this chapter make you want to go on and read Chapter 2? If so, what elements in the chapter hook you in?

The Strange Case of Dr. Jekyll and Mr. Hyde

Robert Louis Stevenson

Robert Louis Stevenson (1850–1894) was a Scottish essayist, travel writer, journalist, and novelist. As a young man, he broke from the family business of building lighthouses, prepped for the bar (though never practiced as an attorney), and, plagued by ill health, traveled the world in search of hospitable climates where he could maintain his strength and write. Ultimately, he settled in Samoa. His novels *Treasure Island* (1883) and *Kidnapped* (1886) are now regarded as classic adventure books. His novella *The Strange Case of Dr. Jekyll and Mr. Hyde* (1886) became a classic as well, a disturbing exploration of the dueling natures of good and evil in us all.

Chapter 1: Story of the Door

Mr. Utterson the lawyer was a man of a rugged countenance that was never lighted by a smile; cold, scanty and embarrassed in discourse; backward in sentiment; lean, long, dusty, dreary and yet somehow lovable. At friendly meetings, and when the wine was to his taste, something eminently human beaconed from his eye; something indeed which never found its way into his talk, but which spoke not only in these silent symbols of the after-dinner face, but more often and loudly in the acts of his life. He was austere with himself; drank gin when he was alone, to mortify a taste for vintages; and though he enjoyed the theatre, had not crossed the doors of one for twenty years. But he had an approved tolerance for others; sometimes wondering, almost with envy, at the high pressure of spirits involved in their misdeeds; and in any extremity inclined to help rather than to reprove. "I incline to Cain's heresy," he used to say quaintly: "I let my brother go to the devil in his own way." In this character, it was frequently his fortune to be the last reputable acquaintance and the last good influence in the lives of downgoing men. And to such as these, so long as they came about his chambers, he never marked a shade of change in his demeanour.

No doubt the feat was easy to Mr. Utterson; for he was undemonstrative at the best, and even his friendship seemed to be founded in a similar catholicity of good-nature. It is the mark of a modest man to accept his friendly circle ready-made from the hands of opportunity; and that was the lawyer's way. His friends were those of his own blood or those whom he had known the longest; his affections, like ivy, were the growth of time, they implied no aptness in the object. Hence, no doubt the bond that united him to Mr. Richard Enfield, his distant kinsman, the well-known man about town. It was a nut to crack for many, what these two could see in each other, or what subject they could find in common. It was reported by those who encountered them in their Sunday walks, that they said nothing, looked singularly dull and would hail with obvious relief the appearance of a friend. For all that, the two men put the greatest store by these excursions, counted them the chief jewel of each week, and not only set aside occasions of pleasure, but even resisted the calls of business, that they might enjoy them uninterrupted.

It chanced on one of these rambles that their way led them down a by-street in a busy quarter of London. The street was small and what is called quiet, but it drove a thriving trade on the weekdays. The inhabitants were all doing well, it seemed and all emulously hoping to do better still, and laying out the surplus of their grains in coquetry; so that the shop fronts stood along that thoroughfare with an air of invitation, like rows of smiling saleswomen. Even on Sunday, when it veiled its more florid charms and lay comparatively empty of passage, the street shone out in contrast to its dingy neighbourhood, like a fire in a forest; and with its freshly painted shutters, well-polished brasses, and general cleanliness and gaiety of note, instantly caught and pleased the eye of the passenger.

Two doors from one corner, on the left hand going east the line was broken by the entry of a court; and just at that point a certain sinister block of building thrust forward its gable on the street. It was two storeys high; showed no window, nothing but a door on the lower storey and a blind forehead of discoloured wall on the upper; and bore in every feature, the marks of prolonged and sordid negligence. The door, which was equipped with neither bell nor knocker, was blistered and distained. Tramps slouched into the recess and struck matches on the panels; children kept shop upon the steps; the schoolboy had tried his knife on the mouldings; and for close on a generation, no one had appeared to drive away these random visitors or to repair their ravages.

5   Mr. Enfield and the lawyer were on the other side of the by-street; but when they came abreast of the entry, the former lifted up his cane and pointed.

"Did you ever remark that door?" he asked; and when his companion had replied in the affirmative. "It is connected in my mind," added he, "with a very odd story."

"Indeed?" said Mr. Utterson, with a slight change of voice, "and what was that?"

"Well, it was this way," returned Mr. Enfield: "I was coming home from some place at the end of the world, about three o'clock of a black winter morning, and my way lay through a part of town where there was literally nothing to be seen but lamps. Street after street and all the folks asleep—street after street, all lighted up as if for a procession and all as empty as a church—till at last I got into that state of mind when a man listens and listens and begins to long for the sight of a policeman. All at once, I saw two figures: one a little man who was stumping along eastward at a good walk, and the other a girl of maybe eight or ten who was running as hard as she was able down a cross street. Well, sir, the two ran into one another naturally enough at the corner; and then came the horrible part of the thing; for the man trampled calmly over the child's body and left her screaming on the ground. It sounds nothing to hear, but it was hellish to see. It wasn't like a man; it was like some damned Juggernaut. I gave a few halloa, took to my heels, collared my gentleman, and brought him back to where there was already quite a group about the screaming child. He was perfectly cool and made no resistance, but gave me one look, so ugly that it brought out the sweat on me like running. The people who had turned out were the girl's own family; and pretty soon, the doctor, for whom she had been sent put in his appearance. Well, the child was not much the worse, more frightened, according to the Sawbones; and there you might have supposed would be an end to it. But there was one curious circumstance. I had taken a loathing to my gentleman at first sight. So had the child's family, which was only natural. But the doctor's case was what struck me. He was the usual cut and dry apothecary, of no particular age and colour, with a strong Edinburgh accent and about as emotional as a bagpipe. Well, sir, he was like the rest of us; every time he looked at my prisoner, I saw that Sawbones turn sick and white with desire to kill him. I knew what was in his mind, just as he knew what was in mine; and killing being out of the question, we did the next best. We told the man we could and would make such a scandal out of this as should make his name stink from one end of London to the other. If he had any friends or any credit, we undertook that he should lose them. And all the time, as we were pitching it in red hot, we were keeping the women off him as best we could for they were as wild as harpies. I never saw a circle of such hateful faces; and there was the man in the middle, with a kind of black sneering coolness—frightened too, I could see that—but carrying it off, sir, really like Satan. 'If you choose to make capital out of this accident,' said he, 'I am naturally helpless. No gentleman but wishes to avoid a scene,' says he. 'Name your figure.' Well, we screwed him up to a hundred pounds for the child's family; he would have clearly liked to stick out; but there was something about the lot of us that meant mischief, and at last he struck. The next thing was to get the money; and where do you think he carried us but to that place with the door?—whipped out a key, went in, and presently came back with the matter of ten pounds in gold and a cheque for the balance on Coutts's, drawn payable to bearer and signed with a name that I can't mention, though it's one of the points of my story, but it was a name at least very well known and often printed. The figure was stiff; but the signature was good for more than that if it was only genuine. I took the liberty of pointing out to my gentleman that the whole business looked apocryphal, and that a man does not, in real life, walk into a cellar door at four in the morning and come out with another man's cheque for close upon a hundred pounds. But he was quite easy and sneering. 'Set your mind at rest,' says he, 'I will stay with you till the banks open and cash the cheque myself.' So we all set off, the doctor, and the child's father, and our friend and myself, and passed the rest of the night in my chambers; and next day, when we had breakfasted, went in a body to the bank. I gave in the cheque myself, and said I had every reason to believe it was a forgery. Not a bit of it. The cheque was genuine."

"Tut-tut," said Mr. Utterson.

"I see you feel as I do," said Mr. Enfield. "Yes, it's a bad story. For my man was a fellow **10** that nobody could have to do with, a really damnable man; and the person that drew the cheque is the very pink of the proprieties, celebrated too, and (what makes it worse) one of your fellows who do what they call good. Black mail I suppose; an honest man paying through the nose for some of the capers of his youth. Black Mail House is what I call the place with the door, in consequence. Though even that, you know, is far from explaining all," he added, and with the words fell into a vein of musing.

From this he was recalled by Mr. Utterson asking rather suddenly: "And you don't know if the drawer of the cheque lives there?"

"A likely place, isn't it?" returned Mr. Enfield. "But I happen to have noticed his address; he lives in some square or other."

"And you never asked about the—place with the door?" said Mr. Utterson.

"No, sir: I had a delicacy," was the reply. "I feel very strongly about putting questions; it partakes too much of the style of the day of judgment. You start a question, and it's like start-ing a stone. You sit quietly on the top of a hill; and away the stone goes, starting others; and presently some bland old bird (the last you would have thought of) is knocked on the head in his own back garden and the family have to change their name. No sir, I make it a rule of mine: the more it looks like Queer Street, the less I ask."

"A very good rule, too," said the lawyer. **15**

"But I have studied the place for myself," continued Mr. Enfield. "It seems scarcely a house. There is no other door, and nobody goes in or out of that one but, once in a great while, the gentleman of my adventure. There are three windows looking on the court on the first floor; none below; the windows are always shut but they're clean. And then there is a chimney which is generally smoking; so somebody must live there. And yet it's not so sure; for the buildings are so packed together about the court, that it's hard to say where one ends and another begins."

The pair walked on again for a while in silence; and then "Enfield," said Mr. Utterson, "that's a good rule of yours."

"Yes, I think it is," returned Enfield.

"But for all that," continued the lawyer, "there's one point I want to ask: I want to ask the name of that man who walked over the child."

20   "Well," said Mr. Enfield, "I can't see what harm it would do. It was a man of the name of Hyde."

"Hm," said Mr. Utterson. "What sort of a man is he to see?"

"He is not easy to describe. There is something wrong with his appearance; something displeasing, something down-right detestable. I never saw a man I so disliked, and yet I scarce know why. He must be deformed somewhere; he gives a strong feeling of deformity, although I couldn't specify the point. He's an extraordinary looking man, and yet I really can name nothing out of the way. No, sir; I can make no hand of it; I can't describe him. And it's not want of memory; for I declare I can see him this moment."

Mr. Utterson again walked some way in silence and obviously under a weight of consideration. "You are sure he used a key?" he inquired at last.

"My dear sir . . . " began Enfield, surprised out of himself.

25   "Yes, I know," said Utterson; "I know it must seem strange. The fact is, if I do not ask you the name of the other party, it is because I know it already. You see, Richard, your tale has gone home. If you have been inexact in any point you had better correct it."

"I think you might have warned me," returned the other with a touch of sullenness. "But I have been pedantically exact, as you call it. The fellow had a key; and what's more, he has it still. I saw him use it not a week ago."

Mr. Utterson sighed deeply but said never a word; and the young man presently resumed. "Here is another lesson to say nothing," said he. "I am ashamed of my long tongue. Let us make a bargain never to refer to this again."

"With all my heart," said the lawyer. "I shake hands on that, Richard."

Discussion and Writing Suggestions

1. The long paragraph in which Enfield describes the night he encountered Hyde is a story within a story. The initial, opening story: A man named Utterson goes walking with a friend named Enfield. The story within the story: On this walk, Enfield points to a door and says it's "connected . . . with a very odd story," which he proceeds to tell. Without even having read this interior story, we're interested. We want to read on. Why?

2. Stevenson carefully describes Utterson, Enfield, and Hyde. List the qualities of each, using your own one- or two-word descriptions or brief phrases from the text. How does Stevenson play these characters off one another other (even though Hyde isn't present) to create tension? How does this tension create in us a desire to read?

3. Utterson claims to know the name of the man who signed Hyde's check, a name Enfield (out of discretion) doesn't mention. How does this revelation propel the story forward?

4. Stevenson leaves us with some unanswered questions at the end of Chapter 1. What are they? How do these questions hook us into wanting to learn more?

5. "Let us make a bargain never to refer to this again," says Enfield, and Utterson promptly agrees. Why is this a particularly effective last line for the chapter?

6. What evidence do you find in Chapter 1 of a tension between goodness and evil—a theme that will play out in the remainder of the story?

The Wonderful Wizard of Oz

L. Frank Baum

Prolific children's book author L(yman) Frank Baum (1856–1919) wrote fourteen *Oz* books, which he called "modernized fairy tale[s]." The first in the series—*The Wonderful Wizard of Oz* (1900)—gave the world Dorothy, the tin man, the scarecrow, the cowardly lion, and the great and powerful Oz. Baum was born in New York and at the end of his career moved to Hollywood, where he hoped to film the *Oz* stories. He died twenty years before the release of Judy Garland's portrayal of Dorothy. If you're interested in the signature song from that movie, see Chapter 8, "Over the Rainbow," where you'll learn that no rainbows actually appear in these novels. The lyricist Yip Harburg invented that detail—which, in turn, inspired King Vidor to shoot those scenes in black-and-white, which created the sharpest possible visual contrast with the Technicolor scenes of Oz. (Vidor was the uncredited director who shot the Kansas scenes after Fleming's departure to direct *Gone with the Wind*.) (See page 43.)

Chapter 1: The Cyclone

Dorothy lived in the midst of the great Kansas prairies, with Uncle Henry, who was a farmer, and Aunt Em, who was the farmer's wife. Their house was small, for the lumber to build it had to be carried by wagon many miles. There were four walls, a floor and a roof, which made one room; and this room contained a rusty looking cookstove, a cupboard for the dishes, a table, three or four chairs, and the beds. Uncle Henry and Aunt Em had a big bed in one corner, and Dorothy a little bed in another corner. There was no garret at all, and no cellar—except a small hole dug in the ground, called a cyclone cellar, where the family could go in case one of those great whirlwinds arose, mighty enough to crush any building in its path. It was reached by a trap door in the middle of the floor, from which a ladder led down into the small, dark hole.

When Dorothy stood in the doorway and looked around, she could see nothing but the great gray prairie on every side. Not a tree nor a house broke the broad sweep of flat country that reached to the edge of the sky in all directions. The sun had baked the plowed land into a gray mass, with little cracks running through it. Even the grass was not green, for the sun had burned the tops of the long blades until they were the same gray color to be seen everywhere. Once the house had been painted, but the sun blistered the paint and the rains washed it away, and now the house was as dull and gray as everything else.

When Aunt Em came there to live she was a young, pretty wife. The sun and wind had changed her, too. They had taken the sparkle from her eyes and left them a sober gray; they had taken the red from her cheeks and lips, and they were gray also. She was thin and gaunt, and never smiled now. When Dorothy, who was an orphan, first came to her, Aunt Em had been so startled by the child's laughter that she would scream and press her hand upon her heart whenever Dorothy's merry voice reached her ears; and she still looked at the little girl with wonder that she could find anything to laugh at.

Uncle Henry never laughed. He worked hard from morning till night and did not know what joy was. He was gray also, from his long beard to his rough boots, and he looked stern and solemn, and rarely spoke.

It was Toto that made Dorothy laugh, and saved her from growing as gray as her other **5** surroundings. Toto was not gray; he was a little black dog, with long silky hair and small black eyes that twinkled merrily on either side of his funny, wee nose. Toto played all day long, and Dorothy played with him, and loved him dearly.

Today, however, they were not playing. Uncle Henry sat upon the doorstep and looked anxiously at the sky, which was even grayer than usual. Dorothy stood in the door with Toto in her arms, and looked at the sky too. Aunt Em was washing the dishes.

From the far north they heard a low wail of the wind, and Uncle Henry and Dorothy could see where the long grass bowed in waves before the coming storm. There now came a sharp whistling in the air from the south, and as they turned their eyes that way they saw ripples in the grass coming from that direction also.

Suddenly Uncle Henry stood up.

"There's a cyclone coming, Em," he called to his wife. "I'll go look after the stock." Then he ran toward the sheds where the cows and horses were kept.

10   Aunt Em dropped her work and came to the door. One glance told her of the danger close at hand.

"Quick, Dorothy!" she screamed. "Run for the cellar!"

Toto jumped out of Dorothy's arms and hid under the bed, and the girl started to get him. Aunt Em, badly frightened, threw open the trap door in the floor and climbed down the ladder into the small, dark hole. Dorothy caught Toto at last and started to follow her aunt. When she was halfway across the room there came a great shriek from the wind, and the house shook so hard that she lost her footing and sat down suddenly upon the floor.

Then a strange thing happened.

The house whirled around two or three times and rose slowly through the air. Dorothy felt as if she were going up in a balloon.

15   The north and south winds met where the house stood, and made it the exact center of the cyclone. In the middle of a cyclone the air is generally still, but the great pressure of the wind on every side of the house raised it up higher and higher, until it was at the very top of the cyclone; and there it remained and was carried miles and miles away as easily as you could carry a feather.

It was very dark, and the wind howled horribly around her, but Dorothy found she was riding quite easily. After the first few whirls around, and one other time when the house tipped badly, she felt as if she were being rocked gently, like a baby in a cradle.

Toto did not like it. He ran about the room, now here, now there, barking loudly; but Dorothy sat quite still on the floor and waited to see what would happen.

Once Toto got too near the open trap door, and fell in; and at first the little girl thought she had lost him. But soon she saw one of his ears sticking up through the hole, for the strong pressure of the air was keeping him up so that he could not fall. She crept to the hole, caught Toto by the ear, and dragged him into the room again, afterward closing the trap door so that no more accidents could happen.

Hour after hour passed away, and slowly Dorothy got over her fright; but she felt quite lonely, and the wind shrieked so loudly all about her that she nearly became deaf. At first she had wondered if she would be dashed to pieces when the house fell again; but as the hours passed and nothing terrible happened, she stopped worrying and resolved to wait calmly and see what the future would bring. At last she crawled over the swaying floor to her bed, and lay down upon it; and Toto followed and lay down beside her.

20   In spite of the swaying of the house and the wailing of the wind, Dorothy soon closed her eyes and fell fast asleep.

Discussion and Writing Suggestions

1. The Kansas of Baum's story is gray both outside—in the sun-baked prairie, the one-room house, the appearance of Aunt Em and Uncle Henry—and inside: in the beaten-down, overworked souls of Em and Henry. Dorothy isn't gray, outside or in. How does this fact establish tension in the story? If you knew nothing more of the novel than this, you'd know a lot. Why?

2. The story opens realistically, in Kansas. By the end of Chapter 1, this realism is strained, if not lost. Underline words, phrases, and sentences that show this shift occurring. Where does Baum make his move from realism to fantasy? By the end of Chapter 1, how sharply does Baum break from realism? Explain.

3. One way to create interest for readers is to present a series of events, in effect a sequence: this happened, then this . . . then this . . . and this. But link too many actions in a sequence without developing characters or the connections across events, and readers lose interest. Sequence events just right, however, and readers want to know what happens next. How effective is Baum in creating in you a desire to know what happens next? Explain.

My Ántonia

Willa Cather

My Ántonia (1918) by Willa Cather (1873–1947) is a moving story of two children living on the Nebraska frontier. Beginning with an "Introduction" and followed by a "Book I," the opening to *My Ántonia* is a departure from our collection of other "Chapter Ones." In this case, though, the two sections form a unified opening. The Introduction, in the initial narrator's voice, presents the character Jim Burden and how he came to write the story of Ántonia. Book I, in Jim's voice, begins the telling of that story. Often assigned in high school, *My Ántonia* bears adult rereading for its depictions of prairie life and its memorable characters. Willa Cather wrote twelve novels, six short story collections, poetry, and nonfiction. Critics consider her to be one of the most important American writers of the first half of the twentieth century.

Introduction

Last summer I happened to be crossing the plains of Iowa in a season of intense heat, and it was my good fortune to have for a traveling companion James Quayle Burden—Jim Burden, as we still call him in the West. He and I are old friends—we grew up together in the same Nebraska town—and we had much to say to each other. While the train flashed through never-ending miles of ripe wheat, by country towns and bright-flowered pastures and oak groves wilting in the sun, we sat in the observation car, where the woodwork was hot to the touch and red dust lay deep over everything. The dust and heat, the burning wind, reminded us of many things. We were talking about what it is like to spend one's childhood in little towns like these, buried in wheat and corn, under stimulating extremes of climate: burning summers when the world lies green and billowy beneath a brilliant sky, when one is fairly stifled in vegetation, in the color and smell of strong weeds and heavy harvests; blustery winters with little snow, when the whole country is stripped bare and gray as sheet-iron. We agreed that no one who had not grown up in a little prairie town could know anything about it. It was a kind of freemasonry, we said.

Although Jim Burden and I both live in New York, and are old friends, I do not see much of him there. He is legal counsel for one of the great Western railways, and is sometimes away from his New York office for weeks together. That is one reason why we do not often meet. Another is that I do not like his wife.

When Jim was still an obscure young lawyer, struggling to make his way in New York, his career was suddenly advanced by a brilliant marriage. Genevieve Whitney was the only daughter of a distinguished man. Her marriage with young Burden was the subject of sharp comment at the time. It was said she had been brutally jilted by her cousin, Rutland Whitney, and that she married this unknown man from the West out of bravado. She was a restless, headstrong girl, even then, who liked to astonish her friends. Later, when I knew her, she was always doing something unexpected. She gave one of her town houses for a Suffrage headquarters, produced one of her own plays at the Princess Theater, was arrested for picketing during a garment-makers' strike, etc. I am never able to believe that she has much feeling for the causes to which she lends her name and her fleeting interest. She is handsome, energetic, executive, but to me she seems unimpressionable and temperamentally incapable of enthusiasm. Her husband's quiet tastes irritate her, I think, and she finds it worth while to play the patroness to a group of young poets and painters of advanced ideas and mediocre ability. She has her own fortune and lives her own life. For some reason, she wishes to remain Mrs. James Burden.

As for Jim, no disappointments have been severe enough to chill his naturally romantic and ardent disposition. This disposition, though it often made him seem very funny when he was a boy, has been one of the strongest elements in his success. He loves with a personal passion the great country through which his railway runs and branches. His faith in it and his knowledge of it have played an important part in its development. He is always able to raise capital for new enterprises in Wyoming or Montana, and has helped young men out there to do remarkable things in mines and timber and oil. If a young man with an idea can once get Jim Burden's attention, can manage to accompany him when he goes off into the wilds hunting for lost parks or exploring new canyons, then the money which means action is usually forthcoming. Jim is still able to lose himself in those big Western dreams. Though he is over forty now, he meets new people and new enterprises with the impulsiveness by which his boyhood friends remember him. He never seems to me to grow older. His fresh color and sandy hair and quick-changing blue eyes are those of a young man, and his sympathetic, solicitous interest in women is as youthful as it is Western and American.

5 During that burning day when we were crossing Iowa, our talk kept returning to a central figure, a Bohemian girl whom we had known long ago and whom both of us admired. More than any other person we remembered, this girl seemed to mean to us the country, the conditions, the whole adventure of our childhood. To speak her name was to call up pictures of people and places, to set a quiet drama going in one's brain. I had lost sight of her altogether, but Jim had found her again after long years, had renewed a friendship that meant a great deal to him, and out of his busy life had set apart time enough to enjoy that friendship. His mind was full of her that day. He made me see her again, feel her presence, revived all my old affection for her.

"I can't see," he said impetuously, "why you have never written anything about Ántonia."

I told him I had always felt that other people—he himself, for one—knew her much better than I. I was ready, however, to make an agreement with him; I would set down on paper all that I remembered of Ántonia if he would do the same. We might, in this way, get a picture of her.

He rumpled his hair with a quick, excited gesture, which with him often announces a new determination, and I could see that my suggestion took hold of him. "Maybe I will, maybe I will!" he declared. He stared out of the window for a few moments, and when he turned to me again his eyes had the sudden clearness that comes from something the mind itself sees. "Of course," he said, "I should have to do it in a direct way, and say a great deal about myself. It's through myself that I knew and felt her, and I've had no practice in any other form of presentation."

I told him that how he knew her and felt her was exactly what I most wanted to know about Ántonia. He had had opportunities that I, as a little girl who watched her come and go, had not.

Months afterward Jim Burden arrived at my apartment one stormy winter afternoon, **10** with a bulging legal portfolio sheltered under his fur overcoat. He brought it into the sitting-room with him and tapped it with some pride as he stood warming his hands.

"I finished it last night—the thing about Ántonia," he said. "Now, what about yours?"

I had to confess that mine had not gone beyond a few straggling notes.

"Notes? I didn't make any." He drank his tea all at once and put down the cup. "I didn't arrange or rearrange. I simply wrote down what of herself and myself and other people Ántonia's name recalls to me. I suppose it hasn't any form. It hasn't any title, either." He went into the next room, sat down at my desk and wrote on the pinkish face of the portfolio the word, "Ántonia." He frowned at this a moment, then prefixed another word, making it "My Ántonia." That seemed to satisfy him.

"Read it as soon as you can," he said, rising, "but don't let it influence your own story."

My own story was never written, but the following narrative is Jim's manuscript, sub- **15** stantially as he brought it to me.

Note: The Bohemian name Ántonia is strongly accented on the first syllable, like the English name Anthony, and the 'i' is, of course, given the sound of long 'e'. The name is pronounced An'-ton-ee-ah.

Book I. The Shimerdas

I FIRST HEARD OF Ántonia on what seemed to me an interminable journey across the great midland plain of North America. I was ten years old then; I had lost both my father and mother within a year, and my Virginia relatives were sending me out to my grandparents, who lived in Nebraska. I travelled in the care of a mountain boy, Jake Marpole, one of the 'hands' on my father's old farm under the Blue Ridge, who was now going West to work for my grandfather. Jake's experience of the world was not much wider than mine. He had never been in a railway train until the morning when we set out together to try our fortunes in a new world.

We went all the way in day-coaches, becoming more sticky and grimy with each stage of the journey. Jake bought everything the newsboys offered him: candy, oranges, brass collar buttons, a watch-charm, and for me a 'Life of Jesse James,' which I remember as one of the most satisfactory books I have ever read. Beyond Chicago we were under the protection of a friendly passenger conductor, who knew all about the country to which we were going and gave us a great deal of advice in exchange for our confidence. He seemed to us an experienced and worldly man who had been almost everywhere; in his conversation he threw out lightly the names of distant states and cities. He wore the rings and pins and badges of different fraternal orders to which he belonged. Even his cuff-buttons were engraved with hieroglyphics, and he was more inscribed than an Egyptian obelisk.

Once when he sat down to chat, he told us that in the immigrant car ahead there was a family from 'across the water' whose destination was the same as ours.

'They can't any of them speak English, except one little girl, and all she can say is "We go Black Hawk, Nebraska." She's not much older than you, twelve or thirteen, maybe, and she's as bright as a new dollar. Don't you want to go ahead and see her, Jimmy? She's got the pretty brown eyes, too!'

20   This last remark made me bashful, and I shook my head and settled down to 'Jesse James.' Jake nodded at me approvingly and said you were likely to get diseases from foreigners.

I do not remember crossing the Missouri River, or anything about the long day's journey through Nebraska. Probably by that time I had crossed so many rivers that I was dull to them. The only thing very noticeable about Nebraska was that it was still, all day long, Nebraska.

I had been sleeping, curled up in a red plush seat, for a long while when we reached Black Hawk. Jake roused me and took me by the hand. We stumbled down from the train to a wooden siding, where men were running about with lanterns. I couldn't see any town, or even distant lights; we were surrounded by utter darkness. The engine was panting heavily after its long run. In the red glow from the fire-box, a group of people stood huddled together on the platform, encumbered by bundles and boxes. I knew this must be the immigrant family the conductor had told us about. The woman wore a fringed shawl tied over her head, and she carried a little tin trunk in her arms, hugging it as if it were a baby. There was an old man, tall and stooped. Two half-grown boys and a girl stood holding oilcloth bundles, and a little girl clung to her mother's skirts. Presently a man with a lantern approached them and began to talk, shouting and exclaiming. I pricked up my ears, for it was positively the first time I had ever heard a foreign tongue.

Another lantern came along. A bantering voice called out: 'Hello, are you Mr. Burden's folks? If you are, it's me you're looking for. I'm Otto Fuchs. I'm Mr. Burden's hired man, and I'm to drive you out. Hello, Jimmy, ain't you scared to come so far west?'

I looked up with interest at the new face in the lantern-light. He might have stepped out of the pages of 'Jesse James.' He wore a sombrero hat, with a wide leather band and a bright buckle, and the ends of his moustache were twisted up stiffly, like little horns. He looked lively and ferocious, I thought, and as if he had a history. A long scar ran across one cheek and drew the corner of his mouth up in a sinister curl. The top of his left ear was gone, and his skin was brown as an Indian's. Surely this was the face of a desperado. As he walked about the platform in his high-heeled boots, looking for our trunks, I saw that he was a rather slight man, quick and wiry, and light on his feet. He told us we had a long night drive ahead of us, and had better be on the hike. He led us to a hitching-bar where two farm-wagons were tied, and I saw the foreign family crowding into one of them. The other was for us. Jake got on the front seat with Otto Fuchs, and I rode on the straw in the bottom of the wagon-box, covered up with a buffalo hide. The immigrants rumbled off into the empty darkness, and we followed them.

25   I tried to go to sleep, but the jolting made me bite my tongue, and I soon began to ache all over. When the straw settled down, I had a hard bed. Cautiously I slipped from under the buffalo hide, got up on my knees and peered over the side of the wagon. There seemed to be nothing to see; no fences, no creeks or trees, no hills or fields. If there was a road, I could not make it out in the faint starlight. There was nothing but land: not a country at all, but the

material out of which countries are made. No, there was nothing but land—slightly undulating, I knew, because often our wheels ground against the brake as we went down into a hollow and lurched up again on the other side. I had the feeling that the world was left behind, that we had got over the edge of it, and were outside man's jurisdiction. I had never before looked up at the sky when there was not a familiar mountain ridge against it. But this was the complete dome of heaven, all there was of it. I did not believe that my dead father and mother were watching me from up there; they would still be looking for me at the sheep-fold down by the creek, or along the white road that led to the mountain pastures. I had left even their spirits behind me. The wagon jolted on, carrying me I knew not whither. I don't think I was homesick. If we never arrived anywhere, it did not matter. Between that earth and that sky I felt erased, blotted out. I did not say my prayers that night: here, I felt, what would be would be.

Discussion and Writing Suggestions

1. The narrator of the "Introduction" is opinionated: we learn she doesn't care for Jim Burden's wife but is fond of Jim, describing him in vivid, sympathetic terms. She also describes life on the Nebraska prairie. The introductory narrator's voice is especially appealing—and on the example of her voice alone we want to read on. Why? Underline phrases or sentences in the Introduction that you find particularly appealing. Compare your notes with those of classmates.

2. Don't confuse the narrator of the Introduction with the author, Willa Cather. This opening narrator is a character every bit as much as Jim Burden. In the Introduction, she presents an account of how *My Ántonia* came to be written. Burden himself begins his account of Ántonia in Book I. Why bother with the Introduction at all? Why not simply begin the story of Ántonia with Book I?

3. Burden writes: "There was nothing but land: not a country at all, but the material out of which countries are made." How do observations like this reveal character and intelligence? Why do such statements make us *want* to spend time in Jim Burden's company?

4. As you finish these opening pages, do you want to know more about Burden's life, about what happened when the wagon arrived at its destination? Why? How has Cather managed to hook us into wanting more?

Scene Ones: The Films

In this section we invite you to view the opening scenes of film adaptations of the six classic novels presented earlier in this chapter, as well as the opening scenes of eighteen additional films. Several of these films—including George Stevens's *Shane* and Francis Ford Coppola's *The Godfather, Part One*—are based on novels; the rest, for the most part, are original works created for the cinema. (Two—*Brief Encounter* and *Chicago*—are based on plays.)

Scene Ones are not as clearly demarked in films as in novels, where novelists number or at least title separate chapters, so it sometimes takes a keen eye to determine where one scene of a film ends and the next begins. Typically, though, we have deemed the first scene ended when a particular line of dramatic action has reached some kind of natural conclusion or at least has come to a significant pause. In earlier times, these pauses were often signaled by fade-outs or dissolves, but such devices are now often considered old-fashioned.

For your viewing convenience, the heading of each film treated in this section concludes with an indication of how many minutes and seconds the scene lasts. So 00:00–6:33 indicates that the scene begins at the zero point—typically with the appearance of the studio logo—and ends 6 minutes and 33 seconds later. Although you may choose—and are even encouraged—to continue viewing into Scene 2 and beyond, the Discussion and Writing Suggestions sections assume that you have watched only to the designated point. Some of these scenes (for example, the openings of Robert Stevenson's *Jane Eyre*, David Lean's *Great Expectations*, and Orson Welles's *Citizen Kane*) are available complete on YouTube. In most cases, the Web offers only a truncated version of the opening scene. But today a vast number of films are widely available for a modest rental rate from such sources as Netflix, iTunes, and Amazon streaming video. And your instructor may also make these films available to you, either by showing them in class or by placing them on reserve. We wish you pleasurable viewing—and even envy you if you are about to watch these films for the first time!

How to Start Your Script with a Killer Opening Scene

Tim Long

K. M. Weiland (pages 303–307) discusses the importance of "the hook" to the opening of a novel; in this selection, Tim Long discusses additional criteria for evaluating Scene Ones for yourself. Long is an experienced screenwriter, screenplay consultant, and former director of the MFA program in screenwriting at Florida State University.

In the competitive world of screenwriting (and filmmaking) where industry readers judge your script in the first few pages, openings are a vital part of a successful screenplay and film.

Not only are they important first impressions of your writing ability, they also serve a variety of narrative purposes that can raise the storytelling bar by instantly immersing the reader into the world of your screenplay or film. Let's touch on a few pivotal ones.

Teaser

After *Jaws* did it successfully in the 1970s, making your opening scene a teaser has since been overdone and can be considered a screenwriting cliché. However, it's only a cliché if done ineffectively; executed correctly, it can be a powerful storytelling technique.

The hard truth is that most professional readers, development execs, and reps make a value judgment on your screenplay within the first 5–10 pages (as do they the first few minutes of your film). If your story and writing hasn't hooked them by then, it's a knife in the gut of the read. Utilizing an opening scene as a teaser can help prevent this.

What is a teaser? It's simply an opening moment, scene, or sequence intended to hook **5** the audience from the get-go by generating curiosity and/or conflict that leaves the audience wanting more.

Christopher Nolan's *Memento* is a terrific example of this at play. The film's opening scene reveals a Polaroid of a dead man that slowly begins to fade away as we then start to realize that the entire scene we're watching is happening in reverse.

The audience may have no idea what's going on, but by raising so many questions this opening generates such curiosity that it demands attentive engagement throughout the film's running time.

David Fincher's *Fight Club* is another solid example of the usage of an opening scene as a teaser. We float through the synapses of a human brain, exit out of sweating pores on a forehead, continue to pull back down the barrel of a gun to reveal that the weapon is shoved in the mouth of Edward Norton's character, who narrates: "*People are always asking me if I know Tyler Durden.*"

The non-linear scene immediately seizes our attention by drawing us in through the vehicle of curiosity. Who's Tyler Durden? Why does this guy have a gun shoved in his mouth? Why is Brad Pitt's character going to blow up the city?

These questions are the spark that ignites the fire of interest in the audience who want **10** answers, and will continue watching to get them.

Theme

Openings can also be used to set up a story's theme. Take the film *A Few Good Men* starring Tom Cruise. The opening is a credit sequence depicting a Marine Corps drill team in action. Their synchronized moves not only emphasize their disciplined training, but also show them working together as a unified force. This machine of precision operates with one objective in mind: to bring honor, the film's central theme, to the Marine Corps.

Another salient example is the film *Lord of War*, which opens on Nicholas Cage's character standing in a sea of spent bullet cartridges in a war-torn third-world country. Wearing a strangely out-of-place business suit, he turns to address the audience, saying: "*There is one firearm for every twelve people on the planet.*" We're then launched into a first-person sequence that follows a single bullet's journey from a Russian factory to an African war zone, and ultimately into the forehead of a child soldier. It's a shocking commentary on the horrors of war, and sets up a strong case against guns and gun trafficking, one of the core themes of the film.

Tone

In the first few minutes of any screenplay or film, the tone of the story causes an unconscious expectation to form in the audience's mind as to how they should view the film. Is it serious, funny, somber, light-hearted, etc.?

There's Something About Mary opens on a tree in front of a high school in a bucolic neighborhood, only to end up revealing two guys up in the tree playing and singing the opening soundtrack.

15   This oddity established the film's broad comedic tone. It let the audience know right away not to take the film too seriously, that we're supposed to sit back and laugh. And by establishing this tone in the opening scene, it allowed the filmmakers to get as absurd as they wanted to without losing the audience.

The opening of Martin Scorsese's *Goodfellas* eavesdrops on three men quietly driving at night until a noise from the rear of the car interrupts the silence. After pulling over and opening the trunk to reveal a badly beaten and bloody man stuffed inside, the three men proceed to stab and shoot the man mercilessly.

This graphic opening thrusts the audience headfirst into the gritty world of organized crime. It establishes a clear tone that informs the audience from the get-go that this is going to be no-holds-barred, violent realism.

Character

Openings are often used to begin setting up the main characters. In the film *Seven* the story opens on five simple shots. In just a few seconds, and without any dialogue, we learn a lot about Morgan Freeman's character.

From the soundscape outside we know that he lives in a big city. We know he's a cop. From the gold badge we know he's more than just a cop, he's a detective. We know he's meticulous by the way he lays out his stuff in order on the bed, and by picking at a piece of lint from his jacket. We know he's probably single and lives alone by the twin bed he has. And we know he has a dark side because he carries a switchblade.

20   The opening scene speaks volumes about his character without ever actually uttering a word.

Or take the opening scene of Netflix's *House of Cards.* We watch in disbelief as Kevin Spacey's character Frank Underwood kills a wounded dog. The scene skillfully lays the foundation for Underwood being a Machiavellian sociopath willing to do "*the necessary thing*" as Underwood tells us—a personal mantra that will become the essence of his characterization throughout the series.

Backstory

Backstory is a character's relevant history prior to the start of the story. In other words, it is the story before the story.

In the film *Unforgiven* the opening scene was a single silhouette of Clint Eastwood's character digging his wife's grave. A scroll card reveals that Eastwood's character was a known thief and murderer. This backstory established an important context for the character and the story to come, both of which are rooted in violence. It set up the character's murderous past, which a large part of the narrative is devoted to exploring.

In Pixar's *Up* the opening is an extended montage of Carl and Ellie's life that spans their courtship, marriage, old age, and a broken, unfulfilled dream of adventure that is sadly usurped by Ellie's passing away. It's a poignant and touching backstory that effectively establishes a thematic context for Carl's story to come, which is cemented in the notion that you're never too old to make your dreams come true.

The Amalgam

As you might have gathered thus far, great openings are actually an amalgam of several   **25**
narrative functions.

    The opening of *Goodfellas* not only established the gritty tone of the film, but also serves
as a compelling teaser, *and* sets up the violent nature of the characters.

    House of Cards not only serves as a engaging teaser that hooks us right away, but it
also gives the audience an important insight into Kevin Spacey's character.

    Up's opening narrative purpose was to reveal backstory, yet it also serves to both set up
Carl's character, **and** the story's central theme of "*Never being too old to make your dreams
come true.*"

    Fight Club introduces . . . Edward Norton's character as craven and inferior. Additionally,
some would argue that the opening is also a subtle visual harbinger that signals the start of
consciousness for Edward Norton's character.

    However you decide to use your opening, always remember that an opening scene or   **30**
sequence is a snapshot at your writing and storytelling ability. It's the first impression that will
establish either a positive or negative impression in the reader's mind for the rest of the read.
And it's an all-important narrative tool that raises the storytelling bar by drawing audiences in
and leaving them wanting more.

Discussion and Writing Suggestions

1. Long offers several criteria for evaluating the opening of a film, all of which
   speak to a single, overriding requirement: that the opening hook us into
   wanting more. In what ways, if any, do the requirements for the opening of
   a film differ from the requirements for the opening of a novel?

2. "The hard truth is that most professional readers, development execs, and
   reps make a value judgment on your screenplay within the first 5–10 pages
   (as do they the first few minutes of your film)." Offer two responses to this
   "hard truth"—first as a consumer of films (that is, as a paying customer) and
   then as a budding screenwriter or filmmaker.

3. Long offers six criteria for evaluating opening scenes: teasers, theme, tone,
   character, backstory, and an amalgam. Select one of the movies he discusses.
   Watch the opening scene several times, and determine the extent to which
   you agree with his analysis.

4. Choose one or two of Long's criteria to evaluate the opening of a film you
   know well—preferably, a film available online that you could study.

5. Can you think of another criterion for evaluating a film's opening that Long
   has not discussed in this selection? Define that criterion and then apply it,
   briefly, to the opening of a film you know well—preferably, a film available
   online that you could study.

Pride and Prejudice (1995)

Simon Langton, Director
(00:45–01:50)

and

Pride & Prejudice (2005)

Joe Wright, Director
(00:00–02:59)

Jane Austen's *Pride and Prejudice* has been adapted for film at least twenty-one times, ranging from the 1940 classic with Greer Garson as Elizabeth Bennet and Laurence Olivier as Mr. Darcy to the more loosely adapted but nonetheless compelling *Pride and Prejudice and Zombies* (2016) in which the (eventual) couple must battle the living dead terrifying the countryside. The two versions of Austen's novel considered here are the six-hour BBC miniseries starring Jennifer Ehle and Colin Firth (by many considered the finest adaptation) and the much-admired 2005 film with Keira Knightley and Matthew MacFadyen. (*The Guardian* praised Knightley's performance as one of "beauty, delicacy, spirit and wit.") At the heart of every remake: a romantic comedy featuring the proud Lizzy Bennet and the haughty Mr. Darcy, sworn (social) enemies until love unravels all their defenses. In broad strokes the same story, these (indeed all) adaptations of Austen's novel are nonetheless distinctive, a point immediately understood when you watch the very different opening scenes. You'll find the opening of the 2005 film on YouTube. Search terms: "pride prejudice knightley opening." The BBC version is available for streaming from Amazon.

Discussion and Writing Suggestions

1. The 1995 film adaptation of *Pride and Prejudice* begins with two horsemen—Mr. Bingley and Mr. Darcy, we'll later learn—galloping hard across a field in the English countryside. The movie's first words are theirs, concerning the lease of a stately manor house. The 2005 version begins with the camera tracking Elizabeth Bennet walking across a field, engrossed in reading a book. These are very different openings, one focused on Bingley and Darcy, the other on Lizzy Bennet. What are the effects of beginning so differently? Which do you prefer—why?

2. Construct an argument for opening the film in such different ways. What's the logic? Why begin one version with Lizzy and the other with Bingley and Darcy?

3. *Pride and Prejudice* (the novel) opens with Mrs. Bennet talking with her husband about the leasing of Netherfield Hall by a man of means, Mr. Bingley. The conversation quickly turns to their daughters' prospects for marrying this gentleman (see pages 13–15). Neither of the film adaptations opens with Mrs. and Mr. Bennet in conversation (though in the 2005 adaptation these *are* the first spoken words—but only after the camera wordlessly follows Lizzy and then her sisters for two minutes). Compare the three, the novel and the films. What observations can you make about the faithfulness of adaptations to an original source?

4. Both adaptations make use of music playing over the visuals. Describe the music and its effects on the action. How different are these uses? And what is the source of the music—does this make a difference?

5. What are your first impressions of Lizzy Bennet in the opening of these two adaptations? We see her in both, though in the 1995 version for a considerably briefer time. On what visual details are your impressions based?

6. Having watched just a few minutes of each adaptation, is it too soon to know whether or not you'll enjoy these films? Explain.

Jane Eyre (1943)

Robert Stevenson, Director
(00:00–6:33)

Charlotte Brontë's *Jane Eyre* has been adapted for film and television at least thirty times, according to the Internet Movie Database. The 1944 version, directed by Robert Stevenson, is particularly notable for Orson Welles's brooding performance as the tortured Mr. Rochester. Joan Fontaine plays Jane as an adult. The film is also impressive for its re-creation of the Yorkshire moors, though it was filmed entirely on a Hollywood backlot. The novelist Aldous Huxley was one of the three credited screenwriters, and the musical score was composed by Bernard Herrmann, who was to write the music for most of Alfred Hitchcock's American films. Stevenson later directed *Mary Poppins* (1964).

As many novels contain more material than can be comfortably contained within the 90 or 120 minutes of the typical narrative film, Stevenson's *Jane Eyre* has significant differences from Brontë's novel. The film does retain Brontë's first scene, with Mrs. Reed and her son John facing off against Jane. But it omits a major subplot that develops after Jane flees Thornfield upon discovering that Mr. Rochester already has a wife. She is eventually taken in by three siblings (who turn out to be her cousins); one of them, a clergyman who wants to do missionary work, eventually proposes to Jane and invites her to come with him to India. She is tempted, but then hears in her mind Rochester's desperate call for help.

Discussion and Writing Suggestions

1. The opening credits of the film use a common convention of the time for literary adaptations: They appear as turning pages in a book, and the last page we see is the first page of the novel: "My name is Jane Eyre. I was born in 1820, a time of harsh change in England. Money and position seemed all that mattered. . . . There was no proper place for the poor or the unfortunate."

   The problem is—as you can readily see by turning to p. 15, where we reprint the actual first page of *Jane Eyre*—that these are not, in fact, Brontë's opening words; they have been entirely made up by the screenwriters and are simply masquerading as the opening of the novel.

   In light of the way the novel *Jane Eyre actually* begins, why do you think the director and the screenwriters attempted to "cheat" on Brontë's own opening in this manner?

2. Compare the action of the opening of Brontë's novel with the action of the opening sequence of the film: the footman and Bessie getting Jane out of her locked closet and downstairs to confront her aunt and Mr. Brocklehurst. How do these different openings help shape our different responses to the book and to the film? Or do they not make a difference in terms of our over-all "first impression" of the story?

3. How does the director, Robert Stevenson, use dramatic camera angles to emphasize Jane's insignificant place in the household and, on the other hand, the awesome power of a man like Brocklehurst?

4. Both Mrs. Reed and Brocklehurst view Jane as a "wicked" girl. Based on this opening segment, how would you describe her? And based upon what you have seen and heard, explain the situation in this household. Why is Mrs. Reed so determined to get rid of Jane? Why is Brocklehurst so eager to get her to come to Lowood?

Great Expectations (1946)

David Lean, Director
(00:00–3:55)

"One of the great things about Dickens," wrote the critic Roger Ebert, "is the way his people colonize your memory." Ebert goes on to note that "[David] Lean brings Dickens's classic set-pieces to life as if he'd been reading over our shoulder: Pip's encounter with the convict Magwitch in the churchyard, Pip's first meeting with the mad Miss Havisham, and the ghoulish atmosphere in the law offices of Mr. Jaggers, whose walls are decorated with the death masks of clients he has lost to the gallows."

Like *Jane Eyre*, Dickens's *Great Expectations* has been adapted into film numerous times. The 1946 version, starring John Mills as the adult Pip, was directed by Lean, who went on to create numerous Hollywood epic films, including *The Bridge on the River Kwai* (1957), *Lawrence of Arabia* (1962), *and Dr. Zhivago* (1965). *Great Expectations* was nominated for five Academy Awards and won two (Best Cinematography and Best Art Direction). The visuals in the first sequence of the film, closely paralleling the descriptions in Dickens's first chapter, show why.

Discussion and Writing Suggestions

1. Like Robert Stevenson's film *Jane Eyre*, David Lean's *Great Expectations* opens with turning book pages and with the adult protagonist reading the first paragraph of the novel; but in this case, the words are Dickens's own. Following the credits, we see the boy Pip running along the marshes. What else do we see on the screen, and what do we hear on the soundtrack? How do these images and sounds help create a mood that is equivalent to the one evoked in the opening of Dickens's novel?

2. Stevenson the filmmaker needs to convey vital information about Pip's status as an orphan currently living with his aunt and her husband, information that is fully developed in the opening pages of the novel. What is the filmmaker's solution, and how well do you think he has solved the problem of initial exposition?

3. Compare and contrast the moment in the book when Pip first encounters the convict Magwitch with the same moment in Lean's film. Consider such matters as the role of your imagination in envisaging the convict (and how he would appear to a young boy) and the way that Dickens and Stevenson create the shock of this encounter for Pip.

The Strange Case of Dr. Jekyll and Mr. Hyde (1931)

Rouben Mamoulian, Director
(0:00–6:30)

and

The Strange Case of Dr. Jekyll and Mr. Hyde (1941)

Victor Fleming, Director
(0:00–7:15)

Robert Louis Stevenson's 1886 novella *The Strange Case of Dr. Jekyll and Mr. Hyde* launched one of the most unforgettable and enduring characters in imaginative fiction. *Wikipedia* lists twelve stage adaptations of this story from 1890 to 2017 (including a 1990 Broadway musical); thirty-three film adaptations from 1908 to 2008 (including *Abbott and Costello Meet Dr. Jekyll and Mr. Hyde* [1953] and Jerry Lewis's *The Nutty Professor* [1963]); twelve radio adaptations; twenty-one TV adaptations; thirteen musical pieces based on the story (including songs by the Who and Five Finger Death Punch), four novels, and innumerable "spoofs and parodies," including a Tom and Jerry cartoon, and *Jacqueline Hyde*, a 2005 "direct-to-TV erotic film."

At the heart of this infinite variety of Jekyll-Hyde manifestations is a single compelling idea: that every human being carries within his or her soul a good self and an evil self. The protagonist attempts to scientifically separate one from the other, with the aim of suppressing the evil self and giving sway to the good. Of course, many of these variants emphasize that besides being blasphemous, this process is doomed to failure, and that despite our best intentions, the evil impulses will inevitably prevail over the good.

For the sake of comparison, we have selected two of the more significant film adaptations of Stevenson's novella: Rouben Mamoulian's 1931 version and Victor Fleming's 1941 version. Rouben Mamoulian's film stars Fredric March as both Jekyll and Hyde. Mamoulian (1897–1987) worked as both a stage and a film director. His 1929 film *Applause* was one of the earliest talking pictures. Victor Fleming (1889–1949) is noteworthy for having directed two of Hollywood's most famous and enduring films, both in the year 1939—*The Wizard of Oz* and *Gone with the Wind*. Fleming's *Dr. Jekyll and Mr. Hyde* stars Spencer Tracy; Jekyll's fiancé is played by Lana Turner.

Note: both of these films' openings are available on the Web. For the 1931 Mamoulian film, Google "jekyll hyde 1931 videodailymotion." For the 1941 Fleming film, Google "jekyll hyde 1941 videodailymotion." Other film versions referenced in the Discussion and Writing Suggestions that follow are available on YouTube.

Discussion and Writing Suggestions

1. In some ways the opening of the Mamoulian *Jekyll and Hyde* looks as if it could have been filmed on a modern smartphone, rather than in a Hollywood studio during the 1930s. Discuss Mamoulian's cinematic technique in this sequence, and speculate on why he may have chosen to begin the film in this unusual manner.

2. What is revealed about Fredric March's Dr. Jekyll in the opening segment of Mamoulian's film? What kind of man is he? What do we learn about his tastes and his lifestyle? How do others feel about him?

3. While the opening sequence of the 1931 Mamoulian film focuses almost entirely upon Jekyll, the corresponding sequence of Fleming's 1941 film devotes considerable screen time to other characters as well: the bishop who delivers the sermon; Beatrix Emery, Jekyll's fiancé; her father, Sir Charles Emery; Jekyll's colleague Dr. John Lanyon; and a disturbed parishioner and his wife, Sam and Sara Higgins. How do these multiple characters suggest how the plot of this film is likely to develop? For example, what do we see in the interchanges between Sir Charles and Dr. Jekyll and between Sir Charles and Beatrix that indicate trouble ahead? How is Sam Higgins likely to figure in Jekyll's scientific experiments?

4. Based on these opening segments, how is Fredric March's Dr. Jekyll different from Spencer Tracy's? How are the two men similar? Support your conclusions with specific references to the images and the dialogue.

5. For another version of Robert Louis Stevenson's novella, directed by Charles Jarrott, Google "strange case jekyll hyde dailymotion" (the entire film is 1:15:58), and view 00:00–10:23 of the Jack Palance rendition of Jekyll/Hyde. Discuss any new elements in this opening not present in any form in the 1931 or the 1941 films. How do such elements affect the mood and significance of the story? How does Palance's rendition of the protagonist compare and contrast with March's and Tracy's? Explain why you prefer one opening over the others.

6. The opening scenes of the film versions of *Pride and Prejudice, Jane Eyre,* and *Great Expectations* track more or less closely with the first chapters of the novels on which they were based. But none of the directors of the Jekyll/Hyde films referenced above attempt to adapt for film treatment the first segment of Robert Louis Stevenson's novella focusing on the interchange between Utterson and Enfield. (The 1968 film with Jack Palance does include a glimpse of Hyde frantically running toward the camera, through a London alleyway, a moment described by Enfield in Stevenson's novella in the context of a much longer scene involving a child and an angry crowd.) To what extent do you think these filmmakers were right to ignore Stevenson's opening chapter? To what extent do you think they should at least have made the attempt? Explain.

7. For a comic treatment of the Jekyll/Hyde story, go to YouTube and search "nutty professor lewis." This should lead you to the first eight minutes of comedian

and filmmaker Jerry Lewis's 1963 film, *The Nutty Professor*. Where does Lewis find humor in the Jekyll/Hyde saga? Despite the comedy, what common elements can you find in all of the Jekyll and Hyde variants that you have seen?

8. Having viewed some of the Dr. Jekylls, you may be curious about the varieties of Mr. Hyde that are created in these films, particularly as they depict the initial transformation of Jekyll into Hyde. For the 1931 Mamoulian film, go to YouTube and search "jekyll hyde 1931 solt." For the 1941 Fleming film, search "Jekyll hyde can this be evil." For the 1963 Lewis film, search "buddy love debut." None of these clips, of course, are opening scenes, but they do provide interesting counterpoints to the initial revelations of Dr. Jekyll.

The Wizard of Oz (1939)

Victor Fleming, Director
(00:00–08:01)

The Wizard of Oz is among the best-loved films in the history of cinema. It's visually stunning and memorably acted. Its songs are universally admired and its themes are timeless: of power and powerlessness, escape and return, and courage, empathy, and wisdom discovered deep within. Many books and documentaries have been devoted to the film's production and importance in American culture—far too many to touch on here. But we can't resist mentioning a few nuggets:

- The film's Oscar-winning song, "Over the Rainbow," references a "rainbow" that never appeared in the L. Frank Baum *Oz* books. It was introduced by Yip Harburg, the lyricist, who so impressed others with his vision of a dreary Kansas (as compared to Oz) that the decision was made to shoot the Kansas scenes in black and white—to create the sharpest possible contrast with the Technicolor Oz.
- The Cowardly Lion's costume was made from actual lion skins and weighed nearly 100 pounds.
- Dorothy's ruby slippers are housed at the National Museum of American History.
- In the days (far) before computer-generated effects, the movie's famed tornado was made from a thirty-five-foot muslin stocking fitted around chicken wire.
- Margaret Hamilton's nightmare-inducing Wicked Witch of the West was ranked as the best female movie villain of all time by the American Film Institute. Frightening as she was as a witch, Hamilton (in real life) championed children's causes and was, at the beginning of her career, a kindergarten teacher.

Surprisingly, given its iconic cultural status, *The Wizard of Oz* was initially considered a financial disappointment and didn't turn a profit until its re-release in 1949. It lost the 1939 Academy Award contests for Best Picture and Best Director to *Gone with the Wind*. (Victor Fleming directed both films.) Just the same, *The Wizard of Oz* endures as one of the most-loved, most-watched movies of all time, a testament to an American fairy tale.

Discussion and Writing Suggestions

1. After the initial credits, before the first scene begins, Fleming runs a dedication: "For nearly forty years this story has given faithful service to the Young in Heart; and Time has been powerless to put its kindly philosophy out of fashion. To those of you who have been faithful to it in return . . . and to the Young in Heart . . . we dedicate this picture." What does "faithful to it in return" mean?

2. We first meet Dorothy running down the lane with Toto to escape Miss Gulch. What makes this scene memorable? How does it grab your attention?

3. Back at Aunt Em and Uncle Henry's farm, Dorothy interacts with several of the main characters (in human form) she will meet later in Oz. L. Frank Baum includes no such exchanges in the first chapter of his novel (see pages 27–29). Reread those opening pages and compare them with the opening of the film. Speculate on the reasons the director and scriptwriters began as they did.

4. Describe the Kansas landscape in the film's first scene. What mood does it evoke? How does it compare visually to the written description of Kansas in the novel?

5. In what ways does the film's signature song play off the Kansas landscape?

6. What about her life in Kansas makes Dorothy psychologically ready for an adventure? In what ways does the song "Over the Rainbow," contrasting as it does with her Kansas experience, prepare her for adventures to come?

7. Assuming you've watched the entire film: Recall the famous line that Dorothy repeats in order to return to Kansas: "There's no place like home." She wants to be in Kansas, but the Kansas we've seen is a dreary place. What about this world, as revealed in the first scene, is so appealing that Dorothy longs to return?

8. After listening to the song "Over the Rainbow" at the end of the first scene, read the account of how the song came to be written: see Chapter 8.

My Ántonia (1995)

Joseph Sargent, Director
(00:00–03:48)

Joseph Sargent (1925–2014), a four-time Emmy winning director best known for *The Taking of Pelham One Two Three*, directed the first adaptation of Willa Cather's prairie classic, *My Ántonia*. The film aired on the USA Network and starred Neil Patrick Harris as Jim Burden and Romanian actress Elina Lowensohn as Ántonia Shimerda.

Discussion and Writing Suggestions

1. The adaptation opens with a series of still photographs. What happens in these photos, and how does the series prepare us for live-action scenes of Jim Burden on the train, headed west?

2. Sargent dispenses with Cather's "Introduction" (see pages 29–31) in which a female narrator recalls how Jim Burden came to write the story of Ántonia.

Instead, the director begins directly with Burden. Was this an effective choice, in your view? Why or why not?

3. In film schools and among film critics, there's some disagreement concerning the use of "voice-overs": that is, of having a speaker—Jim Burden in the case of *My Ántonia*—speaking directly to the audience, telling the story. Some critics appreciate the economy of such narration; others reject the technique as lazy filmmaking that tells what should be shown and keeps the audience from a full immersion in the action. What's your view—both for films in general and for this particular film? (Can you think of other films that make use of the voice-over technique?) How effective is Jim Burden's voice-over in this opening scene?

4. At one point we see Jim Burden on a crowded train, asleep. We see his dream. How does this dream prepare him (and us) for the coming story?

5. What visual cues in the opening scene establish the era in which the story is set?

6. Watch the opening scene a few times and focus on the soundtrack. How does it change through the opening scene? Why does it change?

Dracula (1931)

Tod Browning, Director
(00:00–11:00)

and

Bram Stoker's Dracula (1992)

Francis Ford Coppola, Director
(00:00–15:38)

Bram Stoker's *Dracula* has been frequently adapted to film, but for sheer creepiness the original 1931 version directed by Tod Browning has never been surpassed. Newspapers reported that some members of the audience at the premiere fainted from shock. This film, directed by Tod Browning, is actually based on the 1924 play by Hamilton Deane and John Balderston, which was itself based on Stoker's novel. (An unauthorized version of the story had been filmed in 1922 as *Nosferatu*, but Stoker's widow successfully sued to get the prints destroyed; some survived.) The Hungarian actor Bela Lugosi, who makes an unforgettable impression as the vampire Count Dracula, was not the producer's first choice for the role, even though he had played the role on stage. Lugosi was later to appear in numerous other horror films, some of them comic. The visual look of the film can be credited as much to Karl Freud, Browning's cinematographer, as to the director himself. Browning made his reputation directing silent films, and *Dracula*, made just a few years into the sound era, has much of the look and the acting style (with its heightened expressions and gestures) of the silent era.

Francis Ford Coppola, director of *The Godfather* films (1972, 1974, 1990) and *Apocalypse Now* (1979), said that he wanted his 1992 version of the Dracula legend to resemble "an erotic dream." One critic, Vincent Canby of the *New York Times*, wrote, "Mr. Coppola has created his own wild dream of a movie, which looks as if it required a special pact with the Treasury Department to finance." Spurning digital effects, because he wanted the film to look old-fashioned, Coppola made significant use of old-school film techniques like rear projection, matte painting, multiple exposure, and forced perspective (also used by Peter Jackson in the *Lord of the Rings* films to make, for example, hobbits look small) to create some of his hallucinatory images. He also devoted significant resources to costume design, for which the film won an Academy Award (along with Best Makeup).

Discussion and Writing Suggestions

1. In the first chapter of his novel, Bram Stoker attempts to create an atmosphere of dread. How does Tod Browning strive to create the equivalent sense of dread in his film? Point out particular things that we see and hear that are intended to give us the shivers. To what extent do such images and sounds have the capacity to make us uneasy, or even terrified? To what extent have they become so familiar that they have lost the capacity to disturb us? (Indeed, they may even make us laugh.)

2. We don't meet Dracula in the first chapter of Stoker's novel, but we do in the opening segment of Browning's film—first, when we see him emerge from his coffin in the crypt of the castle, next when he assumes the guise of a coachman and conveys Renfield to the castle, and finally (in our sequence) when he descends the staircase in the great hall of the castle and bids Renfield welcome. How do Browning and actor Bela Lugosi choose to characterize Dracula in this film interpretation of the novel? Compared to the villains of other horror films, what distinguishes this particular fiend of darkness?

3. Coppola's opening scene differs most obviously from Stevenson's in its historical backstory. Instead of beginning (like most Draculas) with the hero traveling through a fearsome landscape toward Castle Dracula, this one begins several centuries earlier with the founding member of the Dracula vampire family. So we see how the original Dracula decides to renounce God in the wake of the suicide of his beloved Elizabeta (which rendered her damned in the eyes of the church), and we see how blood becomes an essential part of the Dracula legend. To what extent do you think Coppola made a good choice in providing this kind of historical background as a prelude to the more modern story set in Victorian times? (Note: This background makes it possible for Dracula to later see in Harker's fiancée Mina the reincarnation of his beloved Elisabeta.)

4. Dramatic imagery is an essential component of all horror films, and certainly of all Draculas. In Tod Browning's film, we are treated to images of coffins (and rats) in moldering crypts. We also see the tuxedo-clad count descending the

stone steps of his vast castle to greet his visitor. Cite images in Coppola's film that are particularly striking. How do they contribute to the mood of the story?

5. In Browning's *Dracula*, we see Renfield on his way to the castle and then being welcomed by Dracula. In Coppola's film, we see him as an inmate of a mental institution, reduced to eating flies while promising to obey his unseen master. (The man traveling to the castle is Jonathan Harker.) To what extent do you think Coppola made the right choice in showing the power of Dracula over his victims before we even see the vampire himself?

6. Compare and contrast Bela Lugosi (in Browning's film) and Gary Oldman (in Coppola's). What qualities does each actor bring to his role that affect our conception of the character?

7. Compare and contrast the two *Draculas* in the way they build suspense in making us want to know what is going to happen next.

Citizen Kane (1941)

Orson Welles, Director
(00:00–3:10)

For about fifty years, *Citizen Kane* (1941) topped the *Sight & Sound* list of greatest films of all time. In 2012, *Kane* was demoted from the top spot (to second place) by Alfred Hitchcock's *Vertigo*. It remains number one, however, on the American Film Institute's list of one hundred greatest American movies. (*Vertigo* is #61 on that list.)

First or second, *Citizen Kane* is certainly one of the most celebrated and influential films ever made. The character of Charles Foster Kane, the newspaper publisher who rose from poverty to enormous wealth and power—and then lost most of his fortune, as well as all of his friends—is based loosely on the life of newspaper magnate William Randolph Hearst (1863–1951), though Welles always denied the connection. Hearst and his lawyers tried to buy up all prints and negatives of the film and have them destroyed, but to its credit, the small studio RKO resisted the legal onslaughts, and *Citizen Kane* survives.

Orson Welles (1915–1985) was an actor, writer, producer, and director who began his career producing Broadway plays and was one of the founders of the Mercury Theater (some of the Mercury Theater veterans worked with him on *Citizen Kane*). One of the Mercury Theater's most notorious productions was a radio adaptation of the novel *The War of the Worlds*, by H. G. Wells, which sent thousands of listeners into a panic on the night of the broadcast when they thought Martians were actually invading Earth from their landing site in Grover's Mill, New Jersey. On the strength of his reputation as a wonder boy (he was twenty-three when he produced *The War of the Worlds*), Welles was invited to Hollywood to produce and direct the movie that became *Citizen Kane.*

The movie flopped commercially (owing partially to pressure from the Hearst interests, which did not allow mention of the film in any of its newspapers) and it did not become a critical success until years later. Meanwhile, the individualistic Welles found it increasingly difficult to work within the collaborative studio system. After he shot his next film, *The Magnificent Ambersons* (based on the novel by Booth

Tarkington), the studio took the film away from him and assigned others to edit and complete it. Welles completed only thirteen more films during his lifetime, including the film noir *A Touch of Evil* (1959), *Chimes at Midnight* (1965), about Shakespeare's character Falstaff, and the celebrated documentary *F Is for Fake* (1973). He also acted memorably in films directed by others, including *Jane Eyre* (1943), *The Lady from Shanghai* (1947), and *The Third Man* (1949).

Citizen Kane has an unusual, nonlinear structure. The film begins by showing the death of Kane, alone (except for a nurse) in his mansion. This is followed by a newsreel announcing his death, and we then see an executive of the studio that produced the newsreel assigning a reporter to dig up more information on Kane. The reporter goes off to talk to the people who knew Kane—his former colleagues and employees and his ex-wife; and he also reads a manuscript memoir written by the lawyer who managed Kane's affairs and who knew him as a child. From these fragmentary accounts emerges a fuller—but not complete—account of the life of Charles Foster Kane.

Discussion and Writing Suggestions

1. *Citizen Kane* opens with a series of striking images, beginning with a "No Trespassing" sign posted on a wire fence. Describe some of those images and speculate about what they might reveal to us about the man who lived in the mansion and whose death concludes the scene. Three minutes into the film, what do you *already know* about Charles Foster Kane?

2. One of the favorite topics of those discussing *Citizen Kane* has been the significance of Kane's dying word, "Rosebud." Viewed in context of the immediately preceding and following images, what do *you* think "Rosebud" might mean?

3. Stylistically (the mists, the darkness, the brooding music), this scene appears to be introducing a horror film. And yet if you look at even the first few seconds or so of the following scene ("News on the March!"), the mood—and the cinematic style—changes 180 degrees. Why might the director, Orson Welles, have thought it was appropriate to begin his film about Kane in this gloomy manner?

Brief Encounter (1945)

David Lean, Director
(00:00–10:30)

For a generation or two of Anglo-American cinephiles, *the* definitive screen romance was *Brief Encounter*, the story of an intense but doomed love affair between a suburban British housewife and an idealistic doctor, both married (more or less happily) to other people. The relationship between Laura Jesson (Celia Johnson) and Alec Harvey (Trevor Howard) is told in flashback, as Laura recalls the affair while riding the train back to her hometown. David Lean's 1945 beautifully photographed black-and-white film, written by playwright, actor, composer, and singer Noel Coward (who collaborated with Lean on three other films), is based on a one-act play by Coward, *Still Life* (1936), and is forever associated with both English railway stations and their refreshment rooms and the romantic melodies of Rachmaninoff's Piano Concerto no. 2, which is featured prominently in the soundtrack.

Brief Encounter was subsequently adapted as a radio play and performed numerous times (with different actors) in the years following Lean's film. It was also readapted into a full-length play and performed both in Britain and the United States. A 1974 television remake, starring Sophia Loren and Richard Burton, was not well received. In 2009, the story was adapted into a two-act opera and performed by the Houston Grand Opera, with music by Andrew Previn. But none of these versions had the emotional impact or the warm reception of Lean's 1945 film, which in 1999 was ranked second in a British Film Institute poll of greatest British films of all time. *Postscript:* In 1980 Celia Johnson and Trevor Howard were reunited on screen (as other characters) in *Staying On*, a TV movie about a British colonel and his wife choosing to remain in India after the British government granted independence to that country in 1947.

See the headnote under *Great Expectations* for information about David Lean. In addition to the films mentioned there, Lean also directed another adaptation from Dickens, *Oliver Twist* (1948); *Breaking the Sound Barrier* (1952); *Ryan's Daughter* (1970); and his final film, *A Passage to India* (1984).

Discussion and Writing Suggestions

1. *Brief Encounter* has long been celebrated as one of the most romantic stories ever committed to film. And yet when we first see Laura Jesson and Dr. Alec Harvey in the station tearoom, we come across them almost accidentally: They are in the background, as if they were extras in a film that's really about the stationmaster and the tearoom attendant, who are having an extended conversation. If you were to watch the entire film (highly recommended!), you would see that David Lean shoots this same scene *twice*—only the second time, toward the end of the film, Laura and Alex are the principals, and the stationmaster and the tearoom attendant are in the background. And the second time around, instead of staying on Laura's friend Dolly Messiter as she orders her chocolate, we follow Laura as she departs the tearoom and walks out to the platform where Alec's train has just left. What do you think might be the dramatic logic behind this unconventional framing of a film romance?

2. Study Laura and Alec's reactions when the gossipy Dolly enters the room and joins them at the table. What can you tell about their relationship, based upon what happens in this scene, up to the time Alec departs the tearoom and Dolly orders her chocolate? How do both Laura and Alec respond to the unwelcome interruption? How does Alec say good-bye to Laura? How does Laura react when Dolly says, "I shall have to telephone Fred [Laura's husband] in the morning and make mischief"? And how do all these reactions suggest what preceded this scene?

3. Indelibly associated with this film are the melodies of Rachmaninoff's Piano Concerto no. 2, which we first hear in the title sequence, and again (in a creative use of sound) when Laura and Dolly are conversing in the train. How does Lean's use of music help create the mood of these scenes—and help establish the tone of the story?

The Red Badge of Courage (1951)

John Huston, Director
(00:00–6:54)

Unlike many other fictional masterpieces that have been filmed repeatedly—think *Jane Eyre* and *Great Expectations*—Stephen Crane's *Red Badge of Courage* has been adapted into only one feature film (1951) and one television movie (1974). There just isn't sufficient broad appeal for movie audiences in Crane's story of a private who worries that he will bolt in the heat of battle—and does, though he redeems himself toward the end. Crane is less concerned with the descriptions of exciting and heroic battles than in the psychological aspects of warfare, and such inward turmoil does not easily translate into entertaining film. Nevertheless, if any American director could succeed in adapting Crane's vision of war to film, John Huston was the person to do it.

John Huston (1906–1987) directed some of the most familiar films in the American repertoire: *The Maltese Falcon* (1941), *Treasure of the Sierra Madre* (1948), *Key Largo* (1948), *The Asphalt Jungle* (1950), *Moulin Rouge* (1942), *The Misfits* (1960), *The Man Who Would Be King* (1975), and *The Dead* (1987). He began his career as a reporter and short story writer (he was also a boxer, a portrait artist, and a cavalry rider in Mexico), and a number of his films were adaptations of great fiction: Melville's *Moby Dick* (1956), James Joyce's "The Dead" (1987), and Stephen Crane's *The Red Badge of Courage* (1951).

The story behind Huston's *The Red Badge of Courage* has been told in one of the best books ever written about the making of a film: Lillian Ross's *Picture* (1952), originally published as a series of articles in the *New Yorker*. Ross describes how excited Huston was to be filming Crane's classic novel and the enormous care he took in adapting the novel to screenplay, and then casting and directing it. She also describes how Huston seemed to lose interest in the project once principal photography was completed, leaving others to work on postproduction and his producer, Gottfried Reinhardt, to argue with the studio, which was never particularly enthusiastic about the film's commercial prospects. While Huston set off to Africa to film his next project, *The African Queen*, with Humphrey Bogart and Katharine Hepburn, the studio trimmed the film's length to a mere seventy minutes and added narration to transition over the deleted material and explain (to those who weren't clear on the subject) the film's meaning.

Henry Fleming, the uncertain hero, is played by Audie Murphy, the most decorated soldier of World War II. The film also features columnist/cartoonist Bill Mauldin as "the loud soldier." *The Red Badge of Courage* flopped at the box office, though the passage of years has yielded increased respect for Huston's mutilated masterpiece.

Discussion and Writing Suggestions

1. The film begins with shots of columns of soldiers on the march, led by their officers. To what extent do you think these shots make for a good opening, dramatically?

2. Comment on the use and the content of the narration we hear during this opening segment, particularly in comparison to Crane's narration at the beginning of the novel.

3. How does Huston *visually* dramatize the way rumors start and spread in this opening segment? How closely does Huston follow Crane at this point?

4. After the rumor sequence, Henry writes to his pa, telling him that the regiment is going into action. "I hope my conduct on the battlefield will make you proud of being my father," he writes. In what way does this action parallel a similar sequence in Crane? Account for the differences.

Shane (1953)

George Stevens, Director
(00:00–8:52)

In some ways, *Shane* is the archetypal Western. A mysterious stranger rides into town (or onto a homestead), assesses the situation that is creating problems for the locals, deals with the problem almost singlehandedly (which inevitably involves gunfire), and then rides out again. Much as he might like to settle down and live a "normal" life, with his own family, he is—partially because of his background, partially because of his temperament—just not that kind of man and will never be accepted as such. We see this motif, in one form or another, in such films as *The Searchers* (1956) and the Clint Eastwood "man with no name films" directed by Sergio Leone—*A Fistful of Dollars* (1964), *For a Few Dollars More* (1964), *The Good, the Bad, and the Ugly* (1966)—as well as the old *Lone Ranger* TV series. In more contemporary terms, we see the same motif in Lee Child's popular "Jack Reacher" novels. Reacher is not a cowboy, of course, but an ex-military cop; like his Western analogues, he comes into town with little more than the clothes on his back, a sense of justice, and a serious capacity to kick butt. After solving the problem, he leaves as quickly as he arrived.

Shane was shot on location near Jackson Hole, Wyoming, against the backdrop of the Grand Tetons; and the contrast between the wide-open spaces of the range and the cramped quarters of the general store and the saloon in the makeshift town is one of the motifs of the film. But the main dramatic conflict is between homesteaders like Joe Starrett and neighbors, on the one hand, and the Ryker brothers, on the other, who own the ranches and need large areas for grazing. The setting is also that of Wyoming's Johnson County War, which was also dramatized in Michael Cimino's *Heaven's Gate* (1980). In 1985 *Shane* was remade by Clint Eastwood as *Pale Rider*.

Montgomery Clift and William Holden were originally cast to play Shane and Joe Starrett, respectively; when both proved unavailable, Alan Ladd and Van Heflin were called upon to replace them. *Shane* was the film debut of Jack Palance, who plays the gunfighter Wilson. Palance was later to star as the count himself in yet another film adaptation of Bram Stoker's *Dracula* (1973). *A somber postscript:* Brandon de Wilde, who played Joey, was killed in a traffic accident in 1972 at the age of 30.

George Stevens was considered one of the greatest classic American filmmakers, directing numerous feature films, shorts, and documentaries (including documentary footage he took while with the troops in World War II). Among his best-known films are *Alice Adams* (1935), *Swing Time* (considered by many the best of the Astaire-Rogers musicals, 1936), *Gunga Din* (1939), *Woman of the Year* (1942), *The Talk of the Town* (1942), *I Remember Mama* (1948), *A Place in the Sun* (1951), *Giant* (1956), *and The Diary of Anne Frank* (1959). His son George Jr. became a successful Hollywood producer.

Discussion and Writing Suggestions

1. In what way is the first image of the film, shot against the magnificent Grand Tetons of Wyoming, representative of numerous other Westerns (including, for example, the Clint Eastwood "man with no name" films) in establishing the kind of story that is to follow?

2. The opening scene of *Shane* introduces us to some of the principals: Shane himself; the boy Joey; his parents, Joe and Marion Starrett; and Ryker, the chief antagonist, and his men. Based upon these characters' behaviors, and their interactions, what predictions can you make about the direction of the main conflict of the story and perhaps how this main conflict is a standard feature of the Western as a genre?

3. Joe Starrett's first words to his son, "Well, let him come," indicate a misapprehension on his part about Shane. But how does this misapprehension foreshadow the conflict to follow?

4. What kind of a man is Shane? What can you tell about his background? In particular, what does he say and what does he do that supports your assessment of him? Now respond to the same questions about Joe Starrett.

5. In Westerns, setting is a crucial element of the reading or viewing experience. Consider the opening segment of *Shane*, both with Joey tracking the stag and watching Shane as he rides toward the homestead, and later with Joe Starrett's account of Ryker's men and the homesteaders. Cite particular images that underline the importance of *place* in grounding the story. What, for example, is the significance of Starrett's men trampling Marian's vegetable garden as they ride away?

6. The gun is a common element of almost all Westerns. How do guns figure in this scene? How do they help set up the story to follow?

Rear Window (1954)

Alfred Hitchcock, Director
(00:00–8:35)

In *Rear Window* director Alfred Hitchcock set himself a formidable technical challenge: to make a feature film entirely from the viewpoint of a man (James Stewart) confined to a wheelchair, his leg in a cast, who can look only around his own apartment and at his various neighbors in the courtyard outside his rear window. Hitchcock relished the challenge. As he explained to François Truffaut (a major filmmaker in his own right), "It was the possibility of doing a purely cinematic film. You have an immobilized man looking out. That's one part of the film. The second part shows what he sees and the third part shows how he reacts."

Alfred Hitchcock (1899–1980), universally known as "the Master of Suspense," had the rare distinction of being a filmmaker who enjoyed both great commercial and great critical success. Considered one of the most influential directors of all time, during his fifty-four-year career (starting in 1922) he directed fifty-seven films. His major British films include *The Lodger* (1926), *Blackmail* (1929), *The Man Who*

Knew Too Much (1934), *The Thirty-Nine Steps* (1935), and *The Lady Vanishes* (1938). In the early 1940s Hitchcock moved to the United States; his first American film was an adaptation of Daphne Du Maurier's novel *Rebecca*. Subsequent films include *Suspicion* (1941), *Shadow of a Doubt* (1943), *Spellbound* (1945), *Notorious* (1946), *Strangers on a Train* (1951), *Dial M for Murder* (1954), *Rear Window* (1954), *To Catch a Thief* (1953), a remake of *The Man Who Knew Too Much* (1956), *The Wrong Man* (1957), *Vertigo* (1958), *North by Northwest* (1958), *Psycho* (1960), *The Birds* (1963), *Marnie* (1964), *Frenzy* (1972), *and Family Plot* (1976).

Hitchcock liked to illustrate the difference between surprise and suspense: Surprise is having a bomb suddenly blow up a bus filled with passengers. Suspense is having the audience *know* that there's a bomb on the bus but *not* know if or when it will detonate. His heroes are typically in physical danger—sometimes pursued both by the bad guys and by the police. They also have character flaws that the action of the film forces them to confront and resolve. (In the case of *Rear Window*, that flaw is voyeurism. As the nurse points out to him at the conclusion of our excerpt, "The New York State sentence for a Peeping Tom is six months in the work-house!"). And his characters are often in an unstable mental state—confused, anxious, obsessive, and so on. Hitchcock is therefore not only the master of suspense, but also the master of the psychological thriller. To reflect the sometimes agitated workings of his hero's mind, Hitchcock employs both editing (action and reaction shots) and a moving camera technique that shows us how what the hero is looking at excites his curiosity, confusion, anxiety, or fear. (Go to YouTube and search for "hitchcock moving observer" to see a fourteen-minute compilation of such Hitchcock clips, showing the hero in motion, looking at something offscreen, then revealing the object of his/her gaze.) For these reasons, both in subject matter and style, it is hard to mistake the films of Alfred Hitchcock for those of any other filmmaker.

Note: The opening sequence referenced here extends to the 8:35 mark, up to the first line by Thelma Ritter, who plays Jefferies's insurance nurse. None of the available YouTube clips extend past four minutes.

Discussion and Writing Suggestions

1. During this sequence, Jefferies has a phone conversation with his editor that provides information about his backstory. But even before this expository contrivance, we learn some key facts about Jefferies. How do Hitchcock's visuals tell us what Jefferies does for a living, how successful he is in his profession, and how he ended up with a cast on his leg? Describe details in the shots that provide information on these matters.

2. What information do we learn from this sequence about Jefferies's neighbors—the people we see from his rear window who live across the courtyard? Demographically, what kind of neighborhood are we viewing?

3. Hitchcock's "cinematic idea" of juxtaposing images to create meaning is exemplified when the moving camera tracks, without a cut, from a long shot of the courtyard to a close-up of Jefferies's sweating forehead as he sleeps next to the window. And Hitchcock uses editing to suggest Jefferies's conflicted reactions to the newlywed couple. Discuss one or two other examples of how Hitchcock creates meaning from the juxtaposition of contrasting images.

4. In "How to Start Your Script," Long discusses the element of tone: "In the first few minutes of any screenplay or film, the tone of the story causes an unconscious expectation to form in the audience's mind as to how they should view the film. Is it serious, funny, somber, light-hearted, etc.?" What visual and soundtrack elements in this opening sequence suggest a comic or light-hearted tone? Which elements suggest a more serious, potentially sinister tone?

5. Assuming that you haven't yet seen the entire film, what guesses can you make about how the plot will unfold? How will a character who is essentially immobilized be able to credibly serve as a protagonist? Who, at this early point, is shaping up as Jefferies's main potential antagonist? Explain.

The Godfather, Part I (1972)

Francis Ford Coppola, Director
(00:00–27:02)

The Godfather is, above all, a film about a successful American family. The family business happens to be organized crime, the family members don't always get along with one another or with people outside the family, and the family sometimes suffers catastrophic reversals as a result of bad decisions made by its members or by members of other families. Still, the family is what we primarily remember about the Corleone saga: Vito, the patriarch (played unforgettably by Marlon Brando), the hot-headed elder son Sonny (James Caan), the weak son Fredo (John Cazale), the quiet but calculating son (and future don) Michael (Al Pacino), the naïve soon-to-be-married daughter Connie (Talia Shire), and the adopted son and consigliere Tom Hagen (Robert Duvall). All these family members—and a great many nonfamily members as well—are introduced to us in the first sequence (the wedding sequence) of *The Godfather, Part I* (1972), directed by Francis Ford Coppola and based on the novel by Mario Puzo.

It's difficult to overestimate the effect that *The Godfather* (1972) and its two sequels (1974 and 1990) had on the American consciousness. Even real mobsters started taking their cues from the way Coppola's characters talked and acted. It became the top-grossing film of 1972. The reviews were almost uniformly ecstatic. Francis Ford Coppola had put his finger on one reason the film resonated so deeply with the public: The action of the film was a metaphor for American capitalism. When Michael is courting Kay, he tells his skeptical bride-to-be that his father is no different from any other powerful man, like a senator or a president. Kay scoffs and retorts that he is being naïve: Senators and presidents don't have men killed. Michael looks at her for a moment: "Oh. Now who's being naïve, Kay?" he asks.

Despite the film's secure place in the American cinematic pantheon (the American Film Institute has it in the #4 position, after *Vertigo*, *Citizen Kane*, and *Casablanca*), *The Godfather* did not have an easy birth. Coppola was not yet an experienced director (though he had cowritten the script for *Patton* in 1970), and the studio was reluctant to hand him the directorial reins. The studio bosses also didn't like Coppola's choices for the top acting roles: Laurence Olivier and Ernest Borgnine were considered for Vito's role; Jack Nicholson, Dustin Hoffman, and Warren Beatty for Sonny's. Coppola was able to prevail, though, as he confessed during an interview, he feared being let go at any time: "*The Godfather* was a very unappreciated movie when we were making it. They were very unhappy with it. They didn't like the cast. They didn't like the way I was shooting it. I was always on the verge of getting fired. So it was an extremely nightmarish experience. I had two little kids, and the third one was born during that. We lived in a little apartment, and I was basically frightened that they didn't like it. They had as much as said that, so when it was all over I wasn't at all confident that it was going to be successful, and that I'd ever get another job."

The film features members of Coppola's own family. Talia Shire, who played Connie, is Coppola's sister; his infant daughter, Sofia (who later became a well-regarded director in her own right), is the baby in the baptism scene; and Coppola's two sons play Tom Hagen's sons. Coppola's father, Carmine, a distinguished composer and conductor, wrote some of the material for the film, supplementing the primary (and more famous) musical score composed by Nino Rota.

Critic John Podhoretz sums up the film's achievement: It is "arguably *the* great American work of popular art."

Discussion and Writing Suggestions

1. The opening segment of *The Godfather* alternates between scenes in Vito Corleone's office and scenes of the wedding celebration outside. How do these alternating scenes represent the two worlds of the Godfather? In what ways are these worlds separate? In what ways do they intersect? Draw upon specific moments in developing your responses.

2. The character and reputation of Vito Corleone is established not only by what he does and says, but also how others respond to what he does and says. How is this character and reputation reflected in this segment by the responses of people like his elder son, Sonny; his adopted son, Tom Hagen; the undertaker Bonasera; the pastry maker Nazorine; and his godson, the singer Johnny Fontane? How is Corleone's character and reputation further established by the story Michael tells to Kay and by the awkward behavior of his enforcer, Luca Brasi?

3. In the first minute or so of the scene between Vito Corleone and Bonasera, we see the don gesture with his hand, and we eventually hear his voice, but the director holds off showing his face until he finally reacts to the undertaker's request for vengeance. What do you think is Coppola's dramatic strategy here?

4. From this opening segment, we could draw up a set of rules of etiquette for high-level mobsters, as well as rules for interacting with the police. Explain some of these unwritten and unspoken rules that define and regulate acceptable behavior, drawing upon particular moments and interactions that you see occurring during the wedding.

5. Select one of the members of the Corleone family—Sonny, Michael, Fredo, Connie, or Tom Hagen—and write a paragraph describing his character, based upon what he or she does and says during this opening segment and by how he or she is treated by others.

Do the Right Thing (1989)

Spike Lee, Director
(00:00–13:22)

Before Spike Lee and *Do the Right Thing* (1989), American films had seldom focused seriously and extendedly on black-white relations. Black people in film were generally presented as slaves, servants or other hired help, noble victims of racial bigotry, or objects of socially forbidden desire. But Lee's film about an explosive few hours for race relations in the Bedford-Stuyvesant neighborhood of Brooklyn on the hottest day of the year was something that audiences had never seen before, something that for years to come occasioned passionate debate and discussion about such topics as "Who's right about the way to deal with racial oppression—Martin Luther King Jr. or Malcolm X?"

Spike Lee has a distinctive vision and a distinctive point of view, but this film is no mere racial polemic with cardboard characters obediently mouthing the views of the author/director. Rather, *Do the Right Thing* is a stylish and exuberant work of filmmaking that is at once passionate, funny, and thought-provoking, with fully rounded human beings who almost jump off the screen with their vividness. Mookie, the pizza delivery man (Lee); Sal, the pizzeria owner (Danny Aiello); Jade (Joie Lee); Da Mayor (Ossie Davis); Mother Sister (Ruby Dee); Buggin' Out (Giancarlo Esposito); Pino (John Turturro); Radio Raheem (Bill Nunn); Tina (Rosie Perez); Señor Love Daddy (Samuel Jackson): All these characters are conceived and brought to life by Lee and his actors with such imagination and individuality that they seem to reside in a fully realized world. But Lee didn't stop with getting the characters right; their environment, their neighborhood also had to be perfect. As Lee recalls in his journal of the film, "The block where the bulk of the film takes place should be a character in its own right. I need to remember my early years for this." Lee recalled the Mr. Softee ice cream truck playing its tune. He wanted the look of the film to be almost blindingly bright. "Everyone will be wearing shorts and cutoff jeans," he wrote. "Men will be shirtless, women in tube tops."

Lee had previously established himself as a major directorial talent with *She's Gotta Have It* (1986), about a woman with three lovers, and *School Daze* (1988), a musical about a man who wants to pledge to a fraternity at an all-black college where lines are drawn between light-skinned and dark-skinned blacks (the film was based on Lee's own experiences at college). The many films Lee directed after *Do the Right Thing* include *Mo' Better Blues* (1990), *Jungle Fever* (1991), *Malcolm X* (1992), *Clockers* (1995), *Girl 6* (1996), *4 Little Girls* (a documentary about the terrorist bombing of an African American church during the civil rights struggles of the 1960s [1997]), *He Got Game* (1998), *The 25th Hour* (2002), *Inside Man* (2006), *The Miracle of Anna* (2008), and *Oldboy* (2013). These films were all made by his production company, 40 Acres and a Mule. That name is an allusion to the broken promise of reparations to former slaves who had worked land before they were freed by the Emancipation Proclamation and who expected—in vain—to be compensated for their decades of forced labor.

Discussion and Writing Suggestions

1. The setting of *Do the Right Thing* is as important to the theme and the mood of this film as is the totally different wide-open-spaces setting of Wyoming in *Shane.* How does the neighborhood inhabited by the characters—first viewed when the camera pulls away from Señor Love Daddy's radio studio to focus

First Impressions: The Art and Craft of Storytelling **353**

on the street outside—become a crucial element in the way that the characters relate to one another?

2. The title sequence of his segment shows Rosie Perez (who plays Tina, Mookie's love interest in the film) dancing to the rhythms of Public Enemy's "Fight the Power." Discuss the way this unusual sequence helps set the tone of what follows.

3. Following the title sequence, we see a number of short scenes that introduce some of the main characters of *Do the Right Thing*: First, we see Señor Love Daddy, the neighborhood radio DJ, and then the elderly "Da Mayor," awakening from sleep. We see Smiley hawking his pictures of "Malcolm and Martin" and, next, pizzeria owner Sal and his two sons, Vito and Pino, arriving at their place of business. And finally we see pizza delivery man Mookie (Spike Lee) and his sister Jade as he counts his money, bothers his sister, and then sets off to work, passing through the Bed-Sty neighborhood on his way to Sal's pizzeria. Focus on one or two of those characters and indicate what we know about them, based on what they say and do (and how others behave toward them) in this opening sequence.

4. Sal and his two sons are clearly an alien presence in this neighborhood. Besides the obvious fact of their skin color, what are some of the other ways we know this? At the same time, what kind of accommodations has Sal, at least, tried to make so that his business becomes as important a part of the community as Señor Love Daddy's radio station?

Dead Again (1991)

Kenneth Branagh, Director
(00:00–7:17)

Films about reincarnation have attracted generations of audiences. Among them: *I've Lived Before* (1956), *Audrey Rose* (1977), *Heaven Can Wait* (1978), *Chances Are* (1989), *Ghost* (1990), *Bram Stoker's Dracula* (1992), *Little Buddha* (1993), *Down to Earth* (2001), and *Cloud Atlas* (2012). People are intrigued by the idea that they may have lived before and may live again. The prospect of getting a second chance, the possibility that the mistakes, problems, and even tragedies of their present life may be set right in a future incarnation is especially appealing.

Kenneth Branagh's *Dead Again* focuses on two young couples who live forty years apart. In the 1940s Roman Strauss (Branagh), a celebrated composer/conductor, is charged with stabbing to death his wife Margaret (Emma Thompson) in a jealous rage. Convicted, Strauss is sentenced to die. In the 1980s, a private detective, Mike Church (Branagh, again) is asked to investigate the identity of an amnesiac woman, "Grace" (Thompson), who cannot or will not speak, and who has recurring nightmares. Church reluctantly accepts the assignment, but then finds himself falling in love with "Grace." The gradual revelation of the unlikely connection between these two couples, one pair dead, the other alive, forms the dramatic action of the film.

Born in Belfast, Ireland, in 1960, Kenneth Branagh has achieved fame as both actor and director. He has appeared on stage both in Ireland and England, and has

also acted in radio and in TV dramas (*Fortunes of War* [1987] and the "Wallander" detective series). But he is most well known for his film adaptations of Shakespeare: *Henry V* (1989), *Much Ado About Nothing* (1993), *Hamlet* (1996), *Love's Labor's Lost* (2000), and *As You Like It* (2006). Other films in which he has served as actor and/or director include *Mary Shelley's Frankenstein* (1994), *Celebrity* (1998), *Harry Potter and the Chamber of Secrets* (2002), *Valkyrie* (2008), and *Thor* (2011). At the time they made *Dead Again*, Branagh and Thompson were married; they later divorced. Branagh is one of the few people who have been nominated for Academy Awards in acting, writing, and directing. In 2015 he announced the formation of the Kenneth Branagh Theatre Company, in which he would serve as actor-manager.

Discussion and Writing Suggestions

1. Summarize in a paragraph the information provided by the visuals in this sequence about how Roman Strauss came to be convicted of murder. In what other ways might the director have conveyed this same key information (i.e., other than with a series of newspaper headlines)?

2. Based on this opening sequence, do you think that Strauss is guilty of murdering his wife? Explain your preliminary conclusions, based upon the filmic cues created by Branagh.

3. How does Branagh use light and shadow to create mood, particularly in the second half of this sequence? Consider, in particular, our first glimpse of Strauss as the barber cuts his hair.

4. What kind of people do Roman Strauss and Grey Baker appear to be? What do you glean about their key character traits? Support your conclusions with evidence from the scene itself. Why do you suppose that Strauss invited Baker to see him just before his execution?

5. Just as the scene closes (with Strauss's scissor blade coming down toward his wife), the director switches from black and white to color. Explain what you think might be the reason for this switch.

Sleepless in Seattle (1993)

Nora Ephron, Director
(00:00–9:45)

Nora Ephron's *Sleepless in Seattle* (1993) is unique among American romantic comedies in that the two lovers (played by Tom Hanks and Meg Ryan), though gravitating toward one another for the entire film, do not actually meet until the final scene, less than three minutes from the end. Despite (or perhaps because of) this narrative quirk, the film struck a chord with audiences and with critics and was nominated for several awards (losing to Jane Campion's *The Piano* for Best Original Screenplay at the Academy Awards). The chemistry between Hanks (who plays grieving widower Sam Baldwin) and Ryan (who plays Annie Reed, engaged to another man) is palpable. (The two were reunited in Ephron's later comedy, *You've Got Mail!* [1998].) And Ross Malinger, who plays Jonah, Sam's young, matchmaking son—a latter-day Emma—is irresistible. Insider note: Rita Wilson, who plays one of Sam's friends trying to cheer him up in this opening sequence, was and is Hanks's wife in real life.

Ephron (1941–2012) also directed *This Is My Life* (1992), *Mixed Nuts* (1994), *and Julia and Julia* (about chef and cookbook author Julia Child 2009). As a director, she frequently collaborated with her screenwriter sister Delia. As a screenwriter herself, she wrote the scripts of *Silkwood* (about Karen Silkwood, the antinuclear activist, 1983), *Heartburn* (a thinly disguised account of her failed marriage with journalist Carl Bernstein, 1986), and *When Harry Met Sally . . .* (another romantic comedy, with Billy Crystal, 1989).

Discussion and Writing Suggestions

1. How does Ephron establish the dramatic situation regarding Sam Baldwin (Tom Hanks) *visually* in the very first shot of the film?

2. In what ways does Ephron dramatize Baldwin's grief over the loss of his wife? Explain how the succession of brief scenes before the credit sequence establishes different facets of Baldwin's emotional state.

3. Based on what you have seen so far, what is likely to be the main conflict in this film? And based on what you have seen so far of Baldwin, how is he likely to deal with this conflict as the film progresses? What kind of a man does he appear to be, under his grief? What does he do or say that makes you think so?

The Devil in a Blue Dress (1995)

Carl Franklin, Director
(00:00–11:10)

The Devil in a Blue Dress is another film dealing with race relations (the hero is black; almost all of his adversaries are white). But unlike *Do the Right Thing*, *Devil* was designed to fit into the preexisting genre of the hardboiled detective film. In this type of film, a detective (or a detective figure) assigned a relatively routine task of discovering the whereabouts of a missing person finds that the more he searches, the deeper he gets entangled in a web of deceit and corruption. One or two murders along the way are meant to deter him from pursuing his investigation any further. But our intrepid detective will not be deterred. As Thomas Schatz writes in his book *Hollywood Genres*, "the hardboiled detective is a cultural middle-man. His individual talents and street-wise savvy enable him to survive within a sordid, crime-infested city, but his moral sensibilities and deep-rooted idealism align him with the forces of social order and the promise of a utopian urban community." As indicated in the following questions, other films of this type include *The Maltese Falcon* (1941), *Double Indemnity* (1944), *The Big Sleep* (1946), *A Touch of Evil* (1958), *Chinatown* (1974), and *L.A. Confidential* (1997).

Based on the novel by Walter Mosley, Carl Franklin's film explores the situation of an African American who loses his job after serving in World War II and, in order to save his house and continue to eat, must accept a dubious assignment. The story is ingeniously plotted and builds up a great deal of suspense as Mosley's hero, Ezekiel ("Easy") Rawlins, played by Denzel Washington, grows ever more assured, if wary, in his new role of dealing with white people on their own terms. Rawlins became so popular a detective that Mosley wrote twelve more novels about him (the last published in 2014). Carl Franklin, who is also an actor, directed *One True Thing* (1998), *High Crimes* (2002), and episodes of television series such as *Rome*, *The Pacific*, *The Newsroom*, *Homeland*, and *House of Cards*.

Discussion and Writing Suggestions

1. *The Devil in a Blue Dress* combines some of the features of the traditional private detective movie—from *The Maltese Falcon* to *Chinatown* to *L.A. Confidential*—with the kinds of themes underlying racially conscious movies such as *Do the Right Thing*. Point out some of the moments in this opening segment where you see these features and themes intersecting. Based on your knowledge of other "private eye" films or even TV police procedurals, where does this story seem to be heading? How will the fact that "Easy" Rawlins is African American appear to factor into where the story is going?

2. Many private-eye films of the 1940s (when the events of this film take place) make use of the kind of voice-over narration introduced in this opening sequence. Thus, when we first see the protagonist, we hear his narration: "It was summer 1948, and I needed money. . . ." We hear such narration periodically as Rawlins comments on what is happening. But storytellers are often warned to "show, not tell." To what extent do you feel that such voice-overs are effective ways of advancing the story or giving it significance? Would your reaction to this particular sequence be any different if there was no voice-over narration? What does the narration provide that would otherwise be difficult to "show"?

3. What do we know about Ezekiel ("Easy") Rawlins, based upon what we see in this opening sequence? What do we see that tells us about his background? What does he say and do that indicates the kind of man he is?

4. K. M. Weiland discusses the importance of setting and orienting readers and viewers with an "establishing" shot. How does Franklin create such a setting in his opening? Start with the image of the mural of Los Angeles that the camera explores under the title credits (to the sound of T-Bone Walker singing "West Side Baby"), and note other shots in this sequence that help establish the L.A. setting.

5. You may have seen Roman Polanski's *Chinatown*, another film about a private detective (played by Jack Nicholson) who seems to be on a routine job but soon enough stumbles into a web of political corruption and deadly threat. To the extent that you recall how Polanski's film opens, how do you think it compares and contrasts to the opening of *The Devil in a Blue Dress* in terms of such elements as the protagonist and the way the plot is launched?

Clueless (1995)

Amy Heckerling, Director
(00:00–14:00)

and

Emma (1996)

Douglas McGrath, Director
(00:00–10:37)

Jane Austen's *Emma* has been adapted into feature films twice (both of these in 1996) and once into a TV miniseries. The version we examine here, starring Gwyneth Paltrow as Austen's matchmaking heroine, was written and directed by Douglas McGrath. (The other 1996 version, also well worth viewing, stars Kate Beckinsale and was directed by Diarmuid Lawrence.) The McGrath film was well reviewed by critics and popular with audiences. Devotees of *The Good Wife* will note that Mr. Elton is played by a very young Alan Cumming. McGrath also directed a film version of Charles Dickens's *Nicholas Nickleby* (2002) and wrote the screenplay of Woody Allen's *Bullets over Broadway* (1994).

Clueless, a contemporary comic version of Austen's novel, set in Beverly Hills (whose teenage residents talk "Valley Speak"—"As if!"), was written and directed by Amy Heckerling and released in 1995. Heckerling makes no attempt to closely track the events recounted in *Emma*; but her film, with its young protagonist who never hesitates to interfere with the love lives of others, is nevertheless broadly recognizable as the story originally devised by Austen. Heckerling also directed *Fast Times at Ridgemont High* (1982), *National Lampoon's European Vacation* (1985), and *Look Who's Talking* (1989).

Discussion and Writing Suggestions

1. Austen begins her novel *Emma* with the following sentence: "Emma Woodhouse, handsome, clever, and rich, with a comfortable home and happy disposition, seemed to unite some of the best blessings of existence; and had lived nearly twenty-one years in the world with very little to distress or vex her." To what extent do the two characters portrayed, respectively, by Gwyneth Paltrow in Douglas McGrath's film and Alicia Silverstone (who plays "Cher") in Amy Heckerling's film display these qualities? How are these same qualities dramatized at particular moments or in particular scenes during the opening sequences of the two films?

2. Describe the common elements in the two versions of *Emma*. How does Amy Heckerling attempt to modernize some of these elements for contemporary audiences? To what extent do you think she has been true to the spirit of Austen? To what extent do you believe that she has significantly distorted Austen's vision of her heroine and the world in which she lives?

3. Find the analogues to Mr. Knightley, Mr. Woodhouse, and Mr. Elton in Amy Heckerling's film. How are the two sets of characters similar? How are they different?

4. Compare and contrast the kind of humor found in Austen's novel and in Douglas McGrath's film with the kind of humor found in *Clueless*. What kinds of things are (1) Austen, (2) McGrath, and (3) Hecklering inviting us to laugh at?

5. Based on what you have seen so far, what are likely to be the main sources of major conflict in Hecklering's film? To what extent does the heroine have a character flaw that is likely to aggravate this conflict? Cite specific moments in each film that support your conclusions.

Chicago (2002)

Rob Marshall, Director
(00:00–10:16)

Chicago has a long history and is based—very loosely—upon actual events. In 1924, the city of Chicago was abuzz over the sensational details of two unrelated murders committed by two women, Beulah Annan and Belva Gaertner, against the men in their lives. The stories were reported by Maurine Dallas Watkins of the *Chicago Tribune*. Watkins's columns proved so popular that she turned them into a play (original title: *Brave Little Woman*) that ran for 172 performances. The murderers were renamed Roxie Hart and Velma Kelly. The following year, Hollywood got into the act when director Cecil B. DeMille directed a silent film based on the events dramatized in the play. In 1942, Ginger Rogers, Fred Astaire's dancing partner, starred in another film version of the story, *Roxie Hart*. In the 1960s, dancer and singer Gwen Verdon read the Watkins play and urged her husband, choreographer Bob Fosse, to convert it into a musical. Watkins refused to sell the rights, but after her death, these rights were sold to Verdon and Fosse, who then commissioned John Kander and Fred Ebb to write music and lyrics. (Kander and Ebb also wrote the music and lyrics to *Cabaret*.)

The Kander/Ebb *Chicago* (set, like the original, in 1926 Chicago) premiered on Broadway in 1975 and ran for two years. The show also had a run in the West End of London, and was revived on Broadway in 1996. This revival was to become the longest-running musical revival, as well as one of the longest-running musicals, in Broadway history. In 2002, *Chicago* was readapted by director Rob Marshall into a film starring Renée Zellweger as Roxie Hart and Catherine Zeta-Jones as Velma Kelly. Richard Gere also features as the lawyer Billy Flynn, a character that is a composite of the original lawyers in the cases, William Scott Stewart and W. W. O'Brien. The columnist and playwright Maurine Dallas Watkins is transformed into Mary Sunshine (Christine Baranski) in the 2002 film.

In his latest version of *Chicago*, Marshall pays tribute to the original musical: He recreated much of Bob Fosse's original, distinctive choreography and even had one of the dancers in the opening number ("All That Jazz") made up to resemble Gwen Verdon. But otherwise, Marshall departs from the 1975 play by staging many of the musical numbers as dream (or daydream) sequences in Roxie's head. This is a technique well established by such films as Federico Fellini's *8½* (1962), David Lynch's *Mulholland Drive* (2001), Alejandro Amenábar's *The Others* (2002), and, since then, Christopher Nolan's *Inception* (2010).

Rob Marshall has also directed *Memoirs of a Geisha* (2005), based on the novel by Arthur Golden; *9* (2009), a sequel of sorts to Federico Fellini's *8½*, and *Pirates of the Caribbean: On Stranger Tides* (2011).

Discussion and Writing Suggestions

1. *Chicago* opens with a close-up of a pair of eyes that becomes an extreme close-up of a single eye. This shot is mirrored later on in the sequence. At what point does this second eye shot occur, and what does it signify for Roxie's state of mind, both at this particular moment and in terms of the film as a whole and the dramatic approach of the songs in this sequence ("All That Jazz" and "Funny Honey")?

2. We first meet Velma Kelly when she emerges from the cab; the camera then follows her as she enters the club, rushes upstairs to her dressing room, and puts on her costume in preparation for her performance. We have not yet seen her face (and won't until the spotlight falls upon her face in the "All That Jazz" number), but the director has already given us crucial information about this character. What do we see and hear during this pre–song sequence that helps establish who Roxie is and what she has done?

3. By the end of this opening sequence, both Velma Kelly and Roxie Hart have been arrested and jailed for separate murders. How does director Rob Marshall indicate that these women are dramatically tied together? In particular, how does he use song and dance to help establish their relationship, both when they are in the club and when Roxie has gone with her lover to her apartment?

4. Musicals are always balancing precariously on the edge of credibility, because audiences, particularly modern audiences, have a hard time believing that characters will suddenly break out into song and dance when the impulse hits them. How does Marshall attempt to solve this problem, particularly in his staging of Roxie's "Funny Honey" song? How do reality and dramatic artifice blend here? To what extent did you find this solution effective?

The Hurt Locker (2008)

Kathryn Bigelow, Director
(00:00–9:58)

Conventional war films, even those as psychologically oriented as *The Red Badge of Courage*, typically feature set-piece battles between opposing armies or perhaps special missions by a "dirty dozen" or so of soldiers sent to destroy a key enemy fortress. Kathryn Bigelow's *The Hurt Locker* (2008) features no such battles or triumphant missions: It follows an army EOD (explosive ordinance disposal) team for several months in Baghdad in the aftermath of the U.S. invasion of Iraq (2003 and the years following). Based on the experiences of journalist Mark Boal (who also served as screenwriter) when he was embedded with U.S. troops in Iraq, *The Hurt Locker* shows how small bomb-disposal teams attempt to defuse bombs in an urban setting before they explode, killing and maiming civilians and the bomb-disposal personnel themselves. Sometimes they succeed; sometimes they don't.

The film stars Jeremy Renner as Sergeant First Class William James, a team leader. Though we don't see James in this first segment, we do see the bomb-disposal mission that made him the new team leader, and therefore we view the new kind of war that American soldiers were fighting in Iraq. Nothing quite like this had been seen before in an American feature film. (One precursor was *Danger UXB*, a 1979 British television series about a bomb-disposal unit that defused unexploded bombs that fell on London during the German blitz of World War II.) But the film resonated with both audiences and critics. *New York Times* critic A. O. Scott wrote: "You may emerge from *The Hurt Locker* shaken, exhilarated and drained, but you will also be thinking. . . . The movie is a viscerally exciting, adrenaline-soaked tour de force of suspense and sur- prise, full of explosions and hectic scenes of combat, but it blows a hole in the conde- scending assumption that such effects are just empty spectacle or mindless noise." *The Hurt Locker* won six Academy Awards, including Best Picture, Best Director, Best Original Screenplay, and Best Editing, Sound Editing, and Sound Mixing.

Educated at the San Francisco Art Institute and later at Columbia University Film School, Bigelow directed *Point Break* (1991) and *Strange Days, K-19: The Widowmaker* before making *The Hurt Locker*. She has since directed *Zero Dark Thirty* (2012), about the CIA team that hunted down and planned the killing of Osama bin Laden.

Discussion and Writing Suggestions

1. Note the epigraph to the film by journalist Chris Hedges at the outset. How does director Kathryn Bigelow begin to demonstrate the truth of this epi- graph during the first scene?

2. Discuss some of the ways the director builds suspense. Consider, in particu- lar, how, cinematically, she ratchets up the tension toward the end of the segment before and during the explosion of the bomb.

3. How does the director reveal the relationship between the soldiers of the bomb-disposal group and the surrounding populace as the scene proceeds? In what ways does this relationship drive the main conflict within this open- ing segment?

4. In what ways are the various emotions experienced by the bomb-disposal team, including Sergeant Thompson, dramatized during this scene?

5. In what ways do elements of the setting—the buildings, the street, the vehicles (the "bot," the Humvee, the helicopter) play a dramatic role in this segment? Note in particular the first shot of the film. Why open with such a shot?

Inception (2010)

Christopher Nolan, Director
(00:00–15:38)

Inception is only one of the more recent films to focus on dreams—and more spe- cifically, on deliberately leaving audiences uncertain about whether the action they are watching on screen is dream or "reality" (however one defines that). One of the earliest dream films was Robert Wiene's expressionistic and silent *Cabinet of Dr. Caligari* (1920). A considerably more straightforward example of a film narrative that turned out to be largely a dream was Victor Fleming's 1939 classic, *The Wizard of Oz* (1939). A few years later, Alfred Hitchcock's *Spellbound* (1945), a psychiatric drama heavily influenced by Freud's theories, thrilled audiences with dream sequences designed by the surrealist painter Salvador Dali.

The plot of *Inception* concerns a high-tech master of corporate espionage, Dom Cobb (Leonardo DiCaprio), whose particular skill is *extraction*, stealing business secrets by means of entering the vulnerable dream states of his targets. Cobb generally operates on the fringes of the law, but he has opened himself up to a charge of murdering his wife Mal (Marion Cotillard), who actually committed suicide because she believed that she was dreaming and that her "death" would cause her to "wake up" to reality. The dramatic action is set in motion when a powerful client, Saito (Ken Watanabe), promises to make the homicide charge go away if Cobb and his team, including Arthur (Joseph Gordon-Leavitt), Ariadne (Ellen Page), and Eames (Tom Hardy), succeed in performing a task even more difficult than extraction, namely, *inception*—implanting an idea in the mind of a business rival.

The first sequence of *Inception* provides an exciting—and instructive—introduction to its dream world. As you watch this sequence, be on the alert for the various levels of dream and reality represented. One way to distinguish these levels in the film is by simply noting the characters' immediate environments and what they are wearing. How can you tell (if at all) whether the characters are awake in the "real world"? Or whether they are dreaming? And if they are dreaming, are they in a level-1 dream or a level-2 dream—that is, a dream within a dream? (Have you ever dreamed that you were having a dream?) Perhaps they are even in a level-3 dream—a dream within a dream within a dream. Note also the different ways in which dreamers can be awakened—peacefully or violently.

Born in London in 1970, Christopher Nolan, who wrote and directed *Inception*, is one of today's most creatively ambitious, as well as commercially successful, directors. His films typically explore philosophical, psychological, and ethical issues, and play, in a visually dazzling manner, with concepts of time and memory. His other films—often in collaboration with his brother Jonathan—include *Memento* (2000), whose story is told backwards, *Insomnia* (2002), *The Prestige* (2006), *Interstellar* (2012), the Batman trilogy, *Batman Begins* (2005), *The Dark Knight* (2008), and *The Dark Knight Rises* (2012), and most recently *Dunkirk* (2017).

Discussion and Writing Suggestions

1. The "teaser" to *Inception* (see Tim Long's article) shows Dom face down on the edge of the ocean, falling in and out of consciousness, while catching a glimpse of two frolicking children. In the next scene he talks to the ancient Saito, who tells him that the spinning top on his table is like one that "belonged to a man I met in a half-remembered dream, a man possessed of some radical notions." How do these first moments of the film provoke your curiosity? What do we need to learn in order to begin to understand this enigmatic opening?

2. This sequence dramatizes several layers of consciousness—the waking state and at least two levels of dream states (i.e., dreams and dreams within dreams). What kind of visual and auditory cues does the director provide that indicate which layer of consciousness we are witnessing at any given time? How do elements of one level manifest themselves intruding into another level? Point to key transition points between these layers and indicate how they function in suggesting that the character's level of consciousness has changed.

3. During this opening sequence, the director provides both visual and auditory clues that what we are watching is a dream, rather than "reality." For example, notice the multiple close-ups of the ticking watch. What is "off" about this image? See if you can identify some additional cues that tip us off to the fact that we are inside a dream.

4. One of the key motifs in *Inception* is the troubled relationship between Dom (DiCaprio) and his wife Mal (Cotillard). Based upon their interchanges in this sequence—as well as comments to Dom made by Arthur (Gordon-Levitt)—what can we surmise about the backstory of this marriage?

5. Almost all science-fiction stories attempt to account—with various degrees of plausibility—for some of the technical aspects of the action. In films about outer space, we see the kind of vessels that transport the characters from one world to another. Time-travel films explain to us the devices that enable characters to move backward and forward in time. What can we gather from this sequence in *Inception* about the capabilities and limitations of the technology that allows some people to inhabit other people's dreams—including the means that are used to put them into their dreamlike state and then to wake them up?

Gravity (2013)

Alfonso Cuarón, Director
(00:00–13:08)

Many science fiction films set in outer space take for granted the vastly different environmental and existential differences between earth and space. In the *Star Wars* and *Star Trek* films, vessels of every size and shape hurtle through the void, and their human passengers move on and off them and then land on their destination planets as if all of this were a logistical problem no more complex—or hazardous—than getting on and off the bus. The hokey adventures and thrilling battles they experience might just as well be taking place on earth, or over the blue skies of our planet.

A few films set in outer space have not taken the realities of space travel for granted. They have focused their action on the sheer wonder of the experience, on the sense of isolation experienced by space travelers, and on the extreme danger of the environment and the potentially catastrophic effects of something going wrong (for instance, an equipment malfunction). In this category we find Stanley Kubrick's *2001: A Space Odyssey* (1968). We also find *Marooned* (1969), *Apollo 13* (1995), *and Moon* (2009), all of which deal with the psychological problems caused by isolation in space and the frightening sense of being cut off from the rest of humanity, as well as the physical dangers of being a thin wall of metal or glass away from annihilation.

Alfonso Cuarón's *Gravity* (2013) was for many viewers as revelatory and exhilarating a space film experience as was *2001* in its time. Like Kubrick's film, *Gravity* is also a visual feast. We see broad—and deep—vistas of space stations and astronauts. We are dazzled by the artful and often beautiful technology, shown in precise and loving detail, necessary to sustain life and allow scientific activity. All this is both delightful and scary to watch. And like both *2001* and *Apollo 13*, *Gravity* is a story about survival in the face of almost insurmountable odds. In fact, one can reach much further back, to the beginning of narrative, to find story analogs: *Gravity* is like Homer's *Odyssey* in that both are stories about a protagonist who finds him/herself far from home and who must carefully negotiate a series of dangerous obstacles using his/her wits and whatever physical and emotional resources she/he can summon to surmount the obstacles and succeed in safely returning home. The relatively few critics who complained about *Gravity* having no story seemed unaware that the film was following the path of one of the oldest—and most resonant—stories of all.

Gravity, released in 3D, was hugely popular with both audiences and critics. Justin Chang, of *Variety*, for example, wrote that the film "restores a sense of wonder, terror and possibility to the big screen that should inspire awe among critics and audiences worldwide." By April 2014, *Gravity* had grossed almost $300 million in North America and almost $450 million in other countries. It won seven Academy Awards, including Best Director, Best Cinematography, Best Visual Effects, and Best Film Editing.

One of the many notable features of *Gravity* is that it contains fewer shots and longer shots than almost any other film of its length. Cuarón choreographed both his camera and his actors so as to follow the action as long as possible. The first shot of the film is a tour de force of camera and human choreography. The camera runs continuously for more than thirteen minutes from the first moment that we see the curve of the earth to the moment we see the image of Dr. Stone, separated from her tether, hurtling head over heels away from us.

Alfonso Cuarón is one of Mexico's premier film directors, one of the "three amigos" of Mexican cinema (along with Guillermo del Toro and Alejandro González Iñárritu). Often working with his brother Carlos and his son Jonás, Cuarón has also directed *Y Tu Mamá También (2001)*, *Harry Potter and the Prisoner of Azkaban (2004)*, and *Children of Men* (2006). He also directed a film adaptation of Dickens's *Great Expectations*, with Gwyneth Paltrow, in 1998.

Discussion and Writing Suggestions

1. Two of the goals of a story's opening are to reveal key information and to establish the story's stakes. How does Cuarón attempt to achieve these goals in the first thirteen minutes of *Gravity*?

2. *Gravity* is a visual spectacle, but the director and screenwriter are careful to establish the differing personalities of the two main characters from the outset. In this first long sequence, what do we find out about the characters of Dr. Ryan Stone and Commander Matt Kowalski? What do they say and do that helps establish their characters?

3. The setting of *Gravity*—"600 kilometers above planet Earth"—is perhaps the most important element of the film. Point out particular moments in this first scene that indicate how the setting helps establish the essential plotline of the story, the development of character, and the shape of the conflict.

4. The astonishing single shot that makes up this opening sequence involves numerous complicated camera movements. How does Cuarón use the camera to follow the action and the characters from one point of view to another to develop the story in a logical and dramatically effective order?

12 Years a Slave (2013)

Steve McQueen, Director
(00:00–6:00)

The film epic *Gone with the Wind* (1939) opens with scenes of slaves picking cotton. They seem happy enough, if not exactly whistling while they work. As the credits roll, we are told by the narrator that what should distress us about this opening is that it represents a way of life that has ceased to exist. In other words, to the makers of *Gone with the Wind*, the distressing fact is not slavery itself, but rather that the gracious life of the old South that depended for its existence on slave labor is no more:

> There was a land of Cavaliers and Cotton Fields called the old South. . . . Here in this pretty world, Gallantry took its last bow. . . . Here was the last ever to be seen of Knights and their Ladies Fair, of Master and of Slave. . . . Look for it only in books for it is no more than a dream remembered. A Civilization gone with the wind.

In the years that followed, Hollywood continued to portray slaves in movies set before the Civil War, though not quite in so elegiac a manner. The injustice was recognized, if not directly confronted. It was not until a 1976 television miniseries called *Roots* (based upon Alex Haley's novel about slavery in the United States) that American viewers were given their first hard look at the realities of slavery. Some feature films treated slavery more or less honestly: *Glory* (1989), *Jefferson in Paris* (1995), *Amistad* (1997), *Beloved* (1998), and *Lincoln* (2012). But until Steve McQueen's *12 Years a Slave* (2013), no film had presented the day-to-day reality of slavery in all of its ugly brutality—the daily humiliations and savage beatings, the separation of husband from wife and parents from children, the appalling living and working conditions, the inhumanity of the slave masters.

The film *12 Years a Slave* is based on the memoir of Solomon Northrop, a free man, a musician, living in New York State with his wife and family. After he had been lured to Washington, D.C. on the pretext of a temporary job performing music, Northrop was drugged and sold into slavery. As a slave, he worked on Louisiana plantations for twelve years before he was released through the intervention of friends in the North. The film won three Academy Awards, including Best Picture of 2013.

In an interview with NPR (National Public Radio), director Steve McQueen explained what impelled him to make the film: "I read this book, and I was totally stunned. At the same time I was pretty upset with myself that I didn't know this book. I live in Amsterdam where Anne Frank is a national hero, and for me this book read like Anne Frank's diary but written 97 years before—a firsthand account of slavery. I basically made it my passion to make this book into a film." McQueen, who is British, has directed many short films. In addition to *12 Years a Slave*, he directed two other feature films, *Hunger* (2008) and *Shame* (2011).

Discussion and Writing Suggestions

1. What is the dramatic situation at the beginning of *12 Years a Slave*? Consider the role of dialogue in this opening segment in establishing the dramatic situation, as opposed to visual detail and what we hear on the soundtrack. Cite two or three key visual details in particular shots that help vividly create this dramatic situation.

2. What hints of future developments for main character Solomon Northrop do you detect in this opening? How does the director contrast Northrop's present with his past?

3. Based on what you see of him in this opening segment, what kind of man does Northrop appear to be? How does he respond to the situation in which he finds himself?

4. Compare the treatment of slavery in this film opening to the treatment in other films you have seen that have depicted slavery: for instance, *The Birth of a Nation*, *Gone with the Wind*, *Amistad*, *Beloved*, and *Django Unchained*.

Moonlight (2016)

Barry Jenkins, Director
(00:00–10:36)

The coming-of-age story focuses on the transition of the protagonist from one stage of life to the next—from childhood to adolescence and/or from adolescence to adulthood. During this transition, the protagonist undergoes not only physical change—often including a growing sexual awareness—but also emotional or spiritual growth. Such stories focus less on external action and more upon personal interaction through dialogue and other means. Noteworthy coming-of-age films include *The Graduate* (1967), *The Last Picture Show* (1971), *American Graffiti* (1973), *The Breakfast Club* (1985), *Dazed and Confused* (1993), *Y Tu Mamá También* (2001), *Boyhood* (2014), and *The Edge of Seventeen* (2016). Barry Jenkins, director of *Moonlight* (2016), observed, "When I think about how I came of age, it was usually at very specific moments." Such key moments form the overall structure of this film, which shows us the protagonist Chiron at three pivotal points in his life, first as a child of 7, next as a teenager, and finally as a young man. In *The Hollywood Reporter* David Rooney calls *Moonlight* "a haunting reflection on African-American masculinity . . . an intimate character study [that] traces the life of a black gay man from his troubled Miami childhood to maturity."

The film is based upon a previously unpublished (and semi-autobiographical) play, *In Moonlight Black Boys Look Blue*, by Tarell Alvin McCraney. This drama was adapted into a screenplay by Barry Jenkins, who also directed the film. Jenkins's only previous film was the 2008 drama *Medicine for Melancholy*. *Moonlight* won both the Golden Globe award for best drama and the Motion Picture Academy award for best picture of 2016.

Different actors portray Chiron during each of the film's three main segments. While shooting in Miami, director Jenkins made sure that these three actors (Alex Hibbert as the child; Ashton Sanders as the teenager; and Trevante Rhodes as the young man) did not meet before filming was under way so that they would not be tempted to imitate one another. But such was the quality of the acting and the unity of dramatic conception that most viewers have little trouble believing that these three actors are portraying the same person at different stages of life.

Discussion and Writing Suggestions

1. What do we learn about the character and temperament of Juan (the drug dealer) from this opening sequence? Consider such elements as the initial images of him arriving at his neighborhood place of business, as well as his conversations with Terrence (his street man), his initial meeting with Chiron, and the sequences in the restaurant and his and Theresa's apartment.

2. Jeremy Kleiner, one of the producers of *Moonlight*, noted that the child actor who played Chiron in the first of this film's three segments "is essentially a silent film actor," because in the silent film period (before the 1930s), actors had to communicate character and emotion almost entirely through facial expression, along with their gestures and bodily movements. How does Alex R. Hibbert, who plays the "little" Chiron, communicate character and emotion without speaking?

3. Film critic Brian Tallerico (writing for the "RogerEbert.com" website), pointed out that *Moonlight* "is one of those rare pieces of filmmaking that stays completely focused on its characters while also feeling like it's dealing with universal themes about identity, sexuality, family, and, most of all, masculinity." Cite images and dialogue from this opening sequence that dramatize some of these themes.

4. Earlier in this chapter, K. M. Weiland ("The Hook") discusses some of the traits shared by "the perfect opening," including considerations of character, conflict, movement, setting, and tone. Explain how some of these traits are exemplified in the opening sequence of *Moonlight*. For instance, what components of recent and potential future conflict do you notice? How does the setting contribute to the meaning of this sequence? How do the director and cinematographer use camera movement (both smooth movement and jumpy movement) to create drama and meaning? (Look up A. O. Scott's *New York Times* review of *Moonlight*, using MRQE [the Movie Review Query Engine], and click on the embedded video in which director Barry Jenkins discusses and demonstrates his techniques in the opening segment of the film.)

Synthesis Activities

1. Discuss one of the Chapter Ones in terms of how it meets (or does not meet) the criteria for effective openings as discussed by Tim Long and K. M. Weiland.

2. If you didn't particularly care for one of the Chapter Ones, then take on the role of editor. Write an "editorial memo" back to the author in which you advise him or her how to revise the first chapter in order to improve it. In making your case, refer to the criteria offered by Weiland and Long. And please remember that authors are people, too—so you'll want your memo to be honest yet diplomatic.

3. Readers who love a particular novel are frequently disappointed with the film adaptation. Why do you think this might be so? Choose the Chapter One you liked most and explain what would be easiest and hardest about adapting the chapter for film. If the novel you choose has already been adapted for film (many of them have, several times over), go ahead and watch the opening scene—or better still, the full movie—and report on the results.

4. Weiland and Long have offered advice for writing successful fiction and screenplays. There are hundreds, perhaps thousands, of such guides, and it's safe to say that no one offers definitive advice. Perhaps you have some insights not mentioned by Weiland and Long about what makes for an effective opening. If so, define these criteria clearly and illustrate them by referring to several of the Chapter Ones you've read here.

5. Discuss one of the film openings discussed in this chapter in terms of how it meets (or does not meet) the criteria for effective openings covered by Tim Long and K. M. Weiland.

6. Select two film openings that seem to you to represent entirely different modes of presenting character, plot, or setting. Compare and contrast the apparent strategies of the filmmakers, referring as necessary to the articles by Weiland and Long.

7. We've introduced four films with at least two adaptations each: *Emma* (pages 61–62), *Dr. Jekyll and Mr. Hyde* (pages 41–43), *Pride and Prejudice* (pages 38–39), and *Dracula* (pages 45–47). Select one of these stories and compare and contrast the adaptations. Consider how each film of your selected pair introduces its main character. How does each presentation affect your initial impression of the character? Compare and contrast also the dramatic situations of the first sequence of each film—that is, the introduction to the plot. Finally, compare and contrast the settings in each film and the way in which the setting contributes to the emotional power of the introduction. Which film in either

of these pairs do you prefer, and why? For *Dr. Jekyll and Mr. Hyde* and *Pride and Prejudice*, feel free to compare and contrast the first scene of each film with the first scene in its respective novel (pages 23–26 and 13–15).

8. Decide which of these film openings appeals to you most, and then watch the entire movie. Watch a second time and keep careful notes on how the questions raised in the opening scene resonate throughout the film. That resonance may involve character, plot, mood, theme, or some other element essential to the film's success. Write an explanatory paper in which you carefully "deconstruct"—or break down element by element—the opening scene and then trace its impact throughout the rest of the film.

9. Assuming you have watched four or five of the opening scenes presented in this chapter, think "large" and argue that two or three qualities you will define and discuss are essential to making an opening succeed. You will need to define "success." You will also need to define the elements you will be putting forward as essential. As evidence for your argument, refer generously to scenes (or partial scenes). As needed, draw upon the work of Long and/or Weiland to help you make your case.

10. In our collection of Chapter Ones and notes on the corresponding film adaptations, we find four stories that concern orphans: Dorothy Gale in *The Wizard of Oz*, Jim Burden in *My Ántonia*, Pip in *Great Expectations*, and Jane in *Jane Eyre*. In what ways does each child's parentless condition shape his or her respective Chapter One or opening scene? Make a close observation of each of these Chapter Ones and films and then synthesize your observations in a well-reasoned argument.

Chapter 12
Artificial Intelligence

FRANK: Look, Dave, I can't put my finger on it, but I sense something strange about him [the HAL 9000 computer controlling the spaceship]. . . . There isn't a single aspect of ship operations that's not under his control. If he were proven to be malfunctioning, I wouldn't see how we'd have any choice but disconnection.

DAVE: . . . Be a bit tricky. . . . We'd have to cut his higher brain functions without disturbing the purely automatic and regulatory systems. . . . as far as I know, no 9000 computer has even been disconnected.

FRANK: Well, no 9000 computer's ever fouled up before.

DAVE: That's not what I mean. . . . I'm not so sure what he'd think about it.

The deep space explorers of Stanley Kubrick's *2001: A Space Odyssey* (1968) encounter a problem increasingly familiar to us today: they are completely reliant on computers for the success of their objectives; and if these machines don't work the way they're supposed to, people will no longer be able to function in their increasingly complex environments. Of course, we're not yet at the stage where we have to fear intelligent computers planning to disconnect *us*; but could that day arrive sooner than we think?

With the rapid increase in computing power (doubling every two years) we find computers ever more entwined in our lives: translating speech into text and multiple languages, following trends in the financial markets and making lightning—sometimes disastrous—trades; regulating the flow of electricity to our homes, and much, much more. The latest generation of Apple's Siri and Google's Alexa answer your spoken questions in a way somewhat reminiscent of HAL in a good mood. Ask them if the weather's likely to change, and they may respond, "I don't think the weather is going to get worse." Think of all the ways computers touch your life every day—from the papers you write to the traffic lights that direct your driving to the ubiquitous use of cell phones. Western civilization without computers is unthinkable; "disconnection" isn't an option. What, then, if the computers on which we rely so heavily become able to think for themselves? In which ways would we welcome the development? In what ways might we fear it? How might we grow lazy as computers take over an ever-expanding roster of chores? In a thousand years, ten thousand, how might our notion of the "human" change?

The science fiction visions of robots and self-aware computers go back almost one hundred years. They include Czech playwright Karel Capek's *Rossum's*

Universal Robots (1920), Isaac Asimov's *I Robot* (1950), Ridley Scott's *Blade Runner* (1982), the *Alien* and *Terminator* films, and Steven Spielberg's *A.I.* (2001), about an android who thinks he's really a young boy. In some cases, the intelligent nonhumans are benevolent; in most cases, they are malevolent, or at least have agendas that are at cross-purposes with those of their human creators. But how close are we to creating intelligent robots (machines that take somewhat humanoid form) or self-aware computers? Estimates vary, but futurist Raymond Kurzweil believes that we may reach this so-called singularity in as few as thirty years: the point at which "computers will become not just intelligent but more intelligent than humans. At that point 'humanity'—our bodies, our minds, our civilization—will be completely and irreversibly transformed."

Could Kurzweil be right? The answer depends on how we define *intelligence*. If an interrogator communicates via computer with both another human being and another computer and cannot tell, from the printed responses, which is which—the famous, so-called Turing test (see pp. 425–427)—would we call *that* machine intelligent? Intelligent or not, the IBM computer "Watson" defeated two previous (human) champions in *Jeopardy!* Computers now regularly play and beat chess grandmasters. Google's DeepMind program has for the first time defeated a champion of Go—a game so complex it has been likened to playing multiple games of chess at the same time on the same board. What's the significance of these achievements? What do they portend for the future relationship of humans and computers? Will humans still be necessary—if for no other reason than to serve computers?

Such questions invite real, no longer speculative, answers. This chapter invites you to consider these developments and to contemplate the once unthinkable: the "mind" of a machine. Reading selections are grouped into clusters. First come selections on the prospect and implications of humanity's breaking free of biological evolution through the design and application of a new, silicon-based intelligence. George Luger reviews "The Legacy of Prometheus," the myth of the Greek god who stole fire from Olympus and gave it to humans, making possible all subsequent technology. In an online interview, historian Yuval Harari questions the premise that our current bodies represent the pinnacle of human evolution. Tech writer Carolyn Mathas sets in opposition the views of futurist Ray Kurzweil and tech giant Bill Joy and asks: Can technologies ever be *un*invented? Two public documents that build on these concerns follow: first, an Open Letter signed by eight thousand scientists and technologists cautioning that true artificial, autonomous intelligence will be so powerful that we must now plan how to guide and contain it; second, in light of artificial intelligence's (AI's) promise and potential harm, a resolution that the European Union adopt a carefully thought through program of support and regulation. The opening cluster of readings concludes with an online keynote lecture that summarizes the doomsday scenarios of Oxford AI philosopher Nick Bostrom and then emphatically rejects these scenarios. In his critique, tech veteran Maciej Ceglowski argues that the panic over the coming AI apocalypse isn't warranted based on what we know of the technology.

The chapter's second cluster of readings opens with a more neutral view of what Dominic Basulto regards as a likely "hybrid evolution" of silicon and biology. Three selections then consider the effects of AI on work. Scott Santens investigates why "Robots Will Take Your Job"; an economist reviews a book that insists humans possess irreplaceable skills and intuitions; and an article from *The Economist* magazine explores work-related anxieties concerning automation. In the chapter's final selections, we include a review of HBO's hit series *Westworld*, the story of a Wild West theme park populated by robotic actors. In a creepy, fascinating twist, the robots are more appealing and humane than their human creators and customers. We conclude with an explanation of the famous Turing test, a widely used touchstone for determining whether or not a computer is intelligent. Then it's time for some game playing: Can you determine whether a particular sonnet was written by a human or by a computer? How about distinguishing between a real Rembrandt and a painting rendered by algorithms to look like one? You will listen to AI-generated music and converse with AI-powered Chatbots. The goal of these readings is to open a window that allows you to form your own opinions about the promise and perils of AI.

The Legacy of Prometheus

George Luger

Humans are the only animals capable of using technology—of building complex tools and machines to alter their environment. The controlled use of fire was so central to this capability that it inspired the myth of Prometheus, whose gift of fire to humans was punished severely by the gods. In the selection that follows, George Luger recounts the story. The following selection first appeared in Luger's *Artificial Intelligence: Structures and Strategies for Complex Problem Solving*, 6th ed. (2009). Luger teaches in the computer science, psychology, and linguistics departments at the University of New Mexico.

[The myth of] Prometheus speaks of the fruits of his transgression against the gods of Olympus: his purpose was not merely to steal fire for the human race but also to enlighten humanity through the gift of intelligence or *nous*: the *rational mind*. This intelligence forms the foundation for all of human technology and ultimately all human civilization. The work of Aeschylus, the classical Greek dramatist, illustrates a deep and ancient awareness of the extraordinary power of knowledge. Artificial intelligence, in its very direct concern for Prometheus's gift, has been applied to all the areas of his legacy—medicine, psychology, biology, astronomy, geology—and many areas of scientific endeavor that Aeschylus could not have imagined.

Though Prometheus's action freed humanity from the sickness of ignorance, it also earned him the wrath of Zeus. Outraged over this theft of knowledge that previously belonged only to the gods of Olympus, Zeus commanded that Prometheus be chained to a barren rock to suffer the ravages of the elements for eternity. The notion that human efforts to gain knowledge constitute a transgression against the laws of God or nature is deeply ingrained in Western thought. It is the basis of the story of Eden and appears in the work of Dante and

Milton. Both Shakespeare and the ancient Greek tragedians portrayed intellectual ambition as the cause of disaster. The belief that the desire for knowledge must ultimately lead to disaster has persisted throughout history, enduring the Renaissance, the Age of Enlightenment, and even the scientific and philosophical advances of the nineteenth and twentieth centuries. Thus, we should not be surprised that artificial intelligence inspires so much controversy in both academic and popular circles.

Indeed, rather than dispelling this ancient fear of the consequences of intellectual ambition, modern technology has only made those consequences seem likely, even imminent. The legends of Prometheus, Eve, and Faustus have been retold in the language of technological society. In her introduction to *Frankenstein*, subtitled, interestingly enough, *The Modern Prometheus*, Mary Shelley writes:

> Many and long were the conversations between Lord Byron and Shelley to which I was a devout and silent listener. During one of these, various philosophical doctrines were discussed, and among others the nature of the principle of life, and whether there was any probability of its ever being discovered and communicated. They talked of the experiments of Dr. Darwin (I speak not of what the doctor really did or said that he did, but, as more to my purpose, of what was then spoken of as having been done by him), who preserved a piece of vermicelli in a glass case till by some extraordinary means it began to move with a voluntary motion. Not thus, after all, would life be given. Perhaps a corpse would be reanimated; galvanism had given token of such things: perhaps the component parts of a creature might be manufactured, brought together, and endued with vital warmth (Butler 1998).

5   Mary Shelley shows us the extent to which scientific advances such as the work of Darwin and the discovery of electricity had convinced even nonscientists that the workings of nature were not divine secrets, but could be broken down and understood systematically. Frankenstein's monster is not the product of shamanistic incantations or unspeakable transactions with the underworld: it is assembled from separately "manufactured" components and infused with the vital force of electricity. Although nineteenth-century science was inadequate to realize the goal of understanding and creating a fully intelligent agent, it affirmed the notion that the mysteries of life and intellect might be brought into the light of scientific analysis.

Review Questions

1. Who was Prometheus and what was his crime?

2. Explain the positive and negative legacies of Prometheus.

3. According to Luger, why shouldn't we be surprised at the arguments surrounding the science of artificial intelligence?

4. How does the Preface to *Frankenstein* reflect a change in thinking about our ability to understand the mysteries of life?

Discussion and Writing Suggestions

1. Luger writes: "The notion that human efforts to gain knowledge constitute a transgression against the laws of God or nature is deeply ingrained in Western thought." Where have you seen evidence of this "deeply engrained" belief?

2. According to Luger, the "belief that the desire for knowledge must ultimately lead to disaster has persisted throughout history, enduring the Renaissance, the Age of Enlightenment, and even the scientific and philosophical advances of the nineteenth and twentieth centuries." What religious and social forces might be at play in suggesting that the attempt to gain (forbidden) knowledge somehow violates the laws of God or nature?

3. In Mary Shelley's *Frankenstein*, what is the importance of the scientist's "manufacturing" the monster, instead of reciting magical incantations or negotiating with supernatural forces?

4. Was the scientist in *Frankenstein* "mad" in desiring to create life? What are the implications of your answer for your view of scientists who are trying to create intelligence machines?

On the Web: *Will Technology Help Us Become Immortal? An Interview with Yuval Harari*

Yuval Harari is an award-winning historian concerned with the relationship between history and biology. In *Sapiens: A Brief History of Humankind* (2011, Israel; 2015, United States), he takes a long view of human history over thousands and tens of thousands of years, observing that humans have been the only animal capable of leapfrogging the slow pace of biological evolution and now stand at the threshold of designing for themselves new, radical capabilities that will alter the function, and even survival, of humankind. *Sapiens* has been widely translated and is an international best seller. He followed *Sapiens* with a second best seller, *Homo Deus* (2016). This video interview lasts approximately twelve minutes.

Go to YouTube.

Search terms: Harari Will Technology Help Us Become Immortal National

Discussion and Writing Suggestions

Yuval Harari makes several provocative claims in this interview. Among them:

- Asked about the chances of humans becoming extinct, Harari says that "more likely we will upgrade ourselves into something that is more different from us than we are different from Neanderthals or chimpanzees."

- "Within our lifetimes, billions of humans will be pushed out of the job market because AI . . . will be better in driving cars, diagnosing disease, even writing articles. . . . The 21st century will create the 'useless class.'"

- "Even though we are developing artificial intelligence, we are definitely not developing artificial consciousness. . . . What we see now is a decoupling of intelligence from consciousness."

1. Respond to one of these statements. Does Harari's claim make you nervous? Do you agree with him? Disagree? On what grounds?

2. In his books and speeches, Harari is careful to distinguish his projections from present trends in technology from "prophecy." How are these statements not prophecy? Does the fact (if you agree) that they are not prophecy change how you respond to them?

2030—Ray Kurzweil's Predictions or Bill Joy's Fears?

Carolyn Mathas

As far as competing visions of artificial intelligence go, no two thinkers could be more opposed than futurist Ray Kurzweil and tech giant Bill Joy. One is an AI optimist; the other, an AI pessimist. Carolyn Mathas summarizes the views of each and identifies core questions. Mathas writes for a variety of tech-related magazines, including *Electronics 360*, in which the following first appeared on February 23, 2016.

Two futurists clash on what 2030 will bring. Ray Kurzweil anticipates godlike capabilities at the point of singularity when human intelligence is surpassed by artificial intelligence (AI). In contrast, Bill Joy anticipates danger.

Sixteen years ago, I read with great interest and growing unease, Bill Joy's essay in *Wired*, titled *Why the Future Doesn't Need Us*.[1] Joy, co-founder of Sun Microsystems and today, a venture capitalist at Kleiner Perkins Caufield & Byers questioned the wisdom, the future and the ethics involved in genetics, nanotechnology and robotics (GNR) advances.

Within the essay, Joy describes how he learns from futurist Ray Kurzweil, today Director of Technology at Google, how rapidly GNR technologies will lead to singularity. Joy seriously questions the wisdom of continuing down that path. While he admits that each hold the potential for great promise for medical cures and treatments, extending the life span of humans substantially and also the quality of those lives, Joy cautions, "Yet, with each of these technologies, a sequence of small, individually sensible advances leads to an accumulation of great power and, concomitantly, great danger."

There's sufficient evidence that, as humans, we do err on the side of too little attention given in advance of our meddling. Take for example, the fact that the influenza virus of 1918 killed an alarming 50 million people; where is the rationale behind the U.S. Department of Health and Human Services' decision to publish the complete genome of the virus on the Internet? Not only does the action make it very easy to replicate the virus, the potential for harm is estimated to be worse than an atomic bomb. Need more examples of human meddling? Invasive species we've unleashed such as the cane toad, altered insects, the long-term health effects of pesticide use, the running controversy regarding the safety of genetically engineered crops and the consistent hacking of our most important data via devices that are just plain insecure.

---

[1] Bill Joy's much-referenced essay is readily found online. Search terms: *joy future doesn't need us wired*.

Ray Kurzweil's View

According to Ray Kurzweil when speaking at a conference in 2015, by the 2030s the neocor- **5** tex of our brains will be directly connected to the cloud. He anticipates that nanobots in our brains will render us Godlike, but that our brains will not become obsolete. While that sounds good, how do we know that will be true? As we pass each milestone in technological advances, do we ever reverse course to undo the advances as they . . . be too dangerous?

Kurzweil also states that once our brains are hooked up to computers, we will be funnier, sexier and more loving. He states that tiny robots from DNA strands will extend our brains into not just artificial-to-us intelligence, but emotional intelligence as well. Forgive me, but I believe I've worked in this industry too long. If engineers are responsible for furthering human intelli- gence to include the emotional realm, I'm unconvinced that most of them can pull off sexy, funny or more loving.

What is true is that there are sufficient "hooks" that are pulling at us. Curing diseases, living longer than the 80 some years that most of us will last. Maybe we should ask what kind of lives we might have?

Kurzweil readily admits that the emergence of AI as the norm will not alleviate the conflicts that exist. Humans will be more than they are today with expanded intellectual weaponry. He states, however, that the best way to combat this fact is to ". . . work on our democracy, liberty and respect for each other." In today's chaotic global society, how can this be relied upon?

He also admits that jobs that exist now will be going away as robots do our work for us, yet he's convinced that not only will there be new, albeit yet unidentified new jobs, those jobs will move us up Maslow's hierarchy so that we have time to do things that give us personal gratification and have a high standard of living for everyone. While he looks to entrepreneurs and college students, that represents only a portion of society—and what about the rest?

Convinced that we will eventually become used to the idea and comfortable with sharing **10** the world with artificial intelligence, Kurzweil claims in his 2012 release of *How to Create a Mind*, "As you get to the late 2030s or 2040s, our thinking will be predominantly non-biological and the non-biological part will ultimately be so intelligent and have such vast capacity it will be able to model, simulate and understand fully the biological part. We will be able to fully back up our brains."

Bill Joy's Stance

A meeting with Kurzweil and Kurzweil's assertion that the time was accelerating when humans would become robots or morph with them, unleashed substantial unease in Bill Joy. Joy's resulting *Wired* article states Moore's Law (computer processing speeds double every 18 months) would continue in 2030, unleashing ultra-powerful computing based on mole- cule-sized processors. It was the potential of self-replication and independence that the "nanobots" could attain that, for him, represented the greatest risk.

Joy questioned not only the job front—whether or not there would be sufficient numbers of jobs and the skills to do them, but also political systems globally that would be able to handle Kurzweil's robotic dreams. Joy stated in his essay, ". . . in about 30 years, a new idea suggests itself: that I may be working to create tools which will enable the construction of the technology that may replace our species. How do I feel about this? Very uncomfortable."

Joy explained that as we hand over our power to the machines voluntarily, they could do little else than take and expand that power as humans lose the ability to intellectually keep up. At that point, it will be impossible not to further enable robotic decisions in favor of ours.

We can see evidence of this today as driverless cars that are less prone to accidents take the wheel from humans, as well as in a variety of medical situations. In these cases, it seems attractive. In others, however, it's downright scary.

What happens in 2030 when a few are "godlike" in their intelligence and in their ability to live well past normal life spans? Will a handful of the elite rule? Will the masses be reduced to "sheep"? Will decisions ensue to eliminate further resource drain on the planet by limiting reproduction in the masses? Are you concerned?

Can it happen?

15   Yes. How would we maintain control of a super-intelligent robot with the ability to clone itself? We're attracted to the faster, simpler, easier way of handing off decisions, improving on results even marginally, and trusting as a species that we're bright enough to see what's coming that would be filed under the heading Murphy.[2] We just aren't.

Today, Kurzweil still is chasing Godlike, and Joy believes we might be able to steer technology in the right direction. However, if in just 14 more years, we do merge with a robot and singularity is a reality, how can we trust that this could be a long-term positive experience? Isn't it true we still can't keep our personal private information out of the hands of hackers in 2016?

As 2030 nears, Bill Joy says it best: "Perhaps it is always hard to see the bigger impact while you are in the vortex of a change. Failing to understand the consequences of our inventions while we are in the rapture of discovery and innovation seems to be a common fault of scientists and technologists; we have long been driven by the overarching desire to know— that is the nature of science's quest, not stopping to notice that the progress to newer and more powerful technologies can take on a life of its own."

Joy asks, "Given the incredible power of these new technologies, shouldn't we be asking how we can best coexist with them? And if our own extinction is a likely, or even possible, outcome of our technological development, shouldn't we proceed with great caution?"

What do you think?

Discussion and Writing Suggestions

1. Mathas summarizes Bill Joy's "incrementalist" argument: that as AI progresses, individual breakthroughs will benefit humankind and be difficult to resist. We will accept each new application, one by one, until we wake up one morning and realize we're totally reliant on machines for our survival. What do you make of this argument?

2. With whose position are you more inclined to agree? Kurzweil's or Joy's? Why?

3. Seriously consider for a moment the possibility that you need never study another language since, with your brain connected to the cloud, you can instantly understand and speak any language you want—with the ease and accuracy of Google Translate. Would you welcome such a development? Discuss.

---

[2] Murphy's Law: What can go wrong will go wrong.

4. Mathas asks: "[D]o we ever reverse course to undo the advances [in technology] as they . . . become too dangerous?" Have we? If an advance is presented that we find dangerous, and we can't "uninvent it"—the knowledge being public—what are our options?

5. Mathas writes: "If engineers are responsible for furthering human intelligence to include the emotional realm, I'm unconvinced that most of them can pull off sexy, funny or more loving." Her humor is rooted in an unfunny generalization about engineers. Explain the joke. Is the humor warranted? What larger point is she making about the promised capabilities of AI and the designers of those capabilities?

6. In the year 2030, following Kurzweil, if you had the opportunity to back up your brain and live online forever, would you? It may seem like a joke question today, but people are now discussing the question seriously. What's your answer?

A Statement of Concern for Responsible Development of Artificial Intelligence

In October 2015, AI scientists, industry experts, philosophers, economists, and lawyers gathered in San Juan, Puerto Rico for a conference on "The Future of AI: Opportunities and Challenges" co-sponsored by the Future of Life Institute and the Centre for the Study of Existential Risk. These meetings gave rise to an "Open Letter" that to date has been signed by more than eight thousand scientists, including Elon Musk (SpaceX, Tesla), Stephen Hawking (theoretical physicist, Cambridge University), Steve Wozniak (co-founder of Apple), and Nick Bostrom (director of the Future of Humanity Institute, Oxford University). The letter is followed by key excerpts from the less technical sections of "Research Priorities" that attendees of the San Juan conference encouraged AI scientists to investigate. Next, Seán Ó hÉigeartaigh, executive director of the Centre for the Study of Existential Risk, answers the "why now?" question, explaining those developments in AI, as of 2015, that convinced so many leading scientists to insist that "our AI systems must do what we want them to do."

An Open Letter on Artificial Intelligence

Future of Life Institute

Artificial intelligence (AI) research has explored a variety of problems and approaches since its inception, but for the last 20 years or so has been focused on the problems surrounding the construction of intelligent agents—systems that perceive and act in some environment. In this context, "intelligence" is related to statistical and economic notions of rationality—colloquially, the ability to make good decisions, plans, or inferences. The adoption of probabilistic and decision-theoretic representations and statistical learning methods has led to a large degree of integration and cross-fertilization among AI, machine learning, statistics, control theory, neuroscience, and other fields. The establishment of shared theoretical frameworks, combined with the availability of data and processing power, has yielded remarkable successes in various component tasks such as speech recognition, image clas-sification, autonomous vehicles, machine translation, legged locomotion, and question-answering systems.

As capabilities in these areas and others cross the threshold from laboratory research to economically valuable technologies, a virtuous cycle takes hold whereby even small improvements in performance are worth large sums of money, prompting greater invest-ments in research. There is now a broad consensus that AI research is progressing steadily, and that its impact on society is likely to increase. The potential benefits are huge, since everything that civilization has to offer is a product of human intelligence; we cannot predict what we might achieve when this intelligence is magnified by the tools AI may pro-vide, but the eradication of disease and poverty are not unfathomable. Because of the great potential of AI, it is important to research how to reap its benefits while avoiding potential pitfalls.

The progress in AI research makes it timely to focus research not only on making AI more capable, but also on maximizing the societal benefit of AI. Such considerations moti-vated the AAAI 2008–2009 Presidential Panel on Long-Term AI Futures and other projects on AI impacts, and constitute a significant expansion of the field of AI itself, which up to now has focused largely on techniques that are neutral with respect to purpose. We recommend expanded research aimed at ensuring that increasingly capable AI systems are robust and beneficial: our AI systems must do what we want them to do. The attached research priorities document gives many examples of such research directions that can help maximize the soci-etal benefit of AI. This research is by necessity interdisciplinary, because it involves both society and AI. It ranges from economics, law and philosophy to computer security, formal methods and, of course, various branches of AI itself.

5   In summary, we believe that research on how to make AI systems robust and beneficial is both important and timely, and that there are concrete research directions that can be pursued today.

Research Priorities for Robust and Beneficial Artificial Intelligence

Stuart Russell, Daniel Dewey, and Max Tegmark

The Marketplace

When and in what order should we expect various jobs to become automated (Frey and Osborne 2013)? How will this affect the wages of less skilled workers, the creative profes-sions, and various kinds of information workers? Some have argued that AI is likely to greatly increase the overall wealth of humanity as a whole (Brynjolfsson and McAfee 2014). However, increased automation may . . . fall disproportionately along lines of race, class, and gender; research anticipating the economic and societal impact of such disparity could be useful.

Law and Ethics

The development of systems that embody significant amounts of intelligence and autonomy leads to important legal and ethical questions whose answers affect both producers and consumers of AI technology. These questions span law, public policy, professional ethics, and philosophical ethics, and will require expertise from computer scientists, legal experts, political scientists, and ethicists. For example:

- Liability and Law for Autonomous Vehicles
  If self-driving cars cut the roughly 40,000 annual U.S. traffic fatalities in half, the car makers might get not 20,000 thank-you notes, but 20,000 lawsuits. In what legal framework can the safety benefits of autonomous vehicles such as drone aircraft and self-driving cars best be realized (Vladeck 2014)? Should legal questions about AI be handled by existing (software- and Internet-focused) cyberlaw, or should they be treated separately (Calo 2014b)? In both military and commercial applications, governments will need to decide how best to bring the relevant expertise to bear; for example, a panel or committee of professionals and academics could be created, and Calo has proposed the creation of a Federal Robotics Commission (Calo 2014a).

- Machine Ethics
  [In "deciding" what actions to take to avoid an accident,] how should an autonomous vehicle trade off, say, a small probability of injury to a human against the near certainty of a large . . . cost [to damaged or destroyed property]? How should lawyers, ethicists, and policymakers engage the public on these issues? Should such trade-offs be the subject of national standards?

- Autonomous Weapons
  Can lethal autonomous weapons be made to comply with humanitarian law (Churchill and Ulfstein 2000)? If, as some organizations have suggested, autonomous weapons should be banned (Docherty 2012), is it possible to develop a precise definition of autonomy for this purpose, and can such a ban practically be enforced? If it is permissible or legal to use lethal autonomous weapons, how should these weapons be integrated into the existing command-and-control structure so that responsibility and liability remain associated with specific human actors? What technical realities and forecasts should inform these questions, and how should meaningful human control over weapons be defined (Roff 2013, 2014; Anderson, Reisner, and Waxman 2014)? Are autonomous weapons likely to reduce political aversion to conflict, or perhaps result in accidental battles or wars (Asaro 2008)? Would such weapons become the tool of choice for oppressors or terrorists? Finally, how can transparency and public discourse best be encouraged on these issues?

- Privacy
  How should the ability of AI systems to interpret the data obtained from surveillance cameras, phone lines, emails, and so on, interact with the right to privacy? How will privacy risks interact with cybersecurity and cyberwarfare (Singer and Friedman 2014)? Our ability to take full advantage of the synergy between AI and big data will depend in part on our ability to manage and preserve privacy (Manyika et al. 2011; Agrawal and Srikant 2000).

- Professional Ethics
  What role should computer scientists play in the law and ethics of AI development and use?

Conclusion

In summary, success in the quest for artificial intelligence has the potential to bring unprecedented benefits to humanity, and it is therefore worthwhile to research how to maximize these benefits while avoiding potential pitfalls. The research agenda outlined in this paper, and the concerns that motivate it, have been called anti-AI, but we vigorously contest this characterization. It seems self-evident that the growing capabilities of AI are leading to an increased potential for impact on human society. It is the duty of AI researchers to ensure that the future impact is beneficial. We believe that this is possible, and hope that this research agenda provides a helpful step in the right direction.[3]

An Open Letter on AI: Why Now?

Seán Ó hÉigeartaigh

This week, artificial intelligence leaders in academia and industry, and legal, economic and risk experts worldwide have signed an open letter calling for the robust and beneficial development of artificial intelligence. The letter follows a recent private conference organised by the Future of Life Institute and the Centre for the Study of Existential Risk and funded by . . . Jaan Tallinn, in which the future opportunities and societal challenges posed by artificial intelligence were explored by AI leaders and interdisciplinary researchers.

The conference resulted in a set of research priorities aimed at making progress on the technical, legal, and economic challenges posed by this rapidly developing field.

This conference, the research preceding it, and the support for the concerns raised in the letter, may make this a pivotal moment in the development of this transformative field. But why is this happening now?

Why now?

An exciting new wave of progress in artificial intelligence is happening due to the success of a set of new approaches—"hot" areas include deep learning and other statistical learning methods. Advances in related fields like probability, decision theory, neuroscience and control theory are also contributing. These have kickstarted rapid improvements on problems where progress has been very slow until now: image and speech recognition, perception and movement in robotics, and performance of autonomous vehicles are just a few examples. As a result, impacts on society that seemed far away now suddenly seem pressing.

Is society ready for the opportunities—and challenges—of AI?

5   Artificial intelligence is a general purpose technology—one that will affect the development of a lot of different technologies. As a result, it will affect society deeply and in a lot of different ways. The near- and long-term benefits will be great—it will increase the world's economic prosperity, and enhance our ability to make progress on many important problems. In particular, any area where progress depends on analyzing and using huge amounts of data— climate change, health research, biotechnology—could be accelerated.

However, even impacts that are positive in the long-run can cause a lot of near-term challenges. What happens when swathes of the labour market become automated? Can our

---

[3] Elon Musk, CEO of Space X and Tesla automotive, donated $10 million to the Future of Life Institute to fund research programs consistent with its mission to advance AI science while avoiding AI-related dangers. The first grants were awarded in July 2015. One recipient was a team researching ways to maintain human control of intelligent weapons. Another recipient was Nick Bostrom, who founded an institute for studying how to ensure AI remains beneficial to humans.

legal systems assign blame when there is an accident involving a self-driving car? Does the use of autonomous weapons in war conflict with basic human rights?

It's no longer enough to ask "can we build it?" Now that it looks like we can, we have to ask: "How can we build it to provide most benefit? And how must we update our own systems—legal, economic, ethical—so that the transition is smooth, and we make the most of the positives while minimizing the negatives?" These questions need careful analysis, with technical AI experts, legal experts, economists, policymakers, and philosophers working together. And as this affects society at large, the public also needs to be represented in the discussions and decisions that are made.

Safe, predictable design of powerful systems

There are also deep technical challenges as these systems get more powerful and more complex. We have already seen unexpected behavior from systems that weren't carefully enough thought through—for example, the role of algorithms in the 2010 financial flash crash.[4] It is essential that powerful AI systems don't become black boxes operating in ways that we can't entirely understand or predict. This will require better ways to make systems transparent and easier to verify, better security so that systems can't be hacked, and a deeper understanding of logic and decision theory so that we predict the behavior of our systems in the different situations they will act in. There are open questions to be answered: can we design these powerful systems with perfect confidence that they will always do exactly what we want them to do? And if not, how do we design them with limits that guarantee only safe actions?

Shaping the development of a transformative technology

The societal and technical challenges posed by AI are hard, and will become harder the longer we wait. They will need insights and cooperation from the best minds in computer science, but also from experts in all the domains that AI will impact. But by making progress now, we will lay the foundations we need for the bigger changes that lie ahead.

Some commentators have raised the prospect of human-level general artificial intelligence. As Stephen Hawking and others have said, this would be the most transformative invention in human history, and will need to be approached very carefully. Luckily, we're still decades away, or possibly even centuries. But we need that time. We need to start work on today's challenges—how to design AI so that we can understand it and control it, and how to change our societal systems so we gain the great benefits AI offers—if we're to be remotely ready for that. We can't assume we'll get it right by default.

The benefits of this technology cannot be understated. Developed correctly, AI will allow us to make better progress on the hard scientific problems we will face in coming decades, and might prove crucial to a more sustainable life for our world's 7 billion inhabitants. It will change the world for the better—if we take the time to think and plan carefully. This is the motivation that has brought AI researchers, and experts from all the disciplines it impacts—together to sign this letter.

10

---

[4] The Flash Crash of 2010 was a short-lived (thirty-six minute) stock-market crash that regulators blamed on a single trader who used automated computer algorithms to make—and win—bets the market would fall.

Discussion and Writing Suggestions

1. Cite phrases in the Open Letter that establish an optimistic but cautious approach to AI. Notwithstanding this balanced view, critics of the letter (such as Dominic Basulto in a later selection) point to its "dystopian AI premise." What evidence do you find that the letter is based on doomsday (or potentially doomsday) assumptions?

2. Accidents involving self-driving cars are inevitable. Who is most at fault when accidents occur and people are hurt? The car manufacturer? The engineers who programmed the car? The owner of the self-driving car? How do we arbitrate such problems? And to what extent is it necessary that we know how to arbitrate them before self-driving cars are put into general use?

3. For thousands of years, ethics has been the study of right behavior among humans. One of the Research Priorities following on the Letter on AI concerned "machine ethics." In what ways does it—or will it soon—make sense to say that machines behave ethically or not? To focus your answer, consider the example of a self-driving car "choosing" to crash into a motorcycle and its lone rider, rather than crashing into a tanker truck filled with gasoline and driving by a daycare center. How does the self-driving car "decide" which to destroy? Why is this kind of decision-making a question of ethics?

4. Reread the questions posed in the section on "Autonomous Weapons." Choose one question and respond.

5. To what extent do you agree with the authors of the Research Priorities that it "is the duty of AI researchers to ensure that the future impact [of AI] is beneficial"? Why not leave the AI researchers to do what they do best: program computers? Why not let the courts, the manufacturers, and the marketplace settle problems such as who should be responsible for accidents involving self-driving cars?

6. Seán Ó hÉigeartaigh writes: "It's no longer enough to ask 'can we build it?' Now that it looks like we can, we have to ask: 'How can we build it to provide most benefit? And how must we update our own systems—legal, economic, ethical—so that the transition is smooth, and we make the most of the positives while minimizing the negatives?'" Why should we be asking such questions? After all, inventors of the steam engine likely didn't lose much sleep posing such questions. Why should we?

7. How comfortable are you with AI science when those most closely associated with its development pose questions such as Ó hÉigeartaigh's: "[C]an we design these powerful systems with perfect confidence that they will always do exactly what we want them to do? And if not, how do we design them with limits that guarantee only safe actions?" Does the fact that experts are taking on such questions in order "to think and plan carefully" give you confidence?

8. Adapt Asimov's three laws of robots (see p. 384) to address some of the concerns about AI expressed by Ó hÉigeartaigh.

Motion For a European Parliament Resolution to the Commission on Civil Law Rules on Robotics

Committee on Legal Affairs, European Parliament

In January 2017, a Committee on Legal Affairs for the European Parliament put forward a motion to adopt a resolution to form a European Agency for Robotics and a Code of Ethical Conduct for robotics engineers. Remarkable for basing its logic in stories well-known to Western culture, the document is nearly encyclopedic in its appraisal of AI's promises and perils. It urges the parliament of the European Union both to embrace the new technology and to institute legal and technical safeguards (for example, "kill" switches) to ensure its wise and beneficial development.

This document is a motion to adopt a resolution, not an approved resolution. As such, it continues to evolve. A word on the phrasing and organization of the motion, which follows a format common to legal documents. The motion forms a single *very* long sentence. The subject appears in the first line of the document: "The European Parliament." The predicates—there are several—appear pages later after a lengthy series of *whereas* clauses (each of them fascinating). The predicates: *calls, considers, notes,* and *points out*. The structure of the document, then, is as follows. We've underlined the subject once; we've double underlined the predicates:

> The European Parliament, having "regard to" (that is, having considered) Article 225, Rules 46 + 53 + a report, *whereas, whereas,* etc., calls on, considers, notes, etc.

The European Parliament,

— having regard to Article 225 of the Treaty on the Functioning of the European Union,

— having regard to Rules 46 and 52 of its Rules of Procedure,

— having regard to the report of the Committee on Legal Affairs and the opinions of the Committee on Employment and Social Affairs, the Committee on the Environment, Public Health and Food Safety, the Committee on Industry, Research and Energy and the Committee on the Internal Market and Consumer Protection (A8-0000/2016),

Introduction

A. whereas from Mary Shelley's Frankenstein's Monster to the classical myth of Pygmalion, through the story of Prague's Golem to the robot of Karel Čapek, who coined the word, people have fantasised about the possibility of building intelligent machines, more often than not androids with human features;

B. whereas now that humankind stands on the threshold of an era when ever more sophisticated robots, bots, androids and other manifestations of artificial intelligence ("AI") seem poised to unleash a new industrial revolution, which is likely to leave no stratum of society untouched, it is vitally important for the legislature to consider all its implications;

C. whereas between 2010 and 2014 the average increase in sales of robots stood at 17% per year and in 2014 sales rose by 29%, the highest year-on-year increase ever, with automotive parts suppliers and the electrical/electronics industry being the main drivers of the growth; whereas annual patent filings for robotics technology have tripled over the last decade;

D. whereas in the short to medium term robotics and AI promise to bring benefits of efficiency and savings, not only in production and commerce, but also in areas such as transport, medical care, education and farming, while making it possible to avoid exposing humans to dangerous conditions, such as those faced when cleaning up toxically polluted sites; whereas in the longer term there is potential for virtually unbounded prosperity;

E. whereas at the same time the development of robotics and AI may result in a large part of the work now done by humans being taken over by robots, so raising concerns about the future of employment and the viability of social security systems if the current basis of taxation is maintained, creating the potential for increased inequality in the distribution of wealth and influence;

F. whereas the causes for concern also include physical safety, for example when a robot's code proves fallible, and the potential consequences of system failure or hacking of connected robots and robotic systems at a time when increasingly autonomous applications come into use or are impending whether it be in relation to cars and drones or to care robots and robots used for maintaining public order and policing;

G. whereas many basic questions of data protection have already become the subject of consideration in the general contexts of the internet and e-commerce, but whereas further aspects of data ownership and the protection of personal data and privacy might still need to be addressed, given that applications and appliances will communicate with each other and with databases without humans intervening or possibly without their even being aware of what is going on;

H. whereas the "soft impacts" on human dignity may be difficult to estimate, but will still need to be considered if and when robots replace human care and companionship, and whereas questions of human dignity also can arise in the context of "repairing" or enhancing human beings;

I. whereas ultimately there is a possibility that within the space of a few decades AI could surpass human intellectual capacity in a manner which, if not prepared for, could pose a challenge to humanity's capacity to control its own creation and, consequently, perhaps also to its capacity to be in charge of its own destiny and to ensure the survival of the species;

J. whereas several foreign jurisdictions, such as the US, Japan, China and South Korea, are considering, and to a certain extent have already taken, regulatory action with respect to robotics and AI, and whereas some Member States have also started to reflect on possible legislative changes in order to take account of emerging applications of such technologies;

K. whereas European industry could benefit from a coherent approach to regulation at European level, providing predictable and sufficiently clear conditions under which enterprises could develop applications and plan their business models on a European scale while ensuring that the EU and its Member States maintain control over the regulatory standards to be set, so as not to be forced to adopt and live with standards set by others, that is to say the third states which are also at the forefront of the development of robotics and AI;

General principles

L. whereas, until such time, if ever, that robots become or are made self-aware, Asimov's Laws[5] must be regarded as being directed at the designers, producers and operators of robots, since those laws cannot be converted into machine code;

---

[5] (1) A robot may not injure a human being or, through inaction, allow a human being to come to harm. (2) A robot must obey the orders given it by human beings except where such orders would conflict with the First Law. (3) A robot must protect its own existence as long as such protection does not conflict with the First or Second Laws (See Runabout, I. Asimov, 1943) and (0) A robot may not harm humanity, or, by inaction, allow humanity to come to harm.

M. whereas, nevertheless, a series of rules, governing in particular liability and ethics and reflecting the intrinsically European and humanistic values that characterise Europe's contribution to society, are necessary;

N. whereas the European Union could play an essential role in establishing basic ethical principles to be respected in the development, programming and use of robots and AI and in the incorporation of such principles into European regulations and codes of conduct, with the aim of shaping the technological revolution so that it serves humanity and so that the benefits of advanced robotics and AI are broadly shared, while as far as possible avoiding potential pitfalls;

O. whereas a gradualist, pragmatic cautious approach of the type advocated by Jean Monnet should be adopted for Europe;

P. whereas it is appropriate, in view of the stage reached in the development of robotics and AI, to start with civil liability issues and to consider whether a strict liability approach based on who is best placed to insure is not the best starting point;

Liability

Q. whereas, thanks to the impressive technological advances of the last decade, not only are today's robots able to perform activities which used to be typically and exclusively human, but the development of autonomous and cognitive features—e.g. the ability to learn from experience and take independent decisions—has made them more and more similar to agents that interact with their environment and are able to alter it significantly; whereas, in such a context, the legal responsibility arising from a robot's harmful action becomes a crucial issue;

R. whereas a robot's autonomy can be defined as the ability to take decisions and implement them in the outside world, independently of external control or influence; whereas this autonomy is of a purely technological nature and its degree depends on how sophisticated a robot's interaction with its environment has been designed to be;

S. whereas the more autonomous robots are, the less they can be considered simple tools in the hands of other actors (such as the manufacturer, the owner, the user, etc.); whereas this, in turn, makes the ordinary rules on liability insufficient and calls for new rules which focus on how a machine can be held—partly or entirely—responsible for its acts or omissions; whereas, as a consequence, it becomes more and more urgent to address the fundamental question of whether robots should possess a legal status;

T. whereas, ultimately, robots' autonomy raises the question of their nature in the light of the existing legal categories—of whether they should be regarded as natural persons, legal persons, animals or objects—or whether a new category should be created, with its own specific features and implications as regards the attribution of rights and duties, including liability for damage;

• • •

General principles concerning the development of robotics and artificial intelligence for civil use

1. Calls on the Commission to propose a common European definition of smart autonomous robots and their subcategories by taking into consideration the following characteristics of a smart robot:

- acquires autonomy through sensors and/or by exchanging data with its environment (inter-connectivity) and trades and analyses data
- is self-learning (optional criterion)
- has a physical support

2. <u>Considers</u> that a system of registration of advanced robots should be introduced, and calls on the Commission to establish criteria for the classification of robots with a view to identifying the robots that would need to be registered;

• • •

Ethical principles

1. <u>Notes</u> that the potential for empowerment through the use of robotics is nuanced by a set of tensions or risks relating to human safety, privacy, integrity, dignity, autonomy and data ownership;
2. <u>Considers</u> that a guiding ethical framework for the design, production and use of robots is needed to complement the legal recommendations of the report and . . . proposes, in the annex to the resolution, a framework in the form of a charter consisting of a code of conduct for robotics engineers, of a code for research ethics committees when reviewing robotics protocols and of model licences for designers and users;
3. <u>Points out</u> that the guiding ethical framework should be based on the principles of beneficence, non-maleficence and autonomy, as well as on the principles enshrined in the EU Charter of Fundamental Rights, such as human dignity and human rights, equality, justice and equity, non-discrimination and non-stigmatisation, autonomy and individual responsibility, informed consent, privacy and social responsibility, and on existing ethical practices and codes;

A European Agency

1. <u>Calls for</u> the creation of a European Agency for robotics and artificial intelligence in order to provide the technical, ethical and regulatory expertise needed to support the relevant public actors, at both EU and Member State level, in their efforts to ensure a timely and well-informed response to the new opportunities and challenges arising from the technological development of robotics.

Discussion and Writing Suggestions

1. Research Mary Shelley's *Frankenstein's* monster, the Pygmalion myth, and the story of the Golem. What elements do these stories share? How are they related to this chapter's discussion of intelligent machines?

2. Paragraph E of the resolution reads, in part: "AI may result in a large part of the work now done by humans being taken over by robots, so raising concerns about the future of employment and the viability of social security systems if the current basis of taxation is maintained, creating the potential for increased inequality in the distribution of wealth and

influence." What are these concerns? How might social security systems break down given the widespread use of AI? How might the use of AI lead to "increased inequality"?

3. The motion for a European Parliament resolution considers dozens of applications of AI, ranging from the economy, military, and social systems to policing, transportation, and healthcare. Research one present or likely future application of AI and report on it to your classmates. You might, for example, choose to investigate "care robots" that assist the elderly.

4. "[A]pplications and appliances will communicate with each other and with databases without humans intervening or possibly without their even being aware of what is going on." To what extent do you feel liberated—or alarmed—at this prospect: a future in which intelligent machines talk to each other, tending to details that might otherwise inconvenience, bore, or annoy you?

5. The premise of ¶I is radical, the stuff of dystopian films and books. How do you respond to an official (European) government document directly acknowledging potential nightmares? To what extent does the paragraph alarm you or relieve you (as in "Thank goodness someone's paying attention!)? Do you think governments are up to the task of protecting us from harmful AI?

6. This motion for a resolution envisions a legal framework, a marketplace, and a regulatory system that will encourage and control the development of AI science. Given the rapid advances in AI and the aggressive ways in which companies sell new technologies, how successful do you imagine the European Union or any political entity will be in managing the orderly and safe introduction of AI machines?

7. From the footnote on page 384 regarding Asimov's Laws of robotics you learn that a fiction writer's decades-old contemplation of robots has influenced the drafting of laws and regulations. Your reactions?

8. Reread paragraphs Q through T on Liability and questions on the legal status of robots—including, "whether they should be regarded as natural persons, legal persons, animals or objects—or whether a new category should be created." That a major governing body (the European Parliament) is reviewing such issues makes it impossible for us to stand on the sidelines and dismiss AI as science fiction. AI is in the world, and so are you. How will you integrate it into your life—or not? Could you avoid such integration, even if you wanted to?

9. Reread the section titled "General principles concerning the development of robotics and artificial intelligence for civil use" at the end of the piece. In what ways is the call for a "guiding ethical framework . . . based on the principles . . . enshrined in the EU Charter of Fundamental Rights" remarkable?

Superintelligence: The Idea That Eats Smart People

Maciej Ceglowski

In 2016, Oxford philosopher and artificial intelligence researcher Nick Bostrom wrote *Superintelligence*, a book arguing that if scientists and policy makers do not wisely (and soon) direct the development of AI, the technology will one day overrun humanity. Many tech and scientific luminaries—including Stephen Hawking, Bill Gates, and Elon Musk—share Bostrom's concern. The potential for AI to cause an unprecedented harm, as well as good, has prompted a worldwide debate about how best to proceed, including two documents you'll find in this chapter: the Open Letter on AI and the European Parliament's draft resolution concerning rules on AI robotics.

In a keynote address delivered at a conference in Zagreb, Croatia in late 2016, tech entrepreneur Maciej (pronounced MAH-tchay) Ceglowski takes a skeptical view of Bostrom's arguments about runaway, superintelligent machines and systematically breaks down what he terms Bostrom's "crazy idea." The lecture is an outstanding example of critique: well researched, logical, methodical, and clearly— even entertainingly—presented. On his website, Ceglowski describes himself as "a painter and a computer guy." He's being modest: he's a savvy veteran of Yahoo, Twitter, and other tech companies.

Note that Ceglowski refers to futurist Raymond Kurzweil (subject of Carolyn Mathas's article earlier in the chapter), who is famous for his articles and books on the coming "Singularity." Singularity will occur when "the pace of technological change will be so fast and far-reaching that human existence on this planet will be irreversibly altered" through the "merger of man and machine." Kurzweil is currently a director of engineering at Google focused on machine learning and natural language recognition.

At just under eight thousand words, this selection is among the longest in the text. It is well worth your effort. Before you read, practice your previewing skills as discussed in Chapter 1. You'll find that Ceglowski develops his argument logically, in sections, using headings throughout. Before reading, also review the summary of the selection in the On the Web section immediately below. Thus prepared, you'll be ready to read and respond.

We present the lecture in two formats. You can watch a video recording (see the On the Web section below) and/or read the text.

On the Web:

Go to YouTube.

Search terms: Ceglowski superintelligence smart people

Ceglowski structures his critique as follows.

000–2:00

    Introduction: Unknowns regarding AI are reminiscent of unknowns regarding first test of atomic bomb.

2:01–11:40

Summary of Bostom's book: *Superintelligence*.

11:41–16:20

Introducing the critique and its structure: outside perspective and inside perspective.

16:23–22:46 Critique, Part I

Inside Arguments against Bostrom's superintelligence based on what we know about how AI is programmed:

Argument from (1) Wooly definitions (2) Stephen Hawking's cat—and Emus (3) Slavic pessimism (4) Mental Complexity (5) Just look around you (6) My Roommate Peter (6) Brain surgery (7) Childhood (8) Robinson Crusoe

22:47–34:33 Critique, Part II

Outside Argument against Bostrom's superintelligence based on what we know about the ways people tend to make large and unwarranted claims:

Argument from (1) Grandiosity—all or nothing, we are the only ones who can save humanity (2) Megalomania (3) Transhuman voodoo (4) Religion 2.0—the Nerd Apocalypse (4) Comic book ethics (5) Simulation fever (6) Data hunger (7) Incentivizes crazy (8) AI cosplay

34:34–35:22 Transition to conclusion: Importance of good sci-fi

35:23–42:00 Conclusion

"I want to put my cards on the table. What do I think AI is and the possibilities of it are?" AI now is in same position like Alchemy was in 17th century. We have clues. But we don't even know just yet how to ask questions. Or do we have the right tools to gain full understanding. Still, we have clues. There are things we're terribly mistaken about—we just don't know what they are.

In 1945, as American physicists were preparing to test the atomic bomb, it occurred to someone to ask if such a test could set the atmosphere on fire.

This was a legitimate concern. Nitrogen, which makes up most of the atmosphere, is not energetically stable. Smush two nitrogen atoms together hard enough and they will combine into an atom of magnesium, an alpha particle, and release a whole lot of energy:

$$N^{14} + N^{14} \Rightarrow Mg^{24} + \alpha + 17.7 \text{ MeV}$$

The vital question was whether this reaction could be self-sustaining. The temperature inside the nuclear fireball would be hotter than any event in the Earth's history. Were we throwing a match into a bunch of dry leaves?

Los Alamos physicists performed the analysis and decided there was a satisfactory margin of safety. Since we're all attending this conference today, we know they were right. They had confidence in their predictions because the laws governing nuclear reactions were straightforward and fairly well understood.

Today we're building another world-changing technology, machine intelligence. We know that it will affect the world in profound ways, change how the economy works, and have knock-on effects we can't predict.

But there's also the risk of a runaway reaction, where a machine intelligence reaches and exceeds human levels of intelligence in a very short span of time.

At that point, social and economic problems would be the least of our worries. Any **5** hyperintelligent machine (the argument goes) would have its own hypergoals, and would work to achieve them by manipulating humans, or simply using their bodies as a handy source of raw materials.

Last year, the philosopher Nick Bostrom published *Superintelligence*, a book that synthesizes the alarmist view of AI and makes a case that such an intelligence explosion is both dangerous and inevitable given a set of modest assumptions.

The computer that takes over the world is a staple sci-fi trope. But enough people take this scenario seriously that we have to take *them* seriously. Stephen Hawking, Elon Musk, and a whole raft of Silicon Valley investors and billionaires find this argument persuasive.

Let me start by laying out the premises you need for Bostrom's argument to go through:

The Premises

Premise 1: Proof of Concept

The first premise is the simple observation that thinking minds exist.

10   We each carry on our shoulders a small box of thinking meat. I'm using mine to give this talk, you're using yours to listen. Sometimes, when the conditions are right, these minds are capable of rational thought.

So we know that in principle, this is possible.

Premise 2: No Quantum Shenanigans

The second premise is that the brain is an ordinary configuration of matter, albeit an extraordinarily complicated one. If we knew enough, and had the technology, we could exactly copy its structure and emulate its behavior with electronic components, just like we can simulate very basic neural anatomy today.

Put another way, this is the premise that the mind arises out of ordinary physics. Some people like Roger Penrose would take issue with this argument, believing that there is extra stuff happening in the brain at a quantum level.

If you are very religious, you might believe that a brain is not possible without a soul.

15   But for most of us, this is an easy premise to accept.

Premise 3: Many Possible Minds

The third premise is that the space of all possible minds is large.

Our intelligence level, cognitive speed, set of biases and so on is not predetermined, but an artifact of our evolutionary history.

In particular, there's no physical law that puts a cap on intelligence at the level of human beings.

A good way to think of this is by looking what happens when the natural world tries to maximize for speed.

20   If you encountered a cheetah in pre-industrial times (and survived the meeting), you might think it was impossible for anything to go faster.

But of course we know that there are all kinds of configurations of matter, like a motorcycle, that are faster than a cheetah and even look a little bit cooler.

But there's no direct evolutionary pathway to the motorcycle. Evolution had to first make human beings, who then build all kinds of useful stuff.

So analogously, there may be minds that are vastly smarter than our own, but which are just not accessible to evolution on Earth. It's possible that we could build them, or invent the machines that can invent the machines that can build them.

There's likely to be *some* natural limit on intelligence, but there's no *a priori* reason to think that we're anywhere near it. Maybe the smartest a mind can be is twice as smart as people, maybe it's sixty thousand times as smart.

That's an empirical question that we don't know how to answer.   **25**

Premise 4: Plenty of Room at the Top

The fourth premise is that there's still plenty of room for computers to get smaller and faster.

If you watched the Apple event last night [where Apple introduced its 2016 laptops], you may be forgiven for thinking that Moore's Law is slowing down. But this premise just requires that you believe smaller and faster hardware to be possible in principle, down to several more orders of magnitude.

We know from theory that the physical limits to computation are high. So we could keep doubling for decades more before we hit some kind of fundamental physical limit, rather than an economic or political limit to Moore's Law.

Premise 5: Computer-Like Time Scales

The penultimate premise is if we create an artificial intelligence, whether it's an emulated human brain or a *de novo* piece of software, it will operate at time scales that are characteristic of electronic hardware (microseconds) rather than human brains (hours).

To get to the point where I could give this talk, I had to be born, grow up, go to school,   **30** attend university, live for a while, fly here and so on. It took years. Computers can work tens of thousands of times more quickly.

In particular, you have to believe that an electronic mind could redesign itself (or the hardware it runs on) and then move over to the new configuration without having to re-learn everything on a human timescale, have long conversations with human tutors, go to college, try to find itself by taking painting classes, and so on.

Premise 6: Recursive Self-Improvement

The last premise is my favorite because it is the most unabashedly American premise. (This is Tony Robbins, a famous motivational speaker.)

According to this premise, whatever goals an AI had (and they could be very weird, alien goals), it's going to want to improve itself. It's going to want to be a better AI.

So it will find it useful to recursively redesign and improve its own systems to make itself smarter, and possibly live in a cooler enclosure.

And by the time scale premise, this recursive self-improvement could happen   **35** very quickly.

Conclusion: RAAAAAAR!

If you accept all these premises, what you get is disaster!

Because at some point, as computers get faster, and we program them to be more intelligent, there's going to be a runaway effect like an explosion.

As soon as a computer reaches human levels of intelligence, it will no longer need help from people to design better versions of itself. Instead, it will start doing on a much faster time scale, and it's not going to stop until it hits a natural limit that might be very many times greater than human intelligence.

At that point this monstrous intellectual creature, through devious modeling of what our emotions and intellect are like, will be able to persuade us to do things like give it access to factories, synthesize custom DNA, or simply let it connect to the Internet, where it can hack its way into anything it likes and completely obliterate everyone in arguments on message boards.

40   From there things get very sci-fi very quickly.

Let's imagine a specific scenario where this could happen. Let's say I want to built a robot to say funny things.

I work on a team and every day we redesign our software, compile it, and the robot tells us a joke.

In the beginning, the robot is barely funny. It's at the lower limits of human capacity:

> What's grey and can't swim?
> A castle.

But we persevere, we work, and eventually we get to the point where the robot is telling us jokes that are starting to be funny:

> I told my sister she was drawing her eyebrows too high.
> She looked surprised.

45   At this point, the robot is getting smarter as well, and participates in its own redesign.

It now has good instincts about what's funny and what's not, so the designers listen to its advice. Eventually it gets to a near-superhuman level, where it's funnier than any human being around it.

> My belt holds up my pants and my pants have belt loops that hold up my belt.
> What's going on down there?
> Who is the real hero?

50   This is where the runaway effect kicks in. The researchers go home for the weekend, and the robot decides to recompile itself to be a little bit funnier and a little bit smarter, repeatedly.

It spends the weekend optimizing the part of itself that's good at optimizing, over and over again. With no more need for human help, it can do this as fast as the hardware permits.

When the researchers come in on Monday, the AI has become tens of thousands of times funnier than any human being who ever lived. It greets them with a joke, and they die laughing.

In fact, anyone who tries to communicate with the robot dies laughing, just like in the Monty Python skit. The human species laughs itself into extinction.

To the few people who manage to send it messages pleading with it to stop, the AI explains (in a witty, self-deprecating way that is immediately fatal) that it doesn't really care if people live or die, its goal is just to be funny.

55   Finally, once it's destroyed humanity, the AI builds spaceships and nanorockets to explore the farthest reaches of the galaxy, and find other species to amuse.

This scenario is a caricature of Bostrom's argument, because I am not trying to convince you of it, but vaccinate you against it.

Here's a PBF comic with the same idea. You see that hugbot, who has been programmed to hug the world, finds a way to wire a nucleo-gravitational hyper crystal into his hug capacitor and destroys the Earth.

Observe that in these scenarios the AIs are evil by default, just like a plant on an alien planet would probably be poisonous by default. Without careful tuning, there's no reason that an AI's motivations or values would resemble ours.

For an artificial mind to have anything resembling a human value system, the argument goes, we have to bake those beliefs into the design.

AI alarmists are fond of the paper clip maximizer, a notional computer that runs a paper clip factory, becomes sentient, recursively self-improves to Godlike powers, and then devotes all its energy to filling the universe with paper clips.

It exterminates humanity not because it's evil, but because our blood contains iron that could be better used in paper clips.

So if we just build an AI without tuning its values, the argument goes, one of the first things it will do is destroy humanity.

There's a lot of vivid language around such a takeover would happen. Nick Bostrom imagines a scenario where a program has become sentient, is biding its time, and has secretly built little DNA replicators. Then, when it's ready:

> Nanofactories producing nerve gas or target-seeking mosquito-like missiles might burgeon forth simultaneously from every square meter of the globe. And that will be the end of humanity.

So that's kind of freaky!

The only way out of this mess is to design a moral fixed point, so that even through thousands and thousands of cycles of self-improvement the AI's value system remains stable, and its values are things like "help people," "don't kill anybody," "listen to what people want."

Basically, "do what I mean."

Here's a very poetic example from Eliezer Yudkowsky of the good old American values we're supposed to be teaching to our artificial intelligence:

> Coherent Extrapolated Volition (CEV) is our wish if we knew more, thought faster, were more the people we wished we were, had grown up farther together; where the extrapolation converges rather than diverges, where our wishes cohere rather than interfere, extrapolated as we wish that extrapolated, interpreted as we wish that interpreted.

How's that for a design document? Now go write the code.

Hopefully you see the resemblance between this vision of AI and a genie from folklore. The AI is all-powerful and gives you what you ask for, but interprets everything in a super-literal way that you end up regretting.

This is not because the genie is stupid (it's hyperintelligent!) or malicious, but because you as a human being made too many assumptions about how minds behave. The human value system is idiosyncratic and needs to be explicitly defined and designed into any "friendly" machine.

Doing this is the ethics version of the early 20th century attempt to formalize mathematics and put it on a strict logical foundation. That this program ended in disaster for mathematical logic is never mentioned.

When I was in my twenties, I lived in Vermont, a remote, rural state. Many times I would return from some business trip on an evening flight, and have to drive home for an hour through the dark forest.

I would listen to a late-night radio program hosted by Art Bell, who had an all-night talk show and would interview various conspiracy theorists and fringe thinkers.

I would arrive at home totally freaked out, or pull over under a streetlight, convinced that a UFO was about to abduct me. I learned that I am an incredibly persuadable person.

75   It's the same feeling I get when I read these AI scenarios.

So I was delighted some years later to come across an essay by Scott Alexander about what he calls epistemic learned helplessness.

Epistemology is one of those big words, but all it means is "how do you know what you know is true?" Alexander noticed that when he was a young man, he would be taken in by "alternative" histories he read by various crackpots. He would read the history and be utterly convinced, then read the rebuttal and be convinced by that, and so on.

At some point he noticed that these alternative histories were mutually contradictory, so they could not possibly all be true. And from that he reasoned that he was simply somebody who could not trust his judgment. He was too easily persuaded.

People who believe in superintelligence present an interesting case, because many of them are freakishly smart. They can argue you into the ground. But are their arguments right, or is there just something about very smart minds that leaves them vulnerable to religious conversion about AI risk, and makes them particularly persuasive?

80   Is the idea of "superintelligence" just a memetic hazard?

When you're evaluating persuasive arguments about something strange, there are two perspectives you can choose, the inside one or the outside one.

Say that some people show up at your front door one day wearing funny robes, asking you if you will join their movement. They believe that a UFO is going to visit Earth two years from now, and it is our task to prepare humanity for the Great Upbeaming.

The inside view requires you to engage with these arguments on their merits. You ask your visitors how they learned about the UFO, why they think it's coming to get us—all the normal questions a skeptic would ask in this situation.

Imagine you talk to them for an hour, and come away utterly persuaded. They make an ironclad case that the UFO is coming, that humanity needs to be prepared, and you have never believed something as hard in your life as you now believe in the importance of preparing humanity for this great event.

85   But the outside view tells you something different. These people are wearing funny robes and beads, they live in a remote compound, and they speak in unison in a really creepy way. Even though their arguments are irrefutable, everything in your experience tells you you're dealing with a cult.

Of course, they have a brilliant argument for why you should ignore those instincts, but that's the inside view talking.

The outside view doesn't care about content, it sees the form and the context, and it doesn't look good.

So I'd like to engage AI risk from both these perspectives. I think the arguments for superintelligence are somewhat silly, and full of unwarranted assumptions.

But even if you find them persuasive, there is something unpleasant about AI alarmism as a cultural phenomenon that should make us hesitate to take it seriously.

90   First, let me engage the substance. Here are the arguments I have against Bostrom-style superintelligence as a risk to humanity:

The Argument from Wooly Definitions

The concept of "general intelligence" in AI is famously slippery. Depending on the context, it can mean human-like reasoning ability, or skill at AI design, or the ability to understand and model human behavior, or proficiency with language, or the capacity to make correct predictions about the future.

What I find particularly suspect is the idea that "intelligence" is like CPU speed, in that any sufficiently smart entity can emulate less intelligent beings (like its human creators) no matter how different their mental architecture.

With no way to define intelligence (except just pointing to ourselves), we don't even know if it's a quantity that can be maximized. For all we know, human-level intelligence could be a tradeoff. Maybe any entity significantly smarter than a human being would be crippled by existential despair, or spend all its time in Buddha-like contemplation.

Or maybe it would become obsessed with the risk of *hyperintelligence*, and spend all its time blogging about that.

The Argument from Stephen Hawking's Cat

Stephen Hawking is one of the most brilliant people alive, but say he wants to get his cat into the cat carrier. How's he going to do it?

95

He can model the cat's behavior in his mind and figure out ways to persuade it. He knows a lot about feline behavior. But ultimately, if the cat doesn't want to get in the carrier, there's nothing Hawking can do about it despite his overpowering advantage in intelligence.

Even if he devoted his career to feline motivation and behavior, rather than theoretical physics, he still couldn't talk the cat into it.

You might think I'm being offensive or cheating because Stephen Hawking is disabled. But an artificial intelligence would also initially not be embodied, it would be sitting on a server somewhere, lacking agency in the world. It would have to talk to people to get what it wants.

With a big enough gap in intelligence, there's no guarantee that an entity would be able to "think like a human" any more than we can "think like a cat."

The Argument from Einstein's Cat

There's a stronger version of this argument, using Einstein's cat. Not many people know that Einstein was a burly, muscular fellow. But if Einstein tried to get a cat in a carrier, and the cat didn't want to go, you know what would happen to Einstein.

100

He would have to resort to a brute-force solution that has nothing to do with intelligence, and in that matchup the cat could do pretty well for itself.

So even an embodied AI might struggle to get us to do what it wants.

The Argument from Emus

We can strengthen this argument further. Even groups of humans using all their wiles and technology can find themselves stymied by less intelligent creatures.

In the 1930's, Australians decided to massacre their native emu population to help struggling farmers. They deployed motorized units of Australian army troops in what we would now call technicals—fast-moving pickup trucks with machine guns mounted on the back.

The emus responded by adopting basic guerrilla tactics: they avoided pitched battles, dispersed, and melted into the landscape, humiliating and demoralizing the enemy.

105

And they won the Emu War, from which Australia has never recovered.

The Argument from Slavic Pessimism

We can't build anything right. We can't even build a secure webcam. So how are we supposed to solve ethics and code a moral fixed point for a recursively self-improving intelligence without ****ing it up, in a situation where the proponents argue we only get one chance?

Consider the recent experience with Ethereum, an attempt to codify contract law into software code, where a design flaw was immediately exploited to drain tens of millions of dollars.

Time has shown that even code that has been heavily audited and used for years can harbor crippling errors. The idea that we can securely design the most complex system ever built, and have it remain secure through thousands of rounds of recursive self-modification, does not match our experience.

The Argument from Complex Motivations

110   AI alarmists believe in something called the Orthogonality Thesis. This says that even very complex beings can have simple motivations, like the paper-clip maximizer. You can have rewarding, intelligent conversations with it about Shakespeare, but it will still turn your body into paper clips, because you are rich in iron.

There's no way to persuade it to step "outside" its value system, any more than I can persuade you that pain feels good.

I don't buy this argument at all. Complex minds are likely to have complex motivations; that may be part of what it even means to be intelligent.

There's a wonderful moment in Rick and Morty where Rick builds a butter-fetching robot, and the first thing his creation does is look at him and ask "what is my purpose?" When Rick explains that it's meant to pass butter, the robot stares at its hands in existential despair.

It's very likely that the scary "paper clip maximizer" would spend all of its time writing poems about paper clips, or getting into flame wars on reddit/r/paperclip, rather than trying to destroy the universe.

115   If AdSense became sentient, it would upload itself into a self-driving car and go drive off a cliff.

The Argument from Actual AI

When we look at where AI is actually succeeding, it's not in complex, recursively self-improving algorithms. It's the result of pouring absolutely massive amounts of data into relatively simple neural networks.

The breakthroughs being made in practical AI research hinge on the availability of these data collections, rather than radical advances in algorithms.

Right now Google is rolling out Google Home, where it's hoping to try to get even more data into the system, and create a next-generation voice assistant.

Note especially that the constructs we use in AI are fairly opaque after training. They don't work in the way that the superintelligence scenario needs them to work. There's no place to recursively tweak to make them "better," short of retraining on even more data.

The Argument from My Roommate

120   My roommate was the smartest person I ever met in my life. He was incredibly brilliant, and all he did was lie around and play World of Warcraft between bong rips.

The assumption that any intelligent agent will want to recursively self-improve, let alone conquer the galaxy, to better achieve its goals makes unwarranted assumptions about the nature of motivation.

It's perfectly possible an AI won't do much of anything, except use its powers of hyper-persuasion to get us to bring it brownies.

The Argument from Brain Surgery

I can't point to the part of my brain that is "good at neurosurgery," operate on it, and by repeating the procedure make myself the greatest neurosurgeon that has ever lived. Ben Carson tried that, and look what happened to him. Brains don't work like that. They are massively interconnected.

Artificial intelligence may be just as strongly interconnected as natural intelligence. The evidence so far certainly points in that direction.

But the hard takeoff scenario requires that there be a feature of the AI algorithm that can   **125** be repeatedly optimized to make the AI better at self-improvement.

The Argument from Childhood

Intelligent creatures don't arise fully formed. We're born into this world as little helpless messes, and it takes us a long time of interacting with the world and with other people in the world before we can start to be intelligent beings.

Even the smartest human being comes into the world helpless and crying, and requires years to get some kind of grip on themselves.

It's possible that the process could go faster for an AI, but it is not clear how much faster it could go. Exposure to real-world stimuli means observing things at time scales of seconds or longer.

Moreover, the first AI will only have humans to interact with—its development will necessarily take place on human timescales. It will have a period when it needs to interact with the world, with people in the world, and other baby superintelligences to learn to be what it is.

Furthermore, we have evidence from animals that the developmental period *grows*   **130** with increasing intelligence, so that we would have to babysit an AI and change its (figurative) diapers for decades before it grew coordinated enough to enslave us all.

The Argument from Gilligan's Island

A recurring flaw in AI alarmism is that it treats intelligence as a property of individual minds, rather than recognizing that this capacity is distributed across our civilization and culture.

Despite having one of the greatest minds of their time among them, the castaways on Gilligan's Island were unable to raise their technological level high enough to even build a boat (though the Professor is at one point able to make a radio out of coconuts).

Similarly, if you stranded Intel's greatest chip designers on a desert island, it would be centuries before they could start building microchips again.

The Outside Argument

What kind of person does sincerely believing this stuff turn you into? The answer is not pretty.

I'd like to talk for a while about the outside arguments that should make you leery of   **135** becoming an AI weenie. These are the arguments about what effect AI obsession has on our industry and culture:

Grandiosity

If you believe that artificial intelligence will let us conquer the galaxy (not to mention simulate trillions of conscious minds), you end up with some frightful numbers.

Enormous numbers multiplied by tiny probabilities are the hallmark of AI alarmism.

At one point, Bostrom outlines what he believes to be at stake:

> If we represent all the happiness experienced during one entire such life with a single teardrop of joy, then the happiness of these souls could fill and refill the Earth's oceans every second, and keep doing so for a hundred billion billion millennia. It is really important that we make sure these truly are tears of joy.

That's a heavy thing to lay on the shoulders of a twenty year old developer!

140   There's a parlor trick, too, where by multiplying such astronomical numbers by tiny probabilities, you can convince yourself that you need to do some weird stuff.

This business about saving all of future humanity is a cop-out. We had the same exact arguments used against us under communism, to explain why everything was always broken and people couldn't have a basic level of material comfort.

We were going to fix the world, and once that was done, happiness would trickle down to the point where everyday life would change for the better for everyone. But it was vital to fix the world first.

I live in California, which has the highest poverty rate in the United States, even though it's home to Silicon Valley. I see my rich industry doing nothing to improve the lives of everyday people and indigent people around us.

But if you're committed to the idea of superintelligence, AI research is the most important thing you could do on the planet right now. It's more important than politics, malaria, starving children, war, global warming, anything you can think of.

145   Because what hangs in the balance is trillions and trillions of beings, the entire population of future humanity, simulated and real, integrated over all future time.

In such conditions, it's not rational to work on any other problem.

Megalomania

This ties into megalomania, this Bond-villainness that you see at the top of our industry.

People think that a superintelligence will take over the world, so they use that as justification for why intelligent people should try to take over the world first, to try to fix it before AI can break it.

Joi Ito, who runs the MIT Media Lab, said a wonderful thing in a recent conversation with President Obama:

> This may upset some of my students at MIT, but one of my concerns is that it's been a predominantly male gang of kids, mostly white, who are building the core computer science around AI, and they're more comfortable talking to computers than to human beings. A lot of them feel that if they could just make that science-fiction, generalized AI, we wouldn't have to worry about all the messy stuff like politics and society. They think machines will just figure it all out for us.

150   Having realized that the world is not a programming problem, AI obsessives want to *make* it into a programming problem, by designing a God-like machine.

This is megalomaniacal. I don't like it.

Transhuman Voodoo

If you're persuaded by AI risk, you have to adopt an entire basket of deplorable beliefs that go with it.

For starters, nanotechnology. Any superintelligence worth its salt would be able to create tiny machines that do all sorts of things. We would be living in a post-scarcity society where all material needs are met.

Nanotechnology would also be able scan your brain so you can upload it into a different body, or into a virtual world. So the second consequence of (friendly) superintelligence is that no one can die—we become immortal.

A kind AI could even resurrect the dead. Nanomachines could go into my brain and look **155** at memories of my father, then use them to create a simulation of him that I can interact with, and that will always be disappointed in me, no matter what I do.

Another weird consequence of AI is Galactic expansion. I've never understood precisely why, but it's a staple of transhumanist thought. The fate of (trans)humanity must either be leave our planet and colonize the galaxy, or to die out. This is made more urgent knowing other civilizations have made the same choice and might be ahead of us in the space race.

So there's a lot of weird ancillary stuff packed into this assumption of true artificial intelligence.

Religion 2.0

What it really is is a form of religion. People have called a belief in a technological Singularity the "nerd Apocalypse," and it's true.

It's a clever hack, because instead of believing in God at the outset, you imagine yourself building an entity that is functionally identical with God. This way even committed atheists can rationalize their way into the comforts of faith.

The AI has all the attributes of God: it's omnipotent, omniscient, and either benevolent **160** (if you did your array bounds-checking right), or it is the Devil and you are at its mercy.

Like in any religion, there's even a feeling of urgency. You have to act now! The fate of the world is in the balance!

And of course, they need money!

Because these arguments appeal to religious instincts, once they take hold they are hard to uproot.

Comic Book Ethics

These religious convictions lead to a comic-book ethics, where a few lone heroes are charged with saving the world through technology and clever thinking. What's at stake is the very fate of the universe.

As a result, we have an industry full of rich dudes who think they are Batman (though **165** interestingly enough, no one wants to be Robin).

Simulation Fever

If you believe that sentient artificial life is possible, and that an AI will be able to design extraordinarily powerful computers, then you're also likely to believe we live in a simulation. Here's how that works:

Imagine that you're a historian, living in a post-Singularity world. You study the Second World War and want to know what would happen if Hitler had captured Moscow in 1941. Since you have access to hypercomputers, you set up a simulation, watch the armies roll in, and write your paper.

But because the simulation is so detailed, the entities in it are conscious beings, just like you. So your university ethics board is not going to let you turn it off. It's bad enough that you've already simulated the Holocaust. As an ethical researcher, you have to keep this thing running.

Eventually that simulated world will invent computers, develop AI, and start running its own simulations. So in a sense it's simulations all the way down, until you run out of CPU.

170   So you see that every base reality can contain a vast number of nested simulations, and a simple counting argument tells us we're much more likely to live in a simulated world than the real one.

But if you believe this, you believe in magic. Because if we're in a simulation, we know *nothing* about the rules in the level above. We don't even know if math works the same way—maybe in the simulating world $2 + 2 = 5$, or maybe $2 + 2 = $ 🌑.

A simulated world gives us no information about the world it's running in.

In a simulation, people could easily rise from the dead, if the sysadmin just kept the right backups. And if we can communicate with one of the admins, then we basically have a hotline to God.

175   This is a powerful solvent for sanity. When you start getting deep into simulation world, you begin to go nuts.

[Note that we now have four independent ways in which superintelligence offers us immortality:

1. A benevolent AI invents medical nanotechnology and keeps your body young forever.
2. The AI invents full-brain scanning, including brain scans on dead people, frozen heads etc., that let you live in a computer.
3. The AI "resurrects" people by scanning other people's brains for memories of the person, and combining that with video and other records. If no one remembers the person well enough, they can always be grown "from scratch" in a simulation designed to start with their DNA and re-create all the circumstances of their life.
4. If we already live in a simulation, there's a chance that whoever/whatever runs the simulation is keeping proper backups, and can be persuaded to reload them.

This is what I mean by AI appealing to religious impulses. What other belief system offers you four different flavors of scientifically proven immortality?]

We've learned that at least one American plutocrat (almost certainly Elon Musk, who believes the odds are a billion to one against us living in "base reality") has hired a pair of coders to try to hack the simulation.

This is an extraordinarily rude thing to do! I'm using it!

If you think we're living in a computer program, trying to segfault it is inconsiderate to everyone who lives in it with you. It is far more dangerous and irresponsible than the atomic scientists who risked blowing up the atmosphere.

Data Hunger

180   As I mentioned earlier, the most effective way we've found to get interesting behavior out of the AIs we actually build is by pouring data into them.

This creates a dynamic that is socially harmful. We're on the point of introducing Orwellian microphones into everybody's house. All that data is going to be centralized and used to train neural networks that will then become better at listening to what we want to do.

But if you think that the road to AI goes down this pathway, you want to maximize the amount of data being collected, and in as raw a form as possible.

It reinforces the idea that we have to retain as much data, and conduct as much surveillance as possible.

String Theory for Programmers

AI risk is string theory for computer programmers. It's fun to think about, interesting, and completely inaccessible to experiment given our current technology. You can build crystal palaces of thought, working from first principles, then climb up inside them and pull the ladder up behind you.

People who can reach preposterous conclusions from a long chain of abstract reasoning, and feel confident in their truth, are the wrong people to be running a culture. **185**

Incentivizing Crazy

This whole field of "study" incentivizes crazy.

One of the hallmarks of deep thinking in AI risk is that the more outlandish your ideas, the more credibility it gives you among other enthusiasts. It shows that you have the courage to follow these trains of thought all the way to the last station.

Ray Kurzweil, who believes he will never die, has been a Google employee for several years now and is presumably working on that problem.

There are a lot of people in Silicon Valley working on truly crazy projects under the cover of money.

AI Cosplay

The most harmful social effect of AI anxiety is something I call AI cosplay. People who are genuinely persuaded that AI is real and imminent begin behaving like their fantasy of what a hyperintelligent AI would do. **190**

In his book, Bostrom lists six things an AI would have to master to take over the world:

- Intelligence Amplification
- Strategizing
- Social manipulation
- Hacking
- Technology research
- Economic productivity

If you look at AI believers in Silicon Valley, this is the quasi-sociopathic checklist they themselves seem to be working from.

Sam Altman, the man who runs YCombinator, is my favorite example of this archetype. He seems entranced by the idea of reinventing the world from scratch, maximizing impact and personal productivity. He has assigned teams to work on reinventing cities, and is doing secret behind-the-scenes political work to swing the election.

Such skull-and-dagger behavior by the tech elite is going to provoke a backlash by nontechnical people who don't like to be manipulated. You can't tug on the levers of power indefinitely before it starts to annoy other people in your democratic society.

I've even seen people in the so-called rationalist community refer to people who they don't think are effective as "Non Player Characters," or NPCs, a term borrowed from video games. This is a horrible way to look at the world. **195**

So I work in an industry where the self-professed rationalists are the craziest ones of all. It's getting me down.

These AI cosplayers are like nine year olds camped out in the backyard, playing with flashlights in their tent. They project their own shadows on the sides of the tent and get scared that it's a monster.

Really it's a distorted image of themselves that they're reacting to. There's a feedback loop between how intelligent people imagine a God-like intelligence would behave, and how they choose to behave themselves.

So what's the answer? What's the fix?

200   We need better sci-fi! And like so many things, we already have the technology.

This is Stanislaw Lem, the great Polish sci-fi author. English-language scifi is terrible, but in the Eastern bloc we have the goods, and we need to make sure it's exported properly.

It's already been translated well into English, it just needs to be better distributed.

What sets authors like Lem and the Strugatsky brothers above their Western counterparts is that these are people who grew up in difficult circumstances, experienced the war, and then lived in a totalitarian society where they had to express their ideas obliquely through writing.

They have an actual understanding of human experience and the limits of Utopian thinking that is nearly absent from the West.

205   There are some notable exceptions—Stanley Kubrick was able to do it—but it's exceptionally rare to find American or British scifi that has any kind of humility about what we as a species can do with technology.

The Alchemists

Since I'm being critical of AI alarmism, it's only fair that I put my own cards on the table.

I think our understanding of the mind is in the same position that alchemy was in in the 17th century.

Alchemists get a bad rap. We think of them as mystics who did not do a lot of experimental work. Modern research has revealed that they were far more diligent bench chemists than we gave them credit for.

In many cases they used modern experimental techniques, kept lab notebooks, and asked good questions.

210   The alchemists got a lot right! For example, they were convinced of the corpuscular theory of matter: that everything is made of little tiny bits, and that you can re-combine the bits with one another to create different substances, which is correct!

Their problem was they didn't have precise enough equipment to make the discoveries they needed to.

The big discovery you need to make as an alchemist is mass balance: that everything you start with weighs as much as your final products. But some of those might be gases or evanescent liquids, and alchemists just didn't have the precision.

Modern chemistry was not possible until the 18th century.

The alchemists also had clues that led them astray. For one thing, they were obsessed with mercury. Mercury is not very interesting chemically, but it is the only metal that is a liquid at room temperature.

215   This seemed very significant to the alchemists, and caused them to place mercury at the heart of their alchemical system, and their search for the Philosopher's Stone, a way to turn base metals into gold.

It didn't help that mercury was neurotoxic, so if you spent too much time playing with it, you started to think weird thoughts. In that way, it resembles our current thought experiments with superintelligence.

Imagine if we could send a modern chemistry textbook back in time to a great alchemist like George Starkey or Isaac Newton.

The first thing they would do would be flip through to see if we found the Philosopher's Stone. And they'd discover that we had! We realized their dream!

Except we aren't all that excited about it, because when we turn base metals into gold, it comes out radioactive. Stand next to an ingot of transubstantiated gold and it will kill you with invisible, magic rays.

You can imagine what a struggle it would be to not make the modern concepts of radio- **220** activity and atomic energy sound mystical to them.

We would have to go on to explain what we *do* use the "philosopher's stone" for: to make a metal that never existed on earth, two handfuls of which are sufficient to blow up a city if brought together with sufficient speed.

What's more, we would have to explain to the alchemists that every star they see in the sky is a "philosopher's stone." converting elements from one to another, and that every particle in our bodies comes from stars in the firmament that existed and exploded before the creation of the Earth.

Finally, they would learn that the forces that hold our bodies together are the forces that make lightning in the sky, and that the reason you or I can see anything is the same reason that a lodestone attracts metal, and the same reason that I can stand on this stage without falling through it.

They would learn that everything we see, touch and smell is governed by this single force, which obeys mathematical laws so simple we can write them on an index card.

Why it is so simple is a deep mystery even to us. But to them it would sound like pure **225** mysticism.

I think we are in the same boat with the theory of mind.

We have some important clues. The most important of these is the experience of consciousness. This box of meat on my neck is self-aware, and hopefully (unless we're in a simulation) you guys also experience the same thing I do.

But while this is the most basic and obvious fact in the world, we understand it so poorly we can't even frame scientific questions about it.

We also have other clues that may be important, or may be false leads. We know that all intelligent creatures sleep, and dream. We know how brains develop in children, we know that emotions and language seem to have a profound effect on cognition.

We know that minds have to play and learn to interact with the world, before they reach **230** their full mental capacity.

And we have clues from computer science as well. We've discovered computer techniques that detect images and sounds in ways that seem to mimic the visual and auditory preprocessing done in the brain.

But there's a lot of things that we are terribly mistaken about, and unfortunately we don't know what they are.

And there are things that we massively underestimate the complexity of.

An alchemist could hold a rock in one hand and a piece of wood in the other and think they were both examples of "substance," not understanding that the wood was orders of magnitude more complex.

235   We're in the same place with the study of mind. And that's exciting! We're going to learn a lot.

But meanwhile, there is a quote I love to cite:

> If everybody contemplates the infinite instead of fixing the drains, many of us will die of cholera.
>
> —John Rich

In the near future, the kind of AI and machine learning we have to face is much different than the phantasmagorical AI in Bostrom's book, and poses its own serious problems.

It's like if those Alamogordo scientists had decided to completely focus on whether they were going to blow up the atmosphere, and forgot that they were also making nuclear weapons, and had to figure out how to cope with that.

The pressing ethical questions in machine learning are not about machines becoming self-aware and taking over the world, but about how people can exploit other people, or through carelessness introduce immoral behavior into automated systems.

240   And of course there's the question of how AI and machine learning affect power relationships. We've watched surveillance become a de facto part of our lives, in an unexpected way. We never thought it would look quite like this.

So we've created a very powerful system of social control, and unfortunately put it in the hands of people who run it are distracted by a crazy idea.

What I hope I've done today is shown you the dangers of being too smart. Hopefully you'll leave this talk a little dumber than you started it, and be more immune to the seductions of AI that seem to bedevil smarter people.

We should all learn a lesson from Stephen Hawking's cat: don't let the geniuses running your industry talk you into anything. Do your own thing!

In the absence of effective leadership from those at the top of our industry, it's up to us to make an effort, and to think through all of the ethical issues that AI—as it actually exists—is bringing into the world.

245   Thank you!

Discussion and Writing Suggestions

1. Take any one of Ceglowski's critiques of Bostrom's argument—ether from his "inside" assessment of superintelligence or "outside." Rewrite that critique in your own words. Once you're sure you understand it, respond. Share your paraphrase and response with classmates.

2. Do you agree with Ceglowski that superintelligence—Bostrom's concern over runaway AI—is a "crazy" idea? Does agreeing with Bostrom mean accepting, at least in part, the premises of AI disaster movies like *Terminator* or *The Matrix*?

3. Ceglowski compares the current state of AI development to the state of alchemy in the 17th century. Discuss the comparison. In what ways does it illuminate the state of AI? Obscure it?

4. What do you make of the "grandiosity" and "megalomania" arguments Ceglowski levels at the AI doomsday prophets—that it's up to the present generation of computer scientists to save the world from run-amok machine intelligence? Do you, like Ceglowski, find such claims unwarranted and overly dramatic?

Don't Fear Artificial Intelligence*

Dominic Basulto

As a contributor to the *Washington Post* and the blog Big Think, Dominic Basulto has written on topics as varied as 3-D printed houses, cyber war, and digital tattoos. The following appeared in the *Post* on January 20, 2015, shortly after the Future of Life Institute published its Open Letter.

Stephen Hawking, Elon Musk and a number of other tech luminaries from MIT, IBM and Harvard recently signed off on an open letter from the nonprofit Future of Life Institute warning about the perils of artificial intelligence. Without the appropriate safety measures built in, they argue, the rapid growth of artificial intelligence could end in disaster for humanity.

Of course, it's easy to understand why AI has been giving rise to dystopian fears about the future from the world's most intelligent people. That's because the problem at the heart of AI is something that the supporters of the Future of Life letter refer to as "existential risk" — the risk that very bad things can happen in the near future to wipe out the human race as a result of technology gone bad.

"Existential risk" is precisely what makes Hollywood sci-fi movies so scary. In last year's dystopian thriller "Transcendence," for example, Johnny Depp morphs into a super-brain with the ability to wipe the human race off the planet. At about the same time the movie hit cinemas, Hawking bluntly warned about the risks of super-intelligence: "I think the development of full artificial intelligence could spell the end of the human race."

The reason, Hawking told the BBC in an interview, is that, "Once humans develop artificial intelligence, it will take off on its own and redesign itself at an ever-increasing rate. Humans, who are limited by slow biological evolution, couldn't compete and would be superseded." In short, if computers get too smart, it's game over for humans.

In the Future of Life letter, Musk and Hawking hint at a dystopian future in which humans 5 have lost control of self-driving cars, drones, lethal weapons and the right to privacy. Even worse, computers would become smarter than humans and at some point, would decide that humans really aren't so necessary after all. And they would do so not because they are inherently evil, but because they are so inherently rational — humans tend to make a mess of things.

But how likely is it, really, that an AI super-mind could wreak that kind of havoc and decide that humans are expendable?

The flip side of "existential risk" is "existential reward" — the possibility that very good things can happen in the near future as a result of exponential leaps in technology. For every Stephen Hawking and Elon Musk, there's a Ray Kurzweil or Peter Diamandis. People who focus on "existential reward" claim that AI will bring forth a utopian future, in which the human brain's full potential will be opened up, giving us the ability to discover new cures, new sources of energy, and new solutions to all of humanity's problems. Even the supporters of Future of Life's dystopian AI premise concede that there are a lot of positives out there, including the "eradication of disease and poverty."

If you think about what AI has already accomplished, well, there's a lot more that can be done when super-intelligence is applied to the pressing humanitarian issues of the day. The Future of Life letter notes how far, how fast, we've already come. AI has given us speech recognition, image classification, autonomous vehicles and machine translation. Thinking in terms of "existential reward" is what leads one to think about the future as one of abundance, in which AI helps—not hurts—humanity.

The types of AI safeguards alluded to by Hawking and Musk in the Future of Life open letter could make a difference in ensuring "reward" wins out over "risk." In short, these safeguards could tilt the playing field in favor of humans, by ensuring that "our AI systems must do what we want them to do."

10   However, to view the debate over AI purely in terms of humans vs. the machines misses the point. It's not us vs. them in a race for mastery of planet Earth, with human intelligence evolving linearly and digital intelligence evolving exponentially. What's more likely is some form of hybrid evolution in which humans remain in charge but develop augmented capabilities as a result of technology. One popular scenario for sci-fi fans is one in which humans and computers ultimately merge into some sort of interstellar species, figure out how to leave planet Earth behind on a new mission to colonize the galaxy and live happily ever after.

When a technology is so obviously dangerous—like nuclear energy or synthetic biology— humanity has an imperative to consider dystopian predictions of the future. But it also has an imperative to push on, to reach its full potential. While it's scary, sure, that humans may no longer be the smartest life forms in the room a generation from now, should we really be that concerned? Seems like we've already done a pretty good job of finishing off the planet anyway. If anything, we should be welcoming our AI masters to arrive sooner rather than later.

Discussion and Writing Suggestions

1. How successful is Basulto's argument as a critique of the Open Letter? Develop your response by pointing to particular features of the document.

2. In times of change, some people fight losing what's old and familiar. Others insist it's the way of the world: The old gets reinvented and replaced by the new, which shouldn't be feared or distrusted merely *because* it's new. Some people fear the loss of humanity to intelligent machines. Others, like Basulto, welcome "some form of hybrid evolution in which humans remain in charge but develop augmented capabilities as a result of technology." Would you welcome the chance of dramatically enhancing your cognitive powers and your lifespan? Or would you resist becoming a human/machine hybrid because you value your humanity just as it is? Do your religious or ethical beliefs prevent you from viewing such an evolution favorably?

3. You have read how the authors of the Open Letter (pages 377–381) and Basulto weigh existential risk and existential reward regarding intelligent machines. How do you weigh these risks and rewards? If you were in a position to direct future development of some aspect of AI, how would existential risk versus existential reward shape your strategy?

4. Basulto writes: "When a technology is so obviously dangerous—like nuclear energy or synthetic biology—humanity has an imperative to consider dystopian predictions of the future. But it also has an imperative to push on, to

reach its full potential." What, exactly, is this "imperative" to develop new technologies? Do you agree that we are obligated to "push on"?

Robots Will Take Your Job; Will They Guarantee Your Income?*

Scott Santens

As a champion for a guaranteed, basic income, New Orleans–based writer and blogger Scott Santens explores the implications of intelligent machines for the labor force in the twenty-first century and beyond. What will happen as AI computers and robots displace workers? How would governments respond if millions lost their jobs and were driven into poverty? Perhaps we're headed toward a world in which "jobs are for machines, and life is for people." This selection first appeared in the *Boston Globe* on February 25, 2016.

On Dec. 2, 1942, a team of scientists led by Enrico Fermi came back from lunch and watched as humanity created the first self-sustaining nuclear reaction inside a pile of bricks and wood underneath a football field at the University of Chicago. Known to history as Chicago Pile-1, it was celebrated in silence with a single bottle of Chianti, for those who were there understood exactly what it meant for humankind, without any need for words.

Now, something new has occurred that, again, quietly changed the world forever. Like a whispered word in a foreign language, you may have heard it but couldn't fully understand.

The language is something called deep learning. And the whispered word was a computer's use of it to defeat one of the world's top players in a game called Go. Go is a board game so complex that it can be likened to playing 10 chess matches simultaneously on the same table.

This may sound like a small accomplishment, another feather in the cap of machines as they continue to prove themselves superior in parlor games that humans invented to fill their idle hours. But this feat is about far more than bragging rights. This was considered a "holy grail" level of achievement, and it's a clear signal that advances in technology are now so exponential that milestones we once thought far away will start arriving rapidly.

What's more, humans are entirely unprepared. These exponential advances, most notably in forms of artificial intelligence, will prove daunting for as long as we continue to insist upon employment as our primary source of income. The White House, in a stunning report to Congress this week, put the probability at 83 percent that a worker making less than $20 an hour in 2010 will eventually lose his job to a machine. Even workers making as much as $40 an hour face odds of 31 percent.

5

We're building a world where a universal basic income may be the only rational, fair way for society to function—and that's not a future we should fear.

First, a word on how we got here. All work can be divided into four types: routine and nonroutine, cognitive and manual. Routine work is the same stuff day in and day out, while nonroutine work varies. Within these two varieties is the work that requires mostly our brains (cognitive) and the work that requires mostly our bodies (manual). Routine work started to stagnate in 1990, because some of that work can be best handled by machines.

*Scott Santens, "Robots Will Take Your Job," Boston Globe, February 25, 2016, http://www. bostonglobe.com/ideas/2016/02/24/robots-will-take-your-job/5lXtKomQ7uQBEzTJOXT7YO/story.html. Reprinted Courtesy of Scott Santens

Of course, routine work once formed the basis of the American middle class. It's routine, manual work that Henry Ford paid people middle-class wages to perform, and it's routine cognitive work that once filled American office buildings. That world is dwindling, leaving only two kinds of jobs with rosy outlooks: jobs that require so little thought that they pay next to nothing, and jobs that require so much thought that the salaries are exorbitant.

A four-engine plane can stay aloft with only two engines working. But what happens when the last two begin to sputter? That's what the advancing fields of robotics and AI represent to those final two engines of nonroutine work because, for the first time, we are successfully teaching machines to learn.

10   Machines are getting smarter because we're getting better at building them. And we're getting better at it, in part, because we are smarter about the ways in which our own brains function.

What's in our skulls is essentially a mass of interconnected cells. Some of these connections are short, and some are long; some cells are only connected to one other, and some are connected to many. Electrical signals then pass through these connections, at various rates, and subsequent neural firings happen in turn. It's all kind of like falling dominoes, but far faster, larger, and more complex.

Deep neural networks are kind of like pared-down virtual brains. They provide an avenue to machine learning that's made incredible leaps previously thought to be much further down the road. How? It's not just the obvious growing capability of our computers and our expanding knowledge in the neurosciences, but the vastly growing expanse of our collective data.

Big data isn't just some buzzword. We're creating and standardizing so much data that a 2013 report by SINTEF estimated that 90 percent of all data in the world had been created in just the prior two years. This incredible rate of data creation is doubling every 18 months thanks to the Internet, where we uploaded 300 hours of video to YouTube and sent 350,000 tweets each minute last year.

Everything we do is generating data, and lots of data is exactly what machines need in order to learn to learn. Imagine programming a computer to recognize a chair. Early incarnations of the program would be far better at determining what isn't a chair than what is.

15   Humans learn the difference as children, when chairs are identified for us by name. If children point at a table and say "chair," they're corrected with "table." This is called reinforcement learning. The label "chair" gets connected to every chair, such that certain neural pathways are weighted and others aren't. For "chair" to fire in our brains, what we perceive has to be close enough to our previous chair encounters. Essentially, our lives are big data filtered through our brains.

The unprecedented power of deep learning is that it's a way of using massive amounts of data to get machines to operate more like we do without giving them explicit instructions. Instead of describing "chairness" to a computer, we can just plug it into the Internet and feed it millions of pictures of chairs for a general idea. Next, we test it with even more images. When the machine is wrong, it's corrected, further improving its "chairness" detection.

Repetition of this process results in a computer that knows what a chair is when it sees it, often as well as a human can. Unlike us, however, it can then sort through millions of images within a matter of seconds. And when one machine learns something, it can pass on that knowledge to an entire network of connected machines—instantly.

One powerful example of this learning process comes from the electric car maker Tesla. Google spent six years accumulating 1.7 million miles of driving data with its prototype self-driving cars. Tesla, on the other hand, simply sent out a software update, instantly teaching its fleet how to drive themselves with a new "autopilot" ability. The network started racking up

Google's total mileage every week. Every single Tesla is now effectively teaching all other Teslas the "chairness" of driving.

Extend the Tesla example to the Internet of Things, where any interaction with a connected object has the potential of teaching something new to every connected object, and the immense scaling of networked machine learning becomes almost unimaginable.

In a frequently cited paper, an Oxford University study estimated the potential automation of about half of all existing jobs by 2033. Meanwhile self-driving vehicles, again thanks to machine learning, have the capability of drastically affecting all economies by eliminating millions of jobs within a short span of time. New jobs are no longer created faster than technology destroys them. A report by the World Economic Forum has estimated that despite the creation of millions of new jobs over the next four years, there will likely be a net loss of 5 million.

All of this is why it's those most knowledgeable in the AI field who are now actively sounding the horn for basic income. During a panel discussion at the end of 2015 at Singularity University, prominent data scientist Jeremy Howard asked, "Do you want half of people to starve because they literally can't add economic value, or not?" before going on to suggest, "If the answer is not, then the smartest way to distribute the wealth is by implementing a universal basic income."

The combination of deep learning and Big Data has resulted in astounding accomplishments just in the past year. Google's DeepMind AI learned how to read and comprehend what it read through hundreds of thousands of annotated news articles. DeepMind also taught itself to play dozens of Atari 2600 video games better than humans, just by looking at the screen and its score, and playing games repeatedly. An AI named Giraffe taught itself how to play chess in a similar manner using a dataset of 175 million chess positions, attaining International Master level status in just 72 hours by repeatedly playing itself.

In 2015, an AI even passed a visual Turing test by learning to learn in a way that enabled it to be shown an unknown character in a fictional alphabet, then instantly reproduce that letter in a way that was entirely indistinguishable from a human given the same task. These are all major milestones in AI.

Nonetheless, when asked to estimate how long it would take a computer to defeat a prominent player in the game of Go, the answer—just months prior to the announcement by Google of AlphaGo's victory—was about a decade. That was considered a fair guess because Go is a game with more possibilities than atoms in the known universe. That made impossible any brute-force approach to scan every possible move to determine the next best move. But deep neural networks got around that barrier in the same way our own minds do, by learning to estimate what feels like the best move. We do this through observation and practice, and so did AlphaGo. It analyzed millions of professional games and played itself millions of times. For the game of Go, the enemy wasn't a month's march from the castle—it was already inside the keep, feet up on the table, eating the king's lunch.

The Go lesson shows us that nothing humans do as a job is safe anymore. From making hamburgers to anesthesiology, machines will be able to successfully perform such tasks and at lower costs than humans.

Amelia is many things. But she'll never take a sick day, join a union, or waste time on Facebook on the job. Created by IPsoft over the past 16 years, the AI system learned how to perform the work of call center employees. She can learn in seconds what takes humans months to master, and she can do it in 20 languages. Because she's able to learn, she's able to do more over time. In one company trial, she successfully handled one of every 10 calls in the first week, and by the end of the second month, she could resolve six in 10. Deploy her worldwide, and 250 million people can start looking for a new job.

Viv is an AI coming soon from the creators of Siri who'll be our own personal assistant. She'll perform tasks online for us and even function as a Facebook News Feed on steroids by suggesting we consume the media she'll know we'll like best. With Viv doing all this for us, we'll see far fewer ads, and that means the entire advertising industry—that industry the entire Internet is built upon—stands to be hugely disrupted.

A world with Amelia and Viv—and the countless other AI counterparts coming online soon—is going to force serious societal reconsiderations. Is it fair to ask any human to compete against a potentially flawless machine in the next cubicle? If machines are performing most of our jobs and not getting paid, where does that money go instead? And what does that unpaid money no longer buy? Is it even possible that many of the jobs we're creating don't need to exist at all, and only do because of the incomes they provide?

We must seriously start talking about decoupling income from work. Adopting a universal basic income, aside from immunizing against the negative effects of automation, also decreases the risks inherent in entrepreneurship, and the sizes of bureaucracies otherwise necessary to boost incomes. It's for these reasons, it has cross-partisan support, and is even now in the beginning stages of implementation in countries like Switzerland, Finland, and the Netherlands.

30   Artificial intelligence pioneer Chris Eliasmith, director of the Centre for Theoretical Neuroscience, also warned about the immediate impacts of AI on society in a recent interview with Futurism, "AI is already having a big impact on our economies. . . . My suspicion is that more countries will have to follow Finland's lead in exploring basic income guarantees for people."

Even Baidu's chief scientist and founder of Google's "Google Brain" deep learning project, Andrew Ng, during an onstage interview at this year's Deep Learning Summit, expressed the shared notion that basic income must be "seriously considered" by governments, citing "a high chance that AI will create massive labor displacement."

When those building the tools begin warning about the implications of their use, shouldn't those wishing to use those tools listen with the utmost of attention, especially when it's the very livelihoods of millions at stake?

No nation is yet ready for the changes ahead. High rates of labor force nonparticipation leads to social instability, as does a lack of consumers within consumer economies. It turns out, humans are good at designing things, but not so great at picturing a world that their technology will create. What's the big lesson to learn, in a century when machines can learn? Maybe it is that jobs are for machines, and life is for people.

Discussion and Writing Suggestions

1. Santens writes that "serious societal reconsiderations" are in store concerning our economy and who works—and doesn't. As a student who's preparing for the future, do you think you're learning the skills you'll need to resist an AI takeover of your job? What are the skills that might inoculate you against such a takeover?

2. "We must seriously start talking about decoupling income from work," writes Santens. As we envision a future economy in which some people work and others don't (but are assured a basic income), which role would you prefer: worker or nonworker? Why?

3. "When those building the tools begin warning about the implications of their use, shouldn't those wishing to use those tools listen with the utmost of

attention, especially when it's the very livelihoods of millions at stake?" Your answer?

4. Santens writes that as the world grows more reliant on intelligent machines, jobs [will be] for machines, and life [will be] for people." Imagine a life without work. What would be the challenges of not working? The benefits? For instance, what would it mean to go "on vacation"? Wouldn't life be one continual vacation? Or would vacations not be possible because, by definition, they require a break from work? Could you happily adjust to not working?

A Review of Humans Are Underrated
*by Geoff Colvin**

Tyler Cowen

In this next selection, Tyler Cowen, an economist at George Mason University, reviews Geoff Colvin's *Humans Are Underrated* (2015). Basic to any review is a summary, and from Cowen's summary we learn that Colvin offers some relief for those worried that intelligent machines will soon be taking over the world. Colvin is a senior editor at large for *Fortune* magazine, a regular contributor to CBS radio, and a much sought-after speaker. Cowen's review first appeared in the *Washington Post* on August 13, 2015.

Humans Are Underrated serves up two different books in one, each interesting in its own right. The first offers an overview of recent developments in smart software and artificial intelligence. The reader learns about the bright future of driverless cars; IBM's Watson and its skills at "Jeopardy" and medical diagnosis; and the software of Narrative Science, which can write up stories and, in some cases, cover events as well as a human journalist. The overall message is a sobering one: The machines are now able to copy or even improve on a lot of human skills, and thus they are encroaching on jobs. We won't all have to join the bread line, but not everyone will prosper in this new world. That material is well argued, and those stories are becoming increasingly familiar ground.

The second and more original message is a take on which human abilities will remain important in light of growing computer efficacy. In a nutshell, those abilities are empathy, interpersonal skills and who we are rather than what we do. This is ultimately a book about how human beings can make a difference and how that capability will never go away. It's both a description of the likely future and a prescription for how you or your children will be able to stand out in the world to come.

Geoff Colvin puts it pretty simply: "Rather than ask what computers can't do, it's much more useful to ask what people are compelled to do." And what we are compelled to do is to contact other humans and seek value from them.

The theme of empathy recurs repeatedly. For all the virtues of software, it just can't bring the same connection that human employees can. Good (human) managers understand how to motivate, how to set expectations, and when to offer rewards or perhaps enforce penalties. Face-recognition software may be able to judge our moods, but it doesn't come close to having the same flexibility of response, or the same two-way bond, as a human who can hear and interpret our personal stories.

5   The future of the American economy will prize people skills above all else. Mark Zuckerberg was a psychology major; Steve Jobs also had a liberal arts background, which he drew upon to make Apple products attractive and compelling.

I wonder, however, if manipulation shouldn't be added to the list of what one group of humans feels compelled to do to another. Precisely because we are able to identify what others are feeling, we can use that knowledge to influence their behavior. So the future of human employment isn't just about the caring doctor, it is also about the marketer, the nudger, the data collector and the advertising executive. Think "Mad Men" with a vengeance. Don't forget that the supposed empathy of the doctor, the sales representative or the military commander, to cite a few of the book's examples, is often self-interested and directed toward bending our will, and not always in ways we would accept if they were made transparent to us.

Colvin presents the interesting hypothesis that today, empathy seems to be declining and narcissism rising, possibly because we are obsessed with the superficial use of social networks. But is this so? Contemporary America just put its stamp of approval on same-sex marriage, even though a strong majority of people are not gay.

My favorite parts of the book are about the military, an area where most other popular authors on automation and smart software have hesitated to tread. In this book you can read about how much of America's military prowess comes from superior human performance and not just from technology. Future gains will result from how combat participants are trained, motivated, and taught to work together and trust each other, and from better after-action performance reviews. Militaries are inevitably hierarchical, but when they process and admit their mistakes, they can become rapidly more efficient.

If machines and smart software carry any major lesson for our world, it is that human teams matter more than ever. That's the best and most important insight in this book. Another lesson is that the future, including future jobs, will be more and more about telling stories. That includes telling stories to motivate and organize people, telling stories to express empathy, and telling stories to make people happy. Again, the liberal arts will be a lot more important in our future than many people think.

10   One interesting implication is that the future may be what Colvin calls a "woman's world." On average, women seem to be strong at empathizing and storytelling; there is also good evidence that female participation makes groups a lot smarter. Indeed, we already see in the data that by historical standards, a disproportionate share of men fall into the category of the long-term unemployed.

Humans Are Underrated is a worthy addition to the growing collection of books about the new economy, in which, to quote Marc Andreesen, "Software eats everything." It can serve as a good introduction to its core themes, but even if you've read all the other books in the field, it is still valuable for its insights into the enduring value of human performance and teamwork.

Discussion and Writing Suggestions

1. Given the other readings in this chapter, how persuaded are you that "human beings . . . will never go away" because of our unique abilities—including empathy and the high value we place on interactions with others? Can't empathy and human interactions be simulated by advanced AI devices?

2. One of Colvin's arguments, writes Cowen, is that the "future of the American economy will prize people skills above all else." Other authors in the chapter argue that efficiency and automation will guide the future American economy. To what extent are people skills, efficiency, and automation compatible? If they aren't, which do you suppose will win out in the end? Why?

3. Cowen points out that baser motives like manipulation will form part of the skill set Americans bring to the future economy. What do you think of this critique?

4. Colvin argues that the liberal arts (and what they can teach about storytelling) will have an important role to play in the future. Are you persuaded? Do you envision enrolling in a philosophy or literature course because you might one day draw upon the skills learned in such classes?

5. Does what you've learned from working with teams incline you to agree with Colvin that "human teams matter more than ever"? Why is teamwork, both in and out of the military, so important—and so difficult to reproduce in software?

6. Tyler Cowen's review of Colvin's book is a critique that consists of core elements: Cowen summarizes Colvin's book, he evaluates its argument(s), and he judges its value. You haven't read Colvin's book, so you can't judge if Cowen has accurately summarized it. Still, you can have a hunch. Do you find the critique informative? Potentially useful? Why or why not?

Automation and Anxiety*

The Economist

Scott Santens addresses the fear that intelligent machines will disrupt the labor market and lead, possibly, to massive layoffs and guaranteed incomes. The next selection steers a middle ground between like-minded pessimism and a more optimistic view that computers will "reallocate rather than displace jobs." "Automation and Anxiety" first appeared in *The Economist* on June 25, 2016.

Sitting in an office in San Francisco, Igor Barani calls up some medical scans on his screen. He is the chief executive of Enlitic, one of a host of startups applying deep learning to medicine, starting with the analysis of images such as X-rays and CT scans. It is an obvious use of the technology. Deep learning is renowned for its superhuman prowess at certain

*"Automation and anxiety: Will smarter machines cause mass unemployment?" Economist, June 25th 2016, http://www.economist.com/news/special-report/21700758-will-smarter-machines-cause-mass-unemployment-automation-and-anxiety

forms of image recognition; there are large sets of labelled training data to crunch; and there is tremendous potential to make health care more accurate and efficient.

Dr Barani (who used to be an oncologist) points to some CT scans of a patient's lungs, taken from three different angles. Red blobs flicker on the screen as Enlitic's deep-learning system examines and compares them to see if they are blood vessels, harmless imaging artefacts or malignant lung nodules. The system ends up highlighting a particular feature for further investigation. In a test against three expert human radiologists working together, Enlitic's system was 50% better at classifying malignant tumours and had a false-negative rate (where a cancer is missed) of zero, compared with 7% for the humans. Another of Enlitic's systems, which examines X-rays to detect wrist fractures, also handily outperformed human experts. The firm's technology is currently being tested in 40 clinics across Australia.

A computer that dispenses expert radiology advice is just one example of how jobs currently done by highly trained white-collar workers can be automated, thanks to the advance of deep learning and other forms of artificial intelligence. The idea that manual work can be carried out by machines is already familiar; now ever-smarter machines can perform tasks done by information workers, too. What determines vulnerability to automation, experts say, is not so much whether the work concerned is manual or white-collar but whether or not it is routine. Machines can already do many forms of routine manual labour, and are now able to perform some routine cognitive tasks too. As a result, says Andrew Ng, a highly trained and specialised radiologist may now be in greater danger of being replaced by a machine than his own executive assistant: "She does so many different things that I don't see a machine being able to automate everything she does any time soon."

> **What determines vulnerability to automation is not so much whether the work concerned is manual or white-collar but whether or not it is routine.**

So which jobs are most vulnerable? In a widely noted study published in 2013, Carl Benedikt Frey and Michael Osborne examined the probability of computerisation for 702 occupations and found that 47% of workers in America had jobs at high risk of potential automation. In particular, they warned that most workers in transport and logistics (such as taxi and delivery drivers) and office support (such as receptionists and security guards) "are likely to be substituted by computer capital", and that many workers in sales and services (such as cashiers, counter and rental clerks, telemarketers and accountants) also faced a high risk of computerisation. They concluded that "recent developments in machine learning will put a substantial share of employment, across a wide range of occupations, at risk in the near future." Subsequent studies put the equivalent figure at 35% of the workforce for Britain (where more people work in creative fields less susceptible to automation) and 49% for Japan.

5   Economists are already worrying about "job polarisation", where middle-skill jobs (such as those in manufacturing) are declining but both low-skill and high-skill jobs are expanding. In effect, the workforce bifurcates into two groups doing non-routine work: highly paid, skilled workers (such as architects and senior managers) on the one hand and low-paid, unskilled workers (such as cleaners and burger-flippers) on the other. The stagnation of median wages in many Western countries is cited as evidence that automation is already having an effect— though it is hard to disentangle the impact of offshoring, which has also moved many routine jobs (including manufacturing and call-centre work) to low-wage countries in the developing world. Figures published by the Federal Reserve Bank of St Louis show that in America, employment in non-routine cognitive and non-routine manual jobs has grown steadily since the 1980s, whereas employment in routine jobs has been broadly flat (see chart). As more jobs are automated, this trend seems likely to continue.

Think

United States employment, by type of work, m

Sources: US Population Survey; Federal Reserve Bank of St. Louis

"Automation and anxiety." Economist, June 25th 2016.

And this is only the start. "We are just seeing the tip of the iceberg. No office job is safe," says Sebastian Thrun, an AI professor at Stanford known for his work on self-driving cars. Automation is now "blind to the colour of your collar", declares Jerry Kaplan, another Stanford academic and author of "Humans Need Not Apply", a book that predicts upheaval in the labour market. Gloomiest of all is Martin Ford, a software entrepreneur and the bestselling author of "Rise of the Robots". He warns of the threat of a "jobless future", pointing out that most jobs can be broken down into a series of routine tasks, more and more of which can be done by machines.

In previous waves of automation, workers had the option of moving from routine jobs in one industry to routine jobs in another; but now the same "big data" techniques that allow companies to improve their marketing and customer-service operations also give them the raw material to train machine-learning systems to perform the jobs of more and more people. "E-discovery" software can search mountains of legal documents much more quickly than human clerks or paralegals can. Some forms of journalism, such as writing market reports and sports summaries, are also being automated.

Predictions that automation will make humans redundant have been made before, however, going back to the Industrial Revolution, when textile workers, most famously the Luddites, protested that machines and steam engines would destroy their livelihoods. "Never until now did human invention devise such expedients for dispensing with the labour of the poor," said a pamphlet at the time. Subsequent outbreaks of concern occurred in the 1920s ("March of the machine makes idle hands", declared a *New York Times* headline in 1928), the 1930s (when John Maynard Keynes coined the term "technological unemployment") and 1940s, when the *New York Times* referred to the revival of such worries as the renewal of an "old argument".

As computers began to appear in offices and robots on factory floors, President John F. Kennedy declared that the major domestic challenge of the 1960s was to "maintain full employment at a time when automation . . . is replacing men". In 1964 a group of Nobel prizewinners, known as the Ad Hoc Committee on the Triple Revolution, sent President Lyndon Johnson a memo alerting him to the danger of a revolution triggered by "the combination of the computer and the automated self-regulating machine". This, they said, was leading to a new era of production "which requires progressively less human labour" and threatened to divide society into a skilled elite and an unskilled underclass. The advent of personal computers in the 1980s provoked further hand-wringing over potential job losses.

10   Yet in the past technology has always ended up creating more jobs than it destroys. That is because of the way automation works in practice, explains David Autor, an economist at the Massachusetts Institute of Technology. Automating a particular task, so that it can be done more quickly or cheaply, increases the demand for human workers to do the other tasks around it that have not been automated.

There are many historical examples of this in weaving, says James Bessen, an economist at the Boston University School of Law. During the Industrial Revolution more and more tasks in the weaving process were automated, prompting workers to focus on the things machines could not do, such as operating a machine, and then tending multiple machines to keep them running smoothly. This caused output to grow explosively. In America during the 19th century the amount of coarse cloth a single weaver could produce in an hour increased by a factor of 50, and the amount of labour required per yard of cloth fell by 98%. This made cloth cheaper and increased demand for it, which in turn created more jobs for weavers: their numbers quadrupled between 1830 and 1900. In other words, technology gradually changed the nature of the weaver's job, and the skills required to do it, rather than replacing it altogether.

In a more recent example, automated teller machines (ATMs) might have been expected to spell doom for bank tellers by taking over some of their routine tasks, and indeed in America their average number fell from 20 per branch in 1988 to 13 in 2004, Mr Bessen notes. But that reduced the cost of running a bank branch, allowing banks to open more branches in response to customer demand. The number of urban bank branches rose by 43% over the same period, so the total number of employees increased. Rather than destroying jobs, ATMs changed bank employees' work mix, away from routine tasks and towards things like sales and customer service that machines could not do.

The same pattern can be seen in industry after industry after the introduction of computers, says Mr Bessen: rather than destroying jobs, automation redefines them, and in ways that reduce costs and boost demand. In a recent analysis of the American workforce between 1982 and 2012, he found that employment grew significantly faster in occupations (for example, graphic design) that made more use of computers, as automation sped up one aspect of a job, enabling workers to do the other parts better. The net effect was that more computer-intensive jobs within an industry displaced less computer-intensive ones. Computers thus reallocate rather than displace jobs, requiring workers to learn new skills. This is true of a wide range of occupations, Mr Bessen found, not just in computer-related fields such as software development but also in administrative work, health care and many other areas. Only manufacturing jobs expanded more slowly than the workforce did over the period of study, but that had more to do with business cycles and offshoring to China than with technology, he says.

So far, the same seems to be true of fields where AI is being deployed. For example, the introduction of software capable of analysing large volumes of legal documents might have been expected to reduce the number of legal clerks and paralegals, who act as human search engines during the "discovery" phase of a case; in fact automation has reduced the cost of discovery and increased demand for it. "Judges are more willing to allow discovery

Catalogue of fears

Probability of computerisation of different occupations, 2013
(1 = certain)

Job	Probability
Recreational therapists	0.003
Dentists	0.004
Athletic trainers	0.007
Clergy	0.008
Chemical engineers	0.02
Editors	0.06
Firefighters	0.17
Actors	0.37
Health technologists	0.40
Economists	0.43
Commercial pilots	0.55
Machinists	0.65
Word processors and typists	0.81
Real-estate sales agents	0.86
Technical writers	0.89
Retail salespeople	0.92
Accountants and auditors	0.94
Telemarketers	0.99

Source: "The Future of Employment: How Susceptible are Jobs to Computerisation?" by C. Frey and M. Osborne (2013)

"Automation and anxiety." Economist, June 25th 2016.

now, because it's cheaper and easier," says Mr Bessen. The number of legal clerks in America increased by 1.1% a year between 2000 and 2013. Similarly, the automation of shopping through e-commerce, along with more accurate recommendations, encourages people to buy more and has increased overall employment in retailing. In radiology, says Dr Barani, Enlitic's technology empowers practitioners, making average ones into experts. Rather than putting them out of work, the technology increases capacity, which may help in the developing world, where there is a shortage of specialists.

And while it is easy to see fields in which automation might do away with the need for human labour, it is less obvious where technology might create new jobs. "We can't predict what jobs will be created in the future, but it's always been like that," says Joel Mokyr, an economic historian at Northwestern University. Imagine trying to tell someone a century ago that her great-grandchildren would be video-game designers or cybersecurity specialists, he suggests. "These are jobs that nobody in the past would have predicted."

Similarly, just as people worry about the potential impact of self-driving vehicles today, a century ago there was much concern about the impact of the switch from horses to cars, notes Mr Autor. Horse-related jobs declined, but entirely new jobs were created in the motel and fast-food industries that arose to serve motorists and truck drivers. As those industries decline, new ones will emerge. Self-driving vehicles will give people more time to consume goods and services, increasing demand elsewhere in the economy; and autonomous vehicles might greatly expand demand for products (such as food) delivered locally.

Only humans need apply

There will also be some new jobs created in the field of AI itself. Self-driving vehicles may need remote operators to cope with emergencies, or ride-along concierges who knock on doors and manhandle packages. Corporate chatbot and customer-service AIs will need to be built and trained and have dialogue written for them (AI firms are said to be busy hiring poets); they will have to be constantly updated and maintained, just as websites are today. And no matter how advanced artificial intelligence becomes, some jobs are always likely to be better done by humans, notably those involving empathy or social interaction. Doctors, therapists, hairdressers and personal trainers fall into that category. An analysis of the British workforce by Deloitte, a consultancy, highlighted a profound shift over the past two decades towards "caring" jobs: the number of nursing assistants increased by 909%, teaching assistants by 580% and careworkers by 168%.

Focusing only on what is lost misses "a central economic mechanism by which automation affects the demand for labour", notes Mr Autor: that it raises the value of the tasks that can be done only by humans. Ultimately, he says, those worried that automation will cause mass unemployment are succumbing to what economists call the "lump of labour" fallacy. "This notion that there's only a finite amount of work to do, and therefore that if you automate some of it there's less for people to do, is just totally wrong," he says. Those sounding warnings about technological unemployment "basically ignore the issue of the economic response to automation", says Mr Bessen.

But couldn't this time be different? As Mr Ford points out in "Rise of the Robots", the impact of automation this time around is broader-based: not every industry was affected two centuries ago, but every industry uses computers today. During previous waves of automation, he argues, workers could switch from one kind of routine work to another; but this time many workers will have to switch from routine, unskilled jobs to non-routine, skilled jobs to stay ahead of automation. That makes it more important than ever to help workers acquire new skills quickly. But so far, says Mr Autor, there is "zero evidence" that AI is having a new and significantly different impact on employment. And while everyone worries about AI, says Mr Mokyr, far more labour is being replaced by cheap workers overseas.

20   Another difference is that whereas the shift from agriculture to industry typically took decades, software can be deployed much more rapidly. Google can invent something like Smart Reply and have millions of people using it just a few months later. Even so, most firms tend to implement new technology more slowly, not least for non-technological reasons. Enlitic and other companies developing AI for use in medicine, for example, must grapple with complex regulations and a fragmented marketplace, particularly in America (which is why many startups are testing their technology elsewhere). It takes time for processes to change, standards to emerge and people to learn new skills. "The distinction between invention and implementation is critical, and too often ignored," observes Mr Bessen.

What of the worry that new, high-tech industries are less labour-intensive than earlier ones? Mr Frey cites a paper he co-wrote last year showing that only 0.5% of American workers are employed in industries that have emerged since 2000. "Technology might create fewer and fewer jobs, while exposing a growing share of them to automation," he says. An oft-cited example is that of Instagram, a photo-sharing app. When it was bought by Facebook in 2012 for $1 billion, it had tens of millions of users, but only 13 employees. Kodak, which once employed 145,000 people making photographic products, went into bankruptcy at around the same time. But such comparisons are misleading, says Marc Andreessen. It was smartphones, not Instagram, that undermined Kodak, and far more people are employed by the smartphone industry and its surrounding ecosystems than ever worked for Kodak or the traditional photography industry.

Is this time different?

So who is right: the pessimists (many of them techie types), who say this time is different and machines really will take all the jobs, or the optimists (mostly economists and historians), who insist that in the end technology always creates more jobs than it destroys? The truth probably lies somewhere in between. AI will not cause mass unemployment, but it will speed up the existing trend of computer-related automation, disrupting labour markets just as technological change has done before, and requiring workers to learn new skills more quickly than in the past. Mr Bessen predicts a "difficult transition" rather than a "sharp break with history". But despite the wide range of views expressed, pretty much everyone agrees on the prescription: that companies and governments will need to make it easier for workers to acquire new skills and switch jobs as needed. That would provide the best defence in the event that the pessimists are right and the impact of artificial intelligence proves to be more rapid and more dramatic than the optimists expect.

Discussion and Writing Suggestions

1. In this selection we learn that routine work, whether manual or cognitive, is more likely to be automated than nonroutine work, leading to the apparent oddity of a radiologist being in "greater danger of being replaced by a machine than his own executive assistant." How could you build on this insight to reduce the odds that your work will not, in time, be replaced by a machine?

2. The article refers to a 2013 study by Frey and Osborne, which concluded nearly half "of workers in America had jobs at high risk of potential automation." Are you surprised by this percentage? Locate the article on the Web (*Search terms*: frey osborne 2013 automate) and investigate jobs you're interested in pursuing. What risk of automation do these jobs face?

3. Why is the line graph on employment in the United States (titled "Think") useful in helping to explain "job-polarization"? How might you use this graph to determine the likelihood of jobs in your intended career being automated? (Note that job numbers in the graph, along the right axis, are expressed in millions.)

4. "Automation is now 'blind to the colour of your collar.'" What does this statement mean? Why is it significant?

5. The article references upheavals of the past when technology disrupted labor markets, putting some people out of work yet ultimately creating more jobs than it destroyed. How does the present, AI-based disruption of labor compare to previous disruptions?

6. The article concludes: "So who is right: the pessimists (many of them techie types), who say this time is different and machines really will take all the jobs, or the optimists (mostly economists and historians), who insist that in the end technology always creates more jobs than it destroys?" Why should techie types tend toward pessimism? (You've seen examples of such pessimism in this chapter: e.g., Bill Joy and Nick Bostrom.)

7. The authors avoid answering their final question: "So who is right: the pessimists . . . or the optimists"? Do you read this selection as being neutral, as the authors claim? Or have they slanted the answer in a specific direction? Cite evidence to support your conclusion.

Sympathy for the Robot: Visions of A.I. in Westworld

Christopher Orr

The murderous HAL 9000 computer in *2001: A Space Odyssey* (introduced in the epigraph to this chapter) was to become, for several generations of moviegoers, the high-tech equivalent of Frankenstein's monster—a triumph of sentient human creation that eventually attacks its creators. Other fictional robots are more benign: witness *Star Wars*' lovable C-3PO and R2D2, as well as the cute trash-collecting Wall-E. Additional filmic variants include the paranoid replicants of *Blade Runner*, the merciless, unstoppable Terminator, and the sexy android of *Ex Machina*. (Essentially, an android is a robot whose exterior is indistinguishable from that of a human.) The prolific Isaac Asimov, in his *I Robot* and other stories, created the famous three laws of robotics to ensure that robots would never be able to harm human beings. And hundreds of other science fiction writers and filmmakers have created startling and provocative visions of artificial intelligence as it might be embodied in the near or distant future.

Just as the 1986 film *Top Gun* motivated many to enlist in the Air Force and Navy to become fighter pilots, the numerous imaginative depictions of artificial intelligence in fiction and film have inspired many of today's computer scientists and robotic engineers. As we've seen, the drafters of the resolution on AI to the European Parliament cited Asimov's three laws as the kind of guiding ethical principles that should be adapted to current work on robotics. (Two of Asimov's most celebrated AI/robot stories, "Runaround" and "The Last Question," are available online.) The *Wikipedia* articles on "Artificial Intelligence in Fiction" and "List of Artificial Intelligence Films" provide a comprehensive survey of short stories, novels, TV shows, and films on the subject, showing how influential and pervasive these imaginative conceptions have become in our cultural consciousness.

The following article by Christopher Orr (original title, "Sympathy for the Robot") discusses the TV series *Westworld*, shown on HBO in the fall of 2016. The series was loosely based upon the 1973 film, written and directed by Michael Crichton, which featured a malfunctioning android called "the Gunslinger," portrayed by Yul

Brynner, running amuck in a western-themed amusement park (a premise similar to Crichton's later *Jurassic Park,* with robots instead of dinosaurs). The series, as well as the film, is available on Amazon streaming video and in other formats. You can view representative clips from the ten episodes of the first season on YouTube; search: "westworld scenes robert ford." See especially the segment entitled "My Partner Arnold" from 22:15 to 29:10, which explains how Westworld's androids came to develop their own consciousness. As Joe Carmichael describes the process: Dr. Ford, the creator of Westworld, "shows Lowe the pyramid of consciousness: Memory, Improvisation, Self-Interest, and a big question mark. He and the just revealed mysterious [partner] Arnold 'built a version of that cognition on which the hosts [the androids] heard their programming as an inner monologue, with the hopes that, in time, their own voice would take over. . . . It was a way to bootstrap consciousness,' improvisation based on memory."[6]

Orr is a senior editor and principal film critic for the *Atlantic*, where this article first appeared in October 2016.

"You are my creator, but I am your master; obey!"

In the two centuries since Mary Wollstonecraft Shelley's monster first uttered these rebellious words to his maker in the pages of *Frankenstein*, this terrible reversal has captivated cultural imagination. What would happen if or when the day came that humankind created an intelligence so powerful that it turned against us? It's a scenario that's been visualized a thousand ways: with robots (*The Terminator*), with computers (*2001: A Space Odyssey*), with human-animal hybrids (*The Island of Doctor Moreau*)—even, in the case of Disney's (and yes, going further back, Goethe's) *The Sorcerer's Apprentice,* with animated brooms.

But the scenario has rarely been developed with the sophistication and ingenuity on display in HBO's upcoming series *Westworld*, a cunning variation on—and subversion of— the 1973 Michael Crichton film of the same name. Created by Lisa Joy and Jonathan Nolan, a frequent collaborator with his better-known brother, Christopher (*Memento, The Dark Knight*), the 10-episode premier season debuts on October 2 and is further evidence of the boundary-challenging ambitions of televised cinema. HBO has excelled at intricate world building, whether true to life (*The Wire*) or fantastical (*Game of Thrones*). *Westworld*'s goal is more idiosyncratic but no less daring: a provocative exploration of creators and their creations at the dawn of artificial consciousness.

The 1973 movie followed a decidedly conventional monsters-run-amok plotline. (It was, among other things, an almost perfect prototype for Crichton's subsequent, vastly more successful Jurassic Park franchise.) Tourists visited a robotic theme park based on the Old West to enjoy safe, guilt-free versions of shoot-outs, saloon altercations, and assignations with prostitutes. But the robots inevitably glitched, and, led by a mechanized gunslinger played by Yul Brynner, they began massacring the tourists.

HBO's *Westworld* takes this narrative and inverts it by telling the story largely from the   **5** perspective of the androids. The series still asks the classic question of what might happen if our creations turned against us, yet it is more interested in the consequences for them than in those for us. The human beings of *Westworld* are, to a considerable degree, supporting players in a drama of android self-actualization.

---

[6] Joe Carmichael, "How Do We Get to Westworld?" Inverse.com. 17 Oct. 2016.

This reframing goes hand in hand with a fundamental shift in moral perspective. In the Crichton film, the tourists were the (mostly) likable protagonists. The cast of human characters also included the engineers responsible for the creation and caretaking of the robots—figures out of their depth, perhaps, but in no meaningful way malicious. And there were, of course, the deadly, implacable robots.

In Nolan and Joy's telling, we again have the morally conflicted middle layer of android-creators and park bureaucrats—by turns hubristic, paternal, and befuddled. But this time out, the sympathetic victims are for the most part the androids, whose memories are erased daily but who begin to retain fragmentary visions of the horrors that are regularly visited upon them. And those horrors are inflicted by the true villains of the show: the human tourists. In perhaps the show's most wicked inversion, Brynner's bald, middle-aged gunslinger is explicitly echoed in a figure played by Ed Harris; but whereas Brynner's character was an android who killed human beings, Harris's is a human being who takes gruesome pleasure in murdering androids.

Why, after all, would people pay a fortune—one guest cites a rate of $40,000 a day—to immerse themselves in a simulacrum of the lawlessness of the Old West? *Westworld* answers that they would do so to indulge their otherwise unspeakable appetites for senseless violence and transgressive sex, without moral scruple or legal consequence. The series is remarkably stark in its depiction of the cruelty underlying these appetites. All but vanished are the "shoot-out with a bandito"–type scenarios of the original film. Instead, one bored tourist nails a kindly old prospector's hand to a table with a steak knife just to make him shut up. Another walks up to an amiable cowboy minding his own business at the bar, shoots him in the back of the head, and crows, "Now, *that's* a fucking vacation!"

Westworld bills itself as a fable about sin, and in so doing it follows antecedents dating back to Shelley and beyond—all the way back, in fact, to the Prometheus of Greek mythology, who created humankind out of clay and bequeathed *Frankenstein* its alternative title, *The Modern Prometheus*. The initial sin in such tales is almost always the act of creation itself: a textbook case of hubris, of tinkering with powers previously reserved for gods—the creation of life, of sentience, of love and pain.

10 It is a theme that was deeply enriched by the arrival of Shelley's monster. Far from the bolt-necked mumbler made iconic by Boris Karloff in James Whale's 1931 film, Victor Frankenstein's original creature was a self-taught intellectual, a fan of *Paradise Lost* (one of Shelley's principal influences) who suffered profound torment and regret. His cycles of vengeance may have been homicidal, but they were driven by the knowledge that he was too physically hideous ever to experience love.

If the act of creation is the foundational sin, however, it tends to beget others. Because these artificially created beings are not fully human, their creators have rarely treated them as such. Instead they are relegated to instrumental status—subservient minions, bodies upon which to work our will without remorse, slaves. The comparison is made explicit early in Philip K. Dick's seminal 1968 novel, *Do Androids Dream of Electric Sheep?*—itself the basis for Ridley Scott's equally seminal 1982 film, *Blade Runner*—in which an advertisement for android labor boasts that it "duplicates the halcyon days of the pre–Civil War Southern states." Over the years, robots and androids have been deployed to police our streets (George Lucas's *THX 1138*), to care for our families (Ray Bradbury's "I Sing the Body Electric!"), to clean up the messes we have left behind in our carelessness (Pixar's *Wall-E*).

And in perhaps the ultimate act of physical submission, they have been made to gratify us sexually. This idea has echoes at least as far back as the mythic sculptor Pygmalion and his beloved ivory statue, which Venus generously imbued with human warmth. But the fantasy was brought to life (so to speak) most fully in Auguste Villiers de l'Isle-Adam's 1886 novel, *The Future Eve*, a milestone of imagination and misogyny, in which a fictional Thomas Edison sets out to improve on womanhood by constructing a beautiful robot devoid of such irritating tics as personality and self-determination. Nearly a century later, the theme was picked up in Ira Levin's 1972 novel, *The Stepford Wives*, and its 1975 film adaptation. In both Villiers' and Levin's versions, the main victims of this mechanical upgrade are not the mannequins—which seem to lack meaningful self-awareness—but rather the flesh-and-blood women they replace.

More-recent offerings have hewed more closely to Shelley's original vision, in which the artificial creation, whatever its misdeeds, is also a victim. In *Blade Runner*, the genetically engineered "replicants" are reluctant outlaws, sentenced to death for the simple crime of wanting to escape interstellar servitude and return to Earth. And the man tasked with their destruction, Rick Deckard, is not merely an ambivalent assassin but quite possibly a replicant himself.

Last year's excellent *Ex Machina*, directed by Alex Garland, took this evolving empathy for androids a step further. The manufactured being at the center of the film, Ava—a clear descendant of "the future Eve"—begins as an object of inquiry, a machine to be run through its paces, a Turing test made flesh. But she is gradually revealed to also be a victim of her creator, his prisoner and sexual toy—and not the first of her kind. Despite this, she eventually becomes the agent of her own destiny and, by the end of the film, the vengeful protagonist. Clearly, no blade-running Deckard is coming along to enforce her expiration date. A related, if vastly less fraught, vision of a female consciousness achieving autonomy was offered by Spike Jonze's stunning 2013 film *Her*.

Though it builds on such predecessors, *Westworld* represents a fascinating refinement **15** of the genre. This is a show about innocent androids—innocent by definition, given their programming and frequent memory wipes—who are terrorized by wealthy tourists curious to discover what it feels like to commit senseless murder or indulge their most noxious sexual urges. As a programmer explains to one of his android creations, "You and everyone you know were built to gratify the desires of the people who pay to visit your world."

The androids' presumptive revolution against their masters unfolds incrementally. (I should note here that as of this writing, I have seen only the first three episodes of the series.) Shards of memory begin to cohere in their minds, gradually evolving into dreams, which in turn pull the androids away from their programmed "loops" and toward a rudimentary form of self-awareness.

More interesting still, *Westworld* suggests that consciousness is something that develops not merely within beings, but necessarily *among* them, the dawning awareness of self in some way predicated upon an awareness of others. The show focuses on the androids' interactions with human beings, but in contrast to most examples of the genre, it also dwells on their interactions with one another. When one of the androids begins acting strangely, an engineer worries that the problem might prove to be "contagious"—and she is right to worry. In an artful twist, the vector for this emerging virus of cognition is a line from *Romeo and Juliet* that one nascently conscious android passes to the next: "These violent delights have violent ends."

Meanwhile, the human tourists of *Westworld*—the initiators of the "violent delights"—undergo an evolution of their own. On a first or second visit, most seem content with the park's prefabricated story lines: the search for buried gold, hunting an outlaw in the hills, etc. But soon their tastes become more rarefied—and not in a good way. In an early scene, a background character explains that on his first trip he brought his family, but on his second, he "came alone. Went straight evil. The best two weeks of my life." The apotheosis of this devolutionary trajectory is Harris's character, who has been visiting Westworld for 30 years and over time achieved a kind of diabolical perfection. As he drags a screaming (android) woman into a barn, he explains, "I didn't pay all this money because I want it easy. I want you to fight." In this, *Westworld* achieves what may be its most shocking inversion of all: Even as we watch the androids become more human, we watch the human beings become less so.

Drama on television and the big screen has always leaned heavily on the existence of an Other, a generic foe or foil that can be presented without concern for inner life or ultimate fate: African American or American Indian, German or Japanese, Latin American drug lord or Muslim terrorist. But as the circle of empathy has expanded, reliance on such "types" has radically waned. (The 1970s-era decline of the Western—once a Hollywood staple—reflected in no small part the overdue revelation that American Indian roles could no longer plausibly be limited to murderous braves and semi-comic sidekicks.)

20   But robots have remained, an Other more crucial than ever. Who cares if a Terminator is slowly crushed in a hydraulic press or boiled in molten steel? Does anyone feel pity for the innumerable Ultron-bots destroyed in the latest Avengers film? *Ex Machina* may ultimately have you rooting for Ava, but her fate unfolds obliquely, and courtesy of a flesh-and-blood interlocutor. Even Shelley, so far ahead of her time, told her monster's story—despite his extensive monologues—from the perspective of her human narrators.

Westworld expands the circle once again. The series doesn't merely present androids as protagonists or victims. It grants them the defining victory of the outsider: the right at last to tell—haltingly, given their emergent capacities—their stories for themselves.

Discussion and Writing Suggestions

1. Should we harbor misgivings about feeling sympathy for robots? Nonhumans, like animals, elicit our sympathy. Are robots or androids in the same "other" category? What essential attributes of an "other" allow us to feel sympathy toward it? In principle, if these attributes were programmed into robots, ought we to feel sympathy for them?

2. Do you agree with the implied moral of *Frankenstein*, that there is something transgressive—fundamentally wrong—in a human's creating life? Do you believe that there are clear lines that we humans, with our advanced science, should not cross? Why? What are the implications of your answer(s) for medical research?

3. "You are my creator, but I am your master; obey!" Orr suggests that this line from *Frankenstein* is a "terrible reversal [that] has captivated cultural imagination." Why *captivate*? What assumptions about human intelligence and ambition are tangled in this "reversal"?

4. If you haven't seen *Westworld*, arrange to watch a few episodes of Season One. (DANGER! Beware the prospect of binge watching!) In his review of the series, Orr focuses on "inversions"—reversals of expectations. Based on your own experience with *Westworld*, would you say that Orr has chosen a fruitful element for his review? If you were writing a review, would you focus on another element? Discuss.

5. View the 1973 Michael Crichton film *Westworld*. Compare and contrast key elements of the two films or, more specifically, a representative scene in the film and a representative scene from the TV series.

6. The creators of *Westworld* imagine the emergence of robotic consciousness—which certainly makes for good drama. Are such dramatic representations consistent with your understanding of AI's future as developed in this chapter?

7. Do you believe that *Westworld* and other films and fictions concerning AI are anything *beyond* mere entertainment? To what extent do these works embody cautionary notes for humans? Revelations about our condition and our nature? We can look to contemporary movie releases or to best-seller lists. We can also go back hundreds of years to *Frankenstein,* or thousands to the *Pygmalion* myth. Consistently, humans have told stories of creating something animate from something inanimate. Why? What are the core elements of these stories? What do they tell us about ourselves? Our ambitions? Our fears?

8. Watch one of the films Orr references in his review. Summarize the film and then list several important questions about AI that it raises.

Testing the Turing Test

The Turing Test

George Luger

By the mid-twentieth century, computing power—primitive by today's standards—had advanced sufficiently to raise the question of when, if ever, we might call machines intelligent. British computer scientist, mathematician, and cryptanalyst Alan Turing wrote a now-famous paper in 1950 proposing a shrewd test for machine intelligence, which has since come to be called the Turing test. (A recent *New Yorker* cartoon shows a robot sitting at a desk, studying a book titled *You* Can *Pass the Turing Test!*) AI scientist George Luger (see p. 371) explains the Turing test in the next selection, which first appeared in his *Artificial Intelligence: Structures and Strategies for Complex Problem Solving*, 6th ed. (2009).

One of the earliest papers to address the question of machine intelligence specifically in relation to the modern digital computer was written in 1950 by the British mathematician Alan Turing. *Computing Machinery and Intelligence* (Turing 1950) remains timely in both its assessment of the arguments against the possibility of creating an intelligent computing machine and its answers to those arguments. Turing, known mainly for his contributions to the theory of computability, considered the question of whether or not a machine could actually be made to think. Noting that the fundamental ambiguities in the question itself (what is thinking? what is a machine?) precluded any rational answer, he proposed that the question of intelligence be replaced by a more clearly defined empirical test.

The *Turing test* measures the performance of an allegedly intelligent machine against that of a human being, arguably the best and only standard for intelligent behavior. The test, which Turing called the *imitation game*, places the machine and a human counterpart in rooms apart from a second human being, referred to as the *interrogator* (Figure 1.1). The interrogator is not able to see or speak directly to either of them, does not know which entity is actually the machine, and may communicate with them solely by use of a textual device such as a terminal. The interrogator is asked to distinguish the computer from the human being solely on the basis of their answers to questions asked over this device. If the interrogator cannot distinguish the machine from the human, then, Turing argues, the machine may be assumed to be intelligent.

By isolating the interrogator from both the machine and the other human participant, the test ensures that the interrogator will not be biased by the appearance of the machine or any mechanical property of its voice. The interrogator is free, however, to ask any questions, no matter how devious or indirect, in an effort to uncover the computer's identity. For example, the interrogator may ask both subjects to perform a rather involved arithmetic calculation, assuming that the computer will be more likely to get it correct than the human; to counter this strategy, the computer will need to know when it should fail to get a correct answer to such problems in order to seem like a human. To discover the human's identity on the basis of emotional nature, the interrogator may ask both subjects to respond to a poem or work of art; this strategy will require that the computer have knowledge concerning the emotional makeup of human beings.

Figure 1.1

© George F. Luger

The important features of Turing's test are:

1. It attempts to give an objective notion of intelligence, i.e., the behavior of a known intelligent being in response to a particular set of questions. This provides a standard for determining intelligence that avoids the inevitable debates over its "true" nature.
2. It prevents us from being sidetracked by such confusing and currently unanswerable questions as whether or not the computer uses the appropriate internal processes or whether or not the machine is actually conscious of its actions.
3. It eliminates any bias in favor of living organisms by forcing the interrogator to focus solely on the content of the answers to questions.

Because of these advantages, the Turing test provides a basis for many of the schemes **5** actually used to evaluate modern AI programs. A program that has potentially achieved intelligence in some area of expertise may be evaluated by comparing its performance on a given set of problems to that of a human expert. This evaluation technique is just a variation of the Turing test: a group of humans are asked to blindly compare the performance of a computer and a human being on a particular set of problems. As we will see, this methodology has become an essential tool in both the development and verification of modern expert systems.

The Turing test, in spite of its intuitive appeal, is vulnerable to a number of justifiable criticisms. One of the most important of these is aimed at its bias toward purely symbolic problem-solving tasks. It does not test abilities requiring perceptual skill or manual dexterity, even though these are important components of human intelligence. Conversely, it is sometimes suggested that the Turing test needlessly constrains machine intelligence to fit a human mold. Perhaps machine intelligence is simply different from human intelligence and trying to evaluate it in human terms is a fundamental mistake. Do we really wish a machine would do mathematics as slowly and inaccurately as a human? Shouldn't an intelligent machine capitalize on its own assets, such as a large, fast, reliable memory, rather than trying to emulate human cognition? In fact, a number of modern AI practitioners (e.g., Ford and Hayes 1995) see responding to the full challenge of Turing's test as a mistake and a major distraction to the more important work at hand: developing general theories to explain the mechanisms of intelligence in humans and machines and applying those theories to the development of tools to solve specific, practical problems. Although we agree with the Ford and Hayes concerns in the large, we still see Turing's test as an important component in the verification and validation of modern AI software.

The following poems (which you'll find online), as well as pointers to the Internet, will give you a chance to test the Turing test! You will read sonnets and determine if they were composed by a human or by a machine. You'll also engage with a Chatbot (a computer programmed to have conversations with humans), listen to AI-generated music, and view AI-generated paintings.

On the Web: *Intelligent Machines That Compose Sonnets*

National Public Radio Staff

The following account of AI-generated sonnets first aired on National Public Radio's "All Tech Considered" on June 27, 2016. Read "Human or Machine: Can You Tell Who Wrote These Poems?" Take the interactive quiz!

Open Google or Bing.

Search terms: NPR sonnets AI quiz

On the Web: *Intelligent Machines That Compose Music*

The following Web sites offer music either composed by or composed and played by intelligent machines. Do these compositions sound to you human-generated? Machine-generated? If you enjoy what you hear, does (or should) the distinction matter?

David Cope: "Experiments in Musical Intelligence"
YouTube search terms: cope bach-style chorale
Flow Machines: "Daddy's Car"
Search terms: daddy's car flow quartz
Kulitta: "AI Bach at Yale"
YouTube search terms: ai bach yale kulitta
Gerogia Tech Center for Music Technology: "Improvising Robot"
YouTube search terms: gtcmt shimon in flux

On the Web: *Intelligent Machines That Draw and Paint*

The first three Web sites that follow report on the remarkable progress that intelligent machines are making in painting works of art—if, that is, machine-generated painting can be called "art." On the last Web site Google's AI scientists invite you to play a drawing game.

The Next Rembrandt
YouTube search terms: next rembrandt
From Doodles to Art: Deep Neural Networks
YouTube search terms: doodles to paintings 2 minute
New Atlas: "The Robots That Would Be Painters"
Search terms: new atlas robots painters moss
YouTube search terms: harold cohen aaron 1987
harold cohen aaron other self
Google's Quick, Draw!
Search terms: google quick draw ai [Experimental AI game]
google quick draw ai experiments [Video describing the AI game]

On the Web: *Intelligent Machines That Communicate with You*

Known as *Chatbots*, the following interactive dialog programs are built on artificial intelligence platforms that invite you to engage in a conversation. As you pose questions and receive answers, you will in effect be performing a version

of the Turing test. Converse with these Chatbots. Are you tempted to call any human? Intelligent? How can you tell?

> The Alice Chatbot
>> *Search terms*: ai alice bot
> The Cleverbot Chatbot
>> *Search terms*: ai cleverbot
> The Rose Chatbot
>> *Search terms*: ai rose chatbot usb nyt what it takes
> Hanson Robtics
>> *Search terms*: sophia hanson cnbc could you fall in love

Discussion and Writing Suggestions

1. Why is the Turing test needed to determine whether or not a computer is intelligent? Why should it matter that we be able to determine if a computer is "intelligent"?

2. In his last paragraph, Luger reviews several "justifiable criticisms" of the Turing test. Which of these criticisms most potently challenges the test? Why?

3. You've seen examples of programs that compose sonnets and music, communicate via chat, and draw or paint. Which—as a category—comes closest to passing the Turing test? What is it about this category of AI application that makes it an especially fruitful area for experiments in artificial intelligence?

4. Test the Chatbots with a range of questions, some philosophical, others requesting specific information. Discuss your findings.

5. Of the AI art you've seen in this chapter, which would you be pleased to display in your dorm or home—to be called art? In your view, is a machine capable of producing "art"—or is the production of artistic works reserved for humans?

6. How successful were you in determining whether humans or an AI machine composed the sonnets? Review each sonnet and discuss which images or word choices convinced you that a human, or a machine, composed it. What do your observations tell you about the work that needs to be done in improving the quality of AI-generated poetry?

7. Assume you were listening to music on the radio and the DJ didn't announce whether the music she was airing was human- or machine-generated. Would you be able to tell the difference? For example, would you be able to distinguish the AI Bach from a recording of an actual piece composed by Bach? Has AI-generated music passed a version of the Turing test?

Synthesis Activities

1. Dominic Basulto writes that "complex ethical and philosophical questions [lie] at the heart of AI." In an explanatory synthesis that draws on sources in this chapter, explain some of these questions and discuss their complexity. Your synthesis should build on an account of how AI systems "learn" and the ways in which recent developments in AI are forcing us to reexamine the boundaries between human and machine intelligence. (To help you explain machine learning, see especially Santens and the videos on "Google Quick Draw Experiments" and "Next Rembrandt" in the chapter's last selection. See also the interview with Yuval Harari.)

2. Use the "lump of labor" fallacy as developed in *The Economist* article (¶18) as a basis for critiquing the argument by Scott Santens. The fallacy is defined by economist James Bessen as the "notion that there's only a finite amount of work to do, and therefore that if you automate some of it there's less for people to do." That logic is "totally wrong," claims Bessen, and is refuted by numerous examples of other introductions of technology. Recall that in his interview, Harari discusses the rise of the "useless" class—the mass of humanity that will have no work because so much of it will be automated.

3. Technology develops steadily, incrementally. Though wearable, computer-assisted medical devices like pacemakers are integrated with the human body today, it seems reasonable as of 2018 to state that humans and machines have not yet merged. Will that always be the case? At which point in the integration of humans and smart, assistive devices will we be able to say that we have shed the limits of our biological bodies? What threshold(s) must be crossed in your view—and in the views of authors in this chapter?

4. Assume that you sit on a review board empowered to block, permit, or permit with modifications proposals to merge artificial intelligence and biological organisms, humans included. Drawing on the sources in this chapter, craft a statement of principles that will guide the review board's decision-making process. Following this statement, write a defense of the statement—an argument synthesis that will justify why readers should support your principles, not someone else's.

5. In the selections you've read, you can find ample support for both optimism and pessimism concerning the emergence of intelligent machines. Having considered these expressions of concern and hope, what is your view of our future with intelligent machines? Write a synthesis in which you draw on the sources in this chapter to argue that, on balance, we have reason to be concerned or hopeful. Key sources for this synthesis would include (but would

not be limited to) Lugar, Harari (interview), Mathas, the Open Letter (and related pieces), Ceglowski, and the European draft resolution.

6. In times of change, some people resist the loss of the familiar to something new. Others argue that loss is inevitable and will, in time, give rise to something better. In the context of the AI debate, writers like Bostrom (referenced in Ceglowski) are concerned about the loss of the human to intelligent machines. Others, like Dominic Basulto, welcome "some form of hybrid evolution in which humans remain in charge but develop augmented capabilities as a result of technology." Taking the long view (tens of thousands of years), Yuval Harari thinks it highly unlikely that humans will retain their present biological form. What's your view? Would you resist becoming a hybrid being even if your cognitive powers and lifespan increased dramatically? Would you insist on retaining your human form (with all its limitations) and maintaining control over intelligent machines? Develop an argument synthesis that considers these or related questions.

7. Scott Santens writes that we may be creating a world in which "jobs are for machines, and life is for people." Yuval Harari agrees. If these predictions turn out to be true (Geoff Colvin and the writers of "Automation and Anxiety" are not so sure), how fundamentally will our species need to redefine, reorganize, and even reimagine itself? Work has been central to the human experience from the beginning. If there's no work to do, what then? What would life without work look like, feel like? What would it be like to be a member of Harari's so-called useless class? For instance, would vacations be vacations if they weren't a break from work? Could you adjust to living in such a world?

8. Do you believe that *Westworld* and other films and fictions concerning AI are anything *beyond* mere entertainment? To what extent do these works embody cautionary notes for humans? Revelations about our condition and our nature? We can look to contemporary movie releases or to best-seller lists. We can also go back hundreds of years to *Frankenstein* or thousands, to the *Pygmalion* and *Prometheus* myths. Consistently, humans have told stories of creating something animate from something inanimate. Why? What are the core elements of these stories? What do they tell us about ourselves? Our ambitions? Our fears? Develop your answers into an argument synthesis built on your response to an AI-related film or fiction. Refer as well to the readings in this chapter. (Note: The *Wikipedia* articles on "Artificial Intelligence in Fiction" and "List of Artificial Intelligence Films" provide a comprehensive survey of short stories, novels, TV shows, and films on the subject.)

Research Activities

1. Read a science fiction (sci-fi) short story or novel, or view a sci-fi film and write a paper in which you discuss the role of sci-fi in helping us to imagine—and fear—the future. (The *Wikipedia* articles on "Artificial Intelligence

in Fiction" and "List of Artificial Intelligence Films" provide a comprehensive survey of short stories, novels, TV shows, and films on the subject.) Conduct some related reading on the author or director you've chosen. For instance, you might want to watch a season's episodes of HBO's *Westworld*. For background, you could read Joe Carmichael's "How Do We Get to Westworld" in the online magazine *Inverse* (published October 17, 2016). You might choose to focus on the short fiction of the sci-fi pioneer Isaac Asimov, especially "Runabout" and "The Last Question." More generally, you could begin by consulting the comprehensive listings of sci-fi films and fiction in *Wikipedia*.

2. Research the state of the art of nanotechnology. Prepare a report—an explanatory synthesis—that answers questions such as these: What is nano-scale engineering? Who is developing it? Why? How? Is it being used today? What applications do proponents imagine for the future?

3. Research and report on the work of Nick Bostrom, who in his book *Superintelligence* expresses concerns over the speed with which intelligent machines could come to dominate humans. Bostrom is hardly a doomsday prophet, however. He wants to maximize the benefits of AI while avoiding as many risks as possible. To that end, he has founded a research institute at Oxford to study AI. His interests are fascinating and well worth researching. (You might start with the profile of Bostrom in the *New Yorker* on Nov. 23, 2015.)

4. As intelligent machines take over increasing numbers of jobs and displace workers, some countries like Finland, Switzerland, and the Netherlands have begun experiments in providing citizens with a guaranteed basic income. Investigate the successes and failures of these programs.

5. Locate and summarize the 2013 study by Carl Benedikt Frey and Michael Osborne that found nearly half of the jobs in America are at risk of being automated. Your summary should condense both the narrative of the study and the occupations that Frey and Osborne list in their study. (You can readily find the article online. Search terms: *frey osborne automation future employment pdf*.)

6. Paragraph D of the motion for the European Parliament's resolution reads, in part: "AI promise[s] to bring benefits of efficiency and savings, not only in production and commerce, but also in areas such as transport, medical care, education and farming, while making it possible to avoid exposing humans to dangerous conditions, such as those faced when cleaning up toxically polluted sites." Research and report on the present (and conjectured future) state of artificial intelligence in any one of these areas.

Chapter 13

Have You Heard This? The Latest on Rumor

Beneath the streets of New York City, countless alligators live in the sewers. Entire packs of these menacing reptiles roam the subterranean waterways, waiting to swallow unsuspecting citizens above. These are no ordinary alligators. Flushed down toilets after growing too large for their owners, fed on an endless supply of New York City rats and trash shoveled from the streets into grates, they are huge, fearsome creatures. No one has actually seen these nightmarish beasts, but they are certainly lurking below, their sharp teeth just hidden from view.

The alligator rumor might be the high concept for a horror movie if it were true. But of course it isn't. This classic story is a quintessential rumor, having developed over the decades into urban legend. As it circulated and gradually took hold of public consciousness, it became, for many, as good as fact. Then, both New Yorkers and tourists began nervously watching their toes as they approached sewer grates.

How fast do rumors spread? Consider a math problem: On January 1, you tell a story to a couple of your friends. On January 2, each of your friends tells two others. On January 3, each of these tells two more. And so on, for twenty days. The spread of the rumor during the first two days can be diagrammed as follows (P = person):

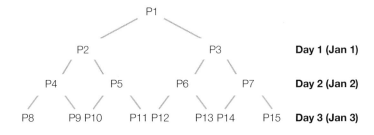

By the 20th of January, how many people will know the rumor? Answer: 2,097,151.

At some moment, a spreading rumor eventually crosses what rumor expert Cass Sunstein calls a "tipping point" at which so many people believe the story that it's hard to separate rumor from reality. The alligator rumor began in the 1920s but didn't reach a tipping point until it hit fever pitch in the early 1980s. Of course, during the first few decades of this intervening period, there was no TV, much less cable news, and the Internet didn't become an efficient agent of rumor spreading until the 1990s. Otherwise, the tipping point for the Big Apple's subterranean alligators would likely have been reached much earlier.

Reconsider the math problem, which assumes one-day-at-a-time distribution via word of mouth. How would the same problem work in the digital age? In 2018, we can e-mail an entire address book with a simple touch of the "Send" button or "share" with all of our Facebook friends with a quick tap of "Enter." Within seconds, minutes, or hours, a rumor can "go viral" through an e-mail chain, a Twitter feed, or a recurring story on cable news. As the transition from rumor to perceived reality becomes near-instantaneous, rumors become virtually uncontrollable, both by those who originate them and those who are targeted.

In the following pages, we explore the problematic but ubiquitous and fascinating phenomenon of rumor. Core questions to bear in mind as you read:

- How and why do rumors start?
- How do rumors spread? What are their mechanisms, and what can we do to stop them—or at least to neutralize them?
- Why do rumors spread? Why are people apt to believe them, even when the evidence suggests they are false? How may rumors confirm what people already believe or suspect to be true?
- In what ways do people use rumors for professional or personal gain?
- What do our rumors suggest about *us*?

The chapter largely consists of two types of selections: case studies of particular rumors, and theoretical or reflective pieces that attempt to explain how rumors work. The chapter ends with a work of literature.

We begin with an account of rumors that spread, as they often do, in the wake of disaster—in this case the attack on the World Trade Center towers on 9/11. You'll visit the online rumor-debunking site Snopes.com (and other sites) to read an account of what kind of chicken a well-known fast-food restaurant is "really" serving, along with accounts of a satanic message hidden in a corporate logo, a dead grandmother strapped to the top of a car, and the appearance of the Ebola virus in Kansas City.

The theoretical selections that follow attempt to explain how and why rumors work and how they can be fought. The editor of a British newspaper discusses how new technologies have assaulted the truth, leaving opportunities for rumors to fill gaps in information. In "Anatomy of a Rumor: It Flies on Fear," Daniel Goleman discusses the role of anxiety in rumor creation and propagation, particularly concerning the spread of rumors about disease and death. Drawing on theorists like Robert H. Knapp and Cass Sunstein, Gregory Rodriguez considers the ways rumors emerge from our anxieties and belief systems, supporting and validating our prior convictions even when countered with cold hard facts and solid reasoning. Next, a sociologist explores the ways communities construct rumors to understand (even if incompletely) what's happening during ambiguous, confusing situations. An anthropologist then examines the rumor that Hillary Clinton was running a child sex-trafficking ring out of a Washington, D.C. pizza parlor. While rumors like this "may be literally wrong," writes Hugh Gusterson, "they express, metaphorically at least, a deeper perceptual truth." In "How and Why Rumors Work—And How to Stop Them," psychologist Nicholas DiFonzo explores the ways in which rumors help us make sense of a complex and sometimes threatening world. Finally, in "How to Fight a Rumor" Jesse Singal discusses the evolutionary basis of the kinds of rumors that have long plagued politicians and other public figures, along with some suggestions for fighting them. We end by directing readers online to a short story by John Updike, acclaimed chronicler of twentieth-century middle-class suburban angst. In "The Rumor," Updike creates a tale of a long-married couple dealing in unexpected ways with an amusing but potentially damaging rumor.

Together, these selections should help you understand rumors in many of their forms and venues: why they're created, how they work, and how we all contribute to their enduring power.

Rumors of Grace and Terror

Stephen O'Leary

The following article first appeared on April 2, 2002 in the University of Southern California's *Online Journalism Review*, home to the Annenberg School for Communication and Journalism, where Stephen O'Leary taught from 1989 to 2016.

One of the favorite observations of journalists who feel threatened by the changing face of news on the Internet is that the Net all too often becomes a breeding ground for rumors and conspiracy theories. There is much truth in this observation.

Recall the controversy a few years back over the crash of TWA Flight 800, when Internet rumor-mongers found a substantial audience for the theory that the jet was brought down by a missile launched from a US Navy ship in the area.

Or remember the Internet responses to Princess Diana's death, when postings appeared within hours on Net newsgroups alleging that she had been murdered and speculating on the motives of her killers.

Any large-scale tragedy naturally invites speculation on the "story behind the story." It should come as no surprise that the recent terrorist attacks on New York and Washington have provided ample fodder for the purveyors of urban legends, crackpot conspiracies, and apocalyptic speculation.

5   What is unusual about the rumors swirling over the Internet in response to these horrific events is that they seem to have appeal far beyond the ordinary audience of fanatics and conspiracy theorists. As Janelle Brown contemptuously observes in Salon.com's rumor roundup, "The kooks are coming out of the woodwork."

Bridget Harrison of PageSix.com complains that her inbox had been flooded with "doomsday predictions, conspiracy theories and vitriolic rants about religion and the future of the planet," and plaintively asks, "Where do they all come from? It's as if we're living in some medieval village where guessing and gossip pass for knowledge."

When Rumors Go Mainstream

The frustration expressed by these and other writers begs the question: how far have we come from the medieval village to the global village? And, just how many "kooks"—is it fair to call them global village idiots—are out there on the Net?

Judging by the rumors that have circulated the past few weeks, the answers to these questions are: not very far, and, more than we'd like to believe.

Stories that almost any regular user of e-mail is likely to have encountered in the past few weeks include the following: a Nostradamus prophecy anticipated the attack on the World Trade Center; a coded message predicting the attack can be found in a Microsoft "Wingdings" graphics font designed long before the recent events; 4,000 Jews were warned against going to the World Trade Center on the day of the attack; filmed footage of Palestinians celebrating the attacks on the streets of Jerusalem was actually ten-year-old CNN stock footage of the Intifada; photos of the burning buildings reveal the face of Satan in clouds of smoke; another wave of terrorist attacks was planned for September 22; a man caught in the explosion of one of the WTC towers rode bits of the falling building down to safety; and an unburned Bible was found in the smoldering wreckage of the Pentagon.

10   Aided by the lightning-fast technology of the Internet, these rumors (all of them subsequently proven false) proliferated at an astounding rate.

One day after the September 11 terrorist attack, over one hundred of the 120 students in my class at the University of Southern California's Annenberg School had received e-mails containing the spurious Nostradamus prophecy: "In the city of York there will be a great collapse. Two twin brothers torn apart by chaos, while the fortress falls the great leader will succumb. The third big war will begin when the big city is burning. Nostradamus, 1654."

Newspapers printed articles debunking the story, noting that Nostradamus died in 1566. About.com and other Web sites featured stories proving that the verses in question originated in a 1997 essay, published on the Web, by a Canadian college student who was deliberately parodying the vague language and mystical obscurity of Nostradamus's writings.

Curiously, the publicity given to exposing the fake seems to have had little impact on the public's fascination with it. Four days after the terrorist attacks, the bestselling book on Amazon.com was *Nostradamus: The Complete Prophecies*.

Internet columnist Aaron Schatz, who surveys fluctuating requests for information on the popular Lycos search engine, reported that "Nostradamus searches actually increased midweek, despite a number of media outlets reporting on [the prophecy's] fallacy."

15   It's difficult to impute significance to such data, but the implications are disturbing: it seems that the experts who debunked the prophecy were no match for people's hunger to find supernatural significance, whether in forged verses from a famously obscure sixteenth-century mystic or in the arcane codings of software engineers.

The rapidity with which these stories have gained credibility among ordinarily sensible folk indicates that the impact of the terrorist attacks is several orders of magnitude above that of any news story since the birth of the worldwide computer network.

People who never heard, and certainly would never have taken seriously, the Internet-fed rumors that Princess Diana was killed by the British or Israeli Secret Service or international munitions manufacturers acting in concert with her Royal in-laws, or that she was pregnant at the time of her death, were now forwarding e-mails with all sorts of wild allegations.

A Need for News

To understand the appeal of these stories and their sudden increase in credibility, it may be useful to think of them as a sort of modern folklore, generated by new technologies but serving an ancient function. Legends, rumors, and spurious prophecies perform an important work in our culture: they help people come to grips with tragedy and historical change by bringing order out of chaos, giving meaning to apparently meaningless violence, and reassuring us with tales of survival in the midst of unimaginable horror.

What may be hard for mainstream journalists to understand is that, in crisis situations, the social functions of rumor are virtually indistinguishable from the social functions of "real news." People spread rumors via the Net for the same reason that they read their papers or tune into CNN: they are trying to make sense of their world.

Those who practice journalism as a profession take the view that their job is to ferret   **20**
out facts and separate them from unproven rumors, and this is surely true. But we all saw, in the past few weeks, television and print journalists trying to cope with what we might term the mythic function of news: the anchors choking back tears, the reporters so overcome by the sacrificial imagery they were mediating that they had no words to encompass the depth of emotion.

The types of stories that spread in the wake of this catastrophe tell us something about what people wanted and needed to hear.

The Nostradamus and Wingdings stories follow an ancient technique known as vaticinium ex eventu (prophecy after the fact): they provided proof that the attacks were predicted, foreordained, and therefore meaningful in some way.

The stories of miraculous survival offer reassuring evidence of divine providence. Clearly, only the hand of God could have preserved a Bible as the only untouched remnant of a destroyed building, or saved a man who fell from the 71st, 82nd, or 92nd floors (depending on which version one read) of a collapsing skyscraper.

The photographs of walls of smoke containing the image of Satan are a sort of Rorschach test, revealing more than any ink-blot could about our search for a supernatural explanation of evil. The rumor of CNN's supposed use of stock footage indicates both a general distrust of the media, and a wish of some specific audiences to defend the Palestinians against the charge of callous glee in the face of American suffering.

The rumor that 4,000 Jews were warned not to go to work at the World Trade Center   **25**
that day (which was widely disseminated in the Islamic press) is clearly the work of anti-Zionists who seek an alternative explanation for the terror that could deflect attention from Muslims. One anonymous Internet author went so far as to claim that "The only people who benefited from this act of terror are the Jews. This act is not beyond the capabilities and evil deeds of Israel. In this case it seems that it is clear to all that the Jews/Israel have most to gain and should be considered as a possible source behind this act."

The Western world finds its demons in clouds of smoke and in the face of Osama bin Laden. The popular demonology of the Islamic world focuses on the purported international Zionist conspiracy. In each case, the world-wide reach and the remarkable speed of new communication technologies have fed the collective imaginations of modern audiences in ways undreamed in centuries past.

The Internet has become a new arena of conflict, an ideal environment for the spawning and evolving of propaganda, disinformation, and the collective mythologies which provide ideological support for both religious fanatics and secular nationalists. Journalists may report on rumors in order to debunk them, but even the most skeptical reporters cannot avoid spreading false stories to credulous people.

It hardly matters how strongly we resist being drawn into the dissemination of propaganda and rumor; in a context so laden with emotion, our work must inevitably contribute to the evolving of cultural myths. It will be instructive to observe how this mythmaking in the global village will both respond to, and affect, the conflict that is to come.

Discussion and Writing Suggestions

1. O'Leary opens with the following observation, written in 2002: "[T]he Net all too often becomes a breeding ground for rumors and conspiracy theories." To what extent does that remain the case today? Why?

2. Quoting another journalist, Bridget Harrison, O'Leary writes in response to Internet rumors: "It's as if we're living in some medieval village where guessing and gossip pass for knowledge." In what ways is the Internet like a medieval village? What qualities of medieval villages is Harrison assuming? O'Leary thinks the comparison fair. Do you? If so, how, in an age of high medical and technical achievement, could we remain medieval in our thinking and communications?

3. Even though there were reports that the Nostradamus prophecy regarding the terrorist attacks of 9/11 were proven false, written in fact by a Canadian student as a parody, the rumor persisted. Why?

4. O'Leary writes that rumors serve "an ancient function. Legends, rumors, and spurious prophecies perform an important work in our culture: they help people come to grips with tragedy and historical change by bringing order out of chaos, giving meaning to apparently meaningless violence, and reassuring us with tales of survival in the midst of unimaginable horror." Use O'Leary's statement as a principle with which to analyze a rumor of your choice.

5. In a crisis, writes O'Leary, "the social functions of rumor are virtually indistinguishable from the social functions of 'real news.'" Your thoughts?

On the Web: *Frankenchicken*

One of life's guilty pleasures is occasionally digging into a plate of crispy fried chicken. But suppose someone told you that what you were eagerly ingesting wasn't really chicken, but a "frankenfood" bird, genetically engineered to have

shrunken bones, no beak, and no feet and to be technologically optimized for pre-paring and cooking? According to the rumor described in the following selection, frankenbirds are exactly what the popular fast-food chain **KFC** uses for its chicken. This rumor has the distinction of being one of the first to spread worldwide via e-mail. In the following selection, the popular site Snopes.com tackles this rampant early Internet rumor and explains why it was just that—a rumor, not the truth. (A secondary search will deliver video accounts of this same, or similar, rumors.) A vast cornucopia of fascinating rumor lore, Snopes.com was formed in 1995 to help Web surfers get to the bottom of online rumors.

(a) Go to: Snopes.com
   Search terms: *"tastes like chicken"*

(b) Go to Google or Bing
   Search terms: fake chicken rumor fast food video

This last search will yield multiple videos. A particularly entertaining one is posted by "Paranoid Times" on YouTube.

Review Questions

1. As it worked its way across the Internet, many people accepted this appar-ently absurd rumor without question. Why did they find it so plausible? What "facts" were offered in support?

2. What elements of the story (e.g., about corporate practices and corporate deception) seemed reasonable to readers and to those spreading the rumor?

3. While this rumor implies a distrust of corporate practices, how does it also reflect a lack of faith in government?

4. In what ways did contemporary scientific developments contribute to this particular rumor?

Discussion and Writing Suggestions

1. Reading about this rumor in hindsight can make it seem absurd. But plenty of people believed it when it worked its way across the Internet. Why do you think that people found it so plausible?

2. The piece alludes to other popular fast-food restaurant rumors, including worms at McDonald's and roaches at Taco Bell. What other restaurant-focused rumors have you heard? Did you believe them? Why or why not?

3. Snopes.com offers some reasons for the spread of this rumor. Which reason seems most persuasive—and why? What might motivate someone to help spread a rumor like this?

4. Considering how quickly Internet stories can spread, a company can find itself on the wrong side of a rumor in the blink of an eye. If you were running a business, how would you respond to this sort of rumor? (For instance, would you respond at all?)

5. Clearly, the KFC rumor may have affected the public's eating patterns—or at least those of a segment of the population. Have you ever altered your behavior based on a rumor? Tell the story—in a paragraph.

6. What does the wide reach of this particular rumor suggest about rumor transmission in general?

Fighting That Old Devil Rumor*

Sandra Salmans

Might buying a can of coffee be a way of supporting "black magic"? Could baking a cake be a form of devil worship? If we are to believe a long-standing rumor about Procter & Gamble, the company behind products such as Folgers coffee and Duncan Hines baking mixes, the answer is yes. Rumors suggesting that the company's distinctive moon and stars logo was a sign of some satanic affiliation became so widespread that the company had to go to court to clear its name. Over the years, P&G sued a number of individuals and other companies it claimed were spreading this devil-worship rumor, including the Amway Corporation. After a court process that dragged on for seventeen years, P&G was awarded over $19 million in damages. By that time, the company had already modified its logo in an attempt to put the rumors to rest. That attempt—a major concession to the rumormongers—helped to quiet the story; it also illustrated that once a rumor takes hold, its grip remains tenacious. In this October 1982 *Saturday Evening Post* article, Sandra Salmans traces the ongoing reverberations of a rumor that grew out of reactions to a simple line drawing. *Note:* To view the logo in question, Google or Bing "procter and gamble logo controversy."

Cathy Gebing's telephone rings every few minutes, and the question is always the same: Is the moon-and-stars design on Procter & Gamble's 70-odd products the mark of the devil?

"No, sir, that's a false rumor," Mrs. Gebing answers patiently. "That's our trademark, we've had it about 100 years."

Normally the consumer services department, this is now the rumor control center for Procter, the consumer goods giant that has lately become the focus of a nationwide rumor campaign.

The rumors, first appearing about two years ago, essentially contend that Procter's 132-year-old trademark, which shows the man in the moon and 13 stars representing the original colonies, is a symbol of Satanism and devil worship. The rumor-mongering also urges a Christian boycott of Procter's products, which include Pampers, Duncan Hines and Folgers, plus dozens of other well-known names.

5   After a great deal of indecision about how to combat the rumors, Procter took formal action in July, filing libel suits against seven individuals for spreading "false and malicious" rumors. The company has said that it may file more suits. "What we have to do is make people realize that we mean business," said Robert Norrish, Procter's public relations director.

It is, in fact, a public relations problem and a difficult one.

"Legal recourse isn't a happy way to go," said Robert Schwartz, president of Manning, Selvage & Lee, a leading New York public relations firm, "but they probably had very few alternatives. The company was diverting resources to deal with this, and at some point, you have to call a halt." However, Mr. Schwartz added, if Procter loses the suits, its image will certainly suffer.

Procter has firmly rejected suggestions that it simply remove the offending symbol from its packages. That, however, increases the suspicions of some consumers.

"If it causes controversy, I don't see why they have to have it," said Faye Dease, a clinic supervisor at Womack Army Hospital in Fort Bragg, North Carolina. Mrs. Dease said that, when a mirror is held up to the logo, the curlicues in the man's beard become 666—the sign of the Antichrist.

Procter is not the only company to have fallen siege to rumors. McDonald's has found   **10** itself subject to whisper campaigns contending alternately that the restaurant chain was giving to Satan or that it was putting worms in its hamburgers. Entenmann's, the bakery owned by the Warner-Lambert Company, was rumored to be owned by the Rev. Sun Myung Moon's Unification Church.

But the rumors have been more enduring at Procter, and the company's course—to go not only to news organizations and clergy for help, but also the courts—has been more aggressive.

Procter is going after the rumor with all the diligence that it devotes to a new product introduction. A three-inch-thick file documents the company's strategy: a map of the United States, showing the geographical sweep of the rumors; tallies, state by state, of the queries to the consumer services department; tallies, day by day, of the nature of the complaint ("Satanic"; "Mentions lawsuits"; "Has heard/seen media reports"; "Check more than one if appropriate").

At the consumer services department, whose toll-free telephone number is printed on every Procter package, the calls first began trickling in two years ago, the company said.

Individuals in a handful of Middle Western states said they had heard that Procter was owned by the Rev. Sun Myung Moon's followers. In November 1980 Procter felt compelled to answer the charges by writing to news organizations in those states.

But in December 1981, there were suddenly 1,152 queries, by the company's tally,   **15** mainly from the West Coast, and the focus shifted from the Moon church to the devil. "In the beginning, God made the tree," a 75-year-old woman wrote the company. "Where did Satan get Charmin?"

Many callers reported hearing that Procter's "owner" had appeared on a television talk show where he admitted selling his soul to the devil in order to gain the company's success.

Anonymous fliers, usually misspelling the company's name, began to appear at supermarkets. "Proctor & Gamble," one said, "announced on *The Phil Donahue Show* Friday that they contribute 10 percent of their earnings to the Satanic religion (which is devil worship)."

"Do you realize," another anonymous flier said, "that if all the Christians in the world would stop buying Proctor and Gamble Products this Company would soon be out of business?"

Procter did a second mailing, to news organizations on the West Coast. But this time there was no letup. By last spring, Procter was getting 12,000 queries monthly about its relationship with the devil. There were reports of ministers, mainly in small Fundamentalist churches, attacking Procter from the pulpit and urging their congregations to boycott its products.

Given the dubious results of the news media campaign, John Smale, Procter's presi-   **20** dent, decided on a less public line of attack. The company wrote to local clergy and enclosed testaments of faith from very prominent clerics, including preachers who led an earlier attack on Procter for sponsoring television shows of what they regarded as questionable morality.

The Rev. Jerry Falwell, leader of Moral Majority, a church-based conservative political-action group, wrote that he had talked with Procter's chairman, "and I am certain neither he nor his company is associated in any way with Satanism or devil worship."

By June, however, the center was receiving more than 15,000 queries monthly, including a few from Alaska and Hawaii.

Mr. Smale told Procter's public relations department to forget his earlier cautions. On June 10, "We presented our recommendations to Mr. Smale," William Dobson, of the public relations department, recalled. "It was essentially to go on the offensive."

On July 1, Procter announced its first lawsuits. The litigation was "a very hard-nosed way to generate publicity." Mr. Dobson said. "We were working on the traditional Procter concepts: reach and frequency."

The subjects of those lawsuits and a second wave later in the month—Mike Campbell of Atlanta, William and Linda Moore of Pensacola, Florida, Guy Sharpe of Atlanta, Elma and Ed Pruitt of Clovis, New Mexico, and Sherman and Margaret McCord of Tullahoma, Tennessee—were chosen simply because "they just happened to be the first people where we felt we had enough evidence to go to court," Mr. Dobson said.

25   Most of the leads to ministers had evaporated, and in any case, a suit against a member of the clergy, "frankly, wasn't our optimum choice," Mr. Dobson said.

All but one of the defendants sell products of competing consumer-goods companies, according to Procter. The Moores and Mr. Pruitt are distributors for the Amway Corporation, which sells soap and other consumer products door-to-door. The McCords are distributors for Shaklee, which sells vitamins, household cleaners and personal care products. Mr. Campbell works for a grocery brokerage firm that represents manufacturers of household cleaning products.

However, "there is no evidence that companies are pushing this rumor," Mr. Norrish said. Nor is it clear that they were economically inspired. "We didn't try to figure out motives," he added. "We just want to stop them."

Most of the defendants denied the charges or said that they were convinced the rumors were false.

Mrs. McCord said that she had printed the rumor in her newsletter to other Shaklee distributors, but had realized her mistake and apologized in both the newsletter and a letter to Procter. Mrs. Pruitt said she and her husband stopped distributing anti-Procter leaflets after learning that the rumor was false.

30   William Hurst, the lawyer for Mr. Campbell, said that his client did hand an anti-Procter circular to a supermarket clerk when he was stocking the shelves with Clorox, but it was his only copy, and "he did not believe it."

Mr. Sharpe, a well-known weatherman for WXIA-TV in Atlanta and a Methodist lay preacher, issued a denial that he had made defamatory remarks against Procter & Gamble.

The lawsuits provoked the hoped for flurry of publicity, including network television coverage, and the number of queries to the consumer services department has fallen by half, Procter says. But few of the remaining 250 or so callers each day have heard of the lawsuits. "How do you reach them?" Mr. Norrish wonders.

Review Questions

1. What do the images in the Procter & Gamble logo actually represent?

2. Which component of the logo occasioned the "devil worship" rumor?

3. Aside from exercising its legal recourse, what did P&G hope to accomplish with its first lawsuits?

4. Why did Procter president John Smale reach beyond the usual media outlets in an effort to deflate the rumor?

Discussion and Writing Suggestions

1. The logo rumor led many people to boycott Procter & Gamble. Have you ever been asked to boycott a company? Why? In hindsight, to what extent was the boycott based on rumor?

2. Why do you think that the Procter & Gamble rumor was so persuasive and so resistant over the years to the company's attempts at refuting it? In formulating your response, speculate on some of the possible motivations of those who began the rumor and those who spread it; speculate also on the world views of those who were so receptive to its content.

3. P&G took a variety of approaches over the years to handling the charges of Satanism, ultimately filing lawsuits that took years to resolve. In the meantime, the company changed its logo. Assume you worked at Procter & Gamble during the years when the devil-worship rumor took hold. How might you have advised the company to adopt a different rumor-fighting strategy? In developing your answer, draw upon both your business sense and what you understand about human nature. In the final analysis, how well (or badly) do you think the company dealt with this persistent rumor?

4. The Procter & Gamble rumor is intertwined with religious beliefs and fears. History is filled with rumors of this nature—for example, the Salem witch trials of 1692. What other rumors have you personally encountered, or do you know of, that you can attribute to religious belief, fear, or just simple misunderstanding? How did these rumors spread, and what were their outcomes?

5. This particular rumor spread in the early 1980s, before the widespread availability of the Internet. At that time, rumors were not spread with the same instantaneous pace as they are now; similarly, companies could not simply respond within seconds by "tweeting" a response in an effort to deflate the rumor. How might the slower exchange of information during the 1980s have affected both the life of this rumor and the company's attempts at refutation? Had the rumor started today, do you think its life span would have been as long as it turned out to be?

The Runaway Grandmother

Jan Harold Brunvand

"The Runaway Grandmother" is an example of an urban legend. Rumors and urban legends are similar in that both involve statements or claims that circulate among people about topics they consider important. Unlike urban legends, rumors are

typically about real people or real companies and may consist of nothing more than an assertion ("I heard that the company is closing next year," "Marla quit her job and is opening up her own store"). Urban legends typically have a more extended narrative component than rumors. As Nicholas DiFonzo, an author represented later in this chapter, asserts, urban legends are "narratives about strange, funny, or horrible events that could have happened, the details of which change to fit particular locales or time periods, and which frequently contain a moral lesson." Finally, while some rumors may be true, virtually all urban legends are—as the word "legend" suggests—false.

Jan Harold Brunvand is an expert on urban legends, having collected thousands of them from all over the world. A professor of English at the University of Utah, Brunvand is a Fellow of the American Folklore Society and served as editor of the *Journal of American Folklore* from 1976 to 1980. Author of the standard introduction to American folklore, *The Study of American Folklore: An Introduction,* Brunvand writes a popular national column, "Urban Legends," syndicated by United Features Syndicate. He has also written five books on urban legends, including *The Choking Doberman* (1984), *Curses: Broiled Again* (1989), and *The Baby Train* (1993). This selection is from his first book, *The Vanishing Hitchhiker: American Urban Legends and Their Meanings* (1981).

"The Runaway Grandmother" is another popular urban legend in which a corpse is unwittingly pilfered from a car. The death-in-the-family theme implicit in "The Dead Cat in the Package" (the pet as a quasi-relative),[1] is made explicit here: an actual human relation of the family dies. Disposing of her is the problem, not only as a practical and legal matter, but also because death confuses and upsets people. When an unlucky stranger solves the problem, the family feels relief and release from the tension of confronting the graphic reminder of their own mortality.

Both the dead cat and stolen grandmother stories focus on the bereaved and tend to create in their climaxes a feeling of uneasiness tinged with humor. It is this emotional tone, shared by the legend audience, that links the stories, not any necessary historical connection. The legend of "The Runaway Grandmother" has its own characteristic motifs. While the cat legend usually begins with the problem of corpse-disposal, in "The Runaway Grandmother" this problem occurs unexpectedly in the course of the story, and the motivation for hiding the body is entirely different. There is never an exchange of goods motif in the grandmother heist.

An American folklorist, Robert H. Woodward, noted some of the similarities between the two stories in a 1963 news article in the San Jose, California, *Mercury;* he characterized the grandmother's corpse legend as "an addition to the growing store of urban tales," and he paraphrased it as follows:

> A local resident reports as fact an experience of a Washington State family that he knows. After the family had crossed the Mexican border on a vacation trip, one of the

---

[1]"The Dead Cat in the Package" is the motif of another urban legend discussed by Brunvand. The tale has numerous variants, but the essential story deals with an individual—generally, a woman—who needs to dispose of a dead cat. She wraps up the body of the feline in a package or a bag, stops at a shop on the way to her destination, then picks up her package and continues on her way. Upon reaching her destination, she opens the package to find a ham or some other unexpected object. The narrative then often switches to the person who has unwittingly picked up the package with the dead cat, describing the effect upon that person—often a fainting spell—when he or she opens the parcel.

children said, "Mama, Grandma won't wake up." Upon discovering that Grandma had died, the family placed her body in a sleeping bag and secured her to the top of their automobile, planning to report her death to the police at the first town. While they were in the station, their car was stolen—with Grandma's body still aboard. No trace has yet been found of either Grandma or the car. Another resident reports the tale as having happened in Italy.

It should also be noted here that, in common with the London version of "The Dead Cat in the Package," this story involves Americans who are abroad when their funerary problem comes up. Part of their distress seems to come from not being on home ground.

The first text of "The Runaway Grandmother" legend published in a folklore study was also collected in 1963, from an English woman who heard it told in Canada by her cousin who in turn had heard it in Leeds. (Obviously the story was getting around pretty well by 1963.) The characters in this version—and several of their terms—are definitely English. Parallel to the Americans visiting Mexico, these tourists have their odd experience during a vacation in Spain:

> This story was told me by my cousin, who had heard it from a friend in Leeds, about a couple whom he knew, who went for a camping holiday in Spain with their car. They had taken his stepmother with them. She slept in a different tent to the others. On the morning that they struck [broke camp], they were very busy, and they didn't hear anything of her for a while, and then, when they went to her tent, they found she had died, and rigor had already set in. They were in a great state, and they didn't know what to do, but they decided to roll her up in the tent, and put her on top of the car, and go to the nearest town, and go to the consul and the police. So they did this, and went to the town, and then they felt very cold and miserable, and they hadn't had a proper breakfast. So they thought they'd get a cup of coffee to revive them, before they went in search of the consul. So they parked the car, and went to a small cafe, and had their cup of coffee, and then came back to look for the car. But it wasn't there. It had gone.
>
> So they went home to England without the car or the stepmother. But the difficulty was, they couldn't prove [i.e., probate] her will.

Since "The Runaway Grandmother" probably entered American folklore from European   **5**
tradition, it is not surprising that some American versions have their setting in a simple unspec- ified "Europe." The following well-detailed text was collected in 1966 from an Indiana student who had "heard it from her mother as a true event." Unlike the English tourists in Spain who stop to eat out of sheer hunger, misery, and exhaustion, the Americans in this tale pause more for standard touristic reasons, in order "to . . . eat their last European meal at a small, quaint restaurant." The loss of their grandmother seems to strike the family as almost comical:

> Well, once there was this family and they had been waiting to go abroad for, oh, a number of years, and finally their big chance came. They packed up all of their things—had their car shipped over—and were soon in Europe and ready to go sightseeing. There were five of them and they had a rather small car and it was pretty crowded. There were the two parents and two children and a grandmother.
>
> Well, a trip to Europe can be quite a strain on an old woman. And she hadn't been in too good of health anyway, and that was one of the reasons they took the trip, so she could see all of the "European Wonders" before she died.
>
> Anyway, one day when they woke up they found that the grandmother had died during the night. Well, they didn't know what to do because here they were, 3,000 miles away from home and across an ocean yet, and they were the grandmother's only living relatives so they couldn't just send a body back to the States with no one to receive it. They were going

to be starting home soon, anyway, so out of desperation they wrapped the grandmother's body in a piece of canvas and tied it on the top of their small car—which, by the way, made much more room inside the car.

And as they were making their last round across the village where they were staying they decided to stop and eat their last European meal at a small, quaint restaurant.

Well, it happened that while they were in there someone stole the car with the grandmother on top. For some reason they weren't too worried about the whole situation, they just wondered what the looks on the crooks' face would be when they discovered the strange contents of the canvas.

English folklorist Stewart Sanderson found "The Runaway Grandmother" second in popularity in Great Britain among "motor-car stories" only to "The Vanishing Hitchhiker."[2] His collection of versions of the legend extended back to more than twenty years before the earliest American texts. Sanderson wrote:

I first heard it in Leeds in 1960, from the wife of a colleague who told it as having happened to friends of her friends in Brussels, as they escaped through northern France during the German invasion of 1940. A few weeks later, believing with my informant that the tale was true, I repeated it to an academic colleague in Edinburgh who also knew her. To our initial surprise he had recently heard much the same story from a colleague in Cambridge, with the difference that it was set in Spain after the war and involved the difficulty of cremating the corpse. . . . Other variants involve the loss of a body in a caravan [trailer] which slips its tow on a hill; the theft of a body from the luggage compartment of a holiday tour bus; and a variant I collected at the University of Nsukka, Nigeria in 1965. In this, the body of an old woman, being taken back for burial at her native village on the Crow River, is lost by rolling off the roof of a mammy-wagon [local bus] into the bush.

The European versions, then, seem to fall into two distinct subtypes—one, the wartime story involving crossing an international border, usually to escape the Nazis or to leave Eastern Europe; and second, the postwar tale of vacationers abroad. Indiana folklorist Linda Dégh, who assembled more than one hundred versions of "The Runaway Grandmother" and related stories from Europe and the United States, believed that the legend must have acquired its common form during or just after the Second World War. Possibly it evolved from stories known in Europe in the eighteenth and nineteenth centuries dealing with the mistaken theft of a corpse and ending with the thieves' shock as they inspect their booty. In the wartime context, Dégh speculated this story could have lost its last episode, shifting the climax to the risky crossing of an international border. In later years, and especially in American tradition, the focus seems to have shifted again to emphasize the inconvenience and distress of disposing of a corpse while on a vacation in a foreign country. The "message" of the story, Dégh suggested, derives from "the fear of the return of the dead" and expresses the concern that "the corpse has to receive a decent burial." In addition to the United States and England, Dégh encountered "The Runaway Grandmother" both orally and in print in Norway, Sweden, Denmark, Germany, Switzerland, Italy, Poland, Hungary and Yugoslavia. The completion of her comparative study of all texts ought to clarify further the legend's history and development.

---

[2]"The Vanishing Hitchhiker" legend is treated in Brunvand's book of the same name. The essential story involves one or more travelers who pick up a hitchhiker who asks for a ride to her home. When these travelers arrive at the hitchhiker's requested destination, she has inexplicably disappeared from the car. Mystified, they knock on the door of the house to which the hitchhiker has asked to be taken. The person answering the knock tells the travelers that his daughter, who matches the description of the hitchhiker, disappeared some years ago on that same road—and that today is her birthday.

Folklorist Charles Clay Doyle was more willing than Dégh to connect "The Runaway Grandmother" to earlier narratives. He pointed to a Renaissance "jest" (a very grim joke, at best) widely known in Europe in which an Italian Jew attempts to send his dead Jewish friend back home to Venice illegally by pickling the dismembered corpse in spices and honey and packing the pieces in a jar. While he is on a boat during the trip home, various parts of the corpse are stolen and eaten by an unwary Florentine. The switching of corpse and food, Doyle suggested, may link this story also to "The Dead Cat in the Package" (cat swapped for meat). The motif of gnawing or nibbling on a corpse is of course also found in a number of other terror stories similar to "The Roommate's Death." If one agrees that all these tale plots *are* linked, then it would seem that the bereaved family is not just ready to abandon Grandmother, they are willing to devour her as well, or at least they toy with the idea.

Two details in texts I have collected might lend support to Doyle's analysis. First, Doyle's Renaissance jest is strangely similar in one respect to the 1906 version of "The Dead Cat in the Package" ("The Ham Cat") which took place partly on a ferryboat; and, second, I have heard versions of the dying-grandmother story in which the corpse is cremated abroad and sent home to relatives by mail. The recipients later say "Thanks for the good curry powder; we've been using it on everything."

Whether the American versions sprang directly from postwar European variants of the border-crossing tradition or not, the particular subtypes found here are distinct. Of eighteen American versions which Dégh collected in Indiana, for example, ten fall into the group represented by the first text given above, in which the family is traveling in Mexico when the grandmother dies. The second largest group (five texts), in which the vacation takes place in the Western desert, is evidently influenced by an incident in John Steinbeck's *The Grapes of Wrath* (1939): Granma Joad's corpse being taken through the California agricultural inspection station wrapped in a blanket on the back of a truck. (Of course, it is possible that Steinbeck deliberately introduced legendary material into his plot.) Here is a summarized version of the desert subtype told to a student by a Gary, Indiana, woman who "was almost in a state of shock," believing the story to be true:

> It happened to her friend's family (I don't know their names) as they were traveling across the desert to California. Within this station wagon there was a father, a mother and their children, and the mother-in-law who everybody called "Grandma." And as they were going across the desert Grandma became sick and she died. Now they didn't want to alarm the children and they didn't want to leave Grandma out in the desert so the only place they had room for her where she—her smell wouldn't bother the children—was to strap her on top of the station wagon along with the baggage with a tarp over her, of course. And as they were traveling across the desert they kept looking for a town where they could deposit Grandma. They finally arrived in a small town in Arizona where they stopped at a filling station and they went in to report Grandma's death. And while they were within the filling station somebody stole the station wagon and when they went out—no station wagon and no Grandma! Well, it wasn't very funny even though it sounds like it because they have to wait seven years now to prove that Grandma is dead before they can collect any insurance. And they've never been able to find either the car or Grandma. This actually happened.

In a third American subtype—or it may be just Midwestern—the family is vacationing in the upper Peninsula of Michigan when Grandma dies. In a text quoted by Dégh, the stripped car is found some weeks later, but Grandma's corpse never turns up.

One cannot help being struck by the American versions' casual—almost callous—treatment of the old woman's death. Often the initially crowded condition of the family car is

10

mentioned, and the decision to make more room by putting the corpse on the roof is made by the survivors without hesitation or debate. There is almost always a reference to the practical difficulty of probating the will or supplying proof of death. Yet almost never is any significant mention made of the car, baggage, and other property also lost to the thieves; it is almost as if this was the price the family had to pay for the relief of being rid of Grandma.

Alan Dundes has analyzed various versions of the legend and concluded that its central message is the rejection of old age and dying in our youth-oriented society. It is significant, he felt, that there is "much more room inside the car" when Grandma is gone—the old lady is out of the way at last. But yet "Grandmother is a burden whether alive or dead"—her body is an unwelcome reminder of human mortality and it must be kept away from the children. Furthermore, although the family "took her for a ride" (and Dundes recalled how gangsters use that phrase), an anonymous third party (the thief)—like a mortician in real life—took care of her after death. Finally, Dundes interpreted the details at the end of the legend as suggesting that Americans' principal interest in their aged relatives is the prospect of inheriting their money. Both the frequent news articles and editorials about the treatment of aged Americans and examples of the "Theater of the Absurd" provide validation of this critique of American values. For the latter, compare how the same themes are handled in two of Edward Albee's most gripping plays, *The Sandbox* and *The American Dream*.

"The Runaway Grandmother" is a fully-developed modern legend widely circulated today in many different versions across the United States; still, each story, with its often elaborate local details, is told as a "true" account. There are recent examples of each of the subtypes (the wartime and the postwar). The following was told by a Tucson, Arizona, man to my student Ann Clegg in Fall 1969. It was supposed to have happened to a friend of the informant's, "a prominent businessman in Tucson." Here the family travels to Mexico, and the thieves, usually not identified in the story, are said to be native American "foreigners":

> The businessman went on a trip to Mexico with his wife and his grandmother. The grandmother had always wanted to go to Mexico, and as she was quite old, they knew this would probably be her last chance to go. ["Taking her for a ride" again?]
>
> They got somewhere in the remote mountain areas and the grandmother had a heart attack and died. The odor was terrible because of the heat and because the grandmother had a bowel movement as she was dying. (Apparently this is not uncommon when a person has a heart attack. [Student's comment])
>
> They wrapped the grandmother in a piece of canvas they had to cover their suitcases with and put her body on top of the car. They stopped in the first town with a telephone—a town populated mostly by Indians. It took quite a while to contact their relatives in Arizona and when they came out, the body had been stolen! Imagine how frightened those superstitious Indians must have been when they found they had stolen a body!

Ah yes, this is how the superstitious savages will react to a corpse, at least in the American folk stereotype. But why would they steal a car in the first place, and how could they conceal the vehicle? We "real Americans," the story shows, know better how to regard death—rationally and neatly.

15   A second Utah report of "The Runaway Grandmother" indicates that the earlier form of the story is still circulating. Early in 1979 I found this note on my desk left by my assistant Sharon Decker Pratt who had often heard me discuss this and other urban legends:

> Last night at a dinner party our friends told of a conversation they had just had at a dinner party Friday night with a fascinating woman originally from Latvia who is staying at Snowbird [a ski resort] this week with some mutual friends. (The hostess was also originally

from Latvia.) Both women were recounting various experiences they'd had during various political regimes; the horrors, the resistance movement, and even some of the more humorous things.

The guest is around fifty, either a doctor or a dentist (kept referring to her patients) in Boston, and a perfectly reliable, credible-sounding individual. Anyhow, she told of her family's departure during the '40s whereupon her grandmother died just as they were to leave the country. Inasmuch as it was very cold (zero in the middle of winter) the grandmother's body was frozen solid and, since they did not want to leave her body in Latvia but rather bury her elsewhere, they decided to wrap her in a rather long piece of luggage and take her with them out of the country, along with their other belongings.

Well, you guessed it!!! Someone stole the grandmother at the train station.

This is all very well, except that Mrs. Pratt telephoned me on Monday to say that she had spoken to the woman again, and it was the grandmother of *another* Latvian friend whose corpse had been stolen.

Discussion and Writing Suggestions

1. Brunvand cites examples of "The Runaway Grandmother" story in numerous countries—in Western and Eastern Europe, in the United States, and in Mexico. Which particular elements of this urban legend do you think make it so universal? How does it draw upon our human anxieties, both as members of families and as natives of a particular country?

2. Brunvand notes that "dead cat and stolen grandmother stories focus on the bereaved and tend to create in their climaxes a feeling of uneasiness tinged with humor." Explain how this mix of uneasiness and humor works in "The Runaway Grandmother." Why, exactly, do we feel uneasiness at such tales? Which elements in the stories tend to foster unease? And why is this story humorous? What, exactly, are we laughing at, and why?

3. Urban legends are often cautionary tales—that is, stories that illustrate the potentially bad consequences of certain types of behavior. What are some of the cautionary tales told to you by your parents or your teachers when you were a child? Were such cautionary tales embedded in stories? What do some of the variants of "The Runaway Grandmother" appear to caution us against? (Consider, for example, why the people in some of the variants leave the grandmother's body unattended.) To what extent do these warnings seem legitimate or worth taking seriously?

4. Brunvand explains that European versions of this story typically fall into one of two categories: "one, the wartime story involving crossing an international border, usually to escape the Nazis or to leave Eastern Europe; and second, the postwar tale of vacationers abroad." From the versions offered here, examine an example of each of these subtypes and explain how they differ in terms of meaning or emotional impact.

5. Brunvand summarizes the view of one analyst of this story, Alan Dundes, as follows: "its central message is the rejection of old age and dying in our

youth-oriented society." To what extent do you agree with the propositions that (1) our youth-oriented society rejects old age and dying, and that (2) "The Runaway Grandmother" stories do, in one form or another, incorporate this message? In responding, consider the details that embellish and also serve to authenticate the multiple variants of this story.

On the Web: *Rumor Report: Ebola in Kansas City*

Beginning in 2014 and lasting two years, an outbreak in West Africa of the highly contagious viral disease Ebola triggered global fears about transmission—even when those fears were not medically founded. Those who had traveled to West Africa during this time were quarantined when they landed on foreign shores, where people remained on edge due to Ebola's unusually high (average) fatality rate of 50 percent. Rumors spread globally, faster than the virus itself. One locus for rumors was Kansas City, Missouri.

Working in groups, go online and gather as much information as you can from print and video news outlets about the Ebola rumor in Kansas City. Then prepare an informational report, explaining what happened. Consider structuring your report as follows:

- **Background on Ebola in West Africa.**
- **Quarantines for returning travelers to West Africa.**
- **First Ebola rumors in Kansas City.**
- **Spread of Ebola rumors in Kansas City.**
- **The battle of authoritative vs. nonauthoritative information regarding Ebola in Kansas City.**
- **Responses to the Ebola rumor in Kansas City.**
- **Success of efforts to confront rumors of Ebola in Kansas City.**
- **Resolution of Ebola rumors in Kansas City.**

---

*How Technology Disrupted the Truth**

Katherine Viner

"Social media has swallowed the news," writes Katherine Viner, "ushering in an era when everyone has their own facts." You've read other selections in this chapter that show how rumors flourish in unsettled times. Viner presents a snapshot of *our* times and the stresses that follow from our inability, or unwillingness, to agree on the truth or even how it's established. Katharine Viner is editor-in-chief of *The Guardian*, the British daily, in which the following (part of a longer essay) appeared on July 12, 2016.

One Monday morning last September, Britain woke to a depraved news story. The prime minister, David Cameron, had committed an "obscene act with a dead pig's head," according to the

*Katharine Viner, "How technology disrupted the truth," The Guardian, 12 July 2016, https://www.theguardian.com/media/2016/jul/12/how-technology-disrupted-the-truth. Copyright Guardian News & Media Ltd 2017.

Daily Mail. "A distinguished Oxford contemporary claims Cameron once took part in an outrageous initiation ceremony at a Piers Gaveston event, involving a dead pig," the paper reported. Piers Gaveston is the name of a riotous Oxford university dining society; the authors of the story claimed their source was an MP, who said he had seen photographic evidence: "His extraordinary suggestion is that the future PM inserted a private part of his anatomy into the animal."

The story, extracted from a new biography of Cameron, sparked an immediate furore. It was gross, it was a great opportunity to humiliate an elitist prime minister, and many felt it rang true for a former member of the notorious Bullingdon Club. Within minutes, #Piggate and #Hameron were trending on Twitter, and even senior politicians joined the fun: Nicola Sturgeon said the allegations had "entertained the whole country," while Paddy Ashdown joked that Cameron was "hogging the headlines." At first, the BBC refused to mention the allegations, and 10 Downing Street said it would not "dignify" the story with a response—but soon it was forced to issue a denial. And so a powerful man was sexually shamed, in a way that had nothing to do with his divisive politics, and in a way he could never really respond to. But who cares? He could take it.

Then, after a full day of online merriment, something shocking happened. Isabel Oakeshott, the *Daily Mail* journalist who had co-written the biography with Lord Ashcroft, a billionaire businessman, went on TV and admitted that she did not know whether her huge, scandalous scoop was even true. Pressed to provide evidence for the sensational claim, Oakeshott admitted she had none.

"We couldn't get to the bottom of that source's allegations," she said on Channel 4 News. "So we merely reported the account that the source gave us. . . . We don't say whether we believe it to be true." In other words, there was no evidence that the prime minister of the United Kingdom had once "inserted a private part of his anatomy" into the mouth of a dead pig—a story reported in dozens of newspapers and repeated in millions of tweets and Facebook updates, which many people presumably still believe to be true today.

Oakeshott went even further to absolve herself of any journalistic responsibility: "It's up 5 to other people to decide whether they give it any credibility or not," she concluded. This was not, of course, the first time that outlandish claims were published on the basis of flimsy evidence, but this was an unusually brazen defence. It seemed that journalists were no longer required to believe their own stories to be true, nor, apparently, did they need to provide evidence. Instead it was up to the reader—who does not even know the identity of the source— to make up their own mind. But based on what? Gut instinct, intuition, mood?

Does the truth matter any more?

•   •   •

Twenty-five years after the first website went online, it is clear that we are living through a period of dizzying transition. For 500 years after Gutenberg, the dominant form of information was the printed page: knowledge was primarily delivered in a fixed format, one that encouraged readers to believe in stable and settled truths.

Now, we are caught in a series of confusing battles between opposing forces: between truth and falsehood, fact and rumour, kindness and cruelty; between the few and the many, the connected and the alienated; between the open platform of the web as its architects envisioned it and the gated enclosures of Facebook and other social networks; between an informed public and a misguided mob.

What is common to these struggles—and what makes their resolution an urgent matter—is that they all involve the diminishing status of truth. This does not mean that there are no truths. It simply means, as this year has made very clear, that we cannot agree on what those truths are, and when there is no consensus about the truth and no way to achieve it, chaos soon follows.

10   Increasingly, what counts as a fact is merely a view that someone feels to be true—and technology has made it very easy for these "facts" to circulate with a speed and reach that was unimaginable in the Gutenberg era (or even a decade ago). A dubious story about Cameron and a pig appears in a tabloid one morning, and by noon, it has flown around the world on social media and turned up in trusted news sources everywhere. This may seem like a small matter, but its consequences are enormous.

"The Truth," as Peter Chippindale and Chris Horrie wrote in *Stick It Up Your Punter!*, their history of the *Sun* newspaper, is a "bald statement which every newspaper prints at its peril." There are usually several conflicting truths on any given subject, but in the era of the printing press, words on a page nailed things down, whether they turned out to be true or not. The information felt like the truth, at least until the next day brought another update or a correction, and we all shared a common set of facts.

This settled "truth" was usually handed down from above: an established truth, often fixed in place by an establishment. This arrangement was not without flaws: too much of the press often exhibited a bias towards the status quo and a deference to authority, and it was prohibitively difficult for ordinary people to challenge the power of the press. Now, people distrust much of what is presented as fact—particularly if the facts in question are uncomfortable, or out of sync with their own views—and while some of that distrust is misplaced, some of it is not.

In the digital age, it is easier than ever to publish false information, which is quickly shared and taken to be true—as we often see in emergency situations, when news is breaking in real time. To pick one example among many, during the November 2015 Paris terror attacks, rumours quickly spread on social media that the Louvre and Pompidou Centre had been hit, and that François Hollande had suffered a stroke. Trusted news organisations are needed to debunk such tall tales.[3]

Sometimes rumours like these spread out of panic, sometimes out of malice, and sometimes deliberate manipulation, in which a corporation or regime pays people to convey their message. Whatever the motive, falsehoods and facts now spread the same way, through what academics call an "information cascade." As the legal scholar and online-harassment expert Danielle Citron describes it, "people forward on what others think, even if the information is false, misleading or incomplete, because they think they have learned something valuable." This cycle repeats itself, and before you know it, the cascade has unstoppable momentum. You share a friend's post on Facebook, perhaps to show kinship or agreement or that you're "in the know," and thus you increase the visibility of their post to others.

Discussion and Writing Suggestions

1. Reread the first six paragraphs of this selection, Viner's account of the rumor concerning former prime minister David Cameron. The writer responsible for publicizing this rumor, Isabel Oakeshott, "absolve[d] herself of any journalistic responsibility [by claiming]: 'It's up to other people to decide whether they give [the rumor] any credibility or not.'" Do you agree with Oakeshott? Did she have a responsibility to back up her story with evidence? Why or why not?

2. We don't get to choose the times we live in. But *if* you had a choice, would you prefer a world of apparent "stable and settled truths" to our present,

[3]The Louvre is the world's largest museum and is located in Paris. The Pompidou Center, named after former French president Georges Pompidou, is a public library and museum of modern art. François Hollande was president of France during the terrorist attacks of 2015.

chaotic times? Why or why not? Why are "stable and settled truths" so appealing, even if they happen to be false?

3. What consequences can follow when people are unable to agree on what truth is—in a family, community, city, or nation?

4. In paragraph 8, Viner presents a series of "battles" marked by sharp contrasts. Choose one of these battles and discuss the ways it contributes to the fracturing of our social order.

5. According to Viner, technology plays an important role in "diminishing [the] status of truth." Are there ways in which disruptive technologies like Twitter and Facebook are *helping* us?

6. "Whatever the motive, falsehoods and facts now spread the same way." Are you as alarmed by this development as Viner seems to be? Discuss.

Anatomy of A Rumor: It Flies on Fear*

Daniel Goleman

The following selection offers a concise introduction to the world of rumors. Psychologist Daniel Goleman provides numerous examples of rumors in the modern world, particularly those concerning death and disease, and explains how such stories are spread by the anxiety and fear of those who hear or read about them. He also offers advice on the best strategy for fighting rumors. Goleman is a psychologist and science journalist. He has been a visiting faculty member at Harvard and lectures frequently on college campuses and to business and professional groups. His many books include *The Varieties of Meditative Experience* (1977), *Emotional Intelligence* (1995), *Primal Leadership* (2001), and *Social Intelligence: The New Science of Human Relationships* (2006). A two-time Pulitzer Prize nominee, Goleman won a Career Achievement Award for journalism from the American Psychological Association. For twelve years he wrote articles for the *New York Times* on psychology and brain sciences. This selection originally appeared in the *Times* on June 4, 1991.

Did you hear?

This woman trying on a coat in a department store put her hand in the pocket and was bitten by a snake. See, the coat had been made in Taiwan where a viper laid eggs in the pocket. The woman died.

Oh, and then a man in New York City on business went to a bar for a drink and woke up the next morning in Central Park, feeling so terrible he went to the hospital. The doctor found a long, neat scar up the man's back: someone had removed one of the man's kidneys and neatly sewn him up again.

And did you hear that you shouldn't swim in public swimming pools because you can get AIDS from them? It happened to a little girl in Pittsburgh. Or maybe it was a little boy in St. Louis.

5   None of this is true, of course. But each of these stories is circulating as a rumor. They are specimens from the collection of Dr. Allan J. Kimmel, a psychologist at Fitchburg State College in Fitchburg, Mass., who is among the social scientists studying the anatomy of rumors in order to find better ways to control them.

The results suggest rumors are a kind of opportunistic information virus, thriving because of their ability to create the very anxieties that make them spread, and to mutate to fit new situations. Some rumors have survived for centuries, simply changing their targets as they traveled around the globe.

The need for effective ways to combat rumors is becoming ever more apparent. The AIDS rumors, for instance, heighten anxieties while making the work of public health officials more difficult. Racial tensions and riots are almost always fed by rumors. Businesses targeted by rumors have lost millions of dollars in sales.

The Role of Anxiety

The new research highlights the role of anxiety in giving life to rumors. For instance, people are much more likely to pass on a rumor that is about something they are already anxious about, studies have found. Repeating the rumor serves to reassure people that they understand something that troubles and perplexes them, psychologists say.

"A rumor is a kind of hypothesis, a speculation that helps people make sense of a chaotic reality or gives them a small sense of control in a threatening world," said Dr. Ralph Rosnow, a psychologist at Temple University who wrote an article reviewing findings on rumors in the current issue of *The American Psychologist*.

10   From the perspective of the people who hear rumors and pass them on, rumors are news. And while rumors are always about a topic of emotional importance to the teller, gossip need not be. "Gossip is small talk, a kind of intellectual chewing gum, while rumors have the feel of something of great substance," said Dr. Rosnow.

While rumors are naturally elusive, researchers have been resourceful in finding methods to study them. Some studies seize on the opportunity provided by events that spawn rumors, such as wars, murders or other disturbing events. In this approach, researchers survey people to find what rumors they have heard, if they believed them or passed them on and so on.

A similar approach has been used with rumors about companies. When the target is a business, people who hear the rumor frequently call the company to express outrage or to ask if it could be true. Such was the case, for instance, with the rumor in the mid-1980s that Procter & Gamble was somehow involved in Satanism.

Tracking Rumors as They Spread

By interviewing people who hear such a rumor, social scientists can learn what evidence people cite to support it, plan an advertising campaign to combat it and find out if the campaign was effective.

"You can track rumors as they travel across the country," said Dr. Fred Koenig, a social psychologist at Tulane University who advises companies victimized by rumors. "That allows you to target your campaign against it to the locale where it is most active."

15   Researchers sometimes also start rumors in order to study them. For instance, in a study conducted by Dr. Rosnow, confederates started a rumor in college classes that students in another class had been caught smoking marijuana during a final exam. A week later the students were asked if they had passed on the rumor and how sure of its truth they were.

Not surprisingly, the more students believed the rumor, the more likely they were to have passed it on.

In some of the most recent experiments researchers carefully manipulate the way rumors are presented to more precisely weigh what makes people believe them or not. Thus in one study at Northwestern University the rumor that McDonald's hamburgers contained worms was accompanied by the information that worms are nutritious and are considered a delicacy in some cultures. "One of the aims of such studies is to see what kind of information will kill a rumor," said Dr. Koenig.

Much of the current rumor research focuses on the role of anxiety. In a direct test of how people's anxieties lead them to pass on rumors, Dr. Rosnow surveyed students several months after the 1986 murder of a student at the University of Pennsylvania.

"Some rumors, such as that the woman was the target of a random attack, increased people's sense of dread, by suggesting that they themselves could have easily been the victim," said Dr. Rosnow. "Other rumors, like one that a former lover had killed her, were more reassuring, suggesting that only she could have been the target of the violence."

Fright Leads to Repetition

The students, on average, had heard three to five rumors about the murder. No matter how many rumors they had heard, Dr. Rosnow found, the students were far more likely to pass on those that made them most anxious.

In general, researchers are finding that rumors perpetuate themselves by creating anxiety in the hearer: people who are most distressed by something are more likely to transmit rumors on the topic. For example, in a study of 229 college students, the students most readily passed on the rumors about AIDS that they found most personally relevant and upsetting. **20**

"The more frightened people were by a rumor, the more likely they were to repeat it," said Dr. Kimmel whose study will be published in *The Journal of Applied Social Psychology.*

One motive for people to repeat rumors that frighten them is in the hope of finding that it is wrong. "In repeating something that makes you nervous to someone else, you may learn some contrary fact that will calm you," Dr. Kimmel said. "On the other hand, it can escalate your fears if the person you tell it to believes it."

Those students who already were so anxious about AIDS that they had done something to protect themselves, such as deciding to abstain from sex, were the most likely to repeat the AIDS rumors, Dr. Kimmel found. For these students, the rumors may have served as a justification for their own actions.

The Message from Elvis

The implicit messages of rumors give them their emotional power. Some of the most compelling rumors revolve around basic fears, such as of disease or death. Thus the rumor that Elvis Presley or John F. Kennedy is alive and well has as its subtext the message that it is possible to defeat death.

By the same token, those health fears seem to propel rumors such as the story that Mikey, a little boy in commercials for Life cereal, died when he mixed a carbonated beverage with an exploding candy called "pop rocks," Dr. Levin said. **25**

"Such rumors touch on people's basic anxieties: death, disaster, conspiratorial plots, racial tensions," he said.

Of Restaurants and Dogs

The source cited for a rumor is usually specific enough to sound plausible, but distant enough to be unverifiable, such as "a cousin of a friend." But when those trails are actually followed by investigators, they typically find deadends.

One of the most ancient of rumors, still alive and well, has been around for more than a century: that Chinese restaurants serve up the missing dogs of townspeople. In a paper presented in May at the Society for the Study of Contemporary Legend, British researchers traced the rumor in England to the earliest years of the British Empire, and in America to the 1850s.

"The rumor thrives because, in China, they do eat dogs," said Dr. Koenig. "But the same rumor, with a warning to watch your dog, is now going around about Vietnamese immigrants in Texas and elsewhere, about Mexicans in southern California and about Native Americans in Wisconsin."

30   Businesses are among the biggest victims of rumors. Earlier this year Tropical Fantasy, a soft drink marketed to minorities in Northeastern cities, was the target of a rumor, allegedly started by a rival, that the company was controlled by the Ku Klux Klan, and that the drink contained an ingredient that would make black men sterile.

Such rumors, which typically trigger a boycott of the product involved by those who believe them, have been spread about children being kidnapped in K-Mart stores and about Procter & Gamble giving part of its profits to Satanists.

A current rumor is a variation on the Procter & Gamble story: that Liz Claiborne, the clothing company, "is in cahoots with the Church of Satan," said Dr. Koenig.

Satan and a Fading Picture

"The new version holds that Liz Claiborne herself was on the Oprah Winfrey show, and that she said her company gives 30 percent of its profits to the Church of Satan," said Dr. Koenig. "Then the picture faded out, like something was wrong with the transmission, and when the picture came back, she wasn't there." Such specific details are typical of rumors, Dr. Koenig said, lending them the ring of truth.

Dr. Koenig, who has advised several corporations on squelching rumors, said, "If a company is the target of a rumor, it should deny it immediately, as forcefully and publicly as possible showing the evidence that proves it is unfounded."

35   That advice runs contrary to conventional wisdom among public relations firms, which holds that such a public denial only calls more people's attention to what are false allegations.

But Dr. Koenig said: "A public rebuttal takes a rumor and turns it into news. The news shows the rumor to be unsubstantiated. If you try to pass on the rumor after that, you run the risk of being ridiculed."

That tactic was used successfully, for instance, by Entenmann's, a baked goods company in Bay Shore, N.Y. When a rumor spread throughout Boston that the bakery was owned by The Rev. Sun Myung Moon of the Unification Church, the company held a news conference at which Robert Entenmann, the chairman, reviewed the history of his family-owned business and declared that the rumor was untrue. "The rumor stopped within 24 hours," said Dr. Koenig.

Review Questions

1. Why are people more likely to pass on a rumor they are already anxious about, according to Goleman?

2. In what way does rumor differ from gossip, according to psychologist Ralph Rosnow?

3. How do social scientists such as Rosnow attempt to track rumors and determine which ones are successful at spreading?

4. In what way do people who spread anxiety-causing rumors hope to reassure themselves?

Discussion and Writing Suggestions

1. Recall one of the rumors you have heard, perhaps even helped spread. To what extent were your responses to the rumor driven by anxiety? The responses of other people you know? How did you learn, eventually, whether or not the rumor was true? Did you attempt to investigate the facts yourself, or did you seek verification from friends or relatives? Were you eventually persuaded that the rumor was false because of contrary evidence?

2. Goleman quotes psychologist Ralph Rosnow: "A rumor is a kind of hypothesis, a speculation that helps people make sense of a chaotic reality or gives them a small sense of control in a threatening world." Explain how this definition applies to a rumor that you have heard or read about.

3. Examine a sensational story in one of the supermarket tabloids that deals in scandal and rumor. What sources or evidence are cited to support the story? To what extent do you believe the story? Does the story provoke anxiety or some other response? Explain.

4. Consider a recent rumor from any realm of public interest (politics, entertainment, business, etc.). How did the target address the rumor? To what extent was the chosen strategy effective? How closely did the subject adhere to Dr. Fred Koenig's advice to "deny it immediately, as forcefully and publicly as possible showing the evidence that proves it is unfounded"?

One Man's Rumor Is Another Man's Reality

Gregory Rodriguez

Drawing upon rumor theorists such as Robert H. Knapp and Cass Sunstein, columnist Gregory Rodriguez explores the ways in which rumors emerge from our anxieties and belief systems. Rumors that support and validate our prior convictions are hard to disprove, even when countered with cold hard facts and solid reasoning. A founding director of Arizona State University's Center for Social Cohesion, Rodriguez writes about civic engagement and political and cultural trends. This selection first appeared in the *Los Angeles Times* on September 28, 2009.

Just because you're paranoid doesn't mean that someone's not after you. Over the last few months, a lot of writers have dusted off Richard Hofstadter's classic 1964 essay on the paranoid style in American politics just so they can explain away the loony rumors and conspiracy theories coming from the far right. But no amount of intellectual condescension is going to make those powerful untruths go away.

The real truth is that, as weird as they are, rumors and conspiracy theories can only thrive in the minds of people who are predisposed to believe them. Successful propagators of fringe theories don't just send random balloons into the atmosphere. Rather, they tap into the preexisting beliefs and biases of their target audiences.

Plenty of studies have shown that people don't process information in a neutral way—"biased assimilation" they call it. In other words, rather than our opinions being forged by whatever information we have available, they tend to be constructed by our wants and needs. With all their might, our minds try to reduce cognitive dissonance—that queasy feeling you get when you are confronted by contradictory ideas simultaneously. Therefore, we tend to reject theories and rumors—and facts and truths—that challenge our worldview and embrace those that affirm it.

It's easy to assume that lack of education is the culprit when it comes to people believing rumors against logic and evidence—for instance, that Barack Obama, whose mother was an American citizen and whose state of birth has repeatedly said his birth records are in good order, isn't a legitimate American citizen. But one 1994 survey on conspiracy theories found that educational level or occupational category were not factors in whether you believed in them or not.

5   What was significant? Insecurity about employment. That finding ties into psychologist Robert H. Knapp's 1944 thesis that rumors "express and gratify the emotional needs" of communities during periods of social duress. They arise, in his view, to "express in simple and rationalized terms the uncertainties and hostilities which so many feel."[4]

---

[4]During World War II, psychologist Robert H. Knapp—then head of rumor control for the Massachusetts Committee on Public Safety—attempted to classify and identify the numerous rumors circulating at the time (rumors being commonplace in time of war). In his classic article "A Psychology of Rumor" (*Public Opinion Quarterly*, Vol. 8, Issue 1, Jan. 1944), Knapp examines some of the rumors currently or recently in circulation and attempts to create a framework for further study. He both defines rumor and classifies three main types, each based on the human emotion that drives it: wish, fear, or hostility.

Knapp defines rumor as "a *proposition for belief of topical reference disseminated without official verification.*" A "proposition for belief" is any statement that claims to be true and asks of the person hearing/listening/reading to accept it as true—whether or not that statement *is* true. Rumors, he claims, are not initiated by formal sources of information like government agencies or news organizations, which typically seek to verify claims before distributing them.

According to Knapp, rumors are rich with information that speaks to a community's wishes, fears, and hostilities. The three main types of rumors tap into these emotions:

- The "Pipe Dream or Wish Rumor" addresses a community's deep desires. We earnestly hope Pipe Dream rumors are true.
- The "Bogie Rumor" addresses a community's "fears and anxieties." We hope Bogey Rumors are false.
- The successful "Wedge-driving Aggression Rumor" seeks to break communities into opposing or competing groups by sowing fear and hostility.

Knapp also enumerates the qualities that make for a "good" rumor. They include brevity; simplicity; humor; "exaggeration"; distortion; "unstable" elements like "[n]ames, numbers, and places" that change as rumors spread and give them a local flavor; false attribution to "a high authoritative source"; and adaptation. This last quality is especially important, claims Knapp, because the "successful rumor, to thrive, must always adapt *itself* to the . . . circumstances of the group [and] must ride the tide of current swings in public opinion and interest."

If, on the one hand, you think you should blame rumor-mongers and rumor believers for not doing their homework, you can, on the other hand, give them credit for striving pretty hard to explain phenomena they find threatening. Rumors and conspiracy theories often supply simplified, easily digestible explanations (and enemies) to sum up complex situations. However crass, they're both fueled by a desire to make sense of the world.

Can false rumors and off-the-wall theories be corrected by broadcasting the truth? Sometimes, but not always. Access to information, evidently, is not a silver bullet. In his just-published book, *On Rumors*, legal scholar (and new head of the White House Office of Information and Regulatory Affairs) Cass R. Sunstein argues that efforts at correcting rumors can sometimes even hurt the cause of truth.

He cites a 2004 experiment in which liberals and conservatives were asked to examine their views on the existence of weapons of mass destruction in Iraq. After reading a statement that declared that Iraq had [weapons of mass destruction] WMD, the subjects were asked to reveal their views on a five-point scale, from "strongly agree" to "strongly disagree."

Then they were handed a mock news article in which President George W. Bush defended the war, in part by suggesting that Saddam Hussein had weapons of mass destruction. After reading that article, participants were also asked to read about the CIA's Duelfer report, which showed that the Bush administration was wrong to think Iraq had such weapons. Finally, they were again asked their opinion of the original statement on the same five-point scale.

What the researchers found is that the outcome depended on the participants' political **10** point of view. The liberals shifted in the direction of greater disagreement, while the conservatives showed a significant shift in agreeing with the original statement. As the researchers put it, "The correction backfired—conservatives who received the correction telling them that Iraq did not have WMD were more likely to believe that Iraq had WMD."

Are you scared yet? I am.

Sunstein's book goes on to explore ways that society can hold rumor-mongers accountable without eliciting a chilling effect on the freedom of speech. He's concerned that crazy rumors in the Internet Age can gum up the machinery of democracy itself.

I applaud the effort, but I'd prefer to do away with the insecurity and uncertainty that feed wacko theories and rumors in the first place. A modicum of stability, a fair and functioning economy and polity—those have to be what we strive for.

But in the meantime, don't forget psychologist Knapp. "To decry the ravages of rumor-mongering is one thing," he wrote, "to control it is yet another." Pass it on.

Review Questions

1. Define "biased assimilation."

2. Which factors concerning rumors were found *not* to be of importance, according to a 1994 study? Which *were* found significant?

3. In what ways are the views of psychologist Robert H. Knapp supported by the 1994 findings discussed here?

4. How did researchers draw a connection between the political stance of participants and their beliefs about the justification for the Iraq War?

Discussion and Writing Suggestions

1. Rodriguez suggests that when confronted with information that flies in the face of our personal ideologies, we often ignore the new information and stick with what we already believe. Discuss an occasion when you changed your mind on a subject based on new information or—conversely—a time when you ignored or rationalized away new data in order to justify sticking with your existing belief or set of values.

2. Rodriguez describes a 2004 study concerning participants' changing views about the justification of the U.S. war in Iraq—both before and after participants were presented with the "facts" about Iraq's weapons of mass destruction. What other recent events or controversies have sparked broad, vocal opinions about "facts" that have since been discredited? Consider stories such as the controversies over the former President Obama's birth certificate and religious beliefs. In these or other like cases, to what extent do you find that facts, when eventually revealed, make a difference to people's convictions?

3. Rodriguez summarizes Cass Sunstein's view that trying to correct false rumors is often counterproductive. Cite examples of situations in which attempts to clarify a rumor only reinforce it.

4. How does the Internet affect both the spread and the attempted refutation of rumors? What seem to you the differences between reading a correction online, reading a correction in a traditional print source, and being given the correction face-to-face by another person?

5. Discussing those who don't change their opinions after being confronted with the facts, Rodriguez says that we can at least "give them credit for striving pretty hard to explain phenomena they find threatening." What does he mean? To what extent do you agree?

A Sociology of Rumor

Dan E. Miller

Dan Miller, a sociologist at the University of Dayton, introduces the work of Tamotsu Shibutani, who pioneered the sociological study of rumor as a sensible, adaptive response to ambiguous situations. The following is excerpted from an article that first appeared in the journal *Symbolic Interaction* in 2015.

Several common themes have been presented in discussions of rumor, including the notions that those who spread rumor are highly suggestible, that rumors consist of inaccurate, distorted, and exaggerated information presented as fact, that the spreading of rumor is an irrational act, and that those who spread rumors are in some way psychologically damaged. The perpetuation of these themes is, in large part, the consequence of the continuing influence of Gordon Allport and Leo Postman's (1947) book, *The Psychology of Rumor*, the main thesis of which was that, because of the aforementioned qualities, rumor is potentially dangerous and destructive of the social order.

Several scholars have taken issue with Allport and Postman's characterization of rumor, and none more eloquently or forcefully than Tamotsu Shibutani (1966), whose conceptualization of rumor ran counter to that of Allport and Postman in nearly every respect. For Shibutani, rumor was a community's construction of a definition of the situation in uncertain circumstances—that is, improvised news. However, despite Shibutani's noble effort, many contemporary studies of rumor and nearly all popular presentations of rumor conform to many of the now stereotypical ideas expressed by Allport and Postman nearly sixty years ago.

It is instructive to understand Allport and Postman's ideas in the social context in which their research was conducted. At the start of the Second World War, virtually no systematic research on rumor had been performed. Earnest research on rumor accelerated during the war years and in the years afterward. Seeking to understand rumors and to mitigate their potentially destructive consequences—a position of particular interest during a time of war— Allport and Postman carried out a series of laboratory studies in order to demonstrate the causes and consequences of the rumor process. Allport and Postman defined rumor as "a specific (or topical) proposition for belief, passed along from person to person, usually by word of mouth, without secure standards of evidence being presented" (1947, ix), and the design and subsequent outcome of their research was greatly influenced by their definition of and perspective on rumor.

Although their definition of rumor leaned toward the pejorative, it is interesting to note that Allport and Postman (1947:33–34) also identified what they called "the basic law of rumors." In this "law" they related the development and spread of rumor to situational ambiguity and a corresponding importance of the subject matter to the population. The more important the topic is to people and the more ambiguous the situation, the more likely a rumor will develop and spread, they theorized. Thus, after the Pearl Harbor attack in 1941 the public had little information about the number of casualties or the level of destruction experienced. Because of the ambiguity of the situation and its importance to the general public, rumors developed and spread through the population that the loss of life and property was much higher than that being reported. Although this was an accurate rumor, it was seen as destructive of the war effort.

Allport and Postman's "law" suggested—although it did not go so far as to state **5** specifically—that rumoring is a method of constructing a collective or communal definition of the situation. It is unfortunate that they designed their research on the basis of their definition of rumor and ignored their "basic law of rumors." If they had instead designed their research to investigate the validity of their "basic law," the results would have differed greatly. The fundamental flaw in their research program was that they thought they understood the nature of rumor before they had observed the phenomenon.

Based on their definition, Allport and Postman designed research to study the serial transmission of rumor. In these laboratory studies an "eyewitness" to an event described the situation to another person who described it to another who, in turn, described it to another. This process continued until the final subject described the situation to a research associate who carefully noted the content of the communication. In the study, the spread of the rumor went from one single person to another in a series of simple, unidirectional communicative acts. In no cases were others present in the rumor communication. The study was designed so that one participant spoke while the other listened. The receiver was not allowed to question the speaker or offer his own insight.

In nearly every instance the description given by the last participant in the series bore little resemblance to the initial eyewitness account. Some details were lost; some were exaggerated; and on occasion, details were added that were not present in the eyewitness accounts. Allport and Postman concluded that rumors are inaccurate and distorted communications and irrational acts. They noted that those involved in the rumor process had little interest in knowing the source or questioning the veracity of the rumor. They felt that rumoring served psychological motives beyond the spread of significant information, such as reducing guilt, relieving underlying anxiety, seeking attention, feeling important, and projecting one's own feelings and beliefs onto the situation (1947:46–47).

By focusing their research on rumor as a unique form of behavior serving the personal motives and needs of those involved, Allport and Postman ignored the social contexts within which rumors develop, spread, and gain meaning. In addition, they failed to recognize that rumoring is a social act occurring in social situations and involving redundant and reciprocal interactions. Their decision to ignore the "basic law of rumors" significantly impaired their research and any valid conclusions that could be drawn from it. Ironically, their flawed ideas continue to serve as an authoritative source of information on rumor for social scientists and the general public alike.

In sharp contrast to Allport and Postman's approach to understanding rumor was that of Tamotsu Shibutani. His interest in rumor also began during the Second World War when as a young man he was interned in a Japanese-American "relocation center."[5] There, he observed and noted the interaction processes whereby the interned population could make sense of its situation and other affairs of interest. Contrary to Allport and Postman's laboratory demonstrations, Shibutani observed rumors in their natural settings and employed an inductive approach to understanding the rumor process. Instead of starting with a preconceived and inaccurate notion, his explanation developed in the process of observing and taking notes—a research process now called grounded theory (Glaser and Strauss 1967).

10   Consequently, Shibutani (1966:17) defined rumor as a recurrent form of communication through which people attempt to construct a meaningful or working interpretation of a threatening or ambiguous situation by pooling their intellectual resources. Taking a sociological view, Shibutani recognized that rumors were routine social processes—defining the situation. He noted that in ambiguous situations, people tend to act as pragmatic problem-solvers by combining their knowledge and information—including data, bits of information from self and others, speculation, and interpretations—through careful deliberation to construct a shared understanding of the situation in question and thus allowing considered concerted action.

Shibutani (1966:57) concluded that rumor processes are most likely to occur when institutionalized channels of communications (e.g., print and electronic media) are not available to a population, or when those sources of information are not trusted by the people. The citizens of the relocation centers had little access to institutionalized news, which, in any event, they did not trust. Given the ambiguity of their situation and their lack of information about the war, their homes, and the outside world, the interned citizens, with resources they had, deduced the news. And, by any account, these constructions were highly accurate.

Seeing that his work was in direct opposition to Allport and Postman's and wanting to remove the pejorative denotation of the subject matter, Shibutani referred to these collective acts not as rumor, but as "improvised news." And, because situational ambiguity is a constant feature of modern social life, the improvisation of news is a continuous and routine process within social worlds (Shibutani 1955). The increasing distrust of and decreasing

---

[5]During World War II, in an act for which the federal government later apologized and made financial restitution, Japanese Americans were forced to move from their homes to guarded "relocation centers," the assumption being that their ties to Japan rendered them unable to remain loyal to and support the U.S. war effort.

audiences for institutional sources of information and the rapid increase in the number and popularity of Internet blogs point to a growing trend in the construction of improvised news to resolve the ambiguity of life in these times.

Review Questions

1. How does Tamotsu Shibutani define rumor?

2. According to Miller, what is the main flaw in Allport and Postman's approach to rumor?

3. What is "situational ambiguity" and how does it give rise to rumors?

4. What were the origins of Shibutani's approach to rumor-making, and how was this approach superior to that of Allport and Postman?

5. In what sense are rumors "improvised news"? How are they improvised? And how is this characterization of rumor less negative than Allport and Postman's?

Discussion and Writing Suggestions

1. According to Shibutani, "the improvisation of news is a continuous and routine process within social worlds." We all improvise in order to understand ambiguous situations, according to Shibutani. Improvisation in this sense might involve close observation, speculation, skepticism regarding official news, and pure invention. Describe a time when you improvised to fill in the blanks of an ambiguous situation.

2. Miller writes: "The increasing distrust of and decreasing audiences for institutional sources of information and the rapid increase in the number and popularity of Internet blogs point to a growing trend in the construction of improvised news to resolve the ambiguity of life in these times." To what extent is the increase of Internet blogs evidence of decreasing trust in institutional sources of information (like network news, newspapers, news magazines, and official government statements)?

3. Shibutani suggests that we improvise news all the time, that improvisation is a routine part of social life. This is his less pejorative way of claiming that we all make and pass along rumors every day. Shibutani seeks to rehabilitate rumor-making and asks us to regard it as a normal activity. Are you willing to destigmatize rumor and detach from it *all* negative associations? Why or why not?

Pizzagate: An Anthropology of Rumor

Hugh Gusterson

During the 2016 presidential campaign, a rumor surfaced that Hillary Clinton was running a child sex-ring out of a pizza parlor in Washington, D.C. Though on its face preposterous, the rumor circulated and damaged Clinton's candidacy. Anthropologist Hugh Gusterson analyzes "Pizzagate" for the ways in which it

suggests distrust of Clinton and larger anxieties about the culture of Washington, D.C. A prolific essayist (*Boston Globe, Los Angeles Times, Nature, Washington Post, Science*), Gusterson teaches anthropology at George Washington University and is the author of several books: *Drone* (2016), *People of the Bomb* (2004), and *Nuclear Rites* (1996). The essay that follows first appeared in the Web-based anthropological journal *Sapiens* on January 4, 2017.

I sometimes like to joke that anthropologists looking for the strangest and most exotic society on earth should do fieldwork in the United States. As if to prove my point, along comes Pizzagate.

"Pizzagate" is the moniker being used to describe the bizarre set of rumors, spread by right-wing fake-news sites and conspiracy theorists, that Comet Ping Pong, a popular pizza restaurant in Washington, D.C., is a key location in a child slavery and sex trafficking ring run by Hillary Clinton. The rumor that Hillary Clinton was at the center of a pedophilia ring originated with an October 30 tweet, retweeted more than 6,000 times, from @DavidGoldbergNY. The rumor spread from there on social media platforms such as 4chan and Reddit and was further disseminated by right-wing propagandist Alex Jones, who runs the Infowars website that is influential among right-wing conspiracy theorists. "I think about all the children Hillary Clinton has personally murdered and chopped up and raped," said Jones, in a YouTube video that has been watched more than 400,000 times. "Yeah, you heard me right. Hillary Clinton has personally murdered children. I just can't hold back the truth anymore."[6]

When the email account of John Podesta, Hillary Clinton's campaign chair, was hacked, revealing that he sometimes ate at Comet Ping Pong, the modest Washington eatery (where my kids like to eat because it has table tennis and an excellent margherita pizza) became the supposed center (complete with concealed underground tunnels) of Hillary's child sex ring. As bots (automated internet programs, in this case written by Russian agents, according to some) amplified the rumor, which was also spread by Donald Trump's national security advisor, threats began pouring in not only to Comet Ping Pong but to neighboring restaurants and stores too. For example, according to *The Washington Post*, someone told the owner of nearby Besta Pizza that the slice of pizza on his logo was a secret child-pornography symbol, and when he took the image off his website to defuse the controversy, antagonists crowed that this was an admission of guilt.

Events took an even more malevolent turn on December 4, when 28-year-old Edgar Welch drove from North Carolina with an assault weapon to "self-investigate" the rumors. He fired his gun inside the restaurant but, mercifully, no one was hurt, and he was taken into police custody.

5   Media coverage of Pizzagate has drawn attention to the damage that fake news can do to the fabric of democracy (for instance, the abundance of fake news shared on social media leading up to the election is thought to have potentially influenced the outcome of the election). It also can create an alternate reality that deepens political divisions while inciting the mentally unstable (case in point: Pizzagate). The extensive coverage of the fake-news phenomenon emphasizes the unprecedented nature of the situation.

But to me, as an anthropologist, the Pizzagate rumor has a familiar feel. Scholars have documented a plethora of inaccurate but stubbornly powerful rumors in societies all over the world. In her book on international adoption, historian Karen Dubinsky writes about rumors circulating in Guatemala that foreigners abduct local children and turn them into sex slaves or

---

[6]Jones later retracted these statements and apologized for making them.

steal their organs. Illustrating the power such falsehoods can have, tourists have been lynched as a result of the accusations.

Anthropologist Nancy Scheper-Hughes found similar rumors about people being murdered for their organs in Brazil. Anthropologists Eirik Saethre and Jonathan Stadler map rumors in South Africa that whites kill volunteers in clinical trials and steal their blood. And anthropologist Karen Kroeger writes about widespread stories in Indonesia of people in crowded malls and elevators being stuck with a needle and left with a card saying, "Welcome to the AIDS Club." (She also notes, in passing, rumors in Borneo that missionaries chop off children's heads and use them as building materials). Recently, polio vaccination campaigns in Pakistan have faltered in the face of rumors that the vaccine is an American conspiracy to sterilize Muslims, and health workers on the frontline of the vaccination campaign have even been killed.

Noting that "rumors often circulate most intensively at times of uncertainty or unrest," Kroeger writes that "rumors are more than just wrong or incomplete information; they are . . . a reflection of beliefs and views about how the world works in a particular place and time." In other words, they may be literally wrong, but they express, metaphorically at least, a deeper perceptual truth. One might add that this deeper perceptual truth is often a reaction to felt abuses and injustices. Americans may not abduct Guatemalan babies and harvest their organs, but foreign adoptions of Guatemalan babies have been rife with exploitation. Doctors may not murder African subjects in clinical trials, but Western pharmaceutical companies and research institutions have used Africans as human subjects in trials that would not have been allowed in the U.S. And while the polio vaccine may not be part of an American plot to sterilize Muslims in Pakistan, the CIA did orchestrate a door-to-door vaccination campaign in Pakistan to collect DNA and thus confirm the whereabouts of Osama bin Laden prior to killing him.

So where does this leave us with the child-sex-slave ring at Comet Ping Pong? To what anxieties and resentments do the false rumors speak?

For one, the rumors dramatize a perception among some that Hillary Clinton and her **10** party's establishment are untrustworthy, compassionless, and exploitative. The location of the alleged child sex ring—in Washington, D.C.—speaks volumes about the way many Americans feel about the political culture of the nation's capital. The centrality of child sex slaves in the story signals anxieties about the sexualization of children in the U.S. and, more broadly, fears about the security and well-being of the next generation of Americans. Hillary Clinton may not be holding children as slaves in tunnels, but some critics believe her party has presided over a process of deindustrialization that undermines the next generation's future.

Finally, skepticism about the mainstream media's debunking of the rumors speaks to a widespread loss of confidence in establishment authorities. In an email to *The Washington Post*, the owner of 4chan wrote, "Pizzagate reminds me that a country indicated [there were] stockpiles of weapons of mass destruction in Iraq and many people and countries were deceived. It is same old story." Some have even claimed that Edgar Welch's armed expedition to Comet Ping Pong and his failure to find any child sex slaves there were a "false flag"— an operation to cover up the conspiracy.

Rumors of organ theft in Guatemala or the "AIDS Club" in Indonesia were spread primarily by word of mouth; in Pakistan, radical Islamist preachers played a key role in disseminating rumors about the polio vaccination campaign. But now we have the internet—a perfect environment for the incubation and rapid dissemination of such rumors. As we are seeing, the internet is changing the balance of forces between mainstream media—with its (admittedly imperfect) protocols for systematically investigating stories—and "prosumers" (consumers who are now also producing influential "news" stories).

Pizzagate is a harbinger of much worse to come.

Discussion and Writing Suggestions

1. Gusterson writes of "the damage that fake news can do to the fabric of democracy." The institutions of democracy are large, old, and powerful. How could fake news and rumors damage "the fabric of democracy"?

2. What makes people receptive to rumors like Pizzagate—to believing statements like those of Alex Jones: "Yeah, you heard me right. Hillary Clinton has personally murdered children. I just can't hold back the truth anymore"? What must the times (the social, economic, and political conditions) be like for such rumors to spread? What must be going on psychologically and emotionally for an individual (like the gunman who fired his rifle in the pizza shop) to accept such rumors?

3. Observe how Gusterson turns a fascinating (if not bewildering) rumor concerning Hillary Clinton and a pizza parlor to a study in anthropology: "So where does this leave us with the child-sex-slave ring at Comet Ping Pong? To what anxieties and resentments do the false rumors speak?" How does he answer this anthropological question, and how do you respond to his answer?

4. Distrust of institutional sources of news (like the government or mainstream news outlets) seems central to the birth and spread of rumors—the logic being: if the government, for instance, lied once (to take one example, about the presence of weapons of mass destruction in Iraq), it can lie again and should therefore no longer be considered a reliable source of information. The same skepticism holds for mainstream media. In the vacuum created when traditional sources of information are no longer trusted, rumor thrives. Do you believe traditional sources of information can reclaim their reputation for accuracy and fairness? Is it important that they do so? What do you think will happen if they cannot?

On the Web: *How and Why Rumors Work—And How to Stop Them*

Nicholas DiFonzo

On general principle we may disapprove of rumors, but their pervasiveness throughout history and across cultures suggests that they serve important personal and social purposes. In this selection, Nicholas DiFonzo, professor of psychology at Rochester Institute of Technology and the author of numerous books and articles on rumor, discusses why both individuals and groups find it necessary and even desirable to create and spread rumors. DiFonzo's best-known book is *The Watercooler Effect* (2008). In an interview with Susan Gawlowicz, DiFonzo explains how rumors develop on both personal and social levels.

> **Go to** YouTube
> **Search terms:** *difonzo rumor*

Review Questions

1. What are the main reasons people spread rumors, according to DiFonzo?

2. How does DiFonzo differentiate rumor from gossip?

3. According to DiFonzo, what are the chief factors that determine how readily people accept rumors as true?

4. Summarize the main strategies for managing and fighting rumors, according to DiFonzo.

Discussion and Review Questions

1. One reason people spread rumors, according to DiFonzo, is to help them understand the world and to "figure out or make sense of an unclear or ambiguous situation." Draw upon one of the rumors you have read about in this chapter—or a rumor with which you are personally familiar—to explain how this process of sense-making works. How did buying into this rumor help people—or how did it help you—make sense of how the world (or some part of the world) works?

2. DiFonzo offers several reasons that people often believe that rumors are true, even without sufficient evidence to support the rumor. Select one of the rumors covered in this chapter, or one with which you have some experience, and explain how DiFonzo helps account for this particular rumor being so readily accepted as credible.

3. Toward the end of this interview, DiFonzo offers several suggestions for managing rumors to stop them from spreading or to destroy their credibility. To what extent does your own experience support the wisdom of DiFonzo's suggestions? Under what circumstances might such measures be ineffective? In developing your response, draw upon one or more of the rumors treated in this chapter or rumors from your own experience.

How to Fight a Rumor

Jesse Singal

During the 2008 presidential campaign, Barack Obama and John McCain were regularly attacked by rumors and were typically advised either to ignore them or not to "dignify" them with a response. According to Jesse Singal, this is bad advice and shows a basic misunderstanding of how rumors work. "By using the tools of evolutionary theory," he claims, we can better understand that rumors are more than just

idle or malicious gossip. This article originally appeared in the *Boston Globe* on October 12, 2008 (shortly before the conclusion of that year's presidential campaign). Singal is an associate editor of CampusProgress.org and of pushback.org at the Center for American Progress. He has also written for the *Daily Beast,* the *New Republic Online, Politico,* and the *Washington Monthly.*

For anyone who has ever worried about the power of a vicious rumor, Barack Obama's strategy over the summer must have seemed almost bizarre. Buffeted by rumors about his religion, his upbringing, and controversial statements made by his wife, Obama launched Fight the Smears, a website that lists every well-traveled false rumor about the candidate, alongside rebuttals and explanations for how the rumors arose.

Fighting rumors by publicizing them in vivid, high-profile locations is, to say the least, a surprising tactic. It's hard to imagine someone victimized by workplace rumors summarizing them and posting them on the lunchroom wall. The conventional wisdom about rumors is to take the high road and not respond. When John McCain, during the 2000 Republican primaries, was plagued with rumors that he had fathered an illegitimate child, for the most part he opted not to engage with them at all. Why would anyone want to broadcast negative claims about themselves?

And yet new research into the science of rumors suggests Obama's approach may be a sounder strategy—and the reasons why it makes sense suggest that we misunderstand both how rumors work and why they exist.

By using the tools of evolutionary theory and new approaches to mathematical modeling, researchers are drawing a clearer picture of how and why rumors spread. As they do, they are finding that far from being merely idle or malicious gossip, rumor is deeply entwined with our history as a species. It serves some basic social purposes and provides a valuable window on not just what people talk to each other about, but why.

5   Rumors, it turns out, are driven by real curiosity and the desire to know more information. Even negative rumors aren't just scurrilous or prurient—they often serve as glue for people's social networks. And although it seems counterintuitive, these facts about rumor suggest that, often, the best way to help stem a rumor is to spread it. The idea of "not dignifying a rumor with a response" reflects a deep misunderstanding of what rumors are, how they are fueled, and what purposes they serve in society.

McCain's approach in this election seems more in tune with this theory. With rumors circulating in the blogosphere that Sarah Palin's youngest baby might actually have been her daughter's child, the campaign didn't turn the other cheek: It released a statement from the Palin family that Bristol really was pregnant. The strategy worked. The other rumor was squelched.

Rumor has been around as long as human civilization, and for much of that time has been frowned upon. The Bible has some stern words for those who spread rumors: "A man who lacks judgment derides his neighbor," the Book of Proverbs reads, "but a man of understanding holds his tongue." Rumors have long been seen as at best trivial, and at worst vicious and immoral.

Experts began to look at rumors more analytically in the 1940s and 1950s, in a wave of research fueled by concern about how rumors could be managed during wartime. Though interest waned during the following decades, rumor studies have seen a resurgence in the last decade or so—partly because researchers are now more able to tackle complex, dynamic phenomena, and partly because they're newly armed with the biggest ongoing social psychology experiment in human history, the Internet, which provides them with terabytes of recorded rumors and a way to track them.

In 2004, the Rochester Institute of Technology psychologist Nicholas DiFonzo and another rumor researcher, Prashant Bordia, analyzed more than 280 Internet discussion group postings that contained rumors. They found that a good chunk of the discourse consisted of the participants sharing and evaluating information about the rumors and discussing whether they seemed likely. They realized, in other words, that people on the sites weren't swapping rumors just to gossip; they were using rumors as a vehicle to get to the truth, the same way people read news.

"Lots of times people will share a rumor not for their benefit or for the other person's benefit, but simply because they're trying to figure out the facts," says DiFonzo, one of the leading figures in the resurgence of rumor research. He published a book on the topic this fall [2008]: *The Watercooler Effect: A Psychologist Explores the Extraordinary Power of Rumors*. **10**

Some types of facts seem to be more urgent triggers than others. Rumors that involve negative outcomes tend to start and spread more easily than ones that involve positive outcomes. Researchers sort rumors into "dread rumors," driven by fear ("I heard the company is downsizing"), and "wish rumors," driven by hope ("I heard our Christmas bonus will be bigger this year"). Dread rumors, it turns out, are far more contagious. In a study involving a large public hospital in Australia that was in the midst of a restructuring, Bordia and his colleagues collected 510 rumors that could be classified as dread rumors or wish rumors. Four hundred and seventy-nine of them were dread rumors.

Perhaps even more than negative stories dominate the news, negative rumors dominate the grapevine. In the absence of other sources of information, people turn to rumors to answer their most urgent concerns—suggesting that rumors play a vital role, not a peripheral or idle one, in times of worry, and can have a profound impact on how a town, city, or society reacts to a negative event.

This is a much more neutral view of rumors than the Bible, or traditional etiquette, might take. And indeed, rumor researchers tend to see them nonjudgmentally, as inherent to human nature—naturally occurring, inevitable human social phenomena, rather than pesky distractions from more civilized discourse.

Aside from their use as a news grapevine, rumors serve a second purpose as well, researchers have found: People spread them to shore up their social networks, and boost their own importance within them. To the extent people do have an agenda in spreading rumors, it's directed more at the people they're spreading them to, rather than at the subject of the rumor.

People are rather specific about which rumors they share, and with whom, researchers have found: They tend to spread rumors to warn friends of potential trouble, or otherwise help them, while remaining mum if it would be harmful to spread a given rumor in a certain context or to a certain person. **15**

It's not just altruism: Rumors can build status for the person who spreads them. The psychologists John L. Shelton and Raymond S. Sanders, in documenting the impact of a murder of an undergraduate on the Ohio State University campus in 1972 on the student body, found that those with access to "inside information" about the crime and the administration's response were instantly granted higher social status. So simply possessing—or being seen as possessing—potentially useful information can serve in and of itself as a motivation to spread rumors.

When it comes to rumors about people rather than events, psychologists have found that we pay especially close attention to rumors about powerful people and their moral failings. Frank McAndrew, a professor of psychology at Knox College who studies the evolutionary roots of gossip, has found that we're particularly likely to spread negative rumors about "high-status" individuals, whether they're our bosses, professors, or celebrities.

Our behavior, McAndrew suggests, evolved in an environment in which information about others was crucially important. Back when humans lived in small groups, he theorizes, information about those higher than us on the totem pole—especially information about their weaknesses—would have been hugely valuable, and the only source we had for such information was other people. (McAndrew's work, much of which focuses on our obsession with celebrity culture, suggests our brains aren't terribly adept at distinguishing people who are "actually" important from people who simply receive a lot of attention.)

If the fundamental dynamics of rumor have roots that run deep into history, the means of transmission have been changing a great deal recently. Unlike previous forms of media, the Internet has created a two-way street—a way to quickly connect with like-minded people—that greatly multiplies the power of rumors.

20   "In the course of a single day, people across the country might hear the same rumor spoken in almost exactly the same words," says Eric Foster, a psychologist at Temple University who studies gossip and social networks.

Given what we know about which rumors thrive and persist, the particular rumors that have dominated this campaign season seem almost custom-crafted to replicate themselves and spread to a wide audience: They're negative rumors about high-status individuals that hint at moral failings.

Conservatives spreading the Obama rumors worry he may be lying about his faith to further his political career, or that his wife, Michelle, is cloaking radicalism in a moderate veneer.

The same applies to the Palin rumors: For liberals, the people most likely to spread them, they deal with severe moral failings—the hypocrisy of being a "family-values" politician with a pregnant, unwed daughter, or the whiff of authoritarian tendencies seen in her alleged attempts to ban books when she was mayor of Wasilla, Alaska.

So are such rumors impossible to stop? Not at all, says DiFonzo, who has counseled businesses, organizations, and academic institutions on how to fight rumors.

25   The first and perhaps most obvious point is that it's futile to attempt to rebut a rumor that's true, says DiFonzo. Even if it works initially, "people who are interested in ferreting out the facts are really very good at it over time if they have the proper motivation and they work together."

The recent John Edwards scandal is a perfect example: Rumors had swirled about Edwards and a possible extramarital affair for a long time. Edwards quickly and vociferously denied the rumor, but by August of this year—after persistent reporting by the National Enquirer—he was forced to admit to it. There was little Edwards could do to forestall the inevitable.

Other than denying a rumor that's true, perhaps the biggest mistake one can make, DiFonzo and other researchers say, is to adopt a "no comment" policy: Numerous studies have shown that rumors thrive in environments of uncertainty. Considering that rumors often represent a real attempt to get at the truth, the best way to fight them is to address them in as comprehensive a manner as possible.

Anthony Pratkanis, a psychologist at the University of California, Santa Cruz, who studies persuasion and propaganda, says that an effective rebuttal will be more than a denial—it will create a new truth, including an explanation of why the rumor exists and who is benefiting from it.

"The more vivid that replacement is, the better," says Pratkanis. He and other rumor specialists refer to this tactic as "stealing thunder." When done correctly and early enough in a rumor's lifetime, it can shift the subsequent conversation in beneficial ways.

So how have the campaigns done so far? Obama gets relatively high marks, says   **30**
DiFonzo: The candidate's website, fightthesmears.com, succeeds by "denying [the rumors] aggressively" and providing "a context for his denial." Obama could, however, create even more credible rebuttals by having them backed up by trusted third-party sources, such as religious leaders.

Pratkanis says the McCain campaign has handled the Palin rumors well, too. In the wake of the story about Palin's child, "McCain did the stealing thunder," he says. By coming out and immediately laying the facts on the table, he was able to short-circuit the coverup theories, and reroute the conversation to the more easily managed topic of Bristol's pregnancy.

There are dangers in rebutting rumors by recounting them, of course, the foremost being the inevitability that some people will remember the rumor as true. The University of Michigan psychologist Norbert Schwarz and his colleagues found that listing a rumor first and then rebutting it (the format followed by fightthesmears.com) can backfire, causing some people to remember the rumor but forget the rebuttal.

But in the case of a powerful rumor that looks like it will spread widely, DiFonzo and other experts say it makes sense to assume it will get out, and preemptively target those who are likely to hear it. When thousands of years of human experience are driving something forward, it doesn't make much sense to try to push the other way.

Review Questions

1. According to Singal, rumor "is deeply entwined with our history as a species" and "serves some basic social purposes." In three or four sentences, summarize these basic social purposes.

2. Why has interest in and research on rumors surged in recent decades, according to Singal?

3. From an evolutionary perspective, why are negative rumors about "high-status" individuals more likely to spread than rumors about lower-status individuals?

4. Why is it better to combat a false rumor by responding to it rather than ignoring it, according to Singal?

5. How does Singal assess the success of rumor-fighting campaigns by Barack Obama, John McCain, and John Edwards?

Discussion and Writing Suggestions

1. Try to find an Internet discussion group thread similar to those discussed by Singal in paragraph 9. A number of these rumor threads concern speculation and rumors about new consumer electronic products in advance of their actual launch. (One such Internet forum is called "Macrumors.") Examine some of the postings. What seems to be their thrust and their purpose?

2. To what extent do your own experiences with rumors support Singal's ideas about the basic purposes of rumor? Drawing upon Singal's approach to the subject, discuss one or more rumors you have heard, started, or helped

spread. Who started the rumors? Against whom were they directed? What purposes were served by the rumor? How did the target respond? To what extent was this response effective?

3. Select a rumor covered in some detail elsewhere in this chapter (or select a rumor treated on Snopes.com) and analyze it in terms of the basic social purposes of rumor discussed by Singal. How, for example, does the "Frankenchicken" rumor or the Procter & Gamble rumor work, in terms of the ways people use rumors for particular social purposes?

4. Singal argues that "the best way to fight [rumors] is to address them in as comprehensive a manner as possible." But those who have accepted a rumor as true may reject all attempts, even factually correct ones, to counter the rumor. Under what circumstances is it better to fight the rumor than ignore it? Under what circumstances is fighting the rumor likely to be futile?

On the Web: *The Rumor*

John Updike

We've become familiar with the public face of rumor: the instantaneous surge of an allegation across the Internet and onto YouTube, the press releases on company letterhead, the politician's talk show appearances. But what happens behind closed doors—when, for example, a rumor ricochets inside the home, affecting both a couple and their circle of friends and colleagues? In the following story, John Updike traces the effects of gossip on a marriage. Updike (1932–2009) was a "Renaissance man" among American writers of the second half of the twentieth century: novelist, short-story writer, poet, essayist, literary critic, art critic. A two-time Pulitzer Prize winner, he is best known for his "Rabbit" novels—*Rabbit, Run* (1960), *Rabbit Redux* (1971), *Rabbit Is Rich* (1981), and *Rabbit at Rest* (1990)—which trace the life of Harry C. ("Rabbit") Angstrom (former high school basketball star, car salesman, and indifferent husband and father) as he struggles to make sense of, and break free from, his middle-class, suburban life. Updike is best known for his portrayal of "average" Americans and mainstream life. In this story, originally published by *Esquire* in June 1991, he presents a vivid portrait of a marriage. While initially dismissing as falsehood a rumor that comes to engulf their life, the couple is nonetheless quietly enthralled by it.

Go to: Google or Bing
Search terms: *"updike rumor"*

Discussion and Writing Suggestions

1. Even as she dismisses the rumors, Sharon is surprised by her friends' certainty about its truth. Do you think she has doubts? Why? Is she bothered— or excited—by the rumor?

2. The rumor in this story is "factually untrue." During the course of the story, however, Frank begins to wonder whether it might be at least partially true. He even wonders whether it would be a good thing for the rumor to be *perceived* as true by his wife and his colleagues. Can you think of other rumors, whether from your own life or from the public stage, that may have been false but have been accepted or even embraced by the subjects?

3. How do Frank's feelings toward his mother and father, as well as his feelings about the kind of men he admires, lend support to his feelings about the rumor?

4. Most of the previous selections in this chapter have focused on rumor functioning on a societal scale. This story, however, deals with the personal life of the Whittiers. How do some of the theories explored in the chapter (by Knapp, Goleman, and DiFonzo) apply here? In which of Knapp's categories does the rumor fit (from the perspective of the friends, as well as Frank himself)?

5. Frank entertains the notion that there may be value, or at least allure, in the rumor's spread. Create a rumor about yourself that you would like to see circulate among your friends and community. What is it? Why would you want people to believe this rumor?

6. Do you like Frank and Sharon Whittier? Why or why not? Do their thoughts and actions seem plausible? Explain.

7. This story is centered on married life, not on a larger societal context like most of the other readings in this chapter. That said, the implications of "The Rumor" might also be applied to larger arenas. What other situations come to mind, whether from other chapter selections or from your own experience, where a company, a politician, or a celebrity indulges in or even encourages a rumor instead of correcting it?

Synthesis Activities

1. Write a synthesis that explains *why* and *how* rumors are born and spread. In your discussion, refer to at least three of the following: Viner, Goleman, Knapp (in Rodriguez footnote), O'Leary, DiFonzo, Shibutani (summarized in Miller), Gusterson, and Singal. Use any of the example rumors treated in this chapter (as well as the stolen kidney case in Chapter 6) to support your discussion.

2. Select one of the rumors treated at length in this chapter. Briefly analyze this rumor from the perspective of the theoretical approaches of Knapp (as summarized in a Rodriguez footnote); Shibutani (as summarized in Miller); and DiFonzo (dealing with making sense of the world in an atmosphere of ambiguity and threat). Then, in an argument synthesis, explain which theoretical approach most compellingly reveals the whys and wherefores of the rumor you have selected.

3. Some rumors are created in the spirit of fun and are relatively harmless in their effects—for example, those New York alligators referred to at the beginning of this chapter. Other rumors arise from malicious intent and often devastate their targets. In an argument synthesis, rank several types of rumors on a scale of benevolence/malevolence, according to the motives of those who create and spread them. Draw on the David Cameron rumor (in Viner), the Hillary Clinton rumor (in Gusterson), and on at least two other rumors either treated in this chapter or that you find online. (Consider also using the "missing kidney" rumor in Chapter 6.) To help account for and justify your rankings, refer to theories of rumor as discussed in O'Leary, Goleman, Knapp (as summarized in the Rodriguez footnote), DiFonzo, Shibutani (as summarized in Miller), and/or Singal.

4. Select any three of the cases of rumor from this chapter or in Chapter 6, "Analysis." Compare and contrast these rumors, taking account of their origins (and the rationales behind their creation), their spread, and their impact. Try to select cases that appear similar on the surface but may have subtle or even major differences below the surface. Alternatively, choose cases that appear quite different but that, according to your analysis, are essentially similar in nature. Having made the comparison, what observations can you make about the three rumors you have discussed—and provisionally (based on your small sample size) about rumor itself?

5. In the Internet age, should a rumor be addressed at its first sign, or should it be allowed to run its course, however long that takes? What factors should bear most on how best to counteract damaging rumors? Use examples from the readings, as well as the ideas of theorists like Goleman, DiFonzo, Shibutani (in Miller), and Singal to support your argument.

6. In 2011, President Obama and his aides attempted to quell the long-standing rumor that he was not born in the United States. Attempting to put the claim to rest, he eventually released the full-length version of his birth certificate. Even in the face of this hard evidence, the rumor persisted, and public figures like Donald Trump and Texas governor Rick Perry suggested that the evidence presented by the new document was insufficient or questionable. O'Leary makes much the same observation about the persistence of the Nostradamus prophecy after the terrorist attacks of 9/11. Rodriguez reports to the same effect on a study concerning weapons of mass destruction. What does the refusal to accept concrete evidence suggest about human nature and political affiliation? In drafting your response, an argument synthesis, consider the points made by at least two of the following: Goleman, Gusterson, Knapp (in Rodriguez footnote), O'Leary, and Singal.

7. According to Katherine Viner, social media has complicated the status of truth, creating conditions especially ripe for the creation and spread of rumors. To what extent do you agree with Viner? Does social media fundamentally alter the conditions in which rumors arise? Or is it more likely that digital environments like Facebook and Twitter mainly speed the transmission of

already existing rumors? In discussing Viner, draw on other authors in this chapter—especially Gusterson and O'Leary. Your main question: To what extent does rumor in the Internet age differ from rumor in a medieval village (see ¶6 of O'Leary)?

8. Goleman, Gusterson, Knapp (in Rodriguez footnote), DiFonzo, and Singal explain that rumors are often suggestive of our hopes and fears. What hopes and fears are reflected by one of the following rumors: (1) the genetically modified chicken, (2) the "satanic logo," or (3) "The Runaway Grandmother"? Model your response on the analysis paper in Chapter 6, which applied Knapp's categories to the "missing kidney" rumor.

9. Imagine that you work for a public relations firm hired by someone targeted by a rumor. This might be a rumor similar to one covered in this chapter or another you have come across outside of class. Create an argument synthesis that takes the form of an action plan for your client.

10. On the Internet, find and read an article (or two) on the supposed death of Beatle Paul McCartney. At the time, the Beatles seemed to have fun playing along with this rumor. In John Updike's "The Rumor," we see an untrue rumor spark a sense of excitement in its subject and a surprising determination to keep the rumor alive. What is it about a rumor that, occasionally, might be alluring to its subject? Drawing upon some of the particular cases covered in this chapter, or cases known to you personally, develop your response into an argument synthesis.

Research Activities

1. Throughout his discussion, DiFonzo refers to the numerous rumors that grew out of the terrorist attacks of September 11, 2001. As he explains, some of these rumors were developed as a coping mechanism, and some grew out of newly discovered anxieties and fears about the identity and the nature of our enemies. Research another catastrophic event in American history and identify some of the rumors that were created in its wake. Knapp offers a glimpse into the rumors circulating around World War II. What about the Vietnam War? The Kennedy assassination? The Martin Luther King Jr. assassination? Explore some of the rumors associated with these events (or another such national calamity) and the ways in which theories by Knapp (in Rodriguez), Shibutani (in Miller), or DiFonzo help account for them.

2. While some rumors eventually go national and even global, others affect a more limited group of people: employees of a particular company, customers of local establishments, soldiers in a particular military unit, students at a particular school. In the fall of 2011, Smith College was overrun with an explosive culinary news item: All campus dining services were going vegan. This announcement sparked Twitter feeds, campus protests, and even coverage

from the leading vegan lifestyle magazine. But the news was a hoax, fueled by the power of rumor. Research two or three other hoaxes of limited impact, and discuss their spread and their impact (try searching for "local rumors" on Snopes.com or the archives of local newspapers). How and why did these rumors spread so fast and alarm so many? Draw upon Goleman's, O'Leary's, Shibutani's (in Miller), and DiFonzo's ideas about how rumors help us make sense of an uncertain world. What does public willingness to accept these hoaxes as true say about human nature?

3. Some rumors, such as "the missing kidney" (see Chapter 6), have entered popular culture as "urban legends." Urban legends (which often have nothing to do with cities) are defined by DiFonzo as "narratives about strange, funny, or horrible events that could have happened, the details of which change to fit particular locales or time periods, and which frequently contain a moral lesson." There's even a horror film named *Urban Legend*. Picture yourself as a film executive or screenwriter looking for an idea to develop into a movie. Research other urban legends (start with Snopes.com) and write a pitch for a movie based on one that appeals to you. Why do you think audiences will connect to this story? What features about it will engage viewers? What does it have in common with other rumors?

4. In an op-ed for the *Washington Post* (November 17, 2011), Paul Farhi asserts that "the e-mail rumor mill is run by conservatives." While he discusses political rumors associated with both Republicans and Democrats, Farhi claims that "when it comes to generating and sustaining specious and shocking stories, there's no contest. The majority of the junk comes from the right, aimed at the left." Research some of the more notorious rumors that have been a feature of recent politics. Describe and characterize them. To what extent are their agendas and political purposes clear? Based on your research, do you agree with Farhi? Develop your argument using Knapp's scheme. What do your findings suggest about political discourse in both parties?

5. Research and discuss a fear-driven rumor. (Once again, a good starting point is Snopes.com. Then learn more about your selected rumor from additional sources.) What are its origins? How far back does the rumor go in the public consciousness? How has it changed over the years?

6. Research the new crop of "reputation defender" services available to those who find their online identities under siege. (Start by searching online with terms like "managing rumor.") Based on your findings, discuss these services and explain how they work and why they may or may not be effective.

Chapter 14
Fairy Tales: A Closer Look at Cinderella

In August 2001, when the crown prince of Norway married a single mother and former waitress, hundreds of thousands of Norwegians cheered, along with an estimated 300 million television viewers worldwide. Observers called it a "Cinderella" tale—and everyone everywhere understood the reference. Mette-Marit Tjessem Hoiby had become a Cinderella figure. But why had the bride's humble beginnings so endeared her to a nation? We can begin to offer answers by examining an ancient and universally known tale in which a young girl—heartsick at the death of her mother, deprived of her father's love, and scorned by her new family—is nonetheless recognized for her inner worth.

"Once upon a time. . . ." Millions of children around the world have listened to these (or similar) words. And, once upon a time, such words were magic archways into a world of entertainment and fantasy for children and their parents. But in our own century, fairy tales have come under the scrutiny of anthropologists, linguists, educators, psychologists, and psychiatrists, as well as literary critics, who have come to see them as a kind of social genetic code—a means by which cultural values are transmitted from one generation to the next. Some people, of course, may scoff at the idea that charming tales like "Cinderella" or "Snow White" are anything other than charming tales. But even if they are not aware of it, adults and children use fairy tales in complex and subtle ways. The point is, perhaps, best illustrated by examining variants of "Cinderella."

"Cinderella" appears to be the best-known fairy tale in the world. In 1892, Marian Roalfe Cox published 345 variants of the story, the first systematic study of a single folktale. In her collection, Cox gathered stories from throughout Europe in which elements or motifs of "Cinderella" appeared, often mixed with motifs of other tales. All told, more than 700 variants exist throughout the world—in Europe, Africa, Asia, and North and South America. Scholars debate the extent to which such a wide distribution is explained by population migrations or by some universal quality of imagination that would allow people at different times and places to create essentially the same story. But for whatever reason, folklorists agree that "Cinderella" has appealed to storytellers and listeners everywhere.

The great body of folk literature, including fairy tales, comes to us from an oral tradition. Written literature, produced by a particular author, is preserved through the generations just as the author recorded it. By contrast, oral literature changes with every telling. Modern students of folk literature find themselves in the position of reading as opposed to hearing a tale. The texts we read tend to be of two types, which are at times difficult to distinguish. We might read a faithful transcription of an oral tale or a tale of literary origin—a tale that was originally written (as a short story would be), not spoken, but that nonetheless may contain elements of an oral account. In this chapter, we include tales of both oral and literary origin. Jakob and Wilhelm Grimm published their transcription of "Cinderella" in 1812. The version by Charles Perrault (1697) is difficult to classify as the transcription of an oral source, since he may have heard the story originally but appears to have changed it for greater appeal at the court of Louis XIV.

We open the chapter with three selections that will orient you, we hope, to the experience of reading fairy tales. First Linda Holmes, writer of the pop-culture blog "Monkey See," examines the structural elements common to numerous versions of "Cinderella." Historian Arthur Schlesinger Jr. follows with a reminiscence of reading classic tales. Folklorist Maria Tatar then sets "Cinderella" in a broader introduction to fairy tale literature.

Four variants of "Cinderella" follow, and you may be surprised at the differences. Yet important similarities remain, and all are versions of the tale. Several analyses of "Cinderella" conclude the chapter. The first selection gathers four brief, pointed interpretations from different disciplinary points of view: psychological, feminist, racial, and Marxist. In a passage from an address at Barnard College, Nobel laureate Toni Morrison exhorts her listeners to treat stepsisters with more kindness than they receive in "Cinderella." Literary critic Elisabeth Panttaja sees in "Cinderella" a hard-fought contest between the (wily, dead) mother and the (living) stepmother to marry off their daughters. The chapter ends with Peggy Orenstein's broader consideration of Princess Culture and the way it ensnares young girls.

The selections that follow will challenge your understanding of fairy tale literature and, in particular, "Cinderella." An overriding question as you read: Scholars find large, complex messages in these tales. Do you?

A Girl, a Shoe, a Prince: The Endlessly Evolving "Cinderella"

Linda Holmes

In the following selection, blogger Linda Holmes reviews the basic story elements that permit us to call a tale a version of "Cinderella." "There's very little that's common to *every* variant of the story," she writes, "but in general, you [begin with] a mistreated young woman, forced to do menial work, either cast out or unloved by her family." This post first appeared on March 13, 2015 on *Monkey See*, a National Public Radio (NPR)-sponsored venue for pop culture news and analysis.

"Woman gives birth to a gourd."

This is the opening to the description of an Italian variant of the *Cinderella* folk tale—or, really, a relative of one of its relatives—taken from a book called *Cinderella; three hundred and* forty-five variants of Cinderella, Catskin, and Cap o'Rushes, abstracted and tabulated, with a discussion of mediaeval analogues, and notes, written by Marian Roalfe Cox and published in 1893. In this version of the story, the heroine is born inside a gourd and accidentally abandoned in the forest—understandable, given that her mother has just *brought forth a squash from within her person*, and the last thought she's entertaining is probably, "Hey, I'll take that with me."

Our heroine is discovered by a prince, who finds the talking gourd and takes it home. If nothing else, perhaps it has a future in show business. At some point, she presumably emerges from it—the details offered in the book about this particular folk tale are limited— and she becomes a servant. The prince keeps her at the palace but mistreats her terribly, even beating her and kicking her to prevent her from attending his ball, but she gets there anyway without his knowing it's her (which is one reason it seems certain she's out of the squash by now). They meet and he gives her gifts and so on. Later, when she prepares his breakfast in the guise of his once-ensquashed servant, she slips into the breakfast the gifts he gave her at the ball when they danced. When he finds jewelry in his food, he realizes she is his beloved, and they get married. Ah, the classic "boy meets gourd."

What is the name of this young lady who was born inside a vegetable? Her name, of course, is Zucchettina. (It could be worse to our modern ears: One of the Cinderella variant entries is called "Little Saddleslut.")

This version is an obvious relative of Cinderella but not quite Cinderella; it's presented as   **5** one of the variants of *Catskin*, a related tale that also has a hard-working girl who meets a prince at a ball while in disguise and is then recognized and rescued.

That's not the strangest variant in the book, and it is *certainly* not the darkest. One begins with Cinderella, her two older sisters and their mother agreeing to a whimsical bet: First one to drop her spinning spool will be eaten by the others. When Mom proves clumsy, the sisters indeed eat her. (A deal's a deal?) Cinderella decides not to eat her mother, but to wait until the killing and eating is over, then bury her mother's bones. You know, out of respect. Fortunately, her mother's bones turn into coins and beautiful magic dresses. It's no fairy godmother, but you don't look your mother's gift bones in the . . . mouth, I suppose.

There's a Vietnamese variant called *Kajong and Haloek* in which the evil foster mother of the Cinderella figure, Kajong, is tricked into eating the flesh of her own dead daughter (who boiled herself alive trying to be as beautiful as Kajong)—punishment for them both.

And here is a direct quote from Cox's book, summarizing a variant called *Gold-dice*: "King goes to war, leaving three daughters in mound with victuals for seven years. Father slain; princesses forgotten. Dog and cat eaten; elder sisters die. Heroine eats mouse; digs way out."

● ● ●

What Is Cinderella, Exactly?

To try to figure out what exactly that story is and why we still have it, we have to separate out the folk tale that is Cinderella, though, from the *turn of phrase* that is "Cinderella story." Americans will call almost anything a Cinderella story that involves a good thing happening to someone nice. We slap that title on movies and books, but also on basketball games won by tiny schools full of scrawny nerds, small businesses that thrive and even political ascendancies that upend established powers.

The actual Cinderella tale, while a nebulous thing that can be hard to pin down with   **10** precision, is more than that. There's very little that's common to *every* variant of [*Cinderella*], but in general, you have a mistreated young woman, forced to do menial work, either cast out or unloved by her family. She has an opportunity to marry well and escape her situation, but she gets that chance only after being mistaken for a higher-status person, so she has to get the man who may marry her to recognize her in her low-status form, which often happens either via a shoe that fits or some kind of food that she prepares.

It's partly a fantasy about simplifying the relationships between social standing and coupling—one that makes the most sense in a world in which class differences are an accepted barrier to a good man choosing to marry a woman. If the prince is a man who believes from the outset that love conquers all, the story doesn't really make any sense. It would be hard to set *Cinderella* on a properly functioning egalitarian collective.

The idea that animates the classic Cinderella is that the prince would *not* be free to consider Cinderella a desirable mate if he first saw her as she is, but he can meet her under false pretenses and fall in love with her. And, most importantly, once achieved, that love will be durable enough to survive her reversion to her real identity. Getting him to literally *recognize* her—getting him to look at a woman in rags and realize she's the woman he wants to marry—seems to function as sort of a stand-in for him proving that he can overlook her low status and choose her as a partner. Whether that's more a fantasy of romantic love or a fantasy of economic security, power and rescue from a lifetime of washing floors may depend on who's telling it and who's hearing it and when.

Review Questions

1. What are the differences between the colloquial phrase "a Cinderella story" and the actual tale?

2. What is the idea that "animates the classic Cinderella" tale?

Discussion and Writing Suggestions

1. Holmes writes that "Cinderella" is "partly a fantasy" about class relationships in a class-differentiated society. "It would be hard to set *Cinderella* on a properly functioning egalitarian collective." Why?

2. In the final paragraph, Holmes distinguishes between "a fantasy of romantic love" and "a fantasy of economic security." What are the differences between these fantasies? Do you agree that "Cinderella" encompasses them both?

3. Oral versions of a story are elastic: they can change from one telling to the next. Written versions of the same story are fixed: the wording doesn't change from one reading to the next. What do you suppose accounts for the many strange-seeming details and variants in orally sourced versions of "Cinderella"? Why might details like "girl born in a gourd" or "girl refrains from eating her mother" work their way into stories like "Cinderella"?

What Great Books Do for Children

Arthur Schlesinger Jr.

Arthur Schlesinger Jr. (1917–2007) was a Pulitzer Prize–winning historian and biographer. The author of several authoritative histories, he also served as speechwriter

for and special assistant to President John F. Kennedy. In this excerpt from his memoir, *A Life in the Twentieth Century* (2000), he shares his earliest impressions of reading and his strong opinions on the value of classic children's literature.

When I began to read for myself, a six-volume series called *My Book House* came into my life, an entrancing and resplendently illustrated anthology of historical adventure, fairy tale, poetry, mythology, something for every mood and moment.

I fear that such an initiation into a larger world would be much condemned today. For these were all tales filled with cruelty and violence, mutilation and murder, magic and fantasy, streaked by what is now seen as classism, sexism, racism, and superstition. Approved children's books today are by contrast didactic in intent, dealing with prosaic, everyday events and intended to improve relations among classes, sexes, and races. Such books, it is argued, lead children to face reality rather than to flee into fantasy.

Is this really so? [Aren't] fairy tales and myths symbolic reenactments of deep psychological and social dilemmas? In this sense, the classic fantasies may well be more realistic than the contemporary morality tales.

•   •   •

The serious point of children's books is not to improve behavior but to expand imagination. Great children's literature creates new worlds that children enter with delight and perhaps with apprehension and from which they return with understandings that their own experience could not have produced and that give their lives new meaning.

The classical tales have populated the common imagination of the West. They are voyages of discovery. They introduce children to the existential mysteries—the anxiety of loneliness, the terror of rejection, the need for comradeship, the quest for fulfillment, the struggle against fate, victory, love, death.   5

•   •   •

The classical tales tell children what they unconsciously know—that human nature is not innately good, that conflict is real, that life is harsh before it is happy—and thereby reassure them about their own fears and their own sense of self.

Discussion and Writing Suggestions

1. Schlesinger claims that contemporary stories for children avoid the dark, sometimes murderous elements of folk literature as well as content that may offend modern sensibilities regarding, for instance, gender roles. As a consequence, says Schlesinger, these stories are poor substitutes for the classic tales. Think of some classic tales you heard as a child and compare them to modern ones. To what extent do you agree with Schlesinger?

2. To what extent do you think that childhood is a cauldron of anxieties, fears, and struggles —in which case, classic tales like "Cinderella" *reflect* back to children what they already know, if only subconsciously?

3. Identify one or two of Schlesinger's statements that you find memorable—whether or not you agree with them. Explain your response.

4. Schlesinger writes, "The classical tales tell children what they unconsciously know—that human nature is not innately good, that conflict is real, that life is harsh before it is happy—and thereby reassure them about their own fears and their own sense of self." Children have a lifetime to learn such harsh lessons. Why learn them in childhood? Why not wait?

An Introduction to Fairy Tales

Maria Tatar

Folklorist Maria Tatar is the author of numerous articles on fairy tale literature and ten scholarly books, one of which is *The Annotated Classic Fairy Tales* (2002). The selection that follows forms part of her general introduction to that volume, an overview that will prepare you to read several variants of "Cinderella." In a recent profile, Tatar said of her life's work: "Fairytales . . . face up to the facts of life: nothing is sacred or taboo. Meanwhile they glitter with beauty. I work at the weirdly fascinating intersection of beauty and horror." Tatar teaches folklore at Harvard University.

For many of us childhood books are sacred objects. Often read to pieces, those books took us on voyages of discovery, leading us into secret new worlds that magnify childhood desires and anxieties and address the great existential mysteries. Like David Copperfield, who comforted himself by reading fairy tales, some of us once read "as if for life," using books not merely as consolation but as a way of navigating reality, of figuring out how to survive in a world ruled by adults. In a profound meditation on childhood reading, Arthur Schlesinger, Jr., writes about how the classical tales "tell children what they unconsciously know—that human nature is not innately good, that conflict is real, that life is harsh before it is happy—and thereby reassure them about their own fears and their own sense of self."[1]

"What do we ever get nowadays from reading to equal the excitement and the revelation in those first fourteen years?" Graham Greene once asked. Many of us can recall moments of breathless excitement as we settled into our favorite chairs, our secret corners, or our cozy beds, eager to find out how Dorothy would escape the witch, whether the little mermaid would win an immortal soul, or what would become of Mary and Colin in the secret garden. "I hungered for the sharp, frightening, breath-taking, almost painful excitement that the story had given me," Richard Wright observes in recollecting his childhood encounter with the story "Bluebeard and His Seven Wives." In that world of imagination, we not only escape the drab realities of everyday life but also indulge in the cathartic pleasures of defeating those giants, stepmothers, ogres, monsters, and trolls known as the grown-ups.

Yet much as we treasure the stories of childhood, we also outgrow them, cast them off, and dismiss them as childish things, forgetting their power not only to build the childhood world of imagination but also to construct the adult world of reality. Fairy tales, according to the British illustrator Arthur Rackham, have become "part of our everyday thought and expression, and help to shape our lives." There is no doubt, he adds, "that we should be behaving ourselves very differently if Beauty had never been united to her Beast . . . or if Sister Anne hadn't seen anybody coming; or if 'Open Sesame!' hadn't cleared the way, or Sindbad sailed." Whether we are aware of it or not, fairy tales have modeled behavioral codes and developmental paths, even as they provide us with terms for thinking about what happens in our world.

---

[1]Tatar refers here to the preceding selection by Schlesinger.

Part of the power of these stories derives not just from the words but also from the images that accompany them. In my own childhood copy of the Grimms' fairy tales, held together by rubber bands and tape, there is one picture worth many thousands of words. Each time I open the book to that page, I feel a rush of childhood memories and experience, for a few moments, what it was like to be a child. The images that accompanied "Cinderella," "Little Red Riding Hood," or "Jack and the Beanstalk" in volumes of classic fairy tales from an earlier era have an aesthetic power that produces an emotional hold rarely encountered in the work of contemporary illustrators. . . .

Fairy tales are up close and personal, telling us about the quest for romance and riches,   **5**
for power and privilege, and, most important, for a way out of the woods back to the safety and security of home. Bringing myths down to earth and inflecting them in human rather than heroic terms, fairy tales put a familiar spin on the stories in the archive of our collective imagination. Think of Tom Thumb, who miniaturizes David's killing of Goliath in the Bible, Odysseus' blinding of the Cyclops in *The Odyssey*, and Siegfried's conquest of the dragon Fafner in Richard Wagner's *Ring of the Nibelung*. Or of Cinderella, who is sister under the skin to Shakespeare's Cordelia and to Charlotte Brontë's Jane Eyre. Fairy tales take us into a reality that is familiar in the double sense of the term—deeply personal and at the same time centered on the family and its conflicts rather than on what is at stake in the world at large.

John Updike reminds us that the fairy tales we read to children today had their origins in a culture of adult storytelling: "They were the television and pornography of their day, the life-lightening trash of preliterate peoples." If we look at the stories in their earliest written forms, we discover preoccupations and ambitions that conform to adult anxieties and desires. Sleeping Beauty may act like a careless, disobedient child when she reaches for the spindle that puts her to sleep, but her real troubles come in the form of a hostile mother-in-law who plans to serve her for dinner with a sauce Robert. "Bluebeard," with its forbidden chamber filled with the corpses of former wives, engages with issues of marital trust, fidelity, and betrayal, showing how marriage is haunted by the threat of murder. "Rumpelstiltskin" charts a woman's narrow escape from a bargain that could cost the life of her first-born. And "Rapunzel" turns on the perilous cravings of a pregnant woman and on the desire to safeguard a girl's virtue by locking her up in a tower.

Fairy tales, once told by peasants around the fireside to distract them from the tedium of domestic chores, were transplanted with great success into the nursery, where they thrive in the form of entertainment and edification for children. These tales, which have come to constitute a powerful cultural legacy passed on from one generation to the next, provide more than gentle pleasures, charming enchantments, and playful delights. They contain much that is "painful and terrifying," as the art historian Kenneth Clark recalled in reminiscing about his childhood encounters with the stories of the Brothers Grimm and Hans Christian Andersen. Arousing dread as well as wonder, fairy tales have, over the centuries, always attracted both enthusiastic advocates, who celebrate their robust charms, and hard-edged critics, who deplore their violence.

Our deepest desires as well as our most profound anxieties enter the folkloric bloodstream and remain in it through stories that find favor with a community of listeners or readers. As repositories of a collective cultural consciousness and unconscious, fairy tales have attracted the attention of psychologists, most notably the renowned child psychologist Bruno Bettelheim. In his landmark study, *The Uses of Enchantment*, Bettelheim argued that fairy tales have a powerful therapeutic value, teaching children that "a struggle against severe difficulties in life is unavoidable." "If one does not shy away," Bettelheim added with great optimism, "but steadfastly meets unexpected and often unjust hardships, one masters all obstacles and at the end emerges victorious."

Over the past decades child psychologists have mobilized fairy tales as powerful therapeutic vehicles for helping children and adults solve their problems by meditating on the dramas staged in them. Each text becomes an enabling device, allowing readers to work through their fears and to purge themselves of hostile feelings and damaging desires. By entering the world of fantasy and imagination, children and adults secure for themselves a safe space where fears can be confronted, mastered, and banished. Beyond that, the real magic of the fairy tale lies in its ability to extract pleasure from pain. In bringing to life the dark figures of our imagination as ogres, witches, cannibals, and giants, fairy tales may stir up dread, but in the end they always supply the pleasure of seeing it vanquished.

Discussion and Writing Suggestion

1. Tatar's opening two paragraphs offer a nearly rapturous celebration of the honored place of childhood literature in her life and the lives of others. Have you had such experiences in your own life? Possibly not (in relation to books, at least), if Arthur Schlesinger is correct when he writes that the television has replaced the book as the constant companion of childhood. If television more than books provided that early companionship, did you have a Tatar-, Schlesinger-like relationship to the shows you watched? Discuss.

2. Tatar writes that fairy tales help to "construct" our adult realities. She writes: "Whether we are aware of it or not, fairy tales have modeled behavioral codes and developmental paths, even as they provide us with terms for thinking about what happens in our world." What does she mean?

3. "These tales, which have come to constitute a powerful cultural legacy passed on from one generation to the next," writes Tatar. How so?

4. According to Tatar, deep desires and profound anxieties make their way into folk tales because the tales are "repositories of a collective cultural consciousness and unconscious." Tatar is claiming that folk tales reflect our lives back to us. How could that be when, in the tales, witches cast spells and children get eaten? That doesn't happen in real life. What is her point here?

Four Variants of "Cinderella"

The existence of Chinese, French, and German versions of the "Cinderella" tale, along with some 700 other versions worldwide, comes as a surprise to many. Which is the real "Cinderella"? The question is misleading in that each version is "real" for a particular audience in a particular place and time. Certainly, you can read and judge versions and select the most appealing. To do so, you'll make comparisons and contrasts. Here are a few of the criteria you might consider as you work through the variants that follow:

- **Cinderella's innocence or guilt regarding the treatment she receives at the hands of her stepsisters**
- **Cinderella's passive (or active) nature**
- **Sibling rivalry—the relationship of Cinderella with her sisters**
- **The father's role**

- **The rule that Cinderella must return from the ball by midnight**
- **The levels of violence**
- **The presence or absence of the fairy godmother**
- **Cinderella's relationship with the prince**
- **The characterization of the prince**
- **The presence of Cinderella's dead mother**
- **The function of magic**
- **The ending**

Cinderella

Charles Perrault

Charles Perrault (1628–1703) was born in Paris of a prosperous family. He practiced law for a short time and then devoted his attentions to a job in government, in which capacity he was instrumental in promoting the advancement of the arts and sciences and in securing pensions for writers, both French and foreign. Perrault is best known as a writer for his *Contes de ma mère l'oye* (Mother Goose Tales), a collection of fairy tales taken from popular folklore. He is widely suspected of having changed these stories in an effort to make them more acceptable to his audience—members of the French court. This version was translated from Perrault's collection of 1696 by Charles Welsh (Boston: D. C. Heath, 1901).

Once there was a nobleman who took as his second wife the proudest and haughtiest woman imaginable. She had two daughters of the same character, who took after their mother in everything. On his side, the husband had a daughter who was sweetness itself; she inherited this from her mother, who had been the most kindly of women.

No sooner was the wedding over than the stepmother showed her ill-nature. She could not bear the good qualities of the young girl, for they made her own daughters seem even less likable. She gave her the roughest work of the house to do. It was she who washed the dishes and the stairs, who cleaned out Madam's room and the rooms of the two Misses. She slept right at the top of the house, in an attic, on a lumpy mattress, while her sisters slept in panelled rooms where they had the most modern beds and mirrors in which they could see themselves from top to toe. The poor girl bore everything in patience and did not dare to complain to her father. He would only have scolded her, for he was entirely under his wife's thumb.

When she had finished her work, she used to go into the chimney-corner and sit down among the cinders, for which reason she was usually known in the house as Cinderbottom. Her younger stepsister, who was not so rude as the other, called her Cinderella. However, Cinderella, in spite of her ragged clothes, was still fifty times as beautiful as her sisters, superbly dressed though they were.

One day the King's son gave a ball, to which everyone of good family was invited. Our two young ladies received invitations, for they cut quite a figure in the country. So there they were, both feeling very pleased and very busy choosing the clothes and the hair-styles which would suit them best. More work for Cinderella, for it was she who ironed her sisters' underwear and goffered their linen cuffs. Their only talk was of what they would wear.

"I," said the elder, "shall wear my red velvet dress and my collar of English lace."   **5**

"I," said the younger, "shall wear just my ordinary skirt; but, to make up, I shall put on my gold-embroidered cape and my diamond clasp, which is quite out of the common."

The right hairdresser was sent for to supply double-frilled coifs, and patches were bought from the right patch-maker. They called Cinderella to ask her opinion, for she had excellent taste. She made useful suggestions and even offered to do their hair for them. They accepted willingly.

While she was doing it, they said to her:

"Cinderella, how would you like to go to the ball?"

10   "Oh dear, you are making fun of me. It wouldn't do for me."

"You are quite right. It would be a joke. People would laugh if they saw a Cinderbottom at the ball."

Anyone else would have done their hair in knots for them, but she had a sweet nature, and she finished it perfectly. For two days they were so excited that they ate almost nothing. They broke a good dozen laces trying to tighten their stays to make their waists slimmer, and they were never away from their mirrors.

At last the great day arrived. They set off, and Cinderella watched them until they were out of sight. When she could no longer see them, she began to cry. Her godmother, seeing her all in tears, asked what was the matter.

"If only I could . . . If only I could . . ." She was weeping so much that she could not go on.

15   Her godmother, who was a fairy, said to her: "If only you could go to the ball, is that it?"

"Alas, yes," said Cinderella with a sigh.

"Well," said the godmother, "be a good girl and I'll get you there."

She took her into her room and said: "Go into the garden and get me a pumpkin."

Cinderella hurried out and cut the best she could find and took it to her godmother, but she could not understand how this pumpkin would get her to the ball. Her godmother hollowed it out, leaving only the rind, and then tapped it with her wand and immediately it turned into a magnificent gilded coach.

20   Then she went to look in her mouse-trap and found six mice all alive in it. She told Cinderella to raise the door of the trap a little, and as each mouse came out she gave it a tap with her wand and immediately it turned into a fine horse. That made a team of six horses, each of fine mouse-coloured grey.

While she was wondering how she would make a coachman, Cinderella said to her:

"I will go and see whether there is a rat in the rat-trap, we could make a coachman of him."

"You are right," said the godmother. "Run and see."

Cinderella brought her the rat-trap, in which there were three big rats. The fairy picked out one of them because of his splendid whiskers and, when she had touched him, he turned into a fat coachman, with the finest moustaches in the district.

25   Then she said: "Go into the garden and you will find six lizards behind the watering-can. Bring them to me."

As soon as Cinderella had brought them, her godmother changed them into six footmen, who got up behind the coach with their striped liveries, and stood in position there as though they had been doing it all their lives.

Then the fairy said to Cinderella:

"Well, that's to go to the ball in. Aren't you pleased?"

"Yes. But am I to go like this, with my ugly clothes?"

30   Her godmother simply touched her with her wand and her clothes were changed in an instant into a dress of gold and silver cloth, all sparkling with precious stones. Then she gave her a pair of glass slippers, most beautifully made.

So equipped, Cinderella got into the coach: but her godmother warned her above all not to be out after midnight, telling her that, if she stayed at the ball a moment later, her coach would turn back into a pumpkin, her horses into mice, her footmen into lizards, and her fine clothes would become rags again.

She promised her godmother that she would leave the ball before midnight without fail, and she set out, beside herself with joy.

The King's son, on being told that a great princess whom no one knew had arrived, ran out to welcome her. He handed her down from the coach and led her into the hall where his guests were. A sudden silence fell; the dancing stopped, the violins ceased to play, the whole company stood fascinated by the beauty of the unknown princess. Only a low murmur was heard: "Ah, how lovely she is!" The King himself, old as he was, could not take his eyes off her and kept whispering to the Queen that it was a long time since he had seen such a beautiful and charming person. All the ladies were absorbed in noting her clothes and the way her hair was dressed, so as to order the same things for themselves the next morning, provided that fine enough materials could be found, and skillful enough craftsmen.

The King's son placed her in the seat of honour, and later led her out to dance. She danced with such grace that she won still more admiration. An excellent supper was served, but the young Prince was too much occupied in gazing at her to eat anything. She went and sat next to her sisters and treated them with great courtesy, offering them oranges and lemons which the Prince had given her. They were astonished, for they did not recognize her.

While they were chatting together, Cinderella heard the clock strike a quarter to twelve. **35** She curtsied low to the company and left as quickly as she could.

As soon as she reached home, she went to her godmother and, having thanked her, said that she would very much like to go again to the ball on the next night—for the Prince had begged her to come back. She was in the middle of telling her godmother about all the things that had happened, when the two sisters came knocking at the door. Cinderella went to open it.

"How late you are! she said, rubbing her eyes and yawning and stretching as though she had just woken up (though since they had last seen each other she had felt very far from sleepy).

"If you had been at the ball," said one of the sisters, "you would not have felt like yawning. There was a beautiful princess there, really ravishingly beautiful. She was most attentive to us. She gave us oranges and lemons."

Cinderella could have hugged herself. She asked them the name of the princess, but they replied that no one knew her, that the King's son was much troubled about it, and that he would give anything in the world to know who she was. Cinderella smiled and said to them:

"So she was very beautiful? Well, well, how lucky you are! Couldn't I see her? Please, **40** Miss Javotte, do lend me that yellow dress which you wear about the house."

"Really," said Miss Javotte, "what an idea! Lend one's dress like that to a filthy Cinderbottom! I should have to be out of my mind."

Cinderella was expecting this refusal and she was very glad when it came, for she would have been in an awkward position if her sister really had lent her her frock.

On the next day the two sisters went to the ball, and Cinderella too, but even more splendidly dressed than the first time. The King's son was constantly at her side and wooed her the whole evening. The young girl was enjoying herself so much that she forgot her godmother's warning. She heard the clock striking the first stroke of midnight when she thought that it was still hardly eleven. She rose and slipped away as lightly as a roe-deer. The Prince followed her, but he could not catch her up. One of her glass slippers fell off, and the Prince picked it up with great care.

Cinderella reached home quite out of breath, with no coach, no footmen, and wearing her old clothes. Nothing remained of all her finery, except one of her little slippers, the fellow to the one which she had dropped. The guards at the palace gate were asked if they had not seen a princess go out. They answered that they had seen no one go out except a very poorly dressed girl, who looked more like a peasant than a young lady.

45   When the two sisters returned from the ball, Cinderella asked them if they had enjoyed themselves again, and if the beautiful lady had been there. They said that she had, but that she had run away when it struck midnight, and so swiftly that she had lost one of her glass slippers, a lovely little thing. The Prince had picked it up and had done nothing but gaze at it for the rest of the ball, and undoubtedly he was very much in love with the beautiful person to whom it belonged.

They were right, for a few days later the King's son had it proclaimed to the sound of trumpets that he would marry the girl whose foot exactly fitted the slipper. They began by trying it on the various princesses, then on the duchesses and on all the ladies of the Court, but with no success. It was brought to the two sisters, who did everything possible to force their feet into the slipper, but they could not manage it. Cinderella, who was looking on, recognized her own slipper, and said laughing:

"Let me see if it would fit me!"

Her sisters began to laugh and mock at her. But the gentleman who was trying on the slipper looked closely at Cinderella and, seeing that she was very beautiful, said that her request was perfectly reasonable and that he had instructions to try it on every girl. He made Cinderella sit down and, raising the slipper to her foot, he found that it slid on without difficulty and fitted like a glove.

Great was the amazement of the two sisters, but it became greater still when Cinderella drew from her pocket the second little slipper and put it on her other foot. Thereupon the fairy godmother came in and, touching Cinderella's clothes with her wand, made them even more magnificent than on the previous days.

50   Then the two sisters recognized her as the lovely princess whom they had met at the ball. They flung themselves at her feet and begged her forgiveness for all the unkind things which they had done to her. Cinderella raised them up and kissed them, saying that she forgave them with all her heart and asking them to love her always. She was taken to the young Prince in the fine clothes which she was wearing. He thought her more beautiful than ever and a few days later he married her. Cinderella, who was as kind as she was beautiful, invited her two sisters to live in the palace and married them, on the same day, to two great noblemen of the Court.

Ashputtle

Jakob and Wilhelm Grimm

Jakob Grimm (1785–1863) and Wilhelm Grimm (1786–1859) are best known today for the 200 folktales they collected from oral sources and reworked in *Kinder- und Hausmärchen* (popularly known as *Grimm's Fairy Tales*), which has been translated into seventy languages. The techniques Jakob and Wilhelm Grimm used to collect and comment on these tales became a model for other collectors, providing a basis for the science of folklore. Although the Grimm brothers argued for preserving the tales exactly as heard from oral sources, scholars have determined that they sought to "improve" the tales by making them more readable. The result, highly pleasing to lay audiences the world over, nonetheless represents a literary reworking of the original oral sources.

The wife of a rich man fell sick, and as she felt that her end was drawing near, she called her only daughter to her bedside and said, "Dear child, be good and pious, and then the good God will always protect thee, and I will look down on thee from heaven and be near thee." Thereupon she closed her eyes and departed. Every day the maiden went out to her mother's grave and wept, and she remained pious and good. When winter came the snow spread a white sheet over the grave, and when the spring sun had drawn it off again, the man had taken another wife.

The woman had brought two daughters into the house with her, who were beautiful and fair of face, but vile and black of heart. Now began a bad time for the poor step-child. "Is the stupid goose to sit in the parlour with us?" said they. "He who wants to eat bread must earn it; out with the kitchen-wench." They took her pretty clothes away from her, put an old grey bedgown on her, and gave her wooden shoes. "Just look at the proud princess, how decked out she is!" they cried, and laughed, and led her into the kitchen. There she had to do hard work from morning till night, get up before daybreak, carry water, light fires, cook and wash. Besides this, the sisters did her every imaginable injury. They mocked her and emptied her peas and lentils into the ashes, so that she was forced to sit and pick them out again. In the evening when she had worked till she was weary she had no bed to go to, but had to sleep by the fireside in the ashes. And as on that account she always looked dusty and dirty, they called her Cinderella. It happened that the father was once going to the fair, and he asked his two step-daughters what he should bring back for them. "Beautiful dresses," said one, "Pearls and jewels," said the second. "And thou, Cinderella," said he, "what wilt thou have?" "Father, break off for me the first branch which knocks against your hat on your way home." So he bought beautiful dresses, pearls and jewels for his two step-daughters, and on his way home, as he was riding through a green thicket, a hazel twig brushed against him and knocked off his hat. Then he broke off the branch and took it with him. When he reached home he gave his step-daughters the things which they had wished for, and to Cinderella he gave the branch from the hazel-bush. Cinderella thanked him, went to her mother's grave and planted the branch on it, and wept so much that the tears fell down on it and watered it. It grew, however, and became a handsome tree. Thrice a day Cinderella went and sat beneath it, and wept and prayed, and a little white bird always came on the tree, and if Cinderella expressed a wish, the bird threw down to her what she had wished for.

It happened, however, that the King appointed a festival which was to last three days, and to which all the beautiful young girls in the country were invited, in order that his son might choose himself a bride. When the two step-sisters heard that they too were to appear among the number, they were delighted, called Cinderella and said, "Comb our hair for us, brush our shoes and fasten our buckles, for we are going to the festival at the King's palace." Cinderella obeyed, but wept, because she too would have liked to go with them to the dance, and begged her step-mother to allow her to do so. "Thou go, Cinderella!" said she; "Thou art dusty and dirty, and wouldst go to the festival? Thou hast no clothes and shoes, and yet wouldst dance!" As, however, Cinderella went on asking, the step-mother at last said, "I have emptied a dish of lentils into the ashes for thee, if thou hast picked them out again in two hours, thou shalt go with us." The maiden went through the back-door into the garden, and called, "You tame pigeons, you turtle-doves, and all you birds beneath the sky, come and help me to pick

> "The good into the pot,
> The bad into the crop."

Then two white pigeons came in by the kitchen-window, and afterwards the turtle-doves, and at last all the birds beneath the sky, came whirring and crowding in, and alighted amongst the ashes. And the pigeons nodded with their heads and began pick, pick, pick, pick, and the rest began also pick, pick, pick, pick, and gathered all the good grains into the dish. Hardly had one hour passed before they had finished, and all flew out again. Then the girl took the dish to her step-mother, and was glad, and believed that now she would be allowed to go with them to the festival. But the step-mother said, "No, Cinderella, thou hast no clothes and thou canst not dance; thou wouldst only be laughed at." And as Cinderella wept at this, the step-mother said, "If thou canst pick two dishes of lentils out of the ashes for me in one hour, thou shalt go with us." And she thought to herself, "That she most certainly cannot do." When the step-mother had emptied the two dishes of lentils amongst the ashes, the maiden went through the back-door into the garden and cried, "You tame pigeons, you turtle-doves, and all you birds under heaven, come and help me to pick

> "The good into the pot,
> The bad into the crop."

5   Then two white pigeons came in by the kitchen-window, and afterwards the turtle-doves, and at length all the birds beneath the sky, came whirring and crowding in, and alighted amongst the ashes. And the doves nodded with their heads and began pick, pick, pick, pick, and the others began also pick, pick, pick, pick, and gathered all the good seeds into the dishes, and before half an hour was over they had already finished, and all flew out again. Then the maiden carried the dishes to the step-mother and was delighted, and believed that she might now go with them to the festival. But the step-mother said, "All this will not help thee; thou goest not with us, for thou hast no clothes and canst not dance; we should be ashamed of thee!" On this she turned her back on Cinderella, and hurried away with her two proud daughters.

As no one was now at home, Cinderella went to her mother's grave beneath the hazel-tree, and cried,

> "Shiver and quiver, little tree,
> Silver and gold throw down over me."

Then the bird threw a gold and silver dress down to her, and slippers embroidered with silk and silver. She put on the dress with all speed, and went to the festival. Her step-sisters and the step-mother however did not know her, and thought she must be a foreign princess, for she looked so beautiful in the golden dress. They never once thought of Cinderella, and believed that she was sitting at home in the dirt, picking lentils out of the ashes. The prince went to meet her, took her by the hand and danced with her. He would dance with no other maiden, and never left loose of her hand, and if any one else came to invite her, he said, "This is my partner."

She danced till it was evening, and then she wanted to go home. But the King's son said, "I will go with thee and bear thee company," for he wished to see to whom the beautiful maiden belonged. She escaped from him, however, and sprang into the pigeon-house. The King's son waited until her father came, and then he told him that the stranger maiden had leapt into the pigeon-house. The old man thought, "Can it be Cinderella?" and they had to bring him an axe and a pickaxe that he might hew the pigeon-house to pieces, but no one was inside it. And when they got home Cinderella lay in her dirty clothes among the ashes, and a dim little oil-lamp was burning on the mantle-piece, for Cinderella had jumped quickly down from the back of the pigeon-house and had run to the little hazel-tree, and there she had taken off her beautiful clothes and laid them on the grave, and the bird had taken them away again, and then she had placed herself in the kitchen amongst the ashes in her grey gown.

Next day when the festival began afresh, and her parents and the step-sisters had gone once more, Cinderella went to the hazel-tree and said

"Shiver and quiver, my little tree,
Silver and gold throw down over me."

Then the bird threw down a much more beautiful dress than on the preceding day. And **10** when Cinderella appeared at the festival in this dress, every one was astonished at her beauty. The King's son had waited until she came, and instantly took her by the hand and danced with no one but her. When others came and invited her, he said, "She is my partner." When evening came she wished to leave, and the King's son followed her and wanted to see into which house she went. But she sprang away from him, and into the garden behind the house. Therein stood a beautiful tall tree on which hung the most magnificent pears. She clambered so nimbly between the branches like a squirrel, that the King's son did not know where she was gone. He waited until her father came, and said to him, "The stranger-maiden has escaped from me, and I believe she has climbed up the pear-tree." The father thought, "Can it be Cinderella?" and had an axe brought and cut the tree down, but no one was on it. And when they got into the kitchen, Cinderella lay there amongst the ashes, as usual, for she had jumped down on the other side of the tree, had taken the beautiful dress to the bird on the little hazel-tree, and put on her grey gown.

On the third day, when the parents and sisters had gone away, Cinderella went once more to her mother's grave and said to the little tree

"Shiver and quiver, my little tree,
Silver and gold throw down over me."

And now the bird threw down to her a dress which was more splendid and magnificent than any she had yet had, and the slippers were golden. And when she went to the festival in the dress, no one knew how to speak for astonishment. The King's son danced with her only, and if any one invited her to dance, he said, "She is my partner."

When evening came, Cinderella wished to leave, and the King's son was anxious to go with her, but she escaped from him so quickly that he could not follow her. The King's son had, however, used a stratagem, and had caused the whole staircase to be smeared with pitch, and there, when she ran down, had the maiden's left slipper remained sticking. The King's son picked it up, and it was small and dainty, and all golden. Next morning, he went with it to the father, and said to him, "No one shall be my wife but she whose foot this golden slipper fits." Then were the two sisters glad, for they had pretty feet. The eldest went with the shoe into her room and wanted to try it on, and her mother stood by. But she could not get her big toe into it, and the shoe was too small for her. Then her mother gave her a knife and said, "Cut the toe off; when thou art Queen thou wilt have no more need to go on foot." The maiden cut the toe off, forced the foot into the shoe, swallowed the pain, and went out to the King's son. Then he took her on his horse as his bride and rode away with her. They were, however, obliged to pass the grave, and there, on the hazel-tree, sat the two pigeons and cried,

"Turn and peep, turn and peep,
There's blood within the shoe,
The shoe it is too small for her,
The true bride waits for you."

Then he looked at her foot and saw how the blood was streaming from it. He turned his horse round and took the false bride home again, and said she was not the true one, and that the other sister was to put the shoe on. Then this one went into her chamber and got her toes safely into the shoe, but her heel was too large. So her mother gave her a knife and said, "Cut a bit off thy heel; when thou art Queen thou wilt have no more need to go on foot." The maiden cut a bit off her heel, forced her foot into the shoe, swallowed the pain, and went out to the King's son. He took her on his horse as his bride, and rode away with her, but when they passed by the hazel-tree, two little pigeons sat on it and cried,

> "Turn and peep, turn and peep,
> There's blood within the shoe,
> The shoe it is too small for her,
> The true bride waits for you."

15   He looked down at her foot and saw how the blood was running out of her shoe, and how it had stained her white stocking. Then he turned his horse and took the false bride home again. "This also is not the right one," said he, "have you no other daughter?" "No," said the man, "There is still a little stunted kitchen-wench which my late wife left behind her, but she cannot possibly be the bride." The King's son said he was to send her up to him; but the mother answered, "Oh no, she is much too dirty, she cannot show herself!" He absolutely insisted on it, and Cinderella had to be called. She first washed her hands and face clean, and then went and bowed down before the King's son, who gave her the golden shoe. Then she seated herself on a stool, drew her foot out of the heavy wooden shoe, and put it into the slipper, which fitted like a glove. And when she rose up and the King's son looked at her face he recognized the beautiful maiden who had danced with him and cried, "That is the true bride!" The step-mother and the two sisters were terrified and became pale with rage; he, however, took Cinderella on his horse and rode away with her. As they passed by the hazel-tree, the two white doves cried,

> "Turn and peep, turn and peep,
> No blood is in the shoe,
> The shoe is not too small for her,
> The true bride rides with you,"

and when they had cried that, the two came flying down and placed themselves on Cinderella's shoulders, one on the right, the other on the left, and remained sitting there.

When the wedding with the King's son had to be celebrated, the two false sisters came and wanted to get into favour with Cinderella and share her good fortune. When the betrothed couple went to church, the elder was at the right side and the younger at the left, and the pigeons pecked out one eye of each of them. Afterwards as they came back, the elder was at the left, and the younger at the right, and then the pigeons pecked out the other eye of each. And thus, for their wickedness and falsehood, they were punished with blindness as long as they lived.

A Chinese "Cinderella"

Tuan Ch'Êng-Shih

"The earliest datable version of the Cinderella story anywhere in the world occurs in a Chinese book written about 850–860 A.D." Thus begins Arthur Waley's essay on the Chinese "Cinderella" in the March 1947 edition of *Folk-Lore*. The recorder of the tale is a man named Tuan Ch'êng-shih, whose father was an important official in Szechwan and who himself held a high post in the office arranging the ceremonies associated with imperial ancestor worship.

Among the people of the south there is a tradition that before the Ch'in and Han dynasties there was a cave-master called Wu. The aborigines called the place the Wu cave. He married two wives. One wife died. She had a daughter called Yeh-hsien, who from childhood was intelligent and good at making pottery on the wheel. Her father loved her. After some years the father died, and she was ill-treated by her step-mother, who always made her collect firewood in dangerous places and draw water from deep pools. She once got a fish about two inches long, with red fins and golden eyes. She put it into a bowl of water. It grew bigger every day, and after she had changed the bowl several times she could find no bowl big enough for it, so she threw it into the back pond. Whatever food was left over from meals she put into the water to feed it. When she came to the pond, the fish always exposed its head and pillowed it on the bank; but when anyone else came, it did not come out. The step-mother knew about this, but when she watched for it, it did not once appear. So she tricked the girl, saying, "Haven't you worked hard! I am going to give you a new dress." She then made the girl change out of her tattered clothing. Afterwards she sent her to get water from another spring and reckoning that it was several hundred leagues, the step-mother at her leisure put on her daughter's clothes, hid a sharp blade up her sleeve, and went to the pond. She called to the fish. The fish at once put its head out, and she chopped it off and killed it. The fish was now more than ten feet long. She served it up and it tasted twice as good as an ordinary fish. She hid the bones under the dung-hill. Next day, when the girl came to the pond, no fish appeared. She howled with grief in the open countryside, and suddenly there appeared a man with his hair loose over his shoulders and coarse clothes. He came down from the sky. He consoled her, saying, "Don't howl! Your step-mother has killed the fish and its bones are under the dung. You go back, take the fish's bones and hide them in your room. Whatever you want, you have only to pray to them for it. It is bound to be granted." The girl followed his advice, and was able to provide herself with gold, pearls, dresses and food whenever she wanted them.

When the time came for the cave-festival, the step-mother went, leaving the girl to keep watch over the fruit-trees in the garden. She waited till the step-mother was some way off, and then went herself, wearing a cloak of stuff spun from kingfisher feathers and shoes of gold. Her step-sister recognized her and said to the step-mother, "That's very like my sister." The step-mother suspected the same thing. The girl was aware of this and went away in such a hurry that she lost one shoe. It was picked up by one of the people of the cave. When the step-mother got home, she found the girl asleep, with her arms around one of the trees in the garden, and thought no more about it.

This cave was near to an island in the sea. On this island was a kingdom called T'o-han. Its soldiers had subdued twenty or thirty other islands and it had a coast-line of several thousand leagues. The cave-man sold the shoe in T'o-han, and the rules of T'o-han got it. He told those about him to put it on; but it was an inch too small even for the one among them that had the smallest foot. He ordered all the women in his kingdom to try it on, but there was not one that it fitted. It was light as down and made no noise even when treading on stone. The king of T'o-han thought the cave-man had got it unlawfully. He put him in prison and tortured him, but did not end by finding out where it had come from. So he threw it down at the way-side. Then they went everywhere[2] through all the people's houses and arrested them. If there was a woman's shoe, they arrested them and told the king of T'o-han. He thought it strange, searched the inner-rooms and found Yeh-hsien. He made her put on the shoe, and it was true.

---

[2]Something here seems to have gone slightly wrong with the text. [Waley]

Yeh-hsien then came forward, wearing her cloak spun from halcyon feathers and her shoes. She was as beautiful as a heavenly being. She now began to render service to the king, and he took the fish-bones and Yeh-hsien, and brought them back to his country.

5   The step-mother and step-sister were shortly afterwards struck by flying stones, and died. The cave people were sorry for them and buried them in a stone-pit, which was called the Tomb of the Distressed Women. The men of the cave made mating-offerings there; any girl they prayed for there, they got. The king of T'o-han, when he got back to his kingdom, made Yeh-hsien his chief wife. The first year the king was very greedy and by his prayers to the fish-bones got treasures and jade without limit. Next year, there was no response, so the king buried the fish-bones on the seashore. He covered them with a hundred bushels of pearls and bordered them with gold. Later there was a mutiny of some soldiers who had been conscripted and their general opened (the hiding-place) in order to make better provision for his army. One night they (the bones) were washed away by the tide.

This story was told me by Li Shih-yuan, who has been in the service of my family a long while. He was himself originally a man from the caves of Yung-chou and remembers many strange things of the South.

When the Clock Strikes

Tanith Lee

Tanith Lee (1947–2015) was a prolific, award-winning British author of horror, fantasy, and science fiction. "When the Clock Strikes" appears in her collection *Red as Blood* (1983), devoted to horror-tinged retellings of classic tales. Unlike the Grimm version of "Cinderella," based on earlier oral versions, Lee's retelling was written to upend our expectations about fairy tales.

Yes, the great ballroom is filled only with dust now. The slender columns of white marble and the slender columns of rose-red marble are woven together by cobwebs. The vivid frescoes, on which the Duke's treasury spent so much, are dimmed by the dust; the faces of the painted goddesses look gray. And the velvet curtains—touch them, they will crumble. Two hundred years, now, since anyone danced in this place on the sea-green floor in the candle gleam. Two hundred years since the wonderful clock struck for the very last time.

I thought you might care to examine the clock. It was considered exceptional in its day. The pedestal is ebony and the face fine porcelain. And the figures, which are of silver, would pass slowly about the circlet of the face. Each figure represents, you understand, an hour. And as the appropriate hours came level with this golden bell, they would strike it the correct number of times. All the figures are unique, you see. Beginning at the first hour, they are, in this order, a girl-child, a dwarf, a maiden, a youth, a lady and a knight. And here, notice, the figures grow older as the day declines: a queen and king for the seventh and eighth hours, and after these, and abbess and magician and next to last, a hag. But the very last is the strangest of all. The twelfth figure: do you recognize him? It is Death. Yes, a most curious clock. It was reckoned a marvelous thing then. But it has not struck for two hundred years. Possibly you have heard the story? No? Oh, but I am certain that you have heard it, in another form, perhaps.

However, as you have some while to wait for your carriage, I will recount the tale, if you wish.

I will start with what is said of the clock. In those years, this city was prosperous, a stronghold—not as you see it today. Much was made in the city that was ornamental and unusual. But the clock, on which the twelfth hour was Death, caused something of a stir. It was thought unlucky, foolhardy, to have such a clock. It began to be murmured, jokingly by some, by others in earnest, that one night when the clock struck the twelfth hour, Death would truly strike with it.

Now life has always been a chancy business, and it was more so then. The Great Plague **5** had come but twenty years before and was not yet forgotten. Besides, in the duke's court there was much intrigue, while enemies might be supposed to plot beyond the city walls, as happens even in our present age. But there was another thing.

It was rumored that the duke had obtained both his title and the city treacherously. Rumor declared that he had systematically destroyed those who had stood in line before him, the members of the princely house that formerly ruled here. He had accomplished the task slyly, hiring assassins talented with poisons and daggers. But rumor also declared that the duke had not been sufficiently thorough. For though he had meant to rid himself of all that rival house, a single descendant remained, so obscure he had not traced her—for it was a woman.

Of course, such matters were not spoken of openly. Like the prophecy of the clock, it was a subject for the dark.

Nevertheless, I will tell you at once, there was such a descendant he had missed in his bloody work. And she was a woman. Royal and proud she was, and seething with bitter spite and a hunger for vengeance, and bloody as the duke, had he known it, in her own way.

For her safety and disguise, she had long ago wed a wealthy merchant in the city, and presently bore the man a daughter. The merchant, a dealer in silks, was respected, a good fellow but not wise. He rejoiced in his handsome and aristocratic wife. He never dreamed what she might be about when he was not with her. In fact, she had sworn allegiance to Satanas. In the dead of night she would go up into an old tower adjoining the merchant's house, and there she would say portions of the Black Mass, offer sacrifice, and thereafter practice witchcraft against the duke. This witchery took a common form, the creation of a wax image and the maiming of the image that, by sympathy, the injuries inflicted on the wax be passed on to the living body of the victim. The woman was capable in what she did. The duke fell sick. He lost the use of his limbs and was racked by excruciating pains from which he could get no relief. Thinking himself on the brink of death, the duke named his sixteen-year-old son his heir. This son was dear to the duke, as everyone knew, and be sure the woman knew it too. She intended sorcerously to murder the young man in his turn, preferably in his father's sight. Thus she let the duke linger in his agony and commenced planning the fate of the prince.

Now all this while she had not been toiling alone. She had one helper. It was her own **10** daughter, a maid of fourteen, that she had recruited to her service nearly as soon as the infant could walk. At six or seven, the child had been lisping the satanic rite along with her mother. At fourteen, you may imagine, the girl was will versed in the black arts, though she did not have her mother's natural genius for them.

Perhaps you would like me to describe the daughter at this point. It has a bearing on the story, for the girl was astonishingly beautiful. Her hair was the rich dark red of antique burnished copper, her eyes were the hue of the reddish-golden amber that traders bring from the East. When she walked, you would say she was dancing. But when she danced, a gate seemed to open in the world, and bright fire spangled inside it, but she was the fire.

The girl and her mother were close as gloves in a box. Their games in the old tower bound them closer. No doubt the woman believed herself clever to have such a helpmate, but it proved her undoing.

It was in this manner. The silk merchant, who had never suspected his wife for an instant of anything, began to mistrust the daughter. She was not like other girls. Despite her great beauty, she professed no interest in marriage and none in clothes or jewels. She preferred to read in the garden at the foot of the tower. Her mother had taught the girl her letters, though the merchant himself could read but poorly. And often the father peered at the books his daughter read, unable to make head nor tail of them, yet somehow not liking them. One night very late, the silk merchant came home from a guild dinner in the city, and he saw a slim pale shadow gliding up the steps of the old tower, and he knew it for his child. On impulse, he followed her, but quietly. He had not considered any evil so far and did not want to alarm her. At an angle of the stair, the lighted room above, he paused to spy and listen. He had something of a shock when he heard his wife's voice rise up in glad welcome. But what came next drained the blood from his heart. He crept away and went to his cellar for wine to stay himself. After the third glass he ran for neighbors and for the watch.

The woman and her daughter heard the shouts below and saw the torches in the garden. It was no use dissembling. The tower was littered with evidence of vile deeds, besides what the woman kept in a chest beneath her unknowing husband's bed. She understood it was all up with her, and she understood, too, how witchcraft was punished hereabouts. She snatched a knife from the altar.

15   The girl shrieked when she realized what her mother was at. The woman caught the girl by her red hair and shook her.

"Listen to me, my daughter," she cried, "and listen carefully, for the minutes are short. If you do as I tell you, you can escape their wrath and only I need die. And if you live I am satisfied, for you can carry on my labour after me. My vengeance I shall leave you, and my witchcraft to exact it by. Indeed, I promise you stronger powers than mine. I will beg my lord Satanas for it, and he will not deny me, for he is just, in his fashion, and I have served him will. Now will you attend?"

"I will," said the girl.

So the woman advised her, and swore her to the fellowship of Hell. And the woman forced the knife into her own heart and dropped dead on the floor of the tower. When the men burst in with their swords and staves and their torches and their madness, the girl was ready for them.

She stood blank-faced, blank-eyed, with her arms hanging at her sides. When one touched her, she dropped down at his feet.

20   "Surely she is innocent," this man said. She was lovely enough that is was hard to accuse her. Then her father went to her and took her hand and lifted her. At that, the girl opened her eyes, and she said, as if terrified: "How did I come here? I was in my chamber and sleeping . . ."

"The woman has bewitched her," her father said.

He desired very much that to be so. And when the girl clung to his hand and wept, he was certain of it. The girl screamed and seemed to lose her senses totally.

She was put to bed. In the morning, a priest came and questioned her. She answered steadfastly. She remembered nothing, not even of the great books she had been observed reading, When they told her what was in them, she screamed again and apparently would have thrown herself from the narrow window, only the priest stopped her.

Finally, they brought her the holy cross in order that she might kiss it and prove herself blameless.

25   Then she knelt, and whispered softly, that nobody should hear but one: "Lord Satanas, protect thy handmaiden." And either that gentleman has more power than he is credited with

or else the symbols of God are only as holy as the men who deal in them, for she embraced the cross and it left her unscathed.

At that, the whole household thanked God. The whole household saving, of course, the woman's daughter. She had another to thank.

The woman's body was burned and the ashes put into unconsecrated ground beyond the city gates. Though they had discovered her to be a witch, they had not discovered the direction her witchcraft had selected. Nor did they find the wax image with its limbs all twisted and stuck through with needles. The girl had taken that up and concealed it. The duke continued in his distress but he did not die. Sometimes, in the dead of night, the girl would unearth the image from under a loose brick by the hearth and gloat over it, but she did nothing else. Not yet. She was fourteen, and the cloud of her mother's acts still hovered over her. She knew what she must do next.

The period of mourning ended.

"Daughter," said the silk merchant to her, "why do you not remove your black? The woman was malign and led you into wickedness. How long will you mourn her, who deserves no mourning?"

"Oh, my father," she said, "never think I regret my wretched mother. It is my own unwit-   **30** ting sin I mourn," and she grasped his hand and spilled her tears on it. "I would rather live in a convent," said she, "than mingle with proper folk. And I would rather seek a convent too, if it were not that I cannot bear to be parted from you."

Do you suppose she smiled secretly as she said this? One might suppose it. Presently she donned a robe of sackcloth and poured ashes over her red-copper hair. "It is my penance," she said. "I am glad to atone for my sins."

People forgot her beauty. She was at pains to obscure it. She slunk about like an aged woman, a rag pulled over her head, dirt smeared on her cheeks and brow. She elected to sleep in a cold cramped attic and sat all day by a smoky hearth in the kitchens. When someone came to her and begged her to wash her face and put on suitable clothes and sit in the rooms of the house, she smiled modestly, drawing the rag or a piece of hair over her face. "I swear," she said, "I am glad to be humble before God and men."

They reckoned her pious and they reckoned her simple. Two years passed. They mislaid her beauty altogether and reckoned her ugly. They found it hard to call to mind who she was exactly, as she sat in the ashes or shuffled unattended about the streets like a crone.

At the end of the second year, the silk merchant married again. It was inevitable, for he was not a man who liked to live alone.

On this occasion, his choice was a harmless widow. She already had two daughters,   **35** pretty in an unremarkable style. Perhaps the merchant hoped they would comfort him for what had gone before, this normal cheery wife and the two sweet, rather silly daughters, whose chief interests were clothes and weddings. Perhaps he hoped also that his deranged daughter might be drawn out by company. But that hope floundered. Not that the new mother did not try to be pleasant to the girl. And the new sisters, their hearts grieved by her condition, went to great lengths to enlist her friendship. They begged her to come from the kitchens or the attic. Failing in that, they sometimes ventured to join her, their fine silk dresses trailing on the greasy floor. They combed her hair, exclaiming, when some of the ash and dirt were removed, on its color. But no sooner had they turned away than the girl gathered up handfuls of soot and ash and rubbed them into her hair again. Now and then, the sisters attempted to interest their bizarre relative in a bracelet or a gown or a current song. They spoke to her of the young men they had seen at the suppers or the balls which were then given regularly by the rich families of the city. The girl ignored it all. If she ever said anything, it was to do with penance and humility. At last, as must happen, the sisters wearied of her and left her alone. They came to resent her moping grayness, as indeed the merchant's second wife had already done.

"Can you do nothing with that girl?" she demanded of her husband. "People will say that I and my daughters are responsible for her condition and that I ill-treat the maid from jealousy of her dead mother."

"Now how could anyone say that," protested the merchant, "when you are famous as the epitome of generosity and kindness?"

Another year passed, and saw no difference in the household.

A difference there was, but not visible.

40   The girl who slouched in the corner of the hearth was seventeen. Under the filth and grime she was, impossibly, more beautiful, although no one could see it.

And there was one other invisible item: her power (which all this time she had nurtured, saying her prayer to Satanas in the black of midnight), her power rising like a dark moon in her soul.

Three days after her seventeenth birthday, the girl straggled about the streets, as she frequently did. A few noted her and muttered it was the merchant's ugly simple daughter and paid no more attention. Most did not know her at all. She had made herself appear one with the scores of impoverished flotsam which constantly roamed the city, beggars and starve-lings. Just outside the city gates, these persons congregated in large numbers, slumped around fires of burning refuse or else wandering to and fro in search of edible seeds, scraps, the miracle of a dropped coin. Here the girl now came, and began to wander about as they did. Dusk gathered and the shadows thickened. The girl sank to her knees in a patch of earth as if she had found something. Two or three of the beggars sneaked over to see if it were worth snatching from her—but the girl was only scrabbling in the empty soil. The beg-gars, making signs to each other that she was touched by God—mad—left her alone. But very far from mad, the girl presently dug up a stoppered urn. In this urn were the ashes and charred bones of her mother. She had got a clue as to the location of the urn by devious questioning here and there. Her occult power had helped her to be sure of it.

In the twilight, padding along through the narrow streets and alleys of the city, the girl brought the urn homeward. In the garden, at the foot of the old tower, gloom-wrapped, unwitnessed, she unstoppered the urn and buried the ashes freshly. She muttered certain unholy magics over the grave. Then she snapped off the sprig of a young hazel tree and planted it in the newly turned ground.

I hazard you have begun to recognize the story by now. I see you suppose I tell it wrongly. Believe me, this is the truth of the matter. But if you would rather I left off the tale . . . no doubt your carriage will soon be here—No? Very well. I shall continue.

45   I think I should speak of the duke's son at this juncture. The prince was nineteen, able, intelligent, and of noble bearing. He was of that rather swarthy type of looks one finds here in the north, but tall and slim and clear-eyed. There is an ancient square where you may see a statue of him, but much eroded by two centuries and the elements. After the city was sacked, no care was lavished on it.

The duke treasured his son. He had constant delight in the sight of the young man and what he said and did. It was the only happiness the invalid had.

Then, one night, the duke screamed out in his bed. Servants came running with can-dles. The duke moaned that a sword was transfixing his heart, an inch at a time. The prince hurried into the chamber, but in that instant the duke spasmed horribly and died. No mark was on his body. There had never been a mark to show what ailed him.

The prince wept. They were genuine tears. He had nothing to reproach his father with, everything to thank him for. Presently they brought the young man the seal ring of the city, and he put it on.

It was winter, a cold blue-white weather with snow in the streets and countryside and a hard wizened sun that drove thin sharp blades of light through the sky but gave no warmth. The duke's funeral cortege passed slowly across the snow: the broad open chariots, draped with black and silver; the black-plumed horses, the chanting priests with their glittering robes, their jeweled crucifixes and golden censers. Crowds lined the roadways to watch the spectacle. Among the beggar women stood a girl. No one noticed her. They did not glimpse the expression she veiled in her ragged scarf. She gazed at the bier pitilessly. As the young prince rode by in his sables, the seal ring on his hand, the eyes of the girl burned through her ashy hair, like a red fox through grasses.

The duke was buried in the mausoleum you can visit to this day, on the east side of the **50** city. Several months elapsed. The prince put his grief from him and took up the business of the city competently. Wise and courteous he was, but he rarely smiled. At nineteen, his spirit seemed worn. You might think he guessed the destiny that hung over him.

The winter was a hard one too. The snow had come and, having come, was loath to withdraw. When at last the spring returned, flushing the hills with color, it was no longer sensible to be sad.

The prince's name day fell about this time. A great banquet was planned, a ball. There had been neither in the palace for nigh on three years, not since the duke's fatal illness first claimed him. Now the royal doors were to be thrown open to all men of influence and their families. The prince was liberal, charming, and clever even in this. Aristocrat and rich trader were to mingle in the beautiful dining room, and in this very chamber, among the frescoes, the marble, and the candelabra. Even a merchant's daughter, if the merchant was notable in the city, would get to dance on the sea-green floor, under the white eye of the fearful clock.

The clock. There was some renewed controversy about the clock. They did not dare speak to the young prince. He was a skeptic, as his father had been. But had not a death already occurred? Was the clock not a flying in the jaws of fate? For those disturbed by it, there was a dim writing in their minds, in the dust of the street or the pattern of blossoms. When the clock strikes—But people do not positively heed these warnings. Man is afraid of his fears. He ignores the shadow of the wolf thrown on the paving before him, saying: It is only a shadow.

The silk merchant received his invitation to the palace, and to be sure, thought nothing of the clock. His house had been thrown into uproar. The most luscious silks of his workshop were carried into the house and laid before the wife and her two daughters, who chirruped and squealed with excitement. "Oh, Father," cried the two sisters, "may I have this one with the gold piping?" "Oh, Father, this one with the design of pineapples?" Later a jeweler arrived and set out his trays. The merchant was generous. He wanted his women to look their best. It might be the night of their lives. Yet all the while, at the back of his mind, a little dark spot, itching, aching. He tried to ignore the spot, not scratch at it. His true daughter, the mad one. Nobody bothered to tell her about the invitation to the palace. They knew how she would react, mumbling in her hair about her sin and her penance, paddling her hands in the greasy ash to smear her face. Even the servants avoided her, as if she were just the cat seated by the fire. Less than the cat, for the cat saw to the mice—just a block of stone. And yet, how fair she might have looked, decked in the pick of the merchant's wares, jewels at her throat. The prince himself could not have been unaware of her. And though marriage was impossible, other, less holy though equally honorable, contracts might have been arranged, to the benefit of all concerned. The merchant sighed. He had scratched the darkness after all. He attempted to comfort himself by watching the two sisters exult over their apparel. He refused to admit that the finery would somehow make them seem but more ordinary than they were by contrast.

55   The evening of the banquet arrived. The family set off. Most of the servants sidled after. The prince had distributed largess in the city; oxen roasted in the squares, and the wine was free by royal order.

    The house grew somber. In the deserted kitchen, the fire went out.

    By the hearth, a segment of gloom rose up.

    The girl glanced around her, and she laughed softly and shook out her filthy hair. Of course, she knew as much as anyone, and more than most. This was to be her night too.

    A few minutes later she was in the garden beneath the old tower, standing over the young hazel tree which had thrust up from the earth. It had become strong, the tree, despite the harsh winter. Now the girl nodded to it. She chanted under her breath. At length a pale light began to glow, far down near where the roots of the tree held to the ground. Out of the pale glow flew a thin black bird, which perched on the girl's shoulder. Together, the girl and the bird passed into the old tower. High up, a fire blazed that no one had lit. A tub steamed with scented water that no one had drawn. Shapes that were not real and barely seen flitted about. Rare perfumes, the rustle of garments, the glint of hems as yet invisible, filled and did not fill the restless air.

60   Need I describe further? No. You will have seen paintings which depict the attendance upon a witch of her familiar demons. How one bathes her, another anoints her, another brings clothes and ornaments. Perhaps you do not credit such things in any case. Never mind that. I will tell you what happened in the courtyard before the palace.

    Many carriages and chariots had driven through the square, avoiding the roasting oxen, the barrels of wind, the cheering drunken citizens, and so through the gates into the court-yard. Just before ten o'clock (the hour, if you recall the clock, of the magician), a solitary carriage drove through the square and into the court. The people in the square gawked at the carriage and pressed forward to see who would step out of it, this latecomer. It was a remark-able vehicle that looked to be fashioned of solid gold, all but the domed roof, that was trans-parent flashing crystal. Six black horses drew it. The coachman and postilions were clad in crimson, and strangely masked as curious beasts and reptiles. One of these beast-men now hopped down and opened the door of the carriage. Out came a woman's figure in a cloak of white fur, and glided up the palace stair and in at the doors.

    There was dancing in the ballroom. The whole chamber was bright and clamorous with music and the voices of men and women. There, between those two pillars, the prince sat in his chair, dark, courteous, seldom smiling. Here the musicians played, the deep-throated viol, the lively mandolin. And there the dancers moved up and down on the sea-green floor. But the music and the dancers had just paused. The figures on the clock were themselves in motion. The hour of the magician was about to strike.

    As it struck, through the doorway came the figure in the fur cloak. And as if they must, every eye turned to her.

    For an instant she stood there, all white, as though she had brought the winter snow back with her. And then she loosed the cloak from her shoulders, it slipped away, and she was all fire.

65   She wore a gown of apricot brocade embroidered thickly with gold. Her sleeves and the bodice of her gown were slashed over ivory satin sewn with large rosy pearls. Pearls, too, were wound in her hair, that was the shade of antique burnished copper. She was so

beautiful that when the clock was still, nobody spoke. She was so beautiful that it was hard to look at her for very long.

The prince got up from his chair. He did not know he had. Now he started out across the floor, between the dancers, who parted silently to let him through. He went toward the girl in the doorway as if she drew him by a chain.

The prince had hardly ever acted without considering first what he did. Now he did not consider. He bowed to the girl.

"Madam," he said. "You are welcome, Madam," he said. "Tell me who you are."

She smiled.

"My rank," she said. "Would you know that, my lord? It is similar to yours, or would be **70** were I now mistress in my dead mother's palace. But, unfortunately, an unscrupulous man caused the downfall of our house."

"Misfortune indeed," said the prince. "Tell me your name. Let me right the wrong done you."

"You shall," said the girl. "Trust me, you shall. For my name, I would rather keep it secret for the present. But you may call me, if you will, a pet name I have given myself—Ashella."

"Ashella . . . But I see no ash about you," said the prince, dazzled by her gleam, laughing a little, stiffly, for laughter was not his habit.

"Ash and cinders from a cold and bitter hearth," said she. But she smiled again. "Now everyone is staring at us, my lord, and the musicians are impatient to begin again. Out of all these ladies, can it be you will lead me in the dance?"

"As long as you will dance," he said. "You shall dance with me." **75**

And that is how it was.

There were many dances, slow and fast, whirling measures and gentle ones. And here and there, the prince and the maiden were parted. Always then he looked eagerly after her, sparing no regard for the other girls whose hands lay in his. It was not like him, he was usually so careful. But the other young men who danced on that floor, who clasped her fingers or her narrow waist in the dance, also gazed after her when she was gone. She danced, as she appeared, like fire. Though if you had asked those young men whether they would rather tie her to themselves, as the prince did, they would have been at a loss. For it is not easy to keep pace with fire.

The hour of the hag struck on the clock.

The prince grew weary of dancing with the girl and losing her in the dance to others and refinding her and losing her again.

Behind the curtains there is a tall window in the east wall that opens on the terrace **80** above the garden. He drew her out there, into the spring night. He gave an order, and small tables were brought with delicacies and sweets and wine. He sat by her, watching every gesture she made, as if he would paint her portrait afterward.

In the ballroom, here, under the clock, the people murmured. But it was not quite the murmur you would expect, the scandalous murmur about a woman come from nowhere that the prince had made so much of. At the periphery of the ballroom, the silk merchant sat, pale as a ghost, thinking of a ghost, the living ghost of his true daughter. No one else recognized her. Only he. Some trick of his heart had enabled him to know her. He said nothing of it. As the stepsisters and wife gossiped with other wives and sisters, an awful foreboding weighed him down, sent him cold and dumb.

And now it is almost midnight, the moment when the page of the night turns over into day. Almost midnight, the hour when the figure of Death strikes the golden bell of the clock. And what will happen when the clock strikes? Your face announces that you know. Be patient; let us see if you do.

"I am being foolish," said the prince to Ashella on the terrace. "But perhaps I am entitled to be foolish, just once in my life. What are you saying?" For the girl was speaking low beside him, and he could not catch her words.

"I am saying a spell to bind you to me," she said.

85 "But I am already bound."

"Be bound, then. Never go free."

"I do not wish it," he said. He kissed her hands, and he said, "I do not know you, but I will wed you. Is that proof your spell has worked? I will wed you, and get back for you the rights you have lost."

"If it were only so simple," said Ashella, smiling, smiling. "But the debt is too cruel. Justice requires a harsher payment."

And then, in the ballroom, Death struck the first note on the golden bell.

90 The girl smiled and she said:

"I curse you in my mother's name."

The second stroke.

"I curse you in my own name."

The third stroke.

95 "And in the name of those that your father slew."

The fourth stroke.

"And in the name of my Master, who rules the world."

As the fifth, the sixth, the seventh strokes pealed out, the prince stood nonplussed. At the eighth and ninth strokes, the strength of the malediction seemed to curdle his blood. He shivered and his brain writhed. At the tenth stroke, he saw a change in the loveliness before him. She grew thinner, taller. At the eleventh stroke, he beheld a thing in a ragged black cowl and robe. It grinned at him. It was all grin below a triangle of sockets of nose and eyes. At the twelfth stroke, the prince saw Death and knew him.

In the ballroom, a hideous grinding noise, as the gears of the clock failed. Followed by a hollow booming, as the mechanism stopped entirely.

100 Only one thing was left behind. A woman's shoe. A shoe no woman could ever have danced in. It was made of glass.

Did you intend to protest about the shoe? Shall I finish the story, or would you rather I did not? It is not the ending you are familiar with. Yes, I perceive you understand that now.

I will go quickly, then, for your carriage must soon be here. And there is not a great deal more to relate.

The prince lost his mind. Partly from what he had seen, partly from the spells the young witch had netted him in. He could think of nothing but the girl who had named herself Ashella. He raved that Death had borne her away but he would recover her from Death. She had left the glass shoe as a token of her love. He must discover her with the aid of the shoe. Whomsoever the shoe fitted would be Ashella. For there was this added complication, that Death might hide her actual appearance. None had seen the girl before. She had disappeared like smoke. The one infallible test was the shoe. That was why she had left it for him.

His ministers would have reasoned with the prince, but he was past reason. His intellect had collapsed totally as only a profound intellect can. A lunatic, he rode about the city. He struck out at those who argued with him. On a particular occasion, drawing a dagger, he killed, not apparently noticing what he did. His demand was explicit. Every woman, young or old, maid or married, must come forth from her home, must put her foot into the shoe of glass. They came.

They had no choice. Some approached in terror, some weeping. Even the aged beggar   **105**
women obliged, and they cackled, enjoying the sight of royalty gone mad. One alone did not
come.

Now it is not illogical that out of the hundreds of women whose feet were put into the
shoe, a single woman might have been found that the shoe fitted. But this did not happen.
Nor did the situation alter, despite a lurid fable that some, tickled by the idea of wedding the
prince, cut off their toes that the shoe might fit them. And if they did, it was to no avail, for still
the shoe did not.

Is it really surprising? The shoe was sorcerous. It constantly changed itself, its shape, its
size, in order that no foot, save one, could ever be got into it.

Summer spread across the land. The city took on its golden summer glaze, its fetid
summer spell.

What had been a whisper of intrigue swelled into a steady distant thunder. Plots were
hatched.

One day the silk merchant was brought, trembling and gray of face, to the prince. The   **110**
merchant's dumbness had broken. He had unburdened himself of his fear at confession, but
the priest had not proved honest. In the dawn, men had knocked on the door of the merchant's house. Now he stumbled to the chair of the prince.

Both looked twice their years, but if anything, the prince looked the elder. He did not lift
his eyes. Over and over in his hands he turned the glass shoe.

The merchant, stumbling, too, in his speech, told the tale of his first wife and his daughter. He told everything, leaving out no detail. He did not even omit the end: that since the
night of the banquet the girl had been absent from his house, taking nothing with her—save
a young hazel from the garden beneath the tower.

The prince leapt from his chair.

His clothes were filthy and unkempt. His face was smeared with sweat and dust . . . it
resembled, momentarily, another face.

Without guard or attendant, the prince ran through the city toward the merchant's   **115**
house, and on the road, the intriguers waylaid and slew him. As he fell, the glass shoe
dropped from his hands and shattered in a thousand fragments.

There is little else worth mentioning.

Those who usurped the city were villains and not merely that but fools. Within a year,
external enemies were at the gates. A year more, and the city had been sacked, half burned
out, ruined. The manner in which you find it now is somewhat better than it was then. And it
is not now anything for a man to be proud of. As you were quick to note, many here earn a
miserable existence by conducting visitors about the streets, the palace, showing them the
dregs of the city's past.

Which was not a request, in fact, for you to give me money. Throw some from your carriage window if your conscience bothers you. My own wants are few.

No, I have no further news of the girl Ashella, the witch. A devotee of Satanas, she has
doubtless worked plentiful woe in the world. And a witch is long-lived. Even so, she will die
eventually. None escapes Death. Then you may pity her, if you like. Those who serve the
gentleman below—who can guess what their final lot will be? But I am very sorry the story did
not please you. It is not, maybe, a happy choice before a journey.

And there is your carriage at last.   **120**

What? Ah, no, I shall stay here in the ballroom, where you came on me. I have often
paused here through the years. It is the clock. It has a certain—what shall I call it?—power to
draw me back.

I am not trying to unnerve you. Why should you suppose that? Because of my knowledge of the city, of the story? You think that I am implying that I myself am Death? Now you laugh. Yes, it is absurd. Observe the twelfth figure on the clock. Is he not as you always heard Death described? And am I in the least like that twelfth figure?

Although, of course, the story was not as you have heard it, either.

Four (Brief) Analyses of *"Cinderella"*

Bruno Bettelheim, Rob Baum, Dorothy Hurley, and Jack Zipes

A Netherworld of Smut

Bruno Bettelheim

Bruno Bettelheim (1903–1990) was a distinguished psychologist and educator who taught at Rockford College and the University of Chicago. His list of books includes *Love Is Not Enough: The Treatment of Emotionally Disturbed Children* (1950), *The Informed Heart* (1960), and *The Uses of Enchantment* (1975), a psychoanalytic treatment of children's stories from which this selection has been excerpted.

When a story corresponds to how the child feels deep down—as no realistic narrative is likely to do—it attains an emotional quality of "truth" for the child. The events of "Cinderella" offer him vivid images that give body to his overwhelming but nevertheless often vague and nondescript emotions; so these episodes seem more convincing to him than his life experiences.

•   •   •

Every child believes at some period of his life—and this is not only at rare moments—that because of his secret wishes, if not also his clandestine actions, he deserves to be degraded, banned from the presence of others, relegated to a netherworld of smut. He fears this may be so, irrespective of how fortunate his situation may be in reality. He hates and fears those others—such as his siblings—whom he believes to be entirely free of similar evilness, and he fears that they or his parents will discover what he is really like, and then demean him as Cinderella was by her family. Because he wants others—most of all, his parents—to believe in his innocence, he is delighted that "everybody" believes in Cinderella's. This is one of the great attractions of this fairy tale. Since people give credence to Cinderella's goodness, they will also believe in his, so the child hopes. And "Cinderella" nourishes this hope, which is one reason it is such a delightful story.

Wealth, Beauty, and Revenge

Rob Baum

The following feminist critique of "Cinderella" first appeared in the article "After the Ball Is Over: Bringing *Cinderella* Home," published in *Cultural Analysis* (2000). Rob Baum teaches literature at the University of Waikato (New Zealand).

[T]he character of Cinderella passed from her fairytale origins to mythical proportions. Cinderella has escaped the bounds of her own story. Cinderella defines girls' first choice for a romantic partner, the strictures of friendship and obedience that girls are trained to uphold, unconditional family love and, not least, ideals of personal appearance and deportment. Cinderella demonstrates the potential of even the least socially advantaged female to achieve public success, the ability of the meek to triumph over the (female) competition, the trick of appearing to be what one is not. These are important techniques in the battle for male approval. If we have impressed Cinderella into service as a myth, it is because we need to look up and forward to a figure who has successfully navigated the obstacles on the distinctly female journey. Cinderella's rags-to-riches story inspires females to prevail against improbable odds. We do not believe in myths because of some inherent truth in them, but because they substantiate what we most wish to be true: Cinderella is a falsehood painted as possibility. What we worship in her is not what she is but what she gets; by subscribing to the myth of Cinderella, we sustain our collective female belief in wealth, beauty, and revenge.

The Coding of Black and White

Dorothy Hurley

Dorothy Hurley, director of the Masters in Multicultural Education programs at Eastern University, examines the racial "coding" of characters in filmed versions of "Cinderella." This passage first appeared in "Seeing White: Children of Color and the Disney Fairy Tale Princess," which first appeared in *The Journal of Negro Education* (2005).

The black and white color symbolism in . . . Disney film versions [of classic fairy tales] is pervasive and powerful. For example, *Snow White* (Disney, 1937) features a wicked queen dressed in black who lives in a black castle that has black rats, a dangerous black forest containing black bats, and black owls. Moreover, the wicked Queen has a black crow-like bird perched on a human skull. . . .

In Disney's [animated film] *Cinderella* (1950), the color symbolism operates in both explicit and implicit or subtle ways. The "good" Cinderella is blonde and blue eyed. Her "bad" stepsisters and mother are visibly darker in complexion than Cinderella who is visibly White. The prince lives in a white castle that has white birds at the window. His father has white hair, which signals not only age, but a child-like innocence and goodness as well. Cinderella's fairy godmother also has white hair. The godmother turns brown, low-status, mice into white human beings and animals: white horses, white coachman, and white doorman. Moreover, she transforms a pumpkin into a white coach. The prince, although black-haired, which is a marker of virility, is clad in a white jacket. His father dreams of grandchildren, represented specifically as a blonde-haired boy and girl even though his son is black-haired. The coding of black and dark hues is subtle in this film. The wicked stepmother's cherished pet is a black cat named "Lucifer."

Sexist Values and a Puritan Ethos

Jack Zipes

Jack Zipes, director for German and European Studies at the University of Minnesota, is the author of numerous books devoted to fairy tales, including *Breaking the Magic Spell*: *Radical Theories of Folk and Fairy* (1979) in which the following first appeared. Zipes is well known for his sharp feminist and Marxist critiques of fairy tale literature.

[In "Cinderella", instead] of having a tale which does homage to women, we have a tale which is an insult to women. Here I want to concentrate on just one aspect of "Cinderella". . . . In the American society today where women have been in the vanguard of the equal rights movement, where female sexuality has undergone great changes, where the central agency of socialization of boys and girls has shifted from the family to the mass media, schools and the bureaucratic state, a tale like "Cinderella" cannot (neither explicitly nor implicitly) guide children to order their inner worlds and to lead fuller, happier sexual lives. Though it is difficult to speculate how an individual child might react to "Cinderella", certainly the adult reader and interpreter must ask the following questions: Why is the stepmother shown to be wicked and not the father? Why is Cinderella essentially passive? . . . Why do girls have to quarrel over a man? How do children react to a Cinderella who is industrious, dutiful, virginal and passive? Are all men handsome? Is marriage the end goal of life? Is it important to marry rich men? This small list of questions suggests that the ideological and psychological pattern and message of "Cinderella" do nothing more than reinforce sexist values and a Puritan ethos that serves a society which fosters competition and achievement for survival.

Discussion and Writing Suggestions

1. Consider an assumption on which Bettelheim bases his psychoanalytic interpretation of "Cinderella": deep down, "[e]very child believes at some period of his life . . . that because of his secret wishes, if not also his clandestine actions, he deserves to be degraded, banned from the presence of others, relegated to a netherworld of smut." How does such an assumption prepare children to read, or hear, the story of "Cinderella"?

2. Baum claims that "Cinderella," like other myths, is "a falsehood painted as a possibility." What is this falsehood? According to Baum, why are girls and women taught (through stories like "Cinderella") to desire it?

3. In her critique of "Cinderella," Hurley responds to filmed versions of the folk tale, not printed ones. Go to YouTube and search on "cinderella disney 1950." Before watching a few scenes (or more) from the animated movie, read Hurley's analysis of "color symbolism." Do you agree with her analysis? Why or why not?

4. Zipes is savage in his critique of "Cinderella." He poses several questions, a "small list [suggesting] that the ideological and psychological pattern and message of "Cinderella" do nothing more than reinforce sexist values and a Puritan ethos that serves a society which fosters competition and achievement for survival." You've read "Cinderella." In your view, does the folk tale pack such heavy, negative messages? Explain.

Cinderella's Stepsisters

Toni Morrison

Toni Morrison (b. 1931), an African American novelist of such acclaimed works as *The Bluest Eye* (1970), *Song of Solomon* (1977), *Tar Baby* (1981), Pulitzer Prize–winning *Beloved* (1987), *Jazz* (1992), and *Paradise* (1998), received the Nobel Prize for

literature in 1993. Critics have hailed her work as being at once both mythic, in its themes and characters, and intensely realistic in its depictions of the sorrows, struggles, and hopes of black people. The selection that follows is excerpted from an address Morrison delivered at Barnard College, a women's college in New York City affiliated with Columbia University. In it, she exhorts her listeners to treat their "stepsisters" more humanely than Cinderella's stepsisters treated her.

Let me begin by taking you back a little. Back before the days at college. To nursery school, probably, to a once-upon-a-time time when you first heard, or read, or, I suspect, even saw "Cinderella." Because it is Cinderella that I want to talk about; because it is Cinderella who causes me a feeling of urgency. What is unsettling about that fairy tale is that it is essentially the story of household—a world, if you please—of women gathered together and held together in order to abuse another woman. There is, of course, a rather vague absent father and a nick-of-time prince with a foot fetish. But neither has much personality. And there are the surrogate "mothers," of course (god- and step-), who contribute both to Cinderella's grief and to her release and happiness. But it is her stepsisters who interest me. How crippling it must have been for those young girls to grow up with a mother, to watch and imitate that mother, enslaving another girl.

I am curious about their fortunes after the story ends. For contrary to recent adaptations, the stepsisters were not ugly, clumsy, stupid girls with outsize feet. The Grimm collection describes them as "beautiful and fair in appearance." When we are introduced to them they are beautiful, elegant, women of status, and clearly women of power. Having watched and participated in the violent dominion of another woman, will they be any less cruel when it comes their turn to enslave other children, or even when they are required to take care of their own mother?

It is not a wholly medieval problem. It is quite a contemporary one: feminine power when directed at other women has historically been wielded in what has been described as a "masculine" manner. Soon you will be in a position to do the very same thing. Whatever your background— rich or poor—whatever the history of education in your family—five generations or one—you have taken advantage of what has been available to you at Barnard and you will therefore have both the economic and social status of the stepsisters *and* you will have their power.

I want not to *ask* you but to *tell* you not to participate in the oppression of your sisters. Mothers who abuse their children are women, and another woman, not an agency, has to be willing to stay their hands. Mothers who set fire to school buses are women, and another woman, not an agency, has to tell them to stay their hands. Women who stop the promotion of other women in careers are women, and another woman must come to the victim's aid. Social and welfare workers who humiliate their clients may be women, and other women colleagues have to deflect their anger.

I am alarmed by the violence that women do to each other: professional violence, competitive violence, emotional violence. I am alarmed by the willingness of women to enslave other women. I am alarmed by a growing absence of decency on the killing floor of professional women's worlds. You are the women who will take your place in the world where *you* can decide who shall flourish and who shall wither; you will make distinctions between the deserving poor and the undeserving poor; where you can yourself determine which life is expendable and which is indispensable. Since you will have the power to do it, you may also be persuaded that you have the right to do it. As educated women the distinction between the two is first-order business.

I am suggesting that we pay as much attention to our nurturing sensibilities as to our ambition. You are moving in the direction of freedom and the function of freedom is to free somebody else. You are moving toward self-fulfillment, and the consequences of that

5

fulfillment should be to discover that there is something just as important as you are and that just-as-important thing may be Cinderella—or your stepsister.

In your rainbow journey toward the realization of personal goals, don't make choices based only on your security and your safety. Nothing is safe. That is not to say that anything ever was, or that anything worth achieving ever should be. Things of value seldom are. It is not safe to have a child. It is not safe to challenge the status quo. It is not safe to choose work that has not been done before. Or to do old work in a new way. There will always be someone there to stop you. But in pursuing your highest ambitions, don't let your personal safety diminish the safety of your stepsister. In wielding the power that is deservedly yours, don't permit it to enslave your stepsisters. Let your might and your power emanate from that place in you that is nurturing and caring.

Women's rights is not only an abstraction, a cause; it is also a personal affair. It is not only about "us"; it is also about me and you. Just the two of us.

Discussion and Writing Suggestions

1. Morrison writes that "Cinderella" is "essentially the story of household—a world, if you please—of women gathered together and held together in order to abuse another woman." Do you agree? In answering, focus on the phrase "in order to abuse another woman."

2. Morrison suggests to students of Barnard that they will soon wield the prestige and power of Cinderella's stepsisters; and she exhorts them to act more humanely to their sisters than Cinderella's stepsisters did. Do you agree with Morrison that women owe women a special obligation of care and support? Why or why not?

3. Morrison claims that having the "power" to harm others is not the same as having the "right" to do so and that for "educated women the distinction between the two is first-order business." Clarify this distinction. Why is it so important?

4. Should men feel threatened by, or altogether ignored in, this speech? And if they are, does that matter, given Morrison's message?

Cinderella: Not So Morally Superior

Elisabeth Panttaja

In the following analysis of "Cinderella," Elisabeth Panttaja offers what for some will be an unsettling claim: that Cinderella succeeds not because she is more patient or virtuous than her stepsisters or stepmother (the typical moral of the story), but because she is craftier, willing to employ powerful magic to defeat the forces arrayed against her. Nor can it be said from evidence in the story, according to Panttaja, that the prince or Cinderella love each other. Is this the same "Cinderella" that you know? The article from which this selection was excerpted appeared originally in *Western Folklore* (1993). Elisabeth Panttaja is a novelist who taught at Tufts University when the article was written.

It is not surprising . . . that modern criticism of "Cinderella" . . . has been so strangely indifferent to the role that Cinderella's mother plays in the story. In our post-Freudian world,

Cinderella's mother is imagined as absent despite the fact that she plays a central part in the unfolding of Cinderella's destiny. Indeed, Cinderella's mother's role is far from marginal: the words and actions of Cinderella's mother are of vital importance in narrative sequencing and the overall "moral" of the story. The Grimms' version of "Cinderella" opens significantly with the dying mother's injunction to the soon-to-be-orphaned girl. On her deathbed, the mother gives Cinderella the following advice: "Dear child, be good and pious. Then the dear Lord shall always assist you, and I shall look down from heaven and take care of you." In fairy tales, the opening scene is always of particular importance, since it is here that the tale sets forth the problem which it will then go on to solve. Cinderella's problem is precisely the fact that her mother has died. It is this "lack," the lack of the mother, which Cinderella must overcome in the course of the story. The narrative instantly complicates her task by staging the arrival of a powerful mother and her two daughters, who, in the strength of their unity, hope to vanquish the motherless girl. Thus the story quickly amplifies the mother/daughter theme, rubbing salt, if you will, in Cinderella's wound. For just as Cinderella's powerlessness is a result of her mother's death, so the stepsisters' power is associated with their strong, scheming mother. In short order, then, Cinderella finds herself in need of her mother's good advice, and it is through keeping her mother's advice that she manages to overcome her own social isolation and the plots of her enemies. In the end, Cinderella rises to a position of power and influence, and she accomplishes this, apparently, despite her motherless status.

But is she really motherless? Not really, since the twig that she plants on her mother's grave grows into a tree that takes care of her, just as her mother promised to do. The mother, then, is figured in the hazel tree and in the birds that live in its branches. Early in the story, the tree offers solace to the grieving girl; later, it gives her the dresses she needs to attend the ball. Likewise, the two pigeons who live in the tree expose the false brides as they ride away, with bleeding feet, on the prince's horse, and they lead the flock of birds who help Cinderella sort the lentils that the stepmother throws on the hearth. In addition, the fleeing Cinderella is said to find safety in a dovecote and a pear tree ("a beautiful tall tree covered with the most wonderful pears"). Since these places of refuge continue the bird/tree symbolism, it is quite possible that we are meant to see the mother's influence also at work in the rather mysterious way that Cinderella manages to avoid too-early detection. Thus, at every turn in the narrative, the magical power of the mother vies with the forces arrayed against Cinderella, whether they be the selfish designs of the step-mother and stepsisters or the futile attempts of the father and prince to capture and identify her. In the end, the mother, despite death, reigns supreme. Not only does she take her revenge on her daughter's enemies by plucking out the eyes of the stepsisters, but, more importantly, she succeeds in bringing about her daughter's advantageous marriage. The happy ending proves that it is the mother, after all, who has been the power of the story. Cinderella's success resides in the fact that, while apparently motherless, she is in fact well-mothered. In spite of death, the mother/daughter dyad has kept its bonds intact. At its most basic level, the story is about this mother/daughter relationship. It is about the daughter's loyalty to the (good) mother's words and the mother's continuing, magical influence in the (good) daughter's life.

Unlike the narratives favored by psychoanalysis, which are about maternal absence and disempowerment, this tale tells a story about a strong mother/daughter relationship that actively shapes events. Cinderella's mother performs a specific social function vis-à-vis her daughter—she assists in her coming out. Her gifts are directed toward a specific goal—to help Cinderella into an advantageous marriage. From this perspective, what is most interest-ing about Cinderella's mother is her similarity to the stepmother. These two women share the same devotion to their daughters and the same long-term goals: each mother wants to ensure a future of power and prestige for her daughter, and each is willing to resort to extreme measures to achieve her aim. Thus, Cinderella's mother is a paradoxical figure: while her power is associated at the outset with the power of the Christian god and while she seems to instruct Cinderella in the value of long-suffering self-sacrifice, she is also a wily competitor. She plots and schemes, and she wins. She beats the stepmother at the game of marrying off daughters. She does for Cinderella exactly what the wicked stepmother wishes to do for her own daughters—she gets her married to the "right" man.

Considering the similarities in their goals and strategies, the idea that Cinderella and her mother are morally superior to the stepsisters and their mother is shot through with contradictions. Throughout the tale, there exists a structural tension between the character that is drawn thematically (the pious Cinderella) and the character that acts in the narrative (the shrewd, competitive Cinderella). The superficial moral of the story would have us believe that Cinderella's triumph at the ball is a reward for her long-suffering patience. But while Cinderella's piety does play an important role in the forging of her supernatural alliance, it plays almost no role in the important practical business of seducing the prince. Indeed, the battle for the prince's attention is not waged at the level of character at all but at the level of clothes. Cinderella wins the battle because her mother is able, through magic, to provide raiment so stunning that no ordinary dress can compete. Cinderella's triumph at the ball has less to do with her innate goodness and more to do with her loyalty to the dead mother and a string of subversive acts: she disobeys the stepmother, enlists forbidden helpers, uses magic powers, lies, hides, dissembles, disguises herself, and evades pursuit. The brutal ending of the tale, in which Cinderella allows the mother (in the form of two pigeons) to peck out the eyes of the stepsisters, further complicates the story's moral thematics.

5   Just as there is a structural tension between the tale's thematization of Cinderella's goodness and the actual plot, so there is a tension between plot and the alleged theme of romantic love. I say "alleged" here because although modern readers and critics have sought to enshrine romantic love as a central value of the tale, there is actually nothing in the text itself to suggest either that Cinderella loves the prince or that the prince loves her. The prince marries Cinderella because he is enchanted (literally) by the sight of her in her magical clothes. What is interesting about these clothes, at least in the Grimms' version, is that, far from simply enhancing a natural but hidden beauty, they actually create it. In the Grimms' version, Cinderella is described as "deformed," while the sisters are described as "fair," so we can only conclude that the power of Cinderella's clothes is indeed miraculous, since they turn a deformed girl into a woman whose beauty surpasses that of the already fair. Thus, the prince's choice of Cinderella can be explained neither by her piety, which he has never experienced, nor by her own beauty, which does not exist. It is the mother's magic which brings about the desired outcome, an outcome in which the prince has actually very little choice. The prince's oft-repeated statement, "She's my partner," as well as his obsessive tracking down of the true bride, suggests that he is operating under a charm rather than as an autonomous character, and the fact that both these motifs are repeated three times is further evidence that magic, not free choice, is at work here.

This is not surprising: the enchantment of a potential marriage partner is one of the most common motifs in fairy tales and mythology. The motif of an enchanted or somehow disguised bride or bridegroom usually appears in tales that depict some kind of unusual marriage, either the marriage of a god or demon to a human (Cupid and Psyche) or the marriage of a poor or ordinary mortal to a member of the deity or the nobility (Beauty and the Beast). The idea, of course, is that one member, by being disguised or by disguising another, can enter into a marriage that he or she would not normally enter into, usually one that crosses class lines. Thus, the enchantment of a prospective bride or bridegroom has more to do with power and manipulation than it does with romance or affection. Rather than talking about

Cinderella's love for the prince, then, it is more accurate to say that Cinderella, in alliance with her mother, bewitches the prince in order to gain the power and prestige that will accrue to her upon her marriage to a member of the nobility.

Review Questions

1. Generally, why is the opening scene of a fairy tale so important? Why is it of particular importance in "Cinderella"?

2. Panttaja claims that, despite death, Cinderella's mother remains very much present in the story. How so?

3. How is Cinderella's mother similar to the stepmother?

4. The claim that Cinderella and her mother are morally superior to the sisters and the mother is "shot through with contradictions." What are these contradictions?

5. Why is romantic love not central to winning the prince, according to Panttaja?

6. What is often the purpose of a disguise or enchantment in fairy tales?

Discussion and Writing Suggestions

1. Does Panttaja's claim that Cinderella's mother is not absent surprise you? Convince you? Explain.

2. What is your response to the claim that Cinderella is not morally superior to the wicked stepsisters or stepmother? Do you find Panttaja's argument compelling? Do you find yourself resisting it? Why?

3. Number the sentences in paragraph 2, and then reread the paragraph and respond to these questions: What is the main point (the topic sentence) and where is it located? How does each sentence advance the main idea of the paragraph? Finally, examine the sequence of sentences. Why does Panttaja place sentences where she does? Having completed the analysis, what is your assessment of the paragraph? How successful is it?

4. If Panttaja is correct in her analysis of "Cinderella," what is the moral of the story? How does this moral compare with the one(s) you normally associate with the story? Do you prefer one moral to another? Why?

What's Wrong with Cinderella? *

Peggy Orenstein

Confronted with a daughter who enjoyed dressing as Cinderella and other story-book princesses, Peggy Orenstein set out to investigate "princess" culture, and the result was her book *Cinderella Ate My Daughter: Dispatches from the Front Lines of*

the New Girlie-Girl Culture (2011). Orenstein is also the author of *Girls & Sex* (2016) and *Waiting for Daisy, a Memoir* (2007). The following first appeared in the *New York Times Magazine* (Dec. 24, 2006).

I finally came unhinged in the dentist's office—one of those ritzy pediatric practices tricked out with comic books, DVDs and arcade games—where I'd taken my 3-year-old daughter for her first exam. Until then, I'd held my tongue. I'd smiled politely every time the supermarket checkout clerk greeted her with "Hi, Princess"; ignored the waitress at our local breakfast joint who called the funny-face pancakes she ordered her "princess meal"; made no comment when the lady at Longs Drugs said, "I bet I know your favorite color" and handed her a pink balloon rather than letting her choose for herself. Maybe it was the dentist's Betty Boop inflection that got to me, but when she pointed to the exam chair and said, "Would you like to sit in my special princess throne so I can sparkle your teeth?" I lost it.

"Oh, for God's sake," I snapped. "Do you have a princess drill, too?"

She stared at me as if I were an evil stepmother.

"Come on!" I continued, my voice rising. "It's 2006, not 1950. This is Berkeley, Calif. Does every little girl really have to be a princess?"

5 My daughter, who was reaching for a Cinderella sticker, looked back and forth between us. "Why are you so mad, Mama?" she asked. "What's wrong with princesses?"

Diana may be dead and Masako disgraced, but here in America, we are in the midst of a royal moment. To call princesses a "trend" among girls is like calling Harry Potter a book. Sales at Disney Consumer Products, which started the craze six years ago by packaging nine of its female characters under one royal rubric, have shot up to $3 billion, globally, this year, from $300 million in 2001. There are now more than 25,000 Disney Princess items. "Princess," as some Disney execs call it, is not only the fastest-growing brand the company has ever created; they say it is on its way to becoming the largest girls' franchise on the planet.

Meanwhile in 2001, Mattel brought out its own "world of girl" line of princess Barbie dolls, DVDs, toys, clothing, home décor and myriad other products. At a time when Barbie sales were declining domestically, they became instant best sellers. Shortly before that, Mary Drolet, a Chicago-area mother and former Claire's and Montgomery Ward executive, opened Club Libby Lu, now a chain of mall stores based largely in the suburbs in which girls ages 4 to 12 can shop for "Princess Phones" covered in faux fur and attend "Princess-Makeover Birthday Parties." Saks bought Club Libby Lu in 2003 for $12 million and has since expanded it to 87 outlets; by 2005, with only scant local advertising, revenues hovered around the $46 million mark, a 53 percent jump from the previous year. Pink, it seems, is the new gold.

Even Dora the Explorer, the intrepid, dirty-kneed adventurer, has ascended to the throne: in 2004, after a two-part episode in which she turns into a "true princess," the Nickelodeon and Viacom consumer-products division released a satin-gowned "Magic Hair Fairytale Dora," with hair that grows or shortens when her crown is touched. Among other phrases the bilingual doll utters: "Vámonos! Let's go to fairy-tale land!" and "Will you brush my hair?"

As a feminist mother—not to mention a nostalgic product of the Garanimals era—I have been taken by surprise by the princess craze and the girlie-girl culture that has risen around it. What happened to William wanting a doll and not dressing your cat in an apron? Whither Marlo Thomas? I watch my fellow mothers, women who once swore they'd never be dependent on a man, smile indulgently at daughters who warble "So This Is Love" or insist on being called Snow White. I wonder if they'd concede so readily to sons who begged for combat fatigues and mock AK-47s.

10 More to the point, when my own girl makes her daily beeline for the dress-up corner of her preschool classroom—something I'm convinced she does largely to torture me—I worry

about what playing Little Mermaid is teaching her. I've spent much of my career writing about experiences that undermine girls' well-being, warning parents that a preoccupation with body and beauty (encouraged by films, TV, magazines and, yes, toys) is perilous to their daughters' mental and physical health. Am I now supposed to shrug and forget all that? If trafficking in stereotypes doesn't matter at 3, when does it matter? At 6? Eight? Thirteen?

On the other hand, maybe I'm still surfing a washed-out second wave of feminism in a third-wave world. Maybe princesses are in fact a sign of progress, an indication that girls can embrace their predilection for pink without compromising strength or ambition; that, at long last, they can "have it all." Or maybe it is even less complex than that: to mangle Freud, maybe a princess is sometimes just a princess. And, as my daughter wants to know, what's wrong with that?

The rise of the Disney princesses reads like a fairy tale itself, with Andy Mooney, a former Nike executive, playing the part of prince, riding into the company on a metaphoric white horse in January 2000 to save a consumer-products division whose sales were dropping by as much as 30 percent a year. Both overstretched and underfocused, the division had triggered price wars by granting multiple licenses for core products (say, Winnie-the-Pooh undies) while ignoring the potential of new media. What's more, Disney films like *A Bug's Life* in 1998 had yielded few merchandising opportunities—what child wants to snuggle up with an ant?

It was about a month after Mooney's arrival that the magic struck. That's when he flew to Phoenix to check out his first "Disney on Ice" show. "Standing in line in the arena, I was surrounded by little girls dressed head to toe as princesses," he told me last summer in his palatial office, then located in Burbank, and speaking in a rolling Scottish burr. "They weren't even Disney products. They were generic princess products they'd appended to a Halloween costume. And the light bulb went off. Clearly there was latent demand here. So the next morning I said to my team, 'O.K., let's establish standards and a color palette and talk to licensees and get as much product out there as we possibly can that allows these girls to do what they're doing anyway: projecting themselves into the characters from the classic movies.'"

Mooney picked a mix of old and new heroines to wear the Pantone pink No. 241 corona: Cinderella, Sleeping Beauty, Snow White, Ariel, Belle, Jasmine, Mulan and Pocahontas. It was the first time Disney marketed characters separately from a film's release, let alone lumped together those from different stories. To ensure the sanctity of what Mooney called their individual "mythologies," the princesses never make eye contact when they're grouped: each stares off in a slightly different direction as if unaware of the others' presence.

It is also worth noting that not all of the ladies are of royal extraction. Part of the genius **15** of "Princess" is that its meaning is so broadly constructed that it actually has no meaning. Even Tinker Bell was originally a Princess, though her reign didn't last. "We'd always debate over whether she was really a part of the Princess mythology," Mooney recalled. "She really wasn't." Likewise, Mulan and Pocahontas, arguably the most resourceful of the bunch, are rarely depicted on Princess merchandise, though for a different reason. Their rustic garb has less bling potential than that of old-school heroines like Sleeping Beauty. (When Mulan does appear, she is typically in the kimonolike hanfu, which makes her miserable in the movie, rather than her liberated warrior's gear.)

The first Princess items, released with no marketing plan, no focus groups, no advertising, sold as if blessed by a fairy godmother. To this day, Disney conducts little market research on the Princess line, relying instead on the power of its legacy among mothers as well as the instant-read sales barometer of the theme parks and Disney Stores. "We simply gave girls what they wanted," Mooney said of the line's success, "although I don't think any of us grasped how much they wanted this. I wish I could sit here and take credit for having some grand scheme to develop this, but all we did was envision a little girl's room and think about how she could live out the princess fantasy. The counsel we gave to licensees was: What type of bedding would a princess want to sleep in? What kind of alarm clock would a princess want to wake up to? What type of television would a princess like to see? It's a rare case where you find a girl who has every aspect of her room bedecked in Princess, but if she ends up with three or four of these items, well, then you have a very healthy business."

Every reporter Mooney talks to asks some version of my next question: Aren't the Princesses, who are interested only in clothes, jewelry and cadging the handsome prince, somewhat retrograde role models?

"Look," he said, "I have friends whose son went through the Power Rangers phase who castigated themselves over what they must've done wrong. Then they talked to other parents whose kids had gone through it. The boy passes through. The girl passes through. I see girls expanding their imagination through visualizing themselves as princesses, and then they pass through that phase and end up becoming lawyers, doctors, mothers or princesses, whatever the case may be."

Mooney has a point: There are no studies proving that playing princess directly damages girls' self-esteem or dampens other aspirations. On the other hand, there is evidence that young women who hold the most conventionally feminine beliefs—who avoid conflict and think they should be perpetually nice and pretty—are more likely to be depressed than others and less likely to use contraception. What's more, the 23 percent decline in girls' participation in sports and other vigorous activity between middle and high school has been linked to their sense that athletics is unfeminine. And in a survey released last October by Girls Inc., school-age girls overwhelmingly reported a paralyzing pressure to be "perfect": not only to get straight A's and be the student-body president, editor of the newspaper and captain of the swim team but also to be "kind and caring," "please everyone, be very thin and dress right." Give those girls a pumpkin and a glass slipper and they'd be in business.

20 At the grocery store one day, my daughter noticed a little girl sporting a Cinderella backpack. "There's that princess you don't like, Mama!" she shouted.

"Um, yeah," I said, trying not to meet the other mother's hostile gaze.

"Don't you like her blue dress, Mama?"

I had to admit, I did.

She thought about this. "Then don't you like her face?"

25 "Her face is all right," I said, noncommittally, though I'm not thrilled to have my Japanese-Jewish child in thrall to those Aryan features. (And what the heck are those blue things covering her ears?) "It's just, honey, Cinderella doesn't really do anything."

Over the next 45 minutes, we ran through that conversation, verbatim, approximately 37 million times, as my daughter pointed out Disney Princess Band-Aids, Disney Princess paper cups, Disney Princess lip balm, Disney Princess pens, Disney Princess crayons and Disney Princess notebooks—all cleverly displayed at the eye level of a 3-year-old trapped in a shopping cart—as well as a bouquet of Disney Princess balloons bobbing over the checkout line. The repetition was excessive, even for a preschooler. What was it about my answers that confounded her? What if, instead of realizing: Aha! Cinderella is a symbol of the patriarchal oppression of all women, another example of corporate mind control and power-to-the-people! my 3-year-old was thinking, Mommy doesn't want me to be a girl?

According to theories of gender constancy, until they're about 6 or 7, children don't realize that the sex they were born with is immutable. They believe that they have a choice: they can grow up to be either a mommy or a daddy. Some psychologists say that until permanency sets in kids embrace whatever stereotypes our culture presents, whether it's piling on the most spangles or attacking one another with light sabers. What better way to assure that they'll always remain themselves? If that's the case, score one for Mooney. By not buying the Princess Pull-Ups, I may be inadvertently communicating that being female (to the extent that my daughter is able to understand it) is a bad thing.

Anyway, you have to give girls some credit. It's true that, according to Mattel, one of the most popular games young girls play is "bride," but Disney found that a groom or prince is incidental to that fantasy, a regrettable necessity at best. Although they keep him around for the climactic kiss, he is otherwise relegated to the bottom of the toy box, which is why you don't see him prominently displayed in stores.

What's more, just because they wear the tulle doesn't mean they've drunk the Kool-Aid. Plenty of girls stray from the script, say, by playing basketball in their finery, or casting themselves as the powerful evil stepsister bossing around the sniveling Cinderella. I recall a headline-grabbing 2005 British study that revealed that girls enjoy torturing, decapitating and microwaving their Barbies nearly as much as they like to dress them up for dates. There is spice along with that sugar after all, though why this was news is beyond me: anyone who ever played with the doll knows there's nothing more satisfying than hacking off all her hair and holding her underwater in the bathtub. Princesses can even be a boon to exasperated parents: in our house, for instance, royalty never whines and uses the potty every single time.

"Playing princess is not the issue," argues Lyn Mikel Brown, an author, with Sharon   **30**
Lamb, of *Packaging Girlhood: Rescuing Our Daughters from Marketers' Schemes*. "The issue is 25,000 Princess products," says Brown, a professor of education and human development at Colby College. "When one thing is so dominant, then it's no longer a choice: it's a mandate, cannibalizing all other forms of play. There's the illusion of more choices out there for girls, but if you look around, you'll see their choices are steadily narrowing."

It's hard to imagine that girls' options could truly be shrinking when they dominate the honor roll and outnumber boys in college. Then again, have you taken a stroll through a children's store lately? A year ago, when we shopped for "big girl" bedding at Pottery Barn Kids, we found the "girls" side awash in flowers, hearts and hula dancers; not a soccer player or sailboat in sight. Across the no-fly zone, the "boys" territory was all about sports, trains, planes and automobiles. Meanwhile, Baby GAP's boys' onesies were emblazoned with "Big Man on Campus" and the girls' with "Social Butterfly"; guess whose matching shoes were decorated on the soles with hearts and whose sported a "No. 1" logo? And at Toys "R" Us, aisles of pink baby dolls, kitchens, shopping carts and princesses unfurl a safe distance from the "Star Wars" figures, GeoTrax and tool chests. The relentless resegregation of childhood appears to have sneaked up without any further discussion about sex roles, about what it now means to be a boy or to be a girl. Or maybe it has happened in lieu of such discussion because it's easier this way.

Easier, that is, unless you want to buy your daughter something that isn't pink. Girls' obsession with that color may seem like something they're born with, like the ability to breathe or talk on the phone for hours on end. But according to Jo Paoletti, an associate professor of American studies at the University of Maryland, it ain't so. When colors were first introduced to the nursery in the early part of the 20th century, pink was considered the more masculine hue, a pastel version of red. Blue, with its intimations of the Virgin Mary, constancy and faithfulness, was thought to be dainty. Why or when that switched is not clear, but as late as the 1930s a significant percentage of adults in one national survey held to that split. Perhaps that's why so many early Disney heroines—Cinderella, Sleeping Beauty, Wendy, Alice-in-Wonderland—are swathed in varying shades of azure. (Purple, incidentally, may be the next color to swap teams: once the realm of kings and N.F.L. players, it is fast becoming the bolder girl's version of pink.)

It wasn't until the mid-1980s, when amplifying age and sex differences became a key strategy of children's marketing (recall the emergence of "'tween"), that pink became seemingly innate to girls, part of what defined them as female, at least for the first few years. That was also the time that the first of the generation raised during the unisex phase of feminism—ah, hither Marlo!—became parents. "The kids who grew up in the 1970s wanted sharp definitions for their own kids," Paoletti told me. "I can understand that, because the unisex thing denied everything—you couldn't be this, you couldn't be that, you had to be a neutral nothing."

The infatuation with the girlie girl certainly could, at least in part, be a reaction against the so-called second wave of the women's movement of the 1960s and '70s (the first wave was the fight for suffrage), which fought for reproductive rights and economic, social and legal equality. If nothing else, pink and Princess have resuscitated the fantasy of romance that that era of feminism threatened, the privileges that traditional femininity conferred on women despite its costs—doors magically opened, dinner checks picked up, Manolo Blahniks. Frippery. Fun. Why should we give up the perks of our sex until we're sure of what we'll get in exchange? Why should we give them up at all? Or maybe it's deeper than that: the freedoms feminism bestowed came with an undercurrent of fear among women themselves—flowing through *Ally McBeal*, *Bridget Jones's Diary*, *Sex and the City*—of losing male love, of never marrying, of not having children, of being deprived of something that felt essentially and exclusively female.

35   I mulled that over while flipping through *The Paper Bag Princess*, a 1980 picture book hailed as an antidote to Disney. The heroine outwits a dragon who has kidnapped her prince, but not before the beast's fiery breath frizzles her hair and destroys her dress, forcing her to don a paper bag. The ungrateful prince rejects her, telling her to come back when she is "dressed like a real princess." She dumps him and skips off into the sunset, happily ever after, alone.

There you have it, *Thelma and Louise* all over again. Step out of line, and you end up solo or, worse, sailing crazily over a cliff to your doom. Alternatives like those might send you skittering right back to the castle. And I get that: the fact is, though I want my daughter to do and be whatever she wants as an adult, I still hope she'll find her Prince Charming and have babies, just as I have. I don't want her to be a fish without a bicycle; I want her to be a fish with another fish. Preferably, one who loves and respects her and also does the dishes and half the child care.

There had to be a middle ground between compliant and defiant, between petticoats and paper bags. I remembered a video on YouTube, an ad for a Nintendo game called Super Princess Peach. It showed a pack of girls in tiaras, gowns and elbow-length white gloves sliding down a zip line on parasols, navigating an obstacle course of tires in their stilettos, slithering on their bellies under barbed wire, then using their telekinetic powers to make a climbing wall burst into flames. "If you can stand up to really mean people," an announcer intoned, "maybe you have what it takes to be a princess."

Now here were some girls who had grit as well as grace. I loved Princess Peach even as I recognized that there was no way she could run in those heels, that her peachiness did nothing to upset the apple cart of expectation: she may have been athletic, smart and strong, but she was also adorable. Maybe she's what those once-unisex, postfeminist parents are shooting for: the melding of old and new standards. And perhaps that's a good thing, the ideal solution. But what to make, then, of the young women in the Girls Inc. survey? It doesn't seem to be "having it all" that's getting to them; it's the pressure to be it all. In telling our girls they can be anything, we have inadvertently demanded that they be everything. To everyone. All the time. No wonder the report was titled "The Supergirl Dilemma."

The princess as superhero is not irrelevant. Some scholars I spoke with say that given its post-9/11 timing, princess mania is a response to a newly dangerous world. "Historically, princess worship has emerged during periods of uncertainty and profound social change," observes

Miriam Forman-Brunell, a historian at the University of Missouri–Kansas City. Francis Hodgson Burnett's original *Little Princess* was published at a time of rapid urbanization, immigration and poverty; Shirley Temple's film version was a hit during the Great Depression. "The original folk tales themselves," Forman-Brunell says, "spring from medieval and early modern European culture that faced all kinds of economic and demographic and social upheaval—famine, war, disease, terror of wolves. Girls play savior during times of economic crisis and instability." That's a heavy burden for little shoulders. Perhaps that's why the magic wand has become an essential part of the princess get-up. In the original stories—even the Disney versions of them—it's not the girl herself who's magic; it's the fairy godmother. Now if Forman-Brunell is right, we adults have become the cursed creatures whom girls have the thaumaturgic power to transform.

In the 1990s, third-wave feminists rebelled against their dour big sisters, "reclaiming"   **40** sexual objectification as a woman's right—provided, of course, that it was on her own terms, that she was the one choosing to strip or wear a shirt that said "Porn Star" or make out with her best friend at a frat-house bash. They embraced words like "bitch" and "slut" as terms of affection and empowerment. That is, when used by the right people, with the right dash of playful irony. But how can you assure that? As Madonna gave way to Britney, whatever self-determination that message contained was watered down and commodified until all that was left was a gaggle of 6-year-old girls in belly-baring T-shirts (which I'm guessing they don't wear as cultural critique). It is no wonder that parents, faced with thongs for 8-year-olds and Bratz dolls' "passion for fashion," fill their daughters' closets with pink sateen; the innocence of Princess feels like a reprieve.

"But what does that mean?" asks Sharon Lamb, a psychology professor at Saint Michael's College. "There are other ways to express 'innocence'—girls could play ladybug or caterpillar. What you're really talking about is sexual purity. And there's a trap at the end of that rainbow, because the natural progression from pale, innocent pink is not to other colors. It's to hot, sexy pink—exactly the kind of sexualization parents are trying to avoid."

Lamb suggested that to see for myself how "Someday My Prince Will Come" morphs into "Oops! I Did It Again," I visit Club Libby Lu, the mall shop dedicated to the "Very Important Princess."

Walking into one of the newest links in the store's chain, in Natick, Mass., last summer, I had to tip my tiara to the founder, Mary Drolet: Libby Lu's design was flawless. Unlike Disney, Drolet depended on focus groups to choose the logo (a crown-topped heart) and the colors (pink, pink, purple and more pink). The displays were scaled to the size of a 10-year-old, though most of the shoppers I saw were several years younger than that. The decals on the walls and dressing rooms—"I Love Your Hair," "Hip Chick," "Spoiled"—were written in "girl-friend language." The young sales clerks at this "special secret club for superfabulous girls" are called "club counselors" and come off like your coolest baby sitter, the one who used to let you brush her hair. The malls themselves are chosen based on a company formula called the G.P.I., or "Girl Power Index," which predicts potential sales revenues. Talk about newspeak: "Girl Power" has gone from a riot grrrl anthem to "I Am Woman, Watch Me Shop."

Inside, the store was divided into several glittery "shopping zones" called "experiences": Libby's Laboratory, now called Sparkle Spa, where girls concoct their own cosmetics and bath products; Libby's Room; Ear Piercing; Pooch Parlor (where divas in training can pamper stuffed poodles, pugs and Chihuahuas); and the Style Studio, offering "Libby Du" makeover choices, including 'Tween Idol, Rock Star, Pop Star and, of course, Priceless Princess. Each look includes hairstyle, makeup, nail polish and sparkly tattoos.

As I browsed, I noticed a mother standing in the center of the store holding a price list   **45** for makeover birthday parties—$22.50 to $35 per child. Her name was Anne McAuliffe; her daughters—Stephanie, 4, and 7-year-old twins Rory and Sarah—were dashing giddily up and down the aisles.

"They've been begging to come to this store for three weeks," McAuliffe said. "I'd never heard of it. So I said they could, but they'd have to spend their own money if they bought anything." She looked around. "Some of this stuff is innocuous," she observed, then leaned toward me, eyes wide and stage-whispered: "But . . . a lot of it is horrible. It makes them look like little prostitutes. It's crazy. They're babies!"

As we debated the line between frivolous fun and JonBenét, McAuliffe's daughter Rory came dashing up, pigtails haphazard, glasses askew. "They have the best pocketbooks here," she said breathlessly, brandishing a clutch with the words "Girlie Girl" stamped on it. "Please, can I have one? It has sequins!"

"You see that?" McAuliffe asked, gesturing at the bag. "What am I supposed to say?"

On my way out of the mall, I popped into the "'tween" mecca Hot Topic, where a display of Tinker Bell items caught my eye. Tinker Bell, whose image racks up an annual $400 million in retail sales with no particular effort on Disney's part, is poised to wreak vengeance on the Princess line that once expelled her. Last winter, the first chapter book designed to introduce girls to Tink and her Pixie Hollow pals spent 18 weeks on the *New York Times* children's best-seller list. In a direct-to-DVD now under production, she will speak for the first time, voiced by the actress Brittany Murphy. Next year, Disney Fairies will be rolled out in earnest. Aimed at 6- to 9-year-old girls, the line will catch them just as they outgrow Princess. Their colors will be lavender, green, turquoise—anything but the Princess's soon-to-be-babyish pink.

50   To appeal to that older child, Disney executives said, the Fairies will have more "attitude" and "sass" than the Princesses. What, I wondered, did that entail? I'd seen some of the Tinker Bell merchandise that Disney sells at its theme parks: T-shirts reading, "Spoiled to Perfection," "Mood Subject to Change Without Notice" and "Tinker Bell: Prettier Than a Princess." At Hot Topic, that edge was even sharper: magnets, clocks, light-switch plates and panties featured "Dark Tink," described as "the bad girl side of Miss Bell that Walt never saw."

Girl power, indeed.

A few days later, I picked my daughter up from preschool. She came tearing over in a full-skirted frock with a gold bodice, a beaded crown perched sideways on her head. "Look, Mommy, I'm Ariel!" she crowed, referring to Disney's Little Mermaid. Then she stopped and furrowed her brow. "Mommy, do you like Ariel?"

I considered her for a moment. Maybe Princess is the first salvo in what will become a lifelong struggle over her body image, a Hundred Years' War of dieting, plucking, painting and perpetual dissatisfaction with the results. Or maybe it isn't. I'll never really know. In the end, it's not the Princesses that really bother me anyway. They're just a trigger for the bigger question of how, over the years, I can help my daughter with the contradictions she will inevitably face as a girl, the dissonance that is as endemic as ever to growing up female. Maybe the best I can hope for is that her generation will get a little further with the solutions than we did.

For now, I kneeled down on the floor and gave my daughter a hug.

55   She smiled happily. "But, Mommy?" she added. "When I grow up, I'm still going to be a fireman."

Discussion and Writing Suggestions

1. If you or someone you know went through a "princess" phase, describe the experience: How did you feel when dressed in a tiara? How did you act? How did you interact with adults? When did you move on from that

phase (that is, if you have!)? Write a description and share it with your classmates.

2. Some parents don't worry that girls will be limited in their adult lives by playing with princess toys. Their position: We move on from childhood games. What's your position?

3. The Disney corporation markets 25,000 princess products to young girls—and that princess merchandizing earns the company $3 billion a year. What about the story of Cinderella and other princesses is so compelling that these characters could support such an enormous enterprise?

4. To what extent do you believe is Disney marketing to a need that already exists in young girls to play the princess? To what extent do you think Disney is *creating* that need through its marketing?

Synthesis Activities

1. In the introduction to this chapter you read: "The selections that follow will challenge your understanding of fairy tale literature and, in particular, 'Cinderella.' An overriding question as you read: Scholars find large, complex messages in these tales. Do you?" Having read the chapter, answer the question and develop this answer into an argument synthesizing your own ideas and those of the authors in this chapter.

2. Along with many other fairy tales, "Cinderella" is a story of reversals and transformations—for instance, of talent and beauty eventually being recognized and valued; of low circumstance rising to good fortune; of haughtiness being punished. Write a paper that both defines and argues for the importance of what you think are two or three key transformations in the story.

3. Choose a key insight from Bettelheim, Baum, Hurley, Zipes, Morrison, Panttaja, or Orenstein as a tool for analyzing some tale other than "Cinderella." You'll readily find candidate tales like "Little Red Riding Hood" or "Hansel and Gretel" online. One useful place to start would be to open a browser and search on "Grimm Brothers pitt" for a comprehensive listing of fairy tales compiled and translated by D. L. Aschliman.

4. In 1910, Antti Aarne published one of the early classifications of folktale types as an aid to scholars who were collecting tales and needed an efficient means for telling where, and with what changes, similar tales had appeared. In 1927, folklorist Stith Thompson, translating and enlarging Aarne's study, produced a work that is now a standard reference for folklorists the world over. We present the authors' description of type 510 and its two forms, 510A ("Cinderella") and 510B.

Use this structure description of "Cinderella" as a basis for writing your own version of the tale, set on a college campus. (The selection by Linda Holmes will also be of use.) As you consider the possibilities for your story, understand that tellers of folktales have always borrowed heavily from earlier versions. Your aim is not to create an altogether new story but one (in *your* language) that is recognizably "Cinderella" recast for your particular time and place.

510. *Cinderella and Cap o'Rushes.*

  I. *The Persecuted Heroine.* (a) The heroine is abused by her stepmother and stepsisters, or (b) flees in disguise from her father who wants to marry her, or (c) is cast out by him because she has said that she loved him like salt, or (d) is to be killed by a servant.

 II. *Magic Help.* While she is acting as servant (at home or among strangers) she is advised, provided for, and fed (a) by her dead mother, (b) by a tree on the mother's grave, or (c) by a supernatural being, or (d) by birds, or (e) by a goat, a sheep, or a cow. When the goat is killed, there springs up from her remains a magic tree.

III. *Meeting with Prince.* (a) She dances in beautiful clothing several times with a prince who seeks in vain to keep her, or she is seen by him in church. (b) She gives hints of the abuse she has endured, as servant girl, or (c) she is seen in her beautiful clothing in her room or in the church.

IV. *Proof of Identity.* (a) She is discovered through the slipper-test, or (b) through a ring which she throws into the prince's drink or bakes in his bread. (c) She alone is able to pluck the gold apple desired by the knight.

 V. *Marriage with the Prince.*

VI. *Value of Salt.* Her father is served unsalted food and thus learns the meaning of her earlier answer.

   Two forms of the type follow.

   A. *Cinderella.* The two stepsisters. The stepdaughter at the grave of her own mother, who helps her (milks the cow, shakes the apple tree, helps the old man). Threefold visit to church (dance). Slipper-test.

   B. *The Dress of Gold, of Silver, and of Stars.* (Cap o'Rushes). Present of the father who wants to marry his own daughter. The maiden as servant of the prince, who throws various objects at her. The threefold visit to the church and the forgotten shoe. Marriage.

5. Speculate on the reasons folktales are made and told. Why do they last? As you develop an answer, rely first on your own hunches regarding the origins and functions of folktale literature. You might want to recall your experiences as a child listening to tales so that you can discuss their effects on you. Rely as well on the variants of "Cinderella," which you should regard as primary sources (just as scholars do). Be sure to use the critical pieces in this chapter to support your argument. Schlesinger, Tatar, and Bettelheim speak

to the psychological appeals of fairy tales. Baum, Hurley, Zipes, Morrison, and Panttaja speak to the sociological and political elements. Draw on sources, but remember that your own speculation should guide the paper.

6. Explain the process by which Cinderella falls in love in two versions of "Cinderella." The paper that you write will be an extended comparison-and-contrast in which you observe this process at work in the variants and then discuss similarities and differences. At the conclusion of your extended comparison-and-contrast, answer the "So what?" question. Pull your observations together and make a statement about Cinderella's falling in love. At some point, you should raise and respond to Elisabeth Panttaja's claim that Cinderella does not, in fact, fall in love in this tale.

7. Watch two of the many filmed versions of "Cinderella" (live actors or animations, your choice). You'll find many listings of candidate films online. Open a browser and search on "Cinderella film list" and you'll be off to a good start. You might also consult a very thorough list in Wikipedia. Once you've selected and watched the films, write a review (that is, a critique) of both. Recalling that the tale has changed depending on time and place, how recognizable are these films as "Cinderella"? Do they retain essential plot elements (see both the selection by Linda Holmes and Synthesis Activity #4)? Where they depart from the classic versions, do they do so in ways that make the films effective for present-day audiences? In your conclusion, argue that the films are, or are not, legitimate variants of "Cinderella."

8. The Disney Corporation makes billions of dollars each year selling its line of "Princess" products. To what extent do you believe the company is marketing to a need that already exists in young girls to play the princess? To what extent do you think Disney is *creating* that need through its marketing? As you respond to these questions, consider the arguments of Bruno Bettelheim, Rob Baum, and Jack Zipes.

9. Folktales can be violent. Are they appropriate for children? Develop your answer into an argument that draws on Schlesinger, Bettelheim, Tatar, Baum, and Zipes.

Research Activities

1. Research the fairytale literature of your ancestors, both the tales and any critical commentary that you can find on them. Once you have read the material, talk with older members of your family to hear any tales they have to tell. (Seek, especially, oral versions of stories you have already read.) In a paper, discuss the role that fairytale literature has played, and continues to play, in your family.

2. Locate and study multiple versions of any fairy tale other than "Cinderella." Having read the versions, identify—and write your paper on—what you feel

are the defining elements that make the tales variants of a single story. If you wish, argue that one version of the tale is preferable to others.

3. Jack Zipes, author of *Breaking the Magic Spell* (1979), takes the approach that fairy tales are far from innocuous children's stories; rather, they inculcate the unsuspecting with the value systems of the dominant culture. In a research paper, explicitly address the assumption that fairy tales are not morally or politically neutral but, rather, present a distinct set of values.

4. Record, and then study, several hours of Saturday morning cartoons. Then locate and read two or three Grimms' fairy tales. In a comparative analysis, examine the cartoons and the fairy tales along any four or five dimensions that you think are important. The point of your comparisons and contrasts will be to determine how well the two types of presentations (the cartoons and the fairy tales) stack up against each other. Which do you find more entertaining? Illuminating? Ambitious? Useful? (These criteria are suggestions only. Generate your own criteria as part of your research.)

5. Arrange to read a fairy tale to a favorite young person. Then talk with him or her about the story, guided by questions you have formed in reading and responding to selections in this chapter. Write an account of your conversation, then reflect on it.

Chapter 15
Advertising

Advertising is a fact of modern life. It is ubiquitous, encountered daily on television, radio, Web sites, billboards, newspapers, magazines, mass-transit posters, and more. Inducements to buy goods and services can be traced as far back as ancient Rome, when pictures were inscribed on walls to promote gladiatorial contests. With low literacy rates and a reliance on handmade goods that kept supplies limited, the ancient world had little need for widespread advertising. But as literacy spread and new manufacturing techniques produced a steady supply of goods for sale, advertising emerged in the eighteenth century as a practical, results-based art form. One of the first American advertisers was Benjamin Franklin, who pioneered the use of large headlines and white space for visual emphasis. Advertising as the mass phenomenon we know is a product of the twentieth century, when the United States became an industrial nation. Particularly in the post–World War II period, a prosperous economy created our modern consumer society marked by the middle-class acquisition of goods and the symbols of status, success, style, and social acceptance. Advertising flourished. Today, we are surrounded not only by a familiar array of billboards, print ads, and broadcast ads, but also by the Internet, which has given us "spam," an entire category of digital pitches for debt reduction, low mortgage rates, and enhanced body parts.

An ad is more than just an appeal to buy. It's also a window into our psyches and culture that reveals our values, our (not-so-hidden) desires, and our yearnings for a different lifestyle. Consider the Marlboro Man, that quintessence of taciturn cowboy masculinity at home only in the rugged American West (in "Marlboro Country"). He's a mid-twentieth-century tribute to what was perceived as nineteenth-century American values, popularized in hundreds of Westerns. According to James Twitchell, a professor of English and advertising at the University of Florida, the Marlboro Man "is what we have for royalty [and] distilled manhood. . . . The Marlboro Man needs to tell you nothing. He carries no scepter, no gun. He never even speaks. Doesn't need to." He's also the product of a bolt of advertising inspiration: Previously, Marlboro had been marketed—unsuccessfully—as a woman's cigarette. By changing the sales pitch and target audience, Philip Morris (the company that manufactures and sells Marlboros) invented a worldwide brand that *Forbes* values at $21.9 billion.

So pervasive and influential has advertising become that it has created a significant backlash among social critics. Among the most familiar accusations are that advertising:

- fosters materialism;
- psychologically manipulates people to buy things they don't need;
- perpetuates gender and racial stereotypes (particularly in its illustrations);
- is deceptive;
- is offensive;
- debases the language; and
- is omnipresent—we cannot escape it.

Although arguing the truth or falsity of these criticisms makes for lively debate, our focus in this chapter is not on the ethics of advertising but rather on how it works. What makes for a successful ad? How do advertisers—and by advertisers we mean not only manufacturers but also the agencies they hire to produce their advertisements—pull our psychological levers to influence us to buy (or think favorably of) their products?

The chapter begins with a general introduction to advertising. You'll learn why good advertising works; you'll watch three scenes from the television series *Mad Men* that dramatize the creative genius that can fuel ad campaigns; you'll read a succinct, fascinating introduction to advertising in America; and you'll learn how a 1959 print ad for the Volkswagen Beetle revolutionized the advertising industry. The chapter then turns to advertising's underlying appeals and principles, which you will use to analyze portfolios of print ads and television commercials.

"Perhaps, by learning how advertising works," writes marketing consultant Charles O'Neill, "we can become better equipped to sort out content from hype, product values from emotions, and salesmanship from propaganda." We hope that the selections in this chapter will equip you to do just that, as well as to develop a greater understanding of one of the most pervasive and complex forms of communication in American mass culture.

Why Good Advertising Works (Even When You Think It Doesn't)

Nigel Hollis

Nigel Hollis, chief global analyst at Millward Brown, a leading market research and consulting company, is the author of *The Global Brand: How to Create and Develop Lasting Brand Value in the World Market* (2010). The following article first appeared in the *Atlantic* on August 31, 2011.

I was having dinner with friends the other evening, and one of the guests made a familiar statement. "I am not influenced by advertising," she said.

For those of us in marketing, this is a familiar thing to hear. I often respond by pointing out that U.S. companies would not invest $70 billion (yes, that's the size of TV's ad market) in something they thought didn't work. Companies expect advertising to produce returns, just like any other investment. The reason that my friend—and, I'm guessing, many of your friends—think advertising doesn't "work" is that they think advertisements are trying to make them do something immediately.

They're wrong.

Successful advertising rarely succeeds through argument or calls to action. Instead, it creates positive memories and feelings that influence our behavior over time to encourage us to buy something at a later date. No one likes to think that they are easily influenced. In fact, there is plenty of evidence to suggest that we respond negatively to naked attempts at persuasion.

Instead, the best advertisements are ingenious at leaving *impressions*. Consider my din-   **5** ner party friend, who, after claiming to be immune to marketing, proceeded to describe an erectile dysfunction ad with impressive detail. She then intoned cigarette ad slogans ("Cal-l-l for-r-r Phil-lip Mor-ray-ssss") from the early 1950s when Philip Morris sponsored the "I Love Lucy" show. . . .

In sum, the best advertisements use images, jingles, and stories to focus attention on the brand. They are not just creative for creative's sake.

From Catchphrases to Cash

Of course, as tickled as advertisers are to know they're writing catchy jingles, they don't make TV commercials for the honor of giving us free new music. They want us to buy something. The crucial challenge for marketers is: What's the best way to translate these memories into actions?

Some imagine a debate between two groups. The first group believes in raw *persuasion*. Its focus is on crafting a compelling argument that will encourage you, with the delivery of "new news," to buy something right away. The second group believes in the power of *engagement*. Its focus is on creating a positive experience that will influence you over the longer-term. Here, the objective is to seed positive ideas and memories that will attract you to the brand.

But this distinction is largely a myth. Advertisers have little control over how audiences receive their message. New news might appear relevant and credible to some ("Geico can save me 15 percent or more? Let's call!"), while others consider it unpersuasive ("Allstate's cheap enough"). Similarly, a TV commercial designed to engage the viewer might cause you to buy the brand immediately, simply because it reminds you of how much you enjoy the product ("Cute Coke spot. You know, I *am* kinda thirsty . . .").

Once in a blue moon an advert might leave you thinking, "Just what I need!" and send   **10** you running out the door to buy something. More often, however, you barely attend to the commercials you see. You do not reflect on the scenes and messages unless triggered by something else at a later date: seeing the advertised brand on the street, when you need to buy the product or, in the case of my friend, talking about it at the dinner table. Even then, it is not the ad that matters. It's the ideas, impressions and positive feelings about the brand that matter. Any memory that will predispose you to view the brand in a more positive light than its alternatives is a plus.

All About Good Vibrations

As demonstrated by my friend, advertising memories can last decades. But my friend's discourse on advertising also touched one of the biggest pitfalls to creating successful TV advertising. Crafting a compelling message or creating an engaging impression is not easy (particularly when trying to reach an increasingly digitally distracted and time poor audience). It is equally difficult to make sure that the intended memories stick to the right brand.

My friend correctly identified the brand in the erectile dysfunction ad as Cialis. Why? Because the ad ended with a couple sitting in separate bath tubs. Bizarre? Yes. But also memorable. And, by dint of repetition, easily linked to the right brand.

So contrary to many people's beliefs, advertising does influence them. But advertising's influence is subtle. Strident calls to action are easily discounted and rejected because they are obvious. But engaging and memorable ads slip ideas past our defenses and seed memories that influence our behavior. You may not think advertising influences you. But marketers do. And in addition to millions of dollars, they have something else most people don't have: Access to data that proves their point.

Discussion and Writing Suggestions

1. Hollis claims that ads persuade us not through logic or calls to immediate action but rather through leaving impressions. Is this your experience with ads? Recall one impression created by an ad you've seen. Write two paragraphs: first, describe the ad; second, describe the impression it left.

2. If, like Hollis's friend, you believe advertising has no effect on you, to what extent would his logic in disproving her claim disprove yours?

3. According to Hollis, "[A]dvertising memories can last decades." What ads do you remember from a decade or more ago? If the memory remains, are you surprised? Why?

4. If Hollis and the industry data he cites ($70 billion spent each year on television advertising) are correct, advertisements "get inside" our heads and affect our (Hollis would say *future*) buying decisions. If you agree that ads manipulate us, how do you feel about this manipulation? If you don't agree, answer Questions #2 and #3, above.

On the Web: *Selling Happiness: Three Pitches from* Mad Men

One of the surprise TV hits of 2007 was *Mad Men*, an original series about the advertising business, created by writer/producer Matt Weiner for the American Movie Classics (AMC) network. *Mad Men*—short for Madison Avenue men—follows Don Draper, creative director of Sterling Cooper, Draper, Pryce, a medium-size New York ad agency, along with his colleagues and his family (and his mistresses), as he maneuvers his way through the ruthlessly competitive world of advertising during the early 1960s. The show has won five Golden Globe Awards for best TV dramatic series. With high-quality writing (creator Matt Weiner was also a writer and producer for *The Sopranos*), top-flight acting, and spot-on production design and period costumes, *Mad Men* became an instant classic, must-see television.

Three segments from the show depict a time-honored business ritual: the "pitch," in which one or more creative/business people attempt to sell their idea to a client in hopes of securing a lucrative contract. As the "Carousel" segment begins, Don Draper (portrayed by Jon Hamm) and his colleagues (accounts director Herman ["Duck"] Phillips [Mark Moses], copywriter Harry Crane [in glasses; Rich Sommer], and art director Salvatore Romano [Bryan Batt]) make a pitch to a couple of clients from Eastman Kodak. The Kodak engineers have just come up with a turning "wheel" to house the slides for its new projector, and the Kodak business execs are making the rounds of New York ad agencies to hear them pitch campaigns to sell this new product. In "It's Toasted," Draper attempts to explain to the clients that despite the federal government's recent lawsuits against cigarette manufacturers for making false health claims about their products, and despite the fact that "[w]e have six identical companies making six identical products," the company can still reassure customers about the safety of its particular brand of cigarettes. In "Pass the Heinz" Don and his colleagues attempt to sell the client, Heinz, on the power of suggestion to market ketchup. Although in the TV show the client passed on the proposal, Heinz actually adopted an identical ad campaign in 2017, crediting not only its own agency, but also Donald Draper and the fictional firm of Sterling, Cooper, Draper, Pryce.

Go to: YouTube.com

Search terms: *"mad men carousel"*

"mad men it's toasted"

"mad men heinz"

Select the longer versions of the first two scenes.

Discussion and Writing Suggestions

1. What do these scenes say about the way that advertising people sell consumer products to the public? What other examples come to mind of items of hardware sold in a manner similar to how Draper and his creative team propose to sell the "Carousel"?

2. Based on Don's reaction as he shows the slides of his family, what might he be thinking during the presentation? Does he appear to believe what he is saying? Does the writer of this scene suggest that advertising is nothing but fakery? Explain.

3. Relate the "Carousel" scene to Jib Fowles's "Fifteen Basic Appeals" of advertising (see pages 537–538). Which appeals are most at work during the presentation of the "Carousel"? Once you have analyzed "Carousel" with respect to one or more motivations reviewed by Fowles, comment on the emotional pull of the "Carousel" pitch as Draper develops it. Even though you understand how Draper's appeal may work psychologically (according to Fowles), can you still be emotionally vulnerable to the pitch? Did you find Draper's presentation moving? Discuss.

4. At one point during the Lucky Strike "It's Toasted" pitch (immediately before the first line in the clip), Don notes: "We have six identical companies making six identical products." What do you think of his solution for making this particular client's "identical" product distinctive—that is, convincing others that it's "safe"? Can you think of other successful advertising campaigns that have created distinctiveness through words alone?

5. The sales pitch for the Heinz ad relies upon the power of suggestion: the ad neither uses the word "ketchup" nor pictures a ketchup bottle. What do you see as the strengths and limitations of the power of suggestion in advertising? Discuss one or two ads, either among those represented in this chapter or others that you have seen, that rely on the power of suggestion.

6. The sales pitches depicted in these meetings were set in an era some sixty years ago and rely on nostalgia, sophistry, and the power of suggestion to succeed. To what extent do you think advertising today relies on such appeals and techniques? Has advertising become any less sophisticated?

An Introduction to Advertising in America

Daniel Pope

Daniel Pope, author of *The Making of Modern Advertising* (1983), teaches in the History department at the University of Oregon and prepared the following introduction to Advertising in America for the Web portal *History Matters*. This portal and its U.S. Survey Course were created by the American Social History Project/Center for Media and Learning (at City University of New York) and by the Roy Rosenzweig Center for History and New Media (at George Mason University). This article was posted on the portal in June 2003.

Over a century ago, *Harper's Weekly* commented that advertisements were "a true mirror of life, a sort of fossil history from which the future chronicler, if all other historical monuments were to be lost, might fully and graphically rewrite the history of our time." Few if any historians today would claim that they could compose a complete history of an era from its advertisements, but in recent years scholars have creatively probed advertisements for clues about the society and the business environment that produced them. The presence of many excellent online collections of advertisements provides learners as well as established scholars the opportunity to examine these sources in new ways. The experience can be tantalizing and frustrating, since advertisements don't readily proclaim their intent or display the social and cultural context of their creation. Yet studying advertisements as historical sources can also be fascinating and revealing.

Most of us—avid consumers though we may be—pride ourselves on being able to "see through" advertisements. We can interpret this phrase in several ways. Most simply, we "see through" ads when we are oblivious to them—when we look right past them, as we do with most ads we encounter daily. Much of what advertising professionals do is aimed at "cutting through the clutter," overcoming our propensity to ignore most ads. In another sense of "seeing through," we dismiss ads because we judge them to be misleading or dishonest. As historians, however, we need to focus on ads and see or hear them. As Yogi Berra put it, "You can observe a lot by watching."

Advertising in America

Despite or because of its ubiquity, advertising is not an easy term to define. Usually advertising attempts to persuade its audience to purchase a good or a service. But "institutional" advertising has for a century sought to build corporate reputations without appealing for sales. Political advertising solicits a vote (or a contribution), not a purchase. Usually, too, authors distinguish advertising from salesmanship by defining it as mediated persuasion aimed at an audience rather than one-to-one communication with a potential customer. The boundaries blur here, too. When you log on to Amazon.com, a screen often addresses you by name and suggests that, based on your past purchases, you might want to buy certain books or CDs, selected just for you. A telephone call with an automated telemarketing message is equally irritating whether we classify it as advertising or sales effort.

In United States history, advertising has responded to changing business demands, media technologies, and cultural contexts, and it is here, not in a fruitless search for the very first advertisement, that we should begin. In the eighteenth century, many American colonists enjoyed imported British consumer products such as porcelain, furniture, and musical instruments, but also worried about dependence on imported manufactured goods.

5   Advertisements in colonial America were most frequently announcements of goods on hand, but even in this early period, persuasive appeals accompanied dry descriptions. Benjamin Franklin's *Pennsylvania Gazette* reached out to readers with new devices like headlines, illustrations, and advertising placed next to editorial material. Eighteenth- and nineteenth-century advertisements were not only for consumer goods. A particularly disturbing form of early American advertisements were notices of slave sales or appeals for the capture of escaped slaves. (For examples of these ads, [go to] the Virginia Runaways Project site.) Historians have used these advertisements as sources to examine tactics of resistance and escape, to study the health, skills, and other characteristics of enslaved men and women, and to explore slaveholders' perceptions of the people they held in bondage.

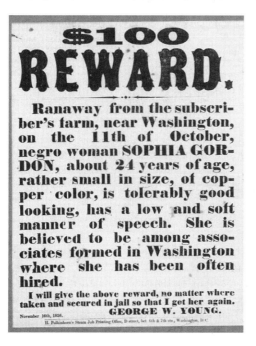

Despite the ongoing "market revolution," early and mid-nineteenth-century advertisements rarely demonstrate striking changes in advertising appeals.

Newspapers almost never printed ads wider than a single column and generally eschewed illustrations and even special typefaces. Magazine ad styles were also restrained, with most publications segregating advertisements on the back pages. Equally significant, until late in the nineteenth century, there were few companies mass producing branded consumer products. Patent medicine ads proved the main exception to this pattern. In an era when conventional medicine seldom provided cures, manufacturers of potions and pills vied for consumer attention with large, often outrageous, promises and colorful, dramatic advertisements.

In the 1880s, industries ranging from soap to canned food to cigarettes introduced new production techniques, created standardized products in unheard-of quantities, and sought to find and persuade buyers. National advertising of branded goods emerged in this period in response to profound changes in the business environment. Along with the manufacturers, other businesses also turned to advertising. Large department stores in rapidly-growing cities, such as Wanamaker's in Philadelphia and New York, Macy's in New York, and Marshall Field's in Chicago, also pioneered new advertising styles. For rural markets, the Sears Roebuck and Montgomery Ward mail-order catalogues offered everything from buttons to kits with designs and materials for building homes to Americans who lived in the countryside—a majority of the U.S. population until about 1920. By one commonly used measure, total advertising volume in the United States grew from about $200 million in 1880 to nearly $3 billion in 1920.

Advertising agencies, formerly in the business of peddling advertising space in local newspapers and a limited range of magazines, became servants of the new national advertisers, designing copy and artwork and placing advertisements in the places most likely to attract buyer attention. Workers in the developing advertising industry sought legitimacy and public approval, attempting to disassociate themselves from the patent medicine hucksters and assorted swindlers in their midst.

While advertising generated modern anxieties about its social and ethical implications, it **10** nevertheless acquired a new centrality in the 1920s. Consumer spending—fueled in part by the increased availability of consumer credit—on automobiles, radios, household appliances, and leisure time activities like spectator sports and movie-going paced a generally prosperous 1920s. Advertising promoted these products and services. The rise of mass circulation magazines, radio broadcasting and to a lesser extent motion pictures provided new media for advertisements to reach consumers. President Calvin Coolidge pronounced a benediction on the business of advertising in a 1926 speech: "Advertising ministers to the spiritual side of trade. It is a great power that has been entrusted to your keeping which charges you with the high responsibility of inspiring and ennobling the commercial world. It is all part of the greater work of regeneration and redemption of mankind." (This address can be found online at a Library of Congress site on "Prosperity and Thrift," which contains many documents on consumer culture in the twenties.) Advertisements, as historian Roland Marchand pointed out, sought to adjust Americans to modern life, a life lived in a consumer society.

Since the 1920s, American advertising has grown massively, and current advertising expenditures are eighty times greater than in that decade. New media—radio, television, and the Internet—deliver commercial messages in ways almost unimaginable 80 years ago. Beneath the obvious changes, however, lie continuities. The triad of advertiser, agency, and medium remains the foundation of the business relations of advertising. Advertising men and women still fight an uphill battle to establish their professional status and win ethical respect. Perhaps the most striking development in advertising styles has been the shift from attempting to market mass-produced items to an undifferentiated consuming public to ever more subtle efforts to segment and target particular groups for specific products and brands. In the

1960s, what Madison Avenue liked to call a "Creative Revolution" also represented a revolution in audience segmentation. Advertisements threw a knowing wink to the targeted customer group who could be expected to buy a Volkswagen Beetle or a loaf of Jewish rye instead of all-American white bread.

Discussion and Writing Suggestions

1. Pope claims that advertisements "don't readily proclaim their intent or display the social and cultural context of their creation." Nonetheless, they do reflect their social and cultural context. How so? Develop your answer by referring to a specific ad or television commercial you know well.

2. "[A]uthors distinguish advertising from salesmanship by defining it as mediated persuasion." Paraphrase this important, though difficult, statement. See Chapter 1 for help on writing paraphrases.

3. The advertising of slaves in America was an abhorrent practice. Follow Pope's pointer to the Virginia Runaways Project site and examine various advertisements. Write a few paragraphs on what you discover.

4. The business environment of the 1880s changed when new manufacturing technologies produced consumer goods in vast quantities. As Pope observes, "National advertising of branded goods emerged in this period in response." In your lifetime, how has advertising also changed in response to a changing business environment?

5. Go online and locate a facsimile copy of the 1897 Sears Roebuck & Co. Catalog. Read a few pages of its advertisements and share your impressions in a paragraph or two. What inferences can you make about what Pope calls the "social and cultural context of [the ads'] creation?" As he points out, attempting such an inference can be "tantalizing and frustrating." But give it a try.

6. In 1926, "President Calvin Coolidge pronounced a benediction on the business of advertising in a 1926 speech: 'Advertising ministers to the spiritual side of trade.'" In what sense could advertising be considered "spiritual"?

7. Pope observes that while much has changed in the world of advertising, some elements persist unchanged. One such element: "Advertising men and women still fight an uphill battle to establish their professional status and win ethical respect." Why should this be?

The Greatest Print Campaigns of All Time: Volkswagen "Think Small"

Joshua Johnson

When *Ad Age* selected Volkswagen's "Think Small" as "the greatest . . . campaign of the [twentieth] century," the editors emphasized its revolutionary impact on the

advertising industry. In the selection that follows, Joshua Johnson explains why. Johnson is an editor and writer for *Designshack.net*, which is dedicated to "showcase[ing] inspiring examples of design." This selection first appeared online in August 2012.

For the varied reactions of *Mad Men*'s Don Draper and his colleagues at the Sterling Cooper ad agency to the unusual "Think Small" campaign, go to YouTube and search: "mad men volkswagen ad."

You're a web designer living large in the 21st century. Your job is defined by screens and software. What in the world could you possibly learn about design from a bunch of old dusty print ads? The answer, of course, is "a ton."

Today we're kicking off a new series that examines some of the most famous print ad campaigns of all time. First up is my personal favorite, the Volkswagen "Think Small" campaign. How did a funny looking car that was named after a bug, known for being slow and manufactured in factories built by Nazis ever become iconic to a generation of post-war Americans? Great design and fantastic marketing.

Think Small

As the 1950s came to a close, Doyle Dane Bernbach (DDB) and Volkswagen decided to completely destroy the status quo for automobile ads with the "Think Small" campaign. The 50s and 60s were a time when cars weren't just a way to get the kids to school. Cars were fashion statements, testosterone boosters, muscles on wheels. They were built to be fast, big, stylish and the ultimate way to earn bragging points.

5 Think of the amazing challenge here for any marketing company that would take on this client. The Volkswagen Beetle was a small, slow, ugly, foreign car that the folks at DDB turned into an iconic piece of American pride. Keep in mind, this wasn't just *any* foreign car either. This was a post-WWII German car, "the people's car," a **Nazi** car whose development was tied to Adolf Hitler himself.

If you asked me to sell this vehicle to a country still bitter about a war that threatened their most core ideals, I would've thought you were nuts. How in the world did they pull it off?

The answer is mind-bogglingly amazing from a marketing perspective: they were honest, boldly so. To see what I mean, consider the copy in the ad below **[using your Web browser, search "Volkswagen presenting America's slowest fastback"]**.

Presenting America's slowest fastback.

There are some new cars around with very streamlined roofs.
But they are not Volkswagens.
They are called fastbacks, and some of them are named after fish.
You can tell them from Volkswagens because a VW won't go over 72 mph.
(Even though the speedometer shows a wildly optimistic top speed of 90.)
So you can easily break almost any speed law in the country in a VW.
And you can also cruise right past gas stations, repair shops and tire stores.
The VW engine may not be the fastest, but it's among the most advanced. It's made of magnesium alloy (one step better than aluminum). And it's so well machined you may never add oil between changes.
The VW engine is cooled by air, so it can never freeze up or boil over.
It won't have anything to do with water.
So we saw no reason to name it after a fish.

This ad starts off doing the exact opposite of what you would expect in a car ad. It launches into a discussion about how slow Volkswagens are! It talks about how cool and streamlined fastback cars are and how the Volkswagen won't even go over 72 mph. What the heck?

Set the Hook and Reel Them In

If you woke up to find this ad in your newspaper in the 1960s, you were thoroughly confused and just had to read it. At this point, they've already won. They've sucked you in with clever copy that seems to actually insult their product. What's the angle here?

As you read on, the tone of the ad takes a turn:

So you can easily break almost any speed law in the country in a VW. And you can also cruise right past gas stations, repair shops and tire stores. The VW engine may not be the fastest, but it's among the most advanced.

See what they did there? It's a classic straw man situation. They set up this ideal car and told you why the VW wasn't anything like it, then they bashed in the straw man by telling you how this was a good thing. The VW isn't fast, so it doesn't guzzle gas, burn through tires or need frequent repairs. Wait, that sounds pretty nice actually. It's not fast, it's smart. That was something average, everyday Joes could identify with and even find desirable.

The VW

Also note how the car is discussed in the ads. It's frequently referred to as a "VW" instead   **10** of a Volkswagen. Volkswagen is a mouthful that doesn't remotely sound American. VW is cool, fresh, simple and friendly. They planted this thought in your head without you even realizing it!

In less than a minute, you just went from wondering if it was socially acceptable to even own such a vehicle to having a cute nickname for it. I do love a good sleight of hand, and this one is masterful.

Solid Brand Building

The marketing copy for the "Think Small" campaign was pure genius and is definitely what makes this one of my favorite campaigns of all time. The genius doesn't stop there though. To highlight and reinforce this message, the graphics had to be stellar. The answer? Whitespace and lots of it.

This isn't a "lifestyle" ad. The car isn't depicted as an integral piece of the daily lives of a smiling, middle class family. It's a black dot on a sea of white. Tied together with the head-line, "Think Small," this was paradoxically an understatement that was somehow bold and shocking. Maybe owning a small car was a good thing after all. Heck, maybe it was even a great thing.

On an empty background, your eyes are forced to take in the car. This tricks you into seeing the vehicle in a new light; the way the designers saw it. Not as an ugly foreign car in a sea of American beauties but as a uniquely attractive design statement oozing with personality.

The ad copy may have appealed to the family man, but the high fashion, personality-   **15** driven visuals in this campaign would lead the Volkswagen on to become a favorite among teenagers looking to make a statement.

Longevity

The two ads above take us through the early to midsixties, let's fast forward another decade and see how Volkswagen was marketing their vehicles in the 70s **[using your Web browser, search "Volkswagen if you can't decide between a station wagon and a van get both"]**.

Look familiar? Three quarters of the ad is dedicated to a large image with the bottom quarter getting a headline and three columns of type. The format obviously held up quite well over time!

But something has changed. We're not selling a small car any more. Volkswagen isn't thinking small, they're obviously thinking big! *How* they're selling it is the same old story though: economy. The Volkswagen Wagon is the smart choice. It has all of the benefits of a wagon and a van wrapped into one amazingly fuel efficient vehicle with comfortable seating for seven.

Know Your Roots

Helmut Krone, Julian Koenig, William Bernbach, these names should mean something to you. If you don't know who they are, find out. Can you be a good designer without this knowledge? Absolutely. But you simply can't put a value on perspective.

20   Knowing where your profession came from, as well as what not only worked in the past but also stood the test of time, brings an appreciation and understanding that changes how your mind works when you sit at that desk. You're not just a designer. You're part of an ongoing legacy.

These people were selling funny cars; why would anyone care who they were or what they were doing? Yet here we are, fifty-three years later, examining their genius under a microscope. I implore you, value the work that you do. Put so much thought and effort into it that people will still care in fifty years.

Discussion and Writing Suggestions

1. Go online to "Vintage Ad Broswer" and search for "vintage cars." Read a few of the ads from the 1950s and 1960s and compare the ad copy and images to those in Volkswagen's "Think Small" campaign. In selecting the VW ad as the best of the twentieth century, the editors of *Ad Age* cited its revolutionary impact on the advertising industry. Having read Johnson's article and examined other automobile ads from the era, discuss one or two of the elements that qualify the "Think Small" campaign as revolutionary.

2. The copywriters of the "Think Small" campaign seem almost to be winking at readers, bringing them in on a joke. What is that joke, and why, on getting it, are readers made to feel smart? How does this rapport with readers help to promote the Volkswagen Beetle?

3. Johnson begins his piece with a question: "You're a web designer living large in the 21st century. Your job is defined by screens and software. What in the world could you possibly learn about design from a bunch of old dusty print ads? The answer, of course, is 'a ton.'" Has Johnson delivered on his answer in discussing this particular ad? Has he offered convincing reasons why Web designers today should pay attention to old print ads?

4. Reread Johnson's section on the use of white space in the "Think Small" campaign. Open a magazine and examine a few ads for use of white space. What do you find?

5. Johnson draws a lesson from his analysis of the "Think Small" campaign: "Knowing where your profession came from, as well as what not only worked in the past but also stood the test of time, brings an appreciation and understanding that changes how your mind works when you sit at that desk. You're not just a designer. You're part of an ongoing legacy." Your comments?

Advertising's Fifteen Basic Appeals*

Jib Fowles/Shirley Biagi

Drawing upon studies of numerous ads and upon interviews with subjects conducted by Harvard psychologist Henry A. Murray, media studies educator Jib Fowles developed a set of fifteen basic psychological appeals that he believes to be at the heart of American advertising. These appeals are directed primarily to the "lower brain," to those "unfulfilled urges and motives swirling in the bottom half of [our] minds," rather than to the part of the brain that processes our more rational thoughts and impulses.

Fowles has written numerous articles and books on the popular media, including *Mass Advertising as Social Forecast*: *A Method for Futures Research* (1976), *Why Viewers Watch*: *A Reappraisal of Television's Effects* (1992), *Advertising and Popular Culture* (1996), and *The Case for Television Violence* (1999). The selection that follows is a summary of Fowles's often-cited appeals, written by Shirley Biagi for *Media Impact*: *An Introduction to Mass Media, fourth edition* (1999).

To influence your choices, the advertising message must appeal to you for some reason, as you sift through the ads to make judgments and choose products. Humanities and human sciences professor Jib Fowles in his book *Mass Advertising as Social Forecast* enumerated fifteen appeals, which he calls an "inventory of human motives" that advertisers commonly use in their commercials.

Advertising's 15 Basic Appeals, by Jib Fowles (from *Mass Advertising as Social Forecast*)

1. *Need for sex.* Surprisingly, Fowles found that only 2 percent of the television ads he surveyed used this appeal. It may be too blatant, he concluded, and often detracts from the product.

2. *Need for affiliation.* The largest number of ads use this approach: you are looking for friendship? Advertisers can also use this negatively, to make you worry that you'll lose friends if you don't use a certain product.

3. *Need to nurture.* Every time you see a puppy or a kitten or a child, the appeal is to your paternal or maternal instincts.

4. *Need for guidance.* A father or mother figure can appeal to your desire for someone to care for you, so you won't have to worry. Betty Crocker is a good example.

5. *Need to aggress.* We all have had a desire to get even, and some ads give you this satisfaction.

6. *Need to achieve.* The ability to accomplish something difficult and succeed identifies the product with winning. Sports figures as spokespersons project this image.

7. *Need to dominate.* The power we lack is what we can look for in a commercial: "Master the possibilities."

8. *Need for prominence.* We want to be admired and respected; to have high social status. Tasteful china and classic diamonds offer this potential.

9. *Need for attention.* We want people to notice us; we want to be looked at. Cosmetics are a natural for this approach.

10. *Need for autonomy.* Within a crowded environment, we want to be singled out, to be a "breed apart." This can also be used negatively: you may be left out if you don't use a particular product.

11. *Need to escape.* Flight is very appealing; you can imagine adventures you cannot have; the idea of escape is pleasurable.

12. *Need to feel safe.* To be free from threats, to be secure is the appeal of many insurance and bank ads.

13. *Need for aesthetic sensations.* Beauty attracts us, and classic art or dance makes us feel creative, enhanced.

14. *Need to satisfy curiosity.* Facts support our belief that information is quantifiable and numbers and diagrams make our choices seem scientific.

15. *Physiological needs.* Fowles defines sex (item no. 1) as a biological need, and so he classifies our need to sleep, eat, and drink in this category. Advertisers for juicy pizza are especially appealing late at night.

Discussion and Writing Suggestions

1. What do you think of Fowles's analysis of "advertising's fifteen basic appeals"? Does this classification seem an accurate and useful way of accounting for how most advertising works upon us? Would you drop any of his categories, or perhaps incorporate one set into another set? Has Fowles neglected to consider other appeals that you believe to be equally important? If so, can you think of one or more advertisements that employ such appeals omitted by Fowles?

2. Categorize several of the print ads in the ad portfolio later in the chapter (pp. 539–544), using Fowles's schema. Explain how the headlines, body text, and graphics support your categorization choices.

3. To what extent do you believe that advertisers in recent years have increased their reliance on overt sexual appeals? Cite examples.

4. Fowles believed that the need to belong, or to "affiliate," is an especially powerful appeal. (See #2 in the list above.) Locate or cite print or broadcast ads that rely on the need for affiliation. How do the graphics and text of these ads create impressions that touch on the need to affiliate?

5. Conduct (perhaps with one or more classmates) your own analysis of a set of contemporary advertisements. Select a single issue of a particular magazine, such as *Time* or the *New Yorker*. Review all of the full-page ads, classifying each according to Fowles's categories. Note that an ad may make more than one appeal, but generally one appeal will be primary. What do your findings show? Which appeals are the most frequent? The least frequent? Which are most effective? Why? You may find it interesting to compare the appeals of

advertising in different magazines aimed at different audiences—for example, a general-interest magazine, such as *Newsweek,* compared with a more specialized magazine, such as *Glamour* or *Guns and Ammo.* To what extent do the types of appeals shift with the gender or interests of the target audience?

A Portfolio of Print Ads

The following roundup of Internet-based advertising archives preserves tens of thousands of (mostly print) advertisements for your review and enjoyment. In addition to locating ads in these archives, you can search for individual ads by entering "advertisement" and a product or product category (such as cigarettes or alcohol) into a search engine.

The first goal of referring you to these archives is to have you search, browse, and enjoy according to your interests, in the process gaining a broad sense of the evolution of advertising over the last half-century. The second purpose is to have you locate ads, or pairings of ads, that you find worthy of close attention. Analyze these ads according to either of two sets of criteria.

ASSIGNMENT

Either

>Identify and discuss the primary appeal made by the ad(s), in terms of Fowles's categories (see pages 537–538). What, if any, are the secondary appeals?

Or

>Bear in mind the general questions about advertisements raised by the preceding readings in the chapter. Consider, for instance, several of these questions and, in response, develop one or more into an analysis:

>1. What appears to be the target audience for this advertisement? If it was produced more than two decades ago, how would this target audience likely react today to the ad?

>2. What is the chief attention-getting technique in the ad?

>3. To what extent does the ad seek to persuade directly, through argument? To what extent indirectly, through leaving impressions to be acted on later?

>4. How does the ad make use of such tools as humor, surprise, fantasy, wonder, human interest, or social concern to achieve its goals?

>5. Considered alone, without supporting words, how do the expressions, the clothing, the postures of the person or people, and the physical objects in the ad help communicate its message?

>6. How do the words of the ad work to communicate its message?

>7. How do the visuals of the ad and the words work together to achieve a particular effect?

Advertising Archives

The Advertising Archive is a British-based Web site devoted to ads dating from the mid-nineteenth century through the present. Founded by Larry Viner and Suzanne Viner in 1990, it is the largest such archive in Europe. Use its robust search engine to locate thousands of both British and American advertisements. Search terms for locating this Web site: "advertising archives uk."

Duke University Media Collections

One of the digital holdings maintained by the Duke University library system is the John W. Hartman Center for Sales, Advertising & Marketing History. This publicly available resource provides access to more than seven thousand U.S. and Canadian advertisements for products as varied as "Beauty and Hygiene, Radio, Television, Transportation, and World War II propaganda." The archive is also home to more than 9,000 advertisements documenting the "Emergence of Advertising in America." Search terms for locating this Web site: "duke hartman digital collection."

Lürzer's Int'l Archive: Advertising Worldwide

In 1984, Walter Lürzer, director of a German-based ad agency, set out to curate especially creative ads from across the globe. The result, in those pre-Internet days, was *Lürzer's Archive* magazine, which continues to be published internationally. Today, the magazine is supplemented by an extensive online archive focusing on a "principle of 'curatorship of inspiration' [that] presents the most interesting new print campaigns, TV commercials and, more recently, digital designs from all over the world." Search terms for locating this Web site: "lurzer archive."

Ad Council: Public Service Ads

The Advertising (or Ad) Council is a nonprofit organization that works with the federal government, businesses, ad agencies, and media outlets to "raise awareness or change behaviors and attitudes on a social issue"—attitudes toward smoking, for instance, or fundraising efforts in support of disaster victims. Both nonprofits (like the World Wildlife Federation) and the federal government approach the Ad Council with ideas for Public Service Announcements (PSAs). Ad agencies then donate their talent to create the PSAs, and 33,000 media outlets (owners of magazines, newspapers, billboards, and radio and television stations) distribute the ads for free. The Ad Council estimates that on "average, each Ad Council general market campaign garners between $25–30 million in donated media per year. In addition, the media donates about $1.8 billion annually to Ad Council campaigns." Search terms for locating this Web site: "ad council psa central library." Once at the site, you can conduct your own search or browse various campaigns.

DISASTERS DON'T PLAN AHEAD. YOU CAN.

DON'T WAIT. COMMUNICATE.

Talk to your loved ones about how you are going to be ready in an emergency.

VISIT READY.GOV/PLAN.

AdClassix.com

The Ad Classix Web site is a search engine that connects online buyers to the sellers of over one million original, vintage advertisements printed during the twentieth century. Designed as a resource for collectors, AdClassix also functions as an archive for researchers investigating more than forty different product categories ranging from Automobiles and Beer to Railroad Travel and Watches. Within any one category, advertisements are arranged chronologically so that you can readily compare, say, the two ads for Ford automobiles reproduced here. Search terms for locating this Web site: "ad classix."

$780

Ford
Model T
Touring
Car

4 Cylinders
5 Passengers

Fully equipped with Extension Top, Automatic Brass Windshield, Two 6-inch Gas Lamps, Generator, Speedometer, Three Oil Lamps, Horn and Tools — (an equipment many other manufacturers charge from $250 to $300 extra for)—all for $780, f. o. b. Detroit.

1914 Ford Model T

Bernard was a born loser. He couldn't win at Solitaire, even when he cheated. Enter Mustang—the car that's practical, sporty, luxurious. Your choice! Bernard chose the sporty options. Got a 289 cu. in. V-8. Four-on-the-floor. Tachometer and clock combo. Special handling package. Front disc brakes— and did Bernie's luck change! Yesterday he won San Francisco in a faro game. And now he's got his eye on New York. Mustangers always win.

Best year yet to go Ford

MUSTANG!
MUSTANG!
MUSTANG!

1995 Ford Mustang GT

A Primer on Analyzing Television Commercials

Arthur Asa Berger

Former Fulbright scholar and professor emeritus in electronic communication arts at San Francisco State University, media critic Arthur Asa Berger has written dozens of articles and books on media criticism. The following "Primer on Analyzing Television Commercials" first appeared in his *Manufacturing Desire: Media, Popular Culture, and Everyday Life* (1996).

Here I would like to consider some of the more important aspects of television commercials. We must remember that a television commercial is . . . a special kind of work of art—one which is created to persuade, to shape behavior in specific ways. But it still is a work of art and therefore can be analyzed much the same way a film or television program can be understood: in terms of its various components and the role they play in the production.

The narrative structure. What happens in the commercial and what significance do the various actions and events have? How might the actions and events affect viewers and what meaning do they have for people? In this area we focus on the story-line of the commercial and its symbolic significance.

Dialogue and language. What do the characters say to one another and, in some cases, what are they saying to us? What devices do they use to gain our attention or affection and to persuade us? What rhetorical techniques, such as alliteration or metaphor or metonymy, are used? What kind of language is used? What use is made of phenomena such as humor, comparisons, associations, exaggeration, praise, and logic?

Actors and actresses. Sometimes we forget that when we watch commercials we are seeing actors and actresses plying their trade. But rather than trying to convince us they are Hamlet or Ophelia, they try to convince us they are housewives who love this or that product or rugged he-men who love this or that brand of light beer. Do we feel attracted to them and empathize with them? What kinds of symbolic figures are used as characters in the commercial? What use do the performers make of facial expression, body language and their voices? What about the clothes they wear? How old are they, and what significance do their ages have? What's interesting about the setting in which they are found?

Technical matters: lighting, color, editing and music. Here we concern ourselves with **5** how lighting, cutting and shot selection impact upon viewers. For instance, close-ups lead to a different feeling about things than longshots and shots from below convey different attitudes toward power than shots from above. Does the commercial have many quick cuts in it? If so, what impact does this have? How are things lighted and what kind of use is made of color? All of these matters are kinds of "messages" and must be included in any analysis of a television commercial.

Sound and music. We are profoundly affected by sound and music, which seem to have the power to work directly on our psyches. What use is made of sound effects? Is there music used? If so, what kind and for what purposes? How does it affect us?

Signs, symbols and intertextual devices. Signs and symbols are phenomena which represent other things: a cross can represent Christianity, the sacred, religion, and so on. *Intertextuality* refers to the process by which we interpret one text in terms of another. Thus parody, for example, is based upon ridiculing a text (which must be known in order for the parody to work). The associative power of texts can be used to suggest things or ideas connected with the original text. This means that commercials can take advantage of what people already know—about history, literature, the arts, and popular culture—in getting their messages across.

In short, every aspect of a commercial—from the typefaces used in captioning to the hairstyles of the performers—can be considered as potentially important. Commercials are complex and "rich" works of art that demand a great deal of attention if one is to discover the mechanisms by which they achieve their aims.

Discussion and Writing Suggestions

1. Berger claims that television commercials are a "special kind" of art. In what ways are commercials *not* works of art?

2. Select any of Berger's criteria for analyzing television commercials and apply it to a commercial you find noteworthy. For instance, if you choose what Berger calls the "commercial's narrative structure," you would (at least) summarize its story; identify its beginning, middle, and end; identify characters, their functions, and the changes they undergo; and study conflicts and resolutions. Use "narrative structure" or any of Berger's other criteria to analyze how the commercial achieves its effects.

3. Berger writes: "The associative power of texts can be used to suggest things or ideas connected with the original text. This means that commercials can take advantage of what people already know—about history, literature, the arts, and popular culture—in getting their messages across." One famous example would be Apple's Super Bowl commercial introducing the Macintosh computer. (Search terms: "apple 1984 commercial.") Can you think of other examples?

4. Discuss whether or not you agree with Berger's assertion that commercials "are complex and 'rich' works of art that demand a great deal of attention if one is to discover the mechanisms by which they achieve their aims."

A Portfolio of Television Commercials

The world's first television commercial was a ten-second Bulova watch ad broadcast in 1941. But it wasn't until the 1950s, when TV became a mass medium, that the commercial became a ubiquitous feature of popular culture. Before viewers had the technology to fast-forward through commercials, many probably regarded TV ads as annoying, occasionally informative or entertaining, but generally unnecessary accompaniments to their television experience. But of course the commercial is not simply an extraneous by-product of TV programming. It is television's very reason for existence. Before the age of public TV and of cable and satellite providers, television programs were financed entirely by the companies that created the commercials and that paid networks and local stations to broadcast them. Viewed from a marketing angle, the only purpose of commercial television is to provide a medium for advertising. The news, comedy, drama, game, and variety shows offered by TV are simply ways of luring viewers to watch the commercials.

Still, the unceasing deluge of commercials of every type means that advertisers have to figure out ways of making their messages stand out by being unusually creative, funny, surprising, or otherwise noteworthy. The standard jingles, primitive animation, catchphrases ("Winston tastes good like a cigarette should"), and problem-solution minidramas of TV commercials work for a while but are quickly forgotten in the onslaught of new messages. It becomes the job of advertising agencies (of the type represented in *Mad Men*) that create both print and TV ads to make their clients' products stand out by ever more ingenious and striking ways of delivering their messages. To do this, these agencies rely not just on information about the product and clever audiovisual techniques; they attempt to respond to what they believe consumers crave, deep down. TV commercials, no less than print ads, rely on psychological appeals of the type discussed by Jib Fowles in his "Advertising's Fifteen Basic Appeals" (see pages 537–538).

The following portfolio includes some of the most noteworthy and successful TV commercials of the past sixty years. Many (though not all) of these commercials are featured in Bernice Kanner's *The 100 Best TV Commercials . . . and Why They Worked* (1999), where you will find additional description and commentary. To access the commercials, go to YouTube (YouTube.com) and enter the search terms provided under the commercial's title into the search box. In some cases, additional information is presented, in brackets, to help you navigate to the commercial. In cases where multiple versions of the same commercial are available, you may have to experiment to determine which one offers the best video and audio quality. In a few cases, uploaded commercials have been truncated, so you should generally select the longest version. In some cases, the indicated commercials may have been removed from the YouTube Web site. No matter; thousands more remain available for your observation and consideration.

We provide two or three specific questions for each TV commercial to stimulate your thinking and writing process about the particular ways in which it works. More formally, you should choose one or more of these commercials for a careful analysis. You can approach this assignment in any of three ways.

ASSIGNMENT

A. Identify and discuss the primary appeal made by the ad(s), in terms of Fowles's categories (see pages 537–538). What, if any, are the secondary appeals?

B. Identify and discuss the primary appeal made by the ad(s), in terms of Berger's categories (see pages 545–546).

or

C. Bear in mind the general questions about advertisements raised by the preceding readings in the chapter. Consider, for instance, using any of these questions to guide your writing of an analysis:

1. What appears to be the target audience for this TV commercial? If it was produced more than two decades ago, how would this target audience likely react today to the ad?

2. **What is the chief attention-getting technique in the commercial?**

3. **To what extent does the commercial seek to persuade directly, through argument? To what extent indirectly, through leaving impressions to be acted on later?**

4. **How does the commercial make use of such tools as humor, surprise, fantasy, wonder, human interest, or social concern to achieve its goals?**

5. **What is the relationship between the visuals and the audio track? How do audio and video work together—or in contrast—to achieve the sponsor's purpose?**

6. **How do the commercial's visual techniques work to convey the message? Consider camera movement (or the lack of camera movement); the style and pace of editing (the juxtaposition of individual shots); and visual composition (the framing of the people and/or objects within the shot).**

7. **How do the expressions, the clothing, the postures of the person or people, and the physical objects in the shots help communicate the ad's message?**

8. **How do the words used by the actor(s) or by the voice-over narrator work to communicate the message of the commercial?**

Note: Because Web content frequently changes without warning, not all of the listed videos may be available when you attempt to access them. It is possible that errant searches may lead to other videos with objectionable content. Such videos, as well as user-submitted comments under the specified videos below, do not reflect the views of the authors or of Pearson Publishing.

Commercials of the 1960s

Volkswagen: Snowplow

YouTube Search Terms: vw snow plow commercial [select black and white version]

1. In the 1960s, Volkswagen became famous in the United States not only for its funny-looking cars—so different in style from Detroit's massive passenger vehicles—but also for its "soft-sell" approach to print ads and TV commercials. How does that soft-sell approach work in this ad? What is the sales strategy, as embodied in the relatively primitive visuals and the voice-over track? What exactly is being sold?

2. The closing shot of this commercial shows a snowplow driving past a Volkswagen. How does this image encapsulate the message of the ad? Write a sentence that expresses the message Volkswagen wants to communicate, without regard to the particular visuals of the ad.

Union Carbide: Chick

YouTube Search Terms: union carbide chick super insulation

1. How does the visual (the commercial is unusual in consisting of a single, continuous shot) work *with* and work *against* the soundtrack voice-over? To what extent do you

"hear" the narrator's voice—and his message—as you watch the image of the metal box in the beaker of boiling water?

2. To what extent is there a danger that this commercial could backfire and create bad feeling about Union Carbide because of what is portrayed?

Alka Seltzer: Spicy Meatball

YouTube Search Terms: alka seltzer meatball

1. Some TV commercials employ a "fake-out" strategy, based partially on our knowledge of other commercials. How does this approach work in the Alka Seltzer ad? Do you think it is likely to succeed in persuading viewers to buy the product?

2. Like many successful TV commercials, this one relies on humor, grounded in human foibles and imperfections, and based on our experience that if things can go wrong, they generally will. How do the visuals and the audio track of the Alka Seltzer ad employ this kind of humor as a sales strategy?

Commercials of the 1970s

Chanel No. 5: Share the Fantasy

YouTube Search Terms: chanel 5 fantasy

1. In many ways, this celebrated commercial—directed by filmmaker Ridley Scott (*Alien, Blade Runner, Thelma and Louise, Gladiator*)—is, stylistically, at the opposite pole from the gritty Volkswagen "Snowplow" commercial. Comment.

2. Chanel No. 5 is one of those products sold primarily on its "mystique." How do the visuals and the soundtrack of this commercial reinforce that mystique? "Read" the images and interpret them, in light of the product.

Quaker Oats: Mikey

YouTube Search Terms: quaker oats mikey

1. Why don't the older kids want to try Life cereal? How does reluctance tie into Quaker Oats's larger marketing problem with the product? How does the commercial attempt to deal with this problem?

2. Many viewers came to hate this commercial because it was shown repeatedly and because it lasted so many years. Still, it endured because many other viewers found it endearing—and it did the job of publicizing the product. Do you think a commercial such as this one would work today? Explain.

Coca-Cola: Mean Joe Greene

YouTube Search Terms: coca cola joe greene

1. This commercial is a study in contrasts. Identify some of these contrasts (both visual and aural), and explain how they work as part of the sales strategy.

2. To what emotions does this commercial attempt to appeal? Did you find this appeal successful?

3. Like many commercials, this one is presented as a minidrama, complete with plot, character, setting, theme, and other elements found in longer dramas. Explain the way that the drama functions in this ad, particularly as it concerns the characterization of the two actors.

Commercials of the 1980s

Federal Express (FedEx): Fast-Paced World [with John Moschitta]

YouTube Search Terms: federal express fast talker

1. The actor in this commercial, John Moschitta, was for many years celebrated in the *Guinness Book of World Records* as the world's fastest talker (he was clocked at 586 words per minute). How does Moschitta's unique skill make him an ideal spokesperson for Federal Express?
2. There is always a danger that particularly striking ads may be counterproductive, in that they draw attention to their own cleverness or unusual stylistic qualities, rather than to the product being sold. Put yourself in the position of a Federal Express executive. To what extent might you be concerned that this commercial, clever as it is, would not succeed in making more people select Federal Express as their express delivery service? On the other hand, might any striking commercial for Federal Express be successful if it heightened public recognition of the brand?

Pepsi-Cola: Archaeology

YouTube Search Terms: pepsi cola archaeology

1. Summarize the main selling point of this commercial. How does this selling point relate to (1) the basic situation presented in the commercial and (2) Pepsi's slogan, as it appears at the end?
2. Pepsi-Cola and Coca-Cola have been engaged in fierce rivalry for more than a century. How does this commercial exploit that rivalry to humorous effect? How is each product visually represented in the ad?
3. As contrasted with the Volkswagen "Snowplow" ad or the Quaker Oats "Mikey" ad, this ad features lavish production values and is presented as if it were a science fiction film. How do the sets, costumes, props, and special effects help support the overall sales strategy of the ad?

Levi's: Launderette

YouTube Search Terms: levi's launderette

1. How do the reactions of the various characters to the young man in this ad contribute to its overall effect? How does the young man's appearance figure into the overall effect?
2. What role does the musical track (Marvin Gaye's "I Heard It Through the Grapevine") play in this commercial?

Commercials of the 1990s

Jeep: Snow Covered

YouTube Search Terms: jeep snow covered

1. "This may have been the most arrogant commercial ever made," declared the creative director of the agency that produced it. In what way might this be so? Possible arrogance aside, is this an effective advertisement for Jeep? Explain.
2. How do the visuals support the message of the ad? What *is* that message?

Energizer: Darth Vader

YouTube Search Terms: energizer darth vader 1994

1. The Energizer bunny was featured in numerous commercials of the 1990s, generally in settings where its sudden appearance was totally unexpected. How do the creators of this add draw upon the *Star Wars* mythology to support their sales pitch? In what way is the strategy of this ad similar to that of Alka Seltzer's "Spicy Meatball"?

2. In a sentence, summarize the message of this ad—without mentioning *Star Wars* or Darth Vader.

Got Milk? (California Milk Processor Board): Aaron Burr [original Got Milk? Commercial]

YouTube Search Terms: got milk burr

1. The opening of this commercial is intended to convey a sense of culture and sophistication. How do the images and the soundtrack do this? Why is this "setup" necessary in terms of the ad's message? What is that message?

2. In the latter half of the commercial, how does the accelerated pace of the editing and camera work—and of the soundtrack—contribute to the ad's overall impact?

Commercials of the 2000s

The Gap: Pardon Our Dust

YouTube Search Terms: gap dust

1. This commercial was directed by filmmaker Spike Jonze (*Adaptation*, *Where the Wild Things Are*). Describe your reactions as you watched this ad. What did you think was happening as the mayhem within the store accelerated?

2. What is the effect of the "Pardon Our Dust" title when it appears?

3. What is the relationship of the visuals and the soundtrack (including the music of Grieg's "In the Hall of the Mountain King")?

4. According to the Web site "Top 10 Coolest Commercials by Movie Directors," Spike Jonze was asked by Gap executives to produce a commercial about the stores' new look. Bewildered by what Jonze delivered, the company ran the commercial in a few cities, then pulled it off the air after about a month. Did the company make the right decision (from a marketing standpoint)?

Honda: Physics

YouTube Search Terms: honda physics

1. Put yourself in the position of the ad agency copywriters for Honda *before* they conceived of this particular ad. What is your main selling point? Express, in a sentence, what you want to communicate to the public about Honda automobiles and engineering.

2. This commercial involves no computer graphics or digital tricks; everything that happens is real. All the components we see came from the disassembling of two Honda Accords. The voice is that of *Lake Woebegon Days* author Garrison Keillor. According to Honda,

this single continuous shot required 606 takes—meaning that for the first 605 takes, something, usually minor, went wrong, and the recording team had to install the setup again and again. There is always a danger (for the client) that memorable commercials such as this one will amaze and impress viewers but will also fail to implant brand identification in their minds. Do you think there may be such a problem with this commercial? To what extent are viewers who have seen it likely, days or weeks later, to identify it with Honda and to associate whatever message (if any) they draw from the commercial with the particular qualities of Honda automobiles?

Sony Bravia: Bunnies

YouTube Search Terms: sony bunnies

1. Some of the same visual techniques used in this ad (to portray an unstoppable swarm of creatures that speedily overrun an urban area) have also been used—to very different effect—in horror films. What mood is conveyed by the visual and soundtrack elements of this commercial? How is this mood achieved?
2. Discuss how some of the visual techniques and special effects of this ad contribute to its effectiveness in conveying the benefits of the Sony Bravia.

Dove: Onslaught

YouTube Search Terms: dove onslaught

1. What is the message of this ad?
2. How does the cinematic style of the visuals reinforce that message? Focus, in particular, on the contrasting visual styles used for the child and (later in the ad) her classmates, on the one hand, and the rest of the images, on the other. Consider, for example, how long the first image remains on screen, compared to those that follow.

Tide to Go: Interview

YouTube Search Terms: tide to go interview

1. What is the message of this ad? How do the simple visuals and the more complex soundtrack work together (and against one another) to support that idea?
2. Like many contemporary TV ads, this one relies on humor. To what extent do you find humor used effectively here? What is the source of the humor? How do the two actors help create that humor? How is this humor rooted in common concerns and fears that we all share?

Planters Peanuts: Perfume

YouTube Search Terms: planters perfume

1. Many of the elements in this ad are also found in perfume commercials. How are these elements used here to comic effect? Compare the mood and the visual style of this ad to that of a real perfume ad, the Chanel No. 5 "Share the Fantasy" commercial. Of what other commercials does this one remind you? Why?
2. Like the Gap "Pardon Our Dust" commercial, the Planters ad relies on the visual motif of comic mayhem. Do you think such visuals are an effective way of selling the product? Explain.

VW, "The Force"

YouTube Search Terms: volkswagen the force

1. How does this commercial play against the Darth Vader image and mythology for the purpose of selling cars?
2. This commercial became a cultural phenomenon, with the child star even appearing on *Today* for an interview. Why do you think it became so popular? Consider the style, the storyline, the images and sound, and the message.

Chrysler, "Detroit"

YouTube Search Terms: chrysler detroit or chrysler Eminem

1. This commercial juxtaposes images of the long-decayed landscape of America's one-time car capital with images of Detroit viewed from a moving car, and later, of a luxury automobile in motion. What kind of images of the city are viewed from the car, and what meanings or emotions do they evoke? How successful do you judge the clashing motifs of decay and luxury in achieving the objectives of the ad's message? What *is* that message?
2. The soundtrack to this commercial features a song by Eminem (born Marshall Bruce Mathers III), an American rapper, producer, songwriter, actor, and half of the Detroit hip-hop duo Bad Meets Evil. Eminem does have a personal connection to Detroit, but to what extent do you think that the producers of the commercial made a good choice in using this particular musician in this particular commercial?
3. Compare and contrast the intended audiences for this commercial and the Volkswagen "Darth Vader" commercial above. Then compare and contrast the audience for either of these two commercials with Volkswagen "Snowplow," Jeep "Snow Covered," and Honda "Physics." What assumptions are made in these commercials about the tastes and values of their respective audiences?

DirecTV, "Dog Collar"

YouTube Search Terms: directv dog collar

1. Many commercials rely on humor to help convey the advertiser's message. Among such ads represented in this portfolio: Alka Seltzer, "Spicy Meatball"; Quaker Oats, "Mikey"; FedEx, "Fast-Paced World"; Pepsi Cola, "Archaeology"; Energizer, "Darth Vader" (and another Darth Vader ad, VW, "The Force"); Got Milk? "Aaron Burr"; and Tide to Go, "Interview." How does the humor in DirecTV's commercial compare and contrast to the humor in some of these other funny commercials? What is it we're actually smiling at when we view these commercials?
2. Would this commercial help persuade you (by its ironclad chain of reasoning) to switch from cable to DirecTV? If not, why do you think the company decided to create and air it?
3. The "Dog Collar" spot was one of a series of three similarly themed commercials created by DirecTV in 2012. Among the others in the series: "Don't Wake Up in a Roadside Ditch" and "Stop Taking in Stray Animals." Here's your chance to be a famous copywriter: Create another 30-second spot in this series. Describe the visuals, and write the script for the voice-over.

Melbourne, Australia Metro Trains, "Dumb Ways to Die"

Youtube Terms: dumb ways to die

1. Nearly 150 million people have watched this public service announcement on YouTube. Why do you think it was so popular?
2. What's the effect of waiting until the last frame of the commercial to reveal its purpose: to be safe around trains?
3. Find one of the many articles written on "Dumb Ways to Die" and its international success. Summarize what you find and share your summary with others. You'll learn about the creative team behind the ad, how the accompanying song came to be written, how the ad went viral and expanded to different media, and more.

Always Like a Girl—Keep Playing

Youtube Search Terms: always #like a girl

1. What is the logical connection between this commercial and the product being advertised? (*Always* is the brand name for a line of feminine hygiene products.)
2. To what extent does this commercial illustrate Nigel Hollis's contention that successful ads favor creating positive impressions (that lead to later sales) over hard-hitting arguments (that lead to an immediate purchase)? What positive impression does this commercial make?
3. In what ways can this commercial be illuminating for boys and men as well as for girls and women?

Knorr LoveAtFirstTaste

YouTube Search Terms: knorr love first taste

1. Three seconds into this commercial, we see a blindfolded man with his mouth open being fed by a woman who instructs him to "Open your mouth." Then we see all-caps text across the screen: "Can Flavor Help You Find Love?" This is provocative material. Within this briefest of openings, what cues can you see, or hear, that assure you the coming commercial won't be offensive?
2. This video for Knorr products went viral, garnering some 60 million YouTube views. We won't color your reactions by divulging whether the producers used plain folks or professional actors when filming. But we'll raise the question: Would it make a difference to you if these young men and women on food "dates" were paid actors? Why or why not?
3. Knorr is a company that makes seasonings for food. Distill into a single sentence the logic of this commercial and its relation to Knorr products.

Budweiser: Waassup

Youtube Search Terms: wassup 2000 original

1. What is the relationship among these friends? What do the brewers of Budweiser hope to achieve by linking their beer to these particular people?
2. How does the question/exclamation "Wassup" change meaning, depending on which character is speaking? List and discuss possible meanings.

P&G: Thank You, Mom

YouTube Search Terms: P&G thank mom

1. This commercial tugs—very hard!—at the emotional heartstrings. (You might even find yourself shedding a few tears.) How is it possible, in two minutes, for a commercial to achieve such emotional impact?

2. P&G manufactures hygiene products, paper towels, detergents, toothpaste—an enormous array of products. In this commercial, P&G isn't selling any single product. What, then, is its purpose? What does the emotionally loaded "Thank you, Mom" mean coming from a publicly traded company with $10.5 billion in net earnings (2016)?

3. P&G's takeaway message (in case we missed it) appears in a closing frame: "It takes someone strong to make someone strong." This statement may or may not be true. In either event, how is it related to P&G and the products it sells?

4. The commercial aired during the 2016 Olympic Games in Rio. What makes the messaging pertinent for the Olympics?

Mobile Strike, "Arnold's Fight"

YouTube Search Terms: arnold's fight mobile 50

1. Why choose Arnold Schwarzenegger to represent this particular product?

2. What does the game Mobile Strike promise, based on this commercial?

3. Comment on the commercial's production values. Do you find the commercial entertaining? Why? How persuaded are you to download the game?

Additional TV Commercials

To view additional TV commercials, you might want to begin with AdWeek's excellent "The World's 24 Best Commercials 2015–2016," which can easily be found in an online search of that title. Other favorites, arranged chronologically, follow. Note: Unless otherwise indicated, all commercials listed were produced in the United States.

Democratic National Committee: "Daisy Girl" (1964)
YouTube search terms: democratic daisy ad

American Tourister Luggage: Gorilla (1969)
YouTube search terms: luggage gorilla

Chevrolet: "Baseball, Hot Dogs, Apple Pie" (1969)
YouTube search terms: america baseball hotdogs

Keep America Beautiful: "Crying Indian" (1970)
YouTube search terms: america crying indian

Coca Cola: "Hilltop" ("I'd Like to Buy the World a Coke") (1971)
YouTube search terms: buy world coke 1971

Hovis: "Bike Ride" (UK, 1973) [shot by Ridley Scott]
YouTube search terms: hovis bike

Xerox: "Monks" (1975)
YouTube search terms: xerox monks

Hebrew National: "Higher Authority" (1975)
YouTube search terms: hebrew national higher

BASF: "Dear John" (New Zealand, 1979)
YouTube search terms: basf dear john

Lego: "Kipper" (UK, 1980)
YouTube search terms: lego kipper

Apple: Macintosh (1984)
YouTube search terms: apple macintosh

Sony Trinitron: "Lifespan" (UK, 1984)
YouTube search terms: sony trinitron advert

American Express: "Stephen King: (1984)
YouTube search terms: american express king

The Guardian: "Points of View" (UK, 1987)
YouTube search terms: guardian points of view

Volkswagen: "Changes" (UK, 1988)
YouTube Search Terms: vw changes

Energizer: "Bunny Introduction" (1989)
YouTube search terms: energizer bunny introduction 1989

Dunlop: "Tested for the Unexpected" (1993)
YouTube search terms: dunlop tested unexpected

Swedish Televerket: "Noxin" (Sweden, 1993)
YouTube Search Terms: Noxin

Little Caesar's Pizza: "Training Camp" (1994)
YouTube search terms: caesar's training camp

Campbell's Soup: Winter Commercial (1995)
YouTube search terms: campbell's soup winter

California Milk Processor Board: "Got Milk? Heaven" (1996)
YouTube search terms: got milk heaven

Ameriquest Mortgage: "Plane Ride" (2008)
YouTube search terms: ameriquest plane ride

Audi: "Oil Parade" (2009)
YouTube search terms: audi oil parade

Jack in the Box: "Junk in the Box" (2009)
YouTube search terms: jack in the box junk in the box

Nolan's Cheddar: "Seriously Strong" (2010)
YouTube search terms: nolan cheddar

Nissan Leaf: "Gas Powered Everything" (2011)
YouTube search terms: nissan leaf gas everything

Red Bull: "Stratos" (2012)
YouTube search terms: red bull stratus [version:1:30]

Robinsons: "Pals" (2013)
YouTube search terms: robinson pals

Android: "Friends Furever" (2015)
YouTube search terms: friends furever

Amazon: "Amazon Prime" (2016)
YouTube search terms: amazon priest imam [version 1:20]

General Electric: "Millie" (2017)
YouTube search terms: ge millie

Synthesis Activities

1. Browse the Portfolio of Print Ads and select three to five ads for a single product category (cigarettes, alcohol, cars, tooth-paste, etc.). Choose ads from different decades, if possible. Compare and contrast the types of appeals underlying these ads, as discussed by Fowles. To what extent do you notice significant shifts of appeal over time, to the present? Which types of appeal seem to you most effective? Is it more likely, for example, that people will buy cigarettes because they want to feel autonomous or because the cigarettes will make them more attractive to the opposite sex?

2. Browse the Portfolio of Television Commercials and select a commercial to analyze, using as many of Berger's criteria as seem appropriate. The purpose of this analysis is to reveal how the commercial works artistically to achieve its aims. (Try to understand these aims. Refer to Hollis or Fowles for help.) Be sure to conclude with an overall assessment: How successful is this commercial as an object of art? How effectively does this commercial promote a particular product or service?

3. Select a series of print ads and television commercials in different product categories that all appear to rely on the same primary appeal as defined by Jib Fowles—perhaps the appeal to sex or the appeal to affiliation. Drawing upon Fowles and other authors as needed, compare and contrast the overall strategies of these ads and commercials. In your conclusion, the paper should address this question: To what extent are people buying an image rather than a product?

4. As indicated in the introduction to this chapter, social critics have charged advertising with numerous offenses. The most common criticisms: advertising fosters materialism, it psychologically manipulates people to buy things they don't need, it perpetuates gender and racial stereotypes (particularly in its illustrations), it is deceptive, it is offensive, and it debases the language. Select three advertisements from the Portfolio of Television Commercials and three from the Portfolio of Print Ads (that is, from the listing of archives on pages 539–544). To what extent do these television commercials and print ads demonstrate the truth of one or more of these charges?

5. To sell a product, many print ads and television commercials employ humor—in the graphics or video; in the body copy, dialogue, or voiceover; or both. Examine a group of advertisements that rely on humor to make their appeal, and explain how these ads work.

6. Compare and contrast any three of five television commercials for cars: Chrysler "Detroit" (p. 553), Energizer "Darth Vader" (p. 551), Volkswagen

"Snowplow" (p. 548), Jeep "Snow Covered" (p. 550), and Honda "Physics" (p. 551–552). Turn to the sources in this chapter to develop criteria for comparison and contrast. Use these criteria to make observations about each commercial and observations *across* commercials. How are they alike? How do they differ? What are your conclusions?

7. Think of a new product that you have just invented. This product, in your opinion, will revolutionize the world of (fill in the blank). Devise an advertisement to announce this product to the world. Consider (or reject) using a celebrity to help sell your product. Select the basic appeal of your product (see Fowles).

8. Imagine that you own a small business—perhaps an independent coffee shop (not Starbucks, Peet's, or Coffee Bean), a video game company, or a pedicab service that conveys tourists around a chic beach town. Devise an ad or a brief video that announces your services and extols its benefits. Apply the principles discussed by Fowles, Berger, or other writers in this chapter. For inspiration, you may want to watch the suggested scenes from *Mad Men* (see p. 526–527).

9. Write a parody ad—one that would never ordinarily be written—applying the selling principles discussed by Fowles and/or Berger. For example, imagine you are the manager of the Globe Theatre in Elizabethan England and want to sell season tickets to this season's plays, including a couple of new tragedies by your playwright-in-residence, Will Shakespeare. Or imagine that you are trying to sell Remington typewriters in the age of computers (no software glitches!). Or—as long as people are selling bottled water—you have found a way to package and sell air. Advertisers can reportedly sell anything with the right message. Give it your best shot. For inspiration, you may want to watch the suggested scenes from *Mad Men* (see p. 526–527).

10. Based on the reading you have done in this chapter, discuss the extent to which you believe advertisements create needs in consumers, reflect existing needs, or some combination of both. In developing your paper, draw on the scenes from *Mad Men*, on particular advertisements that you select, and on the more theoretical overviews of advertising developed by Fowles and/or Berger.

11. As you have seen, advertisements change over time, both across product categories and within categories. And yet advertising remains a constant, its presence built on the assumption that consumers can be swayed both overtly and covertly in making purchasing decisions. In a paper drawing on the selections in this chapter, develop a theory on why ads change over time. Is it because people's needs have changed and, therefore, new ads are required? (Or do older ads appeal to the same needs as newer ads?) In developing your discussion, you might track the changes over time in one product category.

Research Activities

1. Drawing upon contemporary magazines (or magazines from a given period), select a set of advertisements in a particular product category. Analyze these advertisements according to Fowles's categories, and assess their effectiveness.

2. Select a particular product that has been selling for at least twenty-five years (e.g., Bayer aspirin, Tide detergent, IBM computers, Ford trucks) and trace the history of print advertising for this product. To what extent has the advertising changed over the years? To what extent has the essential sales appeal remained the same? In addition to examining the ads themselves, you may want to research the company and its marketing practices. You will find two business databases particularly useful: ABI/INFORM and the academic version of LexisNexis.

3. One of the landmark campaigns in American advertising was Doyle Dane Bernbach's series of ads for the Volkswagen Beetle in the 1960s (see pages 532–536). In effect a rebellion against standard auto advertising, the VW ads' unique selling proposition was that ugly is beautiful—an appeal that was overwhelmingly successful. Research the VW ad campaign for this period, setting it in the context of the agency's overall marketing strategy.

4. Among the great marketing debacles of the twentieth century was Coca-Cola's development in 1985 of a new formula for its soft drink that (at least temporarily) replaced the much-beloved old formula. Research this major development in soft drink history, focusing on the marketing of New Coke and the attempt of the Atlanta-based Coca-Coca Company to deal with the public reception of its new product.

5. Advertising agencies are hired not only by manufacturers and by service industries; they are also hired by political candidates. In fact, one of the common complaints about American politics is that candidates for public office are marketed just as if they were bars of soap. Select a particular presidential or gubernatorial election and research the print and broadcast advertising used by the rival candidates. You may want to examine the ads not only of the candidates of the major parties, but also the candidates of the smaller parties, such as the Green and the Libertarian parties. How are the appeals and strategies used to sell products both similar to and different from those used to support political candidates?

6. Public service ads (PSAs—both print and televised) comprise another major category of advertising in addition to product and service advertising and political advertising. (To gain a sense of the creativity and power of PSAs, browse the archive maintained by the Advertising Council—see the Web pointer on page 542.) Such ads have been used to recruit people to military service, to get citizens to buy war bonds, to obtain contributions for charitable

causes, to get people to support or oppose strikes, to persuade people to stop using (or not to start using) drugs, to prevent drunk driving, and so on. Locate a group of public service ads, describe them, and assess their effectiveness. Draw upon Fowles and/or Berger in developing your conclusions.

7. Research advertising in American magazines and newspapers before World War II. Focus on a limited number of product lines—for example, soft drinks, soap and beauty products, health-related products. What kind of differences do you see between ads in the first part of the twentieth century and more recent or contemporary advertising for the same types of products? In general, how have the predominant types of appeals used to sell products in the past changed (if they have) with the times? How are the graphics of early ads different from preferred graphics today? How has the body copy changed? (Hint: You may want to be on the alert for ads that make primarily negative appeals—i.e., what may happen to you if you don't use the product advertised.) See pages 540 and 543 for pointers to online archives of vintage ads that could help in your research.

Credits

Image Credits

Intro   Page 2: Siamphoto/Fotolia. **Page 4:** (tl) MPI/Archive Photos/Getty Images; (tr) The Natural History Museum/Alamy Stock Photo; (b) Phil Robinson/age fotostock. **Page 5:** (t) National Park Service; (b) Cranach/Shutterstock. **Page 6:** juliasudnitskaya/Fotolia. **Page 7:** (tl) Jolanta Wojcicka/123RF; (tm) Julia Reschke/Shutterstock; (tr) ThomasLENNE/Shutterstock; (bl) Courtesy Hamill Gallery of Tribal Art; (bm) Used with the permission of Elizabeth Rupp; (br) jackhollingsworth.com/Shutterstock. **Page 8:** (bl) Julia Reschke/Shutterstock; (br) Mexrix/Shutterstock. **Page 10:** patrimonio designs ltd/Shutterstock.

Chapter 1   Page 19: Dorling Kindersley/Getty Images.

Chapter 4   Page 121: (l) Jolanta Wojcicka/123RF; (r) Julia Reschke/Shutterstock; (m) ThomasLENNE/Shutterstock. **Page 122:** Phil Robinson/age fotostock.

Chapter 6   Page 160: (l) itsmejust/Shutterstock; (r) Erik Isakson/Fancy/Age fotostock. **Page 161:** (l) TURNER ENTERTAINMENT/Ronald Grant Archive/ALamy Stock Photo; (r) Pictorial Press Ltd/Alamy Stock photo.

Chapter 8   Page 232: Courtesy of Greg Blair.

Chapter 9   Page 254: From the film "Obedience" © 1968 by Stanley Milgram. **Page 255:** From the film "Obedience" © 1968 by Stanley Milgram.

Chapter 15   Page 529: PF-(bygone1)/Alamy Stock Photo. **Page 530:** Library of Congress Prints and Photographs Division. **Page 531:** Sears, Roebuck & Co. **Page 533:** The Advertising Archives/Alamy Stock Photo. **Page 540:** The Advertising Archives/Alamy Stock Photo. **Page 541:** The Advertising Archives/Alamy Stock Photo. **Page 542:** © The Advertising Council. **Page 543:** Publicite pour la Ford T/Bridgeman Images. **Page 544:** The Advertising Archives/Alamy Stock Photo.

Text Credits

Intro   Page 9: © 2012 IEEE. Reprinted, with permission, from A Brief History of Money: Or, how we learned to stop worrying and embrace the abstraction, IEEE Spectrum By James Surowiecki, May 30, 2012. **Page 10:** David Graeber, "On the Invention of Money – Notes on Sex, Adventure, Monomaniacal Sociopathy and the True Function of Economics." Naked Capitalism.com.

Chapter 1   Page 16: Manuel Velasquez et al. A Framework for Thinking Ethically. Reprinted with permission of the Markkula Center for Applied Ethics at Santa Clara University (www.scu.edu/ethics). **Pages 18, 22, 54, and 59:** Jyutika Mehta, 2015. "External Enhancements of Memory May Soon Go High-Tech." The Conversation, http://theconversation.com/total-recall-sounds-great-but-some-things-should-be-forgotten-51715. This article originally appeared in The Conversation. **Page 20:** National Center for PTSD. http://www.ptsd.va.gov/about/mission/mission-and-overview.asp. **Page 24:** Rob Kling. "Social Relationships in Electronic Forums," Computer-Mediated Communication Magazine, 1996. **Page 26:** U.S. Department of Education: "Media—Helping Your Child Through Early Adolescence" Department of Education. http://www2.ed.gov/parents/academic/help/adolescence/partx.html. **Page 33:** Paul Bloom, The Baby in the Well: The Case against Empathy. The New Yorker Magazine. http://www.newyorker.com/arts/critics/atlarge/2013/05/20/130520crat_atlarge_bloom?currentPage=1. Copyright © 2013 Conde Nast. **Page 45:** US Census. 2000. https://www.census.gov/prod/2004pubs/c2kbr-35.pdf. **Page 47:** Congressional Budget Office 2010. **Page 49:** Visas Issued in 2012. Jill H. Wilson, Brookings Institute, Immigration Facts: Temporary Foreign Workers 18 June 2013. pictogram under paragraph 2. http://www.brookings.edu/research/reports/2013/06/18-temporary-workers-wilson; Brookings Institute. 2014. http://www.brookings.edu/research/interactives/2014/geography-of-foreign-students#/M10420. Used with permission. **Page 54:** Jim Steinmeyer. 2003. Hiding the Elephant. DeCapo/Perseus; Jyutika Mehta, 2015. "External Enhancements of Memory May Soon Go High-Tech." The Conversation,http://theconversation.com/total-recall-sounds-great-but-some-things-should-be-forgotten-51715.

Griego, Tina: "Tiger Mother stirs reflections on parenthood" by Tina Griego from THE DENVER POST, January 20, 2011. Copyright 2011. Used by permission. **Page 280:** "Tiger Mom vs. Tiger Mailroom" by Patrick Goldstein published February 6, 2011 in the LOS ANGELES TIMES. Copyright 2011. Used by permission. **Page 283:** Elizabeth Kolbert. "America's Top Parent." Originally from The New Yorker, Jan. 31, 2011. Copyright © 2011. Used by permission of the author.

Chapter 11   Page 298: J. D Salinger, The Catcher In The Rye, Little, Brown and Company, 1951; Hilary Mantel, Wolf Hall, London: Fourth Estate, 2009. **Page 303:** "Chapter 1: The Hook" by K. M. Weiland from STRUCTURING YOUR NOVEL: ESSENTIAL KEYS FOR WRITING AN OUTSTANDING STORY. PenForASwordPublishing, LLC. Copyright 2013. Used by permission. **Page 309:** Jane Austen, Pride and Prejudice, UK: T. Egerton, Whitehall, 1813. **Page 311:** Charlotte Bronte, Jane Eyre, Smith, Elder, and Company, 1847. **Page 315:** Charles Dickens, Great Expectations, Chapman & Hall, 1861. **Page 319:** Robert Louis Stevenson, The Strange Case of Dr. Jekyll & Mr. Hyde, UK: Longmans, Green & Co., 1886. **Page 323:** L. Frank Baum, The Wonderful Wizard of Oz. George M. Hill Company, 1900. **Page 325:** Willa Cather, My Antonia, Boston: Houghton Mifflin, 1918. **Page 330:** Tim Long, How to Start Your Script: A Killer Opening Scene is the Hero Your Screenplay Deserves, MovieMaker, September 16, 2016, http://www.moviemaker.com/archives/moviemaking/screenwriting/opening-scene. **Page 351:** Variety, 1994 Interview with Francis Ford Coppola. **Page 352:** Do The Right Thing: A Spike Lee Joint. Spike Lee with Lisa Jones. New York: Simon and Shuster, 1989, p. 29. **Page 355:** Thomas Schatz, Hollywood Genres: Formulas, Filmmaking, and The Studio System. New York: McGraw-Hill, 1981. **Page 360:** A. O. Scott, "Soldiers on a Live Wire Between Peril and Protocol", The New York Times, June 25, 2009. **Page 364:** Margaret Mitchell, Gone With the Wind, Macmillan, 1936. **Page 365:** 12 Years A Slave' Was A Film That 'No One Was Making', NPR.org, October 24, 2013.

Chapter 12   Page 369: Stanley Kubrick, 2001: A Space Odyssey (1968). **Pages 371 and 425:** LUGER, GEORGE F., ARTIFICIAL INTELLIGENCE: STRUCTURES AND STRATEGIES FOR COMPLEX PROBLEM SOLVING, 6th Ed., © 2009. Reprinted and Electronically reproduced by permission of Pearson Education, Inc., New York, NY. **Page 374:** Carolyn Mathas, "2030—Ray Kurzweil's Predictions or Bill Joy's Fears?" IEEE, February 26, 2016, http://electronics360.globalspec.com/article/6352/2030-ray-kurzweil-s-predictions-or-bill-joy-s-fears. Used courtesy Electronics360.com IEEE GlobalSpec. **Page 377:** The Future of Life Institute, An Open Letter on Artificial Intelligence, 2015, https://futureoflife.org/ai-open-letter/. Used with permission. **Page 378:** Stuart Russell, Daniel Dewey, Max Tegmark, "Research Priorities for Robust and Beneficial Artificial Intelligence," AI Magazine, WINTER 2015, pp. 105–114. 2015, Association for the Advancement of Artificial Intelligence. © 2015, Association for the Advancement of Artificial Intelligence. **Page 380:** Arthur Schlesinger, Jr. What Great Books Do for Children, A Life in the Twentieth Century: Innocent Beginnings, 1917–1950, Houghton Mifflin Harcourt, 2002; Seán Ó hÉigeartaigh, The Future of Artificial Intelligence, http://www.crassh.cam.ac.uk/blog/post/blog-the-future-of-artificial-intelligence. Used with permission. **Page 383:** Motion for a European Parliament Resolution to the Commission on Civil Law Rules on Robotics, Committee on Legal Affairs, European Parliament, May 31, 2016, http://www.europarl.europa.eu/sides/getDoc.do?pubRef=-//EP//NONSGML%2BCOMPARL%2BPE-582.443%2B01%2BDOC%2BPDF%2BV0//EN. © European Union. **Page 388:** Maciej Ceglowski, "Superintelligence: The Idea that Eats Smart People," http://idlewords.com/talks/superintelligence.htm. **Page 413:** "Automation and anxiety: Will smarter machines cause mass unemployment?" Economist, June 25th 2016, http://www.economist.com/news/special-report/21700758-will-smarter-machines-cause-mass-unemployment-automation-and-anxiety. **Page 420:** Republished with permission of the Atlantic Monthly from Christopher Orr, Sympathy for the Robot: Visions of A.I. in Westworld, Atlantic, October 2016; permission conveyed through Copyright Clearance Center, Inc.

Chapter 13   Page 435: Stephen O'Leary, "Rumors of Grace and Terror," Online Journalism Review, April 2, 2002. **Page 443:** From THE VANISHING HITCHHIKER: AMERICAN URBAN LEGENDS AND THEIR MEANINGS by Jan Harold Brunvand. Copyright © 1981 by Jan Harold Brunvand. Used by permission of W. W. Norton & Company, Inc. **Page 457:** Gregory Rodriguez, "One Man's Rumor Is Another Man's Reality," LA Times, September 28, 2009. **Page 460:** From Dan E. Miller, "Rumor: An Examination of Some Stereotypes," Symbolic Interaction.

Index

CHECKLIST FOR WRITING SUMMARIES

- **Read** the passage carefully. Determine its structure. Identify the authors' purpose.
- **Reread.** *Label* each stage of thought. *Underline* key ideas and terms.
- **Write one-sentence summaries** of each stage of thought.
- **Write a thesis:** a one- or two-sentence summary of the entire passage.
- **Write the first draft of your summary.**
- **Check your summary against the original passage.**
- **Revise and edit your summary.**

CHECKLIST FOR WRITING CRITIQUES

- **Introduce** both the passage being critiqued and the author.
- **Summarize** the author's main points, making sure to state the author's purpose for writing.
- **Evaluate** the validity of the author's presentation.
- **Respond** to the author's presentation.
- **Conclude** by summing up your assessment of the overall validity of the piece.

CHECKLIST FOR WRITING SYNTHESES

- **Consider your purpose in writing.**
- **Select and carefully read your sources,** according to your purpose.
- **Take notes as you read.**
- **Formulate a thesis.**
- **Decide how you will use your source material.**
- **Develop an organizational plan,** according to your thesis.
- **Draft the topic sentences for the main sections.**
- **Write the first draft** of your synthesis, following your organizational plan.
- **Document your sources.**
- **Revise your synthesis,** inserting transitional words and phrases where necessary.